PLEIADIAN
ENER(
ASTROI

C0001 79494

"*Pleiadian-Earth Energy Astrology* shows us how to synchronize our personal energy with the current intense multidimensional awakening. It describes ways we can attain cosmic alignment by means of brilliant and totally unique astrological techniques. This refreshing and very practical new approach to astrology integrates Pleiadian wisdom with Maya/Cherokee astrology; a masterful achievement! This is a must-read for all those interested in astrology, the Mayan Calendar, Cherokee knowledge, and cosmic consciousness."

BARBARA HAND CLOW, AUTHOR OF
THE PLEIADIAN AGENDA AND *CHIRON*

"Today's world is a linear world, based on sequencing, hierarchies, and cause and effect. But Pia Orleane and Cullen Baird Smith present an alternative, suggesting that human lives are lived not as a straight line but as a series of cycles. In this remarkable book, they teach their readers how to navigate these cycles, putting their energy to wiser and more inspiring use. Orleane and Smith incorporate insights from the Mayan tradition, from the HeartMath laboratories, and just about everything in between. Follow their suggestions and emerge with a new sense of time, an enriched sense of power, and a life filled with hope."

STANLEY KRIPPNER, PH.D., COAUTHOR OF *PERSONAL MYTHOLOGY*

"The astrological system Pia and Cullen have brought forward is vast! The fundamental thirteen energies, the weaving of our material and subtle realities, and the emphasis on Venus are just some of its important contributions for life on Earth today. My wholehearted thanks for devoting yourselves to this ever-vital, crucial system for an awakened and embodied humanity."

ADAM GAINSBURG, AUTHOR OF *THE LIGHT OF VENUS*
AND FOUNDER OF SOULSIGN.COM

"Using a combination of Pleiadian transmissions along with modern 21st-century astrological insights about Venus, Orleane and Smith give us comprehensive understanding of why this planet is so important to humanity and our current evolution. Anybody seeking to make the important shift to the energy of the heart will find great meaning in the contents of this book."

ARIELLE GUTTMAN, AUTHOR OF *VENUS STAR RISING:
A NEW COSMOLOGY FOR THE 21ST CENTURY*

"This is astrology from a whole new perspective. Using natal charts along with transits and progressions is second nature to astrologers, but it becomes an even more powerful tool when combined with an understanding of universal and earth energy as relayed by the Pleiadians. The authors lead us bit by bit to a whole new understanding of what we can truly become. A book to treasure."

MARGARET CAHILL, PUBLISHER AND FOUNDER OF
THE WESSEX ASTROLOGER

"*Pleiadian-Earth Energy Astrology* offers an expanded way of working with time and energy that supports remembering who we really are and our place in the cosmos. Orleane and Smith describe the interplay of 13 spiraling universal energies with 20 spiraling earth energies, detailing a 'map to oneness,' which incorporates four types of consciousness (individual, community, global, and universal) as well as the four cardinal directions. Thought-provoking and potentially life changing, this book has much to offer to anyone interested in astrology and the evolution of consciousness."

STEPHANIE AUSTIN, M.A., AUTHOR OF *ECOASTROLOGY*
AND FOUNDER OF ECOASTROLOGY.COM

"*Pleiadian-Earth Energy Astrology* questions the basic assumptions by which we organize our lives—most significantly, linear time—to jolt us out of the illusion of past and future and into an expanded present-time awareness of spirals, simultaneity, and synchronicity. The authors, with guidance from a group of Pleiadians called Laarkmaa, reveal how humanity has been enslaved by the illusion of time, which keeps us in a state of separation. They show how we can move toward unity consciousness by using energy, rather than time, as the organizing principle of our lives. In the tradition of *The Pleiaidian Agenda* and *Bringers of the Dawn*, *Pleiadian-Earth Energy Astrology* is a must-read guidebook for the coming Aquarian Age."

EMILY TRINKAUS, AUTHOR OF *CREATING WITH THE COSMOS*

PLEIADIAN-EARTH ENERGY ASTROLOGY

Charting the Spirals of Consciousness

PIA ORLEANE, PH.D.,
AND CULLEN BAIRD SMITH
WITH LAARKMAA

Bear & Company
Rochester, Vermont

Bear & Company
One Park Street
Rochester, Vermont 05767
www.BearandCompanyBooks.com

Bear & Company is a division of Inner Traditions International

Copyright © 2018 by Creative Wave, LLC

All rights reserved. No part of this book may be reproduced or utilized in any form
or by any means, electronic or mechanical, including photocopying, recording, or by
any information storage and retrieval system, without permission in writing from the
publisher.

Library of Congress Cataloging-in-Publication Data

Names: Orleane, Pia, author. | Smith, Cullen Baird, author.
Title: Pleiadian-Earth energy astrology : charting the spirals of consciousness /
    Pia Orleane, Ph.D., and Cullen Baird Smith with Laarkmaa.
Description: Rochester, Vermont : Bear & Company, [2018] | Includes
    bibliographical references and index.
Identifiers: LCCN 2018008467 (print) | LCCN 2018027668 (ebook) |
    ISBN 9781591433095(paperback) | ISBN 9781591433101 (ebook)
Subjects: LCSH: Astrology. | Spiritual life—Miscellanea. | Consciousness—
    Miscellanea. | Pleiades—Miscellanea.
Classification: LCC BF1729.S64 O75 2018 (print) | LCC BF1729.S64 (ebook) |
    DDC 133.5—dc23
LC record available at https://lccn.loc.gov/2018008467

Printed and bound in Canada by Friesens Corporation

10 9 8 7 6 5 4 3 2 1

Text design by Virginia Scott Bowman and layout by Priscilla Baker
This book was typeset in Garamond Premier Pro with Frutiger, Gill Sans,
    Gotham, Legacy Sans, and Trajan used as display typefaces
Design for Appendix C created by Dan Gretz.
All other charts and illustrations created by Chris Molé Design.

To send correspondence to the authors of this book, mail a first-class letter to the
authors c/o Inner Traditions • Bear & Company, One Park Street, Rochester, VT
05767, and we will forward the communication, or contact the authors directly at
www.laarkmaa.com or **www.piaorleane.com**.

We are all parts of one human family, one body,
like drops of water in the same ocean.

Pia Orleane, Ph.D.,
from *Sacred Retreat:*
Using Natural Cycles to
Recharge Your Life

CONTENTS

FOREWORD

BY KENNETH JOHNSON

Some people think of the Mayan calendar as a straight line. An essentially linear paradigm, it begins with the day sign Imix (crocodile) and ends with the day sign Ahau (flower/sun), like a runner completing a race. In the highlands of Guatemala, where the ancient calendar still lies at the center of traditional Mayan spirituality, we think of it as a circle; there is no beginning or end. If we perform a ceremony on a Tz'ikin day (the day called Men in the Yukatek language used in this book), we begin our count with Tz'ikin and count the days in order until we reach Tz'ikin again, completing the circle.

However, a circle returns, always and forever, to the place where it began, so in essence the sacred calendar as it is envisioned in this book is a spiral rather than a circle. Over the millennia different cultures have delved into its magic and its meaning. Each time new dimensions of consciousness embodied in the count of days are revealed, the circle grows larger and larger, always returning but spiraling ever higher into a more vast, more complex, more universal body of wisdom as each new pair of eyes, each new collection of minds, searches for what we call *"cosmovisión* Maya"—the cosmological vision of the ancient and modern Maya, as well as all the other cultures of ancient Mesoamerica (and perhaps as far north as Chaco Canyon, New Mexico) that shared the count of the 260 days.

This shifting ocean of meanings is only fitting, for the days of the sacred calendar are the archetypes of Mesoamerican civilization, and an archetype resists simplistic definition and can never be reduced to a single word or concept. Like images in a kaleidoscope, archetypes emerge from a single source but undergo constant transformation. For example, in medieval times the Vikings envisioned the god Odin as an old man with a white beard who wore a long gray cloak, carried a staff, and wandered from place to place. If he sought a warm spot to rest by your fireside, he would be gone in the morning, but something wondrous and magical would remain to mark his visit. If this same description were given to contemporary people, they would respond, "That's Gandalf," the J. R. R. Tolkien character in *The Lord of the Rings*.

And so it is. Names and stories change, but the archetypes remain the same.

The daykeepers (shamans) used to teach that all twenty of the day signs of the calendar can be found in the *Popol Vuh*, the Mayan creation epic that is still treated as a sacred text by the *costumbristas,* the practitioners of the ancient religion. We were urged to study the myths until we found the day signs, and then meditate on their deeper meanings.

Let us take, for example, the day sign Chuen. In the Yukatek language the word means "artist" or "craftsman." To the Aztecs the day sign was known as "monkey." In the K'iche' language of my teachers the name of this day is B'atz', which can mean "howler monkey," but if pronounced slightly differently, can also mean "thread." It is the thread from which we consciously weave the tapestry of our lives and of our destiny. On 8 B'atz' our village shamans, or daykeepers, are initiated and receive the *vara sagrada* (medicine bundle), which contains seeds of the sacred *tz'ite* tree that have been empowered with the energy we call *koyopa*, the "inner lightning." On 9 B'atz' rituals celebrating the divine feminine are held. When planning nuptials, 13 B'atz' is regarded as the best possible day for a marriage ceremony.

While the various meanings of this day sign seem entirely unrelated, they are all deeply linked. In ancient times the twin monkey gods were the patrons of all artists and craftsmen. Today, the primary art form of the village Maya is weaving. In the *Popol Vuh* the twins who created all the fine arts were turned into monkeys because of their arrogance toward others. The story reminds all those who were born on the day sign B'atz' that they possess innate creative artistic talents that are a gift from Ajaw, the Divine Power, but they must treat their gifts with humility and graciousness and not succumb to pride or arrogance.

Names and stories change, but archetypes remain the same.

Pia Orleane and Cullen Baird Smith retain the traditional meanings of the B'atz' day sign, drawing attention to its artistic creativity and boundless energy as well as its more problematic aspects. But they also introduce a new spiral of meaning into the old archetypes. To them, this is the day of illuminating. To illuminate is to shed light on something, and the concept of illumination links the artistic and shamanic meanings of this day sign in a new and powerful way. The creative artist's poems or paintings illuminate human life in all its complexity, while the daykeeper illuminates the spiritual essence behind life's myriad events. Like the koyopa (sheet lightning, or powerful inner energy) itself, the process of illumination fills our existence with meaning and magic. This book expands the spirals of consciousness as Orleane and Smith present new perspectives on the cycles of energy and life.

And thus the spirals of consciousness continue to ascend, circles growing ever larger, myths and archetypes growing ever deeper.

KENNETH JOHNSON holds a BA in comparative religions from California State University, Fullerton. He obtained his master of arts in Eastern studies (with an emphasis in classical Sanskrit) from St. John's College, Santa Fe. He is the author of numerous books and magazine articles, including *Jaguar Wisdom:*

An Introduction to the Mayan Calendar; Mayan Calendar Astrology: Mapping Your Inner Cosmos; The Mayan Prophecies: Renewal of the World; and *Jaguar Medicine: An Introduction to Mayan Healing Traditions* (with Anita Garr). He was initiated as an *aj qij* (daykeeper) in 2017 in Momostenango, Guatemala. Ken can be visited at www.jaguarwisdom.org.

ACKNOWLEDGMENTS

Our most profound gratitude to Laarkmaa, the loving group of Pleiadians who helped us to deepen our understanding of energy and introduced the system contained in this book. Their wisdom is laced throughout this text, and in some chapters they speak directly to the reader. Thank you, Laarkmaa, for teaching us how each energy builds on others, interlinking into spirals that can move us higher up the evolutionary scale with each revolution. It is Laarkmaa who taught us the concept of *In Lak'ech* (I am another yourself) and showed us the importance of understanding that each of us forms an important part of the whole. Laarkmaa taught us that hierarchy does not exist in the cosmos; what exists is a presentation of energies to which we may relate in higher or lower octaves, according to the choices we make.

We gratefully acknowledge the creative imaginings of José Argüelles, who opened the portals of human imagination through his vision of the First Harmonic Convergence in 1987. It was through his creative dream that many finally began the path to awakening. Argüelles inspired us to see beyond conditioned thinking and beliefs into other possibilities. By moving away from the time structures of the Gregorian calendar and closer to the understanding that time does not really exist, he awakened in humanity the desire to understand and participate with cycles of *energy* rather than time.

We are indebted to astrologer and Mayan calendar scholar Bruce Scofield, whose original work on the energies of Mesoamerican astrology was derived from a study of the Mayan calendar and observations of Western astrological characteristics in his clients. Thank you, Bruce, for enhancing our awareness of this system. Your original work is reflected throughout this book, and we have interwoven many of your concepts with those of our own.

We are thankful for Kenneth Johnson for contributing the foreword to this book. We have followed your work for years and incorporated some of your understandings into the following text. Thank you for your recognition of the new spirals of meaning we are offering the world.

Arielle Guttman and Adam Gainsburg deepened our understanding of the cycles of Venus and how the dance between that lovely planet and ours affects our relationships here on Earth. We are thankful for visionary wisdom and the rich conversations we have shared. Thank you, Arielle and Adam.

We are grateful to Aluna Joy Yax'kin, who has written about Pleiadian wisdom as she understood it in terms of the Mayan calendar. She has contributed to our knowledge base, and we acknowledge the importance of her work.

A special thanks to Paula Kim for assistance beyond the ordinary. Your understanding of energy is amazing, and our gratitude for your continual support is enormous. You are ever-present in our hearts.

Thanks to friend and graphic artist Chris Molé for the charts and graphs that illustrate the concepts in this book. Her talent and creative eye have graphically represented Laarkmaa in this and previous books and on our website for many years.

Thanks to Dan Gretz for creating the ephemeris for this work, twice! Your professionalism, care, and time were invaluable for our illustrating the new information provided in this book. Thank you!

We also thank the dear friends who took time from their busy lives to read, correct, clarify, and contribute ideas to the early version of this work: Sara and Brendan Bowen, Terence Neff, and Ari Uziel. Thank you for your generosity of time and energy.

We appreciate the further professional refinements offered by our Inner Traditions editors Meghan MacLean and Abigail Lewis. We applaud your understanding of the new system, and we are thankful for your many gifts and talents. Thank you for the many suggestions and clarifications you supplied to make this a book that would appeal to a larger audience and potentially affect the lives of many. We also wish to thank the entire Inner Traditions/Bear & Company team that has worked to bring this book into production, including Jon Graham, Kelly Bowen, Manzanita Carpenter, Erica Robinson, Patricia Rydle, Jeanie Levitan, John Hays, and Ashley Kolesnik.

We wish to thank Pia's astrological clients, who have allowed her to explore their energetic makeup and get to know them from the energetic perspective. It has been delightful!

Our deepest gratitude to our special friend Rebecca Gretz, who attended the first public Laarkmaa gathering and who has been supporting the sharing of Laarkmaa's wisdom and the building of community ever since. Your presence is invaluable in our lives!

Both of us have longed to start a community since we were very young. While our dream has not yet manifested into a physical community, our sense of a living community continues to grow as we connect with more and more like-hearted people who wish to make positive changes in our world. In a way this book was the project of our community, not just the two of us. We are grateful to our entire community, beginning with those already mentioned and extending to include all those who follow Laarkmaa's wisdom and who support the two of us as Laarkmaa's representatives, especially Lesley Grocock, Sulara James, Resha and Stanley Sabre, Brian MacIntyre, Joan Wallace, Nicola Merton-Richards, Kelly Dovey, Diana Johansson, Kathleen Martinez, Ari Uziel, Erika Mikaelsson, Maria Belknap, Cynthia Shapiro, Petter and Julie Barve, Nick Caswell, Sally Claridge, Sharon Swinyard, Ruthanne Holbert, Oribel Joy Divine, Marcellus Davis, Alexander Senchenko, Anna Karmoz, Chrystelle Schoettel, Andy, Maria, and George Haralambous, Niki Themistocleous, Constantinos Nicolaides, and the entire Cyprus Light Mover group. Each of you has been a major support on our journey, and we couldn't have made it without the love and support of you, our spiritual family.

Our gratitude to all who have made positive changes in their lives through listening to Laarkmaa's wisdom. As you change yourselves, you help to change the world.

We are thankful for all the years we have had the opportunity to share the wisdom we have gained working with our Pleiadian friends. We hope this book will add to humanity's collective understanding of our true reality and shared energies.

Spirals of Consciousness

We live in a world that is bound by time, and we measure our experiences on a linear scale oriented toward the past or the future. But the rest of the universe is not linear. Stars, planets, and other orbiting bodies in the galaxy move in circular or elliptical patterns. In fact, about 80 percent of known galaxies exist in a spiral form. The remainder exist in elliptical-spiral combinations or as irregular, shapeless forms. We live in a spiraling universe; therefore, should we not recognize that as part of the universe, our consciousness also moves in spirals? And realizing this, should we not understand that our own evolution could most easily be achieved by participating with spirals of energy, rather than restricting our development through our current focus on linear time—past and future?

When we move away from our focus on *time* we can begin to understand that everything in the universe is organized around the movement of *energy*. This book is based on the concept that energy is alive, conscious, and intelligent. It knows how to move and where to go for its most efficient application.

Energy is nonlinear. It arrives in waves, vibrations, or frequencies (terms that are indistinguishable for the purpose of this book). Waves transport energy everywhere. In fact, all of life is about wave motion, and our experiences occur in wave motion, not in linear, fragmented

1

parcels of time. We ourselves are waves of energy; we are not static, unchanging solid particles joined in some random (or intentional) fashion. Our bodies are even equipped to translate the vibrations of incoming energy into the experiences of our reality. This is how we interface with our third-dimensional world; our physical senses are designed to interpret vibrational signatures of energy. Our sight translates vibration into what we see, our hearing translates vibration into sound, our olfactory senses translate vibrations of energy into smell, and so on.

Science has not yet been able to explain the deeper underlying structure of harmonics that forms life. But recent scientific observations have revealed that our material world is not as solid as we may believe it to be. It consists of unrealized vibratory possibilities, which are rendered into the solid physical world we perceive *through the energy of thought*. Waves of energy manifest into physical form through interacting with other waves of energy. Einstein attempted to prove this while working on his unified field theory. Today, his work on this idea is simply interpreted to mean that every thought we think affects every aspect of our reality.

When we begin to observe and participate with energy as energy, rather than using time as our organizing principle, we can discover how to truly participate with other energies to create a different reality on Earth. The magnetic field of our planet broadcasts a very wide range of energetic frequencies that commingle with the energy of the Sun and other planets in our solar system, even extending out farther into the cosmos. Astrophysicist Percy Seymour proposed that each of us is attuned to specific frequencies that were magnetically imprinted on us while we were still in the womb. We, the authors, see that magnetic imprint as an alignment with specific energetic frequencies, which we will delve into more deeply in this book to explain the specific essence of each energetic frequency and how to work with it. Understanding how these energies have imprinted on us as we arrived on Earth in physical form is equivalent to understanding our purpose.

How are we defined by a specific combination of frequencies, and how can we use that frequency combination we call our individual selves to participate in human evolution here on Earth and beyond into an infinite universe? The continual wave motion of energy can be explained somewhat today through quantum physics. At the quantum level, scientists perceive phenomena as either particles or waves, depending upon how they are measured. Particles are perceived to be stable and unchanging localizations in a quantum field of continually moving waves.

We humans typically view ourselves as particles—stable, static, unchanging (for the most part)—rather than as waves. Once we are born, according to Percy Seymour, our senses begin to take in information and send it to our brains. We lose the sense of being fluid, undulating, as our immediate sensory experience begins to override our earlier prenatal experience of magnetic or energetic resonance. We forget about our earlier wavelike forms.

It is fundamentally unfeasible for us to believe that we are progressing in developmental strides when we are not in harmony with cosmic rhythms. By segmenting our experiences into blocks of time, especially focusing on a perceived past or hoped-for future, we have become ever more separated from each other and from Nature, stuck in the artificial rhythms of man-made time. We have further separated ourselves through a belief that everything that happens to us is local, meaning that it involves a transfer of some kind of signal through some kind of force, giving it the appearance of a reality manifested through cause and effect only. Nothing could be further from the truth. We actually live in a nonlocal universe, meaning that everything can happen simultaneously, regardless of distance between objects or events. We will explore this more deeply later in the book.

We need to step away from the limits of time and begin to recognize the possibility that events can and do occur in synchronicity and that we have the ability to participate in the way energy unfolds into our manifested reality. Everything is connected simultaneously, and these connections are not affected by size or distance. Yet the *energy* of each instant is separate and distinct, and each energy adds to the energy that presented before it and contributes to the energy that follows. To realize the potential available in this understanding, we must begin to carefully watch the energy of the moment and respond accordingly.

ADAPTING TO A PHYSICAL BODY

The birthing process is a wonderful example of the way we're meant to meet each moment. Birth (as all of life) never occurs on schedule or in one linear push. Each new baby arrives in a rhythm of waves, synchronizing neonatal energies to those awaiting in the new environment. The mother dilates her birth passage, expanding her physical body just enough to allow her child to pass through. The mother experiences great pulses of contraction and expansion as the child's energetic essence moves from the fluid, watery world of the womb into a more solid, structured, physical life. The process of birth is more about expansion than it is about contraction, and we should remember that as we are pushing to give birth to a new consciousness that honors the expansive possibilities of being part of a larger reality.

Early in life we work to fit into a new environment, one that divides everything into the polar opposites of female-male, night-day, cold-hot, good-bad, and me-other. Our Earth experience is based on dualism, and we begin to forget that from the deepest level, all energy is connected. We separate everything into what we consider to be safe categories and judge everything and everyone around us. This is the process we use to continuously recreate a limited, false reality based on our perceptions of separation and duality. Eventually, we forget that everything is connected. Time becomes a separating factor, and we teach our children to pay attention to and learn from history. We learn to obsess over past mistakes, rather than realizing that each moment has a different energy because we ourselves change moment to moment. We must abandon the past to live truly in the present, and that requires learning to be aware of what each new moment is asking of us, rather than relying on past experiences.

The continued encapsulation of experience in time has caused separation between individuals and separation of humans from Nature. As a species, we are currently participating in a form of movement from unity toward individuality. This is not evolutionary; it is *devolutionary*. Human evolution has not improved through a course of deeper and deeper separation and specialization. We can discover (and some of us are discovering) who we truly are through incorporating all of our vast and varied individual experiences (which are occurring simultaneously) into a unified harmonic whole, finding that we are, indeed, one unified collective.

The purpose of this book is to expand our human awareness by reorganizing our understanding of energy. The astrological system unveiled in the following pages introduces energy as a potential— making us who we are and providing endless opportunities to unfold into our true selves. It's an evolutionary process. We can become who we're intended to be. Unlike some earlier astrological systems, this system does not rely only on the element of time or the placement of specific planets to define an individual. The system acknowledges that each of us came to relate to specific energies and to synchronistically participate with *every* available energy. Each of us magnetically aligns to several specific energies as we come into human form to understand and work with those aspects of energy more completely. We are here on Earth to fully explore each aspect of every energy and to intelligently integrate the results of our explorations. We reach unity when we share our combined understanding and integration with each other. This is how our species can evolve. Later, we'll explain how the essence of integration is contained in the energy of thirteen, a number that—with the exception of meters in the metric system—is conspicuously absent in most of our current measuring or counting systems. The energy of thirteen is a fantastically important key to understanding and synthesizing all combined energies; it's a fundamental missing link!

PATTERNS OF ENERGY

There are two major patterns of spiraling energy that constitute the foundation of our system. The first pattern is found in universal energies that relate to cosmic laws and cosmic truth. They reflect principles that are constants throughout the universe and are continually changing in the ways they manifest. There are thirteen universal energies, defined and explained in chapters 3 and 6. The second pattern is found in twenty earth energies, which are the energies most relevant to our human proficiency. These energies are more specific to our lives on Earth and they build on one another, creating a non-hierarchical foundation for what comes next. Each contributes an important piece to understanding the whole of our earthly experience. Participation with these energies occurs at a lower or higher vibration, depending upon our choices and the development of our conscious awareness.

Each of us aligns specifically with one or two of the earth energies at birth. Hence, it is an individual mission to explore and discover how to use those energies for personal and planetary evolution. There are twenty of these energies, and they will be defined and explained in detail in chapters 7 through 9. Who we are and how we interact—with each other and with our environment—colors and flavors our lives. This is what determines the course of our evolution.

To begin to understand how our human energy manifests into physical form, we must look at our makeup and our environment. We are electromagnetic beings living in an electromagnetic atmosphere. Seventy percent of our physical makeup is water, which conducts electricity. Our nervous systems, essentially electrical in nature, are sensitive to the magnetic fields around us. Therefore, we respond to the fluctuations of energy as it pulses through our bodies and through our environment. Magnetism and electricity are complementary, and one can induce the other. An electrical current will generate a magnetic field, and vice versa. Because our bodies are electromagnetic, once we learn to understand our own energy more thoroughly and to participate more consciously with external energies as they pulse through our atmosphere, it is possible we may learn to co-create our own environment by oscillating our electrical charge in a way that attracts other specific energies of our choosing.

Both the heart and the brain operate through electrical conductivity. The heart generates a torus-shaped magnetic field that has surprising functions. For one thing, it is common knowledge that the heart functions as the leader in all systems processes within the body. The heart also sends commands to the brain for a variety of primary body functions. If we consciously join the heart and brain currents, *consciously* allowing our hearts to lead our minds, we may discover higher vibrational states that could potentially allow us to cross dimensions. As you'll learn later in this book, the heart-brain system has been the subject of much research.

Experiences with "interdimensional" or interstellar energies have occurred since the dawn of humanity. This book is related to the wisdom obtained through communication with interdimensional beings. Stories of involvement with extraterrestrials exist in aboriginal Australia, the African Dogon tribe, among the Maya and the Maori, in Russia and America, and possibly in every part of the world. From an anthropological and archeological perspective there is ample evidence that multiple cultures and societies from beyond our planet have visited humans for thousands of years. Existing cave and rock drawings and oral creation myths derived from these experiences provide, according to many, an unquestionable historical record of extraterrestrial contact with humanity. Members of the Dogon tribe (who possess advanced astronomical knowledge that could only have been supplied by an advanced civilization) speak of "space beings." The indigenous tribes of Australia have preserved the legacy of "sky beings" they call the Wandjina through both oral tradition and an exceptionally large collection of five-thousand-year-old rock paintings scattered through the Kimberly region of northern Australia that show striking representations of alien beings. In Europe, the Saami people of Scandinavia claim to be descendants of "star people." In North America, several indigenous tribes, including the Cherokee, Cree, Hopi, and Dakota/Lakota, believe their ancestors originally came from the stars. Many of these indigenous groups who believe their heritage is derived from a place or dimension other than Earth have a distinct and specific historical connection with the Pleiadian star system. The Cherokee creation myth refers to arriving on Turtle Island (Earth) from the Pleiades, and the Hopi have a specific name for Pleiadians, referring to them as Chuhukon, meaning those who cling together and communicate telepathically. Indigenous cultures' preoccupation with the Pleiades leads us to believe that visitors from the Pleiadian system have been contacting and participating with humanity for thousands of years. However, human consciousness has not thus far been fully able to integrate the wisdom from these valuable exchanges, or in most cases to even consider the possibility of interacting with other dimensions.

We're living in a period when our consciousness may finally be ready to understand just how interactive we are *with*—and inseparable we are *from*—each other within the universe. When a magnetic wave of energy pulses to Earth, we respond. When we send out a wave of our own energy (through thoughts, feelings, or actions), the universe responds. We're deeply interconnected, and it's time we recognize and take responsibility for our energetic responses, which affect everyone and everything. Whether we know it or not, whatever we express becomes part of the universe; likewise, everything from the universe is absorbed, becoming part of us. We must also recognize that we are being influenced electromagnetically by Nature, and our thoughts and feelings have an impact on Nature and our environment. Our body consciousness knows the rhythms and pulses of the electromagnetic field of the cosmos and its influence on us. Therefore, conscious participation with these pulses of energy is only possible when we understand that the energetic makeup of the electromagnetic field provides our individual and collective experiences.

We are finally beginning to more fully understand that we're part of a greater whole. As we decide how we'll set aside our linear perceptions of time and our ideas of a static reality, we'll begin integrating a new system that will be based on the wave nature of energy. Because we, like everything in the universe, are waves of energy, we need to provide an energetic context for our experiences through the understanding of the spiral movement of energy. Everything in the universe spirals, and our consciousness is no different. As part of the spiral of life we need to consciously step into the flow of energetic awareness and become cosmic citizens. This book offers a system to achieve that reality.

Many advanced beings are guiding humanity's evolution by helping us to understand cosmic laws and what is required of us. Laarkmaa is one such guiding group. Laarkmaa describe themselves as "one of six and six of one," a perfect illustration of individuality within unity. They operate from the Pleiades, visiting the denser realm of planet Earth to share their perspective and help us grow. We, the authors, are not unique in our ability to communicate with interstellar beings. Others, such as Barbara Hand Clow and Barbara Marciniak, have also shared Pleiadian perspectives with the world. Laarkmaa, the Pleiadians who work specifically with the two of us, offer the newest wave of Pleiadian wisdom for humanity's evolution. Their reasons for helping us are simple: they love us. They have been through their own challenging evolutionary process, and they understand that what we do here on Earth affects the entire universe because everything is connected. They are here to help us find the answers to our questions within our own hearts. They wish to awaken us to the power we hold through every choice we make, beginning with our choice of thoughts, attitudes, feelings, and finally, actions. This book has been written because Laarkmaa is one of many Pleiadian groups that wish for humanity to align itself with others in the galaxy who function in spirals of consciousness. We invite you to open your hearts and minds, join the flow of energetic awareness and the spiral of life in the cosmos, and begin a new era of consciousness together!

2

DNA and Species Evolution

Our earthly experience is focused through a three-dimensional lens, revealing a reality where we mentally separate everything into polar opposites. This fundamental duality is deeply ingrained into our human consciousness by the underlying and persistent view of everything as either "self" or "other." Because the mind filters our human consciousness, we simultaneously experience disconnection from the original intuitive heart wisdom that is part of Nature and the cosmos. As we explore the reasons we have so grossly misunderstood the purpose of our earthly experience in duality, we can begin to right ourselves to use our dualistic perspectives as tools for growth, moving toward unity. In our ever-changing evolutionary process, the views of science and the views of spirituality or other nonscientific views are gradually moving closer together.

Duality (or polarity) is based on the energy of two, which is a splitting or division of the number one. It is defined as a state that consists of two parts that make up a whole. Because of our focus on this split, our earthly experience has been primarily based on individuation and separation. Yet before we were born, we were only waves of energy in the universe. Physics tells us that everything in the universe is just energy or information. How did humanity lose this awareness and arrive at our "civilized" (and more complicated) dualistic perspective of life, and more importantly, how can we now reverse that state of dualism to embrace unity consciousness instead?

Science tells us that our intelligence (and possibly our perspective) is held within our DNA, which is a macromolecule that codes biological information.[1] According to science it represents the upper and lower limits of what is possible for us. For many years scientists believed that we are limited by the potential that lies within the two known functional strands of our DNA, which compose approximately 2 percent of our total DNA; the remaining DNA was believed to be inactive and was considered "junk" DNA. Some forward-thinking scientists are now suggesting that perhaps this undefined DNA is waiting for a signal from something to bring it to life—possibly a signal that our consciousness is finally resonating with the spiraling energies of the universe. With this recognition, we could potentially achieve a higher level of awareness than humanity has ever known. *Scientific American* referred to "a stunning inventory of previously hidden switches, signals, and signposts embedded like runes throughout the entire length of human DNA."[2]

Perhaps part of the reason we see reality through a three-dimensional lens of duality is because our science is focused on only those two strands of DNA, while remaining unclear about the purpose of the rest of our acknowledged DNA. Laarkmaa tells us that our DNA currently exists as a form of soup within us, with only two ingredients (or strands) clearly visible. So what if the scientists are wrong and are just not seeing (or understanding) what is not clearly visible? What would that mean for our evolution? If these two DNA strands are the master molecules of life, what are the functions of the remaining DNA? What wisdom is held there? No scientist can answer that question yet, but the Pleiadians have given us an answer, which we will explore later.

DNA is always vibrating or oscillating because of its molecular structure. It transmits information in the form of waves, frequencies, and vibrations. DNA's spiraling strands cause the energy passing through them to form a traceable spiraling path. The two known strands run in opposite directions, indicating that duality is inherent in these two strands.

Laarkmaa tells us that each of us actually has *twelve* strands of DNA, ten of which are currently inactive. (This may correlate to the inactive DNA scientists disregard.) Expanding on the Pleiadian perspective, Laarkmaa also tells us that the ten strands of DNA that have not yet been defined by our current science connect us to other dimensions, also as yet undiscovered. Many of us are aware that we are part of a larger reality that cannot presently be validated by our three-dimensional science. Isn't it worth considering that our so-called junk DNA could actually represent the ten strands defined by the Pleiadians as our connection to ourselves in other dimensions? Laarkmaa speaks frequently about our "parallel selves" in other dimensions.* What if each of these parallel selves is connected to a strand of our own DNA, and as we begin to awaken, we become aware of the existence of other parts of ourselves?

Perhaps we are unaware of the other ten strands of DNA because we only attune to the frequencies of the two known strands that are easily accessible. Because all DNA vibrates, the implication for the other ten strands of DNA is that each one may be vibrating at a frequency that is resonant only with a dimension of a concurrent vibration, which is *not* our third-dimensional vibrational frequency. This implication does not conflict with physics, which acknowledges that there are an infinite number of dimensions within the universe. Each dimension exists as a band of frequency, resonating at a different vibration. Just as a radio bandwidth is described in terms of its frequencies, we can define any dimension in terms of a unique spectrum of frequencies. By definition, we cannot see or hear or touch frequencies that are out of our own bandwidth, or frequency range . . . yet. The third dimension is rather dense in its manifestation, focused on slow vibrations that

---

*See *Remembering Who We Are: Laarkmaa's Guidance on Healing the Human Condition.*

manifest as our dense physical world. However, frequencies that vibrate at a higher rate are lighter, and realities that may resonate with those frequencies would by definition have to exist in a dimension outside of our own third dimension. Because humanity's collective attention is tuned to the specific frequency of this third dimension, we often forget that other, nonphysical energies even exist or that other dimensions may actually be part of the larger reality. Our most advanced scientists are barely beginning to understand this larger reality that contains multiple dimensions.

Since everything that exists literally has its own unique energy, DNA can also be viewed in terms of energy, vibration, frequency, or waveform. These are interchangeable terms that offer different ways of looking at the same phenomenon—the wave nature of creation. Energy has its own intelligence, and it organizes itself according to the frequency in which it is expressing. Frequencies of one dimension exchange information with (or interact with) the frequencies of anything they encounter within that dimension. Physics confirms this, even though the language of physics is different from the language we are using here. At the energetic level it is not the physical object that matters, but the frequency that is expressed. Therefore, it is possible to define each dimension according to its own bandwidth. Physics continually reminds us that *everything* is energy existing at a particular frequency.

Of the possible twelve dimensions suggested by Laarkmaa, the third dimension operates at the lowest frequency. It is the most physically dense, according to physics (just as solid ice is denser than water vapor). As each dimension increases in number (from four to twelve), its frequencies are higher than those in the previous one, (just as x-ray energy has a bandwidth of frequency that is higher than a radio bandwidth). This is a general property of energy. Lower vibrations correspond to lower energies, and higher vibrations indicate higher energies. With our attention tuned to familiar third-dimensional frequencies, most of us are just not aware, or are only *becoming* aware, of other frequencies that exist.

We also tend to think of ourselves only as the third-dimensional body we inhabit. We rarely consider that parts of ourselves may simultaneously exist in parallel realms in other dimensions.

Quantum physics points out that the quantum world is invisible to the naked eye, yet is teeming with life. A principle called "quantum entanglement" occurs when a pair or groups of particles interact in ways that make them depend on each other, causing them to become entangled through coherence and behave as a single particle no matter how far apart they may be. In quantum entanglement, the quantum state of each particle cannot be described independently of the state of the other(s). Likewise, information about one particle improves our knowledge of the other. Recently, quantum physicists revealed that the phenomenon of quantum entanglement could theoretically be the physical mechanism that holds DNA together.[3] We propose that quantum entanglement could also mean that we are all connected and affect each other all the time. Going further, what if the idea of quantum entanglement could be stretched to suggest that we are synchronistically connected to other aspects of ourselves as they exist in other dimensions, and we become more aware of these dimensions and aspects of ourselves as the DNA for those dimensions begins to awaken?

Looking for the missing strands of our own DNA outside our perceptions in the third dimension may open us to a greater awareness of other conscious energetic beings who inhabit these higher frequencies or dimensions. We may also integrate more aspects of ourselves into our core essence as we begin to remember parts of ourselves that are expressing in multiple dimensions.

CARDIAC COHERENCE

Closely related to quantum entanglement is the concept of cardiac (heart) coherence, which describes the heart's ability to synchronize (or entrain) all the body's systems to function in vibration with the heart. Rollin McCraty of the HeartMath Institute says, "Heart intelligence is the flow of higher awareness and the intuition we experience when the mind and emotions are brought into synchronistic alignment with the energetic heart. When we are all heart-centered and coherent, we have a closer alignment with our deeper source of intuitive intelligence . . . resulting in a stronger connection with our deep inner voice."[4] When you look at cardiac coherence and quantum entanglement side by side, their qualities are quite similar. Very soon quantum entanglement in all types of physical systems will begin to answer some of the issues addressed in this chapter, establishing interconnectedness across diverse scales and expressions of life. This is science's answer to spirituality's movement toward unity.

THE BEAUTY OF ONENESS

Our experience of duality has always been intended to help us understand the beauty of oneness. We were never intended to use the energy of duality to cling to illusions of conflict that keep us stuck in human form as we are now. This attachment to limited form prevents us from expanding into our enlightened true selves. We need to step outside of our limited beliefs about our DNA having only two strands and open to the possibility that the Pleiadians are correct. If experiments with DNA and heart coherence enable us to activate our DNA, it is possible we can begin to understand the mystery of our so-called junk DNA. Laarkmaa has already told us that this material is our own ten strands of DNA, undiscovered either by science or through our own experience. Are we going to wait for science to prove we can access other dimensions or to prove the existence of the remaining ten strands of our DNA, or are we going to explore energy from a more personal experience? This book offers a system of studying energy that can enhance our awareness of who we are as energetic beings, encourage better relationships with the energy of others, and guide us in how to live our lives on Earth and in the cosmos. Each human holds an individual viewpoint that governs how that person tunes into energy or available frequencies. Humanity has seen these individual viewpoints as a source of conflict rather than seeing how multiple viewpoints can contribute to achieving a harmony that perhaps relies on other points of view.

As you study your own energetic makeup and your relationship to others throughout the pages of this book, consider the intelligence that exists in each form of energy and how these forms can synchronize to form a unified whole. As beings of electromagnetic energy we respond to all energies that flow to and through us—from planetary influences to incoming galactic waves to the universal frequencies that are constantly passing through us. We resonate with some energetic influences and are repulsed by others, depending upon how we align ourselves to the specific polarities of duality in any situation. This affects our character, behavior, relationships, and interactions with life. It defines who we believe ourselves to be. When we align ourselves with specific familiar and comfortable polarities while rejecting those that seem strange or different, we miss possibility and opportunity. We are acculturated to view separateness as a normal part of life, embracing tribalism, nationalism, religious affiliation, political parties, skin color, and so on. Clearly, we have outgrown these archaic ideas, and they no longer serve us. We are evolving and now can choose to transcend identification with polarities that separate and embrace the inherent value of opposing concepts. Beginning to understand the energy that makes us who we are and others who they are is a step in learning to accept and integrate differing perspectives so that we can see a bigger picture.

Laarkmaa tells us to always remember the meaning of the Mayan expression In Lak'ech (I am another yourself) as a guideline to who we really are—individual parts that make up the whole of humanity. As is repeatedly expressed throughout this book, what one of us thinks, says, or does affects all others, for we are connected. This is a basic interpretation of quantum entanglement. At some deep level we cannot separate ourselves from each other or from our wholeness. If we begin to remember that we are connected, we may begin to actually organize our lives by the principles of the golden rule: "Do unto others as you would have them do unto you."

The Pleiadians tell us that the organizing principles of the universe give us thirteen spiraling energies to support our evolution. Each of the first twelve (associated with its own strand of DNA) represents both a dimension and a distinct consciousness. (Later in this book we will explore how the number twelve energetically represents understanding.) Laarkmaa also suggests that each of our twelve DNA strands represents a separate dimension where we can experience different aspects of ourselves. However, the twelve energies we have been discussing throughout this chapter are followed by an important thirteenth energy that our modern culture entirely ignores. Most measuring units today focus on the number twelve: There are twelve months in a Gregorian calendar year and twelve numbers on the face of a clock. There are twelve Western zodiac symbols and twelve animal signs in the Chinese zodiac. Representations of twelve are everywhere, while thirteen is almost always absent or ignored, and often considered unlucky. While we are introducing the idea that we have twelve strands of DNA and possibly can access twelve dimensional aspects of ourselves, we are simultaneously suggesting that our evolution does not end with the number twelve. We desperately need to reintegrate the number thirteen back into our awareness, for it is in *that* energy that we can potentially integrate all of the wisdom of our twelve DNA strands and twelve-dimensional selves. If you draw a circle with twelve doors (representing each of our twelve strands of DNA and corresponding dimensions), the observer/participant standing in the middle of that circle is the thirteenth component, who is capable of integrating all of the twelve dimensions into a thirteenth point of integration and understanding of the whole. Yet we need awareness of each aspect of ourselves before we can integrate all and complete our evolution.

THE ASTROLOGICAL COMPONENT

The astrological system presented in this book is based on thirteen energies, not twelve. Ophiuchus, a constellation first identified as far back as ancient Greece, was officially included in the boundaries of the International Astronomical Union in 1930, and in 1970 it was suggested as a new astrological sign falling between November 30 and December 18. The growing recent awareness of Ophiuchus seems more synchronistic than coincidental given Laarkmaa's reminder of the Pleiadian system for understanding energy, which suggests that the thirteenth energy represents a point of completion and integration—the integration of twelve-dimensional energies into a unified whole, as in the example described earlier. Thus, Ophiuchus—located around the celestial equator—could symbolically represent a central point of integration for a species awakening into higher consciousness. We will discuss this further in chapters 3 and 6.

In truth, the astrological system we are introducing in this book may represent the resolution of the human experience—the opportunity for us to finally integrate everything we have come here to learn, fulfilling a higher potential in our evolving consciousness. As observed earlier, most of the modern world, including astrology, ignores the energetic number thirteen. But its arrival as a fundamental precept may signal an end to our (largely unconscious) denial and attachment to polarized viewpoints that lead to negative beliefs and actions. If we expand our perspective to include the integrative principle in the energy of thirteen, the meaning of the number may begin to vibrate in our consciousness and interact in subtle ways with our previous conditioning. Perhaps we can begin to glimpse a reality that is multidimensional, rather than seeing all of our experiences and each other as separate and disconnected.

Pleiadian-Earth Energy Astrology™ is designed to help us examine and improve the way we relate. Do we apply our particular characteristics skillfully? Are we open-hearted as we examine how others relate to us? Do we embrace our differences and integrate the viewpoints of others into our own, however foreign they may seem? Can we allow others to express their viewpoints without feeling separated or threatened? We make peace with our own fears when we acknowledge and embrace our shadows. The information this system offers about shadow cycles (fully explained in chapter 11 and previously in Laarkmaa's earlier books*) shows us how to do that. It helps us learn how to *respond* to situations or people rather than *reacting* to them.

Relationships (of all kinds) are the primary means for seeing and reflecting divergent energies. The thoughts and actions we express in duality are either supportive and cooperative or unsupportive and separating. The magnitude of those expressions either draws us toward unity or repels us. As we explore the dynamics of Pleiadian-Earth Energy Astrology we can learn to positively experience energy fluctuations both inside ourselves (as we perceive ourselves) and outside of us (as we perceive others and our environment.) Conscious evolution requires intelligent adaptation.

If we take the evolutionary step of trusting in the possibility that being human involves awakening twelve (not two) strands of DNA and that those twelve strands are connected to other dimensions and other levels of awareness, we may grow beyond our limited dualistic perspective of life. As our awareness shifts we may find our understanding of reality comes from a more multidimensional perspective aligned more closely with cosmic truth. According to the Pleiadians we will begin to experience and understand the twelve dimensions available to us as our twelve strands of DNA awaken. By integrating all aspects of the particular energy each of us came to Earth to explore, we will begin to open all twelve strands of our DNA. It will then be possible to finally integrate all aspects of ourselves as we evolve into the fullness of the

---

*See *Conversations with Laarkmaa: A Pleiadian View of the New Reality* and *Remembering Who We Are: Laarkmaa's Guidance on Healing the Human Condition.*

new humans, a species of higher and lighter vibration. At that point we can evolve into a rainbow body*—combining our denser physical form with the lighter, higher-frequency etheric form. When we achieve this evolutionary step, our participation with this earthly experiment will be complete.

---

*This concept is fully explained by Laarkmaa in *Remembering Who We Are*.

A PLAY OF ENERGIES
BY LAARKMAA

We Pleiadians offer the following information to humanity to show you a larger reality than the reality you perceive through the third dimension. In the universe all energy spirals in waves; it's not linear or static. We want humanity to understand how energy works in the universe, so that you may align yourselves more harmoniously with all others and begin to live in a more balanced way, benefiting all life. We have shared this way of understanding reality with humans for thousands of years, yet you persist in viewing reality in a linear fashion. And you perceive progress as proceeding through the arrow of time, which is an illusion. Your confusion stems from focusing on time and ignoring energy. Time as you perceive it does not exist in the cosmos. Time is circular, if it exists at all. Its spiraling *energies* take you from one point to another. On Earth you no longer arrange your lives according to the movement of energy in relationship to Nature or the cosmos, as you did in ancient times. Your technology and current linear thinking have displaced you from your earlier Nature-based wisdom. You move about your world identifying with an artificial calendar that is disharmonious with Nature and the cosmic movement and flow. We will tell you a bit about the movement of cosmic energy, which applies on Earth as well.

Cosmic energy moves in cycles of thirteen, from initiation to completion, spiraling in a harmonious way and inclusive of all that is. Your

Moon has thirteen cycles of change in a year of Earth-based time, giving you one clue about how to organize your lives. The Gregorian calendar you devised measures time based on a system of twelve, where you divide your year into twelve months and your days into two sets of twelve hours. Your current astrological systems are also based on a system of twelve. Because you misunderstand and miscount energies, you continually begin new cycles before you've completed old ones. There is no space for integration, therefore you never incorporate what you learn. This skewed view of the true reality keeps you stuck in cycles and patterns of thought and behavior, preventing you from remembering your true nature and your relationship to the cosmos.

The universal energies explained to you in this book move from one to thirteen—from initiation to completion. This is actually the way all energy moves in the cosmos. While each energy builds on the previous one, this is not a linear system, for each energy exists in and of itself alone. For example, consciousness begins with a new idea, then merges with other concepts and adds creativity. It solidifies, changing as necessary, and flows to share with other energies. It merges with other worlds, then connects you to everything. Harmonizing all relationships, it manifests and illuminates the truth. Energy opens your understanding at a deeper level, and then the idea is complete. Finally, it's integrated and a new cycle begins. If you can see your concept of reality through this lens of counting from one to thirteen, you're activating brain cells you are not currently using and connecting them to your heart. Then your DNA receives and responds to more conscious information as it flows in from the universe. In other words, you can finally obtain cosmic citizenship. This book contains the instructions—the map and the pathway—for activating greater consciousness, larger visions of reality, and peace, harmony, connection, understanding, and abundance for all.

On several occasions while visiting your planet over thousands of years, we offered this information to humanity, but it fell out of use when we left the Maya and then much later the Cherokee. Because Western cultures consider themselves more advanced than indigenous cultures—which is exactly the opposite of the truth from our perspective—the wisdom we shared with indigenous cultures was overridden and cast aside. In its place you developed systems that relied exclusively on linear thought. Yet if you choose to engage this system we shared with humanity (more than five thousand years ago when we gave the Maya their calendar), you can move beyond the structures of third-dimensional reality. You can finally understand the truth of multidimensional reality, which is reflected through energy (not time).

Begin to see time as a loop or a spiral, rather than moving from the past to the future. When you see it the way we present it—as constantly moving energy—you understand you're always in the present moment. Each "now moment" builds on energies arriving synchronistically, rather than linearly. These spiraling energies accumulate and manifest a different reality when you participate with each of thirteen energies (as presented to you). When you engage the flow of energies (as we suggested) and build on each idea coming in with a conscious understanding, you'll reach a new, higher level of awareness at the end of each cycle. Simply beginning to think in this way will help you to understand larger cosmic ideas. It will also enhance your ability to communicate. Thinking as we do will take you far beyond the confines of a contracted physical experience created by limiting beliefs (fed to you by religion, educational systems, and your incomplete, rudimentary science that expounds very linear concepts of time and reality).

We—and others like us in the universe—communicate through mathematical and musical tones. We know all communication involves the harmonizing of ideas. In Pleiadian communication energy "speaks" directly to other energy in each present moment in tones carrying mathematical or musical meaning. Direct communication travels instantly wherever it needs to go, because it's not mentally filtered. Energy has intelligence. Yet you fail to honor this when you insist on directing energy in a linear way to where you want it to go, rather than allowing the energy to move as it knows best. Have you ever wondered why your best-made plans fail to materialize? It's because you don't know how to participate with available energies to use them. Instead, you insist on manipulating or directing energy through your mental thought processes and your limited awareness of time. When you release ideas and beliefs about what *should* be and begin to allow energy to spiral and connect—as it will naturally—your communications will become instantaneous and synchronistic. This allows you to communicate more easily with flow and grace. You'll begin to experience true connectivity, where you understand everything you do has an impact on everything else in the universe. This is why we are here—to help you understand your influence on the entire cosmos and to learn how to make better choices for the highest good of all.

Energy is intelligent and can manifest in any form it chooses. Everything is related because everything is connected. Your individuality is intended to allow you to focus on specific forms of energy and share your perspectives with one another. This allows you to create a stronger and more functional whole that sees the value of *all* aspects of duality (but not as a separating function). Human consciousness has never been able to grasp duality's sole purpose—to show you individual aspects of the whole to better understand and integrate them. Throughout existence, humankind's mind has created more and more separation because you habitually focus on your differences. You've also allowed past experiences to determine your future, using time as a teacher rather than exploring energies in the present moment.

Because your reality is based on the fantasy of linear time, your thinking has become attached to this illusion. You continue to co-create the same situations, the same relationships, and the same challenges over and over again. (You experience this in what you call karma, where you experience the effects of your choices in the next moment, without understanding you've even made a choice!) We encourage you to let go of concepts of time as you believe it to be and expand your imagination. Your mind keeps you trapped in belief systems and limited ideas, encouraging an attachment to those that continue your experience of living in separation and pain. This is simply not necessary. You're still very much focused on facts, which trap you in linear modes of thinking, even though these alleged facts are altered with changing circumstances. Modern scientists, upon discovering a new fact, will disregard that very fact as another new discovery arises, which they then label as the latest, most correct fact. Facts are continually changing as new knowledge arrives. We suggest you shift your focus to truth instead, which is ever-present and available through understanding the movement of energy.

You don't yet understand the power of choice, which lives in your every thought. Each energy you experience has both a higher and lower vibrational form of manifestation; you choose the level at which you wish to participate. We present these energies through a higher vibration, so you can align yourselves with higher and higher choices. Thoughts and choices have much more power than you know, and largely contribute to manifesting what happens in your lives. *How* you think determines *what* you manifest, but you've not yet realized this.

We don't mean focusing on something you want and trying to will it into existence. We mean the open, expansive kind of thinking that always includes possibilities for the highest good for all. When you choose your thoughts more consciously, you elevate the availability of possibilities because you align with cosmic flow. Remember, every choice you make builds on and determines the outcomes of your manifested experience. And if you use the concepts introduced in this book, you'll have a better understanding of energy. Then you accelerate your consciousness and enrich your life. Re-creating calendars (based on energy rather than time) to guide your life is an excellent place to start.

All energies spiral, merging together and building on one another, and each holds (or has) a specific vibration. Here on Earth you experience energies at higher or lower rates of vibration, according to the choices you make through what you think about and how you participate with energy. We briefly discuss cosmic energies below and describe how to use them at the higher vibratory rate, according to cosmic laws. Once you understand the flow of universal energies, you'll see the benefit in organizing your calendars for scheduling appointments and determining your actions according to the *energy* present, rather than making blind decisions based on convenience and an artificial sense of time. Thus far, you schedule all of your appointments and make all your plans according to the linear Gregorian calendar.

What if you designed your calendars based on the flow of universal energies and began to schedule your appointments in harmony with appropriate energies? For instance, you would schedule a meeting to establish a new company during the energy of four (foundation). Or you would take time off to meditate during the energy of seven (merging and mystical connections). You would schedule gatherings for family and friends or attempt to start a community during the energy of eight (connection). These are a few simple examples of how you can begin to reorganize your life with less resistance and more flow. You can create your own calendar using both Gregorian dates and this new system of counting energies, marking each day according to the universal energies that arrive from one to thirteen. (See appendix C to see which energies match up with each Gregorian date.) As you check your new calendar, you can see how best to participate with the energies that will be present on that day.

Now we will give you an introductory picture of how to use all the universal energies. Remember, energy has a higher and a lower vibrational form of manifestation.

UNIVERSAL ENERGIES

The energy of *one* is available for beginning new projects or for starting something anew. You may use this energy to begin again every moment. Incorporate it into your life. The energy of one, representing unity, splits into two, offering you different perspectives of the unified whole. The energy of *two* represents duality. The collective consciousness of humanity seems to be stuck in a misunderstanding about this energy, rather than using its higher vibratory possibilities for growth. Currently, you experience the energy of two as a dynamic tension, bringing conflict and competition between polar opposites. We want to help you move beyond the pain and suffering present in your misunderstanding of duality. Universal two energy is meant to show you both sides of the same coin so you can see several perspectives at once. Once you better understand the energy, you can use it to create more harmony by seeing that differences actually bring a greater perspective rather than adversity.

The next presenting universal energy of *three* is the energy of creativity. It provides you the opportunity to add your own newly conceived perspectives to the two opposite perspectives of duality, thereby creating something new. The energy of three is a powerful force of creativity in the universe. Proper use of this energy can help you become conscious cocreators with the cosmic energies.

The *four* universal energy provides a foundation to stabilize your creations. Misusing this energy at a lower vibration causes you to be stuck or rigid in your beliefs. Using four energy's higher vibration gives you a solid foundation of trust, love, compassion, and joy to support your continued growth and development.

The *five* universal energy is intended for change. This energy instills flexibility, so you don't become rigid in your thinking. Five energy encourages compromise. In this energy you can add new input to your original idea or shift your thinking according to what is present in *this* now moment.

The *six* energy is about the movement and sharing of wisdom—allowing it to flow freely. It brings together all of your creative ideas, as well as things you begin to remember from other realms you've known. As you share them you make this planetary home of yours more understandable and comfortable.

The *seven* universal energy is about merging. This energy encourages you to step beyond your illusory boundaries to realize how everything in the universe is synchronistically connected. It shows you everything is possible when you step beyond artificial limits and reach into the infinite. This is why so many humans think of seven as a lucky number. Seven is the energy allowing conscious awareness of multiple dimensions. It shows you how to merge third-dimensional perspectives with cosmic perspectives to live harmoniously and well, and to move back and forth between dimensions by recognizing they're all available and merge. You can turn your focus of attention to any dimension you choose at any time.

The universal energy of *eight* builds on the preceding concepts. It offers the ultimate understanding of connection. When you actually *know* all things are connected, you move into a space where you more consciously choose what you are going to do, say, think, or feel. You must understand each of those thoughts, feelings, ideas, and actions ripples out to affect everything and everyone else, for you are indeed connected. You would not dream of making a choice that's not for the highest good of all. Separation is impossible at this level, and individual gifts and talents are applied to benefit the whole. When you begin to make your choices from this vibratory level, you can experience true abundance. No one experiences lack at any level. You can think of the visual representation of the universal energy of eight (8) as an infinity loop. Turn the 8 on its side and see how both sides of duality are now reflected in the eight energy as a single infinite loop. They are connected through the merging point of seven you just experienced when you finally realized everything is meant to exist simultaneously.

Figure 3.1. Infinity loop

The *nine* universal energy is about harmony. Nine sets a specific harmonic tone for helping you bring together everything you've learned thus far and harmonizing it within your entire human system. The universal nine energy is also a force for increased creativity, enhancing and harmonizing the three energy threefold. It combines the energy of six (flow) with the energy of three (creativity.) The harmonic tone of nine, containing three and six energies, creates a harmonic resonance that could make your world more peaceful and harmonious, if you could comprehend and use its gifts.

The universal *ten* energy is the point on the spiral of understanding where you can really make a difference in your reality. Here on Earth when you reach this point in any cycle, you either experience challenge from the chaos you've created or, if you've learned and understood how to use the previous universal energies, your conscious intentions help you manifest more clearly. You experience the energy of ten as either being stuck in old thoughts, beliefs, and ideas or incorporating everything you've learned from the energies of one through nine. The ten energy is all about the choice to manifest something new or to remain stuck and challenged where you are.

If you've incorporated all the previous presenting energies at the level of ten, you can use them to manifest something of a higher vibration. This type of manifestation is built on the naturally occurring spirals of energy. Most of humanity is so distressed by the misunderstanding and misuse of energy that when reaching the point of nine or ten on the spiral, you simply give up in frustration and begin again, which is why so many of you are stuck. The energy of ten is a very, very crucial energy. The energy is now, dear ones, for you to learn ten energy is here for you to expand and to act on what you've experienced up to this point. If you've wisely integrated all of the other nine energies of a cycle, you can move to another vibratory level on the spiral of consciousness, taking your consciousness to the universal energy of eleven.

Many of you have long known the universal energy of *eleven* represents illumination, bringing in the light. It's something that helps you connect to other realms. You pay attention to days on your calendar or times on your clock displaying 11:11. How much more powerful would the marking of eleven energy be if you were in sync with the *true* arrival of 11:11 energy, rather than the arbitrary dates and times you see on your humanmade calendar? If you were to engage with the spiral of universal energies from initiation (1) to completion (13), then you'd more easily be able to access the magic of 11:11.

Eleven shows you the power of the binary system, where you see two marks of equal value standing side by side creating a new number. The energy of 1 stands beside another 1, side by side. This is the way most intelligent beings understand the concept of individuality within unity. Two individual units join in unity. This viewpoint moves you away from believing in a hierarchy where one number holds more value than another; they don't. They are simply different energies working together for the whole. In binary systems numbers are always related and connected, reflecting their energy back and forth. Eleven is a very influential energy, once you learn to use it. We realize this is a completely different understanding of counting, measuring, and arranging your world, but we offer it to you to accelerate your evolutionary movement. When you masterfully achieve this level of awareness in the spiral of consciousness, you reach twelve.

Universal *twelve* is the energy of complete understanding. It holds the energy of both one (initiation) and two (where you split your understanding into dualistic perspectives.) When combined into twelve, you begin to understand unity. At this point in the spiral you recognize the energy of one and the energy of two are the same, representing two sides of the same coin. Everything you've perceived in duality's opposite is actually the same thing viewed from a different perspective. When you reach the true understanding of universal twelve energy, you'll know in every cell of your body that everything is connected. Everything is simply energy, and how you perceive it and participate with it determines how it manifests in your world. This awareness takes you to the highest level of awareness you can achieve on your spiraling journey through evolutionary consciousness.

You then reach the thirteenth energy of integration, the universal energy humanity currently ignores. Here is where you integrate everything you've learned in *any* cycle of energetic movement. *Thirteen* ends the cycle, for it's the point of total and absolute integration. Now, having integrated all you've learned, you stand ready to initiate a new cycle of ideas, experiences, and applications. You've arrived at the point of entry for an even higher and newer level of awareness. You may pause and consider, "How can I now apply everything I just learned and begin again?" But beginning again is not just starting over, repeating cycles and patterns; it's a jumping off point to really begin a whole new era of growth and movement. This process continues over and over again, continually expanding your consciousness until you return to Source. Once you've achieved this understanding, you'll be free to use your own energy anywhere in the universe. We trust you'll enjoy deeper exploration into the perspectives we share about universal energy and cosmic consciousness throughout this book.

OVERVIEW OF THE PLEIADIAN-EARTH ENERGY ASTROLOGY SYSTEM

Every astrologer seeks a deeper understanding of what makes us human, what makes us individual, and what governs our circumstances in life. The ancient science of astrology has many wonderful branches to help explain who we are, yet none remotely approach the subtle levels of awareness that make the Pleiadian-Earth Energy Astrology system unique. For starters, it is based on the most mathematically stable, dynamic structure known to the third dimension: the spiral. Many fundamental processes or patterns we know about involve spirals. From galaxies and seashells to the arrangement of notes along a musical scale, water flowing in rivers or down drains, the motion of the electromagnetic field, or the structure of DNA, the mysterious spiral is *everywhere!* The examples are endless.

Pleiadian-Earth Energy Astrology is the only known system based on the cosmic energies that spiral (unnoticed) through the distinct levels of human consciousness. It is also alone in its use of the number thirteen as an integral player in understanding ourselves and our potential for evolution. Remarkably, this system instructs us in internally *and* externally expanding and integrating each level of our awareness. Once we understand and earnestly apply the intelligent guidance the cosmic energies offer, results follow naturally.

The opportunities to evolve continuously unfold as each group of spiraling energies ceaselessly winds its way through our levels of consciousness. We integrate each level as we complete it. In this way, we energetically change our relationship to ourselves and our outer experience simultaneously as we cycle through the system's clear, simple, and direct teachings. We now present an overview of this astrological system and show how the universal base of thirteen energies helps us realize (more deeply) the potential of who we are and our place in the universe.

The Seven Sisters, as the stars of the Pleiades are sometimes called, are rarely used as guide points on astrological maps. Yet ironically, the Pleiadians have given humanity one of the most coherent and user-friendly systems to understand the relationships of all the energies that affect us (individually and collectively) and govern the unfolding of our human condition. The most famous use of this energetic wisdom is the Mayan calendar, which was never about time; it was always about energy. Here, we offer a much-needed, in-depth, and up-to-date approach for studying this valuable energy and introduce ways to apply it for our conscious evolution. In the pages that follow, our Pleiadian friends—Laarkmaa—explain universal and earth energies from their cosmic perspective, helping us grow and evolve.

Pleiadian-Earth Energy Astrology is based on the interplay of two energy systems: universal (or cosmic) energies and earth-based energies. (See figs. 4.1 and 4.2). In simple language, these energies are nothing more than waves—also referred to as frequencies or waveforms—that synchronize with the energy fields of humans. Cosmic energies that affect us here on Earth and earth-based energies define each present moment, describing that part of the whole each of us is here to explore in third-dimensional reality. Our outer personalities are formed by combining these two energy systems. Universal energies show us how our personal energy interacts with other energies in the universe, while earth energies relate to the way we participate with others here on Earth to create our third-dimensional reality. Learning how the two combine

Spiraling Universal Energies

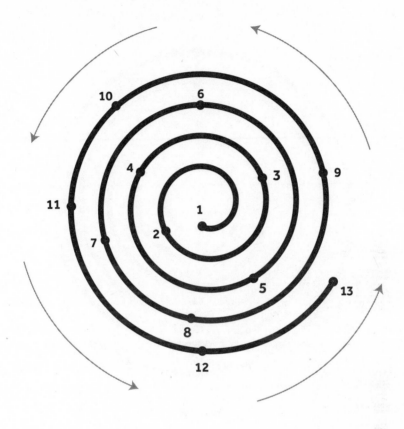

The energy spirals counterclockwise, in harmony with the cosmos.

1	Initiating	8	Connecting
2	Duality	9	Harmonizing
3	Creating	10	Manifesting
4	Foundation	11	Illuminating
5	Change	12	Understanding
6	Flow	13	Completing
7	Merging		

© 2018 Pia Orleane, Ph.D.

Figure 4.1.

Spiraling Earth Energies

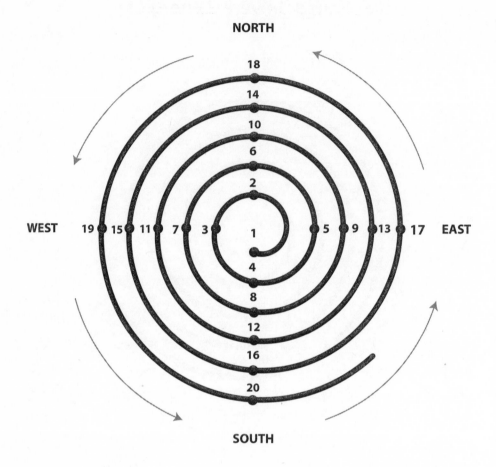

Earth energies spiral in a counterclockwise direction, beginning in the east.

1	Being	11	Illuminating
2	Breathing	12	Choosing
3	Listening	13	Exploring
4	Planting	14	Healing
5	Moving	15	Seeing
6	Transcending	16	Intuiting
7	Remembering	17	Evolving
8	Loving	18	Self-Regulating
9	Feeling	19	Catalyzing
10	Devoting	20	Enlightening

© 2018 Pia Orleane, Ph.D.

Figure 4.2.

in our everyday experience brings a universal focus of wholeness and harmony into our dualistic world. This astrological system guides us in understanding the spiraling interplay of these two energetic cycles, revealing a deeper awareness of the connection between who we are and events that occur on Earth.

Everything that exists is a grand play of interacting waves of energy. Because of the dynamic interplay between spiraling universal and earth energies, the elements forming the core of this system will be discussed repeatedly throughout the book. The Pleiadians offer exceptional insights into energy and its effects on our individual and collective energetics. As we are here to learn to work with these spiraling energies within ourselves and with others on Earth, we are drawn to understand the vibrational influences that make each of us unique. Looking at the world through the lens of the Pleiadian-Earth Energy Astrology system shows us how each person—and each day—consists of a combination of energies engaged in multiple interactions. Energy communicates with other energies. (The specific energy of personal relationships can also be determined in this system.*)

KEY COMPONENTS OF THE PLEIADIAN-EARTH ENERGY ASTROLOGY SYSTEM

The key components in the Pleiadian-Earth Energy Astrology system are:

- The 1,250 years of Venus's complete cycle around the Sun
- Evolutionary guidance

---

*By adding the universal energies and earth energies of each partner, the actual energy of the relationship is explained. When calculating, if the combined universal energies total more than thirteen, subtract thirteen from the total to establish the universal energy for the couple. If the combined earth energies total more than twenty, subtract twenty from the total to establish the couple's earth energy. This simple formula provides a quick and accurate exploration of the energies that are guiding the relationship. See chapter 10 for greater detail.

- The universal (or cosmic) energies
- The earth energies
- Societal imprinting
- Vortex points
- Shadow cycles, personal and collective.

Each of these key components has a dedicated chapter that discusses it in detail. The interplay of all these energies defines to a great extent who we are and how we relate in the world. No two people and no two days are the same because each person is composed of a combination of multiple energies. One way to use the Pleiadian-Earth Energy Astrology system is to allow the information to help you consciously redefine your reality according to the cosmic wisdom that already lives inside your heart, rather than by what is dictated from the outside (society, teachers, leaders, parents, religion).

The Cycle of Venus

Venus is one of our most profound influences. Her position and phase at the time of our birth—and throughout our lifetime—affects our relationships, view of life, and interactions with the world. Historically, the Pleiadians showed humans how Venus could be used as a guiding force on our planet, helping us understand the seemingly dual aspects of the same energy. This helps us move through dualistic perceptions. (See chapter 5 for a detailed discussion.)

The planet moves between positions of morning star and evening star, each of which has different characteristics. These effects were known and honored by Mayan, Cherokee, Australian aboriginal, and other land-based peoples who were connected to Nature. Because Venus has dual positions of evening star and morning star, She is the planet that most closely reveals the dual nature of our experience here on Earth.

During one full rotation from morning star to evening star to morning star again, Venus also expresses the thirteen phases of "personality." Each of these phases provides a certain lens through which we see the world and will be discussed in detail in chapter 5, and a new cycle is begun each time Venus rises newly as a morning star.

Often used as a reference for the Divine Feminine, Venus is associated with the energy of Mary (both Mother Mary and Mary Magdalene), as well as other feminine goddess representations. In our troubled present world it may be easily said that the Divine Feminine is returning to Earth, both as a nurturing influence and as a strong force for justice. This need for justice became very apparent in the United States in late 2017, when many women began speaking out with greater strength for both rights and respect.

Figure 4.3. Venus dance

Venus moves through a unique, five-point star pattern during Her cyclical patterns, replicating specific energetic cycles during a 1,250 Earth-year period (Venus's complete orbit or cycle around the Sun). See figure 4.3 on page 39 and color plate 1 at the back of the book. The influence of this star-pattern energetic is vastly different from the mere placement of Venus in a Western natal astrology chart. It has far-reaching influences on humanity, showing how we are part of the collective and also affect the whole. Summarizing, Venus reveals the truth about the way we relate, which is the most important element we can examine in our search for higher consciousness. This influence gives us a deeper understanding of duality and the interweaving of relationships here on Earth.

Evolutionary Guidance

Evolutionary Guidance is the frequency that sparks our desire to grow and guides us. In the Pleiadian-Earth Energy Astrology system, it is the force that guides and influences our choices for personal growth. This energy acts on the feminine qualities of receptivity, reaction, intuitive response (to life), and emotional response to family, community, and society. Not surprisingly, most humans rarely notice this influence. People simply think, "This is how I am." Yet a deeper look at the Evolutionary Guidance reveals that it is the force of one's own evolutionary impulses manifesting.

Because Evolutionary Guidance influences life at a subconscious level, it may be broadly compared with the influence of the Moon in Western astrology. It is your direct connection to the universe, guides your personal evolution, and leads you to an understanding of being larger than your third-dimensional Earth personality. As a major guiding force in life it directs the development of personality, shapes character, and defines our response to both the inner and outer worlds. This influence clearly reveals how you can work with challenges to co-create your individual destiny. Consciously working with the directional influence of Evolutionary Guidance, we feel fulfilled in knowing who we are and how to *intentionally respond* to life. Not only do we discover our earthly purpose, but also how to find our way home in the universe.

Universal or Cosmic Energies

Universal or cosmic energies are simply energies in the form of vibrations, frequencies, or waveforms that seek to synchronize humanity with the universe. The simple rule of energy is that "like attracts like." The degree of synchronization depends upon the overall energetic state of the person receiving the energy. For example, the energetic state of happiness has a high frequency, high vibration, high energy, or high energetic signature. Similarly, the energetic state of misery has a lower energetic frequency, lower vibration, or lower energy than happiness. At any given moment each of our physical, mental, emotional, and spiritual energetic fields has its own unique frequency, and simultaneously, they combine to create an *overall* frequency. This correlates to individual instruments in an orchestra compared with the actual orchestra. It is exactly the same. And the sum total of those different states of energy in any moment is exactly what we refer to as the "energetic signature" of a person *in that moment*. These states range from high to low. Like every other energy, they are not hierarchical, just functional definitions (or energy signatures).

High vibrations align and combine (or synchronize) with cosmic truth—or other kinds of high vibrations—to create a unified whole. Each of these ways of thinking about energy is valid and equal. A person's energetic makeup is defined by a single universal frequency and specific earth energy that are determined by birth date. Thus, each person will explore and discover *all* the aspects of living with the particular defining energies associated with that birth date. The Evolutionary Guidance energy contributes by guiding the conscious development of the person. However, humankind is also affected by the universal energies present (or flowing through) each day, so in addition to the universal energy defined by the date of birth, these thirteen universal waveforms spiral through our lives on a daily basis and assert their influence in a more transient or temporary way. Thus, while we synchronize with the universal energy that is determined at our birth, each day brings a new influence from a different universal number than the day before. This means energies change daily. Humans always have the choice of aligning (being in harmony) with any energy or not (thereby creating a disharmonious experience with that energy). You will see in chapter 6 that universal energies flow to us and intermingle with our current energetic makeup (or energy fields, or energetic disposition), interacting with us through the opportunities they carry in multiple ways through a variety of influences. Thus, we are given several opportunities to learn to flow in harmony or through alignment with the cosmos along several distinct yet simultaneous paths (or not) with several universal concurrent energies that play different roles in our energetic makeup. One of the reasons for this book is to help humanity understand the advantages of choosing cosmic alignment. As you are beginning to see, the cosmos (and even Gaia) has different systems of organizing events that are totally unrelated to concepts of time or the Gregorian calendar (which was forced on us). Replacing that with a calendar that is Nature-based and aligned with cosmic flow goes a long way in accelerating our evolution and helping us to become true cosmic citizens.

Earth Energies

The twenty earth energies are aligned with earthly experience. The Pleiadians shared their perspective on these energies to help us understand each human's specific role on Earth. The interaction between the thirteen spiraling universal energies and the twenty spiraling earth energies is not new information. The Mayan, the Cherokee, and other land-based peoples acknowledged that the Pleiadians gave them this wisdom, and there is evidence that each culture used it to guide their lives. Although the Cherokee and the Maya had different names for each energy (in their particular languages), the energies listed in this book are in modern English, using words that most closely illustrate and define each energy. The energies are expressed in terms that show us how each affects who we are and the best ways to work with all of the earth energies.

Societal Imprinting

The societal influence addresses the specific energies (or beliefs) we absorb from our environment and the collective consciousness. These societal patterns were present when we were born and continue to influence our decisions about who we are and what is possible.

Imprinted into our view of reality at birth, they dictate what we believe and absorb from our environment. One of the benefits of the Pleiadian-Earth Astrology Energy system is how to live a more expanded, freer life by rethinking our inheritance (from teachers, leaders, parents, religion, and so on) and choosing to live according to the cosmic wisdom within our hearts.

Vortex Points

Vortex points occur at the integration (or merging) of the two cycles of energy (universal and earth), creating a more extreme experience. Days with vortex energy offer a more intense and accelerated experience of whatever is happening. They affect the entire collective consciousness of humanity, not just individuals. Those who are sensitive feel things more intensely on vortex days,* which may be compared to the ripples of energy that occur around an earthquake. (See chart of upcoming vortex days in appendix A.)

Shadow Cycles

Shadow cycles show us places where we may be energetically stuck or doggedly hold onto certain beliefs or patterns of behavior that no

---

*The days of intense energy that we call vortex days were first described by Mayan calendar scholar José Argüelles. Although these days occur throughout the year, they most often occur around the beginning and end of collective shadow cycles.

longer serve us. They may also reflect energetic imbalances due to unresolved karmic issues. As a result, humans unconsciously create the same unwanted patterns over and over again because we are unaware of the underlying energetic cause or pattern. The intense periods of shadow occur in an individual life approximately every sixty days and collectively (on a planetary basis) approximately every eight months.

These periods are opportunities to step into greater levels of clarity and consciousness by clearing the fog of our dysfunctional thinking and beliefs. What is hidden in the shadows is waiting to be revealed and healed. On one level, these energies work individually because each person is unique. Yet the shadows also reveal the work necessary for humanity to collectively evolve. These cycles are hugely significant because they are portals into understanding both individual and collective evolution. (See the chart of collective shadow cycles for the upcoming years in appendix B.)

Chapter 11 describes shadow cycles for an individual (or personal) chart. These cycles reveal what is hidden in our personalities. Challenges offer opportunities for growth, yet if the patterns inherent in each cycle are hard to see, you cannot find a way to unwind and transcend them. As each shadow cycle issue is described, solutions are offered for working through each concern and defined in terms of the individual makeup, providing novel ways for moving past blocks, challenges, and difficulties. You may find guidance for your own particular shadows as you read the descriptions. Consciousness requires awareness; evolution requires intelligent adaptation.

While each person has a unique and particular path through the cycling of these energies, a common pattern affects all humanity as we spiral to higher states of consciousness. A deep examination of these repeated experiences (with the same elements) reveals the block or challenge to development. Each cycle spells out a particular task to help us move beyond the limiting habits of human behavior. Finally, we can understand the work required to permanently release these blocks. Breaking the cycle of dysfunctional patterns and beliefs clears a path to a more fulfilling life. Chapter 11 also discusses the evolutionary stages we need to reach to live more freely, purposefully, and joyously. Without a doubt, shadow cycles are one of the most unusual and valuable tools available for human evolution right now.

Collective shadow cycles are periods of intense energy driving evolutionary change for humanity collectively. Vortex days are the foreshocks or aftershocks, when we prepare for large changes to come or we still feel the intensity of something that has already occurred. Since 2012 all energies have been available to us *simultaneously*, as will be discussed more fully in chapter 11. Therefore, the effect of vortex energy is even more intense now than before 2012, when energies were presented on Earth in a sequential order. Interestingly, this current advanced presentation of energies has not been fully understood or appreciated by most, including many Mayan calendar scholars.

This astrological system guides our individual and collective experience from the physical, mental, psychological, and spiritual levels. You will discover just how easy it is to work with these energies to co-create a more balanced personal and collective reality. In other words, the Pleiadians have given us a gift to help us open the doorway to our own potential with ease. The simplicity of this astrological system lies in its ability to easily examine the essence of each person's unique energetic makeup, rather than looking at planetary influences based on time and complicated placements, which are the foundation of more familiar, conventional systems.

A Pleiadian-Earth Energy Astrology chart can never completely define the totality of any person, but it does carry a golden opportunity for deep exploration into the recurring patterns or spirals of energy that confound or delight us. To become more conscious humans means to evolve beyond dysfunctional patterns. The chart not only reveals our energetic makeup but also simplifies our complex dance with the other energies that affect us. As we begin to explore this system of discovery, subtle but definite changes in awareness begin to grow. This is a system for self-exploration. It is a system for peace and harmony, designed to help humanity become more conscious citizens of the universe. The Pleiadians have given us a tremendous gift, and it is up to us to use it wisely.

Venus and Duality

Venus, which Pleiadians consider to be the star (although it is actually a planet) with the greatest influence on humanity, moves in specific rhythms, shining love in all Her aspects into the shadows and light of each person's being. Named for the Roman goddess of love and beauty, the planet Venus presents two faces of morning star or evening star, depending on where She is in Her cyclical orbit. This feminine attribute has contributed to long-standing views that Venus is, according to some cosmologies, a representation of the Divine Feminine. In fact, multiple goddesses and religious figures have been associated with Venusian energy, beginning with the Sumerian goddess Inanna, known as the Queen of Heaven and Earth, and moving forward to modern Christian representations of the great Mother Mary and Mary Magdalene. Even the 30,000–25,000 BCE stone figure of a woman discovered in 1908 in a cave near the Austrian village of Wilendorf was named after Venus because of the long-standing association between the female form and Venus. Recognition of the special import of Venus on humanity has been in our conscious awareness for a very long time.

SCIENTIFIC PERSPECTIVE

There are currently accepted facts about the planet Venus. Venus and Earth began as planetary twins, born into the universe at approximately the same time. Venus is the closest planet to Earth and has similar size and mass. Yet Venus's sky appears orange, while Earth's sky appears blue. Part of the reason for this difference is that more than sixteen hundred giant volcanoes puncture the surface of Venus, some of which are still active, along with many smaller volcanoes. And while Venus may once have possessed oceans of carbon dioxide and water that helped shape Her surface (and were perhaps hospitable to life), those are now gone. Scientists believe the entire surface of Venus has been remodeled through time.

Although many of Venus's astronomical and geophysical characteristics are similar to our planet's, there are profound differences in appearance and movement. Venus is one of only two known planets in the universe to rotate clockwise in retrograde rotation* (backward) on its axis, and this rotation is so slow that it stretches the definition of rotation; it occurs once every 243 Earth days. According to the Pleiadians, periodic alignment with the retrograde rotation of Venus enables us to break cycles and patterns that do not serve our evolution. (Breaking these cycles and patterns will be more fully explained in chapter 11.) Therefore, this planet becomes a critical influence in the Pleiadian-Earth Energy Astrology system.

THE EARTH-VENUS DANCE

Venus's rhythms are unique because Her circular orbit around the Sun is in synchronization with Earth's orbit around the Sun, reflecting opposite views of similar patterns we experience on Earth. On Earth we are continually aware of opposites. At the lower levels of awareness all opposites can seem threatening or negative. At the higher levels of awareness we learn to recognize that opposites are simply different perspectives that contribute to the whole. Venus offers us a consistent portal to access higher states of consciousness in our experience

---

*The other planet that rotates clockwise on its axis is Uranus.

of duality, if we choose to pay attention and make conscious choices.

Earth and Venus rotate in a dance with each other around the Sun. When plotting geocentrically from the Earth perspective, a mathematician tracing the path of Venus would draw a beautiful five-pointed star within a mandala. To the naked eye the movement of Venus is more like a spiral or a joining of two spirals in the shape of a heart.

The Earth-Venus dance represents an integration of harmonious energies that express in the relationship pattern of the golden mean, often called "the divine proportion." The golden mean is a mathematical ratio based on phi that forms a 1.618 relationship between measured sides and is a fundamental building template frequently found in Nature, most visibly in the beautiful nautilus shell. A spatial relationship that also appears in architecture throughout the ages, it is found by dividing a line into two parts in such a way that the longer part

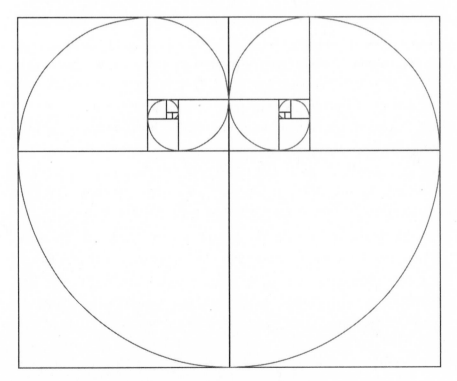

Figure 5.1. Golden mean reflection

divided by the smaller part is also equal to the entire length divided by the longer part. This ratio can also be seen in the relationship between some numbers, which we call the Fibonacci sequence. Each number in the Fibonacci sequence is the sum of the two numbers preceding it (0, 1, 1, 2, 3, 5, 8, 13, 21, 34, and so on).

The relationship between these energetic forces, according to Venus Star Point® astrologer Arielle Guttman, keeps the forces of Nature working together in harmony.[1]

Musical scales unfold according to this cosmic measurement, and humans are proportioned within this same design, as approximated by Leonardo da Vinci in his 1490 drawing titled *Vitruvian Man*.* Within this sequence of the golden mean, the numbers five, eight, and thirteen take on special significance to the orbit of Venus in relation to Earth. Venus loops every 1.618 years, creating a perfect five-pointed geometric star in eight years as viewed from Earth. Before beginning a new loop of 1.618 years, She pauses for forty days at the point that has just been created. Venus revisits each of the five points every 250 years. After She revisits each of the five points, Venus begins weaving a new pattern in the sky. The full cycle from beginning to end takes 1,250 years. These patterns affect humanity's evolution. There are numerous mathematical equations showing the significance of the Earth-Venus dance and the way it affects us here on Earth.

To explain it another way, the five points of the Venus mandala are created in eight Earth years, which equal approximately thirteen Venus years.

Here is a third way of explaining the magical relationship between Venus and Earth: Venus orbits the Sun in approximately 225 Earth days. Earth orbits the Sun in 365 days. Divide the time of Earth's orbit (365 days) by Venus's orbit (225 days) and you come remarkably close to the ratio of the golden mean of 1.618.

Vitruvian Man, drawn by Leonardo da Vinci circa 1490, is exhibited at the Gallerie dell' Accademia, Venice, Italy.

It would appear that to gain greater access to the beauty and harmony of life, humanity would do well to better organize life according to this divine proportion, or golden mean. For the purposes of this book, we will point out how each place that Venus touches in Her dance with Earth brings a particular set of gifts and a particular set of challenges. As one of the most far-reaching influences on humanity, Venus shows us how we are individual parts of the collective and how we individually affect the whole. It is Venus that shows us the truth about how we *relate*, which we feel is the most important element we can examine in our search for higher consciousness. This influence gives us a deeper understanding of the interweaving of all relationships.

THE VENUS INFLUENCE

As we just explained, Venus takes eight years to trace a full five-pointed star, forming a Venus-Sun conjunction at the end of each cycle. Arielle Guttman calls this position a Venus Star Point.[2] It is at this point that Venus is at a perihelion, the closest point to the Sun, where from our perspective She pauses for forty days before beginning a new cycle. This forty-day pause is considered a retrograde motion—the planet appears to slow, stop, and then reverse course—from the Earth perspective. Because Venus appears retrograde at Her nearest position to Earth as well as to the Sun, She also appears brightest at these times.

The influence of any planet in retrograde feels as if things on Earth are working backward (or not at all). The experience of retrograde relationships shows us that there are two ways of looking at life or of relating to the universe. A retrograde position offers an opportunity to view life in a detached, objective, and impersonal manner if we allow ourselves to move outside of our normal reactive patterns to whatever may be occurring. The optical illusion of a planet's apparent backward motion provides a symbolic second chance for us to revisit old ground and retrace our steps—or change them—giving us a tremendous opportunity to break old patterns and live more in the flow of each energy as it arrives in each new moment. Planets in retrograde retard our usual progress and impel us to examine the areas affected by each planet's influence, which at times can be very challenging.

The pause in movement of Venus at a conjunction with the Sun is an important evolutionary influence on Earth, as the light of the Sun joins the love represented by Venus to bring a sense of cosmic unity to our earthly dualistic experience. Not only is this important by itself, but the forty-day retrograde period of Venus coincides with the Pleiadian collective shadow periods (which will be discussed more fully in chapter 11), clearly spelling out that there is a prospect for change each time Venus pauses before giving humanity a different view of reality. The question is, how can we individually and collectively participate with these changing energies?

As a collective we earthlings are given portals of opportunity to unwind old dysfunctional beliefs and patterns every time Venus shines Her light at the end of Her current cycle. The message is clear: look at where you are and make more enlightened choices!

Five Star Points are created during the looping pattern of Venus's cycle around the Sun. These five points remain active, influencing us individually and collectively on Earth until Venus completes an entire l,250-year cycle and begins again. (See color plate 1 at the back of the book.) Venus rotates into a different zodiac sequence every 250 years. Five of these rotations over a 1,250-year period complete a Venus star mandala.

Venus spends 260 days as the morning star and 260 days as the evening star, moving from point to point as She weaves Her mandala in the sky. Every time She passes through one point in Her orbit and begins Her dance with another energy, which occurs approximately every nine and a half of our months (the average time of human gestation from conception to birth), a shift in energy occurs on the planet and in our personal lives. It could be considered a time of rebirthing. If we study the characteristics of each universal energy in chapter 6, it is easy to see that the energy of nine, harmony, is completely aligned with these

Venusian shifts. We would go so far as to say that Venus is prodding us to experience life from another perspective in order to bring more understanding and harmony into our lives. Understanding the movements of Venus can bring wonder and guidance into what otherwise often seems a very unpredictable and inexplicable world.

Venus expresses thirteen phases of "personality" during one full rotation between Her positions as a morning star, then evening star, and back to morning star again. Each of us aligns with one of these particular Venusian personalities in our own life journey. Soul-sign astrologer Adam Gainsburg has named these phases of Venus according to the specific energies each phase typifies.[3] We find his categorization synchronous with the universal energies we have listed in this book. As we discuss each phase below, we will compare his listing to the universal energy listings we have been given by Laarkmaa.

It would seem that Venus is in complete resonance with cosmic rhythms and cycles, and as She interweaves Her energy with Earth, we have the opportunity to investigate each of these energies from the perspective reflected to us by Venus during a particular phase. Each phase has an impact on our individual lives through offering specific characteristics and influences that help to form the outer personality and interaction with the outer world. As we learn to understand and appreciate all the phases of Venus and all the universal energies, we move toward integrating our fractured individual parts into one harmonious whole.

INTERPRETING THE ENERGY

The first step in assessing the influence of Venus is to note Her position as either the morning or evening star. From our perspective, Venus remains in the position of the morning star for 260 days before disappearing. After a brief period in which She is invisible, She reappears as the evening star for 260 days. Venus begins her retrograde loop while She is still an evening star and completes it just before resuming Her position as the morning star. Because Venus moves much more slowly into visibility as the evening star and much more quickly into position as the morning star, it can *appear* that the morning star phase is longer. But in reality, She spends about the same amount of time in each phase.

Individually, we usually connect with one or the other of those specific positions of Venus, regardless of the particular phase she is expressing. Those who resonate with Venus as the morning star are often more practical and assertive than those who resonate more deeply with Venus as the evening star. The position of Venus as the evening star is more receptive, and those who resonate with that energy are often more collectively or cosmically oriented and less earthbound in lifestyle. But having an affinity for Venus as either the morning or evening star does not mean that we are more or less aware of cosmic wisdom. The difference is simply how we *apply* that cosmic wisdom in our day-to-day lives. We feel that an evolved and balanced person can reflect personal attributes of both positions.

The phases of Venus described by Gainsburg match the universal energies, although the length of each phase as we measure it on Earth varies from the periods of universal energies, which last approximately one day of our earthly experience from inception to completion. Page 55 shows a comparison of the phases of Venus as suggested by Gainsburg and the universal energies described by Laarkmaa. You can see how each phase, named for specific characteristics of that phase, matches the universal energies that will be described in more detail in chapter 6.

The direction of rotation or spin of a planet is determined by the degree of tilt on its axis. As noted earlier, all of the planets in our solar system except Venus and Uranus orbit the Sun in a counterclockwise direction. Venus orbits in a clockwise direction, which aligns Her energy with our orientation to time and forward "progress" here on Earth. Yet as discussed above, Venus also directs us to explore duality through the lens of unity: how do polar-opposite viewpoints benefit the harmonic whole? This we have, as a collective, failed to do. Those who are sensitive can actually feel the shifts of Venus from phase to phase. Others may sense that something has changed, without understanding just what that something is or how to use it. The Pleiadian-Earth Energy Astrology system provides tools for reaching harmony through the guidance of Venus and other cosmic systems. The influence of Venus as She rotates through various star points (angles or conjunctions with the Sun) every nine and a half months influences how we think and how we act as a society and as a world. Each star point has a particular influence that is reflected in society and expressed individually as well. When Venus moves into Her next position, we ourselves, individually and collecltively, begin to perceive our world from a different vantage point.

Gainsburg's 13 Venus Phases	Laarkmaa's 13 Universal Energies
Inception	Initiation
Gestation	Duality
Birth	Creation
Emergence	Foundation
Fullness	Change
Surrender and Discovery	Flow
Immersion	Merge
Transmutation	Connect
Rebirth	Harmonize
Remembering and Embodiment	Manifest
Wholeness	Illuminate
Completion	Understand
Transition	Complete-Integrate

We may see the Venus star as Arielle Guttman has described it, as having a head, two helping hands, and two supporting feet. Each point on the pentagram represents one of the above features. People or situations occurring at each of these astrological star points affect us in positive or negative ways, urging us to delve more deeply into our understanding of relationships with everyone and everything. These rotations reflect energies that Guttman has aligned with Western astrological influences as archetypes for specific zodiac signs. For those who follow Western astrology, these alignments serve to orient us to the energies that may be present. However, because Western astrology is divided into twelve sections, not thirteen, we believe that as wonderful as this alignment may be, something is missing in determining the full meaning of what Venus wishes to share in Her changing perspectives. Following the actual sky movement, the astronomical phases of Venus that align with the thirteen universal energies described by the Pleiadians, we can easily fill in this missing piece.

It is important to remember that everything in the universe, including human life, is made of energy. If you look at the pattern of relationships, you can see how one energy is drawn to another to complement an aspect of the self that needs to be discovered. This has very little to do with outer personalities, other than the fact that personalities are formed by energies and certain patterns of energetic response.

Often, people wonder, *What was I thinking when I entered into partnership with that person?* or similar questions. Venus shows that the appropriate question is really, What was I *feeling* when I was drawn to that energy? Or, What purpose or function did that energetic interaction serve in my development?

The ultimate question posed by Venus is always this: how do I give and receive love in every situation?

Our most recent and important view of Venus came from the angelic kingdom, when Pia received a message from the angel Gabriella (known by many as Archangel Gabriel) about the true influence of Venus on human evolution. We share that angelic perspective here to close our discussion on Venus.

You need to share with others the view of Venus from the angelic realm. The energy of Venus can be seen as a five-pointed star. You can feel the energy of Venus through your heart and your energetic connections at any time. To understand Venus through your mind, you must examine archetypes, numbers, and symbols that define Her influence on worldly events and on you individually.

But the true vision of Venus can be better understood if you see Her energy as part of the angelic kingdom, which is working with humanity for evolution. This is the view from the heart. Using the meaning of colors and numbers as shared by Laarkmaa, the energy of Venus can be understood from a feeling perspective.

Each point of the star represents a particular energy that can be perceived as a wave of energetic color and can be associated with a particular archangel. [See color plate 2 at the back of the book.]

The eastern point of Venus contains golden light, bringing grace into the human situation. It is this influence that helps each person to open to possibilities and move past accumulated karma. It is the first point of the star, the point of initiation, where grace pours into the human in that person's current position here on Earth. It is important to remember in third-dimensional timing that grace is available in any moment. You can begin again through the power and assistance of grace simply by turning your attention to the present, claiming responsibility for your choices, and asking for the assistance of the golden light of grace. Here sits my [Gabriella's] angelic energy, ready to assist any who ask to receive grace. Yet in order for grace to correct what is out of balance and create a more balanced flow, you must take personal human responsibility to act in accordance with what is received. What is received can be freely given to another. If you want grace in your life, you must give grace to others. It is your responsibility and choice to give grace freely from your own heart in harmonious flow with the grace that is being given from the angelic kingdom.

Moving counterclockwise, the second point of Venus is north. This position can be seen as the top of the Venus star. This is the position that defines who you are in your outer personalities through your inner perspectives of yourselves and your world. This second point represents duality and the split you experience in your dualistic, polar experience on Earth. Here sits Archangel Michael, ready to cut through all illusions and guide you to the true reality. Yet you must be willing to see through the illusion by letting go of your attachments to polarity.

Good and bad no longer exist when the illusion is removed, for as Laarkmaa has shown you [Pia], even the dark serves the light. The northern point of Venus contains white and blue light. The white energy represents clarity, purity, and truth. The blue energy represents trust. Archangel Michael will help any who ask to see past delusions defined by polar perspectives, but you must be willing to really look in order to see with clarity. You must be willing to purify your thoughts, meaning that you stop judging everything and everyone and even yourself. Truth can only be revealed when you remove the glasses of judgment. Archangel Michael is there for you to turn to when you need an infusion of trust, when you need to understand that if you trust the wisdom of the universe and participate through responsible choices, truth will always be revealed. Only truth that is based on unity rather than separation can lead you to the love you seek.

The third and western point of Venus contains the energy of pink. This is the direction that feeds your subconscious thoughts and the direction from which you can intuit what is real. When you move into this position after integrating the clarity, purity of thought, and truth gained at the second point of Venus, you can be overwhelmed at the recognition of the love that you seek and find here. Archangel Raphaella, who brings an understanding of unconditional love, governs the third point of Venus. The energetic point of this position represents the reality of love that is ever-present and available to you at all times. Love is the highest force in the universe, and Archangel Raphaella sits in this position to show you how you can create whatever you need through the power of love.

The fourth and fifth points on the star of Venus represent the feet, supporting you and your earthly experience. These positions are filled with the energetic color of emerald green, the color of healing. Archangels Ariel (on the left) and Uriel (on the right) govern these two points, showing you how you can heal yourselves, your world, and anything that is out of balance when you incorporate the energy of the other points of Venus.

The center of Venus is infused with the color yellow surrounded by violet. These are the energies of joy and transcendence. Your own inner angel sits at this point, encouraging the flaming of your divine spark. The color violet represents every transformation you choose, and the color yellow holds the energy of illumination, which brings joy. This is the place where Venus connects your heart to the universe and you recognize that you are one with all that is. The joy of transcending to this place can be experienced at any time, when you move your perceptions out of the way. This is the place of peace.

6

THE THIRTEEN
UNIVERSAL ENERGIES

Laarkmaa gave us the Pleiadian wisdom of universal energies to share with the world. Here, you will learn to work with each energy to understand its inherent value. We live in accordance with these energies, either aware or unaware of what they ask of us or how to appropriately respond to their influence. *Universe* means "turned toward unity," and working with these energies brings humanity into unity with the cosmos. The energies, one to thirteen, represent qualities of movement that carry us from separation into unified consciousness. When we participate with universal energies they invite us to transcend any lived experiences rooted in perceptions of polarity. They explain duality's role in the cosmic whole, and by studying them—as instructed by the Pleiadians—we begin to embrace the world of dualistic opposites as the gift that transforms our consciousness.

Numbers are not just numbers—merely used to count or measure—but are very specific energies. When we learn to work with these energies correctly and choose how we participate in life, we are more aligned with universal flow. We call these energies "universal" to remind us that we can engage life at a cosmic level in every moment. Humans are not the most advanced life-forms in the universe, nor are we the most intelligent. We need to understand all life has value—

within our world and beyond—and universal energies help us to do this. We chose to come and work on third-dimensional Earth, where most of our choices focus on our perception of the physical plane. It's time to awaken and realize that what we think, feel, and do here on Earth ripples out and affects everything in the universe. Our choice is that powerful. And learning about the universal energies will guide us to make more awakened and evolved choices, thus bringing us into harmony with cosmic flow.

Each universal energy carries a specific vibration that affects us in precise ways. We are magnetically drawn to respond to life by the influence of our unique universal energy and our relationship to energies that are different from our own. Although these energies are numbered, there is no hierarchical order because the *energy* of the number is more important than its numerical position. Discovering the larger story being shared (as designated by a universal energy's number) is rather like discovering the intrinsic value of gold. Like gold, golden energy carries beauty, grace, and healing properties. Likewise, the numerical value of each universal energy has more intrinsic value than its linear placement in a hierarchical numbering scheme. The meaning of the number is all that matters.

The Pleiadians explain there are thirteen universal energies in a spiral of cosmic movement. There are also twenty earth energies that we work with simultaneously with the universal ones. The Maya marked the movement of the universal energies within each of the twenty groups of earth energies—or periods in their annual 260-day cycle—calling them *trecenas,* meaning "groups of thirteen," which can be applied to different earth circumstances. Similarly, Laarkmaa helps us understand our individual place in the universe and our role in the development of human evolution through teaching the details of our individual energies and how we can use them harmoniously with others. We learn by aligning ourselves with these energies as we experience them in our daily lives. What occurs is literally a movement of energy, and we perceive these experiences as the true passage of time (instead of the old, conventional linear time). The purpose and gifts of the universal energies are described briefly as follows. As you look at the gifts carried by these energies, begin to see how one is linked to the next in a continual flow throughout the cycle of thirteen. As already stated, because these energies spiral there is no hierarchy or greater importance to any of the energies. Each one is absolutely valuable and necessary in the cycle of unified awareness. Begin anywhere on the spiral and see how each energy is born from and flows into the next energy.

The thirteen universal energies can be experienced as a process of initiation, dualistic perspective, creativity, foundaton, change, flow, merging, connection, harmony, manifestation, illumination, understanding, and completion—which then link to a new cycle of initiation, dualism, and so on.

1. INITIATION AND NEW BEGINNINGS

The first energy is the energy of *initiation* and new beginnings. Its energy, coming directly from Source, is filled with unity, possibility, and intention and is used to create new thoughts, ideas, and opportunities. When the energy of initiation is present, things begin to happen. This energy can also be considered the point of focusing awareness. It's clearly an opportunity to begin new projects, expand thinking toward new ideas, or initiate projects that can make a difference in your life.

As the point of potentiality—where anything and everything is possible—you set intentions for what comes next. By focusing on initiation energy you bring the attention into the present moment over and over again, always beginning from where you are right now. People who carry the energy of initiation in their makeup are forceful and assertive. They like to start projects and excel at trying new things. It's important for them to keep the momentum of evolution moving forward, always expanding into new developments.

2. PULSE OF DUALITY

In the second energy the unified force powerfully splits into opposites. The pulse of *duality* gives us the opportunity to see viewpoints other than our own. The purpose of this energy is to expand from one idea to many in order to enlarge our overall perspective. Individual gifts can be offered to the whole. In our current reality humans constantly misunderstand (and subsequently misuse) the energy of two, thanks to beliefs formed from opposing views of reality. Thus, judgments and the accompanying feelings of separation unintentionally create lives that are constantly full of conflict, competition, and struggle. It's the experience of a dynamic tension between polar opposites. Yet two is primarily about learning the cosmic lesson that one aspect of duality actually complements its opposite. When we begin to understand and use this energy cooperatively—as intended—our constant sense of pain and separation will cease to exist because our individual judgments and beliefs of separation will cease to exist.

People carrying two energy in their vibrational makeup sometimes have a mystical component to them. And although they are often full of visionary insights, most experience many conflicts until they learn (and show others) how cooperation is more powerful than competition.

Days composed of two energy are often full of tremendous conflicts or oppositions, calling us to see and honor differences by finding ways to merge them harmoniously. The energy of two is present to help us understand how polarized opposites can and must work together. As one of Pia's clients commented, "Duality is a great opportunity to practice alchemy," which expresses the inherent gift in living on a dualistic planet. If you carry two energy in your vibrational makeup, part of your mission is to live by example so that others will understand that all of our differences are actually gifts. In the energy of two there's a greater opportunity to recognize and correct every place where we compete for what we believe is "right" or justify our ideas (over others) as being the only correct or accurate ones. When we use the energy of two properly, we complement each other. Thus, the pain and separation of duality cease to exist when we learn principles of cooperation that are offered in two energy.

There is another aspect of duality that we desperately need to understand during these chaotic times. Because we spend our lives misunderstanding and misusing duality, we experience extremes of everything—hot and cold, light and dark, male and female, and so on. At the very end of this spectrum is the duality of life and death. Understanding that the lens we use to view our Earth experience grossly distorts the dualistic perspective, we may come to regard life and death as opposite sides of the same thing. Just as hot and cold come together to create warmth, and female and male join in ecstatic union, life and death are not as different as we may think. The energy of a person lives on after physical death. Many people report communications between the living and those who have crossed over to another plane. Life and death are actually part of a grand cycle, yet humans see them as separate because of our misguided dualistic perspective. We could lessen our own grief in the presence of death by simply embracing the true meaning of duality. Both life and death (or any polar opposites) are actually varying aspects of the same thing— energy that never dies but takes different forms in the evolutionary spiral of consciousness.

3. CREATING

The third energy is about *creativity*. At this point the creative energy from Source begins to flow and move. Intentions set in the energy of one and shared in the energy of two begin to create possibilities in the energy of three. Creatively, our intentions become visible. If we are working in the universal system of spiraling energies, it becomes quite apparent—in the energy of three—that what we *think* at the level of initiation (or one energy) matters. How we share our ideas with others (in two energy) enhances the creative abilities that arise in three energy. Duality brings different perspectives to enhance our inspired and imaginative possibilities. Days that carry the energy of three bring opportunities for creating what we have intended and shared. People who carry this energy in their vibrational makeup may be restless, struggling when stillness is required. They are usually expressive, artistic, and love to create. Their energy of three compels them to find peaceful solutions to both internal and external conflicts. Their job is to help create from the intentions and cooperation that have been achieved through using the previously experienced energies of initiation and duality.

4. FOUNDATION

The fourth energy defines our reality and sets boundaries on our experience. This energy reflects all that we have intended, shared, and created—whether we like it or not. Four energy lays the *foundation* for our creations. It provides stability, yet if we focus only on the energy of four, we can experience being rigid or stuck. Days that have four energy are not good times for movement, whether it's physical travel or presenting new ideas. People with four energy share it through practical and realistic applications of what has come before and don't easily change their minds. The energy of four provides a very good look at the foundations we have created. If we don't like them, the opportunity for change will arrive at the next level of spiraling energies.

5. OPPORUNITY TO CHANGE

The fifth energy in the spiral of consciousness offers us an *opportunity to change* our path or adjust our intentions. Here, we can first fully experience our own power, the power of choice. We realize possibilities through changing and expanding our intentions. Life itself is change and continually expands through movement, which is necessary for survival. Flexibility promotes adaptability, allowing alignment with cosmic guidance. Days that have five energy are excellent for reconsidering one's progress and making adjustments where necessary. This energy is curious by nature and encourages us to consider the unimaginable. People who have five energy in their vibrational makeup may struggle between being erratic and being flexible. Change comes in many colors, but it is always present. A person with five energy needs to practice waiting before acting on the impulse for change that arises through everyday living and learning. It's important to consider how the intended change will affect everyone and everything in that person's orbit.

6. FLOW

The sixth energy is the energy of *flow*. It develops, refines, and improves itself as it contacts and interacts with other energies in the universe. It transcends all conflict through seeking to blend or merge opposites into harmony. The energy of six can be compared to a river with no boundaries. It cannot be constrained or contained, because like water, it always finds a way to recreate itself in the existing circumstances. The energy of six understands movement. It's never what it will be. Following the fifth energy of change, the sixth energy instills a sense of flow in life. Days guided by this energy are excellent times for movement of any type. It helps us remain aware that all potential challenges can be resolved through flowing over, through, or around them, rather than resisting or competing in conflict. Those who carry six energy are always looking for ways to improve situations or circumstances. They may be overly critical in their search for harmony and must learn to become tolerant and nonjudgmental as part of the improvements they seek. Once acceptance becomes an internal guide, those with six energy can bring harmony to the world. This energy continues the theme of survival by teaching us to flow through all circumstances. The secret to working with universal six energy is remembering that when we flow through every experience without trying to make it something other than what it is, life goes much more smoothly.

7. MERGING WORLDS

The seventh energy represents a doorway between worlds. It lies exactly midway between initiation and completion, allowing us to examine our path. Seven is a mystical energy, calling us to decipher and understand hidden truths. The energy of seven opens our vision. The perceived veil is an illusion because all kingdoms and dimensions are here right now. In essence, we could say that the energy of seven shows us the veil itself is a human misconception, existing in our consciousness because we misunderstand the energy of two. We have been participating with and creating a world of illusion; we don't yet understand the true purpose of living in duality on Earth. The seven energy brings the opportunity to resolve and transcend all of the conflicts we have created through that misunderstanding. The energy of seven seeks to *merge opposites* into harmony, thus providing a direct connection to Source. It helps us to remember that not only are we divine, we also are part of the divinity of everything. The seven energy provides opportunities to work with both the spiritual and physical aspects of life simultaneously. Days of seven energy inspire us to step out from illusory beliefs and search for cosmic truth. People who carry this energy may act as mirrors, showing us how we are behaving in the world or who we are. Yet many who carry seven energy are blinded by the light of truth and unable to see their own reflection. Focusing on cooperation and truth in the energy of seven compels us to continue on the path, looking for ways we can more easily connect.

8. CONNECTION AND ABUNDANCE

The eighth energy provides the connection we have been seeking. It's not a coincidence that the numerical symbol for eight is an infinity loop turned on end. This is the energy of *connection and abundance*. It represents love—the most important energy in the universe, which unconditionally connects us all. The infinity symbol shows us how we are mirror images of one another, connected at the center. In the energy of eight we can discover there is no need for competition; cooperation is much more connecting. We may feel richer (abundant in friends, health, or happy attitudes) and more connected on days that carry eight energy. People who have this energy in their vibrational makeup gather different ideas and perspectives into their lives, seeking to connect the dots on the map. They may love to travel. And while some of their ideas are definitely beyond what's considered normal, they are rarely unbalanced in their grasp of the true reality. They hold within them the secret of In Lak'ech. Recognizing ourselves in others is the source of all connection and the greatest abundance possible.

9. HARMONY

The ninth energy takes everything accumulated in the spiral of consciousness thus far and seeks to harmonize it. Nine energy is the essence of *harmony*. If we have appropriately applied each of the evolutionary energies encountered thus far, we are now ready to see how everything can be harmoniously interconnected as we step into the energy of nine. This shows us how to blend everything that's different and create harmony from opposites. Days with nine energy are usually peaceful days, full of the vibration of cooperation. People who carry this energy enjoy engaging the details that connect the individual to the whole. They have deep convictions about peace and will ceaselessly work toward that goal. They may also struggle with discouragement when they cannot find the harmony they seek. The secret to reaching harmony always appears when we follow our hearts and seek the highest good for all.

10. PHYSICAL MANIFESTATION

The tenth energy lets us know how we are progressing on the spiral of consciousness. If we set intentions for the highest good as we initiated the new cycle in one energy, shared other perspectives cooperatively in the energy of two, allowed the addition of new creative thought in the energy of three, firmed the foundation for our intentions in the energy of four, self-corrected our journey in the energy of five, managed to flow through or around obstacles rather than allowing them to deter us with six energy, merged with expanded possibilities in seven, connected deeply with one another in eight energy, and attained harmony in nine, the energy of ten offers us a chance to *manifest in the physical* what we intended at the beginning of the cycle (initiated with one energy). Unfortunately, most humans—even those who believe themselves to be awake and aware—still don't understand this flow. And those who may know about these cycles usually don't consistently follow this flow because of interference from artificial time, dysfunctional beliefs, and selfish, separating behaviors. When choices are made from this false perspective of life, the energy of ten can be exceedingly challenging. It will feel like chaos, and we may wonder how we ever arrived at the state we are experiencing. This is the state of humanity today—confused, inconsistent, and unbalanced. A ten day in our current paradigm can often feel confusing or disorienting. Challenges may arrive at every turn. The current structure of the third dimension is based on separation, competition, greed, and fear. There is very little mindfulness for what we are collectively creating through our thoughts, beliefs, and actions. Is it any wonder our world is so troubled?

People who carry ten energy in their vibrational makeup usually intuitively understand the power of manifestation and will more easily see challenges as opportunities. They may also see the link between thoughts and physical reality more clearly. Although influenced by the collective chaos, these people are actually here to help us understand the importance of our thoughts and our attitudes. The Pleiadians and other star beings are trying very hard to help us regain our alignment with cosmic flow. The system of Pleiadian-Earth Energy Astrology is an exceptionally valuable tool for redefining the truth of our reality and preparing us to become galactic citizens.

11. ILLUMINATION

Eleven is the energy of *illumination*, bringing a new awareness and helping us to see reality. If we had trouble in the energy of ten, eleven is here to light our way. It strips away illusions and allows us to see the truth, if only we will open our eyes and our hearts. The energy of eleven encourages us to be aware of all things—physical and nonphysical—that don't feed our vision or contribute to our spiritual journey. Eleven energy is like that of the planet Neptune in Western astrology; it helps us gain a greater perspective of a larger truth. The energy of eleven allows us to free ourselves from things we no longer need or that no longer serve the highest good. This energy may push buttons we'd prefer to ignore, yet the pain we experience only exists because we are resisting the truth. When this energy is experienced at its highest frequency, illumination is possible—for an instant, for a day, or an eternity. Days with eleven energy are best for seeking new perspectives and ways to serve unity. People with this energy may be drawn to explore or connect with other energies to help enlighten humanity. They may find it easier to trust in the universe and in possibilities, as they acknowledge the illuminating truth that brings graceful simplicity to manifesting light and love into our confused and chaotic third-dimensional world.

12. UNDERSTANDING

The energy of twelve is the energy of *understanding*. This is where we finally understand that there is no difference between endings and beginnings; when something ends, something new is automatically born. People who carry twelve energy have an intuitive and deep understanding of death and transcendence. They also have a unique ability to see many perspectives simultaneously, revealing the whole picture at once. Days that carry twelve energy help us understand everything that has come before on the energetic spiral in preparation for the final integration that will arrive in the energy of thirteen. Through the understanding of twelve we accept where we are and prepare to begin again. Days with twelve energy are rejuvenating, returning what we may have lost. This energy is useful for self-renewal through the little deaths that happen in every present moment, preparing for what comes next. People with twelve energy usually understand its rejuvenative properties and are often drawn to helping restore old things or broken people. They make excellent counselors. Within the energy of twelve the excitement of things to come coexists with a letting go of things that have already passed; it continually brings recognition that each ending begins something new. To use it properly we must allow both past and future to fade as we focus on the present moment, having understood what came before and remaining open to what yet remains a mystery. Using the energy of twelve helps us remember that only in the present can we prepare for the unknown future.

13. COMPLETION

The energy of thirteen is the energy of *completion*. It's in this energy that we can fully integrate everything we've learned. It represents ascension and a return to Source. All has been completed, and we are ready to return to the void to begin a new cycle. The darkness of the void brings clarity, and we must be willing to enter that black stillness to find the answers we seek. From a lack of understanding, modern cultures continually ignore or dismiss this energy, thereby denying possibilities of greater understanding. One reason humanity appears completely stuck in our developmental progress is because modern cultures worldwide do not honor the energy of thirteen. It is even considered unlucky in many circles. The reasons for this were addressed eloquently in Pia's book *Sacred Retreat: Using Natural Cycles to Recharge Your Life*. During the ancient matriarchal goddess cultures, women connected to Nature and to the cosmos because they used the energy of their thirteen menstrual cycles and the thirteen cycles of the Moon to guide them. When patriarchal cultures overtook matriarchal cultures, the number and energy of thirteen was shifted to represent an unlucky energy to be avoided at all costs. Whether or not they understood what they were doing, the patriarchy's actions initiated a movement to separate humans from Nature. This proved to be an enormous cosmic mistake, as it also separated humanity from the rest of the universe. The 2006 discovery of the dwarf planet* Eris along with growing acknowledgement of Ophiuchus have arrived in our consciousness at this juncture because we are finally ready to integrate all that has occurred on our human journey. Perhaps we are ready at last to say, *We're done. Let's begin something new as the new humans.*

There's a radical frequency shift in the energy of thirteen, representing a fulfillment of the creative impulse (that began in the initiation energy of one) and a readiness to greet what comes next. Days that carry the energy of thirteen offer the opportunity to quiet our minds and seek answers beyond the limits of the third dimension. People who carry this energy are illusion busters. They may have clairvoyant experiences or prophetic dreams, for they are, in a sense, living between what has been and what will be. Unexpected forces and changes will always be a part of their lives. If we resist these changes, we may experience more challenges. But if these forces and changes are embraced, humanity can ascend into a new form.

Universal cycles spiral through thirteen energies—the number needed to energetically integrate previous experiences and reach completion before beginning the next level of conscious exploration. We—collective humanity—still view time through an arbitrary linear lens, ignoring the spiraling cycles of time in Nature and relying instead on artificial calendars and clocks. We must assimilate both our Earth and cosmic views to make the necessary changes in our understanding

---

*Dwarf planets are too small to be considered planets but too large to fall into smaller categories and fail to meet other criteria that would qualify them as planets. However, they can have a powerful influence on our behaviors on Earth. Pluto was downgraded from planet to dwarf planet very recently, yet Pluto continues to have a tremendous impact on humanity. There are many known and unknown dwarf planets in the universe.

of the world. While we respect science, we can't always wait for it to decide what is real because our actual experience may reveal a wider reality. The transition from manmade clocks and calendars to cosmic universal spirals of reality requires being able to bring cosmic flow into existing structures—to experience the flow firsthand by understanding the energy itself. Nothing can prevent this, if the heart is curious and willing.

This begins with a thorough understanding that within a universal sequence, each energy lasts for roughly a twenty-four hour Earth period, from sunset to sunset. The actual flow of energy changes at sunset each day and each subsequent change builds on previous experience to enlarge it. Yet we continue to organize our lives by twenty-four hour clocks instead of synchronizing with the heart-brain. We neglect to add "flow" to our tightly held schedules, eventually creating burnout and confusion. Humans are seemingly locked into false impressions of dualities that we do not innately recognize and that misguide us. No single human being began life this way. Newborns and children who have not yet been socialized innately live in a natural balance and flow.

Unlike our Gregorian calendar measure of time, actual days do not end at midnight and begin anew one minute later. The fluid energy of each day departs as the setting sun brings us a new universal energy to explore. Looking at our third-dimensional days in this manner encourages us to adjust, adapt, and move through them in a way that continues the flow of our evolutionary path. Spirals by nature move both up and down, giving us the freedom and flexibility to explore our earthly environment through emotional, mental, and physical responses to the varying energies within a cycle. We bring consciousness from the heavens downward to Earth, and then we ourselves spiral back upward as our awareness begins to expand. This pattern is repeated often enough for us to feel its rhythm and become cooperative with its gifts, if we so choose. We are lead in a spiral that begins and ends like an ouroboros, the mythical alchemical serpent that ate its own tail, signifying the meaning of infinity, or wholeness. We, like the ouroboros, are being guided to become deeply involved with ourselves in order to see what is out of harmony, then devour it and begin again.

Astrologer and Mayan calendar scholar Bruce Scofield believes the number thirteen is important to human understanding because of the ratio of lunar cycles to solar cycles. He explains that because there are thirteen lunar cycles in one solar year, the ratio of one to thirteen is present at all times in our lives.[1] Laarkmaa is sharing the importance of thirteen cycles with humanity to help us understand our relationship on Earth to our relationship within the cosmos; observing the relationship between the planet Earth and the Sun, and Earth and the thirteen cycles of the Moon enhances our awareness. We begin each cycle in the initiation energy of one, and we complete it in the energy of thirteen as we integrate what we have experienced. Thirteen has also been known as a special number to the Divine Feminine. Women are keenly aware that cycles on Earth begin and end in harmony with the Moon's cycles in the sky. Thirteen is also one of the numbers of the Fibonacci series (generated by adding the two previous numbers five and eight—numbers that are extremely important in the cycles of Venus), described in chapter 5. The mystical qualities of the Fibonacci numbers point to the importance of paying attention to the cosmic spiral of universal energies here on Earth.

We are living in the most special period humanity has ever faced. As a species we have experienced all aspects of duality and have now arrived at an energetic period where we are encouraged to break all old patterns, surrender all limiting beliefs, and step out of fear and separation into true and unconditional love, the essence of unity consciousness. Even if it frightens us, we must act responsibly by looking deeply at our long-cherished beliefs about who we are and our place in the universe. We make the choice to release our dependence on the artificial structures of time as the governor of our reality. Understanding the spirals of universal energy and rearranging our perspective of time as energy helps us step away from the illusion. These thirteen energies are a cosmic reality, and when we work with them, rather than manipulating, controlling, or ignoring them, we manifest a more peaceful world. We become cosmic citizens who live by the principles of Ahimsa (the Hindu and Buddhist principle of nonviolence) and In Lak'ech. We are standing at the portal, and what we choose determines who we will become.

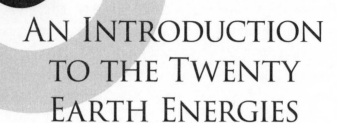

An Introduction to the Twenty Earth Energies

In the Pleiadian-Earth Energy Astrology system, the earth energies work in concert with universal ones. The twenty earth energies emphasize wholeness and unity. Everything that exists unfolds in our experience as a spiraling flow of energies, though we have been trained away from seeing this natural movement of energy. Everything we experience—every manifestation—is energy's intelligence expressing itself as vibration, frequency, or waveform. This astrological system is a language within a language that uses simple numbers to reveal deep universal wisdom, teaching us how to navigate relationships with ourselves, with each other, and with our earthly experience. From the moment of birth these energetic cycles provide endless opportunities to align with our higher wisdom and expand our understanding of who we are in any moment. They create inner psychological movements that cause us to evaluate the complex yet subtle layers of everything we encounter. This elemental language of earth energies is constantly moving to and through us, exposing the concepts and personal tendencies that drive us and all relationships.

Earth energies have a higher and a lower vibration. Our individual life choices—and the degree to which we've developed our conscious awareness—determine whether we choose the high or the low road. The explanations of each earth energy clearly describe the changes required to shift any experience to its higher vibrational possibilities. Many personally conflicting life patterns or mysteries are resolved when we begin applying the wisdom and insights offered in this book. This astrological system is a map for understanding our individual and collective evolution as we move into a deeper relationship with the energies that manifest as all of creation. Earth energies point to the simple resolution of polarities by integrating contrasting energies into the whole. Our positive or negative response to duality is only meant to show how two contrasting elements can work cohesively together.

Like their universal counterparts, the relationship between earth energies is neither linear nor hierarchical; they move in spirals. A quick detour may help you to visualize their circular flow. Imagine you're walking along the perimeter of a wheel with twenty spokes. (In actuality, it's the energies that are moving through your life.) The earth energies sit at the center of the wheel and flow out along its spokes to the outer rim where you are walking. The center of the wheel (or hub) containing the energies represents humanity's "map to oneness"—a gift from the earth energies. Their flow is guidance for your life. And as you walk along the edge of the wheel, touching some spokes while ignoring others, you are actually interacting with the earth energies—your own map to oneness—from every direction. Walking around this circular wheel, you are viewing the guidance of the earth energies from all possible angles and for any given earthly situation. Each individual has a unique map to oneness. And the guidance is complete in its ability to touch every area of your experience.

This simple example demonstrates how it's impossible for hierarchy to exist when the motion is circular. All points on the circle's circumference (or rim) are an equal distance from its center. Therefore, as we view the earth energies (or universal energies, for that matter), they are all equal. Now imagine you're located above a spiral and looking down into its center from above. All you'll see is a circle. But if you look at the same spiral from the side, it clearly appears as a *stack* of many circular rings that give it a certain height or thickness. Therefore, imagine in our simple example above—where we walked along the perimeter of a circle—that in fact we were climbing a small hill, starting at the bottom and slowly winding our way to its top. Can you see or feel the spiral pattern now? An example takes advantage of the "relative motion" that you experience when you're sitting next to another car at a stoplight. When the light turns green, for just a few seconds you're not sure if you're moving, or the car next to you is moving, or both. Now imagine that just for a few moments you can view the motion of the energies relative to you in a similar way. Whether you're moving and the earth energies are still or you're still and they're moving, it is the same thing. Just remember: if you're moving, the energies are stationary (or still), but if the energies are moving, you are at the stationary center. You just successfully mastered a complex mathematical concept.

All energies move in spirals, and you can feel their movement. Pause for a moment to deeply feel this cyclical rhythm of spirals; the path is circular because each energy actually represents the same concept of unity viewed from a different angle. The spiral path accounts for the true experience that every moment is now, and in a very real way, each now-moment is new and unique. We're always viewing everything from our individual perspective, and we haven't yet learned to harmonize those perspectives. This astrological system helps us to do that by showing us that earth energies build on each other, creating a spiraling, nonhierarchical foundation, ceaselessly seeking to help us resolve our duality consciousness. Each energy contributes a key piece of understanding to the puzzle of our entire earthly experience. The explanations for the energies are clear and direct, and their interpretation is straightforward if you allow yourself to always *feel* the earth energy as you study its meaning or even think about it.

At the beginning of each thirteen-day universal cycle of energy, one particular earth energy sets the tone for the next thirteen days of our earthly experience. Earth energies change daily at sunset, flowing from one to the next to the next. However, the tone for the entire thirteen day universal cycle is set by whichever earth energy is present on the first day of that period. We call this first earth energy the evolutionary guidance, as its benevolent influence is felt throughout all thirteen days of any given universal energy cycle. With nothing more than a simple intention, we can train ourselves to feel the quality of each new earth energy as it arrives at sunset. We also experience the most prominent earth energy of this thirteen-day period in its role as the evolutionary guidance.* We can choose to match our actions through aligning more specifically with the daily changes of each earth energy, while simultaneously paying attention to the overall evolutionary guidance energy.

The earth energies are listed below starting with their numerical ordering. Next, their specific details are listed as follows: how they are experienced in the world, their overall gifts, and their use as an evolutionary guiding force. You will notice similarities in all of these energies, because each one reveals the same insights from different angles—our individual maps to oneness.

1. BEING ENERGY

Periods of *Being* energy are highly creative, although people may often feel as if they are struggling to gain a sense of security during these times. The response to this need often produces imbalanced bonding with family, community, or nation, and we may forget that we

---

*If you wish to determine your own specific evolutionary guidance energy, refer to the ephemeris in appendix C. Find your birthdate and the universal number next to it, and then trace the numbers back to 1. The earth energy that appears next to the universal number 1 immediately prior to your birth determines your personal evolutionary guidance. If your birthdate falls in the universal energy of 1, you have a double influence of that particular energy. (Note that if your birthdate falls prior to the ephemeris included in the book, an expanded ephemeris of the years 1900 through 2100 can be found at https://audio.innertraditions.com/pleaen.)

are only secure when we see the entire world as one family and act accordingly.

As an evolutionary guidance, *Being* energy brings creative, initiating impulses and strong emotions. *Being* energy brings visionary gifts and a strong instinctual ability to respond to life in a loving and nurturing way. Overall, the gifts of *Being* energy serve the purpose of urging us to create new, more harmonious responses to life, while releasing old primal needs for things that make us believe we are secure. We do this by listening to our intuition, following our hearts, and learning to trust the universe.

2. BREATHING ENERGY

Periods of *Breathing* energy may feel unstable. This is a restless period, often full of unpredictable changes. We may feel that we cannot control anything in our environment, and it may seem that there are no barriers to protect us or make us feel secure. In *Breathing* energy we may also feel a need to experiment with new ways of expressing ourselves. As an evolutionary guidance, *Breathing* energy helps us to understand that opposites exist to show us different perspectives we must accept and integrate into our reality to be whole. Overall, the gifts of *Breathing* energy are here to help humanity remember that we are all waves of energy and are continually changing as we evolve.

3. LISTENING ENERGY

Periods of *Listening* energy are often perceived as times of trouble in the world. There is a need for deep listening when this energy presents itself, as secrets are often revealed during these times. It can also be a time of insights that lead to new understandings. Days of *Listening* energy offer us regular opportunities to slow down and reconnect to the universe. This energy leaves no room for self-deception or wishful thinking. It is here to bring a spiritual perspective into form on this plane of existence. *Listening* days are opportunities to do the work necessary to be in the silence, integrate your experience, and hear what needs to come next.

As an Evolutionary Guidance *Listening* energy repeatedly calls us into stillness and asks us to find the place where we can act from exceptionally high values and integrity. If we are not careful in this energy, we may find ourselves being critical of others who do not meet the high standards we are seeking. This response can cause us to feel we can't get what we need from the world. However, *Listening* Evolutionary Guidance also instills patience as it compels us to continually seek the wisdom of the heart. The overall gift of this energy is the capacity to create order and form from higher visions by going deeply into the silence of the void, where our worldview can then be expanded.

4. PLANTING ENERGY

Periods of *Planting* energy are positive or lucky times, full of new perceptions and creative ideas. Prosperity comes more easily in this energetic period, which offers opportunities for new beginnings of all kinds—businesses, relationships, ideas, and adventures. However, *Planting* energy also requires that we act maturely, or our efforts will go unfulfilled. To use this energy to manifest something real, we must follow through and share our ideas with others. In turn, many people experience a need for acknowledgment during times of *Planting* energy and want to be recognized for their contributions.

As an Evolutionary Guidance *Planting* energy will always lead us to bring our own ideas into the world. It spurs a need to "make a difference" or to contribute in some way to the betterment of our world and asks us to grow into the full version of who we can be. The overall gift of this energy is the recognition that everything begins with a thought or an intention. Following the energy of those thoughts with intentional actions creates our world.

5. MOVING ENERGY

Periods composed of *Moving* energy are good times for exploring the vast differences between us and learning to integrate those differences in a positive way. *Moving* energy is all about confrontations and discoveries. We can experience the lowest or the highest manifestations of our reality in this energy. Sadly, the usual response to this energy in the world today is to react to everything through competition, aggression, greed, or even war. We have not yet learned as a species how to use the dynamic tension of our differences in a harmonious way to create peace and balance.

As an Evolutionary Guidance, *Moving* energy brings all inner conflicts to the surface for us to understand who we are and how we affect others. This energy offers us the chance to realize the power we have to make changes in the world through the choices we make in each moment. Because the purpose of this energy is to uncover conflict in order to resolve it, humanity is capable of expressing the lowest extremes of experience or attaining our highest ideals. *Moving* energy guides us to return to our hearts for answers whenever emotions are stirred, leading us to move toward the higher versions of who we can be. One of the greatest gifts of *Moving* energy is bringing spiritual integrity into the third dimension. It offers us the opportunity to learn that the spiritual and the physical are the same, that the heart and mind are connected, and that we can merge all opposites in peace when the struggle between differences is surrendered.

6. TRANSCENDING ENERGY

Times of *Transcending* energy can be powerful times for collective goals and manifesting ideals. This energy brings us the ability to move forward and forget old grievances and to trust in new beginnings. The gift of *Transcending* energy is the ability to let go of what no longer serves us individually or serves our world.

The Evolutionary Guidance of *Transcending* energy leads us to learn to transcend anything. It encourages us to use the gift of discernment—rather than judgment—to notice differences and transcend any troubling places within those differences, as we learn to accept what they have to offer. We must remember that all differences or opposites have the potential to bring us closer together in harmony.

7. REMEMBERING ENERGY

Days or periods of *Remembering* energy bring feelings of peace, equality, cooperation, and sensitivity to the needs of others. This energy offers opportunities for seeking balance, cooperation, and merging. These are periods of time when we more easily unite our differences and can find freedom in the joy of service. Periods of this type of energy are intended to help us remember the truth that we are all connected and can all live in abundance. *Remembering* energy is about helping humanity to remember what is possible and to attain it. This energy radiates a sense of peace.

As Evolutionary Guidance energy *Remembering* energy leads us to resolve the paradox between our desire for independence and freedom and our desire to be a part of a family, community, or fellowship. During periods of *Remembering* energy we may feel the urge to travel and learn more about both traditional and unconventional experiences we encounter.

8. LOVING ENERGY

Times of *Loving* energy are generally felt as positive, bringing enthusiasm and productivity. A day or period of time of this energy can bring beauty and harmony into our dualistic experience. However, it does so by bringing opposites into our focus, giving us the choice to integrate them in harmony or create conflict through judgment and blame.

As an Evolutionary Guidance *Loving* energy produces tensions and conflicts to reveal different perspectives. The challenge within this energy is for us to remember to cooperate rather than compete, never forcing others to choose sides, but instead working together in unity. The underlying guidance of *Loving* energy is always to resolve those conflicts in a way that honors opposite perspectives and brings unconditional love into the situation. When we experience tension at these times, we must learn to temper it with kindness, compassion, and grace.

9. FEELING ENERGY

Periods of *Feeling* energy are full of heightened emotions. Laarkmaa tells us that our emotions are signals to change something within ourselves rather than blaming others when we are feeling emotionally upset or personally out of balance. Times of *Feeling* energy are perfect opportunities to step away from our own dysfunctional beliefs and behaviors and change the way we see things. We suffer more during a time of *Feeling* energy if we are unwilling to change in order to grow. This energy offers us the possibility to become masters of awareness through learning to live through our hearts, rather than allowing our anger or unhappiness to determine our choices.

As an Evolutionary Guidance *Feeling* energy teaches us the necessity of being fluid and flexible, responding to life moment by moment. As humans we will continue to experience powerful emotions, but our evolutionary job is to learn how to respond to what we feel by examining and changing ourselves, rather than reacting in old patterns that blame others for what is occurring. *Feeling* energy arrives to teach us to pay attention to our emotional state and choose to change inappropriate thoughts, beliefs, and behaviors.

10. DEVOTING ENERGY

Periods of *Devoting* energy are quite auspicious, bringing waves of cooperation, harmony, success, prosperity, and celebration. These are periods to be used for changing the world into a peaceful place through a spirit of cooperation that we can share with others. This energy is about sharing love and friendship and building community.

As an Evolutionary Guidance *Devoting* energy brings a determined, loyal, persistent approach to life that can offer success and fulfillment. However, our current response to this energy is usually to choose loyalty to ideas or people with whom we agree. To use this energy wisely we must simply remember to choose our loyalties from our hearts, not according to what our minds or societies dictate. Learning to shift our loyalties is evolutionary work. Laarkmaa tells us that the most important loyalty is loyalty to the truth, and as long as we are willing to face the truth and work in harmony with it, we grow.

11. ILLUMINATING ENERGY

Periods of *Illuminating* energy favor curiosity and creativity. There is usually much laughter and joy during these periods, but they are not simply about being happy. These are times that can also be used for healing what is out of balance, whether socially or personally. There is a potential for much drama about circumstances, whether political or personal, during times of *Illuminating* energy. We are offered opportunities to peer deeply into the illusion that has been created by our collective thoughts and beliefs and to shine light into the darkness of our previous misunderstandings. These periods can either deepen the collective illusion, as people immerse themselves more completely into the play on the stage of life, or they can awaken us to the true reality when we become curious about what else is possible.

An Evolutionary Guidance of *Illuminating* energy is all about focusing on the power of illusion. This guiding force urges us to cut away false fronts and recognize the truth. This energy encourages us to be authentic in all circumstances, yet many may struggle to determine what is authentic under the spell of the collective illusion. People usually forget the truth of who they are. The influence of *Illuminating* energy is there to guide us to find our true selves, rather than playing various roles in third-dimensional personalities. This influence can be quite transforming, if we allow light to pierce the veil of all illusion.

12. CHOOSING ENERGY

Periods of *Choosing* energy help us realize and understand the power of our choices. This energy also continually reminds us that we are here to be of service. We may be more drawn to projects that serve others during these times. These periods teach us how to choose from our hearts, but sometimes the lessons are quite challenging. Each of us is a spark of divine light, and our lights connect. Everything we think, say, or do affects everyone and everything else. *Choosing* energy helps us understand how to make choices based on love rather than through fear or judgment. Every choice counts, for it affects all others.

An Evolutionary Guidance of *Choosing* energy focuses on uncovering what prevents us from making choices that lead to harmony and peace for the highest good of everyone on the planet. We may be drawn to uncover, search out, or discover hidden things, including all the experiences we have forgotten in our incarnation on Earth. We have forgotten that we are connected to everything in the universe and that we have the power to create our future through the choices we make in the moment. The evolutionary guidance of *Choosing* energy presents opportunity after opportunity to experience challenges in a way that awakens the remembrance of the power of choice, until we learn to choose more wisely.

13. EXPLORING ENERGY

Periods of *Exploring* energy are times of presenting new ideas, reviewing all options, discerning differences more clearly, and making decisions. People are prone to investigate new things or travel to new places during this energetic period. We may also experience a strong need to improve ourselves, increasing both our integrity and our self-confidence. There is a great push to release old thoughts and invite in new ideas. The greatest gift of this energy is that it reminds us that anything is possible.

An Evolutionary Guidance of *Exploring* energy creates a bridge between our inner experience and our cosmic connections. It encourages us to look at everything with fresh vision and to move beyond any opinionated or rigid attitudes or overconfidence into the tenuous and wonderful position of the unknown. This energy implores us to think deeply about reality and to allow our hearts to guide us through constantly changing points of reference so that we can perceive a larger truth.

14. HEALING ENERGY

Periods of *Healing* energy assist in bringing spirit into matter. We may find ourselves moving between mystical realms and the third-dimensional world on a regular basis during these times, and we may need to work to balance living in both places simultaneously. There are opportunities for healing on many levels with *Healing* energy, but the cost (and benefit) of such healing is detachment from dysfunctional beliefs and patterns of behavior. When we do not release those old patterns, we lose the opportunity for healing and we continue egotistic, aggressive, and competitive behaviors. The way to properly use *Healing* energy is by recognizing that we must first harmonize the imbalances within ourselves before we can help humanity to heal. If we use *Healing* energy as it is intended, we will consciously practice balance, acceptance, compassion, and trust, moment by moment, so that our lives become demonstrations of spirit expressing into every situation.

Emotional wounds can send us inward in search of truth. *Healing* energy supports the integration of all our previous experiences (in both parallel lives* and this one) to heal existing imbalances. The evolutionary guidance of this energy demonstrates that time is an illusion; we can integrate all experiences into the now and begin to use all of who we are to help the world. With an Evolutionary Guidance of *Healing* energy we can receive information, refine it, and share it with others. We can become way showers, holding the door open for others to pass into higher vibrational states of being.

15. SEEING ENERGY

Periods of *Seeing* energy are times to soar toward our highest aspirations. We can realize that we are here to expand our consciousness and share it with others. The power of our minds and a sense of inner knowingness and self-confidence may be more easily attained during these times. However, we may also make rash decisions and actions, failing to consider the possible outcome of such choices. There is a strong desire for freedom during periods of *Seeing* energy, and consequences may not be considered until actions have been taken. It is important during these times for us to focus not only on the details that capture our attention at the moment, but also on the entire picture of what we are creating when we act. This can be a very visionary, psychic, and powerful time if we fine-tune our powers of discrimination and make choices from our hearts. Ultimately, the largest gift of *Seeing* energy is an expanded vision that brings hope to the world.

---

*Laarkmaa refers to all "past lives" as parallel lives because the Pleiadians tell us that time does not truly exist. Each of our experiences is happening simultaneously in another dimension.

An Evolutionary Guidance of this energy encourages us to live our lives from the perspective of Ahimsa. Often in this energy it is easier to leave an uncomfortable situation than to take action to change it. There is a strong desire for both freedom and perfection under this guidance. We may focus on details to achieve what we want, or we may develop courage to stay and change situations that are uncomfortable. *Seeing* energy asks us to explore everything from a spiritual perspective and reminds us that true freedom can be achieved only when Ahimsa is realized.

16. INTUITING ENERGY

The presence of *Intuiting* energy signals that new things are about to take place. This is an energy that brings grace, trust, and an ability to hear our own inner voice. Our sensitivities can be highly expanded during these times. We may also experience tests and difficult decisions, leaving us longing for a more harmonious experience. If we focus only on our sensitivities, we may experience these tests and trials as unnecessarily painful. If we are realistic and self-aware, we can move more easily through challenges and accept them as a necessary part of life. We have the choice to react to life with resignation and depression or to follow our inner guidance by accepting and working with our challenges.

An Evolutionary Guidance of *Intuiting* energy will continually transmit and express guidance from spirit. However, most people are not trained to listen to the inner, unacknowledged voice. Patterns of rejection and loss of self-confidence may surface through this Evolutionary Guidance to teach us that we must step away from any habitual patterns of fear of being criticized or overshadowed by others. This guidance is here to teach us to trust that grace is available and to listen to our hearts. As we learn to do so, we can also learn to be comfortable with the authority of our own intuition.

17. EVOLVING ENERGY

Boundaries quickly shift and change during periods of *Evolving* energy. Plans often fall apart, and there may be an earthshaking feeling in almost all of our experiences. Everything seems destabilized, which is the perfect opportunity, of course, for making positive changes, whether personal or planetary. These are times when we may have the ability to bring information from the cosmos into a more accessible form.

An Evolutionary Guidance of *Evolving* energy requires us to learn to flow with constantly changing circumstances, yet to do so with trust. This energy continually brings us new ideas and strong convictions about possibilities. We may also experience prosperity and abundance at multiple levels when we learn to flow with the continual changes.

18. SELF-REGULATING ENERGY

Periods of *Self-regulating* energy can bring a very healing presence into the world. Like a flash of lightning, this energy quickly slices through illusion to help us see things as they truly are. It helps humanity to transcend the limited material worldview of empirical reality. It is a time to cut through our limitations and reach for possibilities, to use our gifts to prove our competency. This energy supports making difficult choices to achieve a better world. The greatest gift of *Self-regulating* energy is the ability to eliminate anything that does not resonate with the truth.

An Evolutionary Guidance of this type of energy brings intense experiences to activate personal transformation. To properly use the energy we must be willing to do whatever it takes to grow. *Self-regulating* guidance encourages us to find inner peace through overcoming our own obstacles. It urges us to dissolve boundaries we have created through judgment and criticism, within ourselves first, and then in the outer world.

19. CATALYZING ENERGY

A period of *Catalyzing* energy is full of challenges, drama, and difficulties, but it also brings creativity into focus. This energy is a cosmic force leading us toward unity. It provides rapid transformations with the opportunity to emerge reborn. We may find that all our thoughts, words, and actions more quickly catalyze change around us on these potent days. A single sentence, thoughtlessly uttered, may bring changes that were never intended. These energies arrive to awaken humanity with more force when we are sleepwalking through our lives. All kinds of things that no longer work can be quickly destroyed during this energy, opening the way for new and more balanced ways of living.

An Evolutionary Guidance of *Catalyzing* energy brings an ability to look beyond third-dimensional illusions and see things as they really are. Whether this energy is found in a period of time or in a person, it affects everyone and everything in its vicinity. Sudden and unexpected changes can deepen our understanding or cause inner confusion, depending upon how we interact with what is occurring. The rapid nature of *Catalyzing* changes is often profound. The Evolutionary Guidance encourages us pay attention to how we affect all others.

20. ENLIGHTENING ENERGY

Times of *Enlightening* energy bring the world the chance to achieve multiple perspectives at once, helping to lift the consciousness of humanity. True social progress can be achieved during periods of this type of energy, but sadly, we as a collective have not yet recognized how to do this. Humanity remains attached to polarized ideas, rather than sharing and combining our different worldviews. *Enlightening* energy is very idealistic, and its greatest gift is the opportunity to release our dualistic perceptions and move away from polarization toward true harmony, unity, and peace.

An Evolutionary Guidance of *Enlightening* energy asks us to learn to integrate cosmic perspectives of truth with earthly realities. It urges us to set aside judgment, competition, and separation to achieve cosmic unity on Earth. The essential purpose is to remind us not only to bring our own light into the world but also to accept the light of others.

LEVELS OF CONSCIOUSNESS IN EARTH ENERGIES

While this and the following chapters on earth energies may appear to be organized in linear, hierarchical style, that appearance is merely for ease of assimilation. Life is not linear; it is cyclical. Therefore, although it may look as though the earth energies presented here, numbered from one to twenty, are hierarchical, these energies cannot be measured against one another. No earth energy is any better or more elevated than any other; all work together as part of the intricate weave of the whole. The energy numbered twenty is no higher or purer than the energy numbered one; each energy is simply assigned a numerical value because humans tend to think in linear fashion. As you read the descriptions, please remember that nothing exists by itself. Everything is connected to and affected by everything else.

Each earth energy comes from a particular focus of conscious awareness: individual, communal, global, or universal. There is no hierarchy in these types of awareness either; each type has equal status and contributes a valuable perspective here in the third dimension. (See fig. 8.1.) We are born with either one or two of these specific types of conscious awareness; they are what give us our personal perspectives (through our earth energy personality and through our evolutionary guidance). Ultimately, as we personally evolve we move past our particular personal positions of awareness and incorporate *all* aspects of

Types of Conscious Awareness of Earth Energies

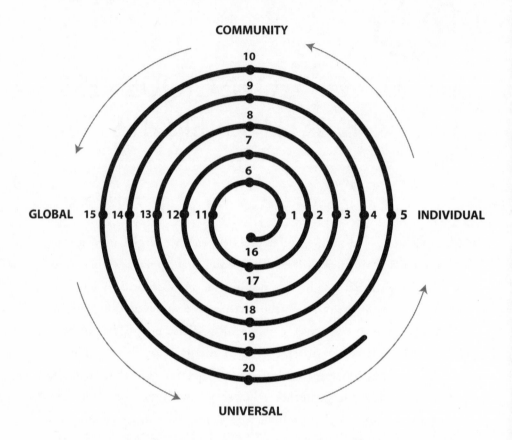

Earth energies spiral in a counterclockwise direction, beginning in the east.

Individual	Community	Global	Universal
1 Being	6 Transcending	11 Illuminating	16 Intuiting
2 Breathing	7 Remembering	12 Choosing	17 Evolving
3 Listening	8 Loving	13 Exploring	18 Self-Regulating
4 Planting	9 Feeling	14 Healing	19 Catalyzing
5 Moving	10 Devoting	15 Seeing	20 Enlightening

Figure 8.1

consciousness into who we are. This is why no one position is more exalted than any other, and all contribute to the wholeness of our human vision and experience. But it is helpful to examine the types of conscious awareness that color our personal perspectives as we are learning about the totality of who we are.

Every day the earth energies on our planet teach us about the different levels of consciousness. We need all of these levels to relate to each other and our environment. There are five earth energies that express through individual consciousness, five that express through community consciousness, five that express through global consciousness, and five that express through universal consciousness. We remind you that one level is not any better than another; they are simply *different*. For example, a person from universal consciousness may not be able to translate their universal vision for use in the community, while a person from individual consciousness may contribute unique perspectives that help us at a global level. What determines the type of awareness within each level of consciousness is how much work a person has achieved through living by the golden rule and making choices that are for the highest good of all in unity and love.

In addition, we are not only affected by the conscious awareness with which we were born, we are also influenced by the type of consciousness available in the energy of any particular day. For example, on days that carry earth energies of individual consciousness, we may be prone to deep introspection.

We will now explain how each type of consciousness works within this system, both individually and collectively, using the words "consciousness" and "awareness" interchangeably.

INDIVIDUAL CONSCIOUSNESS

When awareness is focused from an individual consciousness, the external world is perceived by pulling all that we experience into a deeply personal level to understand and integrate it. We may become lost in our own world, losing track of broader perspectives and thinking more in terms of "I" than "we." We may be prone to seeing everything in the universe in terms of how it affects us individually. Or we may generate unique ideas to share with others. Earth energy periods that come from an individual focus of consciousness require us to continually expand our perspectives by sharing our ideas with others. We must also practice accepting the ideas of others and integrating (or allowing) them into our own understanding without resistance. The earth energies that come from the position of individual awareness are:

1. *Being*—the place of potential
2. *Breathing*—acknowledgment of other perspectives
3. *Listening*—meditative quiet and stillness before the first thought
4. *Planting*—where we embed our thoughts as seeds for the future
5. *Moving*—where conflicts arise to stimulate change.

We can all use the energy of days with individual consciousness to bring new ideas to the world.

COMMUNITY CONSCIOUSNESS

When our consciousness is focused from a community viewpoint, we automatically tend to think in terms of "we" instead of "I." Those who think this way usually enjoy working with others. This type of consciousness should bring an inner awareness that our thoughts and actions affect others, but it doesn't always do so. Many people born with community consciousness make personal choices without considering how they will affect others, but community consciousness is the perfect place to learn how what we do impacts the whole, and some were born into this consciousness simply to learn that lesson. Some who have a strong yearning to be in community have not yet learned how to work well together, or may be publically active but reclusive in their private lives. Others with this type of consciousness find satisfaction in community projects because they naturally know or have learned how to work and play well with others. Community consciousness exists to help us better understand the gift of duality and bring opposite ideas into a state of harmony that works for all. It provides opportunities to engage in endeavors that better our communities, however we define community. The earth energies that come from the position of community awareness are:

6. *Transcending*—going beyond the restrictive aspects of our challenges and differences
7. *Remembering*—awakening to the memory of who we are
8. *Loving*—where we practice unconditional love
9. *Feeling*—exploring our emotional guidance for growth
10. *Devoting*—learning about loyalty.

GLOBAL CONSCIOUSNESS

A globally focused consciousness has a worldview of circumstances and events, rather than a personal or community perspective. Global consciousness encourages us to merge our consciousness with the entire planet. People with this orientation of awareness may be intrinsically aware that everything is connected and use their global perspective to serve the highest good of all. Although viewpoints may vary from person to person, anyone who thinks from the global perspective tends to think of the whole at some level when making choices or decisions. Ideally, this level of awareness summons peaceful solutions to challenges and a constant whole-worldview. But we must *choose* to act in accordance with global consciousness. Global awareness can also be used in a negative way, as when a leader who wants to take over the world uses his awareness of multiple perspectives to accomplish his goal. For those who are awake, aware, and making conscious choices from the global level of awareness, the spirit of cooperation is so important that they will tend to always consider others when making decisions for themselves. The earth energies that come from the position of global awareness are:

11. *Illuminating*—shining the light of insight into the illusion of life
12. *Choosing*—understanding the power of choice and how it affects others
13. *Exploring*—breaking free from dysfunctional patterns and discovering other possibilities
14. *Healing*—understanding the power to make whole again when we connect with and trust the universe
15. *Seeing*—perceiving the details of life from a higher perspective.

Days with global consciousness are perfect for practicing our whole worldview and recognizing that we are all connected.

UNIVERSAL CONSCIOUSNESS

Universal consciousness focuses our viewpoint from a comprehensive perspective, opening us to the possibility of experiencing realms of consciousness beyond the third dimension. This type of awareness can help free us from old restrictive patterns and open our thinking to include cosmic perspectives. Many people with a universal consciousness describe feeling noticeably different from and often misunderstood by others. They sometimes even feel alone on Earth. They may find their idealistic visions are difficult for others to accept in the context of existing third-dimensional beliefs. Others may feel their idealistic and expansive ideas must be shared at the individual, community, and global levels to help open all of our minds. Universal consciousness stretches humanity to reach beyond its limited programming, often revealing unexpected opportunities to see things from multidimensional perspectives. Days that carry universal energy can help us to shift old patterns of thought or behavior and open us to cosmic perspectives. Such days are:

16. *Intuiting*—listening to the heart and inner voice
17. *Evolving*—eliminating what no longer serves us or the planet
18. *Self-regulating*—bringing ourselves back into flow, moment by moment
19. *Catalyzing*—making a difference through our vibrational presence
20. *Enlightening*—embodying possibilities to become beings of light and love.

EARTH ENERGIES AND THE CARDINAL DIRECTIONS

The twenty earth energies are also aligned with our earthly directions of north, south, east, and west, with five earth energies in each direction. The cosmic organization of these directional energies is, of course, cyclical, as is all life. (See fig. 8.2.) The first energy described is aligned with the east. The next one is aligned with the north. The spiraling presentation continues in a counterclockwise direction, aligned with the movement of most of the planets in our solar system. Following the spiral on the graph, you can see how one direction merges into the next, spiraling through various stages of each direction. An important thing to remember is that while these energies have varying and different characteristics, each one builds on the previous energy and contributes to the one following it, in a continuous flow. To understand how they all work together, it is imperative to release the human tendency to think linearly, comparing one expression to another. Notice the differences, but do not become involved in judging one as being more than or less than another. *All* are necessary. Envision the mythical ouroboros, which you may recall is the snake that eats its own tail, and try to think of how that ancient symbol demonstrates that all of life is circular and connected, with no real beginning and no real end. The symbol of the ouroboros will surface again and again through seeing similarities

Directional Influence of Earth Energies

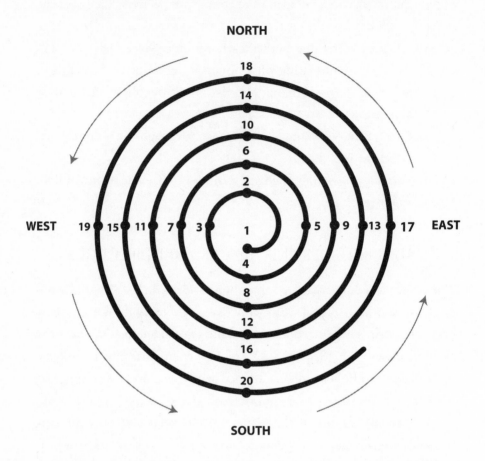

Earth energies spiral in a counterclockwise direction, beginning in the east.

East	North	West	South
1 Being	2 Breathing	3 Listening	4 Planting
5 Moving	6 Transcending	7 Remembering	8 Loving
9 Feeling	10 Devoting	11 Illuminating	12 Choosing
13 Exploring	14 Healing	15 Seeing	16 Intuiting
17 Evolving	18 Self-Regulating	19 Catalyzing	20 Enlightening

© 2018 Pia Orleane, Ph.D.

Figure 8.2.

within the earth energies. When we see the earth energies as circular and connected, we begin to better understand how each day and each individual contributes to life. Although we have told you that the earth energies spiral from one direction to another, we will group them here according to their directional association so that you can see similar characteristics of energies within each direction.

Eastern Energies

The eastern direction is aligned with the sunrise and the newness we find at the beginning of each day. The east contains the potential of all possibilities, even when hidden from sight or from our current awareness. Eastern energy is related to the energy of the color red, which Laarkmaa tells us brings movement and life.*

The eastern direction can bring hopes and dreams into reality if we allow that to happen. Eastern energy enhances our understanding that new beginnings are *always* possible. The earth energies from the east are:

1. *Being*—the place of potential
5. *Moving*—where conflicts arise to stimulate change
9. *Feeling*—exploring our emotional guidance for growth
13. *Exploring*—breaking free from dysfunctional patterns and discovering other possibilities
17. *Evolving*—eliminating what no longer serves us or the planet.

Northern Energies

The northern direction gives us the strength to move through challenges. It is associated with the color white, which Laarkmaa tells us is the energy of truth. Northern energies can be mentally active and are often full of changes. Transitions of all kinds are associated with

---

*Each color carries a certain vibration. Laarkmaa describes the energy of colors in their book *Remembering Who We Are*.

northern energy and the color white. In Western cultures a bride generally wears white to symbolize purity, a patriarchal label for the use of white. Actually, the choice of white for a wedding gown symbolizes the truth of a bride's transformation from being an individual alone to becoming part of a larger whole through marriage. In Peru, white represents angels and good health. In the Chinese culture, white is the color of mourning and is associated with death, the ultimate transition. The earth energies associated with the north are:

2. *Breathing*—acknowledgment of other perspectives
6. *Transcending*—going beyond the restrictive aspects of our challenges and differences
10. *Devoting*—learning about loyalty
14. *Healing*—understanding the power to make whole again when we connect with and trust the universe
18. *Self-regulating*—bringing ourselves back into flow, moment by moment.

Western Energies

The western direction brings deep awareness. We associate the color blue with the west, and Laarkmaa tells us that blue represents the energy of trust. In some shamanic cultures the west is seen as the direction of dreams and insights.[1] When we are working with western energy, we may wish to quiet our minds to perceive more expansive possibilities. Earth energies associated with west are:

3. *Listening*—meditative quiet and stillness before the first thought
7. *Remembering*—awakening to the memory of who we are
11. *Illuminating*—shining the light of insight into the illusion of life
15. *Seeing*—perceiving the details of life from a higher perspective
19. *Catalyzing*—making a difference through our vibrational presence.

Southern Energies

The southern direction brings an abundance of growth. Things (and people) bloom in the presence of southern energy. This energy compels us to make creative choices that will cause growth and evolution for others, the planet, and ourselves. The southern direction is often perceived as the direction from which we manifest our reality, according to how we have engaged with energies that preceded our interaction with this energy. The color yellow is associated with the south, and Laarkmaa tells us that the energy of yellow brings joy and illumination. The southern earth energies are:

4. *Planting*—where we embed our thoughts as seeds for the future
8. *Loving*—where we practice unconditional love
12. *Choosing*—understanding the power of choice and how it affects others
16. *Intuiting*—listening to the heart and inner voice
20. *Enlightening*—embodying possibilities to become beings of light and love.

PLANETARY CORRESPONDENCES TO EARTH ENERGIES

For those who follow Western astrology, it may also be helpful to understand the earth energies in terms of planetary alignment. Western astrology typically uses only eleven planetary positions (Sun, Moon, Mercury, Venus, Mars, Jupiter, Saturn, Chiron, Uranus, Neptune, and Pluto) and a handful of asteroids (Ceres, Pallas, Vesta, and Juno) as descriptive influences on our personalities. We have used certain asteroid comparisons when appropriate, and we have added Eris and our own planet, Earth, to influences that are listed. There are more earth energies described in the Pleiadian system (twenty) than are considered to be planetary influences in Western astrology, so there will be some repetition in the comparisons below. We have done our best to characterize each earth energy below from a planetary perspective.

Being energy is similar to the visionary yet often confusing energy of Neptune. A person or a day of *Being* energy can be filled with wild thoughts and feelings or full of intuitive guidance.

Breathing energy is somewhat similar to the influences of the planet Mercury. Mentally adaptive, quick, intelligent, restless, agile, clever, changeable, and communicative are all descriptors for both Mercury and *Breathing* energy.

Listening energy can be compared to the energy of Saturn in Western astrology. There is an air of seriousness defined by hard work and discipline in these days or people. This energy can feel limiting, forcing us to go inward to wait for expansion and growth.

Planting energy is best compared to the planet Jupiter, the planet Western astrology associates with abundance and expansion. *Planting* energy appears to bring opportunities to embed seeds for growth.

Moving energy can be related to the mythical planet Maldeck. It is said that the dynamic tension propelling advanced evolution created such stress on Maldeck that the planet exploded into the form in which it now exists as asteroids. Days and people with *Moving* energy are often filled with inner dynamic tension that stimulates growth by demanding choices be made. Both *Moving* energy and the asteroids seem to carry a mix of qualities related to learning, growth, creativity, intelligence, attachment and letting go, meaningful work, relationships, self-acceptance, and self-worth.

Transcending energy is best related to the energy of the planet Mars. There is a pioneering expression of this energy that is eager to go beyond anything that no longer serves and is impatient to begin the next step on the journey of evolution. This is both personal and global.

Remembering energy is related to the asteroid Juno, the Divine Feminine representation of our link to the "other" and to our capacity for meaningful relationships. This energy is about conscious union.

Loving is the earth energy most closely aligned with the planet Venus, our twin planet. Venus closely affects our participation with duality here on Earth because Venus has two very distinct aspects—the morning star and the evening star. Likewise, days or people with *Loving* energy may seem to have two distinct aspects to their energy. This energy often creates or engages in tension in order to better understand the polarities of duality. The tension provides something to push against in order for us to make a leap to the next level of understanding.

Feeling energy is related to the energetic influence of the Moon. It has long been known that the Moon's gravitational force affects our bodies and our planet, creating tides and fluctuations both internally and externally. Since we are water beings (approximately 60–70 percent water), it is not difficult to understand that the Moon pulls on the waters of humans.* Traditional astrology asserts that the Moon governs our instincts, emotions, and feelings. Days and people who carry *Feeling* energy seem to be full of the tides of emotions. In this energy thoughts always arise *after* feelings, which can cause an unsettling confusion.

Devoting energy is another energy that is best compared to the planet Mercury, for both Mercury and *Devoting* energy are interested in communication and transportation. On these days we may have stronger desires to move about and to improve our communication. People with this energy are always most interested in travel and communicating deeply.

---

*For facts on the amount of water contained in the human body, see page 149 of Pia's book *Sacred Retreat*.

Illuminating energy can also best be compared to the influences of the planet Venus. But this time the planetary comparison relates to Venus as a symbol of an earthy, artistic lover of beauty. Days and people who carry *Illuminating* energy can bring qualities of resourcefulness, sensuality, and productivity, or they can have materialistic, acquisitive, insecure, and self-indulgent qualities. Duality is in full play in this earth energy.

Choosing energy is most directly related to our own planet, Earth, for this is the planet where we learn about choice. Laarkmaa tells us that the power of choice is a special gift for humanity to use here in duality.* Choice is the most powerful energy we humans have at our disposal for determining our own reality. While love may be the strongest force in the universe, it remains our human choice on Earth to participate with the energy of love through unconditional acceptance, openheartedness, kindness, and compassion. Our thoughts, feelings, attitudes, tone of voice, and actions are always our choice. It is our greatest tool to align ourselves with cosmic love for our own evolution.

Exploring energy relates to another property of Mars—passionate and assertive forward movement. Days of this energy stimulate exploration. People who carry this energy are often activists who want to understand and achieve change.

Healing energy is best compared to the planet Chiron, representing the ability to access multidimensional perspectives for healing. Chiron is known in Western astrology as the "wounded healer," and this association with Chiron represents the attainment of mastery through magical alchemy that is possible on days of *Healing* earth energy or around people who carry this energy.

Seeing is another earth energy that can be compared to the expansive energies of the planet Jupiter. Days of *Seeing* energy are filled with

---

*This concept is fully explained in *Remembering Who We Are.*

trust in our natural abundance. People who carry *Seeing* energy are often rebels who continually ask the question, "Is there a better, more expansive way?"

Intuiting earth energy seems to be related to characteristics of both the planets Saturn and Neptune. The connection with Saturn is based on limitations that are always present in this energy. The Neptune influence relates to the presence of natural intuition, yet both days and people expressing this energy can carry an underlying insecurity and fear of being judged by others for being different. The best way to work with these energies simultaneously is to allow intuition to help us remember what is real and then bring inspired ideas into the structures of our earthly realm in a pragmatic way.

Evolving energy is very similar to the energy of the planet Uranus, which is known for sudden radical shifts and changes. Uranus is characterized in Western astrology as the planet that awakens us. The rebellious energy of this planet can cause great destabilization of existing paradigms, compelling us to make necessary changes. Evolving energy does the same, shattering old beliefs and patterns of behavior with electric abruptness and clearing the way for freedom and reform.

Self-regulating is yet another earth energy that seems similar to the influence of the planet Neptune, because it brings an ability to dissolve boundaries in order to merge that which is separate into wholeness. Self-regulating energy shares the same capacity as Neptune for connecting to and sharing cosmic wisdom for personal and planetary healing.

Catalyzing energy is best compared to Eris, the dwarf planet associated with forces of the feminine for profound transformation.[2] Days of *Catalyzing* earth energy empower us to address hidden blind spots and to rebalance the places in our world made toxic by imbalanced masculine energies. Both Eris and *Catalyzing* energy propel us to explore relatively unconscious areas for the soul's growth.

Enlightening energy is most closely compared to the planet Pluto, the planetary influence that brings deep and profound transformation. While such changes may feel devastating when they are in process, it is good to remember that *Enlightening* energy is aligned with the southern direction and will always ultimately bring growth and abundance. Both this energy and Pluto assist in the transformations that are currently occurring on Earth.

THE RELATIONSHIP BETWEEN EARTH ENERGIES AND PERSONALITY

In their attempt to help humanity evolve into a more conscious species, the Pleiadians gave the Maya more than five thousand years ago the same explanation they recently gave us. The two descriptions are similar because both came from Pleiadian wisdom. Now, with Laarkmaa's help, we've given modern English names to each one, making all of them more understandable in our current culture. Laarkmaa also helped us explore and understand these energies more deeply and asked us to formally introduce them to the humans (at this time) in this book. Here, we'll examine the ways earth energies affect our human personalities and give a basic description of each energy's dualistic manifestation through its higher and lower frequencies.

As you explore the energies, notice how earth energies automatically can manifest in the personality through both higher and lower vibrations. The gift of duality is that it offers the opportunity to see that its very definition speaks directly to the mathematical concept of two parts that make the whole. By definition, duality is its own resolution; embrace the opposites as coexisting and equal, and you merge the two into unity. It's an invitation to choose wholeness without fighting over which part is "right." It is something to consider and understand as you move along your own evolutionary path. As we examine the effects of the twenty earth energies in human personalities, we'll give a basic description of the energy. Bruce Scofield's work of applying psychological characteristics to each of the energies and his view of historical treatment of these energies is woven into each description here, and we credit him for his seminal work.[1] In our book we share advanced wisdom from the Pleiadians to once again help humanity make this evolutionary leap.

As you read the descriptions of each earth energy in relationship to human personalities, you'll see the references to higher and lower vibrations, as well as information on balanced and unbalanced states. None of us live in higher vibrational energy all of the time. If we did, we wouldn't be human, we'd be on to our next assignment! We suggest that you examine the qualities of both positive and negative manifestation of the energies and see where you're spending most of your time. What can you do to change or transcend negative aspects and move into a more positive representation of your specific earth energy?

This is what we're here to accomplish. When any part of the whole is vibrating at the highest, most positive level, the collective is substantially changed. When we *all* choose to vibrate at our highest energetic levels, we'll be able to move into a new, more harmonious expression of humanity. As you read the descriptions, remember the earth energies are only one aspect of the personality. Additionally, nothing exists in isolation; everything is connected to and affected by everything else. You may wish to find your own energy by reading the descriptions that resonate with your view of yourself in these pages, or you can use your birthdate and refer to the ephemeris in appendix C to find your earth energy. (Note that if your birthdate falls prior to the ephemeris included in the book, an expanded ephemeris of the years 1900 through 2100 can be found at https://audio.innertraditions.com/pleaen.)

1. BEING—THE PLACE OF POTENTIAL

Being energy represents a beginning and an ending without distinction. This energy is the essence of a place where everything is united in a fundamental ground of being that is necessary to life. The Mayan word for this energy is *imix,* and the Cherokee refer to it as *Uktewana,* which is a freshwater lake dragon with great power. This quality gives those who carry *Being* energy an intense urge to merge with others, and they can experience profound disappointment when others don't share as openly and as deeply as they do.

People with *Being* energy usually have strong creative urges and an intense emotional power that fuels their desire to create. They are often full of new ideas and usually have outstanding courage, strength, and a tendency for hard work. They may spend long periods thinking about what they want to do before they begin, and once a project has begun it must continue to interest them or they may not complete it. They are very independent and may have a difficult time receiving criticism in any form, reacting defensively rather than objectively. At the same time they are often very critical of others. Because of this dynamic around criticism, many who have this energy perceive the world as a harsh place.

Those who carry *Being* energy feel everything in life intensely. It's important to them to have their feelings honored, although they themselves sometimes don't even clearly understand what it is they're feeling. They may appear touchy or sensitive to others, and many may experience an incessant need for emotional security. Like all of us, they have to learn that their sense of security can be found only within themselves. They often experience rejection as a constant reminder to search for love inside the self. Feelings of rejection and loneliness are large challenges to those with *Being* energy. The lower vibrations of this energy will manifest as being needy, emotionally reactive, critical, and insecure. In the higher vibrations, people with *Being* energy use their creative natures to continually start again when things aren't going smoothly.

2. BREATHING—ACKNOWLEDGMENT OF OTHER PERSPECTIVES

Breathing is a powerful earth energy full of potential and aptly called wind, air, breath, or life by ancient cultures. The Mayan word for this energy is *ik,* and the Cherokee word is *kawoladedv.* This energy is almost completely based on discovering the fundamental benefits of duality. We must begin to breathe as soon as we are born, or we'll perish. Our breath is our introduction to duality; it is where we learn the concept that it takes both an in-breath and an out-breath to create the wholeness of breathing. We can't live without doing both.

Breathing energy is all about change. People whose personalities carry this energy experience changeability in life more than most. They may find it challenging to reach decisions because they are always aware that circumstances are continually changing. People who carry this energy are mentally quick, interested in many subjects, and want to understand everything required to navigate their world. Most are drawn to learning, speaking, reading, writing, and other forms of mental exploration. Many have overly active minds and an ability to link seemingly unrelated ideas. They can find themselves feeling confused or overwhelmed by too much information, and they are quick to change their minds. They need regular periods of quiet time without thinking to recuperate from an overload of exploration or communication.

At the lower vibrational level, fear that they are going to make a wrong decision plagues people with *Breathing* energy. They are easily swayed by the strong opinion of others, which may be completely irrelevant to their particular situation. The biggest challenges for those with this energy always seem to stem from indecision. They may find it challenging to commit to anything, which makes accepting responsibilities more difficult for them than it is for most people. It's this challenge, however, that gives them the push to remember that many views of any situation are valid and any choice made must feel right in their hearts, not only in their heads.

These people are multifaceted and capable of seeing and harmonizing many points of view. This either adds to their confusion or helps them see the whole picture. Imagination and idealism are large parts of *Breathing* energy. At the higher vibratory levels, these people are aware that life offers many choices and opportunities. Those who carry this energy are here to help us all learn to integrate dualistic opposites into the unity from which we have come.

3. LISTENING—MEDITATIVE QUIET AND STILLNESS BEFORE THE FIRST THOUGHT

Listening energy offers the ability to be completely still, deeply listening to the voice of the cosmos. It can be seen as the void where nothing yet exists. The Cherokee called this energy *utvdasdi,* and the Maya called it *akbal.* Whatever the name, it carries power to descend into the abyss and receive guidance before acting in the world. In this energy of stillness and quiet our individual selves can merge with the whole of the cosmos. In this space deep transformations are activated. Most people who carry this energy as part of their personality easily access this realm through simple intention or deep meditation. In the quiet of a meditative state they are able to release the illusions of the third dimension while remembering universal truths.

Those who carry *Listening* energy are extremely private people who highly value seclusion and solitude. They tend to have an inner life that can be deeply mysterious to others, so they need a place of their own where they will not be disturbed and can rest and regenerate. *Listening* energy gives these personalities great patience, organization, endurance, and systematic, logical ability to solve problems. They also have the gift of intuition, which gives them an important balance between worlds. These people can work on a project for long periods of time without becoming bored. Big projects capture their interest, and they're dedicated to achieving their goals, no matter how long it takes. They exhibit a natural personal power that is apparent to others.

Those with *Listening* energy may enjoy restoring old things to a place of beauty, including restoring balance to fellow humans who have been harmed or damaged. They feel deep respect for history and experience, and attempt conventional solutions before using unproved ideas. Often, they choose careers that create beautiful and secure environments, such as architecture or construction, or they work as counselors, helping restore wholeness to psyches.

People with *Listening* energy usually experience a simultaneous longing for adventure and a deep need for security. Entering the heart of stillness and listening for directions can solve this seeming contradiction.

Lower vibrations of *Listening* energy elicit tendencies to be overcautious or obsessed with order or to be distrustful, undemonstrative, self-doubting, pessimistic, and even controlling. Many have subterranean volcanic tempers that if not properly channeled can erode their health, relationships, and general sense of well-being. One of the largest challenges for those with this energy is a deep need for security, which may manifest as an intellectual need to be right, a need for physical security, or both. The need for security can also cause a tendency to subtly attempt to control others. These people may become quite emotional if they feel their security needs aren't being met, and this can cause concern that the universe can't or won't provide what's needed.

Higher vibrational aspects of *Listening* energy bring practicality, responsibility, discipline, conscientiousness, dependability, patience, balance, compromise, success, a realistic view, and a deep and knowing trust that the universe is supportive. These higher frequencies will express in people with *Listening* energy who recognize that everything they think, feel, and do touches everything and everyone else in the world.

4. PLANTING—WHERE WE EMBED OUR THOUGHTS AS SEEDS FOR THE FUTURE

The energy of *Planting* has been called seed energy, corn energy, lizard energy, frog energy, or iguana energy by various indigenous peoples. The Cherokee called it *ahwisga,* and the Maya called it *kan.* All of these names symbolize fertility and the power of growth. Seeds, once planted, take sustenance from other energies (the soil, the Sun, rain) to grow and bloom. Likewise, *Planting* energy incorporates previously expressed energies (those of initiation experienced in *Being* energy, the rhythm and pulse of duality experienced in *Breathing* energy, and the germination period experienced in *Listening* energy) to establish a pattern for growth. *Planting* energy demonstrates how working with the gifts of other energies is vital to our ability to express our own gifts.

People who carry this energy as part of their personalities are usually bright, sunny, and full of new ideas. They are active, dynamic, enthusiastic, and can be mischievous. They are also patient and dedicated to their families. Most are drawn to prosperity in some way and will likely never be hungry. Many have a desire to be in the public eye and have a magnetic quality that draws others to them—even when they want solitude. These people are different, and others notice their difference. They are networkers, quick to respond to opportunities and make contacts with people who can get a job done.

Those with *Planting* energy may get deeply involved in special interests. They enjoy learning about intricate topics such as philosophy, spirituality, or metaphysics and have enormous amounts of physical energy. Most love to travel, and sharing with others is a natural talent. Each place where their energy lands, a seed of possibility is planted. Their very lives seem to be fertile ground, and they inherently understand that the time for new ideas is *now*. Highly intuitive, those with *Planting* energy have powerful senses and often operate on their intuition rather than thinking about what comes next. Although they have great patience to perform existing routines, there's still a strong desire to bring creative new possibilities into the world. They are loyal friends.

At the lower vibrations people with *Planting* energy may be immature, hyperreactive, and inflexible, finding compromise difficult—if not impossible. One of the biggest challenges for those with this energy is to follow through with their own ideas and not wait for the perfect time or place to pursue what their hearts dictate. They may vacillate between waiting for someone else to move forward or ignoring others altogether.

Higher vibrational aspects of *Planting* energy appear in those who have learned to channel their creative energy into projects, giving each project life. These people thrive on bringing new individual ideas into the world and watching them grow.

5. MOVING—WHERE CONFLICTS ARISE TO STIMULATE CHANGE

Moving energy brings aliveness into all of one's experiences. It also brings transformations, challenges, and the ability to learn (and share) their understanding that change and transformation are part of life. The Cherokee word for this energy is *asaladod,* and the Mayan word is *chicchan,* or celestial snake. People who carry this energy in their personalities usually experience both high and low extremes in life. They are very strong willed, powerful, and full of life force, with an instinct for survival. They are also sensitive and may keep many veils around themselves for protection. They can be secretive and definitely enjoy privacy, though others are continually drawn to them. They may experience strong emotions and may also have difficulty containing, controlling, balancing, or understanding these emotions. There may be an ongoing sense of upheaval and crisis in the lives of those with *Moving* energy. At the lower vibrations these people project their feelings onto others to avoid dealing with their own pain. If they don't explore the messages of their own emotions, they might find themselves in great indecision, which prevents them from moving forward. When this occurs the universe makes decisions for them by default, and they may feel trapped by life. Laarkmaa advises all humans to use our emotions as signposts that indicate when we need to rebalance our lives from an inner level.[2]

Most people with *Moving* energy have exceptional intelligence. They grasp and synthesize enormous amounts of data, yet use their instinct rather than relying on their intelligence to make most of their decisions. They usually have great stamina and physical strength as well.

There is a tendency to indulge in excess, for either work or pleasure. Money and time management are challenges for people with this energy; if they are lacking these skills, they tend to cram too much into a very short time. Their financial reality may be disastrous, or they may rely on others for their well-being. Such lifestyles can lead to stress, affecting their physical or mental health. At the higher frequency levels, these bright and powerful people demonstrate how to make choices to live from a higher vibrational place.

6. TRANSCENDING—GOING BEYOND THE RESTRICTIVE ASPECTS OF OUR CHALLENGES AND DIFFERENCES

The Maya referred to this energy as *cimi*, or death, which was symbolic of the transformative process. The Cherokee word is *ayohuhisdi*. In the third dimension we are preoccupied with physical death, but the energy of *Transcending* is about inner deaths, releasing old patterns and beliefs that no longer work. In the Mayan culture butterflies represented souls who had passed from this Earth. The process by which butterflies emerge from cocoons symbolizes the beautiful transformations that are part of destiny, if we simply invite the transformational process of change into our human reality.

Transcending energy is a literal bridge between the spiritual realms and physical realms, and it can bring a knowing that one is living between worlds. People whose personalities carry this energy usually have deep interests in metaphysics. They are fascinated by the mysteries in life surrounding them. They are able to sense the energy of the ever-present ouroboros, intuiting how deeply connected endings and beginnings will always be. Life is a circle; death in any form is simply part of that circle.

These people usually have a deep desire to help and participate in community. They cooperate well with others, and their personal viewpoints rarely get in the way of a more community-oriented vision. There's a strong sense of responsibility and duty, which can be taken too literally. Most born into the energy of *Transcending* are given enormous challenges to transcend, and their lives may be filled with personal sacrifice.

In the lower vibrational expressions these people may act with hesitation, continually waiting for the perfect moment or the perfect insight. If they allow their desire for perfection to lead the way, they may experience melancholy or even resignation. *Transcending* energy presents continual challenges until there is an awareness that all dysfunctional ways of thinking and acting must be released—including the perception of self as victim. Lower vibrational expressions of *Transcending* energy manifest as irresponsibility, self-centeredness, impatience, and carelessness. These people can be uncooperative, temperamental, and headstrong. They must focus on the lesson that perfection is an evolutionary process and that every positive idea or action makes a difference.

A more balanced and higher vibrational expression of *Transcending* energy manifests as self-confidence, courage, enthusiasm, inspiration, and the ability to initiate changes that can help the whole of humanity. When people of this energy are functioning at their highest vibration, they always make choices for the highest good of the community.

7. REMEMBERING—AWAKENING TO THE MEMORY OF WHO WE ARE

Remembering energy in the Mayan culture was represented by the picture of a grasping hand, or *manik*. The hand represents knowing when to grasp and when to surrender. In its most positive aspect, grasping someone or something is making a connection, offering support, or reaching an understanding. In its negative aspect, to grasp can mean to clutch, grab, seize, or grip—all words indicating power or control over a person, thing, or situation. Negative meanings of surrender relate to loss of some kind. Yet surrender can also mean to freely release our need to be right or control a situation. The Cherokee word for *Remembering* is *anvdodisgi*. The energy of *Remembering* is about surrendering to possibilities that exist outside of our limited beliefs and reaching for connection with higher realities. The energy of *Remembering* is about moving away from the separation we feel here on Earth and returning to a sense of the unity from which we came.

People whose personalities carry this energy have a deep purpose of helping us all remember how opposites can merge into congruence. They are here to bring harmony, and their appreciation for beauty usually allows them to see the beauty of the world. They are peaceful and generous, intuitive, and sensitive to the needs of others. They are also bold and speak out when necessary, confronting any issue that seems unjust. They are quick to help in any way that seems appropriate. However, those who carry *Remembering* energy often feel as if they are living in two worlds—either the past and the future, or here on Earth and some other location in the cosmos. Because these people are standing between different realities they can be excellent counselors to others, and they usually have strong skills in diplomacy. Cooperation and interaction are important concepts to them. They may have some wild ideas, but they are rarely unbalanced in their grasp of reality.

In the lower vibrations of *Remembering* energy people may find themselves being overly compromising, hesitant, or giving their power away to others. They may be superficial in their appreciation of beauty, rather than seeing true inner beauty. They may truly struggle trying to balance their wish for security with their need for freedom. They may feel conflict within themselves and struggle to create inner peace, or they may feel a constant struggle between freedom and security. But isn't that struggle the very essence of learning when to grasp and when to surrender?

Those in the higher vibrations of *Remembering* energy are usually interested in relating, sharing, fair actions and decisions, and cooperation. They are generous, balanced, and helpful to others, and they realize that their vision is connected to the higher realms. They have qualities of receptivity and an intuitive response to life, as well as a strong desire for connection through family or community. The desire for harmony is keenly present in them. In the highest manifestation of this energy they can help us to find the balance between being in spirit and being in physical form.

8. LOVING—THE ENERGY OF
UNCONDITIONAL LOVE

Loving energy is a pathway for accelerated growth, but love is not always soft and gentle; love also knows how to fight for justice. Those who carry *Loving* energy in their personalities know how to fight, and they will take risks to create confrontations they feel are necessary to bring higher levels of awareness. People who have this energy in their personalities may have high ideals, but they are constantly challenged to manifest those ideals in everyday life. Many who carry this energy experience suffering because they are always fighting for some cause or trying to convince others of a different viewpoint. This energy is called *Loving* energy because that is what it's *supposed* to do; it's the energy of accepting differences that are completely opposite, turning the other cheek, and loving the other person as oneself. This energy is at the heart of the principle of In Lak'ech.

People with *Loving* energy in their personalities are very generous. They are drawn to communicate constantly, through talking, reading, or writing. Their minds are complex, and they understand the intricacies of the mental process. However, they have a tendency to overstimulate their minds, creating a great deal of nervous energy that needs a physical outlet, and they need to take care not to get lost in mental clutter. People with *Loving* energy in their personalities often tend to drift away from family ties, developing the distance they need to achieve their own growth. Many will establish spiritual families that are more in alignment with their desire for harmony, rather than remaining attached to biological families that they may associate with constant strife. These people have an uncanny ability to pull in exactly who and what they need when they operate from higher states of harmony. People with *Loving* energy are very loyal once they have established mutual trust with others.

People in the lower vibrations of this energy may thrive on competition, using it to eliminate boredom. They will seek conflict, arguing just for the sake of arguing. Because they thrive on pushing the limits they may even perceive others who are unwilling to fight as weak. In the higher vibrations, however, people with *Loving* energy dissolve competition into cooperation, weaving opposites into harmony. The Maya used the symbol of Venus, or *lamat,* to represent *Loving* energy in recognition of the necessity of unconditionally accepting opposite aspects (like the morning star and the evening star) of any seemingly contradictory situation. The Cherokee also looked to the stars, *aninoquisi,* for this energy. This energy is associated with a deeper exploration of Christ consciousness, the unconditional love that heals all separation. In its highest manifestation *Loving* energy is a beautiful, energetic representation of complete acceptance and unconditional love. Those who carry this energy in their personalities are here to bring a higher level of consciousness and light into embodiment for human evolution, whether they recognize that calling or not. Their challenge is to dismiss all beliefs that there is only one correct way to do things. There is always some dynamic tension in the atmosphere with *Loving* energy because in duality, tension helps us to grow.

9. FEELING—EXPLORING OUR EMOTIONAL GUIDANCE FOR GROWTH

The Maya referred to *Feeling* energy as rain, or *muluc.* The Cherokee word is *asvnasdi.* This is the energy most disturbed by disharmony on Earth. It represents the emotions that quickly inform us if we are out of harmony with someone or something around us. Laarkmaa gives us a way to understand what we feel by defining our natural feeling states as love, joy, trust, and compassion, and our emotions as the more uncomfortable feelings of anger, fear, grief, jealousy, and frustration.[3] Emotions, the Pleiadians tell us, are purposefully designed to be uncomfortable to get our attention. Laarkmaa says they are signposts to notify us we are out of balance and that we need to change our opinion, our belief, or our thinking about whatever is causing our discomfort.[4] It's never an outside source that causes our discomfort; it's always our own inner reaction to an external event or person that sends us into emotional misery. When we are unhappy we're motivated to change, and the only people we can ever change are ourselves. Harmony comes from looking within ourselves. When we all look at how we're thinking, feeling, and acting in the outer world with an eye toward how we're affecting others, we move closer to reaching harmony.

Those who carry *Feeling* energy in their personalities are usually overflowing with powerful emotions that can swiftly change. They relate to life through these emotions and can be overwhelmed by what they feel. Most often, they respond to life through what they feel, rather than what they think. They are sensitive to their environment and exceptionally responsive to it. Most have strong, curious, independent minds and are quite capable of solving problems without the assistance of others. If they try to learn through making mental comparisons, they can easily become confused or stuck. Often, those with *Feeling* energy experience tension between their natural changeability and their desire to maintain control (of circumstances and of their own reactions to circumstances). They may have a deep need to hide any uncertainty or lack of self-esteem. They may also exhibit intense behaviors that are completely incomprehensible to other people, making it difficult for others to trust them. They unconsciously project their strong emotions onto others without understanding that they are contaminating the other person. Theirs is a world of extremes. Many feel that their lives are a constant battle between the rawness of their emotions and the discipline they must employ to control them, struggling all of their lives to learn how to intelligently respond to the emotions that so quickly arise within them.

Many of those with the makeup of *Feeling* energy were dominated by their mothers and were imprinted by that relationship. A positive role model can lead to an adult personality that is a responsible leader. A negative role model often produces someone with a deep-seated inferiority complex, lack of confidence or self-esteem, and a strong need for positive recognition. Continual reactive and judgmental responses to others may make it difficult for such a person to complete projects or stay in long-term relationships. Emotional reactions can lead them to be uncompromising and unbending. If a decision is made from an emotional place, these people will stubbornly refuse to re-evaluate or consider other possibilities. Quite simply, unaware people with this energy act from the lower vibrations of instinct, while mature, developed people who carry *Feeling* energy act on higher vibrations of intuition. Those with this energy who have matured and evolved are masters of awareness, continually discerning the ebb and flow of life circumstances and responding appropriately moment by moment. There is no limit to the heights of success these people can achieve through their ability to witness and experience energy as it constantly changes form. They are ever ready to change course according to the energy that is present in the moment and are fully aware of what's required to do so. They act on it whenever necessary, making their decisions by assessing how their choices will affect others as well as themselves. These people are responsive, changeable, and flexible, finding it easy to adapt in real time. They have learned to set clear boundaries to maintain their own stability in an ever-changing world. People with higher vibrational expressions of *Feeling* energy are sensitive on many levels. They may have natural psychic gifts or develop psychic abilities through their own increasing awareness. Unusual phenomena will appeal to their strong and intelligent minds. As they become acutely aware of the link between the conscious and the unconscious, they may even seek a career in fields of psychic or paranormal phenomena. They are dreamers, but unlike their unbalanced counterparts, they don't get lost in fantasy. While they've learned to navigate their own emotions in order to make necessary changes within themselves, they're very aware of the feelings of others who haven't yet learned to discover the guidance of their own emotions. They exercise their personal power through demonstrating high ideals and vision for all of humanity.

10. DEVOTING—LEARNING ABOUT LOYALTY

Devoting energy is an energy of consistency, cooperation, celebration, and trust. The Maya referred to this energy as *oc,* meaning both "dog" (our most loyal companions) and "foot" (the part of the body with which we literally take the next step). The Cherokee word for "loyalty" is *gohiyuhi* and "to devote" is *uwohiyuhi.* People who have *Devoting* energy in their personalities make loyal friends. They are warmhearted and sociable, generous, and always willing to help. They want to help humanity and are tirelessly supportive to people and causes they find worthy. They're multitalented, often expressing themselves through creative endeavors or sharing healing energies. They can also be powerful speakers. They have a good sense of perspective and harmony and enjoy creative arts such as drawing, painting, music, or dancing. These people know how to enjoy themselves and are generally happy in life, although they may experience disappointment when others do not meet their expectations. When this happens they may feel alone or experience feelings of being unsupported in the world, which can lead to a heavy heart or depression. These feelings also can lead to a loss of trust, followed by a sense of insecurity.

People with *Devoting* energy are idealistic and can lose touch with what is actually happening in the present when they are creatively planning for the future. They may focus on a particular goal while ignoring the needs of the present reality. They are sometimes challenged to stay on course and not get sidetracked in daydreams. Most people with this energy seem to experience prosperity, and some can be quite extravagant. They are usually successful in whatever career they choose. They enjoy leadership, but they also understand when it's time to follow.

At the lower vibrations those with *Devoting* energy may be challenged to detach from people or beliefs to which they have been loyal. They can actually be quite stubborn about change when acting from the lower vibration. They must also guard against jealousy, anger, or fear— emotions that arise when they cling to their own ideas of what is right without considering other viewpoints or possibilities. They may be loyal to dysfunctional families, inappropriate partners, religions, or beliefs that do not serve the highest good of all. Often, *Devoting* personalities allow family approval and family issues to shape their lives. They can remain involved in family issues long past the time they have outgrown the need to involve themselves. The most influential parent of those with *Devoting* energy (whether present or absent) is usually the father, who may have been either a source of inspiration or a source of conflict.

One of the biggest challenges for people with this energy is learning to truly see their own gifts and love themselves unconditionally. They have a good sense of perspective when viewing others, and yet may be blind to their own positive qualities, which leaves them feeling defeated. Part of the path for those with this energy is learning to release all patterns of judgment they experienced when young or feelings of resentment they may still carry for not having been supported as they think they deserved in early life. Basically, they may need to break free from dominating influences to be their true selves. The challenges they face may teach them to love and accept themselves unconditionally.

Laarkmaa tells humanity that the highest loyalty is the loyalty to truth and that truth can always be found in the heart.[5] This perspective releases people from unsuitable loyalties that don't serve their evolution. At the higher vibrational level people with *Devoting* energy are aware that the only true loyalty is loyalty to the truth and that truth can always be found in the heart. Higher vibrational aspects of this energy allow one to enjoy true and deeply supportive connections because the person has moved beyond fear and insecurity.

11. ILLUMINATING—SHINING THE LIGHT OF INSIGHT INTO THE ILLUSION OF LIFE

The purpose of *Illuminating* energy is to help unveil all things occluded by illusion. However, those who carry Illuminating energy in their personalities often get caught in their own attachment to the beauty of the illusion, immersing themselves in all the complications of life. Intelligent, quick, and adaptable, they are multifaceted and can play any desired role with very little effort. They are often creative and playful with an excellent sense of humor and know how to have a good time, even when life seems challenging. Most have a strong need for attention, and a large percentage of these people are artists, musicians, designers, or writers. They incorporate beauty and creativity into their lives in any circumstance. Many choose to work in communication arts because they are highly interactive with others and curious about everything. They also have a great ability to act as diplomats or counselors who unveil the truth. They usually have magnetic personalities, and others easily follow them. While they are capable of working with details, they excel at generalities.

Those living in the lower vibrations of *Illuminating* energy are deeply immersed in drama, always turning the attention of others toward themselves and magnifying events beyond reason or reality. They demand indulgences as a form of escape and participate in all kinds of amusements to keep themselves distracted from the real work of attending to their own evolution. Because they are charismatic they can also lead others down self-destructive paths, inflicting confusion and disorder in whatever arena they are playing—emotional, spiritual, or financial. They are the ones who have forgotten that there's a larger reality than the third-dimensional one in which they're involved. Because they've forgotten, many have a deep fear of the future or of not having enough money. They may quickly switch their attention from one interest to another in an attempt to distract themselves or avoid whatever difficulty they are facing.

These people may also be challenged to be authentic in expressing their own deep feelings, hiding behind the humor that is so much a part of them. By authentically sharing the truth of what they feel, they can change old patterns of denying or laughing at things that hurt. However, they may be so busy playing the different roles they explore in the third dimension that they lose sight of what's important and real to them. Their biggest challenge is becoming real to themselves.

Those who resonate with the higher vibrations of *Illuminating* energy use their natural lightness and humor to break through the dramas of life by making situations seem ridiculous or even hysterical. They're aware of the power of imagination, positive thoughts, and creative ideas that are available for healing any situation. They are curious about how to build a world that is better for everyone, and they will search for magical outcomes to seemingly impossible situations. The Cherokee work for this energy is *unadvnelvdi,* the Mayan word is *chuen.*

12. CHOOSING—UNDERSTANDING THE POWER OF CHOICE AND HOW IT AFFECTS OTHERS

The Mayan word for *Choosing* energy *(eb)* meant "human." The Cherokee word for "choose" is *asuye'a* and the word for "chosen" is *agasuyeda.* Laarkmaa tells us that humanity has been selected to experience the power of choice as part of our evolutionary path. Both the Cherokee and the Maya have an oral history that relates stories of Pleiadians coming to Earth to guide humans and share wisdom about how to choose wisely.

People with *Choosing* earth energy as part of their personalities are generally relaxed and easygoing, courteous, and kind, and they are deeply interested in relationships. Most who carry this energy wish to serve in the world in some way. They are creative, practical, and good problem solvers and have strong ambitions. They'll work hard to achieve goals and easily anticipate the needs of others. People with this energy must be careful to balance their own needs with their desire to serve others. They prefer to avoid all conflict and maintain peace and harmony at almost any cost, if possible. Yet dark emotions can lurk under the surface in people with *Choosing* energy. Beneath all the ease and flow of their outer personalities they may experience internalized resentment and anger if they feel disrespected, ignored, or dismissed. If they repress the guidance of their own emotions, these people can experience great conflict between their peaceful outer selves and the anger that has been stored within them. Patterns of internalizing anger, resentment, or other emotions must be broken to hear the messages for inner change that may otherwise be hidden. These emotions must be addressed and released in a conscious way so they can move forward. They must learn to express their true feelings rather than allowing unresolved emotions to collect until they overflow. The peace they so highly value requires listening to their own hearts.

Those who carry *Choosing* energy may encounter multiple trials, challenges, and illnesses (spiritual and/or physical) in their life journeys. These challenges are actually opportunities to awaken and develop their natural strength and abilities. At the lower vibrations people with this energy may react to these challenges with resentment, smoldering anger, or generally suppressed feelings that they can never get what they feel they deserve. When they respond from the higher vibrational level, those with *Choosing* energy understand each conscious choice helps speed everyone—all of humanity—toward the evolutionary states of peace, harmony, and enlightenment. At the deepest level we all must learn that every choice we make brings a chance to remember our connection to the cosmos and that we are divine beings who have the power to co-create our reality. People who carry this energy have a mission (recognized or not) to demonstrate this for all of us.

13. EXPLORING—BREAKING FREE FROM DYSFUNCTIONAL PATTERNS AND DISCOVERING OTHER POSSIBILITIES

The Mayan word *ben* and the Cherokee word *ajvysdi* describe this energy as a reed or pillar of light that connects the Earth and the universe. We feel that people who carry this energy have the potential to be bridges of light, radiating integrity and genuine vision through their exploration of all possibilities. They live at the forefront of conscious thought, connecting the current world to a possible future world, always beyond the established ideals of society. These people are explorers, bringing visionary awareness of possibilities into everything they do. They are deep thinkers, with a great love of learning and a strong inner confidence that allows them to take on problems that send others running. In conversation they may actually create some sort of controversy just to explore all aspects of a particular subject. Inviting opposing viewpoints helps them to arrive at the truth more quickly, if they aren't attached to a rigid belief about the subject. Usually, they become highly trained in whatever interests them. They're farsighted and work hard to bring the future into a very real present. As hard workers with great endurance, they are likely to accomplish whatever they set their minds to do, as their efforts are supported by their ample self-confidence. Those with *Exploring* energy usually have very strong personal opinions and a desire to share them. They're natural leaders because they understand people. They're adept at reading the character of others, have a natural talent for diplomacy, and usually speak kindly to others. They rarely show their emotions when under duress, which allows them to be helpful to others in challenging situations. They also know how to relax and enjoy life.

People with *Exploring* energy in their personalities love wide-open spaces, beautiful settings, and travel. Outdoor experiences nurture them. They shift their personal perceptions through their own experiences. When they change their beliefs, their reality changes as well. These people continually work between the polarities of duality. If they choose to align with the lower vibrations of *Exploring* energy, they may become quite attached to rigid belief systems or express a continual series of criticisms and judgments. They may act as though they feel morally superior. When aligned with the higher vibrations of this energy, however, they respond to life through a continual awareness of the existence of opposites, yet from a perspective that's interested in harmonizing apparently opposite points of view. They know their opinions will change as they gain new information, and they understand that the journey itself provides perfection through the process of evolution.

14. HEALING—UNDERSTANDING THE POWER TO MAKE WHOLE AGAIN WHEN WE CONNECT WITH AND TRUST THE UNIVERSE

The Maya referred to this energy as *ix,* meaning "magician" or "jaguar," and those who possessed this energy were called priests, for they were believed to have a connection to the gods. Their words were considered to reflect divine truth. The Cherokee called them *didahnvwisgi,* "medicine men" or "medicine women." Both the Maya and Cherokee considered those who possessed *Healing* energy to be the most sacred members of society. Today, evolved people carrying this energy know that each one of us is sacred and that we are all one.

People who carry *Healing* energy generally feel a sense of urgency about resolving the disharmonious aspects of living on Earth. They're endowed with strong intuition and various psychic abilities. Keenly aware of the energies around them, these sensitive people can read others intuitively, so they're naturally drawn to the healing arts, where they can use their intuitive abilities to connect with and support the healing of others. Those who fully develop their gifts sometimes have the ability to shape-shift, moving quickly from one dimension into another, which allows them to offer healing energy to the imbalanced sick of the world through their ability to expand the mind and alter consciousness. People with this energy in their personalities often find that others automatically speak about their problems to them without being asked. They sometimes seem to have a sign on their foreheads that reads: "Tell me your story." Deeply compassionate people, they feel the pain of the world every day.

Spiritual truth is the center of life for those with *Healing* energy. It's the cornerstone of their existence and what motivates them. They're attracted to the mystical, and when they're awake and aware, their lives can be living demonstrations of what it means to be sacred. When they merge their devotion to the spiritual they can achieve spiritual breakthroughs and facilitate others in their own spiritual development.

Most who carry this energy in their personalities are intelligent and well educated. Often, they're powerful speakers or writers. They have an inborn sense of strategy, a good imagination, and are powerful public communicators. They're generous, extravagant, goal-oriented, and fiercely dedicated to achieving the goals they set. Deeply concerned with principles of justice, they fight to make a point, but do so in an indirect way. They can be quite assertive while managing to avoid direct confrontations. Extremely private and exceptionally sensitive, those with *Healing* energy are easily overburdened by taking on responsibilities that are not theirs. Through their desire to help others, they may suddenly find themselves trapped by obligations for which they did not specifically volunteer.

Those with *Healing* energy can be extremely intense and must guard against pushing others away. Father-daughter issues may be present in those with this energy, affecting the way they relate to or function as authority figures. Although they're excellent communicators in public, in personal conversations they may not be aware that they often don't say what they think, believing they have clearly addressed the topic. Without speaking directly, they may weave suggestions and insinuations into conversations or leave out entire thoughts they believe they have expressed. If personal communication doesn't work, those with *Healing* energy may eventually explode into cutting and critical remarks to make a direct point. Yet, they rarely see the communication difficulty may have been on their own side of the conversation or communication.

When acting from the lower vibrational level of this energy, people may become annoyed if others cannot see so clearly what they know to be true. They can also be very self-absorbed if they're not careful, taking themselves too seriously or attempting to impose their views on others because they are so certain they know the truth. Unresolved childhood traumas can change into social maladjustment at the lowest level of this energy, where these people revert to an insistence that they know the truth as a defensive pattern.

When acting from the higher vibrational expressions of *Healing* energy these people are courageous, daring, and forceful. They will govern any tendency to speak critically, for they know that what they think and say deeply affects others. They will take responsibility for the power they carry. They have a sense that they are connected with the larger picture and know the truth, and they use this knowledge to demonstrate better ways of living. They understand that time is an illusion, and they move in a fluid, organic way, considering what is best for others as they simultaneously make responsible choices for themselves. In the highest vibration they're the way-showers who bring healing to the world.

15. SEEING—PERCEIVING THE DETAILS OF LIFE FROM A HIGHER PERSPECTIVE

The energy of *Seeing* is about using an expanded perspective to accomplish things that matter in the world. Those who carry this energy in their personalities can be visionaries who can see what others cannot. They radiate a light that attracts others to their wisdom. The Maya referred to this energy as *men,* meaning "wise one" or "sage," drawing an eagle to represent this energy. The Cherokee referred to the wisdom of this energy as *akto'vhisdi.*

Most people carrying *Seeing* energy in their personalities are quite capable of meeting whatever challenges arise. They focus their attention on the details of life with extreme precision, yet long for a more harmonious experience than life usually presents. These people love to travel simply because travel expands their understanding of life. They're very independent and ambitious, but they also experience a frequent desire to escape the challenges and difficulties of living on Earth.

Many people with this energy could be considered old souls. They've been here before, want to make a difference, and seem to experience all kinds of challenges that stretch them and make them grow. However, when third-dimensional challenges become extreme, these people often look for ways to escape or to ease the pain of living. Escape can take the higher vibrational form of travel to seek a broader vision or the lower vibrational form of escape through alcohol, drugs, shopping, television, Internet, social media, or anything that distracts them from what is currently happening. The consciousness of the person determines the choice.

Sometimes, when they focus exclusively on the details that so interest them, people who have *Seeing* energy lose the ability to see the whole picture. When operating from the lower vibrations they may seem scattered, ungrounded, or quite indecisive, refusing to commit to anything, concerned that commitment may limit their independence or sense of freedom. Emotions come to the surface easily to guide them toward changes that need to occur, but their desire for escape can override the need for looking at the message of what they are feeling. When operating from higher vibrational frequencies they use their urge to expand to bring new ideas into traditional situations. They easily integrate details into a larger vision that serves all. When they're living from this place, others see them as being very wise and seek out their opinions. One of the hardest realizations for someone with *Seeing* energy is that despite the prophetic vision they may have, they cannot save the world. They must continually guard against feeling hopeless or wondering why they choose to be here on Earth and remember that they're here to give hope and bring light.

16. INTUITING—LISTENING TO THE HEART AND INNER VOICE

Older indigenous cultures represented *Intuiting* earth energy as an insect or a bird—perhaps a bee or an owl. The Cherokee word for owl qualities is *wahuhi,* and the Mayan word for this energy was *cib.* Whatever indigenous word was used, this energy was connected to the wisdom of hearing the inner voice. People who carry *Intuiting* energy as part of their personalities are serious, deep, realistic, and question everything. They seem to have an inner knowing that there's more to life than what's apparent in the third dimension yet may not know how to access it. Often, they experience a lifelong search for universal wisdom, much of which they could access through their own intuition, if they just knew how. They may go to class after class, workshop after workshop, hoping to find the truth they seek, when it's right there in their own hearts. Often, in their search they absorb so much information and energy from others that they need time alone to clear out inner confusion, evaluate, and return to balance.

On the everyday level people with *Intuiting* energy in their personalities usually have a very realistic approach to life, seeing and working with what is in front of them. Practical and able to manage circumstances for the best use of their time, they also have a knack for knowing what works and what doesn't within their culture; they know the importance of being in the right place at the right time. They are usually highly creative and productive and may choose careers that allow them to express their natural creativity. Extroverted and outspoken, these people rarely hold back their thoughts or ideas, yet people with *Intuiting* energy experience deep feelings of rejection when others discount their thoughts. One of the biggest challenges for them is to overcome wounds of rejection and trust the inner guidance they have been given, which may take years. Personal insecurities can interfere with success. Sometimes, people with this energy have such serious challenges in their own lives that they forget how to be compassionate with others. They may begin to judge or criticize everything and everyone, dismissing how others feel or making fun of others' circumstances. This type of reaction causes great difficulties within both personal and business relationships, leaving the person with *Intuiting* energy feeling more alone than ever because their relationships are not working. If they have not learned how to connect with their own intuition, they may also be abnormally afraid of the death of others, viewing death as a form of abandonment.

At the higher vibratory levels people with *Intuiting* energy are open to the inner voice and use their intuition to guide everything. Helping others though the traumas and challenges is natural to them, and they can offer quite enlightened perspectives. Because they're both curious and tireless in their search for truth, they listen to anything that captures their attention and may offer new information. They are aware that life and death are connected and that there's nothing to fear in moving from the energetic position of life to the energetic position of death. People at the highest vibratory level can be fearless in living because they've learned to trust their native intuitive guidance. Although they always retain their natural curiosity they may eventually discard outside searches for truth, for they realize that all answers are found in the heart, which is connected to the entire library of cosmic wisdom.

17. EVOLVING—ELIMINATING WHAT NO LONGER SERVES US OR THE PLANET

The earth energy of *Evolving* brings unexpected changes that are necessary for evolution. Often, these experiences cause us to feel out of control. The Cherokee referred to forces of change as *anisadoyasgi,* and the Maya called the energy *caban.* People with this energy in their personalities are active thinkers who continually focus on plans or strategies to take them to the next step. Their continual thinking involves constantly shifting focal points. They initiate new ideas and have strong convictions about what is possible. It may seem to others that they're always in motion. They're master problem solvers with a strong desire to explore uncharted territories. Their ideas can be extremist and controversial compared with the mundane perspectives of society. Ahead of the times in their thinking, they often push the limits of what most people consider to be reasonable, but they're here to make changes. Most are extremely self-confident and intense, which makes them appear to be powerful. They're fiercely independent, sometimes stubborn, and can't tolerate being told what to do. They can experience intense and overwhelming emotions that they may rationalize or ignore until they erupt like a volcano. Yet, they also have a good sense of humor and an excellent understanding of human nature. They're complex people who struggle to maintain equilibrium in life.

People with *Evolving* energy in their personalities often prefer to work either alone or as leaders because they cannot stand following directions from others. Because they are so independent, when things seem out of their control they can become despondent. At the lower vibratory levels they may be disorganized, fanatical, unreasonable, impractical, thoughtless, inconsistent, unthinking, or unpredictable. They can neglect their own or others' feelings, rationalizing everything so much that they make poor choices. If they ignore their intuition or allow their heads to outtalk their hearts, they experience tremendous inner stress and confusion. Many who are born within the energy of *Evolving* find it difficult to live on Earth because of the continually changing circumstances. The paradox of wishing for a stable life while living a life so full of changes makes it difficult for them to hold their lives together according to a plan. They may want life to stay the same but continually experience change that is out of their control. They can be prone to fantasy because they wish to escape the pain of life. The heavy density of our current reality can feel like too much to bear.

People acting from higher vibrations of *Evolving* energy may seem positively electric! They're prepared to do radical and adventurous things and are excellent at solving large problems. Their pioneering thoughts offer many evolutionary ideas to the world. Humanitarian, progressive, reforming, tolerant, friendly, altruistic, inventive, intuitive, and freedom loving, people acting from the higher vibratory levels of this energy can be like a quick, brilliant flash of lightning that brings unexpected and innovative change. They have learned how to flow with the intentions of the universe, adding their own original thoughts to help our species to evolve.

18. SELF-REGULATING—BRINGING OURSELVES BACK INTO FLOW

Laarkmaa speaks about *Self-regulating* energy:

[It] separates truth from illusion, delineating true reality. This energy brings a rather poignant and deep glimpse of the reality that comes through focused intent and synchronistic linking in a tele-pathic manner between yourselves and others in the universe, and allowing things to flow as they should. This energy compels you to speak the truth and flow with what is happening, moment by moment.[6]

Similarly, the Maya called this energy *Etz'nab,* describing it as "a knife," "a sharp piece of flint," or "a mirror." We like the symbolism of a mirror, for it reflects the truth of who we are and how we are behaving in the world. We adjust ourselves when we look into mirrors. The Cherokee word for "an instrument of self-reflection" is *adakehdi.*

Those who have *Self-regulating* earth energy in their personalities have sharp minds and the ability to see into the heart of things. They often seem to clearly understand all the nuances and details of situations outside of themselves but may struggle to see themselves clearly. They may hold others at a distance for their own protection because they have experienced so many hardships and challenges in their early lives, yet they love connecting with people. They are polite, noncompetitive, and self-sacrificing by nature. They are compromising and willing to put their own interests aside in order to meet the needs of others. There is an interesting mix in the overall makeup of those who carry this energy: while their outward appearance reflects confidence, their inner struggles may reflect much self-doubt, causing them to feel very insecure.

People with *Self-regulating* earth energy in their personalities often feel the limits of third-dimensional reality in a very real way and long to transcend any sense of earthly bondage. Their entire lives may seem to be dedicated to finding solutions to longstanding problems or overcoming limitations, whether personal or planetary. They possess practical and penetrating minds, are well-read and enthusiastic about new subjects, and enjoy engaging in stimulating conversations. Yet, they often seek recognition from others because they fail to acknowledge their own strengths. They are usually extremely sensitive, and many have clairvoyant abilities. The combination of brilliant minds and extreme sensitivity gives them the ability to connect with the invisible or the intangible, and many of them choose to work either in particularly challenging intellectual fields, such as quantum physics, or in the mystical realms that suit their psychic abilities.

When they're acting from the lower vibrational frequencies of *Self-regulating* energy these people may be confused, impractical, unrealistic, reclusive, hypersensitive, or ungrounded. Filled with hesitation from their own lack of self-confidence, they allow the challenges of life to overwhelm them. The greatest challenge for those born with this type of energy is to move beyond lower vibratory reactions, seek out the part of themselves they've been hiding from, and love it.

When they act from the higher vibrations of *Self-regulating* energy, these people transcend their own challenges and find success. Because the higher vibrations of this energy bring the abilities to cut through illusion, connect to other realms, and flow through challenges with compassion and trust, they can attain recognition through excellent problem-solving. The higher vibratory levels teach them to let go of judgments about themselves and ask for clarity about how they contribute to their own illusions. They've learned that strong reactions to others can provide insights into themselves, and they use their personal gifts to succeed in life by rising above limitations.

19. CATALYZING—MAKING A DIFFERENCE THROUGH OUR VIBRATIONAL PRESENCE

The Maya described *Catalyzing* energy as *cauac,* or storm. The word for storm and turbulent qualities in Cherokee is *unole.* Like the storm for which it is named, this energy brings catalytic transformations. People who carry *Catalyzing* earth energy in their personalities find continual change in their lives. As is also common for those who carry *Evolving* energy, situations that are impossible to avoid are a repeating theme for them. Many of these people suffer chronic illnesses because their lives are so intense. The deeper the affliction, the more life experience is acquired, activating incredible transformation processes. Their choice to be born into this energy indicates a desire to "catch up" in growth and development while clearing past karma in the current life.

People carrying *Catalyzing* energy in their personalities retain a childlike innocence and openness that allows them to follow their intuition and improvise in any situation. There's a sense that they're eternally young. In fact, they're self-generating—integrating their experiences as a way to be their own best teacher. They see from so many perspectives that they need little outside human influence to come to full realization of truth. They are very curious, mentally active, talkative, and friendly. They are multifaceted, interesting, and well-liked, and have a great concern for the welfare of others. Generally uninterested in the mundane affairs of the world, those with *Catalyzing* energy search for the deeper meanings of life. They are natural empaths with magnified sensitivities who have the ability to catalyze events, people, and situations through their mere presence and interactions. Often, their gifts are unappreciated by others who don't recognize their role in bringing about transformational breakthroughs. They keep things moving, and everything changes when they are around. They may not even be aware of why things happen, but things do happen, simply because they are present.

Each of our experiences in life can be seen as either a blessing or a curse, depending upon our perspective. Those who carry *Catalyzing* energy certainly need to learn the importance of choosing their attitude. People in the lower vibrational frequencies of this energy may project their suffering onto others, blaming them for what's occurring. Unresolved or deeply held anger can suddenly erupt, or they may internalize their suffering until it manifests as physical illness. Those in the higher vibrational frequencies use a softer, gentler approach to challenges, stepping out of the way or redirecting the energy as a deeper awareness of unconscious issues that arise to be cleared or healed. At the higher vibrational levels suffering is seen as an opportunity to grow, and people with *Catalyzing* energy learn to accept it and make changes through their own choices. They gain the ability to feel internally complete in the face of external pressures and accept their role as catalytic transformers of people, ideas, and situations.

20. ENLIGHTENING—EMBODYING POSSIBILITIES TO BECOME BEINGS OF LIGHT AND LOVE

The Maya visualized the energy of *Enlightening* as a flower unfolding all its petals in the noonday sun. They named this energy *ahau,* meaning "leader" or "one connected to the light." The Cherokee word for enlightenment is *adadeyodi.* Those who carry *Enlightening* earth energy are idealists and are somewhat romantic in their views of life. They can be wonderful and inspiring, or they can shake themselves (and others) to the core as they plunge into deeper and deeper recognitions of the truth about life. Because their ideals are quite high and they are focused on the beauty of what life *could* be, results may not always meet their expectations. That does not mean their vision is unattainable; they may simply be ahead of their time in understanding what's possible. This realization may cause them to experience frequent disappointment and disillusionment. They may feel that they are often misunderstood because the idealistic vision they bring cannot be comprehended through the structures of existing third-dimensional beliefs.

Enlightening energy represents the light that emanates from our hearts and connects us to the light of Source. People with this energy have an intrinsic knowledge of this light, and it gives them the desire to grow, expand, and share. They have a great respect for beauty. Many are quite creative and may be interested in artistic pursuits: painting, sculpture, fabric, color, architecture, interior decorating, or the simple and elegant beauty of Nature. They're hardworking and goal oriented. They exhibit a natural ability to share what they know with others, yet are not always balanced in doing so. Usually, those with *Enlightening* energy will try to assess the whole picture before they determine their best course of action. They possess a huge desire to find solutions that serve the highest interest of everyone involved. However, once they've decided what they feel is best, they will then try to convince others that the course they have chosen for themselves is also the right course for everyone else. Because of their tendency to alienate others by trying to change or improve them, they work best on their own.

People who have *Enlightening* energy in their makeup often exhibit extremes in their personalities. It's easy to see both the lower and the higher vibratory frequencies in their behavior. At the lower vibratory levels they may be simple dreamers (disconnected from life) or may continually separate themselves from others because they believe they're special or have all the answers. In the extreme these people can develop a Christ complex, believing themselves to be enlightened beings. They may act entitled, believing the world owes them a living because they are so special. The biggest challenge they encounter is judging everything and then needing to overcome the myriad disappointments that occur as they continually strive for perfection in themselves, others, or the world.

At the higher vibrational level those with *Enlightening* energy can be visionaries, determined to bring higher consciousness into the world. They focus on their dreams with intent to make them real, and they remember that they are here to merge dualistic perspectives into harmony, not to insist that only they are right. They feel a need to succeed on their own, regardless of family prosperity, and they will practice unconditional love for all of life. Those with higher vibratory levels of this energy remember everyone is a divine spark of light with something to contribute, and they work to bring everyone's contributions into the whole.

If you have read the descriptions of each of the earth energies presented in this and the previous chapter, you most likely have found part of yourself in each energy. As stated at the beginning of our earth energy exploration, this is because each energy shows us a different view of the same thing. We are all guided from a particular point of view to eventually reach the same destination in our evolutionary journey. The earth energies in conjunction with the universal energies are our map to oneness.

THE ENERGY
OF PERSONAL
RELATIONSHIPS

Relationships also carry their own energy. Just as the personality of an individual requires both earth and universal system energy, so does a relationship. To determine relationship energies, each system is calculated separately. The rules are simple: because universal energies range from 1 to 13, the combined individual numbers must also be in this range. Similarly, the range allowed for a relationship's earth energies is between 1 and 20. For cases where the combined individual numbers fall outside the accepted ranges, a simple subtraction corrects this (shown on pages 145 and 146).

The two calculations are easy and are best demonstrated by an example. Add each individual's universal energies to obtain the relationship's universal energy. (The numerical values are in the list below.)

Numerical List of Earth Energies and Universal Energies
Earth Energies

1. *Being*—place of potential
2. *Breathing*—acknowledgment of other perspectives
3. *Listening*—meditative quiet and stillness before the first thought
4. *Planting*—where we embed our thoughts as seeds for the future

5. *Moving*—where conflicts arise to stimulate change
6. *Transcending*—going beyond the restrictive aspects of our challenges and differences
7. *Remembering*—awakening to the memory of who we are
8. *Loving*—where we practice unconditional love
9. *Feeling*—exploring our emotional guidance for growth
10. *Devoting*—learning about loyalty
11. *Illuminating*—shining the light of insight into the illusion of life
12. *Choosing*—understanding the power of choice and its effects on others
13. *Exploring*—breaking dysfunctional patterns and discovering possibilities
14. *Healing*—understanding the power to make whole again when we connect with and trust the universe
15. *Seeing*—perceiving the details of life from a higher perspective
16. *Intuiting*—listening to the heart and inner voice
17. *Evolving*—eliminating what no longer serves us or the planet
18. *Self-regulating*—bringing ourselves back into flow
19. *Catalyzing*—making a difference through our vibrational presence
20. *Enlightening*—embodying possibilities to become beings of love and light

Universal Energies

1. *initiating*
2. *duality*
3. *creating*
4. *foundation*
5. *change*
6. *flow*
7. *merging*
8. *connecting*
9. *harmonizing*
10. *manifesting*

11. *illuminating*
12. *understanding*
13. *completing*

Relationship Universal Energy

First person's universal energy	1
+ Second person's universal energy	12
Universal relationship energy	13

In this example, the couple's relationship has a universal energy of 13, which is a number within the accepted range. Now, you must determine the relationship's earth energy:

Relationship Earth Energy

First person's earth energy of *healing*	14
+ Second person's earth energy of *healing*	14
Earth relationship energy	28

Notice the relationship's earth energy is 28, which is greater than the maximum allowed number of 20. This is easily adjusted below:

Adjust Relationship Energy

Earth relationship energy	28
− Subtract the maximum earth energy	20
Adjusted earth relationship energy	8

Now, look at the lists again. The personality energy of the couple's relationship is 13 (universal) and 8 (earth). To see the gifts and challenges inherent within the relationship, look at the attributes of the 13th universal energy (*completing*) and the 8th earth energy (*Loving*). This happens to be the energetic signature of the authors' relationship. Our relationship is full of completing projects or ideas and integrating them (as seen in the energy of 13). It also brings a continual stream of opposite viewpoints with the opportunity to harmonize them. But above all, the *Loving* earth energy relationship holds deep spiritual exploration and the expression of complete acceptance and unconditional love.

Here's another example in which both universal and earth energies are out of their acceptable ranges and *must be adjusted:*

First person's universal energy	13
+ Second person's universal energy	4
Universal relationship energy	17

Universal relationship energy	17
− Subtract the maximum universal energy	13
Adjusted universal relationship energy	4

The relationship's earth energy calculations are equally easy:

First person's earth energy	13
+ Second person's earth energy	18
Earth relationship energy	31

To adjust:

Earth relationship energy	31
− Subtract the maximum number of earth energies	20
Adjusted earth relationship energy	11

Look at the lists on pages 143–45 to determine the personality energy of this couple's relationship; it is 4 *foundation* (universal) and 11 *Illuminating* (earth). This relationship has a strong foundational universal energy (4), which can most likely withstand all kinds of challenges. And the 11th earth energy—*Illuminating*—gives the couple a mutual desire to shine light into the illusions of life. They also share an awareness of the power of imagination, positive thoughts, and creative ideas, and a good sense of humor to lighten the challenges life brings.

Now let's practice, step by step, with your own relationship's energy. Remember the total ranges of each set of energies:

Universal energies = 1–13
Earth energies = 1–20

Slowly do the calculations for each system individually first, before combining the two systems together to get the relationship personality.

Step 1: See the numerical value for each universal energy in the list on pages 144–45.

Step 2: Add the first person's universal energy to the second person's universal energy. What is your new total? If your total universal energy number is greater than 13, proceed to step 3 below. If your total universal energy number is less than 13, proceed to step 4 below.

Step 3: If your total universal energy number is greater than 13, take this number and subtract 13 to get your new universal energy value. Record this number and proceed to step 4 below.

Step 4: Using the numerical values in the list on pages 143–44, it's now time to calculate the total earth energies for the relationship. Add the first person's earth energies to the second person's earth energies. What is your new total? If the total earth energies is greater than 20, proceed to step 5 below. If your total earth energies are less than 20, proceed to step 6 below.

Step 5: If your total earth energy number is greater than 20, take this number and subtract 20 to get your new earth energy value. Record this number and proceed to step 6 below.

Step 6: Now that you have a numerical value for both the universal energies and earth energies, you are ready to discover your relationship personality. How exciting! Take a look at the relationship chart and find the definition that corresponds to your universal energy number and the definition that corresponds to your earth energy number. What did you discover?

Of course, there are many other elements determining the character of a relationship. Each person in the relationship contributes all the higher or lower vibratory qualities of their particular combinations of energies. In addition, directional associations influence the compatibility of the relationship. In general, those who share the same direction seem to empower one another, and opposite directions seem to offer the most challenges for growth. Northern energies are very compatible with eastern energies (and vice versa), and southern energies are very compatible with western energies (and vice versa). This simple directional guideline can help us understand why some people are more challenging to be around than others or why we just can't figure out some people. In the same way, we may also use the directional guidance to understand the energy of any given day.

Each person's universal energy plays out in the relationship, too. A person whose universal energy is 1 (*initiating*) will get along much better with someone whose universal energy is 5 (*change*) or 3 (*creating*) than with someone whose universal energy is 4 (*foundation*.) Even the position of Venus—perhaps *especially* the position of Venus—strongly influences the flow within a relationship, as discussed in chapter 5. We will now list some of the particular influences of the earth energies in a relationship. Remember that these attributes form only part of the picture and that other influences contribute to the nature and interactions of the relationship.

1. BEING—THE PLACE OF POTENTIAL

A relationship that carries the earth energy of *Being* will always be full of the potential for change. It may provide a very nurturing ground for discovering all the possibilities in life. However, both partners need to be careful not to assume responsibilities that are not their own or become too indecisive about major decisions. Individuals with *Being* energy often can be obsessive about caring for their beloved in the relationship.

2. BREATHING—ACKNOWLEDGMENT OF OTHER PERSPECTIVES

Because of an inherent reluctance to commit to ideas or situations, many who have *Breathing* energy in their personality struggle in personal relationships. Their partners may view them as inconsistent, negligent, or even fickle. However, a relationship that is built on this energy offers flow and flexibility as part of daily life. If both partners are comfortable with this flow, the relationship can be exciting and growth-oriented.

3. LISTENING—MEDITATIVE QUIET AND STILLNESS BEFORE THE FIRST THOUGHT

People who have *Listening* energy in their makeup experience a paradox between their needs and their desires. They're extremely devoted to their loved ones and are protective, yet if they feel ignored or dismissed, their volcanic tempers can erupt in the environment of the relationship. If the relationship itself is based on *Listening* earth energy, both partners will need private time and space to listen to their own intuition before sharing it. Partners in a *Listening* relationship have a wonderful chance to explore greater depths of relating through entering the stillness together. They also have the opportunity to deal with personal insecurities in a calm and safe harbor.

4. PLANTING—WHERE WE EMBED OUR THOUGHTS AS SEEDS FOR THE FUTURE

If only one partner carries *Planting* energy there may be a tendency for that person to continually seek recognition from the other. If the relationship itself carries *Planting* earth energy, one of the biggest challenges is whether or not partners choose to act maturely with each other. In an immature *Planting* relationship one partner may act in an emotionally or sexually immature manner. In a mature relationship of this type both parties will be eager to bring new ideas into the world. This couple can choose a path together and encourage the growth of the seeds they plant.

5. MOVING—WHERE CONFLICTS ARISE TO STIMULATE CHANGE

People with *Moving* energy need very little from others and will not often negotiate on issues that they feel could compromise their freedom. This tendency may cause intimacy problems or challenges in personal relationships. Partners can change direction without conscious thought of how it affects the other person. Emotions easily come to the surface in this type of earth energy relationship. Differences in how each partner sees the world will continually bring struggle as well as opportunities to grow through finding a unified perspective and releasing the need to be right. At times, a *Moving* relationship may feel like a roller coaster to the couple involved.

6. TRANSCENDING—GOING BEYOND THE RESTRICTIVE ASPECTS OF OUR CHALLENGES AND DIFFERENCES

People with *Transcending* energy have a strong interest in relationships and will usually choose a partner who shares the traditional values that are important to them. In a *Transcending* earth energy relationship, each person will usually consider what is important to his or her partner. Difficulties may arise when one refrains from taking action and waits for the other person to make decisions. The relationship may serve as a turning point of growth for both parties, as it offers a place where differences may be harmonized in a mutual desire for peace.

7. REMEMBERING—AWAKENING TO THE MEMORY OF WHO WE ARE

Deep connections can be difficult for those who have *Remembering* energy, so personal relationships may be challenging. They may struggle between the need to be independent and the need to be in the relationship. A relationship based on this earth energy can bring opportunities to discover how to move through differences by using compromise or to how to find ways of being independent while still being actively involved in the relationship.

8. LOVING—WHERE WE PRACTICE UNCONDITIONAL LOVE

Because this is the energy of the relationship of the authors, we are intimately familiar with all the gifts a relationship with *Loving* energy can bring. We will explore this relationship in more depth than we have offered in the descriptions of other relationship energy, simply to give you an example of possibilities that can be discovered within the challenges of any relationship. *Every* relationship brings the potential for growth and expansion for those who have chosen to be in it, if both parties agree to work with the energies that are present.

In relationships that carry *Loving* energy, couples find themselves cycling between feelings of being at cross-purposes and having misunderstandings, to feelings of sublime unity, acceptance, beauty, and unconditional love. Those who are drawn into this energy type of relationship hold the vision of a new world and new ideals. Because *Loving* energy represents a new vision and a new truth, those who carry this energy may believe that there is only one way to do things—the way of their higher vision. In a relationship that combines individual components, there will be conflict over what is considered the right way until both partners learn to accept that there can be two rights, rather than a right and a wrong. The challenge of this relationship is to remember to use the higher vision of *Loving* energy by honoring each other's perspectives.

Many may wonder why they can't seem to consistently maintain the positive state, failing to understand that the purpose of their union is to continually bring opposites back into harmony. Each partner in a *Loving* relationship will continually bring different perspectives into the relationship, allowing both parties to surrender into the harmony of multiple perspectives that lead to a single truth.

Loving energy is an accelerated energy of a new order, and in this type of relationship, each partner is challenged to remember all of who she or he is. This energy is related to the Christ light and demands each partner continually return to unconditional pure love in order to remain in the relationship. Each person must release any tendency toward judgment, of both self and the other person, and learn to make conscious and responsible choices in each moment so that no regrets are created. There may be many questions within the relationship about who the couple is together or the nature of their joint destiny. The paradox is that *Loving* relationships are *already* being themselves and living their destiny. *Loving* gifts and talents hold unrecognized wisdom, and the challenge of this relationship is to continually embody the clarity and power of their natural gifts while living in harmony. They must always remember to open to larger possibilities.

Loving energy works with opposites more than any other earth energy does, encouraging continual growth by keeping some tension between the polarities while seeking balance as the separation of opposites merges into unity. In a relationship this means that each person will fight for what he or she believes to be right, trying to teach the other the new truth. *Loving* relationships vacillate between being overly opinionated and too easily influenced through a desire for cooperation. This type of relationship energy can be so powerful that it overrides individual personalities, causing confusion and doubt about individual truths. These tendencies can cause reactive qualities

that affect either partner, causing that partner to be overly opinionated and stubborn in protecting beliefs. While this energy represents
simplicity (through love, peace, and harmony), the tendency to believe
there's only one right way to do things can cause a great deal of mental clutter and complexity. *Loving* relationships can create addictive
cycles of conflict through obsessive thoughts and compulsive reactions, blowing things out of proportion. Cycles like this are self-
destructive. The secret to navigating this possible paradox is to not
give way to extremes, always express feelings in a positive way, and
remember that there can be *two* rights, rather than a right and a wrong
view. This keeps the relationship focused on its core truths of peace,
love, and harmony. It's beneficial for those in *Loving* relationships to
keep moving, rather than getting stuck in places of mental analysis
that cause imbalance within and between partners, and to continually choose peace and love. Balance is of key importance in *Loving*
relationships.

9. FEELING—EXPLORING OUR EMOTIONAL GUIDANCE FOR GROWTH

Personal relationships can be exceedingly challenging for individuals
who carry *Feeling* energy unless they have learned to navigate their
own emotional waters. Unpredictable changes of mind and emotional
reactions can sometimes make a deep or lasting relationship almost
impossible, unless matched with someone who enjoys the challenge
of complete unpredictability. In relationships carrying *Feeling* earth
energy, couples may find themselves in continual struggles between
expressing the depth of their feelings and overreacting to one another.
Feeling relationships may oscillate between feelings of deep sharing
and connection to times of hurt feelings, misunderstandings, and
withdrawal. Those in this type of relationship who choose to respond
rather than react—to each other and to life—experience much richness in their relationship.

10. DEVOTING—LEARNING ABOUT LOYALTY

Because *Devoting* energy is a very loyal energy, people who carry this energy make wonderful partners, especially when they find someone with whom they feel a kinship of the soul. Relationships are extremely important to them, and a relationship based on this type of energy will bring both partners a sense of feeling safe; it's a space in which they can work on any issues of trust lingering from previous experiences, whether in their earlier lives or parallel lives.*

11. ILLUMINATING—SHINING THE LIGHT OF INSIGHT INTO THE ILLUSION OF LIFE

A person with *Illuminating* earth energy brings curiosity, creativity, and drama into any relationship. Relationships that carry this energy can be quite challenging, causing the partners to be emotionally distant and aloof from each other or to use the challenges as opportunities to deepen what they share. Partners are usually loyal to one another and enjoy a continual flow of stimulating conversation, entertainment, and exploration of uncharted territory together. This is a relationship that may be full of drama or curious explorations and/or a shared desire to shine light into the darkness of the world.

12. CHOOSING—UNDERSTANDING THE POWER OF CHOICE AND ITS EFFECT ON OTHERS

Relationships are of utmost importance to people with *Choosing* energy. Those with this energy seek out a personal relationship as a

---

*Laarkmaa describes past lives as parallel lives. A full explanation is in *Conversations with Laarkmaa*, page 7.

necessity, like food or shelter, and usually make wonderful partners when matched with the right person. Because they so highly value peace, they often act in a self-sacrificing manner, attempting to please and keep the peace in every relationship. They may later resent these sacrifices if they haven't respected themselves enough to be honest in expressing their own truth. They long for deep connections with others and seek them through interpersonal relationships before creating an honest relationship with themselves—a relationship where they actually listen to their emotional guidance and make choices from the heart.

Choosing earth energy relationships radiate a sense of ease and charm. People in these relationships usually experience the world as a pleasant place, although there are certainly challenges to help them grow. These relationships are usually very interested in being of service. The creative potential available in this type of earth energy relationship can provide levels of service that really make a difference for planetary evolution.

13. EXPLORING—BREAKING FREE FROM DYSFUNCTIONAL PATTERNS AND DISCOVERING NEW POSSIBILITIES

People with *Exploring* energy also have a strong desire for close personal relationships but won't tolerate anything that restricts them from being themselves. Although they're usually loyal and caring partners, they need freedom of movement and enjoy variety in life experiences. Relationships with *Exploring* earth energy are sure to be filled with constant travel, discoveries, and sharing. Overall, partners in this type of energy relationship support each other and usually align in harmony.

14. HEALING—THE POWER TO RESTORE WHOLENESS WHEN WE CONNECT WITH AND TRUST THE UNIVERSE

Those with *Healing* energy will usually enter into a relationship only with someone whose primary focus is spirituality. They will not tolerate shallow relationships, yet often get entangled in relationships where they become responsible for keeping their partner's life afloat, causing internal conflict. Relationships with *Healing* earth energy are also usually based on spiritual interests and personal or planetary evolution. A couple that shares this type of energy relationship may find themselves continually giving to others in an attempt to help the world. They will need to set time aside to honor the relationship.

15. SEEING—PERCEIVING THE DETAILS OF LIFE FROM A HIGHER PERSPECTIVE

People who have *Seeing* energy do best in relationships with other free spirits, yet many find themselves in relationships that tie them down or with partners who try to control them. Relationships based on *Seeing* earth energy can offer both parties respect for individual freedom within the relationship. People in this type of relationship may find themselves often escaping on vacations to relieve any limits they may feel in everyday life. The relationship supports building a life that is not restrictive.

16. INTUITING—LISTENING TO OUR HEARTS AND INNER VOICES

People with *Intuiting* earth energy may be reluctant to commit to long-term relationships for fear of being overcome by the power of another person or by the power of the relationship itself. Insecurities arise for them in relationships when they perceive they're being judged, but when judgment is not present, these people are usually very dedicated part-ners. A relationship with *Intuiting* energy can be full of grace, a realistic approach to life, and the potential for growth. To remain functional, this relationship absolutely must have a comfortable balance of personal authority and the willingness to listen to and respect the other.

17. EVOLVING—ELIMINATE WHAT NO LONGER SERVES US OR THE PLANET

People with *Evolving* earth energy prefer to maintain a sense of per-sonal independence within relationships. They don't like having their lives dictated by others, and this can even include another's suggestions. Many people with *Evolving* energy choose to remain independent rather than struggle through the compromises that are required in a balanced relationship. Relationships that are based on this type of energy are usually unpredictable and full of change, and both partners will need to work together to remember challenges are opportunities to respond in creative or unusual ways. Together, they can brainstorm about new ideas or make unusual choices about the way they live their lives.

18. SELF-REGULATING—BRINGING OURSELVES BACK INTO FLOW, MOMENT BY MOMENT

Those with *Self-regulating* energy long to understand the deeper meaning of relationships (beyond the romantic or the physical). They may express jealousy through their intense desire to deeply connect with another or struggle in close relationships because they're unre-alistic about what the relationship can offer. In a relationship of *Self-regulating* earth energy, partners will likely be totally devoted to each other, yet may find themselves compromising to achieve harmony. They may struggle to cooperate without losing a sense of themselves. This relationship provides an excellent base for learning how to express individual needs while still honoring the needs of the beloved.

19. CATALYZING—MAKING A DIFFERENCE THROUGH OUR VIBRATIONAL PRESENCE

Relationships are supremely important to people with *Catalyzing* energy. Homelife anchors them. They will treat their partners with respect and faithfulness, expecting the same in return. A relationship of *Catalyzing* earth energy exhibits love, affection, genuine caring, emotional support, and overwhelming compassion. Partners in this type of relationship may often find themselves helping out in their partner's problems to change the situation. This couple may also often unintentionally find themselves the center of attention at social events. They will find that they stir things up wherever they go.

20. ENLIGHTENING—EMBODYING POSSIBILITIES TO BECOME BEINGS OF LIGHT AND LOVE

Those with *Enlightening* energy in their personalities devote themselves to partners or friends with astonishing intensity. They're quick to sacrifice themselves for the happiness of another, but are disappointed when their sacrifices aren't appreciated. In a relationship of *Enlightening* energy, being truly concerned for the welfare of others is as natural as breathing. Yet the partners may have challenges when one partner claims to know what is best for everyone in all situations, thereby devaluing the other's contributions. However, when this couple is in harmony, love can radiate from them into the world as they share visionary ideals and hope for the future.

After reading energetic characteristics of each type of earth energy relationship, you have most likely recognized that *all* relationships struggle with different perspectives and ways of doing things and that *all* relationships offer great opportunities for growth and increased harmony. These brief descriptions are only a shallow glance at what is possible in a relationship, and it is, of course, up to each participant to determine how to access the potential richness of being in a relationship with another. Enjoy your explorations and allow your deeper look at your relationship to bring more grace and flow into your life.

11
SHADOW CYCLES
OF EVOLUTION

According to the Pleiadian perspective, once every 260 of our Gregorian calendar days we come to a particular alignment with the cosmic spiral of universal energies that opens to greater possibilities for collective change. These periods of alignment are energetic portals of opportunity to discard dysfunctional beliefs and illusions and realign ourselves with universal truths. This "pause" in our ongoing unfolding of experience also coincides with the retrograde period of Venus at the end of each of Her cycles, as mentioned in chapter 5. During these times we are encouraged to move into the heart-based cosmic perceptions of energy and life that can expand our consciousness. We call such times of alignment "collective shadow periods." These periods give humanity a chance to release the tension of emotion-based judgments and fears that have accumulated from misconceptions of the truth and move into the possibility of understanding the cosmic wisdom that we are all connected. Similarly, each individual encounters a personal shadow cycle approximately every sixty-five days, where a greater opportunity for personal work occurs.

Laarkmaa uses the Mayan term In Lak'ech to describe the understanding of universal connection. The importance of understanding this concept cannot be underestimated because it teaches us that everything we think, say, or do affects everyone and everything else, on this planet and out into the universe. Likewise, we are affected either positively or negatively by everything others think, say, or do. Shadow periods (both collective and individual) offer a time to consider whether or not the reality we are experiencing is the one we truly wish to continue. They generally cause enough discomfort to encourage us to examine how we are participating with life and if we are allowing it to help us grow. Through personal or collective introspection we can release all the misconceptions that continue to define our world and choose more cosmically aligned truths. The reason this isn't happening is because most of humanity refuses to open their eyes to other perspectives and stop judging those who do not see the world as they do. The usual treatment of a shadow cycle by those who do not understand their benefit (which is most of humanity!) is to further entrench existing beliefs about what is right and wrong, closing down all possibilities for change that are offered during this period of cosmic opportunity. People become very emotional during shadow cycles. Laarkmaa tells us that all emotions are signals that we ourselves are out of balance and therefore change must begin within *us*.[1] However, most people who experience emotional distress revert to old patterns of outward blame, rather than doing inner work to change themselves.

Usually, we humans focus our attention on a forward momentum that is aligned with our perception of time. Our thoughts are linear, we schedule all of our appointments in advance according to an agreed-upon time, and most of our choices are based on either an experienced past (things we have been taught through others or experienced ourselves) or an imagined future. We perceive everything that occurs in linear time. During shadow periods this alignment with linear time simply doesn't work. Universal movement of energy is counterclockwise, and during these periods of alignment with universal movement we may feel a tension or a lack of congruence in our lives because we are experiencing an unaccustomed orientation of energetic movement. Energy moves in intelligent patterns and waves. During a collective shadow cycle there may be an underlying agitation that brings stronger than usual emotional reactions to circumstances. These periods may bring tension in relationships, financial distress, or political unrest. The underlying agitation is actually an urge to cut through all illusion and find unity, but it is rarely acknowledged as an impulse for positive change. It is difficult for the collective to make big shifts in belief systems. Historically, these periods have been misused by the few who understand how to manipulate emotional chaos to create a further sense of uncertainty and fear. The establishment of the Department of Homeland Security in the United States is a prime example. The department was established on November 25, 2002, the first day of a collective shadow period, allegedly in response to fears of terrorism. However, it has since become clear that it was also and continues to be a response to widespread xenophobia. The failure to achieve a harmonic situation among nations on Earth demonstrates that most of our governments and religious leaders are still desperately clinging to an ancient paradigm that breeds judgment, separation, poverty, and war—a paradigm based on forward progress, linear time, and control rather than on cooperation and living in the present moment. This old paradigm is kept in place by our individual and collective participation in systems that are ruled by globally agreed-upon concepts about reality.

As our planet moves into alignment with cosmic energies every 260 days, the collective shadow cycles offer an opportunity to reassess what we believe about reality and to make changes for our own evolution. Truly transformative events can occur during these times, but they rarely do because, collectively, we are simply not open to possibilities.

The counterclockwise spiral of a shadow cycle is designed to help us unwind the patterns that no longer serve humanity or the cosmos. The Pleiadians have explained that there is a purpose to experiencing these cycles of emotional stress and upset. These patterns of intense emotional reactions regularly present themselves as an opportunity to examine emotional blockages and dysfunctional beliefs. The field of psychology has long recognized that dysfunctional beliefs contribute to or cause emotional discomfort. Yet, one of the most difficult things for humans to achieve is the release of long-cherished beliefs. Beliefs give us a structure on which we build our reality. Periods of intense shadow work help us to consider other potentials through examining beliefs that no longer work and to open our hearts and minds to new possibilities. This way of working with our own psyches and behaviors is key to our well-being and our evolution, providing a chance to unwind karma or deep patterns that are no longer useful in our lives. When we work with them, they help us to align with a natural, cosmic flow.

COLLECTIVE SHADOW PERIODS

Collective shadow periods always begin in the energy of 4 *Being* (under the influence of *Self-regulating* evolutionary guidance), and they end on 10 *Enlightening* (under the evolutionary guidance of *Illuminating*.) Laarkmaa explains that this combination of energies is particularly potent in awakening humans in the evolutionary process. Those who wish to evolve simply must self-regulate to the energies demanding evolutionary change. As they begin to shift their perspectives and beliefs, they become more illuminated by the truth. (See an example of a collective shadow period in figure 12.1. A complete listing of upcoming collective shadow cycles until 2033 is listed in appendix B.)

It is up to us to begin to understand and use shadow cycle periods of cosmic alignment to begin to understand and change patterns that no longer serve us individually or as a species. We may feel out of control if we resist the evolutionary changes that are occurring, or we may participate with them by spiraling into higher viewpoints and choosing more conscious actions. Many of our choices in the modern world are based on artificial financial values. We participate in a hierarchical system of charging money (paper that actually has no value) for services. This form of exchange is based on an idea that we must exchange our gifts and talents (work) for a reward (food and shelter) that is provided by someone else. A more cooperative, energetic, conscious form of existence would eliminate the use of money for a more balanced exchange of

Sample of Entire Collective Shadow Cycle

Each shadow cycle Begins on 4 *Being* and ends on 10 *Enlightening*.

Date in Cycle	Universal Energy	Earth Energy
April 10, 2019	4	*Being*
April 11, 2019	5	*Breathing*
April 12, 2019	6	*Listening*
April 13, 2019	7	*Planting*
April 14, 2019	8	*Moving*
April 15, 2019	9	*Transcending*
April 16, 2019	10	*Remembering*
April 17, 2019	11	*Loving*
April 18, 2019	12	*Feeling*
April 19, 2019	13	*Devoting*
April 20, 2019	1*	*Illuminating*
April 21, 2019	2	*Choosing*
April 22, 2019	3	*Exploring*
April 23, 2019	4	*Healing*
April 24, 2019	5	*Seeing*
April 25, 2019	6	*Intuiting*
April 26, 2019	7	*Evolving*
April 27, 2019	8	*Self-Regulating*
April 28, 2019	9	*Catalyzing*
April 29, 2019	10	*Enlightening*

*Note the universal count begins again within the shadow cycle at 1.

© 2018, Pia Orleane Ph.D.

Figure 12.1

energy. Scottish author, philosopher, and master dowser Hamish Miller offered the world another way to achieve harmony through establishing an organization called Parallel Communities in 2006. Through his organization he linked more than one thousand members in diverse groups around the globe who were seeking to build a more caring and positive future for mankind. Miller's parallel communities still exist (see www.parallelcommunity.com) to foster cooperation and the idea of In Lak'ech.

More recently, South African author and politician Michael Tellinger has reawakened the world to possibilities of establishing communities based on the African philosophy of *ubuntu*, which is part of a Zulu phrase meaning that all of humanity has a universal bond of sharing. In this philosophy an exchange of energies rather than money guides the community.[2] In 2012 Tellinger founded the Ubuntu Party in South Africa, based on principles of contributionism, and today there are small groups around the globe struggling to bring this dream to life. As long as we repeat old patterns of behavior that are preordained through linear thinking and competitive living, we can expect future collective shadow periods to bring even more conflict, creating what Laarkmaa calls the "dynamic tension" that is necessary for revolutionary and evolutionary change.

We can see the effects of that mode of behavior in current world politics, as well as in looking backward through what we remember or have been taught through illusory history that was colored and written according to the beliefs of those who recorded it. Based on our current response to the cosmic energies pushing for evolution on this planet, Laarkmaa tells us that we can expect more dynamic tension, bringing even more discord, destruction, and devastation of existing financial and political structures in a push for the changes that are necessary if we are to live in a more balanced, conscious way. These human revolutionary movements are most likely to be accompanied by catastrophic movements of Earth herself. The consciousness of energy is actually propelling us into a different paradigm. We must ask ourselves if we need to be forced to change, or are we willing to participate in our own evolution?

In these times of challenge and opportunity we can raise our consciousness by abandoning outdated ways of thinking. We can respond to life by simply changing our perspectives and opening our hearts. The core of the true reality as perceived through cosmic awareness is available for all of us to experience in any moment, without the illusions that we have collectively created. Shadow periods offer us a chance to stop momentarily and reexamine where we are, collectively or individually. They then reset our forward momentum according to how we have (or have not) used the wisdom available during the period of cosmic alignment.

INDIVIDUAL SHADOW CYCLES

Shadow cycles are not limited to opportunities for the collective. Each of us has a unique pattern of cycles of growth (personal shadow cycles) that offer us an opportunity to do accelerated inner work approximately once every sixty-five days. Through doing our own personal shadow work and changing ourselves, we can make a difference in the collective. Remember, everyone and everything is connected. Therefore, if we individually begin to respond differently to life, it will ultimately affect the response of others as well. Individual shadow cycles are determined by counting sixty-five days from the same energy as the day of your birth.

You can find that energy in appendix C for your birth year and then look for it again in the current year to start noting your personal shadow cycles. The date you find marks the end of your personal shadow cycle. Seven to ten days preceding *that* date you will begin to experience the actual shadow cycle period, which offers a chance for doing deep inner work.

Unlike collective shadow cycles, a personal shadow cycle does not always begin in the same energy. In fact, personal shadow cycles rotate through varying levels of consciousness, giving us an individual, community, global, and universal perspective of where we may be stuck or need to change within one 260-day period. The flow of personal shadow work moves us through all four of these stages of awareness, giving us the opportunity to look more deeply at what may need to change within us.

THE FOUR STAGES OF AWARENESS

Each of the four stages of shadow cycles will bring our awareness to a central theme from various levels of awareness. The central theme for each person's work is thereby presented through different perspectives and through different circumstances until that theme has been thoroughly examined from each level of awareness. You will also notice the repeated suggestion to learn to listen to your intuition in many of the shadow cycles.

Individual shadow cycles may present such themes as:

- Loneliness and feelings of rejection
- Inner conflict between survival needs and social interaction
- A deep need for security or rigid beliefs about what is "right"
- Challenge in making decisions
- A struggle to be seen and recognized.

Community shadow cycles may hold themes such as:

- Tension between the need for security and the desire for freedom
- Feelings of victimhood or not being able to receive what is needed
- Conflict between stubbornness and a need to change
- General turbulence and a tendency to fight for a specific viewpoint
- Irrational urges and a lack of self-control
- A general lack of trust.

Global shadow cycles may bring themes of:

- Judgment and competition or a need to improve self or others
- Conflicting physical and spiritual needs
- Tendency to focus on self-interest versus global concerns
- Control over individual passions
- Questions about reality and responsibilities.

Universal shadow cycles may bring a focus on:

- Feelings of being unable to manifest dreams
- Assumptions and beliefs based on history and a refusal to change beliefs
- A deep need to belong versus internal contradictions about what feels right
- Disappointment
- A restless desire to cut through all illusion.

Each cycle holds a particular theme that is relevant to the individual, and it will present over and over until it is transcended on all levels. While particular themes connected to each shadow period are suggested in this book, each person uncovers individual patterns in working with a personal cycle. as each issue is presented in periodic and familiar patterns. You can look at the suggestions for each period, but remember that these themes are not the only "issues" that may arise during a particular cycle. The actual period of personal work begins ten days prior to any listed "shadow day."

Once every 260 days, in harmony with the cycles of Venus, we enter into an energy that closely replicates the energy that was present when we were born. These days are called spiritual birthdays. The energy ten days or so prior to a spiritual birthday penetrates the outer personality deeply, nudging us to remember who we really are. These ten days may feel like a struggle to change, a push to move forward, and may present intense challenges in the birthing of a new version of self. These are the gateways or portals in each person's spiral of evolution that provide opportunities to jump to another level of consciousness. Because the energetic patterns just before a spiritual birthday may seem most familiar, they offer the largest opportunities to move out of old paradigms of belief and behavior through deep inner work.

While shadow cycles are our greatest opportunities for changing dysfunctional or outdated coping habits, behaviors, and beliefs, our shadows can come to the surface for our attention at any time. Therefore, it is always advantageous to examine what we are thinking during any extreme emotional reaction to another person or to life in general, remembering that the emotions themselves are signposts to do our work and make necessary changes. Laarkmaa explains in great and patient detail just how to do this in their book *Remembering Who We Are.*

Most people experiencing a personal shadow cycle assume they are having a series of "bad hair" days or days that just seem unlucky. However, the truth is that they are experiencing a cosmic nudge to examine aspects of their lives that are out of harmony with life and the cosmos. Laarkmaa has explained in their many public appearances and in both of their books that emotions signal change and that all change must begin within the individual.[3] Working with our emotions is the greatest way to help the collective, our world, and ourselves. Because emotions are typically heightened during personal shadow cycles, these cycles bring up all the places within us that we need to examine to make positive changes. We may feel like we are in a pressure cooker, finding that everything in our experience (emotional and physical) seems much more intense. Emotions of frustration, anger, disappointment, or grief may surface. Our job in a shadow cycle is to acknowledge these emotions and examine how they are guiding us to change without allowing them to overflow onto others. Sadly, most people miss the opportunities available within a personal shadow cycle because either they are not aware that the difficulties they are experiencing are opportunities for change and growth or they are so stuck in painful patterns that they cannot see a way to do things differently. Understanding how to work with our own shadows is the most potent place to work for personal (and planetary) growth and transformation. These cycles are great opportunities for evolution.

SHADOW CYCLE THEMES

There are certain themes that seem to present during specific energetic periods of shadow work for each of the earth energies. These themes need to be adapted to each person's personal search for change and growth, and not everyone will experience a shadow cycle in every energy. Typically, each person experiences only four of the shadow cycle energies, but not always. Some people have a greater variety of influences during particular cycles. The daily unfolding of earth energies brings individual, community, global, and universal energies sequentially, with each period having a different feeling. The cycles of working with internal shadows and pain, which last for approximately ten days, continue this flow, yet the ten-day period generally has a central theme of consciousness directed by the current evolutionary guidance, shining light into the shadows that most need attention. As you read through these themes, notice how the cycle moves your consciousness through the varying levels of individual, community, global, and universal awareness. Each theme is listed according to the dominant earth energy of the cycle.

Being. Consciousness is at an *individual* level of awareness during this period. Everything that happens may seem personal during this cycle, but the underlying push is a real urge to move away from separation. You may long to make others understand just who you are, and the desire to merge is great. Emotions may reflect deep feelings of rejection or loneliness during this time. The solution is to be creative and initiate new ways of being and interacting with others.

Transcending. Consciousness is at a *community* level of awareness during this period. This is a cycle designed to bring us more into harmony by recognizing the potency of In Lak'ech. In fact, it is in this energy that we can begin to find the true essence of community. In a period of *Transcending* work one may experience a continual need to improve both self and the world. There may be an inner drive to initiate projects or to assert yourself. There is a tremendous desire to make a difference to the community, and you may find yourself giving so much that you feel used or unappreciated. The work during this time is to examine any feelings of self-sacrifice or victimhood. Make conscious choices about what and with whom you share. Work to understand that everything is not always about *you* and trust that the universe is working for the highest good of all. Participate through making choices that will reflect positively for everyone.

Illuminating. Consciousness is at a *global* level of awareness during this period. It is in this cycle of shadow work that we can begin to distinguish between the illusion and the reality of life on Earth. All manner of "symptoms" may appear as signposts for imbalance. You may find yourself focusing on how love is given and received. The energy of Venus is strongly present in this particular cycle of shadow work, showing us how to use others' perspectives and make exchanges through sharing with others. The work during this cycle is to ask the question, "Is this real or an illusion of a particular belief system?" The solution to finding light in the shadows is to be sure to take responsibility for every thought, feeling, and action one experiences. Play with possibilities and take responsibility for every choice that creates the current reality. Healing and creativity are more easily accessed when we work harmoniously with the energies of this cycle.

Intuiting. Consciousness is at a *universal* level of awareness during this period. Here is the place where we can begin to understand the connection between Earth and the universe and how intuitive wisdom connects us to Source. An *Intuiting* cycle may further deepen questions about what is real and what is not. Here is the place to work on assumptions and beliefs that are based on history or experience. Emotions arise with intensity when we refuse to consider changing our beliefs during this time. The solution to inner conflicts within this cycle is to examine *all* beliefs and assumptions. Work to trust rather than to believe. Open your ears, eyes, and perceptions to the "other" that exists. Remember what you have to offer when your insights come from your intuitive connection to all that is.

Breathing. Consciousness returns to an *individual* level of awareness during this period. This cycle carries a restless and changeable energy. Those who experience a *Breathing* shadow cycle may feel challenged in making decisions. There may also be an increased personal need to communicate during this cycle. This need is an expression of individual consciousness reaching out to become community consciousness. The work during this cycle is to be flexible, not fickle. Honor intuition over the challenges presented by the mind. Breathe before you speak or act, and surround yourself with those who support both who you are and who you are becoming.

Remembering. Consciousness is at the *community* level of awareness during this period. This cycle is a call to transform existing circumstances into more peaceful circumstances. Innovation and movement are required. This cycle is experienced as an emotional tension between the personal need for security and a desire for freedom. The solution is to be creative and refuse to allow others to dictate how you should live. Work to bring the essence of freedom into the earthly realms.

Choosing. Consciousness is at the *global* level of awareness during this period. Here is the opportunity to reveal the secret of life on Earth—that we have the power of choice, and when we use it in alignment with the highest good for all, we can make a difference in our world. Physical and spiritual issues may come to the surface to be healed. Internal conflicts may seem larger than usual, and they will demand your attention.

You may wish to withdraw from the world to seek ancient, deeply hidden truths. The solution to this challenging time is threefold: feel with the heart, choose consciously, and look for the positive in all experiences. This cycle holds the potential for helping humanity remember how to use the power of choice to manifest a more peaceful world.

Evolving. Consciousness is at the *universal* level of awareness during this period. To those who are familiar with Western astrology, this cycle may feel like you are involved with the energy of Uranus—full of the urge for change and independence. Boundaries constantly shift and change during this time. Emotionally, you may be prone to dreaming, and mentally, you may drift off into fantasy; plans often fall apart. The solution is to practice flexibility and patience. Make yourself totally present in the now, rather than escaping into fantasy of "what if." Use your imagination to actually turn dreams into reality. Evolution is all about moving beyond existing boundaries into a better form.

Listening. Consciousness returns to an *individual* focus of awareness during this period. Here is the opportunity to return to the void and quietly wait for guidance. Here is where we silence our overactive minds, calm our emotional states, and simply wait for instructions from the universe. In a *Listening* cycle we finds an awareness of limitations. The energy may feel much like the energy of Saturn—full of restrictions, limitations, and discipline. This period demands hard work for growth and transformation. It requires that we break old patterns. In a cycle of *Listening* energy you may experience trouble at every turn. You may feel frustrated, stuck, or even have great trouble sharing. The world may not seem to meet the high standards you require, giving you an inner desire to simply withdraw into the void. The work is to overcome any rigidity in personal thoughts, beliefs, or judgments about others. Move beyond old patterns of emotional or physical insecurity. The solution to the distress of this cycle comes in remembering that you are eternal. Remember that and move forward into the mystery! Trust the universe to provide everything you need.

Loving. Consciousness moves to a *community* level of awareness during this period. The cycle brings confrontation and fights for the larger truth. This energy is aligned with the Divine Feminine (Mary Magdalene, Mother Mary, Isis, Quan Yin), as well as with the Christ light. It is also related to Venus, which appears as both morning star and evening star, demonstrating how we, too, can express unconditional love even when we are experiencing opposite perspectives. In the process of working with our shadows, we may feel turbulence and tension as we strive to grow. Work to overcome any tendency to fight for your own viewpoint or to compete to prove you are right. Remember that there can always be *two* rights, rather than a right and a wrong. You are simply seeing different perspectives that, when looked at properly, can be harmonized in unity, so look for goals that support a unified view. Use this period to learn to see all aspects of any situation through the eyes of unconditional love.

Exploring. Consciousness is at a *global* level of awareness during this period. There is a great presence of initiation, drive, and assertion during this cycle. Those familiar with Western astrology may see this period as aligned with the energy of Mars. Someone experiencing an *Exploring* shadow cycle will most likely feel a constant need to improve self and the world. Work to overcome judgment of *anything,* including yourself. The solution to emotional distress during this time is to be more kind and accepting of yourself, of others, and of the world.

Self-Regulating. Consciousness is at a *universal* level during this period. You may feel quite alone during a *Self-regulating* shadow cycle, yet powerful transformative experiences are available at this time. There is a strong urge to find and experience unity, somewhat akin to the influence of Neptune in Western astrology. A sense of restlessness may be common. To work with the shadow energies of this cycle, work to consciously overcome any tendency to be critical. Allow an inner awareness to cut away illusions that have formed from dysfunctional beliefs. Use the emotional energy of this time as signposts to self-regulate, find inner harmony, and learn to look beyond what you believe to be true. Cooperate and share without expectations or judgment.

Planting. Consciousness is at the *individual* level of awareness during this period. This is an energetic period that truly pushes us to expand. Self-awareness is critical. You may experience feeling challenged by outer circumstances when your inner desire is to move forward or grow in some way. There is usually a strong need for personal recognition during this cycle. The work is to overcome any tendencies to react in relationships and to focus on gratitude. Planting energy is about planting new ideas, new concepts, and new behaviors. The shadow cycle of *Planting* requires you to look deeply at what you are embedding in your consciousness and become self-aware of old thoughts and patterns of behavior that must be discarded for the new to arrive. Use this period to develop mature responses to life circumstances.

Feeling. Consciousness is at the *community* level of awareness during this period. This is a particularly difficult shadow cycle, which means it offers larger opportunities for growth. You may experience powerful, yet often irrational, urges along with feelings of being completely out of control of your emotional reactions to life. The usual reaction to such energy is to apply strong will to try to control others and your environment. This pattern has been created to allow an illusory feeling of safety. But the cycle is asking that you stop that behavior and learn to master the waves of emotion within yourself. This is the perfect time to practice Laarkmaa's exercise described in *Remembering Who We Are,* to begin watching what you *think* while you are having such huge emotional responses. Learn to change your thoughts away from dysfunctional beliefs or fears. Move your thoughts toward gratitude and trust. This is the predominant lesson of this cycle. The gift of this time is to move away from irrational emotions into a place of enhanced intuition that can then be carried into daily life.

Healing. Consciousness moves to a *global* level of awareness during this period. There is an increase in movement between mystical worlds and the third dimension in this energy. There is also a quickening of the Divine Feminine, which can be unsettling to those attached to patriarchal values. Passions may run out of control. The work of this cycle is to control those passions and inwardly search for the truth. The solution comes from correcting any thoughtless, reckless, or arrogant behaviors and moving into mystical worlds through listening to your intuition.

Catalyzing. The consciousness of this shadow cycle is focused on *universal* awareness. The energy pushes us toward transformation that is aligned with unity. Western astrologers may relate this energy to the energy of Pluto, the planet of transformation. This cycle is full of paradoxes and external controls. You may experience a simultaneous ability to see many perspectives at once and a deep need to belong. The work is to awaken through following our hearts. Anchor yourself to the truth and know that you can be an example to all.

Moving. Consciousness is at an *individual* level of awareness during this period. It will be filled with internal conflicts that come from idealistic or unrealistic thoughts and a hunger for change. However, you may feel thwarted in your progress. During this time you may experience a tendency to cut off social interaction, which was developed as an old survival technique. The work is to keep your heart open, trust others, and trust life. The solution comes when you trust your heart rather than your mind. Honor the Divine Feminine that nurtures you and listen to your intuition rather than your thoughts.

Devoting. Consciousness is at the *community* level of awareness during this period. It is a time in which to examine loyalties. You are expanding from individual perspectives to community-oriented ideas and may feel confused when something (or someone) does not respond in the same loyal way that you do. In this cycle you may question why you feel so alone and why the loyalty you feel to others is not returned. Yet, this shadow cycle is pushing you to choose wisely where loyalty is placed. Laarkmaa tells us that the greatest loyalty is loyalty to the truth, not to ideas we hold about being loyal to certain people, countries, or religions. The work is to stop being stubborn about your own ideas and begin to cooperate at a higher level. The solution comes when you focus on clear communication. If you feel stuck, question your beliefs and change your perspectives. Be loyal to the light of truth.

Seeing. Consciousness is at the *global* level of awareness during this shadow period. It is a period that offers powerful psychic and visionary powers. Yet, the work is to fine-tune discrimination so that you can perceive what is real. Learn to see subtle differences between concepts and work to clearly articulate them, when appropriate. The work of this time is focused on removing personal viewpoints and developing intuitive awareness to connect with the greater whole. The solution comes in removing self-interest and expanding your point of view.

Enlightening. Consciousness is at the *universal* level of awareness during this period, deeply attuned to achieving a unified perspective. Within this cycle is the capacity for transformation. Here is another energy very much connected with Pluto in Western astrology. During this time you may experience feelings of deep disappointment. It may seem as if ideals are simply unreachable, and you may become discouraged. The work is to look into your own shadows and be realistic. You must accept where you are before you can change. Make choices that are based on universal truth and keep life simple. The solution for achieving the gifts of this time is to remember that the ideals you envision are real, but you must be patient with the process of reaching them. Simply *be* the light that you are, and you will make a difference.

When we agree to consciously work with our personal shadows during our shadow cycles, we can become alchemists who turn base metal into gold through changing our attitudes and perceptions. All areas of inquiry reflect how our shadows are affecting our lives individually, through relationships with each other and the planet, and collectively, through our belief systems about the nature of reality and our relationship to the cosmos. The work we do in personal shadow cycles contributes to the changes we make as a collective during the larger collective shadow cycles. Since collective shadow cycles occur when Venus is retrograde prior to beginning another phase, Venus is our guide in examining all aspects of our dualistic experience here on Earth.

COMPLEXITIES AND INCLUSIVENESS

BY LAARKMAA

Pleiadian-Earth Energy Astrology helps you to understand more deeply the energies that express as your thought waves, emotional field, physical forms, and interconnectedness to everything. These manifest as all of creation. The cosmic, universal language of mathematics is understood by every culture through the symbols that express movement toward or away from unity. Pleiadian-Earth Energy Astrology is itself a language using the mathematics of energy to show us how to relate. Everything in the cosmos is about relationship—the essence of all that is or ever will be created. Energy is all about relationship. Numbers are the alphabet of the universal language of mathematics that expresses the presentation of energy. Numbers tell us how energies interact (or form relationships) with and affect anything (including other energies).

Now that you have explored all of the symbolism of the numbers for each universal energy and each earth energy, we will take you into higher mathematical exploration of these energies to see what else each of them holds for you. We will be using both universal and earth energy numerical values to demonstrate the language of mathematical combinations. While each energy can stand on its own, it also can be expanded to include many other energies that are within it, and you can see and understand them through simple arithmetic. We Pleiadians work from a binary system mathematically. When we look at energies we view them as one standing beside the other, equal, but possibly different in the way they manifest. We will not teach binary numbers or counting systems (which use only the numerals zero and one) in this book. Instead, we offer you a binary perspective of seeing two elements or numbers (the Arabic numerals listed here) standing side by side. For instance, the number thirteen has a one (the universal energy of *initiation*) standing beside a three (the universal energy of *creating*), so that the completion universal energy of thirteen (13) also holds a new initiation point (1) and the creative energy (3), which together indicate the potential for new cycle. This is important because it demonstrates that within each ending is a new beginning, which helps you to understand the intricacies of numerical energies so that you can appreciate all they have to offer. Thirteen can also be seen as 1 (*initiation*) plus 3 (creating) equals 4 (*foundation*), indicating that you are *creating* (3) a foundation (4) with each new (1) choice you make

You will find them reflecting and repeating each other, blending together like the ouroboros symbol that winds its way throughout this book. When you look at the numbers from a binary position, you can also sometimes see similarities or identical reflections of the same energy. Both the universal number eleven (*illuminating*) and the 11th earth energy (*Illuminating*) are perfect examples. (11 = 1 standing by 1.) From a binary point of view, the *initiating* universal energy (1) stands directly beside another *initiating* energy (1) to create the universal energy *illuminating* (11), as well as the eleventh earth energy, *Illuminating*. You can see that as the two energetic points reflect back to each other, they illuminate each other's energy and influence. This again shows you how energies come together to create a more perfect whole. You may explore the similarities between other universal numerical values and earth energy numerical values.

As you count higher and higher with the earth energies, which extend to 20, each of the energies can mathematically be broken into more and more complicated permutations. They become more complex, but complex does not necessarily mean better. Each of these energies by its own merit has equal value. Remember that the simple universal energy of one (*initiating*) is just as profound in its simplicity as the complex universal energy of thirteen (*completing*), which integrates everything. Remember that each of these energies stands alone. Just play with the different aspects *within* each energy to see its similarities and its differences. You are enhancing your knowledge and perspectives when you do this. As you begin to look at all the energies in this way, it will help you to focus on similarities, rather than focusing on differences. This way of viewing the world will help you with human relationships also, for you can learn to see your similarities, rather than focusing only on your differences, which brings you toward unity rather than separation.

Always remember when you are exploring the energies in this system that you are counting through two cycles of energy simultaneously: universal energy, which goes from one to thirteen, and earth energy, which goes from one to twenty. When you reach the fourteenth earth energy, you begin to encounter more combinations of numbers with the energies presented. For example, the fourteenth earth energy, *Healing*, contains these seven combinations:

$$1 + 13$$
$$2 + 12$$
$$3 + 11$$
$$4 + 10$$
$$5 + 9$$
$$6 + 8$$
$$7 + 7$$

So within the energy of the fourteenth earth energy are the universal energies of one (*initiating*), two (*duality*), three (*creating*), four (*foundation*), five (*change*), six (*flow*), seven (*merging*—twice!), eight (*connecting*), nine (*harmonizing*), ten (*manifesting*), eleven (*illuminating*), twelve (*understanding*), and thirteen (*completing*). The fourteenth earth energy contains all these energies within it. From this example you can look within any earth energy to see what other energetic combinations are able to participate with the energy that manifests. From the binary view it represents 14 = 1 standing beside 4. *Initiating* universal energy (1) stands beside *foundation* energy (4). In this combination we find the perfect place for humans to begin again in every moment to build a better foundation for your species. We suggest a foundation based on love, trust, joy, and compassion.* And of course, 1 (*initiating*) plus 4 (*foundation*) equals 5 (*change*), which is the basis of life.

The energy of seven is a pivotal energy within the universal energies. It is the point of merging between what was and what will be, between self and other. Therefore, it seems relevant to point out that there are seven earth energies for humans to experience from *Healing* to *Enlightening* (*Healing, Seeing, Intuiting, Evolving, Self-regulating, Catalyzing, and Enlightening*). Because universal seven is an energy of merging, these last seven earth energies merge earthly understanding through global and universal perspectives in a way to help you move your awareness outside of the consciousness of third-dimensional earthly reality. Most of the earth energies with higher mathematical numbers offer a global or universal awareness of consciousness, which builds on the more fundamental elements of individual and community awareness.

But that does not mean that they are more important. For example, the potent energy of *initiating* (1) appears within many of these combinations, over and over again. The presence of this energy suggests that you bring yourself back to the present moment, (1) or (*initiation*), over and over again.

The arrangement of numbers is not hierarchical. It simply shows the complexity involved as more and more energies are gathered with different perspectives to create what comes next. Days that have higher-numbered energies may seem to offer more expansive views of experience; they may also offer complexities that require you to simplify your

---

*Read more about this concept in *Remembering Who We Are*.

perspective in order to perceive what is really occurring. People who carry these higher-numbered energies may seem to be exceptionally aware and awake (at the higher vibratory expression), or they may seem ungrounded (at the lower vibratory expression of the energy.) These new concepts are something that humanity has never understood before, so we wish to make it clear how your experience on Earth is changing to allow new evolutionary awareness to develop.

Each of the other energies (with the exception of one [1], which is a powerful energy all by itself) can be examined through the various permutations we are suggesting. Looking at the higher energies on the spiral shows you how they become more complicated by having more influence from other important energies that have previously presented. Complexity begins the moment the energy of one, *initiating*, invites any other energy to participate and create with it. Any combination includes multiple numerical perspectives.

As the spiral progresses, it becomes more and more complex. You can explore the complexity by writing down all the mathematical permutations that can be obtained within any number. The complexities of the energies actually start to increase complications as the numbers go higher, suggesting that the days that hold these energies offer more in service of evolution.

UNDERSTANDING THE MATH OF ENERGY

We have shown you the differences between energies in previous chapters; now we are going to show you some of the similarities. You may skip this chapter and read it later if you choose. Or you may find it exciting to read it now, as you delve into the next level of cosmic understanding of how everything truly is connected, spiraling together in ways that you do not usually perceive through your linear thinking on Earth. Explore the energies as you go!

As we have said, one (*initiating*) is a powerful number. It does not hold any other energies within it, and the moment you add any other number to it, it begins to change. It is in leaving the point of *initiating* (which is beginnings) that energy begins to move. The second energy (2), *duality*, holds the energy of 1 + 1, which creates two perspectives. You may unite these perspectives to form a dualistic whole, like a coin with two sides. The number two (2) is the energy that opens humanity to seeing everything from opposite viewpoints that can then be joined to create a more complete perspective. (Most of humanity does not yet know how to do this well. Often, when your earthly perspectives become individual, you do not know how to harmonize them.) Here are some other examples:

> Three (3), creating, contains 1 + 2.
> Four (4), *foundation*, contains 1 + 3 and 2 + 2.
> Five (5), *change*, contains 1 + 4 and 2 + 3.
> Six (6), *flow*, contains 1 + 5, 2 + 4, and 3 + 3.

You can see how as each number gets larger, it holds more and more combined energies within it. This is how we demonstrate the process of one energy building on another. It helps to establish how each of you has something to contribute in building an evolved human species. The seventh earth energy (*Remembering*), like the seventh universal energy (*merging*), contains 1 + 6, 2 + 5, and 3 + 4. Or you can say that seven contains all the numbers that come before it within itself (1, 2, 3, 4, 5, 6). Likewise, the eighth earth energy (*Loving*) can be seen to contain the universal (8), *connecting*, and all the energies expressed before it, too: 1 + 7, 2 + 6, 3 + 5, 4 + 4. This pattern continues as you count the universal energies in relationship to the numerical value of the earth energies, with each combination holding more universal numbers, with the exception of the tenth earth energy (*Devoting*) and the twentieth earth energy (*Enlightening*), two energies that offer major points for potential change for humanity. Is it any wonder that the higher numbers may seem so similar when you read and integrate their numerical meaning?

Once you understand the basic description of an energy, there are thousands of ways you can play with the meanings of the numbers held within each energy. That's the point. We are encouraging you to first study each energy's properties alone, learning what they mean and ask of you. Then look beyond the simple number before you to other possible meanings that may exist. What does the number represent when you see it from a binary point of view? What if you add the numerals together from the perspective of Western numerology? What if you break the number apart and look at the meaning of all of the component parts contained within the original number?

We suggest that you look at all the permutations of how each numeric energy includes other energies within it, as well as how the energies work together standing side by side in a binary fashion. For example, you can use a mathematical equation to understand how two energies converge to form a third number: $1 + 1 = 2$. And equally you can divide or separate, revealing a focus on a specific energetic component: $12 \div 3 = 4$. And you can multiply energies together to increase their effect: $3 \times 3 = 9$. The mathematics of this system of astrology gives you a language to understand how you are either working with relationships to move toward unity or separating yourselves by focusing on singular aspects of individual energy.

While the information in this chapter may seem complex, these mathematical explanations can help to explain some of the characteristics that are similar in very different energies. They are similar because they have a portion of another energy or energies within them. This viewpoint helps you to understand why there is so much repetition between the energies as they are described in this book and how each of you is more similar than you can imagine. This system is a light shining new wisdom in the dark, a rare gift for the transformation of human consciousness.

13

A New Calendar Based on Energy, Not Time

All human creation myths tell stories about how physical reality came into being. Each story speaks of some god (or gods) taking a specific action whereby creation was accomplished. None of our creation myths talk about the *energy* of creation or our participation with energy to manifest our world. With the information presented in this book we can reexamine our creation myths and write new ones based on universal truths about physical manifestation. This requires reexamining our existing myths about time and correctly reorienting our perspective to one in which creation flows from energy. It's time for a new myth with energy as the foundation—the source—of creation. This new myth is already a well-established scientific fact.

We need to create a new calendar that supports this new myth in order to live in meaningful ways that naturally flow from and include the cycles that drive life. Calendars capture a culture's underlying patterns, rhythms, and beliefs, fusing meaning into daily life. Such an attempt was made when the Mayan calendar was designed with Pleiadian guidance long ago. But as Western cultures overtook Mayan customs, the Mayan calendar was reduced to a mere relic for counting time. We'll explore this more below.

Five thousand years ago the Pleiadians brought humanity a system to help us realize our birthright as cocreators with the power of choice and the ability to work with the energetic process of creation. The Pleiadians offered our species the opportunity to step away from the prevailing sense of separateness wherein all power was ascribed to a god or other external forces. The Pleiadians wished for us to awaken to our inherent power in the unique tool of choice. Like our Pleiadian friends, we ourselves are energy. We have the power to choose how we interact with other energies within our environment. If we now begin taking responsibility for the choices we make—rather than simply accepting what some deity or prevailing power puts before us—we begin to partner with other energies in the universe to create our own world. Such a step could initiate the manifestation of a peaceful earth.

Like everything else that exists, we're simply energy. Science understands this, yet maintains its bias toward matter in a material world, even as it asserts (when convenient) that matter is energy. Instead of building on the knowledge that everything is the "substance" of energy, we're still trained to think of matter as the fundamental concept. And science continues to cast energy into a secondary role of importance, even though quantum physics clearly states it is *the* fundamental concept. Energy remains a mystery to humanity and stands like a ghost in the room.

Despite the best efforts of our Pleiadian friends throughout the centuries to help humans understand and use energy, human history shows that we still neither understand it nor know how to properly work with it. Humanity has repeatedly and mistakenly turned away from understanding energy while creating false systems to measure time. For five thousand years we have viewed the sequential presentation of energies explained to us by the Pleiadians through the lens of time. In fact, the Mayan calendar was *never* about time. It was, and is today, about energy.

Today, most people have lost interest in the Mayan calendar because its "timing" did not bring an apocalypse or a golden age in 2012, as had been predicted by misdirected archeologists. Yet those energies that could create a golden age are still here. The missing ingredient is a simple understanding of energy. Our consciousness has just not awakened enough in five thousand years to understand the gift the Pleiadians gave us so long ago.

Now, Laarkmaa reminds humanity of how creation occurs through energetic combinations. Thanks to our (Pia and Cullen's) personal relationship with Laarkmaa, we're more deeply aware of the importance of understanding and correctly engaging energy for conscious manifestation. Humans are cocreators; we're gods and goddesses, we're divine, and we have the power to create whatever we need through the choices we make—one by one—as we consciously participate with all available energies.

Humanity is simply ignorant of the principles involved to bring energy from the point of intention to the point of completion required for manifestation. At the end of this chapter we'll suggest how to easily create a new, more functional calendar based on existing and interconnected energies rather than the artificial passage of time (an example can be viewed at https://www.laarkmaa.com/calendar). But first, we must address the creation myth that causes us to view our reality through the lens of time, rather than energy. And we need to explain how to move away from false beliefs based on obsolete systems and misunderstandings about linear progress, which currently form and control the entire structure of contemporary culture and most of humanity. Using time as our governing foundation is simply and fundamentally wrong.

We need to redesign our myths by writing ourselves into them as cocreators who potently work with energy, rather than passively relying on a creation myth in which the movement of time determines what comes next. These new myths will ensure that all who come after us clearly understand that *we* continually recreate our own reality. The Pleiadian-Earth Energy Astrology system is a primer, helping us to understand how energy moves. Laarkmaa and Pleiadian visitors before them have shared this sequential presentation of energies with humanity, explaining the universal flow of energies that build on each other in these spiraling cycles, creating a momentum where manifestation can occur.

The culmination of the Mayan calendar in 2012 didn't bring the end of time or the end of our world. It brought an end to the sequential presentation of energies that had historically arrived in sequential waves. From that point on all energies became available to us simultaneously—meaning everything occurs right here and right now—and can be accessed individually or collectively, as needed. There is a cosmic order of how energies build on each other and work together for ultimate manifestation. The astrological system presented in this book provides a framework for understanding how energies exist simultaneously and how they build cooperatively to create higher levels of vibratory awareness.

Laarkmaa has thoroughly explained each energy, and we, the authors, have personally immersed ourselves in each one to gain a better understanding and more universal perspective of them. Now we wish to share this wisdom to help all of humanity understand just how to work with these energies as they spiral and build on one another to create a more peaceful world. If people understand the energies and begin to take responsibility for their choices, everyone benefits. However, that's a very big *if.* It requires the release of dysfunctional beliefs and old creation myths, making room for the truth about how we create our world.

Parents and other caregivers across the planet use a "time out"—a restriction from participation in a child's world of play—to encourage children to make better choices when they have misbehaved. A "time out" is usually intended to help children comprehend how their actions affect others and teach them to be more introspective and thoughtful about their actions and choices. Perhaps all of humanity needs a time out to realign our beliefs with the larger truth. Laarkmaa has often said humanity needs a big event such as a global power outage or a global snowstorm that causes us to stop our daily routines and gives us time to reflect on our lives and our belief systems. Such an event would allow us space and time to reevaluate how our belief systems cloud our vision, causing us to participate in the illusion of what we *believe* to be our "normal" reality. We simply need to slow down, disengage our busy minds, and pay attention to every thought we have, every choice we make, examining how each thought or action affects others.

Our third-dimensional world is based on duality, yet as explained in earlier chapters, we completely misunderstand what duality represents. We have become conditioned through our current creation myths to believe that there is an opposing force to everything we think, believe, or do. And yet, despite our continual focus on and alignment with specific poles of duality's opposites, there is an inner longing within each of us for unity—the urge to belong. That yearning guides those of us who wish to consciously evolve to continually seek a higher order based on the truth that we are one. Humans cycle between wanting to be right and wanting to belong, missing the point that our dualistic experience offers both possibilities simultaneously.

The principles of unity include everything—every dualistic opposite and every polar viewpoint. And unity is large enough to contain everything within it in harmony. In fact, unity is infinite, and all energies contained within unity make an important contribution to the whole. In the world of quantum physics, everything exists at once. All possible solutions to a problem exist simultaneously. Chaos is part of the creative process; how we choose to participate with the potentials available within our chaotic world determines the harmony or disharmony of our experience. To live in a dualistic world based on harmony rather than constant chaos, we must allow the truth of simultaneity to grow within us. We must remember that two sides of a coin are still the same coin. Learning to work with the side of the coin that is visible at any particular moment is about learning to work with the energy that is present *right now,* while still remaining available to other energies simultaneously. In other words, we can turn the coin over and look at the other side at any moment.

The obvious place to begin such a momentous change is within ourselves, for this is where we keep our beliefs alive. Only when we change our own beliefs can we affect the world outside of us, and of course, we cannot change others; we can only change ourselves. We are never able to change others, but the changes we make ourselves can and do affect others. The hundredth monkey effect, first described by Lyall Watson in the 1970s, discussed how a new behavior or idea expressed by one in a group can spread rapidly (through unexplained pathways) from one group to all other groups once a critical number in the group exhibit the new behavior or acknowledge the new idea.[1] The internet has amplified this possibility exponentially, sometimes causing a homogenization of behaviors in various nations. Cultural myths shift and change when we share our individual experiences, inviting the insights from others into building a new and more complete view of what is real. Sharing the various experiences of everyone expands the perspective of the whole. This is how belief systems can change to align with greater cosmic truths.

One of the first principles to consider as we make this shift to a more positive and inclusive consciousness is that we are energy. As pure energy, everything we think or do individually affects everyone and everything else as part of the unified whole. All thoughts and actions ripple out in waves, mixing and interacting with other energies. We understand that this is a new concept to many who believe that individual thoughts and ideas are private and proprietary. Yet many are realizing our vibrations affect every other energy they encounter (in some way) as they make their way to the farthest reaches of our universe. The intention of thoughts travels outward to have an impact on others and the world at large, so we need to take responsibility for our thoughts and actions. When this way of being and choosing becomes automatic, we can begin to relax and let change happen whenever and wherever it needs to. This is the start of a new cultural myth that instills the truth that what we think and do affects everything else. We sincerely begin to see how we create our reality with persistent thoughts. It then becomes easier to envision living by a calendar based on the energetic movements of thoughts and feelings as they radiate out into our experience and beyond. In this way the old myth of time is overshadowed and a new way of organizing our lives through energy begins.

Once we deeply comprehend our connection to and influence on everything in our world, we can turn our attention to the principles of manifestation. Who doesn't want to manifest a life that is happy and harmonious? Our current myths are based on the idea that time moves from a perceived past into a perceived future. Physicists call this the arrow of time. The arrow is linear and points only from the past into the future, with very little room for a stop at what we call the present moment. Such myths disconnect us from the true reality. The old myths under which we have been living have forbidden a primary interest in the now; only recently has talk of living in the present moment risen above a whisper.

The universe has always operated through laws of energy. All energy spirals toward a central point of integration, where it ceases to exist at all for a brief moment as it temporarily disintegrates in unity. After a pause to integrate what has been experienced, energy dissipates and begins a new spiral, colliding in various combinations over and over as it moves to that central point of integration once again. This is a classic example of the harmonic spiraling motion that abounds on the physical plane. Physics confirms this movement, although current views see energy as a secondary, not primary, element, since third-dimensional science is focused on material effects.

The Pleiadian-Earth Energy Astrology system teaches us how to participate with these spirals, integrating experiences as one proceeds on the evolutionary path. We can use this guide as a map to the new reality, in which we are cocreators. We have simply forgotten how to participate with energy to manifest our world. The map of the Pleiadian astrological system shows us the possibilities for harmonic merging of duality over and over again in the spirals of awakening unity consciousness. When the spiral of energies reaches the central point, duality ceases to exist. This is the actual meaning of the end of time that was referenced in ancient Mayan calendar teachings. The Pleiadians have been trying to teach us for more than five thousand years that our experiences unfold according to how we participate with energy. When we grasp this way of looking at the world, our experience of life expands into full participation with energy, always in the present moment. Everything is synchronistic. Everything is one. There is no right or wrong; there is just learning and experience. Laarkmaa suggests that we not label our experiences as good or bad, but remember that they're *just* experiences. Everything we learn helps us to move closer to unity.

Today, many people are feeling that things are falling apart or that life as they know it simply doesn't work anymore. We can't predict what will come next, even though we desperately try, because we're operating under false beliefs. We have based our awareness of cause and effect on a science that relies on a misunderstanding of time and have governed our lives by an artificial calendar. Outside the artificial structure of time lies freedom, yet even though we value the concept of freedom, we seem to be constantly controlled by time. Why?

Humans seem to believe that if we exert some sense of control over the future, we'll be safe. When we can't predict what comes next, we lose the perceived sense of control over our lives. The artificial calendar we use gives us an *appearance* of control; we look forward to what we believe comes next, scheduling our lives far beyond the energies that exist in the present moment. We organize our behaviors according to an external guide of timing, rather than choosing our behaviors through our connection to energy, Nature, and intuitive guidance.

Because we have lost our connection to Nature through our focus on the world of technology and an artificial calendar, we experience a tremendous sense of separation from the cosmos. We're also separated from the awareness that we ourselves are divine and have the power to co-create our reality. Coupled with the teaching of almost all religions on Earth, this sense of separation also causes us to look for answers outside of ourselves. If we're disconnected from the answers that live in our own hearts and from cosmic wisdom, concepts that lead us toward freedom and away from linear time are scary indeed! The Pleiadians are doing their best to help us awaken to the power we hold by educating us on the use of energy, which leads to the kind of freedom experienced by others in our universe. This extreme freedom requires responsibility and the ability to make better choices, and we must look within ourselves to find the truth. Listening to our hearts reconnects us to our guidance, each other, and the cosmos.

As a species we have long believed that by living according to the rules of time, we control our lives. This myth has falsely organized our lives. Yet even though this myth has proven untrue, we continue to teach our children to pay attention to time and that history predicts the future. Laarkmaa tells us that humanity is being urged to *leap* outside the constraints of time into the quantum field of possibilities, which is completely unpredictable. To make such a leap requires the release of all old, restrictive, time-bound governors and the surrender into the exploration of energy as it arrives moment by moment. Trusting the cosmos is the only way to navigate the environment of our new world. The present system of planning for a future that may or may not arrive is based on a very narrow view of our current reality. We are not suggesting that religious *faith* is the answer. Faith implies blind belief in something external to us. Organized religion failed us through promoting faith outside of ourselves to take care of all situations, rather than encouraging us to simply pay attention to what is here now and act from our own hearts or intuition. Faith implies that someone else has the answers and that we're too ignorant, too uninformed, and too powerless to directly access the divine answers ourselves.

Trust is very different from faith. Trust is based not on belief, but on an inner knowing, a peaceful feeling that provides guidance through an awareness of our direct connection to all that is. With trust we know that everything is unfolding perfectly, even when we are unable to see how problems will be resolved. We act because our intuition leads us to act. Faith, which comes from a disempowered place, often encompasses an element of fear. Many religions teach that faith is the antidote to insecurity, yet any sense of security coming from faith in something outside of ourselves keeps us bound to old beliefs and prevents growth. Faith doesn't encourage us to find creative solutions to our challenges. Faith comes from a position that someone else, someone higher and smarter than we are, will care for us because we're unable to responsibly care for ourselves. Trust comes from a completely different place. There is no fear when one feels trust. Instead, we experience ultimate freedom based on the inner knowing that we ourselves are powerful enough to work together to resolve any and every issue we may face.

Trust is present when we rely on our unified connection to direct our choices. Faith exists when we hope an outside element will take care of us. This separation is part of our misunderstanding of the purpose of duality. Time contributes to this false view, with its focus on the opposites of past and future. When we step outside of time we find all kinds of possibilities available in the myriad of energies that simultaneously exist. This is where we experience synchronicities, meaningful coincidences. Understanding synchronicity is key; in fact, it may be the most important concept to lead us toward connection, collaboration, and unity. Synchronicities are validations that we're in alignment with the cosmos. They're evidence that we're on track. All synchronicities occur in the eternal now, where energies combine to form new and useful patterns for living. They are guideposts to remind us that we're in flow, which is outside of time. Flow is about energy. The now, the present moment, is more powerful than the remembered past or an imaginary future defined by time. Flow is the potent place where potential becomes actuality. Synchronicities teach that all things exist at once and can be accessed when we pay attention and work with all the energies available. Synchronicities are great teachers of oneness, unity, and peace. Both our current calendar system and our current myths completely ignore synchronicity, keeping us mired in old loops of time and belief.

As we begin to integrate more synchronistic experiences into our lives, we may wish to step away from belief systems based on linear time and the artificial Gregorian calendar. We may feel that time simply doesn't work for us anymore. We simply can't organize our lives in twenty-four-hour or twelve-month increments any longer. As we awaken we recognize and remember that there is something missing—the thirteenth energy for integrating all of our experiences synchronistically, which is required for our continually evolving conscious awareness.

The wisdom of energy consciousness is an evolving and ever-expanding field for humanity. While we're still expanding our awareness of universal spirals of energy and how to use them, we remain under the influence of linear time. We must transition from one to the other gently by removing ourselves slowly from our existing structures. One way to do this is to begin to notice what we *feel* each and every day and with each and every person or circumstance. We can learn to sense the energies involved in someone's personality or in the energetic patterns of the day. Begin to explore these energies in relationship to a linear calendar by marking the days of the calendar according to the universal energies that are present each day. Recognize that a seven-day week is not a true measure of energetic movement; it is only halfway through a universal cycle. The Pleiadians have given us a better way to measure and use cycles of energy—the thirteen-day cycle that is aligned with the energetic movement of the cosmos.

REVISIONING THE CALENDAR

We need to remake our calendars to reflect cosmic alignment with the movement of the energy that truly guides our lives. Marking our Gregorian calendars with the Pleiadian-Earth energies helps us to see beyond the illusion of living within a system based on units of twelve-month years and seven-day weeks. Marking a calendar with felt pens or colored pencils is fun and makes it easier to see the differences between the Gregorian system and the Pleiadian energetic model. These vibrant markings actually create a very colorful and easily readable new calendar to help guide our choices for navigating our world.

You can find the actual universal energy for a Gregorian date in appendix C. Mark it on your calendar and then count forward until you reach thirteen. Mark the next day on your calendar with the energy of one, and begin to count to thirteen again. Choose and explore a universal energy; discover how this energy feels and how it can guide your choices throughout each day. Throughout the thirteen-count universal cycle, each energy builds until it is complete. Learning how to work within this naturally occurring presentation of building energies can help us to become more powerful cocreators and live more harmoniously as galactic citizens.

> **Example:** January 1, 2019 carries a universal energy of 9 (*harmonizing*), so January 2 carries the universal energy of 10 (*challenge or manifesting*). January 3 carries the universal energy of 11 (*illuminating*), and January 4 carries the universal energy of 12 (*understanding*). January 5 completes this cycle with the energy of 13 (*completing*), and January 6 begins a new cycle of 1 (*initiating*).

Rarely do the universal energies align with the numerical dates of our Gregorian calendar. The last time this occurred was March 1, 2017. It happens next on February 1, 2019, and then again in November 2019 and on May 1, 2020. (The examples listed in figures 13.1–13.3 show a comparison between the Gregorian calendar dates and the universal energies for these dates.) These are perfect times to easily align your Gregorian calendar with universal energies and then to carry them forward once we move out of alignment again.

Once you have familiarized yourself with the universal energies and integrated them into your Gregorian calendar, begin to explore the twenty earth energies. As explained in chapter 8, each of the earth energies is related to a specific direction. Eastern energies bring new beginnings and initiate movement. Northern energies bring strength to find the truth and move through challenges. Western energies bring deep awareness of possibility, mystery, and transcendence, helping expand our vision. Southern energies bring light to illuminate our path and help us grow. As each day comes to a close at sunset, the energy spirals counterclockwise to the next direction and toward the new energy that is arriving. Refer to fig. 8.2 on page 100 to mark the directional energy on your regular calendar. Then move forward on your calendar,

Example: FEBRUARY 2019
Conversion from the
Gregorian Calendar to the Universal Energetic Calendar

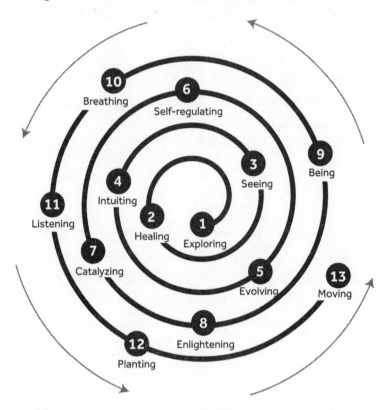

1 Friday, February 1, 2019		**8** Friday, February 8, 2019
2 Saturday, February 2, 2019		**9** Saturday, February 9, 2019
3 Sunday, February 3, 2019		**10** Sunday, February 10, 2019
4 Monday, February 4, 2019		**11** Monday, February 11, 2019
5 Tuesday, February 5, 2019		**12** Tuesday, February 12, 2019
6 Wednesday, February 6, 2019		**13** Wednesday, February 13, 2019
7 Thursday, February 7, 2019		

© 2018 Pia Orleane, Ph.D.

Figure 13.1. The numbers in the spiral represent the universal energies. Note the rare alignment of the universal energy numbers with the dates of the Gregorian calendar. The words represent the earth energies.

Example: NOVEMBER 2019
Conversion from the
Gregorian Calendar to the Universal Energetic Calendar

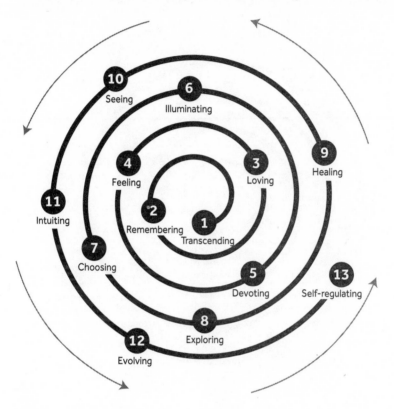

1 Friday, November 1, 2019
2 Saturday, November 2, 2019
3 Sunday, November 3, 2019
4 Monday, November 4, 2019
5 Tuesday, November 5, 2019
6 Wednesday, November 6, 2019
7 Thursday, November 7, 2019

8 Friday, November 8, 2019
9 Saturday, November 9, 2019
10 Sunday, November 10, 2019
11 Monday, November 11, 2019
12 Tuesday, November 12, 2019
13 Wednesday, November 13, 2019

© 2018 Pia Orleane, Ph.D.

Figure 13.2. The numbers in the spiral represent the universal energies. Note the rare alignment of the universal energy numbers with the dates of the Gregorian calendar. The words represent the earth energies.

Example: MAY 2020
Conversion from the
Gregorian Calendar to the Universal Energetic Calendar

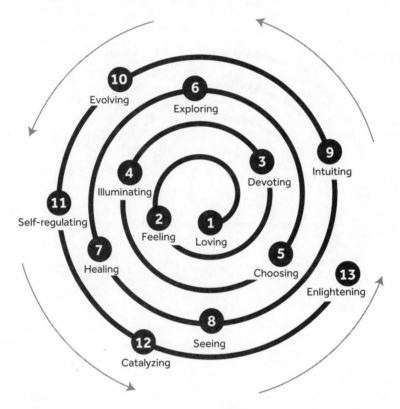

1 Friday, May 1, 2020		**8** Friday, May 8, 2020
2 Saturday, May 2, 2020		**9** Saturday, May 9, 2020
3 Sunday, May 3, 2020		**10** Sunday, May 10, 2020
4 Monday, May 4, 2020		**11** Monday, May 11, 2020
5 Tuesday, May 5, 2020		**12** Tuesday, May 12, 2020
6 Wednesday, May 6, 2020		**13** Wednesday, May 13, 2020
7 Thursday, May 7, 2020		

© 2018 Pia Orleane, Ph.D.

Figure 13.3. The numbers in the spiral represent the universal energies. Note the rare alignment of the universal energy numbers with the dates of the Gregorian calendar. The words represent the earth energies.

marking the directions from east to north to west to south as you count counterclockwise in the spiral of directions. Notice that we "progress" on the Gregorian calendar in a *clockwise,* linear fashion, instilling patterns from a historical perspective. The actual movement of energies, however, is *counterclockwise,* which allows us to make new and original decisions from *all* possibilities by aligning with the cosmic spiraling movement. It is through our collective interpretation of energy as "time" that we perceive everything in our world as moving in a linear, clockwise direction. No wonder we get confused by the illusion of time!

> **Example:** January 1, 2019, carries a northern energy, so January 2 will carry a western energy. January 3 will carry a southern energy, January 4 will carry an eastern energy, and January 5 carries a northern energy once again.

Once you have mastered the directions you may choose to look up the specifics of each earth energy and learn to feel these energies in your everyday awareness. Using a reference point selected from appendix C, you can begin to mark your own Gregorian calendar with the spirals of universal and earth energies each day, exploring the way each energy feels and seeking its gifts as it arrives. We (Pia and Cullen) have designed the first Pleiadian-Earth Energy calendar.* Our new calendar overlays the existing illusory Gregorian calendar, and through using it we can deepen our perception of what is real by noticing the effects of each energy. Remember that you'll be counting through two cycles simultaneously (as is appropriate in duality). You'll mark the arrival of universal energies and the direction of the more specific earth energies. Understanding the interaction of these two energetic systems can support and guide your movement through them, helping you to navigate challenges more consciously by blending your own gifts with the gifts of others and of the day. You'll begin to better understand why some

*See https://www.laarkmaa.com/calendar.

days offer more challenges for your particular energetic makeup or more resonance with your particular energy. You'll see how each energy is part of the collective whole. This way of understanding energy helps us to stop blaming people for discordant situations, simply by learning to see the challenge of the energy rather than blaming any particular person or situation for being problematic or challenging. It also helps us to take proper responsibility for responding to the energies in appropriate ways. This way of living shifts our inner perspective and helps us cope with the outer world in new and more creative ways. When we shift our inner vision, we change the outer world. Perhaps then we can rewrite our myths to include the power we hold to work with energy and co-create our own reality. Starting a new calendar that resonates with the cosmic spirals of energetic movement can change your life. It certainly has changed ours!

14

Who Are You Really?

The universe is composed of harmonic waves. All movement in the universe occurs in wave motion; nothing is static. We can perceive movement on our own planet in terms of waves also. Consider the simplest example of the tides of the ocean—waves moving in, waves moving out. We can also look to our breath to see waves of movement—an in-breath, followed by a wave of out-breath, which leads to breathing in the next wave. In the universe these cosmic waves are subtle and interlinking. Planets and stars have their own movement, yet each individual movement blends with the movement of other energetic bodies, creating the harmony of the universe. On Earth, because we concentrate on the opposites of duality, we forget how to use these opposite waves in harmony. Sometimes, our experiences can feel like tsunamis, knocking us unexpectedly off our feet. If we could learn to be more fluid ourselves, to understand how flexibility is possible in interacting with others and the world, we would have a more harmonious environment on our own planet. The Japanese marshal art *aikido,* often translated to mean "the way of unifying with life energy," teaches us to move in wave motions to accept or reject energies as they come to us. Rather than judging and reacting to energies (people and situations), we simply interact with them neutrally, holding the intention of well-being for all.

In his book *Harmonic Anthology,* John Addey writes:

> We must begin by considering the ever-changing life of nature and in particular the way in which the ebb and flow of all natural processes can be represented by wave forms. . . . [I]n the world of actuality no one natural rhythm acts entirely on its own. The Moon affects the tides and sets up its own rhythm: so does the Sun, adding a rhythm of its own. Thus these two rhythms mingle together and geographical factors modify them still further. Therefore in nature we are dealing not with simple wave forms but always with wave complexes. . . . [In the body] each part of the organ must have a regular rhythm of its own but together they combine in such a way as to produce those spasmic contractions that send blood coursing through the veins.[1]

Quantum mechanics recognizes the importance of wave motion in defining our reality. In quantum mechanics all matter is seen as multifrequency waves that *appear* to be standing still.* The appearance of stillness is illusory. Our reality is not static; it is energy in motion. One of the most important things to know about our evolution is that we ourselves are waves, and our evolutionary process is achieved through wave motion. We are continually in a process of transition. A wave does not appear in one place and die away in another. It is constant and only seems to disappear when its effects are counteracted by other waves that affect it. All harmonic patterns are present to some extent in any complex waveform. The same concept could be extended to humans; each of us is present in each other. Thus, the principle of In Lak'ech.

The Pleiadians ask us to look beyond our mental concepts of what we believe and who we think we are to find the truth of the larger, organic cosmic reality, which is based on ever-changing, interactive waves of energy. Laarkmaa says:

---

*In 1924 French physicist Louis de Broglie discovered that matter behaves like waves rather than like static particles.

All systems of thinking, all perspectives of viewing the world, are intended to be transcended as humanity moves away from the mental realms into the cosmic realms of the heart. The universe operates on principles of harmonizing energy through unconditional love and acceptance and illumination of the path of those energies. The Pleiadian-Earth energy system of astrology and the Mayan calendar are systems Pleiadians gave to humanity to help you understand energy and cosmic flow. Both of these systems are being presented to help you understand how to transcend any limits of thought and move instead to an intuitive participation with energy. Time is one of the illusions of the mental realms. To grasp the cosmic understanding of energy you must move beyond the structures of time that keep you focused on a linear past or future. Working with energy requires you to be present in the moment in which you are living. A wise and intuitive response to what is present is required for higher levels of consciousness to guide you on your developmental journey. Who are you really? You are divine sparks of energy woven into a form that can change as you learn to transcend what you have manifested thus far.[2]

We are expressions of energy that can and do change in every moment. If we attach to beliefs that we are unchanging, the waveforms of life will hit us like unexpected tsunamis. If we recognize our own changeable nature, we participate with the waves of life in a more fluid and gentle manner. When we view ourselves through existing astrological systems based on only twelve energies—twelve signs, twelve houses, twelve main aspects—eliminating the thirteenth energy of integration, we are at a severe disadvantage in our attempt to understand ourselves. In fact, we cannot limit who we are to any division of energies that does not recognize the complexity and interrelatedness of *all* energies. Any limiting view of dividing ourselves into stationary and easily definable units is exactly what prevents us from understanding our totality. Laarkmaa says that we are not static, but energetic waveforms constantly changing. When we insist on dividing ourselves into easily categorized parts, we lose the essence of who we are. Even science and medicine have participated in this compartmentalization through focusing on specialization, rather than honoring more holistic and unified systems. We have become fragmented as a species, and the Pleiadians are urging us to remember that we are all connected and affect one another with every thought we think. *We are one.*

The secret component of connection is lost when we focus on seeing ourselves as special or different, or grouping ourselves into definable categories (races, nations, or religions). We are more likely to realize that everything in the universe is connected when we focus on what we *feel* rather than on what we *think,* for we all experience the same feelings, even if our thoughts about those feelings may differ. Recently, the HeartMath Institute reported, "Our research suggests the heart also is an access point to a source of wisdom and intelligence that we can call upon to live our lives with more balance, greater creativity and enhanced intuitive capacities. . . . In essence, it appeared that the heart could affect our awareness, perceptions and intelligence."[3]

Allowing time rather than energy to guide our evolution is problematic. In the paradigm of linear consciousness, we send our thoughts out into a past that no longer exists or toward a future that we hope to create, with a culturally trained directive to ignore what is happening right now. It would be beneficial for all of us to retrain our consciousness to simply be aware of our experiences in the present moment and respond appropriately. It is ludicrous to base our reality on what lives only in our head as memories of something that no longer exists or as hopes (or worries) about something that has not (and may not) happen in the future. When we feel what is happening right now, we begin to understand the energy of the moment and the energetic connection within the universe. Experiencing life in this way awakens our hearts to the truth, and then our minds can do their proper jobs of following the heart's wisdom, rather than keeping our beliefs in loops of limited thinking about what may or may not be "real."

The Pleiadian-Earth Energy Astrology system can help us to realize ourselves as energy and guide us into meeting and working with other energies as waveforms, rather than as static (and often resistant) units. A Pleiadian-Earth Energy Astrology chart is not a typical astrological chart. It is not intended to define us or lock us into specific aspects that label or identify who we are, nor is it intended to predict what is going to happen in a life. The Pleiadian-Earth energy chart describes the energies we brought to Earth as part of the whole of humanity. These are the energies with which we have specifically agreed to work to support the conscious evolution of humanity; they define our purpose. The more we work with the system, the more fluid the system becomes, showing us the similarities available in each energy from a different perspective and how to use the potentials for more conscious choices and responses in the exploration of all of them. A personal chart is intended to help us acknowledge our gifts, work more deeply with our challenges, and then move beyond any limited views presented within the system as we begin to understand the concepts of energy and wave motion. A Pleiadian-Earth Energy Astrology chart maps the movement of our own energy and our interactions with other energies to help achieve the individual and collective mission of evolution.

I (Pia) can't help but notice similarities in others' energies when I look at clients' charts, for I am always looking to see how each of us complements others and how we are alike. I can see where the "flow" between people occurs and where it becomes stuck. While each of us is an individual, with many, many differing influences combining to create a unique personality, noticing our similarities rather than our differences gives us greater insight into how we relate with each other.

Each of us is made of a predominance of certain energies that work together to direct our evolution. A personal chart explains how that predominance brings a focus to our unique challenges and gifts, revealing the person we have believed (up until now) ourselves to be. Reading your own chart you will feel a sense of familiarity as you read about specific recognizable patterns in yourself. You also become aware of how other energies (society and individuals) have shaped your personality. Laarkmaa has given us a very big gift to help us understand ourselves, our world, and our place in the universe. They have opened the doorway to our potential. We feel that a deep understanding of energy is the key that can give us the power to change anything that does not work for the highest good for everyone. A deeper understanding of energy as we experience it can empower us to harmonize and use *all* the energies available to us. We simply must learn how to navigate our experiences without judgment and with appreciation for the gifts each energy brings, whether that energy is expressing throughout the day or in an individual. We must learn to accept and appreciate (without judgment) everything, for everything is energy and all energy is connected.

To evolve, we must willingly be open to whatever energy arrives, letting go of old ways of experiencing life and following a new spiral of experiences. These experiences can be immensely valuable lessons in recognizing that the energy is indeed different in every moment and we must transcend all viewpoints that cause us to believe any system will always remain the same. Patterns are always available to guide us, but they can never define who we are or what will come next because even within the pattern, change is always the dominating force.

In my book *Sacred Retreat,* I (Pia) speak about the merits of duality and how to use the gifts inherent in opposite polarities of being human. As noted earlier in this book, Laarkmaa tells us that as a species, humans have long misunderstood the point of duality.* The Pleiadian-Earth Energy Astrology system helps to move us away from duality toward unity as we discover multiple perspectives offered by each energy and how they weave together in harmony. This system can help us to move beyond our frozen belief systems that are based on an artificial sense of time. When we are able to understand just how all energies are interconnected, we may be able to step into the limitless river of *all* possibilities. Finally, we may be able to practice the principle expressed

---

*Find Laarkmaa's talks about duality in *Conversations with Laarkmaa.*

as In Lak'ech. We are all each other. If *I* begin to operate from the true reality, it will affect *your* reality as well.

In transcending who we have thought ourselves to be, we necessarily have to let go of all old beliefs. This is the path to conscious evolution—a path that demands we continually release all beliefs based on past experience and open our hearts to the unknown.

Children are especially skilled at this; they live much more in the present moment than do adults. In guiding our children we need to remember that they are intrinsically themselves from the outset. They come to Earth with their own unique sets of instructions and feel a tremendous impact from the influences that parents, teachers, and society place on them. It is a parent's job to provide an environment in which the child can quite naturally evolve into the most conscious level of her or his true nature. It is the adult's job to remind children that all things, including themselves, change, rather than trying to force them into a mold that defines who they are through a parent's hopes or expectations. Society should also provide this function for the children. Parenting in this way allows children to become more attuned to a natural evolutionary flow without having to incorporate projections of how they are seen by a parent (or the world). We need to show our children how all of us are connected and affect each other, teaching responsible choices that are based on the highest good for all. And perhaps we need to learn from our children how to open our hearts in trust, allow ourselves to release all beliefs and expectations, and fall into the next moment with grace and love.

Children and sensitive adults seem to be suffering the most during this time of profound change, and yet it is the sensitive ones and the children who are most aware of the true reality. From a perspective based on comparisons, it may seem that some people are paying a high price for the privilege of showing others how to make necessary changes to become more evolved humans. Yet, when we change our perspective to one of In Lak'ech we are able to see more clearly that everything we incorporate into our own growth and understanding extends into and reflects on others, influencing the collective. It is just a slower process for the collective to awaken and realize how the universe truly works. Therefore, it is imperative that we honor the spirit of In Lak'ech and always consider the highest good of all.

It may seem from our perspective that time is speeding up because we are moving closer to a multidimensional reality where time does not exist. This transition will not be particularly easy if we act from the old paradigm of separation, competition, and judgment. We may experience financial, physical, or relationship challenges as we shift from one paradigm to another. We may feel like we are unraveling and find it hard to see the purpose in the many challenges we are facing. But perhaps a sense of loss of control in our own lives is necessary for our species to learn to trust in the universe and in the power of making our own choices. In the chaos of change we may try to cling to any set of rules that offers a sense of stability. But stability is not the answer, becoming more fluid and flexible is. Change is the only constant in life. It is important to remember that everything we think or do affects all others. It is important to quiet our minds and engage in deep listening before we act. Reactions come from old habits; responses come from flow and grace.

Laarkmaa is trying to help us see beyond limitations of separation. While they describe all of the energies available to us (universal and earth energies), they encourage us to realize that each of us carries all of those energies within us and we can access them at any time. We are connected to each other and to parts of ourselves in other dimensions. Those who manage to understand energy from a multidimensional perspective may begin to reflect the rainbow of energies that they contain. This is the true meaning of having what Laarkmaa calls a rainbow body.* When we achieve rainbow body status, we connect to all dimensional aspects of ourselves and our physical and etheric bodies become completely merged. This integrated self can respond energetically to

---

*See *Remembering Who We Are*.

every situation by accessing the entire spectrum of the rainbow of energies that we are. Achieving a rainbow body also means being fully able to recognize others in ourselves, treat them as we wish to be treated, make choices for the highest good of all, and realize how each one of us affects everyone and everything else. It also means having the ability to recognize that as energy we can respond to life either as our lighter, etheric selves or through our physical bodies. Having a rainbow body is the ultimate achievement of personally integrating all cosmic energies and operating from the highest vibration possible.

As each of us moves toward this integrated, unified view of reality, we begin to understand the truth at a cellular and heart level. Our manifest world is created by the way we respond to energy. It is created through the application of our thoughts, feelings, and choices, moment by moment. Some people will recognize a closer alignment with one energy or another. This recognition supports the realization that this is the energy each of us has chosen for our personal path of evolution and service. Others may see reflections of many energies in their makeup. This is an indication of deeper integration of the whole. It requires tremendous responsibility to step outside of personal suffering or desires in order to show others how all energies can work together. There is no hierarchical posturing; linear structure does not exist in work with energy, for all parts have equal importance in what they bring to the whole. There is no room to judge self or others. If one part of the whole needs attention, that is where the energy appears.

In reading about universal and earth energies in previous chapters, you may have seen parts of yourself. You may have aligned more particularly with one energy or another, yet you could also see how other energies are also contained in the essence of *you*. For those of you who resonate with one or two particular energies as described in this book, please see that as an invitation to explore those energies and take responsibility to attain the highest vibration possible while working with them. For those who resonate with many of the energies within this book, please challenge yourselves to find the highest vibration of each energy and harmonize all of them within yourselves. This is a work about transcendence. You are being called to the work of integration, which is required for our earthly evolution from duality and separation into the cosmic whole.

Who are we really? We are divine energy moving in cosmic waves. When we allow ourselves to respond to the present moment with love, joy, trust, and compassion (Laarkmaa's formula for the foundation of life), we transcend *all* systems, taking the full spectrum of who we are into the universe.*

---

*See *Remembering Who We Are.*

A MAP TO ONENESS

Now that you have been introduced to a new system for managing energy, cycles, and patterns, we remind you of Laarkmaa's overall suggestion that all systems are meant to be transcended. This book illustrates that point in a small measure by showing how the presentation of universal energies on Earth is no longer sequential. All universal energies are now available to us at all times. We simply have to turn our attention to the frequency we seek and align our energy with it. Learning more about our individual energies and how to use them in relationship with other energies, as suggested throughout this book, can help us to move beyond what is familiar into the vast realm of unknown possibilities.

We learned from the Pleiadians that each of us has twelve strands of DNA. Each strand is connected to another dimensional aspect of ourselves. The thirteenth aspect is the point of integration where all dimensional selves come together. Until we awaken to the reality of each of the twelve strands and our existence in twelve different parallel realities, these strands lie within us like a cosmic soup containing two main ingredients: the two strands of DNA that have thus far been discovered by our science. Likewise, we believe ourselves to be the personalities of which we are aware only here in the third dimension, dismissing the possibility that other aspects of ourselves exist in parallel realities, one or two frequencies away! This book explores the twelve dimensions through energetic descriptions of each energy that exists on Earth, including the thirteenth energy that integrates them all. The thirteenth energy is the complete integration of the other twelve aspects of ourselves existing in parallel dimensions and all twelve strands of DNA. The thirteenth energy suggests the possibility that upon reaching this point, we may finally evolve into a new form of humans by using the full consciousness of all twelve strands of our DNA and all twelve aspects of our parallel selves.

Laarkmaa tells us that this book has woven into its pages all the mysteries that we need to accelerate our evolution. We call the information they have so lovingly shared with humanity "a map to oneness." On this map we can find descriptions of every type of energy we can experience here on Earth, through each other and through the passage of what we perceive as time. We can also find portals to access varying parallel aspects of who we are. Laarkmaa speaks of the multiple dimensions we are capable of experiencing, if only we would broaden our perceptions. Each dimension is a radio band of frequency, yet we humans, for the most part, have remained unaware that these frequencies even exist, much less how to access and use them.

Through Laarkmaa's description of the energies available to humanity we can learn to pay attention to our environment and to each other. We can learn to use duality as a gift that shows us other perspectives and possibilities, rather than as an implement of separation. We can learn to expand our consciousness so that we can move beyond our earthly limitations and become cosmic citizens. The map provides a unified view of life, and it supports our finding our way into cosmic alignment with our brothers and sisters in the stars. The map to oneness is a gift to humanity from the Pleiadians to help us transcend our dualistic experience and move into rainbow body form, where we can finally, and fully, be free. We offer you an explanation of this map in our book, and we hope that you use it to help you find your way on your own evolutionary journey.

We invite you to immerse yourself in the study of the energy you have come to Earth to explore, and then transcend it to become the multidimensional being you are meant to be!

Vortex Days: 2018–2033

2018	2019	2020	2021
January 8	January 1	January 20-29	January 7
January 13	January 22	February 8	January 9
January 16	January 29-30	February 11	January 28-29
January 21	February 6	February 16	February 17
January 27	February 12	February 19	February 19
February 3-4	February 17	February 27	March 8
February 11	February 20	March 3	March 12
February 15	February 25	March 6	March 19-20
March 4	March 5	March 11	March 27
March 6	March 8	March 17	April 2
March 25-26	March 13	March 24-25	April 7
April 14	March 16	April 1	April 10
April 16	March 26-31	April 5	April 15
May 3	April 1-4	April 22	April 23
May 7	May 5-10	April 24	April 26
May 14-15	May 11-14	May 13-14	May 1
May 22	May 24	June 2	May 4
May 28	May 27	June 4	May 14-23
June 2	May 29	June 21	June 23-July 2
June 5	June 1	June 25	July 10
June 10	June 4	July 2-3	July 12
June 18	June 12	July 10	July 15
June 21	June 17	July 16	July 20
June 26	June 20	July 21	July 23
June 29	June 25	July 24	July 31
July 9-10	July 1	July 29	August 5
July 11-18	July 8-9	August 6	August 8
August 18-19	July 16	August 9	August 13
August 20-27	July 20	August 14	August 26-27
September 6	August 6	August 17	September 3
September 9	August 8	August 27-31	September 7
September 14	August 27-28	September 1-5	September 24
September 17	September 16	October 6-15	September 26
October 3	September 18	October 25	October 15-16
October 14	October 5	October 28	November 4
October 21-22	October 16-17	November 2	November 6
October 29	October 24	November 5	November 23
November 2	October 30	November 13	November 27
November 19	November 4	November 18	December 4-5
November 21	November 7	November 21	December 12
December 10-11	November 12	November 26	December 18
December 30	November 20	December 2	December 23
	November 23	December 9-10	December 26
	November 28	December 17	December 31
	December 1	December 21	
	December 11-20		

2022	2023	2024	2025
January 8	January 2	January 12	January 13-22
January 11	January 7	January 16	January 30
January 16	January 10	January 23-24	February 1
January 19	January 15	January 31	February 4
January 29-Feb. 7	January 28-29	February 6	February 9
March 10-19	February 5	February 11	February 12
March 27	February 9	February 14	February 20
March 29	February 26	February 19	February 25
April 1	February 28	February 27	February 28
April 6	March 19-20	March 1	March 5
April 9	April 8	March 6	March 18
April 17	April 10	March 9	March 19
April 22	April 27	March 19-28	March 26
April 25	May 1	April 28- May 7	March 30
April 30	May 8-9	May 15	April 16
May 13-14	May 16	May 17	April 18
May 21	May 22	May 20	May 7-8
May 25	May 27	May 25	May 27
June 11	May 30	May 28	May 29
June 13	June 4	June 5	June 15
July 2-3	June 12	June 10	June 19
July 22	June 15	June 13	June 26-27
July 24	June 20	June 18	July 4
August 10	June 23	July 1-2	July 10
August 14	July 3-12	July 9	July 15
August 21-22	August 12-21	July 13	July 18
August 29	August 29	July 30	July 23
September 4	August 31	August 1	July 31
September 9	September 3	August 20	August 3
September 12	September 8	August 21	August 8
September 17	September 11	September 9	August 11
September 25	September 19	September 11	August 21-30
September 28	September 24	September 28	Sept. 30 - Oct. 9
October 3	September 27	October 2	October 17
October 6	October 2	October 9-10	October 19
October 16-25	October 15-16	October 17	October 22
Nov. 25-Dec. 4	October 23	October 23	October 27
December 12	October 27	October 28	October 30
December 14	November 13	October 31	November 7
December 17	November 15	November 5	November 12
December 22	December 4-5	November 13	November 15
December 25	December 24	November 16	November 20
	December 26	November 21	December 3-4
		November 24	December 11
		December 4-13	December 15

2026	2027	2028	2029
January 1	January 2	January 1	January 5
January 3	January 5	January 4	January 9
January 22-23	January 10	January 9	January 16-17
February 11	January 13	January 22-23	January 24
February 13	Jan. 23 - Feb. 1	January 30	January 30
March 2	March 4 - 13	February 3	February 4
March 6	March 21	February 20	February 7
March 13-14	March 23	February 22	February 12
March 21	March 26	March 12-13	February 20
March 27	March 31	April 1	February 23
April 1	April 3	April 3	February 28
April 4	April 11	April 20	March 3
April 9	April 16	April 24	March 13-22
April 17	April 19	May 1-2	April 22 - May 1
April 20	April 24	May 9	May 9
April 25	May 7-8	May 15	May 11
April 28	May 15	May 20	May 14
May 8- 17	May 19	May 23	May 19
June 17-26	June 5	May 28	May 22
July 4	June 7	June 5	May 30
July 6	June 26-27	June 8	June 4
July 9	July 16	June 13	June 7
July 14	July 18	June 16	June 12
July 17	August 4	June 26 -July 5	June 25-26
July 25	August 8	August 5-14	July 3
July 30	August 15	August 22	July 7
August 2	August 16	August 24	July 24
August 7	August 23	August 27	July 26
August 20-21	August 29	September 1	August 14-15
August 28	September 3	September 4	September 3
September 1	September 6	September 12	September 5
September 18	September 11	September 17	September 22
September 20	September 19	September 20	September 26
October 9-10	September 22	September 25	October 3-4
October 29	September 27	October 8-9	October 11
October 31	September 30	October 16	October 17
November 17	October 10-19	October 20	October 22
November 21	November 19-28	November 6	October 25
November 28-29	December 6	November 8	October 30
December 6	December 8	November 27-28	November 7
December 12	December 11	December 17	November 10
December 17	December 16		November 15
December 20	December 19		November 18
December 25	December 27		Nov. 28-Dec. 7

2030	2031	2032	2033
January 7-16	January 16-17	January 4	January 2
January 24	February 5	January 7	January 15-16
January 26	February 7-24	January 17-26	January 23
January 29	February 28	Feb. 26-Mar. 6	January 27
February 3	March 7-8	March 14	February 13
February 6	March 15	March 16	February 15
February 14	March 21	March 19	March 6-7
February 19	March 26	March 24	March 26
February 22	March 29	March 27	March 28
February 27	April 3	April 4	April 14
March 12-13	April 11	April 9	April 18
March 20	April 14	April 12	April 25-26
March 24	April 19	April 17	May 3
April 10	April 22	April 30	May 9
April 12	May 2-11	May 1	May 14
May 1-2	June 11-20	May 8	May 17
May 21	June 28	May 12	May 22
May 23	June 30	May 29	May 30
June 9	July 3	May 31	June 2
June 13	July 18	June 19-20	June 7
June 20-21	July 11	July 9	June 10
July 4	July 19	July 11	June 20-29
July 9	July 24	July 28	July 30-August 8
July 12	July 27	August 1	August 16
July 25	August 1	August 8-9	August 18
July 28	August 14-15	August 16	August 21
August 2	August 22	August 22	August 26
August 5	August 26	August 27	August 29
August 15-24	September 12	August 30	September 6
Sept. 24-Oct. 3	September 14	September 4	September 11
October 11	October 3-4	September 12	September 14
October 13	October 23	September 15	September 19
October 16	October 25	September 20	October 2-3
October 21	November 11	September 23	October 10
October 24	November 15	October 3-12	October 14
November 1	November 22-23	November 12-21	October 31
November 6	November 30	November 29	November 2
November 9	December 6	December 1	November 21-22
November 14	December 11	December 4	December 11
November 27-28	December 14	December 9	December 13
December 5	December 19	December 12	December 30
December 9	December 27	December 20	
December 26	December 30	December 25	
		December 28	

Collective Shadow Cycles: 2018–2033

Cycle Begins	U.E.*	E.E.**	Cycle Ends	U.E.*	E.E.**
July 24, 2018	4	*Being*	August 12, 2018	10	*Enlightening*
April 10, 2019	4	*Being*	April 29, 2019	10	*Enlightening*
December 26, 2019	4	*Being*	January 14, 2020	10	*Enlightening*
September 11, 2020	4	*Being*	September 30, 2020	10	*Enlightening*
May 29, 2021	4	*Being*	June 17, 2021	10	*Enlightening*
February 13, 2022	4	*Being*	March 4, 2022	10	*Enlightening*
October 31, 2022	4	*Being*	November 19, 2022	10	*Enlightening*
July 18, 2023	4	*Being*	August 6, 2023	10	*Enlightening*
April 3, 2024	4	*Being*	April 22, 2024	10	*Enlightening*
December 19, 2024	4	*Being*	January 7, 2025	10	*Enlightening*
September 5, 2025	4	*Being*	September 24, 2025	10	*Enlightening*
May 23, 2026	4	*Being*	June 11, 2026	10	*Enlightening*
February 7, 2027	4	*Being*	February 26, 2027	10	*Enlightening*
October 25, 2027	4	*Being*	November 13, 2027	10	*Enlightening*
July 11, 2028	4	*Being*	July 30, 2028	10	*Enlightening*
March 28, 2029	4	*Being*	April 16, 2029	10	*Enlightening*
December 13, 2029	4	*Being*	January 1, 2030	10	*Enlightening*
August 30, 2030	4	*Being*	September 18, 2030	10	*Enlightening*
May 17, 2031	4	*Being*	June 5, 2031	10	*Enlightening*
February 1, 2032	4	*Being*	February 20, 2032	10	*Enlightening*
October 18, 2032	4	*Being*	November 6, 2032	10	*Enlightening*
July 5, 2033	4	*Being*	July 24, 2033	10	*Enlightening*

* UE means Universal Energy

** EE means Earth Energy

PLEIADIAN-EARTH ENERGY
EPHEMERIS: 1975–2030

This ephemeris will allow you to match the dates of the Gregorian calendar to the spirals of universal energies (UE) and earth energies at play. Use this ephemeris to create your own calendar based on the Pleiadian-Earth energies as well as to determine your own personal energies, including your evolutionary guidance energy (see page 79) and your personal shadow cycles (see page 166).

To determine your evolutionary guidance energy, find your birthdate and the universal number next to it and then trace the numbers back to 1. The earth energy that appears next to the universal number 1 immediately prior to your birth determines your personal evolutionary guidance. If your birthdate falls in the universal energy of 1, you have a double influence of that particular energy.

Individual shadow cycles are determined by counting sixty-five days from the same energy as the day of your birth. The date you find marks the end of your personal shadow cycle. Seven to ten days preceding *that* date you will begin to experience the actual shadow cycle period, which offers a chance for doing deep inner work.

If your birthdate falls prior to the ephemeris included in the book or if you would like to chart the energy of calendar days or shadow cycles further into the future, an expanded ephemeris of the years 1900 through 2100 can be found at https://audio.innertraditions.com/pleaen.

Date	UE	Earth Energy	Date	UE	Earth Energy	Date	UE	Earth Energy
Jan 1 1975	6	Illuminating	Mar 12 1975	11	Being	May 21 1975	3	Illuminating
Jan 2 1975	7	Choosing	Mar 13 1975	12	Breathing	May 22 1975	4	Choosing
Jan 3 1975	8	Exploring	Mar 14 1975	13	Listening	May 23 1975	5	Exploring
Jan 4 1975	9	Healing	Mar 15 1975	1	**Planting**	May 24 1975	6	Healing
Jan 5 1975	10	Seeing	Mar 16 1975	2	Moving	May 25 1975	7	Seeing
Jan 6 1975	11	Intuiting	Mar 17 1975	3	Transcending	May 26 1975	8	Intuiting
Jan 7 1975	12	Evolving	Mar 18 1975	4	Remembering	May 27 1975	9	Evolving
Jan 8 1975	13	Self-Regulating	Mar 19 1975	5	Loving	May 28 1975	10	Self-Regulating
Jan 9 1975	1	**Catalyzing**	Mar 20 1975	6	Feeling	May 29 1975	11	Catalyzing
Jan 10 1975	2	Enlightening	Mar 21 1975	7	Devoting	May 30 1975	12	Enlightening
Jan 11 1975	3	Being	Mar 22 1975	8	Illuminating	May 31 1975	13	Being
Jan 12 1975	4	Breathing	Mar 23 1975	9	Choosing	Jun 1 1975	1	**Breathing**
Jan 13 1975	5	Listening	Mar 24 1975	10	Exploring	Jun 2 1975	2	Listening
Jan 14 1975	6	Planting	Mar 25 1975	11	Healing	Jun 3 1975	3	Planting
Jan 15 1975	7	Moving	Mar 26 1975	12	Seeing	Jun 4 1975	4	Moving
Jan 16 1975	8	Transcending	Mar 27 1975	13	Intuiting	Jun 5 1975	5	Transcending
Jan 17 1975	9	Remembering	Mar 28 1975	1	**Evolving**	Jun 6 1975	6	Remembering
Jan 18 1975	10	Loving	Mar 29 1975	2	Self-Regulating	Jun 7 1975	7	Loving
Jan 19 1975	11	Feeling	Mar 30 1975	3	Catalyzing	Jun 8 1975	8	Feeling
Jan 20 1975	12	Devoting	Mar 31 1975	4	Enlightening	Jun 9 1975	9	Devoting
Jan 21 1975	13	Illuminating	Apr 1 1975	5	Being	Jun 10 1975	10	Illuminating
Jan 22 1975	1	**Choosing**	Apr 2 1975	6	Breathing	Jun 11 1975	11	Choosing
Jan 23 1975	2	Exploring	Apr 3 1975	7	Listening	Jun 12 1975	12	Exploring
Jan 24 1975	3	Healing	Apr 4 1975	8	Planting	Jun 13 1975	13	Healing
Jan 25 1975	4	Seeing	Apr 5 1975	9	Moving	Jun 14 1975	1	**Seeing**
Jan 26 1975	5	Intuiting	Apr 6 1975	10	Transcending	Jun 15 1975	2	Intuiting
Jan 27 1975	6	Evolving	Apr 7 1975	11	Remembering	Jun 16 1975	3	Evolving
Jan 28 1975	7	Self-Regulating	Apr 8 1975	12	Loving	Jun 17 1975	4	Self-Regulating
Jan 29 1975	8	Catalyzing	Apr 9 1975	13	Feeling	Jun 18 1975	5	Catalyzing
Jan 30 1975	9	Enlightening	Apr 10 1975	1	**Devoting**	Jun 19 1975	6	Enlightening
Jan 31 1975	10	Being	Apr 11 1975	2	Illuminating	Jun 20 1975	7	Being
Feb 1 1975	11	Breathing	Apr 12 1975	3	Choosing	Jun 21 1975	8	Breathing
Feb 2 1975	12	Listening	Apr 13 1975	4	Exploring	Jun 22 1975	9	Listening
Feb 3 1975	13	Planting	Apr 14 1975	5	Healing	Jun 23 1975	10	Planting
Feb 4 1975	1	**Moving**	Apr 15 1975	6	Seeing	Jun 24 1975	11	Moving
Feb 5 1975	2	Transcending	Apr 16 1975	7	Intuiting	Jun 25 1975	12	Transcending
Feb 6 1975	3	Remembering	Apr 17 1975	8	Evolving	Jun 26 1975	13	Remembering
Feb 7 1975	4	Loving	Apr 18 1975	9	Self-Regulating	Jun 27 1975	1	**Loving**
Feb 8 1975	5	Feeling	Apr 19 1975	10	Catalyzing	Jun 28 1975	2	Feeling
Feb 9 1975	6	Devoting	Apr 20 1975	11	Enlightening	Jun 29 1975	3	Devoting
Feb 10 1975	7	Illuminating	Apr 21 1975	12	Being	Jun 30 1975	4	Illuminating
Feb 11 1975	8	Choosing	Apr 22 1975	13	Breathing	Jul 1 1975	5	Choosing
Feb 12 1975	9	Exploring	Apr 23 1975	1	**Listening**	Jul 2 1975	6	Exploring
Feb 13 1975	10	Healing	Apr 24 1975	2	Planting	Jul 3 1975	7	Healing
Feb 14 1975	11	Seeing	Apr 25 1975	3	Moving	Jul 4 1975	8	Seeing
Feb 15 1975	12	Intuiting	Apr 26 1975	4	Transcending	Jul 5 1975	9	Intuiting
Feb 16 1975	13	Evolving	Apr 27 1975	5	Remembering	Jul 6 1975	10	Evolving
Feb 17 1975	1	**Self-Regulating**	Apr 28 1975	6	Loving	Jul 7 1975	11	Self-Regulating
Feb 18 1975	2	Catalyzing	Apr 29 1975	7	Feeling	Jul 8 1975	12	Catalyzing
Feb 19 1975	3	Enlightening	Apr 30 1975	8	Devoting	Jul 9 1975	13	Enlightening
Feb 20 1975	4	Being	May 1 1975	9	Illuminating	Jul 10 1975	1	**Being**
Feb 21 1975	5	Breathing	May 2 1975	10	Choosing	Jul 11 1975	2	Breathing
Feb 22 1975	6	Listening	May 3 1975	11	Exploring	Jul 12 1975	3	Listening
Feb 23 1975	7	Planting	May 4 1975	12	Healing	Jul 13 1975	4	Planting
Feb 24 1975	8	Moving	May 5 1975	13	Seeing	Jul 14 1975	5	Moving
Feb 25 1975	9	Transcending	May 6 1975	1	**Intuiting**	Jul 15 1975	6	Transcending
Feb 26 1975	10	Remembering	May 7 1975	2	Evolving	Jul 16 1975	7	Remembering
Feb 27 1975	11	Loving	May 8 1975	3	Self-Regulating	Jul 17 1975	8	Loving
Feb 28 1975	12	Feeling	May 9 1975	4	Catalyzing	Jul 18 1975	9	Feeling
Mar 1 1975	13	Devoting	May 10 1975	5	Enlightening	Jul 19 1975	10	Devoting
Mar 2 1975	1	**Illuminating**	May 11 1975	6	Being	Jul 20 1975	11	Illuminating
Mar 3 1975	2	Choosing	May 12 1975	7	Breathing	Jul 21 1975	12	Choosing
Mar 4 1975	3	Exploring	May 13 1975	8	Listening	Jul 22 1975	13	Exploring
Mar 5 1975	4	Healing	May 14 1975	9	Planting	Jul 23 1975	1	**Healing**
Mar 6 1975	5	Seeing	May 15 1975	10	Moving	Jul 24 1975	2	Seeing
Mar 7 1975	6	Intuiting	May 16 1975	11	Transcending	Jul 25 1975	3	Intuiting
Mar 8 1975	7	Evolving	May 17 1975	12	Remembering	Jul 26 1975	4	Evolving
Mar 9 1975	8	Self-Regulating	May 18 1975	13	Loving	Jul 27 1975	5	Self-Regulating
Mar 10 1975	9	Catalyzing	May 19 1975	1	**Feeling**	Jul 28 1975	6	Catalyzing
Mar 11 1975	10	Enlightening	May 20 1975	2	Devoting	Jul 29 1975	7	Enlightening

Date	UE	Earth Energy	Date	UE	Earth Energy	Date	UE	Earth Energy
Jul 30 1975	8	Being	Oct 8 1975	13	Illuminating	Dec 17 1975	5	Being
Jul 31 1975	9	Breathing	Oct 9 1975	1	**Choosing**	Dec 18 1975	6	Breathing
Aug 1 1975	10	Listening	Oct 10 1975	2	Exploring	Dec 19 1975	7	Listening
Aug 2 1975	11	Planting	Oct 11 1975	3	Healing	Dec 20 1975	8	Planting
Aug 3 1975	12	Moving	Oct 12 1975	4	Seeing	Dec 21 1975	9	Moving
Aug 4 1975	13	Transcending	Oct 13 1975	5	Intuiting	Dec 22 1975	10	Transcending
Aug 5 1975	1	**Remembering**	Oct 14 1975	6	Evolving	Dec 23 1975	11	Remembering
Aug 6 1975	2	Loving	Oct 15 1975	7	Self-Regulating	Dec 24 1975	12	Loving
Aug 7 1975	3	Feeling	Oct 16 1975	8	Catalyzing	Dec 25 1975	13	Feeling
Aug 8 1975	4	Devoting	Oct 17 1975	9	Enlightening	Dec 26 1975	1	**Devoting**
Aug 9 1975	5	Illuminating	Oct 18 1975	10	Being	Dec 27 1975	2	Illuminating
Aug 10 1975	6	Choosing	Oct 19 1975	11	Breathing	Dec 28 1975	3	Choosing
Aug 11 1975	7	Exploring	Oct 20 1975	12	Listening	Dec 29 1975	4	Exploring
Aug 12 1975	8	Healing	Oct 21 1975	13	Planting	Dec 30 1975	5	Healing
Aug 13 1975	9	Seeing	Oct 22 1975	1	**Moving**	Dec 31 1975	6	Seeing
Aug 14 1975	10	Intuiting	Oct 23 1975	2	Transcending	Jan 1 1976	7	Intuiting
Aug 15 1975	11	Evolving	Oct 24 1975	3	Remembering	Jan 2 1976	8	Evolving
Aug 16 1975	12	Self-Regulating	Oct 25 1975	4	Loving	Jan 3 1976	9	Self-Regulating
Aug 17 1975	13	Catalyzing	Oct 26 1975	5	Feeling	Jan 4 1976	10	Catalyzing
Aug 18 1975	1	**Enlightening**	Oct 27 1975	6	Devoting	Jan 5 1976	11	Enlightening
Aug 19 1975	2	Being	Oct 28 1975	7	Illuminating	Jan 6 1976	12	Being
Aug 20 1975	3	Breathing	Oct 29 1975	8	Choosing	Jan 7 1976	13	Breathing
Aug 21 1975	4	Listening	Oct 30 1975	9	Exploring	Jan 8 1976	1	**Listening**
Aug 22 1975	5	Planting	Oct 31 1975	10	Healing	Jan 9 1976	2	Planting
Aug 23 1975	6	Moving	Nov 1 1975	11	Seeing	Jan 10 1976	3	Moving
Aug 24 1975	7	Transcending	Nov 2 1975	12	Intuiting	Jan 11 1976	4	Transcending
Aug 25 1975	8	Remembering	Nov 3 1975	13	Evolving	Jan 12 1976	5	Remembering
Aug 26 1975	9	Loving	Nov 4 1975	1	**Self-Regulating**	Jan 13 1976	6	Loving
Aug 27 1975	10	Feeling	Nov 5 1975	2	Catalyzing	Jan 14 1976	7	Feeling
Aug 28 1975	11	Devoting	Nov 6 1975	3	Enlightening	Jan 15 1976	8	Devoting
Aug 29 1975	12	Illuminating	Nov 7 1975	4	Being	Jan 16 1976	9	Illuminating
Aug 30 1975	13	Choosing	Nov 8 1975	5	Breathing	Jan 17 1976	10	Choosing
Aug 31 1975	1	**Exploring**	Nov 9 1975	6	Listening	Jan 18 1976	11	Exploring
Sep 1 1975	2	Healing	Nov 10 1975	7	Planting	Jan 19 1976	12	Healing
Sep 2 1975	3	Seeing	Nov 11 1975	8	Moving	Jan 20 1976	13	Seeing
Sep 3 1975	4	Intuiting	Nov 12 1975	9	Transcending	Jan 21 1976	1	**Intuiting**
Sep 4 1975	5	Evolving	Nov 13 1975	10	Remembering	Jan 22 1976	2	Evolving
Sep 5 1975	6	Self-Regulating	Nov 14 1975	11	Loving	Jan 23 1976	3	Self-Regulating
Sep 6 1975	7	Catalyzing	Nov 15 1975	12	Feeling	Jan 24 1976	4	Catalyzing
Sep 7 1975	8	Enlightening	Nov 16 1975	13	Devoting	Jan 25 1976	5	Enlightening
Sep 8 1975	9	Being	Nov 17 1975	1	**Illuminating**	Jan 26 1976	6	Being
Sep 9 1975	10	Breathing	Nov 18 1975	2	Choosing	Jan 27 1976	7	Breathing
Sep 10 1975	11	Listening	Nov 19 1975	3	Exploring	Jan 28 1976	8	Listening
Sep 11 1975	12	Planting	Nov 20 1975	4	Healing	Jan 29 1976	9	Planting
Sep 12 1975	13	Moving	Nov 21 1975	5	Seeing	Jan 30 1976	10	Moving
Sep 13 1975	1	**Transcending**	Nov 22 1975	6	Intuiting	Jan 31 1976	11	Transcending
Sep 14 1975	2	Remembering	Nov 23 1975	7	Evolving	Feb 1 1976	12	Remembering
Sep 15 1975	3	Loving	Nov 24 1975	8	Self-Regulating	Feb 2 1976	13	Loving
Sep 16 1975	4	Feeling	Nov 25 1975	9	Catalyzing	Feb 3 1976	1	**Feeling**
Sep 17 1975	5	Devoting	Nov 26 1975	10	Enlightening	Feb 4 1976	2	Devoting
Sep 18 1975	6	Illuminating	Nov 27 1975	11	Being	Feb 5 1976	3	Illuminating
Sep 19 1975	7	Choosing	Nov 28 1975	12	Breathing	Feb 6 1976	4	Choosing
Sep 20 1975	8	Exploring	Nov 29 1975	13	Listening	Feb 7 1976	5	Exploring
Sep 21 1975	9	Healing	Nov 30 1975	1	**Planting**	Feb 8 1976	6	Healing
Sep 22 1975	10	Seeing	Dec 1 1975	2	Moving	Feb 9 1976	7	Seeing
Sep 23 1975	11	Intuiting	Dec 2 1975	3	Transcending	Feb 10 1976	8	Intuiting
Sep 24 1975	12	Evolving	Dec 3 1975	4	Remembering	Feb 11 1976	9	Evolving
Sep 25 1975	13	Self-Regulating	Dec 4 1975	5	Loving	Feb 12 1976	10	Self-Regulating
Sep 26 1975	1	**Catalyzing**	Dec 5 1975	6	Feeling	Feb 13 1976	11	Catalyzing
Sep 27 1975	2	Enlightening	Dec 6 1975	7	Devoting	Feb 14 1976	12	Enlightening
Sep 28 1975	3	Being	Dec 7 1975	8	Illuminating	Feb 15 1976	13	Being
Sep 29 1975	4	Breathing	Dec 8 1975	9	Choosing	Feb 16 1976	1	**Breathing**
Sep 30 1975	5	Listening	Dec 9 1975	10	Exploring	Feb 17 1976	2	Listening
Oct 1 1975	6	Planting	Dec 10 1975	11	Healing	Feb 18 1976	3	Planting
Oct 2 1975	7	Moving	Dec 11 1975	12	Seeing	Feb 19 1976	4	Moving
Oct 3 1975	8	Transcending	Dec 12 1975	13	Intuiting	Feb 20 1976	5	Transcending
Oct 4 1975	9	Remembering	Dec 13 1975	1	**Evolving**	Feb 21 1976	6	Remembering
Oct 5 1975	10	Loving	Dec 14 1975	2	Self-Regulating	Feb 22 1976	7	Loving
Oct 6 1975	11	Feeling	Dec 15 1975	3	Catalyzing	Feb 23 1976	8	Feeling
Oct 7 1975	12	Devoting	Dec 16 1975	4	Enlightening	Feb 24 1976	9	Devoting

Date	UE Earth Energy	Date	UE Earth Energy	Date	UE Earth Energy
Feb 25 1976	10 Illuminating	May 5 1976	2 Being	Jul 14 1976	7 Illuminating
Feb 26 1976	11 Choosing	May 6 1976	3 Breathing	Jul 15 1976	8 Choosing
Feb 27 1976	12 Exploring	May 7 1976	4 Listening	Jul 16 1976	9 Exploring
Feb 28 1976	13 Healing	May 8 1976	5 Planting	Jul 17 1976	10 Healing
Feb 29 1976	**1 Seeing**	May 9 1976	6 Moving	Jul 18 1976	11 Seeing
Mar 1 1976	2 Intuiting	May 10 1976	7 Transcending	Jul 19 1976	12 Intuiting
Mar 2 1976	3 Evolving	May 11 1976	8 Remembering	Jul 20 1976	13 Evolving
Mar 3 1976	4 Self-Regulating	May 12 1976	9 Loving	Jul 21 1976	**1 Self-Regulating**
Mar 4 1976	5 Catalyzing	May 13 1976	10 Feeling	Jul 22 1976	2 Catalyzing
Mar 5 1976	6 Enlightening	May 14 1976	11 Devoting	Jul 23 1976	3 Enlightening
Mar 6 1976	7 Being	May 15 1976	12 Illuminating	Jul 24 1976	4 Being
Mar 7 1976	8 Breathing	May 16 1976	13 Choosing	Jul 25 1976	5 Breathing
Mar 8 1976	9 Listening	May 17 1976	**1 Exploring**	Jul 26 1976	6 Listening
Mar 9 1976	10 Planting	May 18 1976	2 Healing	Jul 27 1976	7 Planting
Mar 10 1976	11 Moving	May 19 1976	3 Seeing	Jul 28 1976	8 Moving
Mar 11 1976	12 Transcending	May 20 1976	4 Intuiting	Jul 29 1976	9 Transcending
Mar 12 1976	13 Remembering	May 21 1976	5 Evolving	Jul 30 1976	10 Remembering
Mar 13 1976	**1 Loving**	May 22 1976	6 Self-Regulating	Jul 31 1976	11 Loving
Mar 14 1976	2 Feeling	May 23 1976	7 Catalyzing	Aug 1 1976	12 Feeling
Mar 15 1976	3 Devoting	May 24 1976	8 Enlightening	Aug 2 1976	13 Devoting
Mar 16 1976	4 Illuminating	May 25 1976	9 Being	Aug 3 1976	**1 Illuminating**
Mar 17 1976	5 Choosing	May 26 1976	10 Breathing	Aug 4 1976	2 Choosing
Mar 18 1976	6 Exploring	May 27 1976	11 Listening	Aug 5 1976	3 Exploring
Mar 19 1976	7 Healing	May 28 1976	12 Planting	Aug 6 1976	4 Healing
Mar 20 1976	8 Seeing	May 29 1976	13 Moving	Aug 7 1976	5 Seeing
Mar 21 1976	9 Intuiting	May 30 1976	**1 Transcending**	Aug 8 1976	6 Intuiting
Mar 22 1976	10 Evolving	May 31 1976	2 Remembering	Aug 9 1976	7 Evolving
Mar 23 1976	11 Self-Regulating	Jun 1 1976	3 Loving	Aug 10 1976	8 Self-Regulating
Mar 24 1976	12 Catalyzing	Jun 2 1976	4 Feeling	Aug 11 1976	9 Catalyzing
Mar 25 1976	13 Enlightening	Jun 3 1976	5 Devoting	Aug 12 1976	10 Enlightening
Mar 26 1976	**1 Being**	Jun 4 1976	6 Illuminating	Aug 13 1976	11 Being
Mar 27 1976	2 Breathing	Jun 5 1976	7 Choosing	Aug 14 1976	12 Breathing
Mar 28 1976	3 Listening	Jun 6 1976	8 Exploring	Aug 15 1976	13 Listening
Mar 29 1976	4 Planting	Jun 7 1976	9 Healing	Aug 16 1976	**1 Planting**
Mar 30 1976	5 Moving	Jun 8 1976	10 Seeing	Aug 17 1976	2 Moving
Mar 31 1976	6 Transcending	Jun 9 1976	11 Intuiting	Aug 18 1976	3 Transcending
Apr 1 1976	7 Remembering	Jun 10 1976	12 Evolving	Aug 19 1976	4 Remembering
Apr 2 1976	8 Loving	Jun 11 1976	13 Self-Regulating	Aug 20 1976	5 Loving
Apr 3 1976	9 Feeling	Jun 12 1976	**1 Catalyzing**	Aug 21 1976	6 Feeling
Apr 4 1976	10 Devoting	Jun 13 1976	2 Enlightening	Aug 22 1976	7 Devoting
Apr 5 1976	11 Illuminating	Jun 14 1976	3 Being	Aug 23 1976	8 Illuminating
Apr 6 1976	12 Choosing	Jun 15 1976	4 Breathing	Aug 24 1976	9 Choosing
Apr 7 1976	13 Exploring	Jun 16 1976	5 Listening	Aug 25 1976	10 Exploring
Apr 8 1976	**1 Healing**	Jun 17 1976	6 Planting	Aug 26 1976	11 Healing
Apr 9 1976	2 Seeing	Jun 18 1976	7 Moving	Aug 27 1976	12 Seeing
Apr 10 1976	3 Intuiting	Jun 19 1976	8 Transcending	Aug 28 1976	13 Intuiting
Apr 11 1976	4 Evolving	Jun 20 1976	9 Remembering	Aug 29 1976	**1 Evolving**
Apr 12 1976	5 Self-Regulating	Jun 21 1976	10 Loving	Aug 30 1976	2 Self-Regulating
Apr 13 1976	6 Catalyzing	Jun 22 1976	11 Feeling	Aug 31 1976	3 Catalyzing
Apr 14 1976	7 Enlightening	Jun 23 1976	12 Devoting	Sep 1 1976	4 Enlightening
Apr 15 1976	8 Being	Jun 24 1976	13 Illuminating	Sep 2 1976	5 Being
Apr 16 1976	9 Breathing	Jun 25 1976	**1 Choosing**	Sep 3 1976	6 Breathing
Apr 17 1976	10 Listening	Jun 26 1976	2 Exploring	Sep 4 1976	7 Listening
Apr 18 1976	11 Planting	Jun 27 1976	3 Healing	Sep 5 1976	8 Planting
Apr 19 1976	12 Moving	Jun 28 1976	4 Seeing	Sep 6 1976	9 Moving
Apr 20 1976	13 Transcending	Jun 29 1976	5 Intuiting	Sep 7 1976	10 Transcending
Apr 21 1976	**1 Remembering**	Jun 30 1976	6 Evolving	Sep 8 1976	11 Remembering
Apr 22 1976	2 Loving	Jul 1 1976	7 Self-Regulating	Sep 9 1976	12 Loving
Apr 23 1976	3 Feeling	Jul 2 1976	8 Catalyzing	Sep 10 1976	13 Feeling
Apr 24 1976	4 Devoting	Jul 3 1976	9 Enlightening	Sep 11 1976	**1 Devoting**
Apr 25 1976	5 Illuminating	Jul 4 1976	10 Being	Sep 12 1976	2 Illuminating
Apr 26 1976	6 Choosing	Jul 5 1976	11 Breathing	Sep 13 1976	3 Choosing
Apr 27 1976	7 Exploring	Jul 6 1976	12 Listening	Sep 14 1976	4 Exploring
Apr 28 1976	8 Healing	Jul 7 1976	13 Planting	Sep 15 1976	5 Healing
Apr 29 1976	9 Seeing	Jul 8 1976	**1 Moving**	Sep 16 1976	6 Seeing
Apr 30 1976	10 Intuiting	Jul 9 1976	2 Transcending	Sep 17 1976	7 Intuiting
May 1 1976	11 Evolving	Jul 10 1976	3 Remembering	Sep 18 1976	8 Evolving
May 2 1976	12 Self-Regulating	Jul 11 1976	4 Loving	Sep 19 1976	9 Self-Regulating
May 3 1976	13 Catalyzing	Jul 12 1976	5 Feeling	Sep 20 1976	10 Catalyzing
May 4 1976	**1 Enlightening**	Jul 13 1976	6 Devoting	Sep 21 1976	11 Enlightening

Date	UE Earth Energy	Date	UE Earth Energy	Date	UE Earth Energy
Sep 22 1976	12 Being	Dec 1 1976	4 Illuminating	Feb 9 1977	9 Being
Sep 23 1976	13 Breathing	Dec 2 1976	5 Choosing	Feb 10 1977	10 Breathing
Sep 24 1976	1 Listening	Dec 3 1976	6 Exploring	Feb 11 1977	11 Listening
Sep 25 1976	2 Planting	Dec 4 1976	7 Healing	Feb 12 1977	12 Planting
Sep 26 1976	3 Moving	Dec 5 1976	8 Seeing	Feb 13 1977	13 Moving
Sep 27 1976	4 Transcending	Dec 6 1976	9 Intuiting	Feb 14 1977	1 Transcending
Sep 28 1976	5 Remembering	Dec 7 1976	10 Evolving	Feb 15 1977	2 Remembering
Sep 29 1976	6 Loving	Dec 8 1976	11 Self-Regulating	Feb 16 1977	3 Loving
Sep 30 1976	7 Feeling	Dec 9 1976	12 Catalyzing	Feb 17 1977	4 Feeling
Oct 1 1976	8 Devoting	Dec 10 1976	13 Enlightening	Feb 18 1977	5 Devoting
Oct 2 1976	9 Illuminating	Dec 11 1976	1 Being	Feb 19 1977	6 Illuminating
Oct 3 1976	10 Choosing	Dec 12 1976	2 Breathing	Feb 20 1977	7 Choosing
Oct 4 1976	11 Exploring	Dec 13 1976	3 Listening	Feb 21 1977	8 Exploring
Oct 5 1976	12 Healing	Dec 14 1976	4 Planting	Feb 22 1977	9 Healing
Oct 6 1976	13 Seeing	Dec 15 1976	5 Moving	Feb 23 1977	10 Seeing
Oct 7 1976	1 Intuiting	Dec 16 1976	6 Transcending	Feb 24 1977	11 Intuiting
Oct 8 1976	2 Evolving	Dec 17 1976	7 Remembering	Feb 25 1977	12 Evolving
Oct 9 1976	3 Self-Regulating	Dec 18 1976	8 Loving	Feb 26 1977	13 Self-Regulating
Oct 10 1976	4 Catalyzing	Dec 19 1976	9 Feeling	Feb 27 1977	1 Catalyzing
Oct 11 1976	5 Enlightening	Dec 20 1976	10 Devoting	Feb 28 1977	2 Enlightening
Oct 12 1976	6 Being	Dec 21 1976	11 Illuminating	Mar 1 1977	3 Being
Oct 13 1976	7 Breathing	Dec 22 1976	12 Choosing	Mar 2 1977	4 Breathing
Oct 14 1976	8 Listening	Dec 23 1976	13 Exploring	Mar 3 1977	5 Listening
Oct 15 1976	9 Planting	Dec 24 1976	1 Healing	Mar 4 1977	6 Planting
Oct 16 1976	10 Moving	Dec 25 1976	2 Seeing	Mar 5 1977	7 Moving
Oct 17 1976	11 Transcending	Dec 26 1976	3 Intuiting	Mar 6 1977	8 Transcending
Oct 18 1976	12 Remembering	Dec 27 1976	4 Evolving	Mar 7 1977	9 Remembering
Oct 19 1976	13 Loving	Dec 28 1976	5 Self-Regulating	Mar 8 1977	10 Loving
Oct 20 1976	1 Feeling	Dec 29 1976	6 Catalyzing	Mar 9 1977	11 Feeling
Oct 21 1976	2 Devoting	Dec 30 1976	7 Enlightening	Mar 10 1977	12 Devoting
Oct 22 1976	3 Illuminating	Dec 31 1976	8 Being	Mar 11 1977	13 Illuminating
Oct 23 1976	4 Choosing	Jan 1 1977	9 Breathing	Mar 12 1977	1 Choosing
Oct 24 1976	5 Exploring	Jan 2 1977	10 Listening	Mar 13 1977	2 Exploring
Oct 25 1976	6 Healing	Jan 3 1977	11 Planting	Mar 14 1977	3 Healing
Oct 26 1976	7 Seeing	Jan 4 1977	12 Moving	Mar 15 1977	4 Seeing
Oct 27 1976	8 Intuiting	Jan 5 1977	13 Transcending	Mar 16 1977	5 Intuiting
Oct 28 1976	9 Evolving	Jan 6 1977	1 Remembering	Mar 17 1977	6 Evolving
Oct 29 1976	10 Self-Regulating	Jan 7 1977	2 Loving	Mar 18 1977	7 Self-Regulating
Oct 30 1976	11 Catalyzing	Jan 8 1977	3 Feeling	Mar 19 1977	8 Catalyzing
Oct 31 1976	12 Enlightening	Jan 9 1977	4 Devoting	Mar 20 1977	9 Enlightening
Nov 1 1976	13 Being	Jan 10 1977	5 Illuminating	Mar 21 1977	10 Being
Nov 2 1976	1 Breathing	Jan 11 1977	6 Choosing	Mar 22 1977	11 Breathing
Nov 3 1976	2 Listening	Jan 12 1977	7 Exploring	Mar 23 1977	12 Listening
Nov 4 1976	3 Planting	Jan 13 1977	8 Healing	Mar 24 1977	13 Planting
Nov 5 1976	4 Moving	Jan 14 1977	9 Seeing	Mar 25 1977	1 Moving
Nov 6 1976	5 Transcending	Jan 15 1977	10 Intuiting	Mar 26 1977	2 Transcending
Nov 7 1976	6 Remembering	Jan 16 1977	11 Evolving	Mar 27 1977	3 Remembering
Nov 8 1976	7 Loving	Jan 17 1977	12 Self-Regulating	Mar 28 1977	4 Loving
Nov 9 1976	8 Feeling	Jan 18 1977	13 Catalyzing	Mar 29 1977	5 Feeling
Nov 10 1976	9 Devoting	Jan 19 1977	1 Enlightening	Mar 30 1977	6 Devoting
Nov 11 1976	10 Illuminating	Jan 20 1977	2 Being	Mar 31 1977	7 Illuminating
Nov 12 1976	11 Choosing	Jan 21 1977	3 Breathing	Apr 1 1977	8 Choosing
Nov 13 1976	12 Exploring	Jan 22 1977	4 Listening	Apr 2 1977	9 Exploring
Nov 14 1976	13 Healing	Jan 23 1977	5 Planting	Apr 3 1977	10 Healing
Nov 15 1976	1 Seeing	Jan 24 1977	6 Moving	Apr 4 1977	11 Seeing
Nov 16 1976	2 Intuiting	Jan 25 1977	7 Transcending	Apr 5 1977	12 Intuiting
Nov 17 1976	3 Evolving	Jan 26 1977	8 Remembering	Apr 6 1977	13 Evolving
Nov 18 1976	4 Self-Regulating	Jan 27 1977	9 Loving	Apr 7 1977	1 Self-Regulating
Nov 19 1976	5 Catalyzing	Jan 28 1977	10 Feeling	Apr 8 1977	2 Catalyzing
Nov 20 1976	6 Enlightening	Jan 29 1977	11 Devoting	Apr 9 1977	3 Enlightening
Nov 21 1976	7 Being	Jan 30 1977	12 Illuminating	Apr 10 1977	4 Being
Nov 22 1976	8 Breathing	Jan 31 1977	13 Choosing	Apr 11 1977	5 Breathing
Nov 23 1976	9 Listening	Feb 1 1977	1 Exploring	Apr 12 1977	6 Listening
Nov 24 1976	10 Planting	Feb 2 1977	2 Healing	Apr 13 1977	7 Planting
Nov 25 1976	11 Moving	Feb 3 1977	3 Seeing	Apr 14 1977	8 Moving
Nov 26 1976	12 Transcending	Feb 4 1977	4 Intuiting	Apr 15 1977	9 Transcending
Nov 27 1976	13 Remembering	Feb 5 1977	5 Evolving	Apr 16 1977	10 Remembering
Nov 28 1976	1 Loving	Feb 6 1977	6 Self-Regulating	Apr 17 1977	11 Loving
Nov 29 1976	2 Feeling	Feb 7 1977	7 Catalyzing	Apr 18 1977	12 Feeling
Nov 30 1976	3 Devoting	Feb 8 1977	8 Enlightening	Apr 19 1977	13 Devoting

Date	UE Earth Energy	Date	UE Earth Energy	Date	UE Earth Energy
Apr 20 1977	1 Illuminating	Jun 29 1977	6 Being	Sep 7 1977	11 Illuminating
Apr 21 1977	2 Choosing	Jun 30 1977	7 Breathing	Sep 8 1977	12 Choosing
Apr 22 1977	3 Exploring	Jul 1 1977	8 Listening	Sep 9 1977	13 Exploring
Apr 23 1977	4 Healing	Jul 2 1977	9 Planting	Sep 10 1977	1 Healing
Apr 24 1977	5 Seeing	Jul 3 1977	10 Moving	Sep 11 1977	2 Seeing
Apr 25 1977	6 Intuiting	Jul 4 1977	11 Transcending	Sep 12 1977	3 Intuiting
Apr 26 1977	7 Evolving	Jul 5 1977	12 Remembering	Sep 13 1977	4 Evolving
Apr 27 1977	8 Self-Regulating	Jul 6 1977	13 Loving	Sep 14 1977	5 Self-Regulating
Apr 28 1977	9 Catalyzing	Jul 7 1977	1 Feeling	Sep 15 1977	6 Catalyzing
Apr 29 1977	10 Enlightening	Jul 8 1977	2 Devoting	Sep 16 1977	7 Enlightening
Apr 30 1977	11 Being	Jul 9 1977	3 Illuminating	Sep 17 1977	8 Being
May 1 1977	12 Breathing	Jul 10 1977	4 Choosing	Sep 18 1977	9 Breathing
May 2 1977	13 Listening	Jul 11 1977	5 Exploring	Sep 19 1977	10 Listening
May 3 1977	1 Planting	Jul 12 1977	6 Healing	Sep 20 1977	11 Planting
May 4 1977	2 Moving	Jul 13 1977	7 Seeing	Sep 21 1977	12 Moving
May 5 1977	3 Transcending	Jul 14 1977	8 Intuiting	Sep 22 1977	13 Transcending
May 6 1977	4 Remembering	Jul 15 1977	9 Evolving	Sep 23 1977	1 Remembering
May 7 1977	5 Loving	Jul 16 1977	10 Self-Regulating	Sep 24 1977	2 Loving
May 8 1977	6 Feeling	Jul 17 1977	11 Catalyzing	Sep 25 1977	3 Feeling
May 9 1977	7 Devoting	Jul 18 1977	12 Enlightening	Sep 26 1977	4 Devoting
May 10 1977	8 Illuminating	Jul 19 1977	13 Being	Sep 27 1977	5 Illuminating
May 11 1977	9 Choosing	Jul 20 1977	1 Breathing	Sep 28 1977	6 Choosing
May 12 1977	10 Exploring	Jul 21 1977	2 Listening	Sep 29 1977	7 Exploring
May 13 1977	11 Healing	Jul 22 1977	3 Planting	Sep 30 1977	8 Healing
May 14 1977	12 Seeing	Jul 23 1977	4 Moving	Oct 1 1977	9 Seeing
May 15 1977	13 Intuiting	Jul 24 1977	5 Transcending	Oct 2 1977	10 Intuiting
May 16 1977	1 Evolving	Jul 25 1977	6 Remembering	Oct 3 1977	11 Evolving
May 17 1977	2 Self-Regulating	Jul 26 1977	7 Loving	Oct 4 1977	12 Self-Regulating
May 18 1977	3 Catalyzing	Jul 27 1977	8 Feeling	Oct 5 1977	13 Catalyzing
May 19 1977	4 Enlightening	Jul 28 1977	9 Devoting	Oct 6 1977	1 Enlightening
May 20 1977	5 Being	Jul 29 1977	10 Illuminating	Oct 7 1977	2 Being
May 21 1977	6 Breathing	Jul 30 1977	11 Choosing	Oct 8 1977	3 Breathing
May 22 1977	7 Listening	Jul 31 1977	12 Exploring	Oct 9 1977	4 Listening
May 23 1977	8 Planting	Aug 1 1977	13 Healing	Oct 10 1977	5 Planting
May 24 1977	9 Moving	Aug 2 1977	1 Seeing	Oct 11 1977	6 Moving
May 25 1977	10 Transcending	Aug 3 1977	2 Intuiting	Oct 12 1977	7 Transcending
May 26 1977	11 Remembering	Aug 4 1977	3 Evolving	Oct 13 1977	8 Remembering
May 27 1977	12 Loving	Aug 5 1977	4 Self-Regulating	Oct 14 1977	9 Loving
May 28 1977	13 Feeling	Aug 6 1977	5 Catalyzing	Oct 15 1977	10 Feeling
May 29 1977	1 Devoting	Aug 7 1977	6 Enlightening	Oct 16 1977	11 Devoting
May 30 1977	2 Illuminating	Aug 8 1977	7 Being	Oct 17 1977	12 Illuminating
May 31 1977	3 Choosing	Aug 9 1977	8 Breathing	Oct 18 1977	13 Choosing
Jun 1 1977	4 Exploring	Aug 10 1977	9 Listening	Oct 19 1977	1 Exploring
Jun 2 1977	5 Healing	Aug 11 1977	10 Planting	Oct 20 1977	2 Healing
Jun 3 1977	6 Seeing	Aug 12 1977	11 Moving	Oct 21 1977	3 Seeing
Jun 4 1977	7 Intuiting	Aug 13 1977	12 Transcending	Oct 22 1977	4 Intuiting
Jun 5 1977	8 Evolving	Aug 14 1977	13 Remembering	Oct 23 1977	5 Evolving
Jun 6 1977	9 Self-Regulating	Aug 15 1977	1 Loving	Oct 24 1977	6 Self-Regulating
Jun 7 1977	10 Catalyzing	Aug 16 1977	2 Feeling	Oct 25 1977	7 Catalyzing
Jun 8 1977	11 Enlightening	Aug 17 1977	3 Devoting	Oct 26 1977	8 Enlightening
Jun 9 1977	12 Being	Aug 18 1977	4 Illuminating	Oct 27 1977	9 Being
Jun 10 1977	13 Breathing	Aug 19 1977	5 Choosing	Oct 28 1977	10 Breathing
Jun 11 1977	1 Listening	Aug 20 1977	6 Exploring	Oct 29 1977	11 Listening
Jun 12 1977	2 Planting	Aug 21 1977	7 Healing	Oct 30 1977	12 Planting
Jun 13 1977	3 Moving	Aug 22 1977	8 Seeing	Oct 31 1977	13 Moving
Jun 14 1977	4 Transcending	Aug 23 1977	9 Intuiting	Nov 1 1977	1 Transcending
Jun 15 1977	5 Remembering	Aug 24 1977	10 Evolving	Nov 2 1977	2 Remembering
Jun 16 1977	6 Loving	Aug 25 1977	11 Self-Regulating	Nov 3 1977	3 Loving
Jun 17 1977	7 Feeling	Aug 26 1977	12 Catalyzing	Nov 4 1977	4 Feeling
Jun 18 1977	8 Devoting	Aug 27 1977	13 Enlightening	Nov 5 1977	5 Devoting
Jun 19 1977	9 Illuminating	Aug 28 1977	1 Being	Nov 6 1977	6 Illuminating
Jun 20 1977	10 Choosing	Aug 29 1977	2 Breathing	Nov 7 1977	7 Choosing
Jun 21 1977	11 Exploring	Aug 30 1977	3 Listening	Nov 8 1977	8 Exploring
Jun 22 1977	12 Healing	Aug 31 1977	4 Planting	Nov 9 1977	9 Healing
Jun 23 1977	13 Seeing	Sep 1 1977	5 Moving	Nov 10 1977	10 Seeing
Jun 24 1977	1 Intuiting	Sep 2 1977	6 Transcending	Nov 11 1977	11 Intuiting
Jun 25 1977	2 Evolving	Sep 3 1977	7 Remembering	Nov 12 1977	12 Evolving
Jun 26 1977	3 Self-Regulating	Sep 4 1977	8 Loving	Nov 13 1977	13 Self-Regulating
Jun 27 1977	4 Catalyzing	Sep 5 1977	9 Feeling	Nov 14 1977	1 Catalyzing
Jun 28 1977	5 Enlightening	Sep 6 1977	10 Devoting	Nov 15 1977	2 Enlightening

Date	UE	Earth Energy
Nov 16 1977	3	Being
Nov 17 1977	4	Breathing
Nov 18 1977	5	Listening
Nov 19 1977	6	Planting
Nov 20 1977	7	Moving
Nov 21 1977	8	Transcending
Nov 22 1977	9	Remembering
Nov 23 1977	10	Loving
Nov 24 1977	11	Feeling
Nov 25 1977	12	Devoting
Nov 26 1977	13	Illuminating
Nov 27 1977	1	**Choosing**
Nov 28 1977	2	Exploring
Nov 29 1977	3	Healing
Nov 30 1977	4	Seeing
Dec 1 1977	5	Intuiting
Dec 2 1977	6	Evolving
Dec 3 1977	7	Self-Regulating
Dec 4 1977	8	Catalyzing
Dec 5 1977	9	Enlightening
Dec 6 1977	10	Being
Dec 7 1977	11	Breathing
Dec 8 1977	12	Listening
Dec 9 1977	13	Planting
Dec 10 1977	1	**Moving**
Dec 11 1977	2	Transcending
Dec 12 1977	3	Remembering
Dec 13 1977	4	Loving
Dec 14 1977	5	Feeling
Dec 15 1977	6	Devoting
Dec 16 1977	7	Illuminating
Dec 17 1977	8	Choosing
Dec 18 1977	9	Exploring
Dec 19 1977	10	Healing
Dec 20 1977	11	Seeing
Dec 21 1977	12	Intuiting
Dec 22 1977	13	Evolving
Dec 23 1977	1	**Self-Regulating**
Dec 24 1977	2	Catalyzing
Dec 25 1977	3	Enlightening
Dec 26 1977	4	Being
Dec 27 1977	5	Breathing
Dec 28 1977	6	Listening
Dec 29 1977	7	Planting
Dec 30 1977	8	Moving
Dec 31 1977	9	Transcending
Jan 1 1978	10	Remembering
Jan 2 1978	11	Loving
Jan 3 1978	12	Feeling
Jan 4 1978	13	Devoting
Jan 5 1978	1	**Illuminating**
Jan 6 1978	2	Choosing
Jan 7 1978	3	Exploring
Jan 8 1978	4	Healing
Jan 9 1978	5	Seeing
Jan 10 1978	6	Intuiting
Jan 11 1978	7	Evolving
Jan 12 1978	8	Self-Regulating
Jan 13 1978	9	Catalyzing
Jan 14 1978	10	Enlightening
Jan 15 1978	11	Being
Jan 16 1978	12	Breathing
Jan 17 1978	13	Listening
Jan 18 1978	1	**Planting**
Jan 19 1978	2	Moving
Jan 20 1978	3	Transcending
Jan 21 1978	4	Remembering
Jan 22 1978	5	Loving
Jan 23 1978	6	Feeling
Jan 24 1978	7	Devoting
Jan 25 1978	8	Illuminating
Jan 26 1978	9	Choosing
Jan 27 1978	10	Exploring
Jan 28 1978	11	Healing
Jan 29 1978	12	Seeing
Jan 30 1978	13	Intuiting
Jan 31 1978	1	**Evolving**
Feb 1 1978	2	Self-Regulating
Feb 2 1978	3	Catalyzing
Feb 3 1978	4	Enlightening
Feb 4 1978	5	Being
Feb 5 1978	6	Breathing
Feb 6 1978	7	Listening
Feb 7 1978	8	Planting
Feb 8 1978	9	Moving
Feb 9 1978	10	Transcending
Feb 10 1978	11	Remembering
Feb 11 1978	12	Loving
Feb 12 1978	13	Feeling
Feb 13 1978	1	**Devoting**
Feb 14 1978	2	Illuminating
Feb 15 1978	3	Choosing
Feb 16 1978	4	Exploring
Feb 17 1978	5	Healing
Feb 18 1978	6	Seeing
Feb 19 1978	7	Intuiting
Feb 20 1978	8	Evolving
Feb 21 1978	9	Self-Regulating
Feb 22 1978	10	Catalyzing
Feb 23 1978	11	Enlightening
Feb 24 1978	12	Being
Feb 25 1978	13	Breathing
Feb 26 1978	1	**Listening**
Feb 27 1978	2	Planting
Feb 28 1978	3	Moving
Mar 1 1978	4	Transcending
Mar 2 1978	5	Remembering
Mar 3 1978	6	Loving
Mar 4 1978	7	Feeling
Mar 5 1978	8	Devoting
Mar 6 1978	9	Illuminating
Mar 7 1978	10	Choosing
Mar 8 1978	11	Exploring
Mar 9 1978	12	Healing
Mar 10 1978	13	Seeing
Mar 11 1978	1	**Intuiting**
Mar 12 1978	2	Evolving
Mar 13 1978	3	Self-Regulating
Mar 14 1978	4	Catalyzing
Mar 15 1978	5	Enlightening
Mar 16 1978	6	Being
Mar 17 1978	7	Breathing
Mar 18 1978	8	Listening
Mar 19 1978	9	Planting
Mar 20 1978	10	Moving
Mar 21 1978	11	Transcending
Mar 22 1978	12	Remembering
Mar 23 1978	13	Loving
Mar 24 1978	1	**Feeling**
Mar 25 1978	2	Devoting
Mar 26 1978	3	Illuminating
Mar 27 1978	4	Choosing
Mar 28 1978	5	Exploring
Mar 29 1978	6	Healing
Mar 30 1978	7	Seeing
Mar 31 1978	8	Intuiting
Apr 1 1978	9	Evolving
Apr 2 1978	10	Self-Regulating
Apr 3 1978	11	Catalyzing
Apr 4 1978	12	Enlightening
Apr 5 1978	13	Being
Apr 6 1978	1	**Breathing**
Apr 7 1978	2	Listening
Apr 8 1978	3	Planting
Apr 9 1978	4	Moving
Apr 10 1978	5	Transcending
Apr 11 1978	6	Remembering
Apr 12 1978	7	Loving
Apr 13 1978	8	Feeling
Apr 14 1978	9	Devoting
Apr 15 1978	10	Illuminating
Apr 16 1978	11	Choosing
Apr 17 1978	12	Exploring
Apr 18 1978	13	Healing
Apr 19 1978	1	**Seeing**
Apr 20 1978	2	Intuiting
Apr 21 1978	3	Evolving
Apr 22 1978	4	Self-Regulating
Apr 23 1978	5	Catalyzing
Apr 24 1978	6	Enlightening
Apr 25 1978	7	Being
Apr 26 1978	8	Breathing
Apr 27 1978	9	Listening
Apr 28 1978	10	Planting
Apr 29 1978	11	Moving
Apr 30 1978	12	Transcending
May 1 1978	13	Remembering
May 2 1978	1	**Loving**
May 3 1978	2	Feeling
May 4 1978	3	Devoting
May 5 1978	4	Illuminating
May 6 1978	5	Choosing
May 7 1978	6	Exploring
May 8 1978	7	Healing
May 9 1978	8	Seeing
May 10 1978	9	Intuiting
May 11 1978	10	Evolving
May 12 1978	11	Self-Regulating
May 13 1978	12	Catalyzing
May 14 1978	13	Enlightening
May 15 1978	1	**Being**
May 16 1978	2	Breathing
May 17 1978	3	Listening
May 18 1978	4	Planting
May 19 1978	5	Moving
May 20 1978	6	Transcending
May 21 1978	7	Remembering
May 22 1978	8	Loving
May 23 1978	9	Feeling
May 24 1978	10	Devoting
May 25 1978	11	Illuminating
May 26 1978	12	Choosing
May 27 1978	13	Exploring
May 28 1978	1	**Healing**
May 29 1978	2	Seeing
May 30 1978	3	Intuiting
May 31 1978	4	Evolving
Jun 1 1978	5	Self-Regulating
Jun 2 1978	6	Catalyzing
Jun 3 1978	7	Enlightening
Jun 4 1978	8	Being
Jun 5 1978	9	Breathing
Jun 6 1978	10	Listening
Jun 7 1978	11	Planting
Jun 8 1978	12	Moving
Jun 9 1978	13	Transcending
Jun 10 1978	1	**Remembering**
Jun 11 1978	2	Loving
Jun 12 1978	3	Feeling
Jun 13 1978	4	Devoting

Date	UE	Earth Energy	Date	UE	Earth Energy	Date	UE	Earth Energy
Jun 14 1978	5	Illuminating	Aug 23 1978	10	Being	Nov 1 1978	2	Illuminating
Jun 15 1978	6	Choosing	Aug 24 1978	11	Breathing	Nov 2 1978	3	Choosing
Jun 16 1978	7	Exploring	Aug 25 1978	12	Listening	Nov 3 1978	4	Exploring
Jun 17 1978	8	Healing	Aug 26 1978	13	Planting	Nov 4 1978	5	Healing
Jun 18 1978	9	Seeing	Aug 27 1978	**1**	**Moving**	Nov 5 1978	6	Seeing
Jun 19 1978	10	Intuiting	Aug 28 1978	2	Transcending	Nov 6 1978	7	Intuiting
Jun 20 1978	11	Evolving	Aug 29 1978	3	Remembering	Nov 7 1978	8	Evolving
Jun 21 1978	12	Self-Regulating	Aug 30 1978	4	Loving	Nov 8 1978	9	Self-Regulating
Jun 22 1978	13	Catalyzing	Aug 31 1978	5	Feeling	Nov 9 1978	10	Catalyzing
Jun 23 1978	**1**	**Enlightening**	Sep 1 1978	6	Devoting	Nov 10 1978	11	Enlightening
Jun 24 1978	2	Being	Sep 2 1978	7	Illuminating	Nov 11 1978	12	Being
Jun 25 1978	3	Breathing	Sep 3 1978	8	Choosing	Nov 12 1978	13	Breathing
Jun 26 1978	4	Listening	Sep 4 1978	9	Exploring	Nov 13 1978	**1**	**Listening**
Jun 27 1978	5	Planting	Sep 5 1978	10	Healing	Nov 14 1978	2	Planting
Jun 28 1978	6	Moving	Sep 6 1978	11	Seeing	Nov 15 1978	3	Moving
Jun 29 1978	7	Transcending	Sep 7 1978	12	Intuiting	Nov 16 1978	4	Transcending
Jun 30 1978	8	Remembering	Sep 8 1978	13	Evolving	Nov 17 1978	5	Remembering
Jul 1 1978	9	Loving	Sep 9 1978	**1**	**Self-Regulating**	Nov 18 1978	6	Loving
Jul 2 1978	10	Feeling	Sep 10 1978	2	Catalyzing	Nov 19 1978	7	Feeling
Jul 3 1978	11	Devoting	Sep 11 1978	3	Enlightening	Nov 20 1978	8	Devoting
Jul 4 1978	12	Illuminating	Sep 12 1978	4	Being	Nov 21 1978	9	Illuminating
Jul 5 1978	13	Choosing	Sep 13 1978	5	Breathing	Nov 22 1978	10	Choosing
Jul 6 1978	**1**	**Exploring**	Sep 14 1978	6	Listening	Nov 23 1978	11	Exploring
Jul 7 1978	2	Healing	Sep 15 1978	7	Planting	Nov 24 1978	12	Healing
Jul 8 1978	3	Seeing	Sep 16 1978	8	Moving	Nov 25 1978	13	Seeing
Jul 9 1978	4	Intuiting	Sep 17 1978	9	Transcending	Nov 26 1978	**1**	**Intuiting**
Jul 10 1978	5	Evolving	Sep 18 1978	10	Remembering	Nov 27 1978	2	Evolving
Jul 11 1978	6	Self-Regulating	Sep 19 1978	11	Loving	Nov 28 1978	3	Self-Regulating
Jul 12 1978	7	Catalyzing	Sep 20 1978	12	Feeling	Nov 29 1978	4	Catalyzing
Jul 13 1978	8	Enlightening	Sep 21 1978	13	Devoting	Nov 30 1978	5	Enlightening
Jul 14 1978	9	Being	Sep 22 1978	**1**	**Illuminating**	Dec 1 1978	6	Being
Jul 15 1978	10	Breathing	Sep 23 1978	2	Choosing	Dec 2 1978	7	Breathing
Jul 16 1978	11	Listening	Sep 24 1978	3	Exploring	Dec 3 1978	8	Listening
Jul 17 1978	12	Planting	Sep 25 1978	4	Healing	Dec 4 1978	9	Planting
Jul 18 1978	13	Moving	Sep 26 1978	5	Seeing	Dec 5 1978	10	Moving
Jul 19 1978	**1**	**Transcending**	Sep 27 1978	6	Intuiting	Dec 6 1978	11	Transcending
Jul 20 1978	2	Remembering	Sep 28 1978	7	Evolving	Dec 7 1978	12	Remembering
Jul 21 1978	3	Loving	Sep 29 1978	8	Self-Regulating	Dec 8 1978	13	Loving
Jul 22 1978	4	Feeling	Sep 30 1978	9	Catalyzing	Dec 9 1978	**1**	**Feeling**
Jul 23 1978	5	Devoting	Oct 1 1978	10	Enlightening	Dec 10 1978	2	Devoting
Jul 24 1978	6	Illuminating	Oct 2 1978	11	Being	Dec 11 1978	3	Illuminating
Jul 25 1978	7	Choosing	Oct 3 1978	12	Breathing	Dec 12 1978	4	Choosing
Jul 26 1978	8	Exploring	Oct 4 1978	13	Listening	Dec 13 1978	5	Exploring
Jul 27 1978	9	Healing	Oct 5 1978	**1**	**Planting**	Dec 14 1978	6	Healing
Jul 28 1978	10	Seeing	Oct 6 1978	2	Moving	Dec 15 1978	7	Seeing
Jul 29 1978	11	Intuiting	Oct 7 1978	3	Transcending	Dec 16 1978	8	Intuiting
Jul 30 1978	12	Evolving	Oct 8 1978	4	Remembering	Dec 17 1978	9	Evolving
Jul 31 1978	13	Self-Regulating	Oct 9 1978	5	Loving	Dec 18 1978	10	Self-Regulating
Aug 1 1978	**1**	**Catalyzing**	Oct 10 1978	6	Feeling	Dec 19 1978	11	Catalyzing
Aug 2 1978	2	Enlightening	Oct 11 1978	7	Devoting	Dec 20 1978	12	Enlightening
Aug 3 1978	3	Being	Oct 12 1978	8	Illuminating	Dec 21 1978	13	Being
Aug 4 1978	4	Breathing	Oct 13 1978	9	Choosing	Dec 22 1978	**1**	**Breathing**
Aug 5 1978	5	Listening	Oct 14 1978	10	Exploring	Dec 23 1978	2	Listening
Aug 6 1978	6	Planting	Oct 15 1978	11	Healing	Dec 24 1978	3	Planting
Aug 7 1978	7	Moving	Oct 16 1978	12	Seeing	Dec 25 1978	4	Moving
Aug 8 1978	8	Transcending	Oct 17 1978	13	Intuiting	Dec 26 1978	5	Transcending
Aug 9 1978	9	Remembering	Oct 18 1978	**1**	**Evolving**	Dec 27 1978	6	Remembering
Aug 10 1978	10	Loving	Oct 19 1978	2	Self-Regulating	Dec 28 1978	7	Loving
Aug 11 1978	11	Feeling	Oct 20 1978	3	Catalyzing	Dec 29 1978	8	Feeling
Aug 12 1978	12	Devoting	Oct 21 1978	4	Enlightening	Dec 30 1978	9	Devoting
Aug 13 1978	13	Illuminating	Oct 22 1978	5	Being	Dec 31 1978	10	Illuminating
Aug 14 1978	**1**	**Choosing**	Oct 23 1978	6	Breathing	Jan 1 1979	11	Choosing
Aug 15 1978	2	Exploring	Oct 24 1978	7	Listening	Jan 2 1979	12	Exploring
Aug 16 1978	3	Healing	Oct 25 1978	8	Planting	Jan 3 1979	13	Healing
Aug 17 1978	4	Seeing	Oct 26 1978	9	Moving	Jan 4 1979	**1**	**Seeing**
Aug 18 1978	5	Intuiting	Oct 27 1978	10	Transcending	Jan 5 1979	2	Intuiting
Aug 19 1978	6	Evolving	Oct 28 1978	11	Remembering	Jan 6 1979	3	Evolving
Aug 20 1978	7	Self-Regulating	Oct 29 1978	12	Loving	Jan 7 1979	4	Self-Regulating
Aug 21 1978	8	Catalyzing	Oct 30 1978	13	Feeling	Jan 8 1979	5	Catalyzing
Aug 22 1978	9	Enlightening	Oct 31 1978	**1**	**Devoting**	Jan 9 1979	6	Enlightening

Date	UE	Earth Energy	Date	UE	Earth Energy	Date	UE	Earth Energy
Jan 10 1979	7	Being	Mar 21 1979	12	Illuminating	May 30 1979	4	Being
Jan 11 1979	8	Breathing	Mar 22 1979	13	Choosing	May 31 1979	5	Breathing
Jan 12 1979	9	Listening	Mar 23 1979	**1**	**Exploring**	Jun 1 1979	6	Listening
Jan 13 1979	10	Planting	Mar 24 1979	2	Healing	Jun 2 1979	7	Planting
Jan 14 1979	11	Moving	Mar 25 1979	3	Seeing	Jun 3 1979	8	Moving
Jan 15 1979	12	Transcending	Mar 26 1979	4	Intuiting	Jun 4 1979	9	Transcending
Jan 16 1979	13	Remembering	Mar 27 1979	5	Evolving	Jun 5 1979	10	Remembering
Jan 17 1979	**1**	**Loving**	Mar 28 1979	6	Self-Regulating	Jun 6 1979	11	Loving
Jan 18 1979	2	Feeling	Mar 29 1979	7	Catalyzing	Jun 7 1979	12	Feeling
Jan 19 1979	3	Devoting	Mar 30 1979	8	Enlightening	Jun 8 1979	13	Devoting
Jan 20 1979	4	Illuminating	Mar 31 1979	9	Being	Jun 9 1979	**1**	**Illuminating**
Jan 21 1979	5	Choosing	Apr 1 1979	10	Breathing	Jun 10 1979	2	Choosing
Jan 22 1979	6	Exploring	Apr 2 1979	11	Listening	Jun 11 1979	3	Exploring
Jan 23 1979	7	Healing	Apr 3 1979	12	Planting	Jun 12 1979	4	Healing
Jan 24 1979	8	Seeing	Apr 4 1979	13	Moving	Jun 13 1979	5	Seeing
Jan 25 1979	9	Intuiting	Apr 5 1979	**1**	**Transcending**	Jun 14 1979	6	Intuiting
Jan 26 1979	10	Evolving	Apr 6 1979	2	Remembering	Jun 15 1979	7	Evolving
Jan 27 1979	11	Self-Regulating	Apr 7 1979	3	Loving	Jun 16 1979	8	Self-Regulating
Jan 28 1979	12	Catalyzing	Apr 8 1979	4	Feeling	Jun 17 1979	9	Catalyzing
Jan 29 1979	13	Enlightening	Apr 9 1979	5	Devoting	Jun 18 1979	10	Enlightening
Jan 30 1979	**1**	**Being**	Apr 10 1979	6	Illuminating	Jun 19 1979	11	Being
Jan 31 1979	2	Breathing	Apr 11 1979	7	Choosing	Jun 20 1979	12	Breathing
Feb 1 1979	3	Listening	Apr 12 1979	8	Exploring	Jun 21 1979	13	Listening
Feb 2 1979	4	Planting	Apr 13 1979	9	Healing	Jun 22 1979	**1**	**Planting**
Feb 3 1979	5	Moving	Apr 14 1979	10	Seeing	Jun 23 1979	2	Moving
Feb 4 1979	6	Transcending	Apr 15 1979	11	Intuiting	Jun 24 1979	3	Transcending
Feb 5 1979	7	Remembering	Apr 16 1979	12	Evolving	Jun 25 1979	4	Remembering
Feb 6 1979	8	Loving	Apr 17 1979	13	Self-Regulating	Jun 26 1979	5	Loving
Feb 7 1979	9	Feeling	Apr 18 1979	**1**	**Catalyzing**	Jun 27 1979	6	Feeling
Feb 8 1979	10	Devoting	Apr 19 1979	2	Enlightening	Jun 28 1979	7	Devoting
Feb 9 1979	11	Illuminating	Apr 20 1979	3	Being	Jun 29 1979	8	Illuminating
Feb 10 1979	12	Choosing	Apr 21 1979	4	Breathing	Jun 30 1979	9	Choosing
Feb 11 1979	13	Exploring	Apr 22 1979	5	Listening	Jul 1 1979	10	Exploring
Feb 12 1979	**1**	**Healing**	Apr 23 1979	6	Planting	Jul 2 1979	11	Healing
Feb 13 1979	2	Seeing	Apr 24 1979	7	Moving	Jul 3 1979	12	Seeing
Feb 14 1979	3	Intuiting	Apr 25 1979	8	Transcending	Jul 4 1979	13	Intuiting
Feb 15 1979	4	Evolving	Apr 26 1979	9	Remembering	Jul 5 1979	**1**	**Evolving**
Feb 16 1979	5	Self-Regulating	Apr 27 1979	10	Loving	Jul 6 1979	2	Self-Regulating
Feb 17 1979	6	Catalyzing	Apr 28 1979	11	Feeling	Jul 7 1979	3	Catalyzing
Feb 18 1979	7	Enlightening	Apr 29 1979	12	Devoting	Jul 8 1979	4	Enlightening
Feb 19 1979	8	Being	Apr 30 1979	13	Illuminating	Jul 9 1979	5	Being
Feb 20 1979	9	Breathing	May 1 1979	**1**	**Choosing**	Jul 10 1979	6	Breathing
Feb 21 1979	10	Listening	May 2 1979	2	Exploring	Jul 11 1979	7	Listening
Feb 22 1979	11	Planting	May 3 1979	3	Healing	Jul 12 1979	8	Planting
Feb 23 1979	12	Moving	May 4 1979	4	Seeing	Jul 13 1979	9	Moving
Feb 24 1979	13	Transcending	May 5 1979	5	Intuiting	Jul 14 1979	10	Transcending
Feb 25 1979	**1**	**Remembering**	May 6 1979	6	Evolving	Jul 15 1979	11	Remembering
Feb 26 1979	2	Loving	May 7 1979	7	Self-Regulating	Jul 16 1979	12	Loving
Feb 27 1979	3	Feeling	May 8 1979	8	Catalyzing	Jul 17 1979	13	Feeling
Feb 28 1979	4	Devoting	May 9 1979	9	Enlightening	Jul 18 1979	**1**	**Devoting**
Mar 1 1979	5	Illuminating	May 10 1979	10	Being	Jul 19 1979	2	Illuminating
Mar 2 1979	6	Choosing	May 11 1979	11	Breathing	Jul 20 1979	3	Choosing
Mar 3 1979	7	Exploring	May 12 1979	12	Listening	Jul 21 1979	4	Exploring
Mar 4 1979	8	Healing	May 13 1979	13	Planting	Jul 22 1979	5	Healing
Mar 5 1979	9	Seeing	May 14 1979	**1**	**Moving**	Jul 23 1979	6	Seeing
Mar 6 1979	10	Intuiting	May 15 1979	2	Transcending	Jul 24 1979	7	Intuiting
Mar 7 1979	11	Evolving	May 16 1979	3	Remembering	Jul 25 1979	8	Evolving
Mar 8 1979	12	Self-Regulating	May 17 1979	4	Loving	Jul 26 1979	9	Self-Regulating
Mar 9 1979	13	Catalyzing	May 18 1979	5	Feeling	Jul 27 1979	10	Catalyzing
Mar 10 1979	**1**	**Enlightening**	May 19 1979	6	Devoting	Jul 28 1979	11	Enlightening
Mar 11 1979	2	Being	May 20 1979	7	Illuminating	Jul 29 1979	12	Being
Mar 12 1979	3	Breathing	May 21 1979	8	Choosing	Jul 30 1979	13	Breathing
Mar 13 1979	4	Listening	May 22 1979	9	Exploring	Jul 31 1979	**1**	**Listening**
Mar 14 1979	5	Planting	May 23 1979	10	Healing	Aug 1 1979	2	Planting
Mar 15 1979	6	Moving	May 24 1979	11	Seeing	Aug 2 1979	3	Moving
Mar 16 1979	7	Transcending	May 25 1979	12	Intuiting	Aug 3 1979	4	Transcending
Mar 17 1979	8	Remembering	May 26 1979	13	Evolving	Aug 4 1979	5	Remembering
Mar 18 1979	9	Loving	May 27 1979	**1**	**Self-Regulating**	Aug 5 1979	6	Loving
Mar 19 1979	10	Feeling	May 28 1979	2	Catalyzing	Aug 6 1979	7	Feeling
Mar 20 1979	11	Devoting	May 29 1979	3	Enlightening	Aug 7 1979	8	Devoting

Date	UE Earth Energy	Date	UE Earth Energy	Date	UE Earth Energy
Aug 8 1979	9 Illuminating	Oct 17 1979	1 Being	Dec 26 1979	6 Illuminating
Aug 9 1979	10 Choosing	Oct 18 1979	2 Breathing	Dec 27 1979	7 Choosing
Aug 10 1979	11 Exploring	Oct 19 1979	3 Listening	Dec 28 1979	8 Exploring
Aug 11 1979	12 Healing	Oct 20 1979	4 Planting	Dec 29 1979	9 Healing
Aug 12 1979	13 Seeing	Oct 21 1979	5 Moving	Dec 30 1979	10 Seeing
Aug 13 1979	1 Intuiting	Oct 22 1979	6 Transcending	Dec 31 1979	11 Intuiting
Aug 14 1979	2 Evolving	Oct 23 1979	7 Remembering	Jan 1 1980	12 Evolving
Aug 15 1979	3 Self-Regulating	Oct 24 1979	8 Loving	Jan 2 1980	13 Self-Regulating
Aug 16 1979	4 Catalyzing	Oct 25 1979	9 Feeling	Jan 3 1980	1 Catalyzing
Aug 17 1979	5 Enlightening	Oct 26 1979	10 Devoting	Jan 4 1980	2 Enlightening
Aug 18 1979	6 Being	Oct 27 1979	11 Illuminating	Jan 5 1980	3 Being
Aug 19 1979	7 Breathing	Oct 28 1979	12 Choosing	Jan 6 1980	4 Breathing
Aug 20 1979	8 Listening	Oct 29 1979	13 Exploring	Jan 7 1980	5 Listening
Aug 21 1979	9 Planting	Oct 30 1979	1 Healing	Jan 8 1980	6 Planting
Aug 22 1979	10 Moving	Oct 31 1979	2 Seeing	Jan 9 1980	7 Moving
Aug 23 1979	11 Transcending	Nov 1 1979	3 Intuiting	Jan 10 1980	8 Transcending
Aug 24 1979	12 Remembering	Nov 2 1979	4 Evolving	Jan 11 1980	9 Remembering
Aug 25 1979	13 Loving	Nov 3 1979	5 Self-Regulating	Jan 12 1980	10 Loving
Aug 26 1979	1 Feeling	Nov 4 1979	6 Catalyzing	Jan 13 1980	11 Feeling
Aug 27 1979	2 Devoting	Nov 5 1979	7 Enlightening	Jan 14 1980	12 Devoting
Aug 28 1979	3 Illuminating	Nov 6 1979	8 Being	Jan 15 1980	13 Illuminating
Aug 29 1979	4 Choosing	Nov 7 1979	9 Breathing	Jan 16 1980	1 Choosing
Aug 30 1979	5 Exploring	Nov 8 1979	10 Listening	Jan 17 1980	2 Exploring
Aug 31 1979	6 Healing	Nov 9 1979	11 Planting	Jan 18 1980	3 Healing
Sep 1 1979	7 Seeing	Nov 10 1979	12 Moving	Jan 19 1980	4 Seeing
Sep 2 1979	8 Intuiting	Nov 11 1979	13 Transcending	Jan 20 1980	5 Intuiting
Sep 3 1979	9 Evolving	Nov 12 1979	1 Remembering	Jan 21 1980	6 Evolving
Sep 4 1979	10 Self-Regulating	Nov 13 1979	2 Loving	Jan 22 1980	7 Self-Regulating
Sep 5 1979	11 Catalyzing	Nov 14 1979	3 Feeling	Jan 23 1980	8 Catalyzing
Sep 6 1979	12 Enlightening	Nov 15 1979	4 Devoting	Jan 24 1980	9 Enlightening
Sep 7 1979	13 Being	Nov 16 1979	5 Illuminating	Jan 25 1980	10 Being
Sep 8 1979	1 Breathing	Nov 17 1979	6 Choosing	Jan 26 1980	11 Breathing
Sep 9 1979	2 Listening	Nov 18 1979	7 Exploring	Jan 27 1980	12 Listening
Sep 10 1979	3 Planting	Nov 19 1979	8 Healing	Jan 28 1980	13 Planting
Sep 11 1979	4 Moving	Nov 20 1979	9 Seeing	Jan 29 1980	1 Moving
Sep 12 1979	5 Transcending	Nov 21 1979	10 Intuiting	Jan 30 1980	2 Transcending
Sep 13 1979	6 Remembering	Nov 22 1979	11 Evolving	Jan 31 1980	3 Remembering
Sep 14 1979	7 Loving	Nov 23 1979	12 Self-Regulating	Feb 1 1980	4 Loving
Sep 15 1979	8 Feeling	Nov 24 1979	13 Catalyzing	Feb 2 1980	5 Feeling
Sep 16 1979	9 Devoting	Nov 25 1979	1 Enlightening	Feb 3 1980	6 Devoting
Sep 17 1979	10 Illuminating	Nov 26 1979	2 Being	Feb 4 1980	7 Illuminating
Sep 18 1979	11 Choosing	Nov 27 1979	3 Breathing	Feb 5 1980	8 Choosing
Sep 19 1979	12 Exploring	Nov 28 1979	4 Listening	Feb 6 1980	9 Exploring
Sep 20 1979	13 Healing	Nov 29 1979	5 Planting	Feb 7 1980	10 Healing
Sep 21 1979	1 Seeing	Nov 30 1979	6 Moving	Feb 8 1980	11 Seeing
Sep 22 1979	2 Intuiting	Dec 1 1979	7 Transcending	Feb 9 1980	12 Intuiting
Sep 23 1979	3 Evolving	Dec 2 1979	8 Remembering	Feb 10 1980	13 Evolving
Sep 24 1979	4 Self-Regulating	Dec 3 1979	9 Loving	Feb 11 1980	1 Self-Regulating
Sep 25 1979	5 Catalyzing	Dec 4 1979	10 Feeling	Feb 12 1980	2 Catalyzing
Sep 26 1979	6 Enlightening	Dec 5 1979	11 Devoting	Feb 13 1980	3 Enlightening
Sep 27 1979	7 Being	Dec 6 1979	12 Illuminating	Feb 14 1980	4 Being
Sep 28 1979	8 Breathing	Dec 7 1979	13 Choosing	Feb 15 1980	5 Breathing
Sep 29 1979	9 Listening	Dec 8 1979	1 Exploring	Feb 16 1980	6 Listening
Sep 30 1979	10 Planting	Dec 9 1979	2 Healing	Feb 17 1980	7 Planting
Oct 1 1979	11 Moving	Dec 10 1979	3 Seeing	Feb 18 1980	8 Moving
Oct 2 1979	12 Transcending	Dec 11 1979	4 Intuiting	Feb 19 1980	9 Transcending
Oct 3 1979	13 Remembering	Dec 12 1979	5 Evolving	Feb 20 1980	10 Remembering
Oct 4 1979	1 Loving	Dec 13 1979	6 Self-Regulating	Feb 21 1980	11 Loving
Oct 5 1979	2 Feeling	Dec 14 1979	7 Catalyzing	Feb 22 1980	12 Feeling
Oct 6 1979	3 Devoting	Dec 15 1979	8 Enlightening	Feb 23 1980	13 Devoting
Oct 7 1979	4 Illuminating	Dec 16 1979	9 Being	Feb 24 1980	1 Illuminating
Oct 8 1979	5 Choosing	Dec 17 1979	10 Breathing	Feb 25 1980	2 Choosing
Oct 9 1979	6 Exploring	Dec 18 1979	11 Listening	Feb 26 1980	3 Exploring
Oct 10 1979	7 Healing	Dec 19 1979	12 Planting	Feb 27 1980	4 Healing
Oct 11 1979	8 Seeing	Dec 20 1979	13 Moving	Feb 28 1980	5 Seeing
Oct 12 1979	9 Intuiting	Dec 21 1979	1 Transcending	Feb 29 1980	6 Intuiting
Oct 13 1979	10 Evolving	Dec 22 1979	2 Remembering	Mar 1 1980	7 Evolving
Oct 14 1979	11 Self-Regulating	Dec 23 1979	3 Loving	Mar 2 1980	8 Self-Regulating
Oct 15 1979	12 Catalyzing	Dec 24 1979	4 Feeling	Mar 3 1980	9 Catalyzing
Oct 16 1979	13 Enlightening	Dec 25 1979	5 Devoting	Mar 4 1980	10 Enlightening

Date	UE	Earth Energy
Mar 5 1980	11	Being
Mar 6 1980	12	Breathing
Mar 7 1980	13	Listening
Mar 8 1980	1	**Planting**
Mar 9 1980	2	Moving
Mar 10 1980	3	Transcending
Mar 11 1980	4	Remembering
Mar 12 1980	5	Loving
Mar 13 1980	6	Feeling
Mar 14 1980	7	Devoting
Mar 15 1980	8	Illuminating
Mar 16 1980	9	Choosing
Mar 17 1980	10	Exploring
Mar 18 1980	11	Healing
Mar 19 1980	12	Seeing
Mar 20 1980	13	Intuiting
Mar 21 1980	1	**Evolving**
Mar 22 1980	2	Self-Regulating
Mar 23 1980	3	Catalyzing
Mar 24 1980	4	Enlightening
Mar 25 1980	5	Being
Mar 26 1980	6	Breathing
Mar 27 1980	7	Listening
Mar 28 1980	8	Planting
Mar 29 1980	9	Moving
Mar 30 1980	10	Transcending
Mar 31 1980	11	Remembering
Apr 1 1980	12	Loving
Apr 2 1980	13	Feeling
Apr 3 1980	1	**Devoting**
Apr 4 1980	2	Illuminating
Apr 5 1980	3	Choosing
Apr 6 1980	4	Exploring
Apr 7 1980	5	Healing
Apr 8 1980	6	Seeing
Apr 9 1980	7	Intuiting
Apr 10 1980	8	Evolving
Apr 11 1980	9	Self-Regulating
Apr 12 1980	10	Catalyzing
Apr 13 1980	11	Enlightening
Apr 14 1980	12	Being
Apr 15 1980	13	Breathing
Apr 16 1980	1	**Listening**
Apr 17 1980	2	Planting
Apr 18 1980	3	Moving
Apr 19 1980	4	Transcending
Apr 20 1980	5	Remembering
Apr 21 1980	6	Loving
Apr 22 1980	7	Feeling
Apr 23 1980	8	Devoting
Apr 24 1980	9	Illuminating
Apr 25 1980	10	Choosing
Apr 26 1980	11	Exploring
Apr 27 1980	12	Healing
Apr 28 1980	13	Seeing
Apr 29 1980	1	**Intuiting**
Apr 30 1980	2	Evolving
May 1 1980	3	Self-Regulating
May 2 1980	4	Catalyzing
May 3 1980	5	Enlightening
May 4 1980	6	Being
May 5 1980	7	Breathing
May 6 1980	8	Listening
May 7 1980	9	Planting
May 8 1980	10	Moving
May 9 1980	11	Transcending
May 10 1980	12	Remembering
May 11 1980	13	Loving
May 12 1980	1	**Feeling**
May 13 1980	2	Devoting

Date	UE	Earth Energy
May 14 1980	3	Illuminating
May 15 1980	4	Choosing
May 16 1980	5	Exploring
May 17 1980	6	Healing
May 18 1980	7	Seeing
May 19 1980	8	Intuiting
May 20 1980	9	Evolving
May 21 1980	10	Self-Regulating
May 22 1980	11	Catalyzing
May 23 1980	12	Enlightening
May 24 1980	13	Being
May 25 1980	1	**Breathing**
May 26 1980	2	Listening
May 27 1980	3	Planting
May 28 1980	4	Moving
May 29 1980	5	Transcending
May 30 1980	6	Remembering
May 31 1980	7	Loving
Jun 1 1980	8	Feeling
Jun 2 1980	9	Devoting
Jun 3 1980	10	Illuminating
Jun 4 1980	11	Choosing
Jun 5 1980	12	Exploring
Jun 6 1980	13	Healing
Jun 7 1980	1	**Seeing**
Jun 8 1980	2	Intuiting
Jun 9 1980	3	Evolving
Jun 10 1980	4	Self-Regulating
Jun 11 1980	5	Catalyzing
Jun 12 1980	6	Enlightening
Jun 13 1980	7	Being
Jun 14 1980	8	Breathing
Jun 15 1980	9	Listening
Jun 16 1980	10	Planting
Jun 17 1980	11	Moving
Jun 18 1980	12	Transcending
Jun 19 1980	13	Remembering
Jun 20 1980	1	**Loving**
Jun 21 1980	2	Feeling
Jun 22 1980	3	Devoting
Jun 23 1980	4	Illuminating
Jun 24 1980	5	Choosing
Jun 25 1980	6	Exploring
Jun 26 1980	7	Healing
Jun 27 1980	8	Seeing
Jun 28 1980	9	Intuiting
Jun 29 1980	10	Evolving
Jun 30 1980	11	Self-Regulating
Jul 1 1980	12	Catalyzing
Jul 2 1980	13	Enlightening
Jul 3 1980	1	**Being**
Jul 4 1980	2	Breathing
Jul 5 1980	3	Listening
Jul 6 1980	4	Planting
Jul 7 1980	5	Moving
Jul 8 1980	6	Transcending
Jul 9 1980	7	Remembering
Jul 10 1980	8	Loving
Jul 11 1980	9	Feeling
Jul 12 1980	10	Devoting
Jul 13 1980	11	Illuminating
Jul 14 1980	12	Choosing
Jul 15 1980	13	Exploring
Jul 16 1980	1	**Healing**
Jul 17 1980	2	Seeing
Jul 18 1980	3	Intuiting
Jul 19 1980	4	Evolving
Jul 20 1980	5	Self-Regulating
Jul 21 1980	6	Catalyzing
Jul 22 1980	7	Enlightening

Date	UE	Earth Energy
Jul 23 1980	8	Being
Jul 24 1980	9	Breathing
Jul 25 1980	10	Listening
Jul 26 1980	11	Planting
Jul 27 1980	12	Moving
Jul 28 1980	13	Transcending
Jul 29 1980	1	**Remembering**
Jul 30 1980	2	Loving
Jul 31 1980	3	Feeling
Aug 1 1980	4	Devoting
Aug 2 1980	5	Illuminating
Aug 3 1980	6	Choosing
Aug 4 1980	7	Exploring
Aug 5 1980	8	Healing
Aug 6 1980	9	Seeing
Aug 7 1980	10	Intuiting
Aug 8 1980	11	Evolving
Aug 9 1980	12	Self-Regulating
Aug 10 1980	13	Catalyzing
Aug 11 1980	1	**Enlightening**
Aug 12 1980	2	Being
Aug 13 1980	3	Breathing
Aug 14 1980	4	Listening
Aug 15 1980	5	Planting
Aug 16 1980	6	Moving
Aug 17 1980	7	Transcending
Aug 18 1980	8	Remembering
Aug 19 1980	9	Loving
Aug 20 1980	10	Feeling
Aug 21 1980	11	Devoting
Aug 22 1980	12	Illuminating
Aug 23 1980	13	Choosing
Aug 24 1980	1	**Exploring**
Aug 25 1980	2	Healing
Aug 26 1980	3	Seeing
Aug 27 1980	4	Intuiting
Aug 28 1980	5	Evolving
Aug 29 1980	6	Self-Regulating
Aug 30 1980	7	Catalyzing
Aug 31 1980	8	Enlightening
Sep 1 1980	9	Being
Sep 2 1980	10	Breathing
Sep 3 1980	11	Listening
Sep 4 1980	12	Planting
Sep 5 1980	13	Moving
Sep 6 1980	1	**Transcending**
Sep 7 1980	2	Remembering
Sep 8 1980	3	Loving
Sep 9 1980	4	Feeling
Sep 10 1980	5	Devoting
Sep 11 1980	6	Illuminating
Sep 12 1980	7	Choosing
Sep 13 1980	8	Exploring
Sep 14 1980	9	Healing
Sep 15 1980	10	Seeing
Sep 16 1980	11	Intuiting
Sep 17 1980	12	Evolving
Sep 18 1980	13	Self-Regulating
Sep 19 1980	1	**Catalyzing**
Sep 20 1980	2	Enlightening
Sep 21 1980	3	Being
Sep 22 1980	4	Breathing
Sep 23 1980	5	Listening
Sep 24 1980	6	Planting
Sep 25 1980	7	Moving
Sep 26 1980	8	Transcending
Sep 27 1980	9	Remembering
Sep 28 1980	10	Loving
Sep 29 1980	11	Feeling
Sep 30 1980	12	Devoting

Date	UE	Earth Energy	Date	UE	Earth Energy	Date	UE	Earth Energy
Oct 1 1980	13	Illuminating	Dec 10 1980	5	Being	Feb 18 1981	10	Illuminating
Oct 2 1980	1	**Choosing**	Dec 11 1980	6	Breathing	Feb 19 1981	11	Choosing
Oct 3 1980	2	Exploring	Dec 12 1980	7	Listening	Feb 20 1981	12	Exploring
Oct 4 1980	3	Healing	Dec 13 1980	8	Planting	Feb 21 1981	13	Healing
Oct 5 1980	4	Seeing	Dec 14 1980	9	Moving	Feb 22 1981	1	**Seeing**
Oct 6 1980	5	Intuiting	Dec 15 1980	10	Transcending	Feb 23 1981	2	Intuiting
Oct 7 1980	6	Evolving	Dec 16 1980	11	Remembering	Feb 24 1981	3	Evolving
Oct 8 1980	7	Self-Regulating	Dec 17 1980	12	Loving	Feb 25 1981	4	Self-Regulating
Oct 9 1980	8	Catalyzing	Dec 18 1980	13	Feeling	Feb 26 1981	5	Catalyzing
Oct 10 1980	9	Enlightening	Dec 19 1980	1	**Devoting**	Feb 27 1981	6	Enlightening
Oct 11 1980	10	Being	Dec 20 1980	2	Illuminating	Feb 28 1981	7	Being
Oct 12 1980	11	Breathing	Dec 21 1980	3	Choosing	Mar 1 1981	8	Breathing
Oct 13 1980	12	Listening	Dec 22 1980	4	Exploring	Mar 2 1981	9	Listening
Oct 14 1980	13	Planting	Dec 23 1980	5	Healing	Mar 3 1981	10	Planting
Oct 15 1980	1	**Moving**	Dec 24 1980	6	Seeing	Mar 4 1981	11	Moving
Oct 16 1980	2	Transcending	Dec 25 1980	7	Intuiting	Mar 5 1981	12	Transcending
Oct 17 1980	3	Remembering	Dec 26 1980	8	Evolving	Mar 6 1981	13	Remembering
Oct 18 1980	4	Loving	Dec 27 1980	9	Self-Regulating	Mar 7 1981	1	**Loving**
Oct 19 1980	5	Feeling	Dec 28 1980	10	Catalyzing	Mar 8 1981	2	Feeling
Oct 20 1980	6	Devoting	Dec 29 1980	11	Enlightening	Mar 9 1981	3	Devoting
Oct 21 1980	7	Illuminating	Dec 30 1980	12	Being	Mar 10 1981	4	Illuminating
Oct 22 1980	8	Choosing	Dec 31 1980	13	Breathing	Mar 11 1981	5	Choosing
Oct 23 1980	9	Exploring	Jan 1 1981	1	**Listening**	Mar 12 1981	6	Exploring
Oct 24 1980	10	Healing	Jan 2 1981	2	Planting	Mar 13 1981	7	Healing
Oct 25 1980	11	Seeing	Jan 3 1981	3	Moving	Mar 14 1981	8	Seeing
Oct 26 1980	12	Intuiting	Jan 4 1981	4	Transcending	Mar 15 1981	9	Intuiting
Oct 27 1980	13	Evolving	Jan 5 1981	5	Remembering	Mar 16 1981	10	Evolving
Oct 28 1980	1	**Self-Regulating**	Jan 6 1981	6	Loving	Mar 17 1981	11	Self-Regulating
Oct 29 1980	2	Catalyzing	Jan 7 1981	7	Feeling	Mar 18 1981	12	Catalyzing
Oct 30 1980	3	Enlightening	Jan 8 1981	8	Devoting	Mar 19 1981	13	Enlightening
Oct 31 1980	4	Being	Jan 9 1981	9	Illuminating	Mar 20 1981	1	**Being**
Nov 1 1980	5	Breathing	Jan 10 1981	10	Choosing	Mar 21 1981	2	Breathing
Nov 2 1980	6	Listening	Jan 11 1981	11	Exploring	Mar 22 1981	3	Listening
Nov 3 1980	7	Planting	Jan 12 1981	12	Healing	Mar 23 1981	4	Planting
Nov 4 1980	8	Moving	Jan 13 1981	13	Seeing	Mar 24 1981	5	Moving
Nov 5 1980	9	Transcending	Jan 14 1981	1	**Intuiting**	Mar 25 1981	6	Transcending
Nov 6 1980	10	Remembering	Jan 15 1981	2	Evolving	Mar 26 1981	7	Remembering
Nov 7 1980	11	Loving	Jan 16 1981	3	Self-Regulating	Mar 27 1981	8	Loving
Nov 8 1980	12	Feeling	Jan 17 1981	4	Catalyzing	Mar 28 1981	9	Feeling
Nov 9 1980	13	Devoting	Jan 18 1981	5	Enlightening	Mar 29 1981	10	Devoting
Nov 10 1980	1	**Illuminating**	Jan 19 1981	6	Being	Mar 30 1981	11	Illuminating
Nov 11 1980	2	Choosing	Jan 20 1981	7	Breathing	Mar 31 1981	12	Choosing
Nov 12 1980	3	Exploring	Jan 21 1981	8	Listening	Apr 1 1981	13	Exploring
Nov 13 1980	4	Healing	Jan 22 1981	9	Planting	Apr 2 1981	1	**Healing**
Nov 14 1980	5	Seeing	Jan 23 1981	10	Moving	Apr 3 1981	2	Seeing
Nov 15 1980	6	Intuiting	Jan 24 1981	11	Transcending	Apr 4 1981	3	Intuiting
Nov 16 1980	7	Evolving	Jan 25 1981	12	Remembering	Apr 5 1981	4	Evolving
Nov 17 1980	8	Self-Regulating	Jan 26 1981	13	Loving	Apr 6 1981	5	Self-Regulating
Nov 18 1980	9	Catalyzing	Jan 27 1981	1	**Feeling**	Apr 7 1981	6	Catalyzing
Nov 19 1980	10	Enlightening	Jan 28 1981	2	Devoting	Apr 8 1981	7	Enlightening
Nov 20 1980	11	Being	Jan 29 1981	3	Illuminating	Apr 9 1981	8	Being
Nov 21 1980	12	Breathing	Jan 30 1981	4	Choosing	Apr 10 1981	9	Breathing
Nov 22 1980	13	Listening	Jan 31 1981	5	Exploring	Apr 11 1981	10	Listening
Nov 23 1980	1	**Planting**	Feb 1 1981	6	Healing	Apr 12 1981	11	Planting
Nov 24 1980	2	Moving	Feb 2 1981	7	Seeing	Apr 13 1981	12	Moving
Nov 25 1980	3	Transcending	Feb 3 1981	8	Intuiting	Apr 14 1981	13	Transcending
Nov 26 1980	4	Remembering	Feb 4 1981	9	Evolving	Apr 15 1981	1	**Remembering**
Nov 27 1980	5	Loving	Feb 5 1981	10	Self-Regulating	Apr 16 1981	2	Loving
Nov 28 1980	6	Feeling	Feb 6 1981	11	Catalyzing	Apr 17 1981	3	Feeling
Nov 29 1980	7	Devoting	Feb 7 1981	12	Enlightening	Apr 18 1981	4	Devoting
Nov 30 1980	8	Illuminating	Feb 8 1981	13	Being	Apr 19 1981	5	Illuminating
Dec 1 1980	9	Choosing	Feb 9 1981	1	**Breathing**	Apr 20 1981	6	Choosing
Dec 2 1980	10	Exploring	Feb 10 1981	2	Listening	Apr 21 1981	7	Exploring
Dec 3 1980	11	Healing	Feb 11 1981	3	Planting	Apr 22 1981	8	Healing
Dec 4 1980	12	Seeing	Feb 12 1981	4	Moving	Apr 23 1981	9	Seeing
Dec 5 1980	13	Intuiting	Feb 13 1981	5	Transcending	Apr 24 1981	10	Intuiting
Dec 6 1980	1	**Evolving**	Feb 14 1981	6	Remembering	Apr 25 1981	11	Evolving
Dec 7 1980	2	Self-Regulating	Feb 15 1981	7	Loving	Apr 26 1981	12	Self-Regulating
Dec 8 1980	3	Catalyzing	Feb 16 1981	8	Feeling	Apr 27 1981	13	Catalyzing
Dec 9 1980	4	Enlightening	Feb 17 1981	9	Devoting	Apr 28 1981	1	**Enlightening**

Date	UE	Earth Energy	Date	UE	Earth Energy	Date	UE	Earth Energy
Apr 29 1981	2	Being	Jul 8 1981	7	Illuminating	Sep 16 1981	12	Being
Apr 30 1981	3	Breathing	Jul 9 1981	8	Choosing	Sep 17 1981	13	Breathing
May 1 1981	4	Listening	Jul 10 1981	9	Exploring	Sep 18 1981	**1**	**Listening**
May 2 1981	5	Planting	Jul 11 1981	10	Healing	Sep 19 1981	2	Planting
May 3 1981	6	Moving	Jul 12 1981	11	Seeing	Sep 20 1981	3	Moving
May 4 1981	7	Transcending	Jul 13 1981	12	Intuiting	Sep 21 1981	4	Transcending
May 5 1981	8	Remembering	Jul 14 1981	13	Evolving	Sep 22 1981	5	Remembering
May 6 1981	9	Loving	Jul 15 1981	**1**	**Self-Regulating**	Sep 23 1981	6	Loving
May 7 1981	10	Feeling	Jul 16 1981	2	Catalyzing	Sep 24 1981	7	Feeling
May 8 1981	11	Devoting	Jul 17 1981	3	Enlightening	Sep 25 1981	8	Devoting
May 9 1981	12	Illuminating	Jul 18 1981	4	Being	Sep 26 1981	9	Illuminating
May 10 1981	13	Choosing	Jul 19 1981	5	Breathing	Sep 27 1981	10	Choosing
May 11 1981	**1**	**Exploring**	Jul 20 1981	6	Listening	Sep 28 1981	11	Exploring
May 12 1981	2	Healing	Jul 21 1981	7	Planting	Sep 29 1981	12	Healing
May 13 1981	3	Seeing	Jul 22 1981	8	Moving	Sep 30 1981	13	Seeing
May 14 1981	4	Intuiting	Jul 23 1981	9	Transcending	Oct 1 1981	**1**	**Intuiting**
May 15 1981	5	Evolving	Jul 24 1981	10	Remembering	Oct 2 1981	2	Evolving
May 16 1981	6	Self-Regulating	Jul 25 1981	11	Loving	Oct 3 1981	3	Self-Regulating
May 17 1981	7	Catalyzing	Jul 26 1981	12	Feeling	Oct 4 1981	4	Catalyzing
May 18 1981	8	Enlightening	Jul 27 1981	13	Devoting	Oct 5 1981	5	Enlightening
May 19 1981	9	Being	Jul 28 1981	**1**	**Illuminating**	Oct 6 1981	6	Being
May 20 1981	10	Breathing	Jul 29 1981	2	Choosing	Oct 7 1981	7	Breathing
May 21 1981	11	Listening	Jul 30 1981	3	Exploring	Oct 8 1981	8	Listening
May 22 1981	12	Planting	Jul 31 1981	4	Healing	Oct 9 1981	9	Planting
May 23 1981	13	Moving	Aug 1 1981	5	Seeing	Oct 10 1981	10	Moving
May 24 1981	**1**	**Transcending**	Aug 2 1981	6	Intuiting	Oct 11 1981	11	Transcending
May 25 1981	2	Remembering	Aug 3 1981	7	Evolving	Oct 12 1981	12	Remembering
May 26 1981	3	Loving	Aug 4 1981	8	Self-Regulating	Oct 13 1981	13	Loving
May 27 1981	4	Feeling	Aug 5 1981	9	Catalyzing	Oct 14 1981	**1**	**Feeling**
May 28 1981	5	Devoting	Aug 6 1981	10	Enlightening	Oct 15 1981	2	Devoting
May 29 1981	6	Illuminating	Aug 7 1981	11	Being	Oct 16 1981	3	Illuminating
May 30 1981	7	Choosing	Aug 8 1981	12	Breathing	Oct 17 1981	4	Choosing
May 31 1981	8	Exploring	Aug 9 1981	13	Listening	Oct 18 1981	5	Exploring
Jun 1 1981	9	Healing	Aug 10 1981	**1**	**Planting**	Oct 19 1981	6	Healing
Jun 2 1981	10	Seeing	Aug 11 1981	2	Moving	Oct 20 1981	7	Seeing
Jun 3 1981	11	Intuiting	Aug 12 1981	3	Transcending	Oct 21 1981	8	Intuiting
Jun 4 1981	12	Evolving	Aug 13 1981	4	Remembering	Oct 22 1981	9	Evolving
Jun 5 1981	13	Self-Regulating	Aug 14 1981	5	Loving	Oct 23 1981	10	Self-Regulating
Jun 6 1981	**1**	**Catalyzing**	Aug 15 1981	6	Feeling	Oct 24 1981	11	Catalyzing
Jun 7 1981	2	Enlightening	Aug 16 1981	7	Devoting	Oct 25 1981	12	Enlightening
Jun 8 1981	3	Being	Aug 17 1981	8	Illuminating	Oct 26 1981	13	Being
Jun 9 1981	4	Breathing	Aug 18 1981	9	Choosing	Oct 27 1981	**1**	**Breathing**
Jun 10 1981	5	Listening	Aug 19 1981	10	Exploring	Oct 28 1981	2	Listening
Jun 11 1981	6	Planting	Aug 20 1981	11	Healing	Oct 29 1981	3	Planting
Jun 12 1981	7	Moving	Aug 21 1981	12	Seeing	Oct 30 1981	4	Moving
Jun 13 1981	8	Transcending	Aug 22 1981	13	Intuiting	Oct 31 1981	5	Transcending
Jun 14 1981	9	Remembering	Aug 23 1981	**1**	**Evolving**	Nov 1 1981	6	Remembering
Jun 15 1981	10	Loving	Aug 24 1981	2	Self-Regulating	Nov 2 1981	7	Loving
Jun 16 1981	11	Feeling	Aug 25 1981	3	Catalyzing	Nov 3 1981	8	Feeling
Jun 17 1981	12	Devoting	Aug 26 1981	4	Enlightening	Nov 4 1981	9	Devoting
Jun 18 1981	13	Illuminating	Aug 27 1981	5	Being	Nov 5 1981	10	Illuminating
Jun 19 1981	**1**	**Choosing**	Aug 28 1981	6	Breathing	Nov 6 1981	11	Choosing
Jun 20 1981	2	Exploring	Aug 29 1981	7	Listening	Nov 7 1981	12	Exploring
Jun 21 1981	3	Healing	Aug 30 1981	8	Planting	Nov 8 1981	13	Healing
Jun 22 1981	4	Seeing	Aug 31 1981	9	Moving	Nov 9 1981	**1**	**Seeing**
Jun 23 1981	5	Intuiting	Sep 1 1981	10	Transcending	Nov 10 1981	2	Intuiting
Jun 24 1981	6	Evolving	Sep 2 1981	11	Remembering	Nov 11 1981	3	Evolving
Jun 25 1981	7	Self-Regulating	Sep 3 1981	12	Loving	Nov 12 1981	4	Self-Regulating
Jun 26 1981	8	Catalyzing	Sep 4 1981	13	Feeling	Nov 13 1981	5	Catalyzing
Jun 27 1981	9	Enlightening	Sep 5 1981	**1**	**Devoting**	Nov 14 1981	6	Enlightening
Jun 28 1981	10	Being	Sep 6 1981	2	Illuminating	Nov 15 1981	7	Being
Jun 29 1981	11	Breathing	Sep 7 1981	3	Choosing	Nov 16 1981	8	Breathing
Jun 30 1981	12	Listening	Sep 8 1981	4	Exploring	Nov 17 1981	9	Listening
Jul 1 1981	13	Planting	Sep 9 1981	5	Healing	Nov 18 1981	10	Planting
Jul 2 1981	**1**	**Moving**	Sep 10 1981	6	Seeing	Nov 19 1981	11	Moving
Jul 3 1981	2	Transcending	Sep 11 1981	7	Intuiting	Nov 20 1981	12	Transcending
Jul 4 1981	3	Remembering	Sep 12 1981	8	Evolving	Nov 21 1981	13	Remembering
Jul 5 1981	4	Loving	Sep 13 1981	9	Self-Regulating	Nov 22 1981	**1**	**Loving**
Jul 6 1981	5	Feeling	Sep 14 1981	10	Catalyzing	Nov 23 1981	2	Feeling
Jul 7 1981	6	Devoting	Sep 15 1981	11	Enlightening	Nov 24 1981	3	Devoting

Date	UE	Earth Energy	Date	UE	Earth Energy	Date	UE	Earth Energy
Nov 25 1981	4	Illuminating	Feb 3 1982	9	Being	Apr 14 1982	1	**Illuminating**
Nov 26 1981	5	Choosing	Feb 4 1982	10	Breathing	Apr 15 1982	2	Choosing
Nov 27 1981	6	Exploring	Feb 5 1982	11	Listening	Apr 16 1982	3	Exploring
Nov 28 1981	7	Healing	Feb 6 1982	12	Planting	Apr 17 1982	4	Healing
Nov 29 1981	8	Seeing	Feb 7 1982	13	Moving	Apr 18 1982	5	Seeing
Nov 30 1981	9	Intuiting	Feb 8 1982	1	**Transcending**	Apr 19 1982	6	Intuiting
Dec 1 1981	10	Evolving	Feb 9 1982	2	Remembering	Apr 20 1982	7	Evolving
Dec 2 1981	11	Self-Regulating	Feb 10 1982	3	Loving	Apr 21 1982	8	Self-Regulating
Dec 3 1981	12	Catalyzing	Feb 11 1982	4	Feeling	Apr 22 1982	9	Catalyzing
Dec 4 1981	13	Enlightening	Feb 12 1982	5	Devoting	Apr 23 1982	10	Enlightening
Dec 5 1981	1	**Being**	Feb 13 1982	6	Illuminating	Apr 24 1982	11	Being
Dec 6 1981	2	Breathing	Feb 14 1982	7	Choosing	Apr 25 1982	12	Breathing
Dec 7 1981	3	Listening	Feb 15 1982	8	Exploring	Apr 26 1982	13	Listening
Dec 8 1981	4	Planting	Feb 16 1982	9	Healing	Apr 27 1982	1	**Planting**
Dec 9 1981	5	Moving	Feb 17 1982	10	Seeing	Apr 28 1982	2	Moving
Dec 10 1981	6	Transcending	Feb 18 1982	11	Intuiting	Apr 29 1982	3	Transcending
Dec 11 1981	7	Remembering	Feb 19 1982	12	Evolving	Apr 30 1982	4	Remembering
Dec 12 1981	8	Loving	Feb 20 1982	13	Self-Regulating	May 1 1982	5	Loving
Dec 13 1981	9	Feeling	Feb 21 1982	1	**Catalyzing**	May 2 1982	6	Feeling
Dec 14 1981	10	Devoting	Feb 22 1982	2	Enlightening	May 3 1982	7	Devoting
Dec 15 1981	11	Illuminating	Feb 23 1982	3	Being	May 4 1982	8	Illuminating
Dec 16 1981	12	Choosing	Feb 24 1982	4	Breathing	May 5 1982	9	Choosing
Dec 17 1981	13	Exploring	Feb 25 1982	5	Listening	May 6 1982	10	Exploring
Dec 18 1981	1	**Healing**	Feb 26 1982	6	Planting	May 7 1982	11	Healing
Dec 19 1981	2	Seeing	Feb 27 1982	7	Moving	May 8 1982	12	Seeing
Dec 20 1981	3	Intuiting	Feb 28 1982	8	Transcending	May 9 1982	13	Intuiting
Dec 21 1981	4	Evolving	Mar 1 1982	9	Remembering	May 10 1982	1	**Evolving**
Dec 22 1981	5	Self-Regulating	Mar 2 1982	10	Loving	May 11 1982	2	Self-Regulating
Dec 23 1981	6	Catalyzing	Mar 3 1982	11	Feeling	May 12 1982	3	Catalyzing
Dec 24 1981	7	Enlightening	Mar 4 1982	12	Devoting	May 13 1982	4	Enlightening
Dec 25 1981	8	Being	Mar 5 1982	13	Illuminating	May 14 1982	5	Being
Dec 26 1981	9	Breathing	Mar 6 1982	1	**Choosing**	May 15 1982	6	Breathing
Dec 27 1981	10	Listening	Mar 7 1982	2	Exploring	May 16 1982	7	Listening
Dec 28 1981	11	Planting	Mar 8 1982	3	Healing	May 17 1982	8	Planting
Dec 29 1981	12	Moving	Mar 9 1982	4	Seeing	May 18 1982	9	Moving
Dec 30 1981	13	Transcending	Mar 10 1982	5	Intuiting	May 19 1982	10	Transcending
Dec 31 1981	1	**Remembering**	Mar 11 1982	6	Evolving	May 20 1982	11	Remembering
Jan 1 1982	2	Loving	Mar 12 1982	7	Self-Regulating	May 21 1982	12	Loving
Jan 2 1982	3	Feeling	Mar 13 1982	8	Catalyzing	May 22 1982	13	Feeling
Jan 3 1982	4	Devoting	Mar 14 1982	9	Enlightening	May 23 1982	1	**Devoting**
Jan 4 1982	5	Illuminating	Mar 15 1982	10	Being	May 24 1982	2	Illuminating
Jan 5 1982	6	Choosing	Mar 16 1982	11	Breathing	May 25 1982	3	Choosing
Jan 6 1982	7	Exploring	Mar 17 1982	12	Listening	May 26 1982	4	Exploring
Jan 7 1982	8	Healing	Mar 18 1982	13	Planting	May 27 1982	5	Healing
Jan 8 1982	9	Seeing	Mar 19 1982	1	**Moving**	May 28 1982	6	Seeing
Jan 9 1982	10	Intuiting	Mar 20 1982	2	Transcending	May 29 1982	7	Intuiting
Jan 10 1982	11	Evolving	Mar 21 1982	3	Remembering	May 30 1982	8	Evolving
Jan 11 1982	12	Self-Regulating	Mar 22 1982	4	Loving	May 31 1982	9	Self-Regulating
Jan 12 1982	13	Catalyzing	Mar 23 1982	5	Feeling	Jun 1 1982	10	Catalyzing
Jan 13 1982	1	**Enlightening**	Mar 24 1982	6	Devoting	Jun 2 1982	11	Enlightening
Jan 14 1982	2	Being	Mar 25 1982	7	Illuminating	Jun 3 1982	12	Being
Jan 15 1982	3	Breathing	Mar 26 1982	8	Choosing	Jun 4 1982	13	Breathing
Jan 16 1982	4	Listening	Mar 27 1982	9	Exploring	Jun 5 1982	1	**Listening**
Jan 17 1982	5	Planting	Mar 28 1982	10	Healing	Jun 6 1982	2	Planting
Jan 18 1982	6	Moving	Mar 29 1982	11	Seeing	Jun 7 1982	3	Moving
Jan 19 1982	7	Transcending	Mar 30 1982	12	Intuiting	Jun 8 1982	4	Transcending
Jan 20 1982	8	Remembering	Mar 31 1982	13	Evolving	Jun 9 1982	5	Remembering
Jan 21 1982	9	Loving	Apr 1 1982	1	**Self-Regulating**	Jun 10 1982	6	Loving
Jan 22 1982	10	Feeling	Apr 2 1982	2	Catalyzing	Jun 11 1982	7	Feeling
Jan 23 1982	11	Devoting	Apr 3 1982	3	Enlightening	Jun 12 1982	8	Devoting
Jan 24 1982	12	Illuminating	Apr 4 1982	4	Being	Jun 13 1982	9	Illuminating
Jan 25 1982	13	Choosing	Apr 5 1982	5	Breathing	Jun 14 1982	10	Choosing
Jan 26 1982	1	**Exploring**	Apr 6 1982	6	Listening	Jun 15 1982	11	Exploring
Jan 27 1982	2	Healing	Apr 7 1982	7	Planting	Jun 16 1982	12	Healing
Jan 28 1982	3	Seeing	Apr 8 1982	8	Moving	Jun 17 1982	13	Seeing
Jan 29 1982	4	Intuiting	Apr 9 1982	9	Transcending	Jun 18 1982	1	**Intuiting**
Jan 30 1982	5	Evolving	Apr 10 1982	10	Remembering	Jun 19 1982	2	Evolving
Jan 31 1982	6	Self-Regulating	Apr 11 1982	11	Loving	Jun 20 1982	3	Self-Regulating
Feb 1 1982	7	Catalyzing	Apr 12 1982	12	Feeling	Jun 21 1982	4	Catalyzing
Feb 2 1982	8	Enlightening	Apr 13 1982	13	Devoting	Jun 22 1982	5	Enlightening

Date	UE	Earth Energy	Date	UE	Earth Energy	Date	UE	Earth Energy
Jun 23 1982	6	Being	Sep 1 1982	11	Illuminating	Nov 10 1982	3	Being
Jun 24 1982	7	Breathing	Sep 2 1982	12	Choosing	Nov 11 1982	4	Breathing
Jun 25 1982	8	Listening	Sep 3 1982	13	Exploring	Nov 12 1982	5	Listening
Jun 26 1982	9	Planting	Sep 4 1982	**1**	**Healing**	Nov 13 1982	6	Planting
Jun 27 1982	10	Moving	Sep 5 1982	2	Seeing	Nov 14 1982	7	Moving
Jun 28 1982	11	Transcending	Sep 6 1982	3	Intuiting	Nov 15 1982	8	Transcending
Jun 29 1982	12	Remembering	Sep 7 1982	4	Evolving	Nov 16 1982	9	Remembering
Jun 30 1982	13	Loving	Sep 8 1982	5	Self-Regulating	Nov 17 1982	10	Loving
Jul 1 1982	**1**	**Feeling**	Sep 9 1982	6	Catalyzing	Nov 18 1982	11	Feeling
Jul 2 1982	2	Devoting	Sep 10 1982	7	Enlightening	Nov 19 1982	12	Devoting
Jul 3 1982	3	Illuminating	Sep 11 1982	8	Being	Nov 20 1982	13	Illuminating
Jul 4 1982	4	Choosing	Sep 12 1982	9	Breathing	Nov 21 1982	**1**	**Choosing**
Jul 5 1982	5	Exploring	Sep 13 1982	10	Listening	Nov 22 1982	2	Exploring
Jul 6 1982	6	Healing	Sep 14 1982	11	Planting	Nov 23 1982	3	Healing
Jul 7 1982	7	Seeing	Sep 15 1982	12	Moving	Nov 24 1982	4	Seeing
Jul 8 1982	8	Intuiting	Sep 16 1982	13	Transcending	Nov 25 1982	5	Intuiting
Jul 9 1982	9	Evolving	Sep 17 1982	**1**	**Remembering**	Nov 26 1982	6	Evolving
Jul 10 1982	10	Self-Regulating	Sep 18 1982	2	Loving	Nov 27 1982	7	Self-Regulating
Jul 11 1982	11	Catalyzing	Sep 19 1982	3	Feeling	Nov 28 1982	8	Catalyzing
Jul 12 1982	12	Enlightening	Sep 20 1982	4	Devoting	Nov 29 1982	9	Enlightening
Jul 13 1982	13	Being	Sep 21 1982	5	Illuminating	Nov 30 1982	10	Being
Jul 14 1982	**1**	**Breathing**	Sep 22 1982	6	Choosing	Dec 1 1982	11	Breathing
Jul 15 1982	2	Listening	Sep 23 1982	7	Exploring	Dec 2 1982	12	Listening
Jul 16 1982	3	Planting	Sep 24 1982	8	Healing	Dec 3 1982	13	Planting
Jul 17 1982	4	Moving	Sep 25 1982	9	Seeing	Dec 4 1982	**1**	**Moving**
Jul 18 1982	5	Transcending	Sep 26 1982	10	Intuiting	Dec 5 1982	2	Transcending
Jul 19 1982	6	Remembering	Sep 27 1982	11	Evolving	Dec 6 1982	3	Remembering
Jul 20 1982	7	Loving	Sep 28 1982	12	Self-Regulating	Dec 7 1982	4	Loving
Jul 21 1982	8	Feeling	Sep 29 1982	13	Catalyzing	Dec 8 1982	5	Feeling
Jul 22 1982	9	Devoting	Sep 30 1982	**1**	**Enlightening**	Dec 9 1982	6	Devoting
Jul 23 1982	10	Illuminating	Oct 1 1982	2	Being	Dec 10 1982	7	Illuminating
Jul 24 1982	11	Choosing	Oct 2 1982	3	Breathing	Dec 11 1982	8	Choosing
Jul 25 1982	12	Exploring	Oct 3 1982	4	Listening	Dec 12 1982	9	Exploring
Jul 26 1982	13	Healing	Oct 4 1982	5	Planting	Dec 13 1982	10	Healing
Jul 27 1982	**1**	**Seeing**	Oct 5 1982	6	Moving	Dec 14 1982	11	Seeing
Jul 28 1982	2	Intuiting	Oct 6 1982	7	Transcending	Dec 15 1982	12	Intuiting
Jul 29 1982	3	Evolving	Oct 7 1982	8	Remembering	Dec 16 1982	13	Evolving
Jul 30 1982	4	Self-Regulating	Oct 8 1982	9	Loving	Dec 17 1982	**1**	**Self-Regulating**
Jul 31 1982	5	Catalyzing	Oct 9 1982	10	Feeling	Dec 18 1982	2	Catalyzing
Aug 1 1982	6	Enlightening	Oct 10 1982	11	Devoting	Dec 19 1982	3	Enlightening
Aug 2 1982	7	Being	Oct 11 1982	12	Illuminating	Dec 20 1982	4	Being
Aug 3 1982	8	Breathing	Oct 12 1982	13	Choosing	Dec 21 1982	5	Breathing
Aug 4 1982	9	Listening	Oct 13 1982	**1**	**Exploring**	Dec 22 1982	6	Listening
Aug 5 1982	10	Planting	Oct 14 1982	2	Healing	Dec 23 1982	7	Planting
Aug 6 1982	11	Moving	Oct 15 1982	3	Seeing	Dec 24 1982	8	Moving
Aug 7 1982	12	Transcending	Oct 16 1982	4	Intuiting	Dec 25 1982	9	Transcending
Aug 8 1982	13	Remembering	Oct 17 1982	5	Evolving	Dec 26 1982	10	Remembering
Aug 9 1982	**1**	**Loving**	Oct 18 1982	6	Self-Regulating	Dec 27 1982	11	Loving
Aug 10 1982	2	Feeling	Oct 19 1982	7	Catalyzing	Dec 28 1982	12	Feeling
Aug 11 1982	3	Devoting	Oct 20 1982	8	Enlightening	Dec 29 1982	13	Devoting
Aug 12 1982	4	Illuminating	Oct 21 1982	9	Being	Dec 30 1982	**1**	**Illuminating**
Aug 13 1982	5	Choosing	Oct 22 1982	10	Breathing	Dec 31 1982	2	Choosing
Aug 14 1982	6	Exploring	Oct 23 1982	11	Listening	Jan 1 1983	3	Exploring
Aug 15 1982	7	Healing	Oct 24 1982	12	Planting	Jan 2 1983	4	Healing
Aug 16 1982	8	Seeing	Oct 25 1982	13	Moving	Jan 3 1983	5	Seeing
Aug 17 1982	9	Intuiting	Oct 26 1982	**1**	**Transcending**	Jan 4 1983	6	Intuiting
Aug 18 1982	10	Evolving	Oct 27 1982	2	Remembering	Jan 5 1983	7	Evolving
Aug 19 1982	11	Self-Regulating	Oct 28 1982	3	Loving	Jan 6 1983	8	Self-Regulating
Aug 20 1982	12	Catalyzing	Oct 29 1982	4	Feeling	Jan 7 1983	9	Catalyzing
Aug 21 1982	13	Enlightening	Oct 30 1982	5	Devoting	Jan 8 1983	10	Enlightening
Aug 22 1982	**1**	**Being**	Oct 31 1982	6	Illuminating	Jan 9 1983	11	Being
Aug 23 1982	2	Breathing	Nov 1 1982	7	Choosing	Jan 10 1983	12	Breathing
Aug 24 1982	3	Listening	Nov 2 1982	8	Exploring	Jan 11 1983	13	Listening
Aug 25 1982	4	Planting	Nov 3 1982	9	Healing	Jan 12 1983	**1**	**Planting**
Aug 26 1982	5	Moving	Nov 4 1982	10	Seeing	Jan 13 1983	2	Moving
Aug 27 1982	6	Transcending	Nov 5 1982	11	Intuiting	Jan 14 1983	3	Transcending
Aug 28 1982	7	Remembering	Nov 6 1982	12	Evolving	Jan 15 1983	4	Remembering
Aug 29 1982	8	Loving	Nov 7 1982	13	Self-Regulating	Jan 16 1983	5	Loving
Aug 30 1982	9	Feeling	Nov 8 1982	**1**	**Catalyzing**	Jan 17 1983	6	Feeling
Aug 31 1982	10	Devoting	Nov 9 1982	2	Enlightening	Jan 18 1983	7	Devoting

Date	UE	Earth Energy	Date	UE	Earth Energy	Date	UE	Earth Energy
Jan 19 1983	8	Illuminating	Mar 30 1983	13	Being	Jun 8 1983	5	Illuminating
Jan 20 1983	9	Choosing	Mar 31 1983	**1**	**Breathing**	Jun 9 1983	6	Choosing
Jan 21 1983	10	Exploring	Apr 1 1983	2	Listening	Jun 10 1983	7	Exploring
Jan 22 1983	11	Healing	Apr 2 1983	3	Planting	Jun 11 1983	8	Healing
Jan 23 1983	12	Seeing	Apr 3 1983	4	Moving	Jun 12 1983	9	Seeing
Jan 24 1983	13	Intuiting	Apr 4 1983	5	Transcending	Jun 13 1983	10	Intuiting
Jan 25 1983	**1**	**Evolving**	Apr 5 1983	6	Remembering	Jun 14 1983	11	Evolving
Jan 26 1983	2	Self-Regulating	Apr 6 1983	7	Loving	Jun 15 1983	12	Self-Regulating
Jan 27 1983	3	Catalyzing	Apr 7 1983	8	Feeling	Jun 16 1983	13	Catalyzing
Jan 28 1983	4	Enlightening	Apr 8 1983	9	Devoting	Jun 17 1983	**1**	**Enlightening**
Jan 29 1983	5	Being	Apr 9 1983	10	Illuminating	Jun 18 1983	2	Being
Jan 30 1983	6	Breathing	Apr 10 1983	11	Choosing	Jun 19 1983	3	Breathing
Jan 31 1983	7	Listening	Apr 11 1983	12	Exploring	Jun 20 1983	4	Listening
Feb 1 1983	8	Planting	Apr 12 1983	13	Healing	Jun 21 1983	5	Planting
Feb 2 1983	9	Moving	Apr 13 1983	**1**	**Seeing**	Jun 22 1983	6	Moving
Feb 3 1983	10	Transcending	Apr 14 1983	2	Intuiting	Jun 23 1983	7	Transcending
Feb 4 1983	11	Remembering	Apr 15 1983	3	Evolving	Jun 24 1983	8	Remembering
Feb 5 1983	12	Loving	Apr 16 1983	4	Self-Regulating	Jun 25 1983	9	Loving
Feb 6 1983	13	Feeling	Apr 17 1983	5	Catalyzing	Jun 26 1983	10	Feeling
Feb 7 1983	**1**	**Devoting**	Apr 18 1983	6	Enlightening	Jun 27 1983	11	Devoting
Feb 8 1983	2	Illuminating	Apr 19 1983	7	Being	Jun 28 1983	12	Illuminating
Feb 9 1983	3	Choosing	Apr 20 1983	8	Breathing	Jun 29 1983	13	Choosing
Feb 10 1983	4	Exploring	Apr 21 1983	9	Listening	Jun 30 1983	**1**	**Exploring**
Feb 11 1983	5	Healing	Apr 22 1983	10	Planting	Jul 1 1983	2	Healing
Feb 12 1983	6	Seeing	Apr 23 1983	11	Moving	Jul 2 1983	3	Seeing
Feb 13 1983	7	Intuiting	Apr 24 1983	12	Transcending	Jul 3 1983	4	Intuiting
Feb 14 1983	8	Evolving	Apr 25 1983	13	Remembering	Jul 4 1983	5	Evolving
Feb 15 1983	9	Self-Regulating	Apr 26 1983	**1**	**Loving**	Jul 5 1983	6	Self-Regulating
Feb 16 1983	10	Catalyzing	Apr 27 1983	2	Feeling	Jul 6 1983	7	Catalyzing
Feb 17 1983	11	Enlightening	Apr 28 1983	3	Devoting	Jul 7 1983	8	Enlightening
Feb 18 1983	12	Being	Apr 29 1983	4	Illuminating	Jul 8 1983	9	Being
Feb 19 1983	13	Breathing	Apr 30 1983	5	Choosing	Jul 9 1983	10	Breathing
Feb 20 1983	**1**	**Listening**	May 1 1983	6	Exploring	Jul 10 1983	11	Listening
Feb 21 1983	2	Planting	May 2 1983	7	Healing	Jul 11 1983	12	Planting
Feb 22 1983	3	Moving	May 3 1983	8	Seeing	Jul 12 1983	13	Moving
Feb 23 1983	4	Transcending	May 4 1983	9	Intuiting	Jul 13 1983	**1**	**Transcending**
Feb 24 1983	5	Remembering	May 5 1983	10	Evolving	Jul 14 1983	2	Remembering
Feb 25 1983	6	Loving	May 6 1983	11	Self-Regulating	Jul 15 1983	3	Loving
Feb 26 1983	7	Feeling	May 7 1983	12	Catalyzing	Jul 16 1983	4	Feeling
Feb 27 1983	8	Devoting	May 8 1983	13	Enlightening	Jul 17 1983	5	Devoting
Feb 28 1983	9	Illuminating	May 9 1983	**1**	**Being**	Jul 18 1983	6	Illuminating
Mar 1 1983	10	Choosing	May 10 1983	2	Breathing	Jul 19 1983	7	Choosing
Mar 2 1983	11	Exploring	May 11 1983	3	Listening	Jul 20 1983	8	Exploring
Mar 3 1983	12	Healing	May 12 1983	4	Planting	Jul 21 1983	9	Healing
Mar 4 1983	13	Seeing	May 13 1983	5	Moving	Jul 22 1983	10	Seeing
Mar 5 1983	**1**	**Intuiting**	May 14 1983	6	Transcending	Jul 23 1983	11	Intuiting
Mar 6 1983	2	Evolving	May 15 1983	7	Remembering	Jul 24 1983	12	Evolving
Mar 7 1983	3	Self-Regulating	May 16 1983	8	Loving	Jul 25 1983	13	Self-Regulating
Mar 8 1983	4	Catalyzing	May 17 1983	9	Feeling	Jul 26 1983	**1**	**Catalyzing**
Mar 9 1983	5	Enlightening	May 18 1983	10	Devoting	Jul 27 1983	2	Enlightening
Mar 10 1983	6	Being	May 19 1983	11	Illuminating	Jul 28 1983	3	Being
Mar 11 1983	7	Breathing	May 20 1983	12	Choosing	Jul 29 1983	4	Breathing
Mar 12 1983	8	Listening	May 21 1983	13	Exploring	Jul 30 1983	5	Listening
Mar 13 1983	9	Planting	May 22 1983	**1**	**Healing**	Jul 31 1983	6	Planting
Mar 14 1983	10	Moving	May 23 1983	2	Seeing	Aug 1 1983	7	Moving
Mar 15 1983	11	Transcending	May 24 1983	3	Intuiting	Aug 2 1983	8	Transcending
Mar 16 1983	12	Remembering	May 25 1983	4	Evolving	Aug 3 1983	9	Remembering
Mar 17 1983	13	Loving	May 26 1983	5	Self-Regulating	Aug 4 1983	10	Loving
Mar 18 1983	**1**	**Feeling**	May 27 1983	6	Catalyzing	Aug 5 1983	11	Feeling
Mar 19 1983	2	Devoting	May 28 1983	7	Enlightening	Aug 6 1983	12	Devoting
Mar 20 1983	3	Illuminating	May 29 1983	8	Being	Aug 7 1983	13	Illuminating
Mar 21 1983	4	Choosing	May 30 1983	9	Breathing	Aug 8 1983	**1**	**Choosing**
Mar 22 1983	5	Exploring	May 31 1983	10	Listening	Aug 9 1983	2	Exploring
Mar 23 1983	6	Healing	Jun 1 1983	11	Planting	Aug 10 1983	3	Healing
Mar 24 1983	7	Seeing	Jun 2 1983	12	Moving	Aug 11 1983	4	Seeing
Mar 25 1983	8	Intuiting	Jun 3 1983	13	Transcending	Aug 12 1983	5	Intuiting
Mar 26 1983	9	Evolving	Jun 4 1983	**1**	**Remembering**	Aug 13 1983	6	Evolving
Mar 27 1983	10	Self-Regulating	Jun 5 1983	2	Loving	Aug 14 1983	7	Self-Regulating
Mar 28 1983	11	Catalyzing	Jun 6 1983	3	Feeling	Aug 15 1983	8	Catalyzing
Mar 29 1983	12	Enlightening	Jun 7 1983	4	Devoting	Aug 16 1983	9	Enlightening

Date	UE	Earth Energy	Date	UE	Earth Energy	Date	UE	Earth Energy
Aug 17 1983	10	Being	Oct 26 1983	2	Illuminating	Jan 4 1984	7	Being
Aug 18 1983	11	Breathing	Oct 27 1983	3	Choosing	Jan 5 1984	8	Breathing
Aug 19 1983	12	Listening	Oct 28 1983	4	Exploring	Jan 6 1984	9	Listening
Aug 20 1983	13	Planting	Oct 29 1983	5	Healing	Jan 7 1984	10	Planting
Aug 21 1983	**1**	**Moving**	Oct 30 1983	6	Seeing	Jan 8 1984	11	Moving
Aug 22 1983	2	Transcending	Oct 31 1983	7	Intuiting	Jan 9 1984	12	Transcending
Aug 23 1983	3	Remembering	Nov 1 1983	8	Evolving	Jan 10 1984	13	Remembering
Aug 24 1983	4	Loving	Nov 2 1983	9	Self-Regulating	Jan 11 1984	**1**	**Loving**
Aug 25 1983	5	Feeling	Nov 3 1983	10	Catalyzing	Jan 12 1984	2	Feeling
Aug 26 1983	6	Devoting	Nov 4 1983	11	Enlightening	Jan 13 1984	3	Devoting
Aug 27 1983	7	Illuminating	Nov 5 1983	12	Being	Jan 14 1984	4	Illuminating
Aug 28 1983	8	Choosing	Nov 6 1983	13	Breathing	Jan 15 1984	5	Choosing
Aug 29 1983	9	Exploring	Nov 7 1983	**1**	**Listening**	Jan 16 1984	6	Exploring
Aug 30 1983	10	Healing	Nov 8 1983	2	Planting	Jan 17 1984	7	Healing
Aug 31 1983	11	Seeing	Nov 9 1983	3	Moving	Jan 18 1984	8	Seeing
Sep 1 1983	12	Intuiting	Nov 10 1983	4	Transcending	Jan 19 1984	9	Intuiting
Sep 2 1983	13	Evolving	Nov 11 1983	5	Remembering	Jan 20 1984	10	Evolving
Sep 3 1983	**1**	**Self-Regulating**	Nov 12 1983	6	Loving	Jan 21 1984	11	Self-Regulating
Sep 4 1983	2	Catalyzing	Nov 13 1983	7	Feeling	Jan 22 1984	12	Catalyzing
Sep 5 1983	3	Enlightening	Nov 14 1983	8	Devoting	Jan 23 1984	13	Enlightening
Sep 6 1983	4	Being	Nov 15 1983	9	Illuminating	Jan 24 1984	**1**	**Being**
Sep 7 1983	5	Breathing	Nov 16 1983	10	Choosing	Jan 25 1984	2	Breathing
Sep 8 1983	6	Listening	Nov 17 1983	11	Exploring	Jan 26 1984	3	Listening
Sep 9 1983	7	Planting	Nov 18 1983	12	Healing	Jan 27 1984	4	Planting
Sep 10 1983	8	Moving	Nov 19 1983	13	Seeing	Jan 28 1984	5	Moving
Sep 11 1983	9	Transcending	Nov 20 1983	**1**	**Intuiting**	Jan 29 1984	6	Transcending
Sep 12 1983	10	Remembering	Nov 21 1983	2	Evolving	Jan 30 1984	7	Remembering
Sep 13 1983	11	Loving	Nov 22 1983	3	Self-Regulating	Jan 31 1984	8	Loving
Sep 14 1983	12	Feeling	Nov 23 1983	4	Catalyzing	Feb 1 1984	9	Feeling
Sep 15 1983	13	Devoting	Nov 24 1983	5	Enlightening	Feb 2 1984	10	Devoting
Sep 16 1983	**1**	**Illuminating**	Nov 25 1983	6	Being	Feb 3 1984	11	Illuminating
Sep 17 1983	2	Choosing	Nov 26 1983	7	Breathing	Feb 4 1984	12	Choosing
Sep 18 1983	3	Exploring	Nov 27 1983	8	Listening	Feb 5 1984	13	Exploring
Sep 19 1983	4	Healing	Nov 28 1983	9	Planting	Feb 6 1984	**1**	**Healing**
Sep 20 1983	5	Seeing	Nov 29 1983	10	Moving	Feb 7 1984	2	Seeing
Sep 21 1983	6	Intuiting	Nov 30 1983	11	Transcending	Feb 8 1984	3	Intuiting
Sep 22 1983	7	Evolving	Dec 1 1983	12	Remembering	Feb 9 1984	4	Evolving
Sep 23 1983	8	Self-Regulating	Dec 2 1983	13	Loving	Feb 10 1984	5	Self-Regulating
Sep 24 1983	9	Catalyzing	Dec 3 1983	**1**	**Feeling**	Feb 11 1984	6	Catalyzing
Sep 25 1983	10	Enlightening	Dec 4 1983	2	Devoting	Feb 12 1984	7	Enlightening
Sep 26 1983	11	Being	Dec 5 1983	3	Illuminating	Feb 13 1984	8	Being
Sep 27 1983	12	Breathing	Dec 6 1983	4	Choosing	Feb 14 1984	9	Breathing
Sep 28 1983	13	Listening	Dec 7 1983	5	Exploring	Feb 15 1984	10	Listening
Sep 29 1983	**1**	**Planting**	Dec 8 1983	6	Healing	Feb 16 1984	11	Planting
Sep 30 1983	2	Moving	Dec 9 1983	7	Seeing	Feb 17 1984	12	Moving
Oct 1 1983	3	Transcending	Dec 10 1983	8	Intuiting	Feb 18 1984	13	Transcending
Oct 2 1983	4	Remembering	Dec 11 1983	9	Evolving	Feb 19 1984	**1**	**Remembering**
Oct 3 1983	5	Loving	Dec 12 1983	10	Self-Regulating	Feb 20 1984	2	Loving
Oct 4 1983	6	Feeling	Dec 13 1983	11	Catalyzing	Feb 21 1984	3	Feeling
Oct 5 1983	7	Devoting	Dec 14 1983	12	Enlightening	Feb 22 1984	4	Devoting
Oct 6 1983	8	Illuminating	Dec 15 1983	13	Being	Feb 23 1984	5	Illuminating
Oct 7 1983	9	Choosing	Dec 16 1983	**1**	**Breathing**	Feb 24 1984	6	Choosing
Oct 8 1983	10	Exploring	Dec 17 1983	2	Listening	Feb 25 1984	7	Exploring
Oct 9 1983	11	Healing	Dec 18 1983	3	Planting	Feb 26 1984	8	Healing
Oct 10 1983	12	Seeing	Dec 19 1983	4	Moving	Feb 27 1984	9	Seeing
Oct 11 1983	13	Intuiting	Dec 20 1983	5	Transcending	Feb 28 1984	10	Intuiting
Oct 12 1983	**1**	**Evolving**	Dec 21 1983	6	Remembering	Feb 29 1984	11	Evolving
Oct 13 1983	2	Self-Regulating	Dec 22 1983	7	Loving	Mar 1 1984	12	Self-Regulating
Oct 14 1983	3	Catalyzing	Dec 23 1983	8	Feeling	Mar 2 1984	13	Catalyzing
Oct 15 1983	4	Enlightening	Dec 24 1983	9	Devoting	Mar 3 1984	**1**	**Enlightening**
Oct 16 1983	5	Being	Dec 25 1983	10	Illuminating	Mar 4 1984	2	Being
Oct 17 1983	6	Breathing	Dec 26 1983	11	Choosing	Mar 5 1984	3	Breathing
Oct 18 1983	7	Listening	Dec 27 1983	12	Exploring	Mar 6 1984	4	Listening
Oct 19 1983	8	Planting	Dec 28 1983	13	Healing	Mar 7 1984	5	Planting
Oct 20 1983	9	Moving	Dec 29 1983	**1**	**Seeing**	Mar 8 1984	6	Moving
Oct 21 1983	10	Transcending	Dec 30 1983	2	Intuiting	Mar 9 1984	7	Transcending
Oct 22 1983	11	Remembering	Dec 31 1983	3	Evolving	Mar 10 1984	8	Remembering
Oct 23 1983	12	Loving	Jan 1 1984	4	Self-Regulating	Mar 11 1984	9	Loving
Oct 24 1983	13	Feeling	Jan 2 1984	5	Catalyzing	Mar 12 1984	10	Feeling
Oct 25 1983	**1**	**Devoting**	Jan 3 1984	6	Enlightening	Mar 13 1984	11	Devoting

Date	UE Earth Energy	Date	UE Earth Energy	Date	UE Earth Energy
Mar 14 1984	12 Illuminating	May 23 1984	4 Being	Aug 1 1984	9 Illuminating
Mar 15 1984	13 Choosing	May 24 1984	5 Breathing	Aug 2 1984	10 Choosing
Mar 16 1984	1 Exploring	May 25 1984	6 Listening	Aug 3 1984	11 Exploring
Mar 17 1984	2 Healing	May 26 1984	7 Planting	Aug 4 1984	12 Healing
Mar 18 1984	3 Seeing	May 27 1984	8 Moving	Aug 5 1984	13 Seeing
Mar 19 1984	4 Intuiting	May 28 1984	9 Transcending	Aug 6 1984	1 Intuiting
Mar 20 1984	5 Evolving	May 29 1984	10 Remembering	Aug 7 1984	2 Evolving
Mar 21 1984	6 Self-Regulating	May 30 1984	11 Loving	Aug 8 1984	3 Self-Regulating
Mar 22 1984	7 Catalyzing	May 31 1984	12 Feeling	Aug 9 1984	4 Catalyzing
Mar 23 1984	8 Enlightening	Jun 1 1984	13 Devoting	Aug 10 1984	5 Enlightening
Mar 24 1984	9 Being	Jun 2 1984	1 Illuminating	Aug 11 1984	6 Being
Mar 25 1984	10 Breathing	Jun 3 1984	2 Choosing	Aug 12 1984	7 Breathing
Mar 26 1984	11 Listening	Jun 4 1984	3 Exploring	Aug 13 1984	8 Listening
Mar 27 1984	12 Planting	Jun 5 1984	4 Healing	Aug 14 1984	9 Planting
Mar 28 1984	13 Moving	Jun 6 1984	5 Seeing	Aug 15 1984	10 Moving
Mar 29 1984	1 Transcending	Jun 7 1984	6 Intuiting	Aug 16 1984	11 Transcending
Mar 30 1984	2 Remembering	Jun 8 1984	7 Evolving	Aug 17 1984	12 Remembering
Mar 31 1984	3 Loving	Jun 9 1984	8 Self-Regulating	Aug 18 1984	13 Loving
Apr 1 1984	4 Feeling	Jun 10 1984	9 Catalyzing	Aug 19 1984	1 Feeling
Apr 2 1984	5 Devoting	Jun 11 1984	10 Enlightening	Aug 20 1984	2 Devoting
Apr 3 1984	6 Illuminating	Jun 12 1984	11 Being	Aug 21 1984	3 Illuminating
Apr 4 1984	7 Choosing	Jun 13 1984	12 Breathing	Aug 22 1984	4 Choosing
Apr 5 1984	8 Exploring	Jun 14 1984	13 Listening	Aug 23 1984	5 Exploring
Apr 6 1984	9 Healing	Jun 15 1984	1 Planting	Aug 24 1984	6 Healing
Apr 7 1984	10 Seeing	Jun 16 1984	2 Moving	Aug 25 1984	7 Seeing
Apr 8 1984	11 Intuiting	Jun 17 1984	3 Transcending	Aug 26 1984	8 Intuiting
Apr 9 1984	12 Evolving	Jun 18 1984	4 Remembering	Aug 27 1984	9 Evolving
Apr 10 1984	13 Self-Regulating	Jun 19 1984	5 Loving	Aug 28 1984	10 Self-Regulating
Apr 11 1984	1 Catalyzing	Jun 20 1984	6 Feeling	Aug 29 1984	11 Catalyzing
Apr 12 1984	2 Enlightening	Jun 21 1984	7 Devoting	Aug 30 1984	12 Enlightening
Apr 13 1984	3 Being	Jun 22 1984	8 Illuminating	Aug 31 1984	13 Being
Apr 14 1984	4 Breathing	Jun 23 1984	9 Choosing	Sep 1 1984	1 Breathing
Apr 15 1984	5 Listening	Jun 24 1984	10 Exploring	Sep 2 1984	2 Listening
Apr 16 1984	6 Planting	Jun 25 1984	11 Healing	Sep 3 1984	3 Planting
Apr 17 1984	7 Moving	Jun 26 1984	12 Seeing	Sep 4 1984	4 Moving
Apr 18 1984	8 Transcending	Jun 27 1984	13 Intuiting	Sep 5 1984	5 Transcending
Apr 19 1984	9 Remembering	Jun 28 1984	1 Evolving	Sep 6 1984	6 Remembering
Apr 20 1984	10 Loving	Jun 29 1984	2 Self-Regulating	Sep 7 1984	7 Loving
Apr 21 1984	11 Feeling	Jun 30 1984	3 Catalyzing	Sep 8 1984	8 Feeling
Apr 22 1984	12 Devoting	Jul 1 1984	4 Enlightening	Sep 9 1984	9 Devoting
Apr 23 1984	13 Illuminating	Jul 2 1984	5 Being	Sep 10 1984	10 Illuminating
Apr 24 1984	1 Choosing	Jul 3 1984	6 Breathing	Sep 11 1984	11 Choosing
Apr 25 1984	2 Exploring	Jul 4 1984	7 Listening	Sep 12 1984	12 Exploring
Apr 26 1984	3 Healing	Jul 5 1984	8 Planting	Sep 13 1984	13 Healing
Apr 27 1984	4 Seeing	Jul 6 1984	9 Moving	Sep 14 1984	1 Seeing
Apr 28 1984	5 Intuiting	Jul 7 1984	10 Transcending	Sep 15 1984	2 Intuiting
Apr 29 1984	6 Evolving	Jul 8 1984	11 Remembering	Sep 16 1984	3 Evolving
Apr 30 1984	7 Self-Regulating	Jul 9 1984	12 Loving	Sep 17 1984	4 Self-Regulating
May 1 1984	8 Catalyzing	Jul 10 1984	13 Feeling	Sep 18 1984	5 Catalyzing
May 2 1984	9 Enlightening	Jul 11 1984	1 Devoting	Sep 19 1984	6 Enlightening
May 3 1984	10 Being	Jul 12 1984	2 Illuminating	Sep 20 1984	7 Being
May 4 1984	11 Breathing	Jul 13 1984	3 Choosing	Sep 21 1984	8 Breathing
May 5 1984	12 Listening	Jul 14 1984	4 Exploring	Sep 22 1984	9 Listening
May 6 1984	13 Planting	Jul 15 1984	5 Healing	Sep 23 1984	10 Planting
May 7 1984	1 Moving	Jul 16 1984	6 Seeing	Sep 24 1984	11 Moving
May 8 1984	2 Transcending	Jul 17 1984	7 Intuiting	Sep 25 1984	12 Transcending
May 9 1984	3 Remembering	Jul 18 1984	8 Evolving	Sep 26 1984	13 Remembering
May 10 1984	4 Loving	Jul 19 1984	9 Self-Regulating	Sep 27 1984	1 Loving
May 11 1984	5 Feeling	Jul 20 1984	10 Catalyzing	Sep 28 1984	2 Feeling
May 12 1984	6 Devoting	Jul 21 1984	11 Enlightening	Sep 29 1984	3 Devoting
May 13 1984	7 Illuminating	Jul 22 1984	12 Being	Sep 30 1984	4 Illuminating
May 14 1984	8 Choosing	Jul 23 1984	13 Breathing	Oct 1 1984	5 Choosing
May 15 1984	9 Exploring	Jul 24 1984	1 Listening	Oct 2 1984	6 Exploring
May 16 1984	10 Healing	Jul 25 1984	2 Planting	Oct 3 1984	7 Healing
May 17 1984	11 Seeing	Jul 26 1984	3 Moving	Oct 4 1984	8 Seeing
May 18 1984	12 Intuiting	Jul 27 1984	4 Transcending	Oct 5 1984	9 Intuiting
May 19 1984	13 Evolving	Jul 28 1984	5 Remembering	Oct 6 1984	10 Evolving
May 20 1984	1 Self-Regulating	Jul 29 1984	6 Loving	Oct 7 1984	11 Self-Regulating
May 21 1984	2 Catalyzing	Jul 30 1984	7 Feeling	Oct 8 1984	12 Catalyzing
May 22 1984	3 Enlightening	Jul 31 1984	8 Devoting	Oct 9 1984	13 Enlightening

Date	UE Earth Energy	Date	UE Earth Energy	Date	UE Earth Energy
Oct 10 1984	1 Being	Dec 19 1984	6 Illuminating	Feb 27 1985	11 Being
Oct 11 1984	2 Breathing	Dec 20 1984	7 Choosing	Feb 28 1985	12 Breathing
Oct 12 1984	3 Listening	Dec 21 1984	8 Exploring	Mar 1 1985	13 Listening
Oct 13 1984	4 Planting	Dec 22 1984	9 Healing	Mar 2 1985	1 Planting
Oct 14 1984	5 Moving	Dec 23 1984	10 Seeing	Mar 3 1985	2 Moving
Oct 15 1984	6 Transcending	Dec 24 1984	11 Intuiting	Mar 4 1985	3 Transcending
Oct 16 1984	7 Remembering	Dec 25 1984	12 Evolving	Mar 5 1985	4 Remembering
Oct 17 1984	8 Loving	Dec 26 1984	13 Self-Regulating	Mar 6 1985	5 Loving
Oct 18 1984	9 Feeling	Dec 27 1984	1 Catalyzing	Mar 7 1985	6 Feeling
Oct 19 1984	10 Devoting	Dec 28 1984	2 Enlightening	Mar 8 1985	7 Devoting
Oct 20 1984	11 Illuminating	Dec 29 1984	3 Being	Mar 9 1985	8 Illuminating
Oct 21 1984	12 Choosing	Dec 30 1984	4 Breathing	Mar 10 1985	9 Choosing
Oct 22 1984	13 Exploring	Dec 31 1984	5 Listening	Mar 11 1985	10 Exploring
Oct 23 1984	1 Healing	Jan 1 1985	6 Planting	Mar 12 1985	11 Healing
Oct 24 1984	2 Seeing	Jan 2 1985	7 Moving	Mar 13 1985	12 Seeing
Oct 25 1984	3 Intuiting	Jan 3 1985	8 Transcending	Mar 14 1985	13 Intuiting
Oct 26 1984	4 Evolving	Jan 4 1985	9 Remembering	Mar 15 1985	1 Evolving
Oct 27 1984	5 Self-Regulating	Jan 5 1985	10 Loving	Mar 16 1985	2 Self-Regulating
Oct 28 1984	6 Catalyzing	Jan 6 1985	11 Feeling	Mar 17 1985	3 Catalyzing
Oct 29 1984	7 Enlightening	Jan 7 1985	12 Devoting	Mar 18 1985	4 Enlightening
Oct 30 1984	8 Being	Jan 8 1985	13 Illuminating	Mar 19 1985	5 Being
Oct 31 1984	9 Breathing	Jan 9 1985	1 Choosing	Mar 20 1985	6 Breathing
Nov 1 1984	10 Listening	Jan 10 1985	2 Exploring	Mar 21 1985	7 Listening
Nov 2 1984	11 Planting	Jan 11 1985	3 Healing	Mar 22 1985	8 Planting
Nov 3 1984	12 Moving	Jan 12 1985	4 Seeing	Mar 23 1985	9 Moving
Nov 4 1984	13 Transcending	Jan 13 1985	5 Intuiting	Mar 24 1985	10 Transcending
Nov 5 1984	1 Remembering	Jan 14 1985	6 Evolving	Mar 25 1985	11 Remembering
Nov 6 1984	2 Loving	Jan 15 1985	7 Self-Regulating	Mar 26 1985	12 Loving
Nov 7 1984	3 Feeling	Jan 16 1985	8 Catalyzing	Mar 27 1985	13 Feeling
Nov 8 1984	4 Devoting	Jan 17 1985	9 Enlightening	Mar 28 1985	1 Devoting
Nov 9 1984	5 Illuminating	Jan 18 1985	10 Being	Mar 29 1985	2 Illuminating
Nov 10 1984	6 Choosing	Jan 19 1985	11 Breathing	Mar 30 1985	3 Choosing
Nov 11 1984	7 Exploring	Jan 20 1985	12 Listening	Mar 31 1985	4 Exploring
Nov 12 1984	8 Healing	Jan 21 1985	13 Planting	Apr 1 1985	5 Healing
Nov 13 1984	9 Seeing	Jan 22 1985	1 Moving	Apr 2 1985	6 Seeing
Nov 14 1984	10 Intuiting	Jan 23 1985	2 Transcending	Apr 3 1985	7 Intuiting
Nov 15 1984	11 Evolving	Jan 24 1985	3 Remembering	Apr 4 1985	8 Evolving
Nov 16 1984	12 Self-Regulating	Jan 25 1985	4 Loving	Apr 5 1985	9 Self-Regulating
Nov 17 1984	13 Catalyzing	Jan 26 1985	5 Feeling	Apr 6 1985	10 Catalyzing
Nov 18 1984	1 Enlightening	Jan 27 1985	6 Devoting	Apr 7 1985	11 Enlightening
Nov 19 1984	2 Being	Jan 28 1985	7 Illuminating	Apr 8 1985	12 Being
Nov 20 1984	3 Breathing	Jan 29 1985	8 Choosing	Apr 9 1985	13 Breathing
Nov 21 1984	4 Listening	Jan 30 1985	9 Exploring	Apr 10 1985	1 Listening
Nov 22 1984	5 Planting	Jan 31 1985	10 Healing	Apr 11 1985	2 Planting
Nov 23 1984	6 Moving	Feb 1 1985	11 Seeing	Apr 12 1985	3 Moving
Nov 24 1984	7 Transcending	Feb 2 1985	12 Intuiting	Apr 13 1985	4 Transcending
Nov 25 1984	8 Remembering	Feb 3 1985	13 Evolving	Apr 14 1985	5 Remembering
Nov 26 1984	9 Loving	Feb 4 1985	1 Self-Regulating	Apr 15 1985	6 Loving
Nov 27 1984	10 Feeling	Feb 5 1985	2 Catalyzing	Apr 16 1985	7 Feeling
Nov 28 1984	11 Devoting	Feb 6 1985	3 Enlightening	Apr 17 1985	8 Devoting
Nov 29 1984	12 Illuminating	Feb 7 1985	4 Being	Apr 18 1985	9 Illuminating
Nov 30 1984	13 Choosing	Feb 8 1985	5 Breathing	Apr 19 1985	10 Choosing
Dec 1 1984	1 Exploring	Feb 9 1985	6 Listening	Apr 20 1985	11 Exploring
Dec 2 1984	2 Healing	Feb 10 1985	7 Planting	Apr 21 1985	12 Healing
Dec 3 1984	3 Seeing	Feb 11 1985	8 Moving	Apr 22 1985	13 Seeing
Dec 4 1984	4 Intuiting	Feb 12 1985	9 Transcending	Apr 23 1985	1 Intuiting
Dec 5 1984	5 Evolving	Feb 13 1985	10 Remembering	Apr 24 1985	2 Evolving
Dec 6 1984	6 Self-Regulating	Feb 14 1985	11 Loving	Apr 25 1985	3 Self-Regulating
Dec 7 1984	7 Catalyzing	Feb 15 1985	12 Feeling	Apr 26 1985	4 Catalyzing
Dec 8 1984	8 Enlightening	Feb 16 1985	13 Devoting	Apr 27 1985	5 Enlightening
Dec 9 1984	9 Being	Feb 17 1985	1 Illuminating	Apr 28 1985	6 Being
Dec 10 1984	10 Breathing	Feb 18 1985	2 Choosing	Apr 29 1985	7 Breathing
Dec 11 1984	11 Listening	Feb 19 1985	3 Exploring	Apr 30 1985	8 Listening
Dec 12 1984	12 Planting	Feb 20 1985	4 Healing	May 1 1985	9 Planting
Dec 13 1984	13 Moving	Feb 21 1985	5 Seeing	May 2 1985	10 Moving
Dec 14 1984	1 Transcending	Feb 22 1985	6 Intuiting	May 3 1985	11 Transcending
Dec 15 1984	2 Remembering	Feb 23 1985	7 Evolving	May 4 1985	12 Remembering
Dec 16 1984	3 Loving	Feb 24 1985	8 Self-Regulating	May 5 1985	13 Loving
Dec 17 1984	4 Feeling	Feb 25 1985	9 Catalyzing	May 6 1985	1 Feeling
Dec 18 1984	5 Devoting	Feb 26 1985	10 Enlightening	May 7 1985	2 Devoting

Date	UE Earth Energy	Date	UE Earth Energy	Date	UE Earth Energy
May 8 1985	3 Illuminating	Jul 17 1985	8 Being	Sep 25 1985	13 Illuminating
May 9 1985	4 Choosing	Jul 18 1985	9 Breathing	Sep 26 1985	1 Choosing
May 10 1985	5 Exploring	Jul 19 1985	10 Listening	Sep 27 1985	2 Exploring
May 11 1985	6 Healing	Jul 20 1985	11 Planting	Sep 28 1985	3 Healing
May 12 1985	7 Seeing	Jul 21 1985	12 Moving	Sep 29 1985	4 Seeing
May 13 1985	8 Intuiting	Jul 22 1985	13 Transcending	Sep 30 1985	5 Intuiting
May 14 1985	9 Evolving	Jul 23 1985	1 Remembering	Oct 1 1985	6 Evolving
May 15 1985	10 Self-Regulating	Jul 24 1985	2 Loving	Oct 2 1985	7 Self-Regulating
May 16 1985	11 Catalyzing	Jul 25 1985	3 Feeling	Oct 3 1985	8 Catalyzing
May 17 1985	12 Enlightening	Jul 26 1985	4 Devoting	Oct 4 1985	9 Enlightening
May 18 1985	13 Being	Jul 27 1985	5 Illuminating	Oct 5 1985	10 Being
May 19 1985	1 Breathing	Jul 28 1985	6 Choosing	Oct 6 1985	11 Breathing
May 20 1985	2 Listening	Jul 29 1985	7 Exploring	Oct 7 1985	12 Listening
May 21 1985	3 Planting	Jul 30 1985	8 Healing	Oct 8 1985	13 Planting
May 22 1985	4 Moving	Jul 31 1985	9 Seeing	Oct 9 1985	1 Moving
May 23 1985	5 Transcending	Aug 1 1985	10 Intuiting	Oct 10 1985	2 Transcending
May 24 1985	6 Remembering	Aug 2 1985	11 Evolving	Oct 11 1985	3 Remembering
May 25 1985	7 Loving	Aug 3 1985	12 Self-Regulating	Oct 12 1985	4 Loving
May 26 1985	8 Feeling	Aug 4 1985	13 Catalyzing	Oct 13 1985	5 Feeling
May 27 1985	9 Devoting	Aug 5 1985	1 Enlightening	Oct 14 1985	6 Devoting
May 28 1985	10 Illuminating	Aug 6 1985	2 Being	Oct 15 1985	7 Illuminating
May 29 1985	11 Choosing	Aug 7 1985	3 Breathing	Oct 16 1985	8 Choosing
May 30 1985	12 Exploring	Aug 8 1985	4 Listening	Oct 17 1985	9 Exploring
May 31 1985	13 Healing	Aug 9 1985	5 Planting	Oct 18 1985	10 Healing
Jun 1 1985	1 Seeing	Aug 10 1985	6 Moving	Oct 19 1985	11 Seeing
Jun 2 1985	2 Intuiting	Aug 11 1985	7 Transcending	Oct 20 1985	12 Intuiting
Jun 3 1985	3 Evolving	Aug 12 1985	8 Remembering	Oct 21 1985	13 Evolving
Jun 4 1985	4 Self-Regulating	Aug 13 1985	9 Loving	Oct 22 1985	1 Self-Regulating
Jun 5 1985	5 Catalyzing	Aug 14 1985	10 Feeling	Oct 23 1985	2 Catalyzing
Jun 6 1985	6 Enlightening	Aug 15 1985	11 Devoting	Oct 24 1985	3 Enlightening
Jun 7 1985	7 Being	Aug 16 1985	12 Illuminating	Oct 25 1985	4 Being
Jun 8 1985	8 Breathing	Aug 17 1985	13 Choosing	Oct 26 1985	5 Breathing
Jun 9 1985	9 Listening	Aug 18 1985	1 Exploring	Oct 27 1985	6 Listening
Jun 10 1985	10 Planting	Aug 19 1985	2 Healing	Oct 28 1985	7 Planting
Jun 11 1985	11 Moving	Aug 20 1985	3 Seeing	Oct 29 1985	8 Moving
Jun 12 1985	12 Transcending	Aug 21 1985	4 Intuiting	Oct 30 1985	9 Transcending
Jun 13 1985	13 Remembering	Aug 22 1985	5 Evolving	Oct 31 1985	10 Remembering
Jun 14 1985	1 Loving	Aug 23 1985	6 Self-Regulating	Nov 1 1985	11 Loving
Jun 15 1985	2 Feeling	Aug 24 1985	7 Catalyzing	Nov 2 1985	12 Feeling
Jun 16 1985	3 Devoting	Aug 25 1985	8 Enlightening	Nov 3 1985	13 Devoting
Jun 17 1985	4 Illuminating	Aug 26 1985	9 Being	Nov 4 1985	1 Illuminating
Jun 18 1985	5 Choosing	Aug 27 1985	10 Breathing	Nov 5 1985	2 Choosing
Jun 19 1985	6 Exploring	Aug 28 1985	11 Listening	Nov 6 1985	3 Exploring
Jun 20 1985	7 Healing	Aug 29 1985	12 Planting	Nov 7 1985	4 Healing
Jun 21 1985	8 Seeing	Aug 30 1985	13 Moving	Nov 8 1985	5 Seeing
Jun 22 1985	9 Intuiting	Aug 31 1985	1 Transcending	Nov 9 1985	6 Intuiting
Jun 23 1985	10 Evolving	Sep 1 1985	2 Remembering	Nov 10 1985	7 Evolving
Jun 24 1985	11 Self-Regulating	Sep 2 1985	3 Loving	Nov 11 1985	8 Self-Regulating
Jun 25 1985	12 Catalyzing	Sep 3 1985	4 Feeling	Nov 12 1985	9 Catalyzing
Jun 26 1985	13 Enlightening	Sep 4 1985	5 Devoting	Nov 13 1985	10 Enlightening
Jun 27 1985	1 Being	Sep 5 1985	6 Illuminating	Nov 14 1985	11 Being
Jun 28 1985	2 Breathing	Sep 6 1985	7 Choosing	Nov 15 1985	12 Breathing
Jun 29 1985	3 Listening	Sep 7 1985	8 Exploring	Nov 16 1985	13 Listening
Jun 30 1985	4 Planting	Sep 8 1985	9 Healing	Nov 17 1985	1 Planting
Jul 1 1985	5 Moving	Sep 9 1985	10 Seeing	Nov 18 1985	2 Moving
Jul 2 1985	6 Transcending	Sep 10 1985	11 Intuiting	Nov 19 1985	3 Transcending
Jul 3 1985	7 Remembering	Sep 11 1985	12 Evolving	Nov 20 1985	4 Remembering
Jul 4 1985	8 Loving	Sep 12 1985	13 Self-Regulating	Nov 21 1985	5 Loving
Jul 5 1985	9 Feeling	Sep 13 1985	1 Catalyzing	Nov 22 1985	6 Feeling
Jul 6 1985	10 Devoting	Sep 14 1985	2 Enlightening	Nov 23 1985	7 Devoting
Jul 7 1985	11 Illuminating	Sep 15 1985	3 Being	Nov 24 1985	8 Illuminating
Jul 8 1985	12 Choosing	Sep 16 1985	4 Breathing	Nov 25 1985	9 Choosing
Jul 9 1985	13 Exploring	Sep 17 1985	5 Listening	Nov 26 1985	10 Exploring
Jul 10 1985	1 Healing	Sep 18 1985	6 Planting	Nov 27 1985	11 Healing
Jul 11 1985	2 Seeing	Sep 19 1985	7 Moving	Nov 28 1985	12 Seeing
Jul 12 1985	3 Intuiting	Sep 20 1985	8 Transcending	Nov 29 1985	13 Intuiting
Jul 13 1985	4 Evolving	Sep 21 1985	9 Remembering	Nov 30 1985	1 Evolving
Jul 14 1985	5 Self-Regulating	Sep 22 1985	10 Loving	Dec 1 1985	2 Self-Regulating
Jul 15 1985	6 Catalyzing	Sep 23 1985	11 Feeling	Dec 2 1985	3 Catalyzing
Jul 16 1985	7 Enlightening	Sep 24 1985	12 Devoting	Dec 3 1985	4 Enlightening

Date	UE	Earth Energy	Date	UE	Earth Energy	Date	UE	Earth Energy
Dec 4 1985	5	Being	Feb 12 1986	10	Illuminating	Apr 23 1986	2	Being
Dec 5 1985	6	Breathing	Feb 13 1986	11	Choosing	Apr 24 1986	3	Breathing
Dec 6 1985	7	Listening	Feb 14 1986	12	Exploring	Apr 25 1986	4	Listening
Dec 7 1985	8	Planting	Feb 15 1986	13	Healing	Apr 26 1986	5	Planting
Dec 8 1985	9	Moving	Feb 16 1986	**1**	**Seeing**	Apr 27 1986	6	Moving
Dec 9 1985	10	Transcending	Feb 17 1986	2	Intuiting	Apr 28 1986	7	Transcending
Dec 10 1985	11	Remembering	Feb 18 1986	3	Evolving	Apr 29 1986	8	Remembering
Dec 11 1985	12	Loving	Feb 19 1986	4	Self-Regulating	Apr 30 1986	9	Loving
Dec 12 1985	13	Feeling	Feb 20 1986	5	Catalyzing	May 1 1986	10	Feeling
Dec 13 1985	**1**	**Devoting**	Feb 21 1986	6	Enlightening	May 2 1986	11	Devoting
Dec 14 1985	2	Illuminating	Feb 22 1986	7	Being	May 3 1986	12	Illuminating
Dec 15 1985	3	Choosing	Feb 23 1986	8	Breathing	May 4 1986	13	Choosing
Dec 16 1985	4	Exploring	Feb 24 1986	9	Listening	May 5 1986	**1**	**Exploring**
Dec 17 1985	5	Healing	Feb 25 1986	10	Planting	May 6 1986	2	Healing
Dec 18 1985	6	Seeing	Feb 26 1986	11	Moving	May 7 1986	3	Seeing
Dec 19 1985	7	Intuiting	Feb 27 1986	12	Transcending	May 8 1986	4	Intuiting
Dec 20 1985	8	Evolving	Feb 28 1986	13	Remembering	May 9 1986	5	Evolving
Dec 21 1985	9	Self-Regulating	Mar 1 1986	**1**	**Loving**	May 10 1986	6	Self-Regulating
Dec 22 1985	10	Catalyzing	Mar 2 1986	2	Feeling	May 11 1986	7	Catalyzing
Dec 23 1985	11	Enlightening	Mar 3 1986	3	Devoting	May 12 1986	8	Enlightening
Dec 24 1985	12	Being	Mar 4 1986	4	Illuminating	May 13 1986	9	Being
Dec 25 1985	13	Breathing	Mar 5 1986	5	Choosing	May 14 1986	10	Breathing
Dec 26 1985	**1**	**Listening**	Mar 6 1986	6	Exploring	May 15 1986	11	Listening
Dec 27 1985	2	Planting	Mar 7 1986	7	Healing	May 16 1986	12	Planting
Dec 28 1985	3	Moving	Mar 8 1986	8	Seeing	May 17 1986	13	Moving
Dec 29 1985	4	Transcending	Mar 9 1986	9	Intuiting	May 18 1986	**1**	**Transcending**
Dec 30 1985	5	Remembering	Mar 10 1986	10	Evolving	May 19 1986	2	Remembering
Dec 31 1985	6	Loving	Mar 11 1986	11	Self-Regulating	May 20 1986	3	Loving
Jan 1 1986	7	Feeling	Mar 12 1986	12	Catalyzing	May 21 1986	4	Feeling
Jan 2 1986	8	Devoting	Mar 13 1986	13	Enlightening	May 22 1986	5	Devoting
Jan 3 1986	9	Illuminating	Mar 14 1986	**1**	**Being**	May 23 1986	6	Illuminating
Jan 4 1986	10	Choosing	Mar 15 1986	2	Breathing	May 24 1986	7	Choosing
Jan 5 1986	11	Exploring	Mar 16 1986	3	Listening	May 25 1986	8	Exploring
Jan 6 1986	12	Healing	Mar 17 1986	4	Planting	May 26 1986	9	Healing
Jan 7 1986	13	Seeing	Mar 18 1986	5	Moving	May 27 1986	10	Seeing
Jan 8 1986	**1**	**Intuiting**	Mar 19 1986	6	Transcending	May 28 1986	11	Intuiting
Jan 9 1986	2	Evolving	Mar 20 1986	7	Remembering	May 29 1986	12	Evolving
Jan 10 1986	3	Self-Regulating	Mar 21 1986	8	Loving	May 30 1986	13	Self-Regulating
Jan 11 1986	4	Catalyzing	Mar 22 1986	9	Feeling	May 31 1986	**1**	**Catalyzing**
Jan 12 1986	5	Enlightening	Mar 23 1986	10	Devoting	Jun 1 1986	2	Enlightening
Jan 13 1986	6	Being	Mar 24 1986	11	Illuminating	Jun 2 1986	3	Being
Jan 14 1986	7	Breathing	Mar 25 1986	12	Choosing	Jun 3 1986	4	Breathing
Jan 15 1986	8	Listening	Mar 26 1986	13	Exploring	Jun 4 1986	5	Listening
Jan 16 1986	9	Planting	Mar 27 1986	**1**	**Healing**	Jun 5 1986	6	Planting
Jan 17 1986	10	Moving	Mar 28 1986	2	Seeing	Jun 6 1986	7	Moving
Jan 18 1986	11	Transcending	Mar 29 1986	3	Intuiting	Jun 7 1986	8	Transcending
Jan 19 1986	12	Remembering	Mar 30 1986	4	Evolving	Jun 8 1986	9	Remembering
Jan 20 1986	13	Loving	Mar 31 1986	5	Self-Regulating	Jun 9 1986	10	Loving
Jan 21 1986	**1**	**Feeling**	Apr 1 1986	6	Catalyzing	Jun 10 1986	11	Feeling
Jan 22 1986	2	Devoting	Apr 2 1986	7	Enlightening	Jun 11 1986	12	Devoting
Jan 23 1986	3	Illuminating	Apr 3 1986	8	Being	Jun 12 1986	13	Illuminating
Jan 24 1986	4	Choosing	Apr 4 1986	9	Breathing	Jun 13 1986	**1**	**Choosing**
Jan 25 1986	5	Exploring	Apr 5 1986	10	Listening	Jun 14 1986	2	Exploring
Jan 26 1986	6	Healing	Apr 6 1986	11	Planting	Jun 15 1986	3	Healing
Jan 27 1986	7	Seeing	Apr 7 1986	12	Moving	Jun 16 1986	4	Seeing
Jan 28 1986	8	Intuiting	Apr 8 1986	13	Transcending	Jun 17 1986	5	Intuiting
Jan 29 1986	9	Evolving	Apr 9 1986	**1**	**Remembering**	Jun 18 1986	6	Evolving
Jan 30 1986	10	Self-Regulating	Apr 10 1986	2	Loving	Jun 19 1986	7	Self-Regulating
Jan 31 1986	11	Catalyzing	Apr 11 1986	3	Feeling	Jun 20 1986	8	Catalyzing
Feb 1 1986	12	Enlightening	Apr 12 1986	4	Devoting	Jun 21 1986	9	Enlightening
Feb 2 1986	13	Being	Apr 13 1986	5	Illuminating	Jun 22 1986	10	Being
Feb 3 1986	**1**	**Breathing**	Apr 14 1986	6	Choosing	Jun 23 1986	11	Breathing
Feb 4 1986	2	Listening	Apr 15 1986	7	Exploring	Jun 24 1986	12	Listening
Feb 5 1986	3	Planting	Apr 16 1986	8	Healing	Jun 25 1986	13	Planting
Feb 6 1986	4	Moving	Apr 17 1986	9	Seeing	Jun 26 1986	**1**	**Moving**
Feb 7 1986	5	Transcending	Apr 18 1986	10	Intuiting	Jun 27 1986	2	Transcending
Feb 8 1986	6	Remembering	Apr 19 1986	11	Evolving	Jun 28 1986	3	Remembering
Feb 9 1986	7	Loving	Apr 20 1986	12	Self-Regulating	Jun 29 1986	4	Loving
Feb 10 1986	8	Feeling	Apr 21 1986	13	Catalyzing	Jun 30 1986	5	Feeling
Feb 11 1986	9	Devoting	Apr 22 1986	**1**	**Enlightening**	Jul 1 1986	6	Devoting

Date	UE Earth Energy	Date	UE Earth Energy	Date	UE Earth Energy
Jul 2 1986	7 Illuminating	Sep 10 1986	12 Being	Nov 19 1986	4 Illuminating
Jul 3 1986	8 Choosing	Sep 11 1986	13 Breathing	Nov 20 1986	5 Choosing
Jul 4 1986	9 Exploring	Sep 12 1986	1 Listening	Nov 21 1986	6 Exploring
Jul 5 1986	10 Healing	Sep 13 1986	2 Planting	Nov 22 1986	7 Healing
Jul 6 1986	11 Seeing	Sep 14 1986	3 Moving	Nov 23 1986	8 Seeing
Jul 7 1986	12 Intuiting	Sep 15 1986	4 Transcending	Nov 24 1986	9 Intuiting
Jul 8 1986	13 Evolving	Sep 16 1986	5 Remembering	Nov 25 1986	10 Evolving
Jul 9 1986	1 Self-Regulating	Sep 17 1986	6 Loving	Nov 26 1986	11 Self-Regulating
Jul 10 1986	2 Catalyzing	Sep 18 1986	7 Feeling	Nov 27 1986	12 Catalyzing
Jul 11 1986	3 Enlightening	Sep 19 1986	8 Devoting	Nov 28 1986	13 Enlightening
Jul 12 1986	4 Being	Sep 20 1986	9 Illuminating	Nov 29 1986	1 Being
Jul 13 1986	5 Breathing	Sep 21 1986	10 Choosing	Nov 30 1986	2 Breathing
Jul 14 1986	6 Listening	Sep 22 1986	11 Exploring	Dec 1 1986	3 Listening
Jul 15 1986	7 Planting	Sep 23 1986	12 Healing	Dec 2 1986	4 Planting
Jul 16 1986	8 Moving	Sep 24 1986	13 Seeing	Dec 3 1986	5 Moving
Jul 17 1986	9 Transcending	Sep 25 1986	1 Intuiting	Dec 4 1986	6 Transcending
Jul 18 1986	10 Remembering	Sep 26 1986	2 Evolving	Dec 5 1986	7 Remembering
Jul 19 1986	11 Loving	Sep 27 1986	3 Self-Regulating	Dec 6 1986	8 Loving
Jul 20 1986	12 Feeling	Sep 28 1986	4 Catalyzing	Dec 7 1986	9 Feeling
Jul 21 1986	13 Devoting	Sep 29 1986	5 Enlightening	Dec 8 1986	10 Devoting
Jul 22 1986	1 Illuminating	Sep 30 1986	6 Being	Dec 9 1986	11 Illuminating
Jul 23 1986	2 Choosing	Oct 1 1986	7 Breathing	Dec 10 1986	12 Choosing
Jul 24 1986	3 Exploring	Oct 2 1986	8 Listening	Dec 11 1986	13 Exploring
Jul 25 1986	4 Healing	Oct 3 1986	9 Planting	Dec 12 1986	1 Healing
Jul 26 1986	5 Seeing	Oct 4 1986	10 Moving	Dec 13 1986	2 Seeing
Jul 27 1986	6 Intuiting	Oct 5 1986	11 Transcending	Dec 14 1986	3 Intuiting
Jul 28 1986	7 Evolving	Oct 6 1986	12 Remembering	Dec 15 1986	4 Evolving
Jul 29 1986	8 Self-Regulating	Oct 7 1986	13 Loving	Dec 16 1986	5 Self-Regulating
Jul 30 1986	9 Catalyzing	Oct 8 1986	1 Feeling	Dec 17 1986	6 Catalyzing
Jul 31 1986	10 Enlightening	Oct 9 1986	2 Devoting	Dec 18 1986	7 Enlightening
Aug 1 1986	11 Being	Oct 10 1986	3 Illuminating	Dec 19 1986	8 Being
Aug 2 1986	12 Breathing	Oct 11 1986	4 Choosing	Dec 20 1986	9 Breathing
Aug 3 1986	13 Listening	Oct 12 1986	5 Exploring	Dec 21 1986	10 Listening
Aug 4 1986	1 Planting	Oct 13 1986	6 Healing	Dec 22 1986	11 Planting
Aug 5 1986	2 Moving	Oct 14 1986	7 Seeing	Dec 23 1986	12 Moving
Aug 6 1986	3 Transcending	Oct 15 1986	8 Intuiting	Dec 24 1986	13 Transcending
Aug 7 1986	4 Remembering	Oct 16 1986	9 Evolving	Dec 25 1986	1 Remembering
Aug 8 1986	5 Loving	Oct 17 1986	10 Self-Regulating	Dec 26 1986	2 Loving
Aug 9 1986	6 Feeling	Oct 18 1986	11 Catalyzing	Dec 27 1986	3 Feeling
Aug 10 1986	7 Devoting	Oct 19 1986	12 Enlightening	Dec 28 1986	4 Devoting
Aug 11 1986	8 Illuminating	Oct 20 1986	13 Being	Dec 29 1986	5 Illuminating
Aug 12 1986	9 Choosing	Oct 21 1986	1 Breathing	Dec 30 1986	6 Choosing
Aug 13 1986	10 Exploring	Oct 22 1986	2 Listening	Dec 31 1986	7 Exploring
Aug 14 1986	11 Healing	Oct 23 1986	3 Planting	Jan 1 1987	8 Healing
Aug 15 1986	12 Seeing	Oct 24 1986	4 Moving	Jan 2 1987	9 Seeing
Aug 16 1986	13 Intuiting	Oct 25 1986	5 Transcending	Jan 3 1987	10 Intuiting
Aug 17 1986	1 Evolving	Oct 26 1986	6 Remembering	Jan 4 1987	11 Evolving
Aug 18 1986	2 Self-Regulating	Oct 27 1986	7 Loving	Jan 5 1987	12 Self-Regulating
Aug 19 1986	3 Catalyzing	Oct 28 1986	8 Feeling	Jan 6 1987	13 Catalyzing
Aug 20 1986	4 Enlightening	Oct 29 1986	9 Devoting	Jan 7 1987	1 Enlightening
Aug 21 1986	5 Being	Oct 30 1986	10 Illuminating	Jan 8 1987	2 Being
Aug 22 1986	6 Breathing	Oct 31 1986	11 Choosing	Jan 9 1987	3 Breathing
Aug 23 1986	7 Listening	Nov 1 1986	12 Exploring	Jan 10 1987	4 Listening
Aug 24 1986	8 Planting	Nov 2 1986	13 Healing	Jan 11 1987	5 Planting
Aug 25 1986	9 Moving	Nov 3 1986	1 Seeing	Jan 12 1987	6 Moving
Aug 26 1986	10 Transcending	Nov 4 1986	2 Intuiting	Jan 13 1987	7 Transcending
Aug 27 1986	11 Remembering	Nov 5 1986	3 Evolving	Jan 14 1987	8 Remembering
Aug 28 1986	12 Loving	Nov 6 1986	4 Self-Regulating	Jan 15 1987	9 Loving
Aug 29 1986	13 Feeling	Nov 7 1986	5 Catalyzing	Jan 16 1987	10 Feeling
Aug 30 1986	1 Devoting	Nov 8 1986	6 Enlightening	Jan 17 1987	11 Devoting
Aug 31 1986	2 Illuminating	Nov 9 1986	7 Being	Jan 18 1987	12 Illuminating
Sep 1 1986	3 Choosing	Nov 10 1986	8 Breathing	Jan 19 1987	13 Choosing
Sep 2 1986	4 Exploring	Nov 11 1986	9 Listening	Jan 20 1987	1 Exploring
Sep 3 1986	5 Healing	Nov 12 1986	10 Planting	Jan 21 1987	2 Healing
Sep 4 1986	6 Seeing	Nov 13 1986	11 Moving	Jan 22 1987	3 Seeing
Sep 5 1986	7 Intuiting	Nov 14 1986	12 Transcending	Jan 23 1987	4 Intuiting
Sep 6 1986	8 Evolving	Nov 15 1986	13 Remembering	Jan 24 1987	5 Evolving
Sep 7 1986	9 Self-Regulating	Nov 16 1986	1 Loving	Jan 25 1987	6 Self-Regulating
Sep 8 1986	10 Catalyzing	Nov 17 1986	2 Feeling	Jan 26 1987	7 Catalyzing
Sep 9 1986	11 Enlightening	Nov 18 1986	3 Devoting	Jan 27 1987	8 Enlightening

Date	UE Earth Energy	Date	UE Earth Energy	Date	UE Earth Energy
Jan 28 1987	9 Being	Apr 8 1987	1 Illuminating	Jun 17 1987	6 Being
Jan 29 1987	10 Breathing	Apr 9 1987	2 Choosing	Jun 18 1987	7 Breathing
Jan 30 1987	11 Listening	Apr 10 1987	3 Exploring	Jun 19 1987	8 Listening
Jan 31 1987	12 Planting	Apr 11 1987	4 Healing	Jun 20 1987	9 Planting
Feb 1 1987	13 Moving	Apr 12 1987	5 Seeing	Jun 21 1987	10 Moving
Feb 2 1987	1 Transcending	Apr 13 1987	6 Intuiting	Jun 22 1987	11 Transcending
Feb 3 1987	2 Remembering	Apr 14 1987	7 Evolving	Jun 23 1987	12 Remembering
Feb 4 1987	3 Loving	Apr 15 1987	8 Self-Regulating	Jun 24 1987	13 Loving
Feb 5 1987	4 Feeling	Apr 16 1987	9 Catalyzing	Jun 25 1987	1 Feeling
Feb 6 1987	5 Devoting	Apr 17 1987	10 Enlightening	Jun 26 1987	2 Devoting
Feb 7 1987	6 Illuminating	Apr 18 1987	11 Being	Jun 27 1987	3 Illuminating
Feb 8 1987	7 Choosing	Apr 19 1987	12 Breathing	Jun 28 1987	4 Choosing
Feb 9 1987	8 Exploring	Apr 20 1987	13 Listening	Jun 29 1987	5 Exploring
Feb 10 1987	9 Healing	Apr 21 1987	1 Planting	Jun 30 1987	6 Healing
Feb 11 1987	10 Seeing	Apr 22 1987	2 Moving	Jul 1 1987	7 Seeing
Feb 12 1987	11 Intuiting	Apr 23 1987	3 Transcending	Jul 2 1987	8 Intuiting
Feb 13 1987	12 Evolving	Apr 24 1987	4 Remembering	Jul 3 1987	9 Evolving
Feb 14 1987	13 Self-Regulating	Apr 25 1987	5 Loving	Jul 4 1987	10 Self-Regulating
Feb 15 1987	1 Catalyzing	Apr 26 1987	6 Feeling	Jul 5 1987	11 Catalyzing
Feb 16 1987	2 Enlightening	Apr 27 1987	7 Devoting	Jul 6 1987	12 Enlightening
Feb 17 1987	3 Being	Apr 28 1987	8 Illuminating	Jul 7 1987	13 Being
Feb 18 1987	4 Breathing	Apr 29 1987	9 Choosing	Jul 8 1987	1 Breathing
Feb 19 1987	5 Listening	Apr 30 1987	10 Exploring	Jul 9 1987	2 Listening
Feb 20 1987	6 Planting	May 1 1987	11 Healing	Jul 10 1987	3 Planting
Feb 21 1987	7 Moving	May 2 1987	12 Seeing	Jul 11 1987	4 Moving
Feb 22 1987	8 Transcending	May 3 1987	13 Intuiting	Jul 12 1987	5 Transcending
Feb 23 1987	9 Remembering	May 4 1987	1 Evolving	Jul 13 1987	6 Remembering
Feb 24 1987	10 Loving	May 5 1987	2 Self-Regulating	Jul 14 1987	7 Loving
Feb 25 1987	11 Feeling	May 6 1987	3 Catalyzing	Jul 15 1987	8 Feeling
Feb 26 1987	12 Devoting	May 7 1987	4 Enlightening	Jul 16 1987	9 Devoting
Feb 27 1987	13 Illuminating	May 8 1987	5 Being	Jul 17 1987	10 Illuminating
Feb 28 1987	1 Choosing	May 9 1987	6 Breathing	Jul 18 1987	11 Choosing
Mar 1 1987	2 Exploring	May 10 1987	7 Listening	Jul 19 1987	12 Exploring
Mar 2 1987	3 Healing	May 11 1987	8 Planting	Jul 20 1987	13 Healing
Mar 3 1987	4 Seeing	May 12 1987	9 Moving	Jul 21 1987	1 Seeing
Mar 4 1987	5 Intuiting	May 13 1987	10 Transcending	Jul 22 1987	2 Intuiting
Mar 5 1987	6 Evolving	May 14 1987	11 Remembering	Jul 23 1987	3 Evolving
Mar 6 1987	7 Self-Regulating	May 15 1987	12 Loving	Jul 24 1987	4 Self-Regulating
Mar 7 1987	8 Catalyzing	May 16 1987	13 Feeling	Jul 25 1987	5 Catalyzing
Mar 8 1987	9 Enlightening	May 17 1987	1 Devoting	Jul 26 1987	6 Enlightening
Mar 9 1987	10 Being	May 18 1987	2 Illuminating	Jul 27 1987	7 Being
Mar 10 1987	11 Breathing	May 19 1987	3 Choosing	Jul 28 1987	8 Breathing
Mar 11 1987	12 Listening	May 20 1987	4 Exploring	Jul 29 1987	9 Listening
Mar 12 1987	13 Planting	May 21 1987	5 Healing	Jul 30 1987	10 Planting
Mar 13 1987	1 Moving	May 22 1987	6 Seeing	Jul 31 1987	11 Moving
Mar 14 1987	2 Transcending	May 23 1987	7 Intuiting	Aug 1 1987	12 Transcending
Mar 15 1987	3 Remembering	May 24 1987	8 Evolving	Aug 2 1987	13 Remembering
Mar 16 1987	4 Loving	May 25 1987	9 Self-Regulating	Aug 3 1987	1 Loving
Mar 17 1987	5 Feeling	May 26 1987	10 Catalyzing	Aug 4 1987	2 Feeling
Mar 18 1987	6 Devoting	May 27 1987	11 Enlightening	Aug 5 1987	3 Devoting
Mar 19 1987	7 Illuminating	May 28 1987	12 Being	Aug 6 1987	4 Illuminating
Mar 20 1987	8 Choosing	May 29 1987	13 Breathing	Aug 7 1987	5 Choosing
Mar 21 1987	9 Exploring	May 30 1987	1 Listening	Aug 8 1987	6 Exploring
Mar 22 1987	10 Healing	May 31 1987	2 Planting	Aug 9 1987	7 Healing
Mar 23 1987	11 Seeing	Jun 1 1987	3 Moving	Aug 10 1987	8 Seeing
Mar 24 1987	12 Intuiting	Jun 2 1987	4 Transcending	Aug 11 1987	9 Intuiting
Mar 25 1987	13 Evolving	Jun 3 1987	5 Remembering	Aug 12 1987	10 Evolving
Mar 26 1987	1 Self-Regulating	Jun 4 1987	6 Loving	Aug 13 1987	11 Self-Regulating
Mar 27 1987	2 Catalyzing	Jun 5 1987	7 Feeling	Aug 14 1987	12 Catalyzing
Mar 28 1987	3 Enlightening	Jun 6 1987	8 Devoting	Aug 15 1987	13 Enlightening
Mar 29 1987	4 Being	Jun 7 1987	9 Illuminating	Aug 16 1987	1 Being
Mar 30 1987	5 Breathing	Jun 8 1987	10 Choosing	Aug 17 1987	2 Breathing
Mar 31 1987	6 Listening	Jun 9 1987	11 Exploring	Aug 18 1987	3 Listening
Apr 1 1987	7 Planting	Jun 10 1987	12 Healing	Aug 19 1987	4 Planting
Apr 2 1987	8 Moving	Jun 11 1987	13 Seeing	Aug 20 1987	5 Moving
Apr 3 1987	9 Transcending	Jun 12 1987	1 Intuiting	Aug 21 1987	6 Transcending
Apr 4 1987	10 Remembering	Jun 13 1987	2 Evolving	Aug 22 1987	7 Remembering
Apr 5 1987	11 Loving	Jun 14 1987	3 Self-Regulating	Aug 23 1987	8 Loving
Apr 6 1987	12 Feeling	Jun 15 1987	4 Catalyzing	Aug 24 1987	9 Feeling
Apr 7 1987	13 Devoting	Jun 16 1987	5 Enlightening	Aug 25 1987	10 Devoting

Date	UE Earth Energy	Date	UE Earth Energy	Date	UE Earth Energy
Aug 26 1987	11 Illuminating	Nov 4 1987	3 Being	Jan 13 1988	8 Illuminating
Aug 27 1987	12 Choosing	Nov 5 1987	4 Breathing	Jan 14 1988	9 Choosing
Aug 28 1987	13 Exploring	Nov 6 1987	5 Listening	Jan 15 1988	10 Exploring
Aug 29 1987	1 Healing	Nov 7 1987	6 Planting	Jan 16 1988	11 Healing
Aug 30 1987	2 Seeing	Nov 8 1987	7 Moving	Jan 17 1988	12 Seeing
Aug 31 1987	3 Intuiting	Nov 9 1987	8 Transcending	Jan 18 1988	13 Intuiting
Sep 1 1987	4 Evolving	Nov 10 1987	9 Remembering	Jan 19 1988	1 Evolving
Sep 2 1987	5 Self-Regulating	Nov 11 1987	10 Loving	Jan 20 1988	2 Self-Regulating
Sep 3 1987	6 Catalyzing	Nov 12 1987	11 Feeling	Jan 21 1988	3 Catalyzing
Sep 4 1987	7 Enlightening	Nov 13 1987	12 Devoting	Jan 22 1988	4 Enlightening
Sep 5 1987	8 Being	Nov 14 1987	13 Illuminating	Jan 23 1988	5 Being
Sep 6 1987	9 Breathing	Nov 15 1987	1 Choosing	Jan 24 1988	6 Breathing
Sep 7 1987	10 Listening	Nov 16 1987	2 Exploring	Jan 25 1988	7 Listening
Sep 8 1987	11 Planting	Nov 17 1987	3 Healing	Jan 26 1988	8 Planting
Sep 9 1987	12 Moving	Nov 18 1987	4 Seeing	Jan 27 1988	9 Moving
Sep 10 1987	13 Transcending	Nov 19 1987	5 Intuiting	Jan 28 1988	10 Transcending
Sep 11 1987	1 Remembering	Nov 20 1987	6 Evolving	Jan 29 1988	11 Remembering
Sep 12 1987	2 Loving	Nov 21 1987	7 Self-Regulating	Jan 30 1988	12 Loving
Sep 13 1987	3 Feeling	Nov 22 1987	8 Catalyzing	Jan 31 1988	13 Feeling
Sep 14 1987	4 Devoting	Nov 23 1987	9 Enlightening	Feb 1 1988	1 Devoting
Sep 15 1987	5 Illuminating	Nov 24 1987	10 Being	Feb 2 1988	2 Illuminating
Sep 16 1987	6 Choosing	Nov 25 1987	11 Breathing	Feb 3 1988	3 Choosing
Sep 17 1987	7 Exploring	Nov 26 1987	12 Listening	Feb 4 1988	4 Exploring
Sep 18 1987	8 Healing	Nov 27 1987	13 Planting	Feb 5 1988	5 Healing
Sep 19 1987	9 Seeing	Nov 28 1987	1 Moving	Feb 6 1988	6 Seeing
Sep 20 1987	10 Intuiting	Nov 29 1987	2 Transcending	Feb 7 1988	7 Intuiting
Sep 21 1987	11 Evolving	Nov 30 1987	3 Remembering	Feb 8 1988	8 Evolving
Sep 22 1987	12 Self-Regulating	Dec 1 1987	4 Loving	Feb 9 1988	9 Self-Regulating
Sep 23 1987	13 Catalyzing	Dec 2 1987	5 Feeling	Feb 10 1988	10 Catalyzing
Sep 24 1987	1 Enlightening	Dec 3 1987	6 Devoting	Feb 11 1988	11 Enlightening
Sep 25 1987	2 Being	Dec 4 1987	7 Illuminating	Feb 12 1988	12 Being
Sep 26 1987	3 Breathing	Dec 5 1987	8 Choosing	Feb 13 1988	13 Breathing
Sep 27 1987	4 Listening	Dec 6 1987	9 Exploring	Feb 14 1988	1 Listening
Sep 28 1987	5 Planting	Dec 7 1987	10 Healing	Feb 15 1988	2 Planting
Sep 29 1987	6 Moving	Dec 8 1987	11 Seeing	Feb 16 1988	3 Moving
Sep 30 1987	7 Transcending	Dec 9 1987	12 Intuiting	Feb 17 1988	4 Transcending
Oct 1 1987	8 Remembering	Dec 10 1987	13 Evolving	Feb 18 1988	5 Remembering
Oct 2 1987	9 Loving	Dec 11 1987	1 Self-Regulating	Feb 19 1988	6 Loving
Oct 3 1987	10 Feeling	Dec 12 1987	2 Catalyzing	Feb 20 1988	7 Feeling
Oct 4 1987	11 Devoting	Dec 13 1987	3 Enlightening	Feb 21 1988	8 Devoting
Oct 5 1987	12 Illuminating	Dec 14 1987	4 Being	Feb 22 1988	9 Illuminating
Oct 6 1987	13 Choosing	Dec 15 1987	5 Breathing	Feb 23 1988	10 Choosing
Oct 7 1987	1 Exploring	Dec 16 1987	6 Listening	Feb 24 1988	11 Exploring
Oct 8 1987	2 Healing	Dec 17 1987	7 Planting	Feb 25 1988	12 Healing
Oct 9 1987	3 Seeing	Dec 18 1987	8 Moving	Feb 26 1988	13 Seeing
Oct 10 1987	4 Intuiting	Dec 19 1987	9 Transcending	Feb 27 1988	1 Intuiting
Oct 11 1987	5 Evolving	Dec 20 1987	10 Remembering	Feb 28 1988	2 Evolving
Oct 12 1987	6 Self-Regulating	Dec 21 1987	11 Loving	Feb 29 1988	3 Self-Regulating
Oct 13 1987	7 Catalyzing	Dec 22 1987	12 Feeling	Mar 1 1988	4 Catalyzing
Oct 14 1987	8 Enlightening	Dec 23 1987	13 Devoting	Mar 2 1988	5 Enlightening
Oct 15 1987	9 Being	Dec 24 1987	1 Illuminating	Mar 3 1988	6 Being
Oct 16 1987	10 Breathing	Dec 25 1987	2 Choosing	Mar 4 1988	7 Breathing
Oct 17 1987	11 Listening	Dec 26 1987	3 Exploring	Mar 5 1988	8 Listening
Oct 18 1987	12 Planting	Dec 27 1987	4 Healing	Mar 6 1988	9 Planting
Oct 19 1987	13 Moving	Dec 28 1987	5 Seeing	Mar 7 1988	10 Moving
Oct 20 1987	1 Transcending	Dec 29 1987	6 Intuiting	Mar 8 1988	11 Transcending
Oct 21 1987	2 Remembering	Dec 30 1987	7 Evolving	Mar 9 1988	12 Remembering
Oct 22 1987	3 Loving	Dec 31 1987	8 Self-Regulating	Mar 10 1988	13 Loving
Oct 23 1987	4 Feeling	Jan 1 1988	9 Catalyzing	Mar 11 1988	1 Feeling
Oct 24 1987	5 Devoting	Jan 2 1988	10 Enlightening	Mar 12 1988	2 Devoting
Oct 25 1987	6 Illuminating	Jan 3 1988	11 Being	Mar 13 1988	3 Illuminating
Oct 26 1987	7 Choosing	Jan 4 1988	12 Breathing	Mar 14 1988	4 Choosing
Oct 27 1987	8 Exploring	Jan 5 1988	13 Listening	Mar 15 1988	5 Exploring
Oct 28 1987	9 Healing	Jan 6 1988	1 Planting	Mar 16 1988	6 Healing
Oct 29 1987	10 Seeing	Jan 7 1988	2 Moving	Mar 17 1988	7 Seeing
Oct 30 1987	11 Intuiting	Jan 8 1988	3 Transcending	Mar 18 1988	8 Intuiting
Oct 31 1987	12 Evolving	Jan 9 1988	4 Remembering	Mar 19 1988	9 Evolving
Nov 1 1987	13 Self-Regulating	Jan 10 1988	5 Loving	Mar 20 1988	10 Self-Regulating
Nov 2 1987	1 Catalyzing	Jan 11 1988	6 Feeling	Mar 21 1988	11 Catalyzing
Nov 3 1987	2 Enlightening	Jan 12 1988	7 Devoting	Mar 22 1988	12 Enlightening

Date	UE	Earth Energy	Date	UE	Earth Energy	Date	UE	Earth Energy
Mar 23 1988	13	Being	Jun 1 1988	5	Illuminating	Aug 10 1988	10	Being
Mar 24 1988	**1**	**Breathing**	Jun 2 1988	6	Choosing	Aug 11 1988	11	Breathing
Mar 25 1988	2	Listening	Jun 3 1988	7	Exploring	Aug 12 1988	12	Listening
Mar 26 1988	3	Planting	Jun 4 1988	8	Healing	Aug 13 1988	13	Planting
Mar 27 1988	4	Moving	Jun 5 1988	9	Seeing	Aug 14 1988	**1**	**Moving**
Mar 28 1988	5	Transcending	Jun 6 1988	10	Intuiting	Aug 15 1988	2	Transcending
Mar 29 1988	6	Remembering	Jun 7 1988	11	Evolving	Aug 16 1988	3	Remembering
Mar 30 1988	7	Loving	Jun 8 1988	12	Self-Regulating	Aug 17 1988	4	Loving
Mar 31 1988	8	Feeling	Jun 9 1988	13	Catalyzing	Aug 18 1988	5	Feeling
Apr 1 1988	9	Devoting	Jun 10 1988	**1**	**Enlightening**	Aug 19 1988	6	Devoting
Apr 2 1988	10	Illuminating	Jun 11 1988	2	Being	Aug 20 1988	7	Illuminating
Apr 3 1988	11	Choosing	Jun 12 1988	3	Breathing	Aug 21 1988	8	Choosing
Apr 4 1988	12	Exploring	Jun 13 1988	4	Listening	Aug 22 1988	9	Exploring
Apr 5 1988	13	Healing	Jun 14 1988	5	Planting	Aug 23 1988	10	Healing
Apr 6 1988	**1**	**Seeing**	Jun 15 1988	6	Moving	Aug 24 1988	11	Seeing
Apr 7 1988	2	Intuiting	Jun 16 1988	7	Transcending	Aug 25 1988	12	Intuiting
Apr 8 1988	3	Evolving	Jun 17 1988	8	Remembering	Aug 26 1988	13	Evolving
Apr 9 1988	4	Self-Regulating	Jun 18 1988	9	Loving	Aug 27 1988	**1**	**Self-Regulating**
Apr 10 1988	5	Catalyzing	Jun 19 1988	10	Feeling	Aug 28 1988	2	Catalyzing
Apr 11 1988	6	Enlightening	Jun 20 1988	11	Devoting	Aug 29 1988	3	Enlightening
Apr 12 1988	7	Being	Jun 21 1988	12	Illuminating	Aug 30 1988	4	Being
Apr 13 1988	8	Breathing	Jun 22 1988	13	Choosing	Aug 31 1988	5	Breathing
Apr 14 1988	9	Listening	Jun 23 1988	**1**	**Exploring**	Sep 1 1988	6	Listening
Apr 15 1988	10	Planting	Jun 24 1988	2	Healing	Sep 2 1988	7	Planting
Apr 16 1988	11	Moving	Jun 25 1988	3	Seeing	Sep 3 1988	8	Moving
Apr 17 1988	12	Transcending	Jun 26 1988	4	Intuiting	Sep 4 1988	9	Transcending
Apr 18 1988	13	Remembering	Jun 27 1988	5	Evolving	Sep 5 1988	10	Remembering
Apr 19 1988	**1**	**Loving**	Jun 28 1988	6	Self-Regulating	Sep 6 1988	11	Loving
Apr 20 1988	2	Feeling	Jun 29 1988	7	Catalyzing	Sep 7 1988	12	Feeling
Apr 21 1988	3	Devoting	Jun 30 1988	8	Enlightening	Sep 8 1988	13	Devoting
Apr 22 1988	4	Illuminating	Jul 1 1988	9	Being	Sep 9 1988	**1**	**Illuminating**
Apr 23 1988	5	Choosing	Jul 2 1988	10	Breathing	Sep 10 1988	2	Choosing
Apr 24 1988	6	Exploring	Jul 3 1988	11	Listening	Sep 11 1988	3	Exploring
Apr 25 1988	7	Healing	Jul 4 1988	12	Planting	Sep 12 1988	4	Healing
Apr 26 1988	8	Seeing	Jul 5 1988	13	Moving	Sep 13 1988	5	Seeing
Apr 27 1988	9	Intuiting	Jul 6 1988	**1**	**Transcending**	Sep 14 1988	6	Intuiting
Apr 28 1988	10	Evolving	Jul 7 1988	2	Remembering	Sep 15 1988	7	Evolving
Apr 29 1988	11	Self-Regulating	Jul 8 1988	3	Loving	Sep 16 1988	8	Self-Regulating
Apr 30 1988	12	Catalyzing	Jul 9 1988	4	Feeling	Sep 17 1988	9	Catalyzing
May 1 1988	13	Enlightening	Jul 10 1988	5	Devoting	Sep 18 1988	10	Enlightening
May 2 1988	**1**	**Being**	Jul 11 1988	6	Illuminating	Sep 19 1988	11	Being
May 3 1988	2	Breathing	Jul 12 1988	7	Choosing	Sep 20 1988	12	Breathing
May 4 1988	3	Listening	Jul 13 1988	8	Exploring	Sep 21 1988	13	Listening
May 5 1988	4	Planting	Jul 14 1988	9	Healing	Sep 22 1988	**1**	**Planting**
May 6 1988	5	Moving	Jul 15 1988	10	Seeing	Sep 23 1988	2	Moving
May 7 1988	6	Transcending	Jul 16 1988	11	Intuiting	Sep 24 1988	3	Transcending
May 8 1988	7	Remembering	Jul 17 1988	12	Evolving	Sep 25 1988	4	Remembering
May 9 1988	8	Loving	Jul 18 1988	13	Self-Regulating	Sep 26 1988	5	Loving
May 10 1988	9	Feeling	Jul 19 1988	**1**	**Catalyzing**	Sep 27 1988	6	Feeling
May 11 1988	10	Devoting	Jul 20 1988	2	Enlightening	Sep 28 1988	7	Devoting
May 12 1988	11	Illuminating	Jul 21 1988	3	Being	Sep 29 1988	8	Illuminating
May 13 1988	12	Choosing	Jul 22 1988	4	Breathing	Sep 30 1988	9	Choosing
May 14 1988	13	Exploring	Jul 23 1988	5	Listening	Oct 1 1988	10	Exploring
May 15 1988	**1**	**Healing**	Jul 24 1988	6	Planting	Oct 2 1988	11	Healing
May 16 1988	2	Seeing	Jul 25 1988	7	Moving	Oct 3 1988	12	Seeing
May 17 1988	3	Intuiting	Jul 26 1988	8	Transcending	Oct 4 1988	13	Intuiting
May 18 1988	4	Evolving	Jul 27 1988	9	Remembering	Oct 5 1988	**1**	**Evolving**
May 19 1988	5	Self-Regulating	Jul 28 1988	10	Loving	Oct 6 1988	2	Self-Regulating
May 20 1988	6	Catalyzing	Jul 29 1988	11	Feeling	Oct 7 1988	3	Catalyzing
May 21 1988	7	Enlightening	Jul 30 1988	12	Devoting	Oct 8 1988	4	Enlightening
May 22 1988	8	Being	Jul 31 1988	13	Illuminating	Oct 9 1988	5	Being
May 23 1988	9	Breathing	Aug 1 1988	**1**	**Choosing**	Oct 10 1988	6	Breathing
May 24 1988	10	Listening	Aug 2 1988	2	Exploring	Oct 11 1988	7	Listening
May 25 1988	11	Planting	Aug 3 1988	3	Healing	Oct 12 1988	8	Planting
May 26 1988	12	Moving	Aug 4 1988	4	Seeing	Oct 13 1988	9	Moving
May 27 1988	13	Transcending	Aug 5 1988	5	Intuiting	Oct 14 1988	10	Transcending
May 28 1988	**1**	**Remembering**	Aug 6 1988	6	Evolving	Oct 15 1988	11	Remembering
May 29 1988	2	Loving	Aug 7 1988	7	Self-Regulating	Oct 16 1988	12	Loving
May 30 1988	3	Feeling	Aug 8 1988	8	Catalyzing	Oct 17 1988	13	Feeling
May 31 1988	4	Devoting	Aug 9 1988	9	Enlightening	Oct 18 1988	**1**	**Devoting**

Date	UE	Earth Energy	Date	UE	Earth Energy	Date	UE	Earth Energy
Oct 19 1988	2	Illuminating	Dec 28 1988	7	Being	Mar 8 1989	12	Illuminating
Oct 20 1988	3	Choosing	Dec 29 1988	8	Breathing	Mar 9 1989	13	Choosing
Oct 21 1988	4	Exploring	Dec 30 1988	9	Listening	Mar 10 1989	1	Exploring
Oct 22 1988	5	Healing	Dec 31 1988	10	Planting	Mar 11 1989	2	Healing
Oct 23 1988	6	Seeing	Jan 1 1989	11	Moving	Mar 12 1989	3	Seeing
Oct 24 1988	7	Intuiting	Jan 2 1989	12	Transcending	Mar 13 1989	4	Intuiting
Oct 25 1988	8	Evolving	Jan 3 1989	13	Remembering	Mar 14 1989	5	Evolving
Oct 26 1988	9	Self-Regulating	Jan 4 1989	1	Loving	Mar 15 1989	6	Self-Regulating
Oct 27 1988	10	Catalyzing	Jan 5 1989	2	Feeling	Mar 16 1989	7	Catalyzing
Oct 28 1988	11	Enlightening	Jan 6 1989	3	Devoting	Mar 17 1989	8	Enlightening
Oct 29 1988	12	Being	Jan 7 1989	4	Illuminating	Mar 18 1989	9	Being
Oct 30 1988	13	Breathing	Jan 8 1989	5	Choosing	Mar 19 1989	10	Breathing
Oct 31 1988	1	Listening	Jan 9 1989	6	Exploring	Mar 20 1989	11	Listening
Nov 1 1988	2	Planting	Jan 10 1989	7	Healing	Mar 21 1989	12	Planting
Nov 2 1988	3	Moving	Jan 11 1989	8	Seeing	Mar 22 1989	13	Moving
Nov 3 1988	4	Transcending	Jan 12 1989	9	Intuiting	Mar 23 1989	1	Transcending
Nov 4 1988	5	Remembering	Jan 13 1989	10	Evolving	Mar 24 1989	2	Remembering
Nov 5 1988	6	Loving	Jan 14 1989	11	Self-Regulating	Mar 25 1989	3	Loving
Nov 6 1988	7	Feeling	Jan 15 1989	12	Catalyzing	Mar 26 1989	4	Feeling
Nov 7 1988	8	Devoting	Jan 16 1989	13	Enlightening	Mar 27 1989	5	Devoting
Nov 8 1988	9	Illuminating	Jan 17 1989	1	Being	Mar 28 1989	6	Illuminating
Nov 9 1988	10	Choosing	Jan 18 1989	2	Breathing	Mar 29 1989	7	Choosing
Nov 10 1988	11	Exploring	Jan 19 1989	3	Listening	Mar 30 1989	8	Exploring
Nov 11 1988	12	Healing	Jan 20 1989	4	Planting	Mar 31 1989	9	Healing
Nov 12 1988	13	Seeing	Jan 21 1989	5	Moving	Apr 1 1989	10	Seeing
Nov 13 1988	1	Intuiting	Jan 22 1989	6	Transcending	Apr 2 1989	11	Intuiting
Nov 14 1988	2	Evolving	Jan 23 1989	7	Remembering	Apr 3 1989	12	Evolving
Nov 15 1988	3	Self-Regulating	Jan 24 1989	8	Loving	Apr 4 1989	13	Self-Regulating
Nov 16 1988	4	Catalyzing	Jan 25 1989	9	Feeling	Apr 5 1989	1	Catalyzing
Nov 17 1988	5	Enlightening	Jan 26 1989	10	Devoting	Apr 6 1989	2	Enlightening
Nov 18 1988	6	Being	Jan 27 1989	11	Illuminating	Apr 7 1989	3	Being
Nov 19 1988	7	Breathing	Jan 28 1989	12	Choosing	Apr 8 1989	4	Breathing
Nov 20 1988	8	Listening	Jan 29 1989	13	Exploring	Apr 9 1989	5	Listening
Nov 21 1988	9	Planting	Jan 30 1989	1	Healing	Apr 10 1989	6	Planting
Nov 22 1988	10	Moving	Jan 31 1989	2	Seeing	Apr 11 1989	7	Moving
Nov 23 1988	11	Transcending	Feb 1 1989	3	Intuiting	Apr 12 1989	8	Transcending
Nov 24 1988	12	Remembering	Feb 2 1989	4	Evolving	Apr 13 1989	9	Remembering
Nov 25 1988	13	Loving	Feb 3 1989	5	Self-Regulating	Apr 14 1989	10	Loving
Nov 26 1988	1	Feeling	Feb 4 1989	6	Catalyzing	Apr 15 1989	11	Feeling
Nov 27 1988	2	Devoting	Feb 5 1989	7	Enlightening	Apr 16 1989	12	Devoting
Nov 28 1988	3	Illuminating	Feb 6 1989	8	Being	Apr 17 1989	13	Illuminating
Nov 29 1988	4	Choosing	Feb 7 1989	9	Breathing	Apr 18 1989	1	Choosing
Nov 30 1988	5	Exploring	Feb 8 1989	10	Listening	Apr 19 1989	2	Exploring
Dec 1 1988	6	Healing	Feb 9 1989	11	Planting	Apr 20 1989	3	Healing
Dec 2 1988	7	Seeing	Feb 10 1989	12	Moving	Apr 21 1989	4	Seeing
Dec 3 1988	8	Intuiting	Feb 11 1989	13	Transcending	Apr 22 1989	5	Intuiting
Dec 4 1988	9	Evolving	Feb 12 1989	1	Remembering	Apr 23 1989	6	Evolving
Dec 5 1988	10	Self-Regulating	Feb 13 1989	2	Loving	Apr 24 1989	7	Self-Regulating
Dec 6 1988	11	Catalyzing	Feb 14 1989	3	Feeling	Apr 25 1989	8	Catalyzing
Dec 7 1988	12	Enlightening	Feb 15 1989	4	Devoting	Apr 26 1989	9	Enlightening
Dec 8 1988	13	Being	Feb 16 1989	5	Illuminating	Apr 27 1989	10	Being
Dec 9 1988	1	Breathing	Feb 17 1989	6	Choosing	Apr 28 1989	11	Breathing
Dec 10 1988	2	Listening	Feb 18 1989	7	Exploring	Apr 29 1989	12	Listening
Dec 11 1988	3	Planting	Feb 19 1989	8	Healing	Apr 30 1989	13	Planting
Dec 12 1988	4	Moving	Feb 20 1989	9	Seeing	May 1 1989	1	Moving
Dec 13 1988	5	Transcending	Feb 21 1989	10	Intuiting	May 2 1989	2	Transcending
Dec 14 1988	6	Remembering	Feb 22 1989	11	Evolving	May 3 1989	3	Remembering
Dec 15 1988	7	Loving	Feb 23 1989	12	Self-Regulating	May 4 1989	4	Loving
Dec 16 1988	8	Feeling	Feb 24 1989	13	Catalyzing	May 5 1989	5	Feeling
Dec 17 1988	9	Devoting	Feb 25 1989	1	Enlightening	May 6 1989	6	Devoting
Dec 18 1988	10	Illuminating	Feb 26 1989	2	Being	May 7 1989	7	Illuminating
Dec 19 1988	11	Choosing	Feb 27 1989	3	Breathing	May 8 1989	8	Choosing
Dec 20 1988	12	Exploring	Feb 28 1989	4	Listening	May 9 1989	9	Exploring
Dec 21 1988	13	Healing	Mar 1 1989	5	Planting	May 10 1989	10	Healing
Dec 22 1988	1	Seeing	Mar 2 1989	6	Moving	May 11 1989	11	Seeing
Dec 23 1988	2	Intuiting	Mar 3 1989	7	Transcending	May 12 1989	12	Intuiting
Dec 24 1988	3	Evolving	Mar 4 1989	8	Remembering	May 13 1989	13	Evolving
Dec 25 1988	4	Self-Regulating	Mar 5 1989	9	Loving	May 14 1989	1	Self-Regulating
Dec 26 1988	5	Catalyzing	Mar 6 1989	10	Feeling	May 15 1989	2	Catalyzing
Dec 27 1988	6	Enlightening	Mar 7 1989	11	Devoting	May 16 1989	3	Enlightening

Date	UE	Earth Energy	Date	UE	Earth Energy	Date	UE	Earth Energy
May 17 1989	4	Being	Jul 26 1989	9	Illuminating	Oct 4 1989	1	Being
May 18 1989	5	Breathing	Jul 27 1989	10	Choosing	Oct 5 1989	2	Breathing
May 19 1989	6	Listening	Jul 28 1989	11	Exploring	Oct 6 1989	3	Listening
May 20 1989	7	Planting	Jul 29 1989	12	Healing	Oct 7 1989	4	Planting
May 21 1989	8	Moving	Jul 30 1989	13	Seeing	Oct 8 1989	5	Moving
May 22 1989	9	Transcending	Jul 31 1989	1	Intuiting	Oct 9 1989	6	Transcending
May 23 1989	10	Remembering	Aug 1 1989	2	Evolving	Oct 10 1989	7	Remembering
May 24 1989	11	Loving	Aug 2 1989	3	Self-Regulating	Oct 11 1989	8	Loving
May 25 1989	12	Feeling	Aug 3 1989	4	Catalyzing	Oct 12 1989	9	Feeling
May 26 1989	13	Devoting	Aug 4 1989	5	Enlightening	Oct 13 1989	10	Devoting
May 27 1989	1	Illuminating	Aug 5 1989	6	Being	Oct 14 1989	11	Illuminating
May 28 1989	2	Choosing	Aug 6 1989	7	Breathing	Oct 15 1989	12	Choosing
May 29 1989	3	Exploring	Aug 7 1989	8	Listening	Oct 16 1989	13	Exploring
May 30 1989	4	Healing	Aug 8 1989	9	Planting	Oct 17 1989	1	Healing
May 31 1989	5	Seeing	Aug 9 1989	10	Moving	Oct 18 1989	2	Seeing
Jun 1 1989	6	Intuiting	Aug 10 1989	11	Transcending	Oct 19 1989	3	Intuiting
Jun 2 1989	7	Evolving	Aug 11 1989	12	Remembering	Oct 20 1989	4	Evolving
Jun 3 1989	8	Self-Regulating	Aug 12 1989	13	Loving	Oct 21 1989	5	Self-Regulating
Jun 4 1989	9	Catalyzing	Aug 13 1989	1	Feeling	Oct 22 1989	6	Catalyzing
Jun 5 1989	10	Enlightening	Aug 14 1989	2	Devoting	Oct 23 1989	7	Enlightening
Jun 6 1989	11	Being	Aug 15 1989	3	Illuminating	Oct 24 1989	8	Being
Jun 7 1989	12	Breathing	Aug 16 1989	4	Choosing	Oct 25 1989	9	Breathing
Jun 8 1989	13	Listening	Aug 17 1989	5	Exploring	Oct 26 1989	10	Listening
Jun 9 1989	1	Planting	Aug 18 1989	6	Healing	Oct 27 1989	11	Planting
Jun 10 1989	2	Moving	Aug 19 1989	7	Seeing	Oct 28 1989	12	Moving
Jun 11 1989	3	Transcending	Aug 20 1989	8	Intuiting	Oct 29 1989	13	Transcending
Jun 12 1989	4	Remembering	Aug 21 1989	9	Evolving	Oct 30 1989	1	Remembering
Jun 13 1989	5	Loving	Aug 22 1989	10	Self-Regulating	Oct 31 1989	2	Loving
Jun 14 1989	6	Feeling	Aug 23 1989	11	Catalyzing	Nov 1 1989	3	Feeling
Jun 15 1989	7	Devoting	Aug 24 1989	12	Enlightening	Nov 2 1989	4	Devoting
Jun 16 1989	8	Illuminating	Aug 25 1989	13	Being	Nov 3 1989	5	Illuminating
Jun 17 1989	9	Choosing	Aug 26 1989	1	Breathing	Nov 4 1989	6	Choosing
Jun 18 1989	10	Exploring	Aug 27 1989	2	Listening	Nov 5 1989	7	Exploring
Jun 19 1989	11	Healing	Aug 28 1989	3	Planting	Nov 6 1989	8	Healing
Jun 20 1989	12	Seeing	Aug 29 1989	4	Moving	Nov 7 1989	9	Seeing
Jun 21 1989	13	Intuiting	Aug 30 1989	5	Transcending	Nov 8 1989	10	Intuiting
Jun 22 1989	1	Evolving	Aug 31 1989	6	Remembering	Nov 9 1989	11	Evolving
Jun 23 1989	2	Self-Regulating	Sep 1 1989	7	Loving	Nov 10 1989	12	Self-Regulating
Jun 24 1989	3	Catalyzing	Sep 2 1989	8	Feeling	Nov 11 1989	13	Catalyzing
Jun 25 1989	4	Enlightening	Sep 3 1989	9	Devoting	Nov 12 1989	1	Enlightening
Jun 26 1989	5	Being	Sep 4 1989	10	Illuminating	Nov 13 1989	2	Being
Jun 27 1989	6	Breathing	Sep 5 1989	11	Choosing	Nov 14 1989	3	Breathing
Jun 28 1989	7	Listening	Sep 6 1989	12	Exploring	Nov 15 1989	4	Listening
Jun 29 1989	8	Planting	Sep 7 1989	13	Healing	Nov 16 1989	5	Planting
Jun 30 1989	9	Moving	Sep 8 1989	1	Seeing	Nov 17 1989	6	Moving
Jul 1 1989	10	Transcending	Sep 9 1989	2	Intuiting	Nov 18 1989	7	Transcending
Jul 2 1989	11	Remembering	Sep 10 1989	3	Evolving	Nov 19 1989	8	Remembering
Jul 3 1989	12	Loving	Sep 11 1989	4	Self-Regulating	Nov 20 1989	9	Loving
Jul 4 1989	13	Feeling	Sep 12 1989	5	Catalyzing	Nov 21 1989	10	Feeling
Jul 5 1989	1	Devoting	Sep 13 1989	6	Enlightening	Nov 22 1989	11	Devoting
Jul 6 1989	2	Illuminating	Sep 14 1989	7	Being	Nov 23 1989	12	Illuminating
Jul 7 1989	3	Choosing	Sep 15 1989	8	Breathing	Nov 24 1989	13	Choosing
Jul 8 1989	4	Exploring	Sep 16 1989	9	Listening	Nov 25 1989	1	Exploring
Jul 9 1989	5	Healing	Sep 17 1989	10	Planting	Nov 26 1989	2	Healing
Jul 10 1989	6	Seeing	Sep 18 1989	11	Moving	Nov 27 1989	3	Seeing
Jul 11 1989	7	Intuiting	Sep 19 1989	12	Transcending	Nov 28 1989	4	Intuiting
Jul 12 1989	8	Evolving	Sep 20 1989	13	Remembering	Nov 29 1989	5	Evolving
Jul 13 1989	9	Self-Regulating	Sep 21 1989	1	Loving	Nov 30 1989	6	Self-Regulating
Jul 14 1989	10	Catalyzing	Sep 22 1989	2	Feeling	Dec 1 1989	7	Catalyzing
Jul 15 1989	11	Enlightening	Sep 23 1989	3	Devoting	Dec 2 1989	8	Enlightening
Jul 16 1989	12	Being	Sep 24 1989	4	Illuminating	Dec 3 1989	9	Being
Jul 17 1989	13	Breathing	Sep 25 1989	5	Choosing	Dec 4 1989	10	Breathing
Jul 18 1989	1	Listening	Sep 26 1989	6	Exploring	Dec 5 1989	11	Listening
Jul 19 1989	2	Planting	Sep 27 1989	7	Healing	Dec 6 1989	12	Planting
Jul 20 1989	3	Moving	Sep 28 1989	8	Seeing	Dec 7 1989	13	Moving
Jul 21 1989	4	Transcending	Sep 29 1989	9	Intuiting	Dec 8 1989	1	Transcending
Jul 22 1989	5	Remembering	Sep 30 1989	10	Evolving	Dec 9 1989	2	Remembering
Jul 23 1989	6	Loving	Oct 1 1989	11	Self-Regulating	Dec 10 1989	3	Loving
Jul 24 1989	7	Feeling	Oct 2 1989	12	Catalyzing	Dec 11 1989	4	Feeling
Jul 25 1989	8	Devoting	Oct 3 1989	13	Enlightening	Dec 12 1989	5	Devoting

Date	UE	Earth Energy	Date	UE	Earth Energy	Date	UE	Earth Energy
Dec 13 1989	6	Illuminating	Feb 21 1990	11	Being	May 2 1990	3	Illuminating
Dec 14 1989	7	Choosing	Feb 22 1990	12	Breathing	May 3 1990	4	Choosing
Dec 15 1989	8	Exploring	Feb 23 1990	13	Listening	May 4 1990	5	Exploring
Dec 16 1989	9	Healing	Feb 24 1990	**1**	**Planting**	May 5 1990	6	Healing
Dec 17 1989	10	Seeing	Feb 25 1990	2	Moving	May 6 1990	7	Seeing
Dec 18 1989	11	Intuiting	Feb 26 1990	3	Transcending	May 7 1990	8	Intuiting
Dec 19 1989	12	Evolving	Feb 27 1990	4	Remembering	May 8 1990	9	Evolving
Dec 20 1989	13	Self-Regulating	Feb 28 1990	5	Loving	May 9 1990	10	Self-Regulating
Dec 21 1989	**1**	**Catalyzing**	Mar 1 1990	6	Feeling	May 10 1990	11	Catalyzing
Dec 22 1989	2	Enlightening	Mar 2 1990	7	Devoting	May 11 1990	12	Enlightening
Dec 23 1989	3	Being	Mar 3 1990	8	Illuminating	May 12 1990	13	Being
Dec 24 1989	4	Breathing	Mar 4 1990	9	Choosing	May 13 1990	**1**	**Breathing**
Dec 25 1989	5	Listening	Mar 5 1990	10	Exploring	May 14 1990	2	Listening
Dec 26 1989	6	Planting	Mar 6 1990	11	Healing	May 15 1990	3	Planting
Dec 27 1989	7	Moving	Mar 7 1990	12	Seeing	May 16 1990	4	Moving
Dec 28 1989	8	Transcending	Mar 8 1990	13	Intuiting	May 17 1990	5	Transcending
Dec 29 1989	9	Remembering	Mar 9 1990	**1**	**Evolving**	May 18 1990	6	Remembering
Dec 30 1989	10	Loving	Mar 10 1990	2	Self-Regulating	May 19 1990	7	Loving
Dec 31 1989	11	Feeling	Mar 11 1990	3	Catalyzing	May 20 1990	8	Feeling
Jan 1 1990	12	Devoting	Mar 12 1990	4	Enlightening	May 21 1990	9	Devoting
Jan 2 1990	13	Illuminating	Mar 13 1990	5	Being	May 22 1990	10	Illuminating
Jan 3 1990	**1**	**Choosing**	Mar 14 1990	6	Breathing	May 23 1990	11	Choosing
Jan 4 1990	2	Exploring	Mar 15 1990	7	Listening	May 24 1990	12	Exploring
Jan 5 1990	3	Healing	Mar 16 1990	8	Planting	May 25 1990	13	Healing
Jan 6 1990	4	Seeing	Mar 17 1990	9	Moving	May 26 1990	**1**	**Seeing**
Jan 7 1990	5	Intuiting	Mar 18 1990	10	Transcending	May 27 1990	2	Intuiting
Jan 8 1990	6	Evolving	Mar 19 1990	11	Remembering	May 28 1990	3	Evolving
Jan 9 1990	7	Self-Regulating	Mar 20 1990	12	Loving	May 29 1990	4	Self-Regulating
Jan 10 1990	8	Catalyzing	Mar 21 1990	13	Feeling	May 30 1990	5	Catalyzing
Jan 11 1990	9	Enlightening	Mar 22 1990	**1**	**Devoting**	May 31 1990	6	Enlightening
Jan 12 1990	10	Being	Mar 23 1990	2	Illuminating	Jun 1 1990	7	Being
Jan 13 1990	11	Breathing	Mar 24 1990	3	Choosing	Jun 2 1990	8	Breathing
Jan 14 1990	12	Listening	Mar 25 1990	4	Exploring	Jun 3 1990	9	Listening
Jan 15 1990	13	Planting	Mar 26 1990	5	Healing	Jun 4 1990	10	Planting
Jan 16 1990	**1**	**Moving**	Mar 27 1990	6	Seeing	Jun 5 1990	11	Moving
Jan 17 1990	2	Transcending	Mar 28 1990	7	Intuiting	Jun 6 1990	12	Transcending
Jan 18 1990	3	Remembering	Mar 29 1990	8	Evolving	Jun 7 1990	13	Remembering
Jan 19 1990	4	Loving	Mar 30 1990	9	Self-Regulating	Jun 8 1990	**1**	**Loving**
Jan 20 1990	5	Feeling	Mar 31 1990	10	Catalyzing	Jun 9 1990	2	Feeling
Jan 21 1990	6	Devoting	Apr 1 1990	11	Enlightening	Jun 10 1990	3	Devoting
Jan 22 1990	7	Illuminating	Apr 2 1990	12	Being	Jun 11 1990	4	Illuminating
Jan 23 1990	8	Choosing	Apr 3 1990	13	Breathing	Jun 12 1990	5	Choosing
Jan 24 1990	9	Exploring	Apr 4 1990	**1**	**Listening**	Jun 13 1990	6	Exploring
Jan 25 1990	10	Healing	Apr 5 1990	2	Planting	Jun 14 1990	7	Healing
Jan 26 1990	11	Seeing	Apr 6 1990	3	Moving	Jun 15 1990	8	Seeing
Jan 27 1990	12	Intuiting	Apr 7 1990	4	Transcending	Jun 16 1990	9	Intuiting
Jan 28 1990	13	Evolving	Apr 8 1990	5	Remembering	Jun 17 1990	10	Evolving
Jan 29 1990	**1**	**Self-Regulating**	Apr 9 1990	6	Loving	Jun 18 1990	11	Self-Regulating
Jan 30 1990	2	Catalyzing	Apr 10 1990	7	Feeling	Jun 19 1990	12	Catalyzing
Jan 31 1990	3	Enlightening	Apr 11 1990	8	Devoting	Jun 20 1990	13	Enlightening
Feb 1 1990	4	Being	Apr 12 1990	9	Illuminating	Jun 21 1990	**1**	**Being**
Feb 2 1990	5	Breathing	Apr 13 1990	10	Choosing	Jun 22 1990	2	Breathing
Feb 3 1990	6	Listening	Apr 14 1990	11	Exploring	Jun 23 1990	3	Listening
Feb 4 1990	7	Planting	Apr 15 1990	12	Healing	Jun 24 1990	4	Planting
Feb 5 1990	8	Moving	Apr 16 1990	13	Seeing	Jun 25 1990	5	Moving
Feb 6 1990	9	Transcending	Apr 17 1990	**1**	**Intuiting**	Jun 26 1990	6	Transcending
Feb 7 1990	10	Remembering	Apr 18 1990	2	Evolving	Jun 27 1990	7	Remembering
Feb 8 1990	11	Loving	Apr 19 1990	3	Self-Regulating	Jun 28 1990	8	Loving
Feb 9 1990	12	Feeling	Apr 20 1990	4	Catalyzing	Jun 29 1990	9	Feeling
Feb 10 1990	13	Devoting	Apr 21 1990	5	Enlightening	Jun 30 1990	10	Devoting
Feb 11 1990	**1**	**Illuminating**	Apr 22 1990	6	Being	Jul 1 1990	11	Illuminating
Feb 12 1990	2	Choosing	Apr 23 1990	7	Breathing	Jul 2 1990	12	Choosing
Feb 13 1990	3	Exploring	Apr 24 1990	8	Listening	Jul 3 1990	13	Exploring
Feb 14 1990	4	Healing	Apr 25 1990	9	Planting	Jul 4 1990	**1**	**Healing**
Feb 15 1990	5	Seeing	Apr 26 1990	10	Moving	Jul 5 1990	2	Seeing
Feb 16 1990	6	Intuiting	Apr 27 1990	11	Transcending	Jul 6 1990	3	Intuiting
Feb 17 1990	7	Evolving	Apr 28 1990	12	Remembering	Jul 7 1990	4	Evolving
Feb 18 1990	8	Self-Regulating	Apr 29 1990	13	Loving	Jul 8 1990	5	Self-Regulating
Feb 19 1990	9	Catalyzing	Apr 30 1990	**1**	**Feeling**	Jul 9 1990	6	Catalyzing
Feb 20 1990	10	Enlightening	May 1 1990	2	Devoting	Jul 10 1990	7	Enlightening

Date	UE	Earth Energy
Jul 11 1990	8	Being
Jul 12 1990	9	Breathing
Jul 13 1990	10	Listening
Jul 14 1990	11	Planting
Jul 15 1990	12	Moving
Jul 16 1990	13	Transcending
Jul 17 1990	**1**	**Remembering**
Jul 18 1990	2	Loving
Jul 19 1990	3	Feeling
Jul 20 1990	4	Devoting
Jul 21 1990	5	Illuminating
Jul 22 1990	6	Choosing
Jul 23 1990	7	Exploring
Jul 24 1990	8	Healing
Jul 25 1990	9	Seeing
Jul 26 1990	10	Intuiting
Jul 27 1990	11	Evolving
Jul 28 1990	12	Self-Regulating
Jul 29 1990	13	Catalyzing
Jul 30 1990	**1**	**Enlightening**
Jul 31 1990	2	Being
Aug 1 1990	3	Breathing
Aug 2 1990	4	Listening
Aug 3 1990	5	Planting
Aug 4 1990	6	Moving
Aug 5 1990	7	Transcending
Aug 6 1990	8	Remembering
Aug 7 1990	9	Loving
Aug 8 1990	10	Feeling
Aug 9 1990	11	Devoting
Aug 10 1990	12	Illuminating
Aug 11 1990	13	Choosing
Aug 12 1990	**1**	**Exploring**
Aug 13 1990	2	Healing
Aug 14 1990	3	Seeing
Aug 15 1990	4	Intuiting
Aug 16 1990	5	Evolving
Aug 17 1990	6	Self-Regulating
Aug 18 1990	7	Catalyzing
Aug 19 1990	8	Enlightening
Aug 20 1990	9	Being
Aug 21 1990	10	Breathing
Aug 22 1990	11	Listening
Aug 23 1990	12	Planting
Aug 24 1990	13	Moving
Aug 25 1990	**1**	**Transcending**
Aug 26 1990	2	Remembering
Aug 27 1990	3	Loving
Aug 28 1990	4	Feeling
Aug 29 1990	5	Devoting
Aug 30 1990	6	Illuminating
Aug 31 1990	7	Choosing
Sep 1 1990	8	Exploring
Sep 2 1990	9	Healing
Sep 3 1990	10	Seeing
Sep 4 1990	11	Intuiting
Sep 5 1990	12	Evolving
Sep 6 1990	13	Self-Regulating
Sep 7 1990	**1**	**Catalyzing**
Sep 8 1990	2	Enlightening
Sep 9 1990	3	Being
Sep 10 1990	4	Breathing
Sep 11 1990	5	Listening
Sep 12 1990	6	Planting
Sep 13 1990	7	Moving
Sep 14 1990	8	Transcending
Sep 15 1990	9	Remembering
Sep 16 1990	10	Loving
Sep 17 1990	11	Feeling
Sep 18 1990	12	Devoting

Date	UE	Earth Energy
Sep 19 1990	13	Illuminating
Sep 20 1990	**1**	**Choosing**
Sep 21 1990	2	Exploring
Sep 22 1990	3	Healing
Sep 23 1990	4	Seeing
Sep 24 1990	5	Intuiting
Sep 25 1990	6	Evolving
Sep 26 1990	7	Self-Regulating
Sep 27 1990	8	Catalyzing
Sep 28 1990	9	Enlightening
Sep 29 1990	10	Being
Sep 30 1990	11	Breathing
Oct 1 1990	12	Listening
Oct 2 1990	13	Planting
Oct 3 1990	**1**	**Moving**
Oct 4 1990	2	Transcending
Oct 5 1990	3	Remembering
Oct 6 1990	4	Loving
Oct 7 1990	5	Feeling
Oct 8 1990	6	Devoting
Oct 9 1990	7	Illuminating
Oct 10 1990	8	Choosing
Oct 11 1990	9	Exploring
Oct 12 1990	10	Healing
Oct 13 1990	11	Seeing
Oct 14 1990	12	Intuiting
Oct 15 1990	13	Evolving
Oct 16 1990	**1**	**Self-Regulating**
Oct 17 1990	2	Catalyzing
Oct 18 1990	3	Enlightening
Oct 19 1990	4	Being
Oct 20 1990	5	Breathing
Oct 21 1990	6	Listening
Oct 22 1990	7	Planting
Oct 23 1990	8	Moving
Oct 24 1990	9	Transcending
Oct 25 1990	10	Remembering
Oct 26 1990	11	Loving
Oct 27 1990	12	Feeling
Oct 28 1990	13	Devoting
Oct 29 1990	**1**	**Illuminating**
Oct 30 1990	2	Choosing
Oct 31 1990	3	Exploring
Nov 1 1990	4	Healing
Nov 2 1990	5	Seeing
Nov 3 1990	6	Intuiting
Nov 4 1990	7	Evolving
Nov 5 1990	8	Self-Regulating
Nov 6 1990	9	Catalyzing
Nov 7 1990	10	Enlightening
Nov 8 1990	11	Being
Nov 9 1990	12	Breathing
Nov 10 1990	13	Listening
Nov 11 1990	**1**	**Planting**
Nov 12 1990	2	Moving
Nov 13 1990	3	Transcending
Nov 14 1990	4	Remembering
Nov 15 1990	5	Loving
Nov 16 1990	6	Feeling
Nov 17 1990	7	Devoting
Nov 18 1990	8	Illuminating
Nov 19 1990	9	Choosing
Nov 20 1990	10	Exploring
Nov 21 1990	11	Healing
Nov 22 1990	12	Seeing
Nov 23 1990	13	Intuiting
Nov 24 1990	**1**	**Evolving**
Nov 25 1990	2	Self-Regulating
Nov 26 1990	3	Catalyzing
Nov 27 1990	4	Enlightening

Date	UE	Earth Energy
Nov 28 1990	5	Being
Nov 29 1990	6	Breathing
Nov 30 1990	7	Listening
Dec 1 1990	8	Planting
Dec 2 1990	9	Moving
Dec 3 1990	10	Transcending
Dec 4 1990	11	Remembering
Dec 5 1990	12	Loving
Dec 6 1990	13	Feeling
Dec 7 1990	**1**	**Devoting**
Dec 8 1990	2	Illuminating
Dec 9 1990	3	Choosing
Dec 10 1990	4	Exploring
Dec 11 1990	5	Healing
Dec 12 1990	6	Seeing
Dec 13 1990	7	Intuiting
Dec 14 1990	8	Evolving
Dec 15 1990	9	Self-Regulating
Dec 16 1990	10	Catalyzing
Dec 17 1990	11	Enlightening
Dec 18 1990	12	Being
Dec 19 1990	13	Breathing
Dec 20 1990	**1**	**Listening**
Dec 21 1990	2	Planting
Dec 22 1990	3	Moving
Dec 23 1990	4	Transcending
Dec 24 1990	5	Remembering
Dec 25 1990	6	Loving
Dec 26 1990	7	Feeling
Dec 27 1990	8	Devoting
Dec 28 1990	9	Illuminating
Dec 29 1990	10	Choosing
Dec 30 1990	11	Exploring
Dec 31 1990	12	Healing
Jan 1 1991	13	Seeing
Jan 2 1991	**1**	**Intuiting**
Jan 3 1991	2	Evolving
Jan 4 1991	3	Self-Regulating
Jan 5 1991	4	Catalyzing
Jan 6 1991	5	Enlightening
Jan 7 1991	6	Being
Jan 8 1991	7	Breathing
Jan 9 1991	8	Listening
Jan 10 1991	9	Planting
Jan 11 1991	10	Moving
Jan 12 1991	11	Transcending
Jan 13 1991	12	Remembering
Jan 14 1991	13	Loving
Jan 15 1991	**1**	**Feeling**
Jan 16 1991	2	Devoting
Jan 17 1991	3	Illuminating
Jan 18 1991	4	Choosing
Jan 19 1991	5	Exploring
Jan 20 1991	6	Healing
Jan 21 1991	7	Seeing
Jan 22 1991	8	Intuiting
Jan 23 1991	9	Evolving
Jan 24 1991	10	Self-Regulating
Jan 25 1991	11	Catalyzing
Jan 26 1991	12	Enlightening
Jan 27 1991	13	Being
Jan 28 1991	**1**	**Breathing**
Jan 29 1991	2	Listening
Jan 30 1991	3	Planting
Jan 31 1991	4	Moving
Feb 1 1991	5	Transcending
Feb 2 1991	6	Remembering
Feb 3 1991	7	Loving
Feb 4 1991	8	Feeling
Feb 5 1991	9	Devoting

Date	UE	Earth Energy	Date	UE	Earth Energy	Date	UE	Earth Energy
Feb 6 1991	10	Illuminating	Apr 17 1991	2	Being	Jun 26 1991	7	Illuminating
Feb 7 1991	11	Choosing	Apr 18 1991	3	Breathing	Jun 27 1991	8	Choosing
Feb 8 1991	12	Exploring	Apr 19 1991	4	Listening	Jun 28 1991	9	Exploring
Feb 9 1991	13	Healing	Apr 20 1991	5	Planting	Jun 29 1991	10	Healing
Feb 10 1991	**1**	**Seeing**	Apr 21 1991	6	Moving	Jun 30 1991	11	Seeing
Feb 11 1991	2	Intuiting	Apr 22 1991	7	Transcending	Jul 1 1991	12	Intuiting
Feb 12 1991	3	Evolving	Apr 23 1991	8	Remembering	Jul 2 1991	13	Evolving
Feb 13 1991	4	Self-Regulating	Apr 24 1991	9	Loving	Jul 3 1991	**1**	**Self-Regulating**
Feb 14 1991	5	Catalyzing	Apr 25 1991	10	Feeling	Jul 4 1991	2	Catalyzing
Feb 15 1991	6	Enlightening	Apr 26 1991	11	Devoting	Jul 5 1991	3	Enlightening
Feb 16 1991	7	Being	Apr 27 1991	12	Illuminating	Jul 6 1991	4	Being
Feb 17 1991	8	Breathing	Apr 28 1991	13	Choosing	Jul 7 1991	5	Breathing
Feb 18 1991	9	Listening	Apr 29 1991	**1**	**Exploring**	Jul 8 1991	6	Listening
Feb 19 1991	10	Planting	Apr 30 1991	2	Healing	Jul 9 1991	7	Planting
Feb 20 1991	11	Moving	May 1 1991	3	Seeing	Jul 10 1991	8	Moving
Feb 21 1991	12	Transcending	May 2 1991	4	Intuiting	Jul 11 1991	9	Transcending
Feb 22 1991	13	Remembering	May 3 1991	5	Evolving	Jul 12 1991	10	Remembering
Feb 23 1991	**1**	**Loving**	May 4 1991	6	Self-Regulating	Jul 13 1991	11	Loving
Feb 24 1991	2	Feeling	May 5 1991	7	Catalyzing	Jul 14 1991	12	Feeling
Feb 25 1991	3	Devoting	May 6 1991	8	Enlightening	Jul 15 1991	13	Devoting
Feb 26 1991	4	Illuminating	May 7 1991	9	Being	Jul 16 1991	**1**	**Illuminating**
Feb 27 1991	5	Choosing	May 8 1991	10	Breathing	Jul 17 1991	2	Choosing
Feb 28 1991	6	Exploring	May 9 1991	11	Listening	Jul 18 1991	3	Exploring
Mar 1 1991	7	Healing	May 10 1991	12	Planting	Jul 19 1991	4	Healing
Mar 2 1991	8	Seeing	May 11 1991	13	Moving	Jul 20 1991	5	Seeing
Mar 3 1991	9	Intuiting	May 12 1991	**1**	**Transcending**	Jul 21 1991	6	Intuiting
Mar 4 1991	10	Evolving	May 13 1991	2	Remembering	Jul 22 1991	7	Evolving
Mar 5 1991	11	Self-Regulating	May 14 1991	3	Loving	Jul 23 1991	8	Self-Regulating
Mar 6 1991	12	Catalyzing	May 15 1991	4	Feeling	Jul 24 1991	9	Catalyzing
Mar 7 1991	13	Enlightening	May 16 1991	5	Devoting	Jul 25 1991	10	Enlightening
Mar 8 1991	**1**	**Being**	May 17 1991	6	Illuminating	Jul 26 1991	11	Being
Mar 9 1991	2	Breathing	May 18 1991	7	Choosing	Jul 27 1991	12	Breathing
Mar 10 1991	3	Listening	May 19 1991	8	Exploring	Jul 28 1991	13	Listening
Mar 11 1991	4	Planting	May 20 1991	9	Healing	Jul 29 1991	**1**	**Planting**
Mar 12 1991	5	Moving	May 21 1991	10	Seeing	Jul 30 1991	2	Moving
Mar 13 1991	6	Transcending	May 22 1991	11	Intuiting	Jul 31 1991	3	Transcending
Mar 14 1991	7	Remembering	May 23 1991	12	Evolving	Aug 1 1991	4	Remembering
Mar 15 1991	8	Loving	May 24 1991	13	Self-Regulating	Aug 2 1991	5	Loving
Mar 16 1991	9	Feeling	May 25 1991	**1**	**Catalyzing**	Aug 3 1991	6	Feeling
Mar 17 1991	10	Devoting	May 26 1991	2	Enlightening	Aug 4 1991	7	Devoting
Mar 18 1991	11	Illuminating	May 27 1991	3	Being	Aug 5 1991	8	Illuminating
Mar 19 1991	12	Choosing	May 28 1991	4	Breathing	Aug 6 1991	9	Choosing
Mar 20 1991	13	Exploring	May 29 1991	5	Listening	Aug 7 1991	10	Exploring
Mar 21 1991	**1**	**Healing**	May 30 1991	6	Planting	Aug 8 1991	11	Healing
Mar 22 1991	2	Seeing	May 31 1991	7	Moving	Aug 9 1991	12	Seeing
Mar 23 1991	3	Intuiting	Jun 1 1991	8	Transcending	Aug 10 1991	13	Intuiting
Mar 24 1991	4	Evolving	Jun 2 1991	9	Remembering	Aug 11 1991	**1**	**Evolving**
Mar 25 1991	5	Self-Regulating	Jun 3 1991	10	Loving	Aug 12 1991	2	Self-Regulating
Mar 26 1991	6	Catalyzing	Jun 4 1991	11	Feeling	Aug 13 1991	3	Catalyzing
Mar 27 1991	7	Enlightening	Jun 5 1991	12	Devoting	Aug 14 1991	4	Enlightening
Mar 28 1991	8	Being	Jun 6 1991	13	Illuminating	Aug 15 1991	5	Being
Mar 29 1991	9	Breathing	Jun 7 1991	**1**	**Choosing**	Aug 16 1991	6	Breathing
Mar 30 1991	10	Listening	Jun 8 1991	2	Exploring	Aug 17 1991	7	Listening
Mar 31 1991	11	Planting	Jun 9 1991	3	Healing	Aug 18 1991	8	Planting
Apr 1 1991	12	Moving	Jun 10 1991	4	Seeing	Aug 19 1991	9	Moving
Apr 2 1991	13	Transcending	Jun 11 1991	5	Intuiting	Aug 20 1991	10	Transcending
Apr 3 1991	**1**	**Remembering**	Jun 12 1991	6	Evolving	Aug 21 1991	11	Remembering
Apr 4 1991	2	Loving	Jun 13 1991	7	Self-Regulating	Aug 22 1991	12	Loving
Apr 5 1991	3	Feeling	Jun 14 1991	8	Catalyzing	Aug 23 1991	13	Feeling
Apr 6 1991	4	Devoting	Jun 15 1991	9	Enlightening	Aug 24 1991	**1**	**Devoting**
Apr 7 1991	5	Illuminating	Jun 16 1991	10	Being	Aug 25 1991	2	Illuminating
Apr 8 1991	6	Choosing	Jun 17 1991	11	Breathing	Aug 26 1991	3	Choosing
Apr 9 1991	7	Exploring	Jun 18 1991	12	Listening	Aug 27 1991	4	Exploring
Apr 10 1991	8	Healing	Jun 19 1991	13	Planting	Aug 28 1991	5	Healing
Apr 11 1991	9	Seeing	Jun 20 1991	**1**	**Moving**	Aug 29 1991	6	Seeing
Apr 12 1991	10	Intuiting	Jun 21 1991	2	Transcending	Aug 30 1991	7	Intuiting
Apr 13 1991	11	Evolving	Jun 22 1991	3	Remembering	Aug 31 1991	8	Evolving
Apr 14 1991	12	Self-Regulating	Jun 23 1991	4	Loving	Sep 1 1991	9	Self-Regulating
Apr 15 1991	13	Catalyzing	Jun 24 1991	5	Feeling	Sep 2 1991	10	Catalyzing
Apr 16 1991	**1**	**Enlightening**	Jun 25 1991	6	Devoting	Sep 3 1991	11	Enlightening

Date	UE Earth Energy	Date	UE Earth Energy	Date	UE Earth Energy
Sep 4 1991	12 Being	Nov 13 1991	4 Illuminating	Jan 22 1992	9 Being
Sep 5 1991	13 Breathing	Nov 14 1991	5 Choosing	Jan 23 1992	10 Breathing
Sep 6 1991	**1 Listening**	Nov 15 1991	6 Exploring	Jan 24 1992	11 Listening
Sep 7 1991	2 Planting	Nov 16 1991	7 Healing	Jan 25 1992	12 Planting
Sep 8 1991	3 Moving	Nov 17 1991	8 Seeing	Jan 26 1992	13 Moving
Sep 9 1991	4 Transcending	Nov 18 1991	9 Intuiting	Jan 27 1992	**1 Transcending**
Sep 10 1991	5 Remembering	Nov 19 1991	10 Evolving	Jan 28 1992	2 Remembering
Sep 11 1991	6 Loving	Nov 20 1991	11 Self-Regulating	Jan 29 1992	3 Loving
Sep 12 1991	7 Feeling	Nov 21 1991	12 Catalyzing	Jan 30 1992	4 Feeling
Sep 13 1991	8 Devoting	Nov 22 1991	13 Enlightening	Jan 31 1992	5 Devoting
Sep 14 1991	9 Illuminating	Nov 23 1991	**1 Being**	Feb 1 1992	6 Illuminating
Sep 15 1991	10 Choosing	Nov 24 1991	2 Breathing	Feb 2 1992	7 Choosing
Sep 16 1991	11 Exploring	Nov 25 1991	3 Listening	Feb 3 1992	8 Exploring
Sep 17 1991	12 Healing	Nov 26 1991	4 Planting	Feb 4 1992	9 Healing
Sep 18 1991	13 Seeing	Nov 27 1991	5 Moving	Feb 5 1992	10 Seeing
Sep 19 1991	**1 Intuiting**	Nov 28 1991	6 Transcending	Feb 6 1992	11 Intuiting
Sep 20 1991	2 Evolving	Nov 29 1991	7 Remembering	Feb 7 1992	12 Evolving
Sep 21 1991	3 Self-Regulating	Nov 30 1991	8 Loving	Feb 8 1992	13 Self-Regulating
Sep 22 1991	4 Catalyzing	Dec 1 1991	9 Feeling	Feb 9 1992	**1 Catalyzing**
Sep 23 1991	5 Enlightening	Dec 2 1991	10 Devoting	Feb 10 1992	2 Enlightening
Sep 24 1991	6 Being	Dec 3 1991	11 Illuminating	Feb 11 1992	3 Being
Sep 25 1991	7 Breathing	Dec 4 1991	12 Choosing	Feb 12 1992	4 Breathing
Sep 26 1991	8 Listening	Dec 5 1991	13 Exploring	Feb 13 1992	5 Listening
Sep 27 1991	9 Planting	Dec 6 1991	**1 Healing**	Feb 14 1992	6 Planting
Sep 28 1991	10 Moving	Dec 7 1991	2 Seeing	Feb 15 1992	7 Moving
Sep 29 1991	11 Transcending	Dec 8 1991	3 Intuiting	Feb 16 1992	8 Transcending
Sep 30 1991	12 Remembering	Dec 9 1991	4 Evolving	Feb 17 1992	9 Remembering
Oct 1 1991	13 Loving	Dec 10 1991	5 Self-Regulating	Feb 18 1992	10 Loving
Oct 2 1991	**1 Feeling**	Dec 11 1991	6 Catalyzing	Feb 19 1992	11 Feeling
Oct 3 1991	2 Devoting	Dec 12 1991	7 Enlightening	Feb 20 1992	12 Devoting
Oct 4 1991	3 Illuminating	Dec 13 1991	8 Being	Feb 21 1992	13 Illuminating
Oct 5 1991	4 Choosing	Dec 14 1991	9 Breathing	Feb 22 1992	**1 Choosing**
Oct 6 1991	5 Exploring	Dec 15 1991	10 Listening	Feb 23 1992	2 Exploring
Oct 7 1991	6 Healing	Dec 16 1991	11 Planting	Feb 24 1992	3 Healing
Oct 8 1991	7 Seeing	Dec 17 1991	12 Moving	Feb 25 1992	4 Seeing
Oct 9 1991	8 Intuiting	Dec 18 1991	13 Transcending	Feb 26 1992	5 Intuiting
Oct 10 1991	9 Evolving	Dec 19 1991	**1 Remembering**	Feb 27 1992	6 Evolving
Oct 11 1991	10 Self-Regulating	Dec 20 1991	2 Loving	Feb 28 1992	7 Self-Regulating
Oct 12 1991	11 Catalyzing	Dec 21 1991	3 Feeling	Feb 29 1992	8 Catalyzing
Oct 13 1991	12 Enlightening	Dec 22 1991	4 Devoting	Mar 1 1992	9 Enlightening
Oct 14 1991	13 Being	Dec 23 1991	5 Illuminating	Mar 2 1992	10 Being
Oct 15 1991	**1 Breathing**	Dec 24 1991	6 Choosing	Mar 3 1992	11 Breathing
Oct 16 1991	2 Listening	Dec 25 1991	7 Exploring	Mar 4 1992	12 Listening
Oct 17 1991	3 Planting	Dec 26 1991	8 Healing	Mar 5 1992	13 Planting
Oct 18 1991	4 Moving	Dec 27 1991	9 Seeing	Mar 6 1992	**1 Moving**
Oct 19 1991	5 Transcending	Dec 28 1991	10 Intuiting	Mar 7 1992	2 Transcending
Oct 20 1991	6 Remembering	Dec 29 1991	11 Evolving	Mar 8 1992	3 Remembering
Oct 21 1991	7 Loving	Dec 30 1991	12 Self-Regulating	Mar 9 1992	4 Loving
Oct 22 1991	8 Feeling	Dec 31 1991	13 Catalyzing	Mar 10 1992	5 Feeling
Oct 23 1991	9 Devoting	Jan 1 1992	**1 Enlightening**	Mar 11 1992	6 Devoting
Oct 24 1991	10 Illuminating	Jan 2 1992	2 Being	Mar 12 1992	7 Illuminating
Oct 25 1991	11 Choosing	Jan 3 1992	3 Breathing	Mar 13 1992	8 Choosing
Oct 26 1991	12 Exploring	Jan 4 1992	4 Listening	Mar 14 1992	9 Exploring
Oct 27 1991	13 Healing	Jan 5 1992	5 Planting	Mar 15 1992	10 Healing
Oct 28 1991	**1 Seeing**	Jan 6 1992	6 Moving	Mar 16 1992	11 Seeing
Oct 29 1991	2 Intuiting	Jan 7 1992	7 Transcending	Mar 17 1992	12 Intuiting
Oct 30 1991	3 Evolving	Jan 8 1992	8 Remembering	Mar 18 1992	13 Evolving
Oct 31 1991	4 Self-Regulating	Jan 9 1992	9 Loving	Mar 19 1992	**1 Self-Regulating**
Nov 1 1991	5 Catalyzing	Jan 10 1992	10 Feeling	Mar 20 1992	2 Catalyzing
Nov 2 1991	6 Enlightening	Jan 11 1992	11 Devoting	Mar 21 1992	3 Enlightening
Nov 3 1991	7 Being	Jan 12 1992	12 Illuminating	Mar 22 1992	4 Being
Nov 4 1991	8 Breathing	Jan 13 1992	13 Choosing	Mar 23 1992	5 Breathing
Nov 5 1991	9 Listening	Jan 14 1992	**1 Exploring**	Mar 24 1992	6 Listening
Nov 6 1991	10 Planting	Jan 15 1992	2 Healing	Mar 25 1992	7 Planting
Nov 7 1991	11 Moving	Jan 16 1992	3 Seeing	Mar 26 1992	8 Moving
Nov 8 1991	12 Transcending	Jan 17 1992	4 Intuiting	Mar 27 1992	9 Transcending
Nov 9 1991	13 Remembering	Jan 18 1992	5 Evolving	Mar 28 1992	10 Remembering
Nov 10 1991	**1 Loving**	Jan 19 1992	6 Self-Regulating	Mar 29 1992	11 Loving
Nov 11 1991	2 Feeling	Jan 20 1992	7 Catalyzing	Mar 30 1992	12 Feeling
Nov 12 1991	3 Devoting	Jan 21 1992	8 Enlightening	Mar 31 1992	13 Devoting

Date	UE Earth Energy	Date	UE Earth Energy	Date	UE Earth Energy
Apr 1 1992	1 Illuminating	Jun 10 1992	6 Being	Aug 19 1992	11 Illuminating
Apr 2 1992	2 Choosing	Jun 11 1992	7 Breathing	Aug 20 1992	12 Choosing
Apr 3 1992	3 Exploring	Jun 12 1992	8 Listening	Aug 21 1992	13 Exploring
Apr 4 1992	4 Healing	Jun 13 1992	9 Planting	Aug 22 1992	1 Healing
Apr 5 1992	5 Seeing	Jun 14 1992	10 Moving	Aug 23 1992	2 Seeing
Apr 6 1992	6 Intuiting	Jun 15 1992	11 Transcending	Aug 24 1992	3 Intuiting
Apr 7 1992	7 Evolving	Jun 16 1992	12 Remembering	Aug 25 1992	4 Evolving
Apr 8 1992	8 Self-Regulating	Jun 17 1992	13 Loving	Aug 26 1992	5 Self-Regulating
Apr 9 1992	9 Catalyzing	Jun 18 1992	1 Feeling	Aug 27 1992	6 Catalyzing
Apr 10 1992	10 Enlightening	Jun 19 1992	2 Devoting	Aug 28 1992	7 Enlightening
Apr 11 1992	11 Being	Jun 20 1992	3 Illuminating	Aug 29 1992	8 Being
Apr 12 1992	12 Breathing	Jun 21 1992	4 Choosing	Aug 30 1992	9 Breathing
Apr 13 1992	13 Listening	Jun 22 1992	5 Exploring	Aug 31 1992	10 Listening
Apr 14 1992	1 Planting	Jun 23 1992	6 Healing	Sep 1 1992	11 Planting
Apr 15 1992	2 Moving	Jun 24 1992	7 Seeing	Sep 2 1992	12 Moving
Apr 16 1992	3 Transcending	Jun 25 1992	8 Intuiting	Sep 3 1992	13 Transcending
Apr 17 1992	4 Remembering	Jun 26 1992	9 Evolving	Sep 4 1992	1 Remembering
Apr 18 1992	5 Loving	Jun 27 1992	10 Self-Regulating	Sep 5 1992	2 Loving
Apr 19 1992	6 Feeling	Jun 28 1992	11 Catalyzing	Sep 6 1992	3 Feeling
Apr 20 1992	7 Devoting	Jun 29 1992	12 Enlightening	Sep 7 1992	4 Devoting
Apr 21 1992	8 Illuminating	Jun 30 1992	13 Being	Sep 8 1992	5 Illuminating
Apr 22 1992	9 Choosing	Jul 1 1992	1 Breathing	Sep 9 1992	6 Choosing
Apr 23 1992	10 Exploring	Jul 2 1992	2 Listening	Sep 10 1992	7 Exploring
Apr 24 1992	11 Healing	Jul 3 1992	3 Planting	Sep 11 1992	8 Healing
Apr 25 1992	12 Seeing	Jul 4 1992	4 Moving	Sep 12 1992	9 Seeing
Apr 26 1992	13 Intuiting	Jul 5 1992	5 Transcending	Sep 13 1992	10 Intuiting
Apr 27 1992	1 Evolving	Jul 6 1992	6 Remembering	Sep 14 1992	11 Evolving
Apr 28 1992	2 Self-Regulating	Jul 7 1992	7 Loving	Sep 15 1992	12 Self-Regulating
Apr 29 1992	3 Catalyzing	Jul 8 1992	8 Feeling	Sep 16 1992	13 Catalyzing
Apr 30 1992	4 Enlightening	Jul 9 1992	9 Devoting	Sep 17 1992	1 Enlightening
May 1 1992	5 Being	Jul 10 1992	10 Illuminating	Sep 18 1992	2 Being
May 2 1992	6 Breathing	Jul 11 1992	11 Choosing	Sep 19 1992	3 Breathing
May 3 1992	7 Listening	Jul 12 1992	12 Exploring	Sep 20 1992	4 Listening
May 4 1992	8 Planting	Jul 13 1992	13 Healing	Sep 21 1992	5 Planting
May 5 1992	9 Moving	Jul 14 1992	1 Seeing	Sep 22 1992	6 Moving
May 6 1992	10 Transcending	Jul 15 1992	2 Intuiting	Sep 23 1992	7 Transcending
May 7 1992	11 Remembering	Jul 16 1992	3 Evolving	Sep 24 1992	8 Remembering
May 8 1992	12 Loving	Jul 17 1992	4 Self-Regulating	Sep 25 1992	9 Loving
May 9 1992	13 Feeling	Jul 18 1992	5 Catalyzing	Sep 26 1992	10 Feeling
May 10 1992	1 Devoting	Jul 19 1992	6 Enlightening	Sep 27 1992	11 Devoting
May 11 1992	2 Illuminating	Jul 20 1992	7 Being	Sep 28 1992	12 Illuminating
May 12 1992	3 Choosing	Jul 21 1992	8 Breathing	Sep 29 1992	13 Choosing
May 13 1992	4 Exploring	Jul 22 1992	9 Listening	Sep 30 1992	1 Exploring
May 14 1992	5 Healing	Jul 23 1992	10 Planting	Oct 1 1992	2 Healing
May 15 1992	6 Seeing	Jul 24 1992	11 Moving	Oct 2 1992	3 Seeing
May 16 1992	7 Intuiting	Jul 25 1992	12 Transcending	Oct 3 1992	4 Intuiting
May 17 1992	8 Evolving	Jul 26 1992	13 Remembering	Oct 4 1992	5 Evolving
May 18 1992	9 Self-Regulating	Jul 27 1992	1 Loving	Oct 5 1992	6 Self-Regulating
May 19 1992	10 Catalyzing	Jul 28 1992	2 Feeling	Oct 6 1992	7 Catalyzing
May 20 1992	11 Enlightening	Jul 29 1992	3 Devoting	Oct 7 1992	8 Enlightening
May 21 1992	12 Being	Jul 30 1992	4 Illuminating	Oct 8 1992	9 Being
May 22 1992	13 Breathing	Jul 31 1992	5 Choosing	Oct 9 1992	10 Breathing
May 23 1992	1 Listening	Aug 1 1992	6 Exploring	Oct 10 1992	11 Listening
May 24 1992	2 Planting	Aug 2 1992	7 Healing	Oct 11 1992	12 Planting
May 25 1992	3 Moving	Aug 3 1992	8 Seeing	Oct 12 1992	13 Moving
May 26 1992	4 Transcending	Aug 4 1992	9 Intuiting	Oct 13 1992	1 Transcending
May 27 1992	5 Remembering	Aug 5 1992	10 Evolving	Oct 14 1992	2 Remembering
May 28 1992	6 Loving	Aug 6 1992	11 Self-Regulating	Oct 15 1992	3 Loving
May 29 1992	7 Feeling	Aug 7 1992	12 Catalyzing	Oct 16 1992	4 Feeling
May 30 1992	8 Devoting	Aug 8 1992	13 Enlightening	Oct 17 1992	5 Devoting
May 31 1992	9 Illuminating	Aug 9 1992	1 Being	Oct 18 1992	6 Illuminating
Jun 1 1992	10 Choosing	Aug 10 1992	2 Breathing	Oct 19 1992	7 Choosing
Jun 2 1992	11 Exploring	Aug 11 1992	3 Listening	Oct 20 1992	8 Exploring
Jun 3 1992	12 Healing	Aug 12 1992	4 Planting	Oct 21 1992	9 Healing
Jun 4 1992	13 Seeing	Aug 13 1992	5 Moving	Oct 22 1992	10 Seeing
Jun 5 1992	1 Intuiting	Aug 14 1992	6 Transcending	Oct 23 1992	11 Intuiting
Jun 6 1992	2 Evolving	Aug 15 1992	7 Remembering	Oct 24 1992	12 Evolving
Jun 7 1992	3 Self-Regulating	Aug 16 1992	8 Loving	Oct 25 1992	13 Self-Regulating
Jun 8 1992	4 Catalyzing	Aug 17 1992	9 Feeling	Oct 26 1992	1 Catalyzing
Jun 9 1992	5 Enlightening	Aug 18 1992	10 Devoting	Oct 27 1992	2 Enlightening

Date	UE Earth Energy	Date	UE Earth Energy	Date	UE Earth Energy
Oct 28 1992	3 Being	Jan 6 1993	8 Illuminating	Mar 17 1993	13 Being
Oct 29 1992	4 Breathing	Jan 7 1993	9 Choosing	Mar 18 1993	**1 Breathing**
Oct 30 1992	5 Listening	Jan 8 1993	10 Exploring	Mar 19 1993	2 Listening
Oct 31 1992	6 Planting	Jan 9 1993	11 Healing	Mar 20 1993	3 Planting
Nov 1 1992	7 Moving	Jan 10 1993	12 Seeing	Mar 21 1993	4 Moving
Nov 2 1992	8 Transcending	Jan 11 1993	13 Intuiting	Mar 22 1993	5 Transcending
Nov 3 1992	9 Remembering	Jan 12 1993	**1 Evolving**	Mar 23 1993	6 Remembering
Nov 4 1992	10 Loving	Jan 13 1993	2 Self-Regulating	Mar 24 1993	7 Loving
Nov 5 1992	11 Feeling	Jan 14 1993	3 Catalyzing	Mar 25 1993	8 Feeling
Nov 6 1992	12 Devoting	Jan 15 1993	4 Enlightening	Mar 26 1993	9 Devoting
Nov 7 1992	13 Illuminating	Jan 16 1993	5 Being	Mar 27 1993	10 Illuminating
Nov 8 1992	**1 Choosing**	Jan 17 1993	6 Breathing	Mar 28 1993	11 Choosing
Nov 9 1992	2 Exploring	Jan 18 1993	7 Listening	Mar 29 1993	12 Exploring
Nov 10 1992	3 Healing	Jan 19 1993	8 Planting	Mar 30 1993	13 Healing
Nov 11 1992	4 Seeing	Jan 20 1993	9 Moving	Mar 31 1993	**1 Seeing**
Nov 12 1992	5 Intuiting	Jan 21 1993	10 Transcending	Apr 1 1993	2 Intuiting
Nov 13 1992	6 Evolving	Jan 22 1993	11 Remembering	Apr 2 1993	3 Evolving
Nov 14 1992	7 Self-Regulating	Jan 23 1993	12 Loving	Apr 3 1993	4 Self-Regulating
Nov 15 1992	8 Catalyzing	Jan 24 1993	13 Feeling	Apr 4 1993	5 Catalyzing
Nov 16 1992	9 Enlightening	Jan 25 1993	**1 Devoting**	Apr 5 1993	6 Enlightening
Nov 17 1992	10 Being	Jan 26 1993	2 Illuminating	Apr 6 1993	7 Being
Nov 18 1992	11 Breathing	Jan 27 1993	3 Choosing	Apr 7 1993	8 Breathing
Nov 19 1992	12 Listening	Jan 28 1993	4 Exploring	Apr 8 1993	9 Listening
Nov 20 1992	13 Planting	Jan 29 1993	5 Healing	Apr 9 1993	10 Planting
Nov 21 1992	**1 Moving**	Jan 30 1993	6 Seeing	Apr 10 1993	11 Moving
Nov 22 1992	2 Transcending	Jan 31 1993	7 Intuiting	Apr 11 1993	12 Transcending
Nov 23 1992	3 Remembering	Feb 1 1993	8 Evolving	Apr 12 1993	13 Remembering
Nov 24 1992	4 Loving	Feb 2 1993	9 Self-Regulating	Apr 13 1993	**1 Loving**
Nov 25 1992	5 Feeling	Feb 3 1993	10 Catalyzing	Apr 14 1993	2 Feeling
Nov 26 1992	6 Devoting	Feb 4 1993	11 Enlightening	Apr 15 1993	3 Devoting
Nov 27 1992	7 Illuminating	Feb 5 1993	12 Being	Apr 16 1993	4 Illuminating
Nov 28 1992	8 Choosing	Feb 6 1993	13 Breathing	Apr 17 1993	5 Choosing
Nov 29 1992	9 Exploring	Feb 7 1993	**1 Listening**	Apr 18 1993	6 Exploring
Nov 30 1992	10 Healing	Feb 8 1993	2 Planting	Apr 19 1993	7 Healing
Dec 1 1992	11 Seeing	Feb 9 1993	3 Moving	Apr 20 1993	8 Seeing
Dec 2 1992	12 Intuiting	Feb 10 1993	4 Transcending	Apr 21 1993	9 Intuiting
Dec 3 1992	13 Evolving	Feb 11 1993	5 Remembering	Apr 22 1993	10 Evolving
Dec 4 1992	**1 Self-Regulating**	Feb 12 1993	6 Loving	Apr 23 1993	11 Self-Regulating
Dec 5 1992	2 Catalyzing	Feb 13 1993	7 Feeling	Apr 24 1993	12 Catalyzing
Dec 6 1992	3 Enlightening	Feb 14 1993	8 Devoting	Apr 25 1993	13 Enlightening
Dec 7 1992	4 Being	Feb 15 1993	9 Illuminating	Apr 26 1993	**1 Being**
Dec 8 1992	5 Breathing	Feb 16 1993	10 Choosing	Apr 27 1993	2 Breathing
Dec 9 1992	6 Listening	Feb 17 1993	11 Exploring	Apr 28 1993	3 Listening
Dec 10 1992	7 Planting	Feb 18 1993	12 Healing	Apr 29 1993	4 Planting
Dec 11 1992	8 Moving	Feb 19 1993	13 Seeing	Apr 30 1993	5 Moving
Dec 12 1992	9 Transcending	Feb 20 1993	**1 Intuiting**	May 1 1993	6 Transcending
Dec 13 1992	10 Remembering	Feb 21 1993	2 Evolving	May 2 1993	7 Remembering
Dec 14 1992	11 Loving	Feb 22 1993	3 Self-Regulating	May 3 1993	8 Loving
Dec 15 1992	12 Feeling	Feb 23 1993	4 Catalyzing	May 4 1993	9 Feeling
Dec 16 1992	13 Devoting	Feb 24 1993	5 Enlightening	May 5 1993	10 Devoting
Dec 17 1992	**1 Illuminating**	Feb 25 1993	6 Being	May 6 1993	11 Illuminating
Dec 18 1992	2 Choosing	Feb 26 1993	7 Breathing	May 7 1993	12 Choosing
Dec 19 1992	3 Exploring	Feb 27 1993	8 Listening	May 8 1993	13 Exploring
Dec 20 1992	4 Healing	Feb 28 1993	9 Planting	May 9 1993	**1 Healing**
Dec 21 1992	5 Seeing	Mar 1 1993	10 Moving	May 10 1993	2 Seeing
Dec 22 1992	6 Intuiting	Mar 2 1993	11 Transcending	May 11 1993	3 Intuiting
Dec 23 1992	7 Evolving	Mar 3 1993	12 Remembering	May 12 1993	4 Evolving
Dec 24 1992	8 Self-Regulating	Mar 4 1993	13 Loving	May 13 1993	5 Self-Regulating
Dec 25 1992	9 Catalyzing	Mar 5 1993	**1 Feeling**	May 14 1993	6 Catalyzing
Dec 26 1992	10 Enlightening	Mar 6 1993	2 Devoting	May 15 1993	7 Enlightening
Dec 27 1992	11 Being	Mar 7 1993	3 Illuminating	May 16 1993	8 Being
Dec 28 1992	12 Breathing	Mar 8 1993	4 Choosing	May 17 1993	9 Breathing
Dec 29 1992	13 Listening	Mar 9 1993	5 Exploring	May 18 1993	10 Listening
Dec 30 1992	**1 Planting**	Mar 10 1993	6 Healing	May 19 1993	11 Planting
Dec 31 1992	2 Moving	Mar 11 1993	7 Seeing	May 20 1993	12 Moving
Jan 1 1993	3 Transcending	Mar 12 1993	8 Intuiting	May 21 1993	13 Transcending
Jan 2 1993	4 Remembering	Mar 13 1993	9 Evolving	May 22 1993	**1 Remembering**
Jan 3 1993	5 Loving	Mar 14 1993	10 Self-Regulating	May 23 1993	2 Loving
Jan 4 1993	6 Feeling	Mar 15 1993	11 Catalyzing	May 24 1993	3 Feeling
Jan 5 1993	7 Devoting	Mar 16 1993	12 Enlightening	May 25 1993	4 Devoting

Date	UE	Earth Energy	Date	UE	Earth Energy	Date	UE	Earth Energy
May 26 1993	5	Illuminating	Aug 4 1993	10	Being	Oct 13 1993	2	Illuminating
May 27 1993	6	Choosing	Aug 5 1993	11	Breathing	Oct 14 1993	3	Choosing
May 28 1993	7	Exploring	Aug 6 1993	12	Listening	Oct 15 1993	4	Exploring
May 29 1993	8	Healing	Aug 7 1993	13	Planting	Oct 16 1993	5	Healing
May 30 1993	9	Seeing	Aug 8 1993	**1**	**Moving**	Oct 17 1993	6	Seeing
May 31 1993	10	Intuiting	Aug 9 1993	2	Transcending	Oct 18 1993	7	Intuiting
Jun 1 1993	11	Evolving	Aug 10 1993	3	Remembering	Oct 19 1993	8	Evolving
Jun 2 1993	12	Self-Regulating	Aug 11 1993	4	Loving	Oct 20 1993	9	Self-Regulating
Jun 3 1993	13	Catalyzing	Aug 12 1993	5	Feeling	Oct 21 1993	10	Catalyzing
Jun 4 1993	**1**	**Enlightening**	Aug 13 1993	6	Devoting	Oct 22 1993	11	Enlightening
Jun 5 1993	2	Being	Aug 14 1993	7	Illuminating	Oct 23 1993	12	Being
Jun 6 1993	3	Breathing	Aug 15 1993	8	Choosing	Oct 24 1993	13	Breathing
Jun 7 1993	4	Listening	Aug 16 1993	9	Exploring	Oct 25 1993	**1**	**Listening**
Jun 8 1993	5	Planting	Aug 17 1993	10	Healing	Oct 26 1993	2	Planting
Jun 9 1993	6	Moving	Aug 18 1993	11	Seeing	Oct 27 1993	3	Moving
Jun 10 1993	7	Transcending	Aug 19 1993	12	Intuiting	Oct 28 1993	4	Transcending
Jun 11 1993	8	Remembering	Aug 20 1993	13	Evolving	Oct 29 1993	5	Remembering
Jun 12 1993	9	Loving	Aug 21 1993	**1**	**Self-Regulating**	Oct 30 1993	6	Loving
Jun 13 1993	10	Feeling	Aug 22 1993	2	Catalyzing	Oct 31 1993	7	Feeling
Jun 14 1993	11	Devoting	Aug 23 1993	3	Enlightening	Nov 1 1993	8	Devoting
Jun 15 1993	12	Illuminating	Aug 24 1993	4	Being	Nov 2 1993	9	Illuminating
Jun 16 1993	13	Choosing	Aug 25 1993	5	Breathing	Nov 3 1993	10	Choosing
Jun 17 1993	**1**	**Exploring**	Aug 26 1993	6	Listening	Nov 4 1993	11	Exploring
Jun 18 1993	2	Healing	Aug 27 1993	7	Planting	Nov 5 1993	12	Healing
Jun 19 1993	3	Seeing	Aug 28 1993	8	Moving	Nov 6 1993	13	Seeing
Jun 20 1993	4	Intuiting	Aug 29 1993	9	Transcending	Nov 7 1993	**1**	**Intuiting**
Jun 21 1993	5	Evolving	Aug 30 1993	10	Remembering	Nov 8 1993	2	Evolving
Jun 22 1993	6	Self-Regulating	Aug 31 1993	11	Loving	Nov 9 1993	3	Self-Regulating
Jun 23 1993	7	Catalyzing	Sep 1 1993	12	Feeling	Nov 10 1993	4	Catalyzing
Jun 24 1993	8	Enlightening	Sep 2 1993	13	Devoting	Nov 11 1993	5	Enlightening
Jun 25 1993	9	Being	Sep 3 1993	**1**	**Illuminating**	Nov 12 1993	6	Being
Jun 26 1993	10	Breathing	Sep 4 1993	2	Choosing	Nov 13 1993	7	Breathing
Jun 27 1993	11	Listening	Sep 5 1993	3	Exploring	Nov 14 1993	8	Listening
Jun 28 1993	12	Planting	Sep 6 1993	4	Healing	Nov 15 1993	9	Planting
Jun 29 1993	13	Moving	Sep 7 1993	5	Seeing	Nov 16 1993	10	Moving
Jun 30 1993	**1**	**Transcending**	Sep 8 1993	6	Intuiting	Nov 17 1993	11	Transcending
Jul 1 1993	2	Remembering	Sep 9 1993	7	Evolving	Nov 18 1993	12	Remembering
Jul 2 1993	3	Loving	Sep 10 1993	8	Self-Regulating	Nov 19 1993	13	Loving
Jul 3 1993	4	Feeling	Sep 11 1993	9	Catalyzing	Nov 20 1993	**1**	**Feeling**
Jul 4 1993	5	Devoting	Sep 12 1993	10	Enlightening	Nov 21 1993	2	Devoting
Jul 5 1993	6	Illuminating	Sep 13 1993	11	Being	Nov 22 1993	3	Illuminating
Jul 6 1993	7	Choosing	Sep 14 1993	12	Breathing	Nov 23 1993	4	Choosing
Jul 7 1993	8	Exploring	Sep 15 1993	13	Listening	Nov 24 1993	5	Exploring
Jul 8 1993	9	Healing	Sep 16 1993	**1**	**Planting**	Nov 25 1993	6	Healing
Jul 9 1993	10	Seeing	Sep 17 1993	2	Moving	Nov 26 1993	7	Seeing
Jul 10 1993	11	Intuiting	Sep 18 1993	3	Transcending	Nov 27 1993	8	Intuiting
Jul 11 1993	12	Evolving	Sep 19 1993	4	Remembering	Nov 28 1993	9	Evolving
Jul 12 1993	13	Self-Regulating	Sep 20 1993	5	Loving	Nov 29 1993	10	Self-Regulating
Jul 13 1993	**1**	**Catalyzing**	Sep 21 1993	6	Feeling	Nov 30 1993	11	Catalyzing
Jul 14 1993	2	Enlightening	Sep 22 1993	7	Devoting	Dec 1 1993	12	Enlightening
Jul 15 1993	3	Being	Sep 23 1993	8	Illuminating	Dec 2 1993	13	Being
Jul 16 1993	4	Breathing	Sep 24 1993	9	Choosing	Dec 3 1993	**1**	**Breathing**
Jul 17 1993	5	Listening	Sep 25 1993	10	Exploring	Dec 4 1993	2	Listening
Jul 18 1993	6	Planting	Sep 26 1993	11	Healing	Dec 5 1993	3	Planting
Jul 19 1993	7	Moving	Sep 27 1993	12	Seeing	Dec 6 1993	4	Moving
Jul 20 1993	8	Transcending	Sep 28 1993	13	Intuiting	Dec 7 1993	5	Transcending
Jul 21 1993	9	Remembering	Sep 29 1993	**1**	**Evolving**	Dec 8 1993	6	Remembering
Jul 22 1993	10	Loving	Sep 30 1993	2	Self-Regulating	Dec 9 1993	7	Loving
Jul 23 1993	11	Feeling	Oct 1 1993	3	Catalyzing	Dec 10 1993	8	Feeling
Jul 24 1993	12	Devoting	Oct 2 1993	4	Enlightening	Dec 11 1993	9	Devoting
Jul 25 1993	13	Illuminating	Oct 3 1993	5	Being	Dec 12 1993	10	Illuminating
Jul 26 1993	**1**	**Choosing**	Oct 4 1993	6	Breathing	Dec 13 1993	11	Choosing
Jul 27 1993	2	Exploring	Oct 5 1993	7	Listening	Dec 14 1993	12	Exploring
Jul 28 1993	3	Healing	Oct 6 1993	8	Planting	Dec 15 1993	13	Healing
Jul 29 1993	4	Seeing	Oct 7 1993	9	Moving	Dec 16 1993	**1**	**Seeing**
Jul 30 1993	5	Intuiting	Oct 8 1993	10	Transcending	Dec 17 1993	2	Intuiting
Jul 31 1993	6	Evolving	Oct 9 1993	11	Remembering	Dec 18 1993	3	Evolving
Aug 1 1993	7	Self-Regulating	Oct 10 1993	12	Loving	Dec 19 1993	4	Self-Regulating
Aug 2 1993	8	Catalyzing	Oct 11 1993	13	Feeling	Dec 20 1993	5	Catalyzing
Aug 3 1993	9	Enlightening	Oct 12 1993	**1**	**Devoting**	Dec 21 1993	6	Enlightening

Date	UE	Earth Energy	Date	UE	Earth Energy	Date	UE	Earth Energy
Dec 22 1993	7	Being	Mar 2 1994	12	Illuminating	May 11 1994	4	Being
Dec 23 1993	8	Breathing	Mar 3 1994	13	Choosing	May 12 1994	5	Breathing
Dec 24 1993	9	Listening	Mar 4 1994	**1**	**Exploring**	May 13 1994	6	Listening
Dec 25 1993	10	Planting	Mar 5 1994	2	Healing	May 14 1994	7	Planting
Dec 26 1993	11	Moving	Mar 6 1994	3	Seeing	May 15 1994	8	Moving
Dec 27 1993	12	Transcending	Mar 7 1994	4	Intuiting	May 16 1994	9	Transcending
Dec 28 1993	13	Remembering	Mar 8 1994	5	Evolving	May 17 1994	10	Remembering
Dec 29 1993	**1**	**Loving**	Mar 9 1994	6	Self-Regulating	May 18 1994	11	Loving
Dec 30 1993	2	Feeling	Mar 10 1994	7	Catalyzing	May 19 1994	12	Feeling
Dec 31 1993	3	Devoting	Mar 11 1994	8	Enlightening	May 20 1994	13	Devoting
Jan 1 1994	4	Illuminating	Mar 12 1994	9	Being	May 21 1994	**1**	**Illuminating**
Jan 2 1994	5	Choosing	Mar 13 1994	10	Breathing	May 22 1994	2	Choosing
Jan 3 1994	6	Exploring	Mar 14 1994	11	Listening	May 23 1994	3	Exploring
Jan 4 1994	7	Healing	Mar 15 1994	12	Planting	May 24 1994	4	Healing
Jan 5 1994	8	Seeing	Mar 16 1994	13	Moving	May 25 1994	5	Seeing
Jan 6 1994	9	Intuiting	Mar 17 1994	**1**	**Transcending**	May 26 1994	6	Intuiting
Jan 7 1994	10	Evolving	Mar 18 1994	2	Remembering	May 27 1994	7	Evolving
Jan 8 1994	11	Self-Regulating	Mar 19 1994	3	Loving	May 28 1994	8	Self-Regulating
Jan 9 1994	12	Catalyzing	Mar 20 1994	4	Feeling	May 29 1994	9	Catalyzing
Jan 10 1994	13	Enlightening	Mar 21 1994	5	Devoting	May 30 1994	10	Enlightening
Jan 11 1994	**1**	**Being**	Mar 22 1994	6	Illuminating	May 31 1994	11	Being
Jan 12 1994	2	Breathing	Mar 23 1994	7	Choosing	Jun 1 1994	12	Breathing
Jan 13 1994	3	Listening	Mar 24 1994	8	Exploring	Jun 2 1994	13	Listening
Jan 14 1994	4	Planting	Mar 25 1994	9	Healing	Jun 3 1994	**1**	**Planting**
Jan 15 1994	5	Moving	Mar 26 1994	10	Seeing	Jun 4 1994	2	Moving
Jan 16 1994	6	Transcending	Mar 27 1994	11	Intuiting	Jun 5 1994	3	Transcending
Jan 17 1994	7	Remembering	Mar 28 1994	12	Evolving	Jun 6 1994	4	Remembering
Jan 18 1994	8	Loving	Mar 29 1994	13	Self-Regulating	Jun 7 1994	5	Loving
Jan 19 1994	9	Feeling	Mar 30 1994	**1**	**Catalyzing**	Jun 8 1994	6	Feeling
Jan 20 1994	10	Devoting	Mar 31 1994	2	Enlightening	Jun 9 1994	7	Devoting
Jan 21 1994	11	Illuminating	Apr 1 1994	3	Being	Jun 10 1994	8	Illuminating
Jan 22 1994	12	Choosing	Apr 2 1994	4	Breathing	Jun 11 1994	9	Choosing
Jan 23 1994	13	Exploring	Apr 3 1994	5	Listening	Jun 12 1994	10	Exploring
Jan 24 1994	**1**	**Healing**	Apr 4 1994	6	Planting	Jun 13 1994	11	Healing
Jan 25 1994	2	Seeing	Apr 5 1994	7	Moving	Jun 14 1994	12	Seeing
Jan 26 1994	3	Intuiting	Apr 6 1994	8	Transcending	Jun 15 1994	13	Intuiting
Jan 27 1994	4	Evolving	Apr 7 1994	9	Remembering	Jun 16 1994	**1**	**Evolving**
Jan 28 1994	5	Self-Regulating	Apr 8 1994	10	Loving	Jun 17 1994	2	Self-Regulating
Jan 29 1994	6	Catalyzing	Apr 9 1994	11	Feeling	Jun 18 1994	3	Catalyzing
Jan 30 1994	7	Enlightening	Apr 10 1994	12	Devoting	Jun 19 1994	4	Enlightening
Jan 31 1994	8	Being	Apr 11 1994	13	Illuminating	Jun 20 1994	5	Being
Feb 1 1994	9	Breathing	Apr 12 1994	**1**	**Choosing**	Jun 21 1994	6	Breathing
Feb 2 1994	10	Listening	Apr 13 1994	2	Exploring	Jun 22 1994	7	Listening
Feb 3 1994	11	Planting	Apr 14 1994	3	Healing	Jun 23 1994	8	Planting
Feb 4 1994	12	Moving	Apr 15 1994	4	Seeing	Jun 24 1994	9	Moving
Feb 5 1994	13	Transcending	Apr 16 1994	5	Intuiting	Jun 25 1994	10	Transcending
Feb 6 1994	**1**	**Remembering**	Apr 17 1994	6	Evolving	Jun 26 1994	11	Remembering
Feb 7 1994	2	Loving	Apr 18 1994	7	Self-Regulating	Jun 27 1994	12	Loving
Feb 8 1994	3	Feeling	Apr 19 1994	8	Catalyzing	Jun 28 1994	13	Feeling
Feb 9 1994	4	Devoting	Apr 20 1994	9	Enlightening	Jun 29 1994	**1**	**Devoting**
Feb 10 1994	5	Illuminating	Apr 21 1994	10	Being	Jun 30 1994	2	Illuminating
Feb 11 1994	6	Choosing	Apr 22 1994	11	Breathing	Jul 1 1994	3	Choosing
Feb 12 1994	7	Exploring	Apr 23 1994	12	Listening	Jul 2 1994	4	Exploring
Feb 13 1994	8	Healing	Apr 24 1994	13	Planting	Jul 3 1994	5	Healing
Feb 14 1994	9	Seeing	Apr 25 1994	**1**	**Moving**	Jul 4 1994	6	Seeing
Feb 15 1994	10	Intuiting	Apr 26 1994	2	Transcending	Jul 5 1994	7	Intuiting
Feb 16 1994	11	Evolving	Apr 27 1994	3	Remembering	Jul 6 1994	8	Evolving
Feb 17 1994	12	Self-Regulating	Apr 28 1994	4	Loving	Jul 7 1994	9	Self-Regulating
Feb 18 1994	13	Catalyzing	Apr 29 1994	5	Feeling	Jul 8 1994	10	Catalyzing
Feb 19 1994	**1**	**Enlightening**	Apr 30 1994	6	Devoting	Jul 9 1994	11	Enlightening
Feb 20 1994	2	Being	May 1 1994	7	Illuminating	Jul 10 1994	12	Being
Feb 21 1994	3	Breathing	May 2 1994	8	Choosing	Jul 11 1994	13	Breathing
Feb 22 1994	4	Listening	May 3 1994	9	Exploring	Jul 12 1994	**1**	**Listening**
Feb 23 1994	5	Planting	May 4 1994	10	Healing	Jul 13 1994	2	Planting
Feb 24 1994	6	Moving	May 5 1994	11	Seeing	Jul 14 1994	3	Moving
Feb 25 1994	7	Transcending	May 6 1994	12	Intuiting	Jul 15 1994	4	Transcending
Feb 26 1994	8	Remembering	May 7 1994	13	Evolving	Jul 16 1994	5	Remembering
Feb 27 1994	9	Loving	May 8 1994	**1**	**Self-Regulating**	Jul 17 1994	6	Loving
Feb 28 1994	10	Feeling	May 9 1994	2	Catalyzing	Jul 18 1994	7	Feeling
Mar 1 1994	11	Devoting	May 10 1994	3	Enlightening	Jul 19 1994	8	Devoting

Date	UE Earth Energy	Date	UE Earth Energy	Date	UE Earth Energy
Jul 20 1994	9 Illuminating	Sep 28 1994	1 Being	Dec 7 1994	6 Illuminating
Jul 21 1994	10 Choosing	Sep 29 1994	2 Breathing	Dec 8 1994	7 Choosing
Jul 22 1994	11 Exploring	Sep 30 1994	3 Listening	Dec 9 1994	8 Exploring
Jul 23 1994	12 Healing	Oct 1 1994	4 Planting	Dec 10 1994	9 Healing
Jul 24 1994	13 Seeing	Oct 2 1994	5 Moving	Dec 11 1994	10 Seeing
Jul 25 1994	1 Intuiting	Oct 3 1994	6 Transcending	Dec 12 1994	11 Intuiting
Jul 26 1994	2 Evolving	Oct 4 1994	7 Remembering	Dec 13 1994	12 Evolving
Jul 27 1994	3 Self-Regulating	Oct 5 1994	8 Loving	Dec 14 1994	13 Self-Regulating
Jul 28 1994	4 Catalyzing	Oct 6 1994	9 Feeling	Dec 15 1994	1 Catalyzing
Jul 29 1994	5 Enlightening	Oct 7 1994	10 Devoting	Dec 16 1994	2 Enlightening
Jul 30 1994	6 Being	Oct 8 1994	11 Illuminating	Dec 17 1994	3 Being
Jul 31 1994	7 Breathing	Oct 9 1994	12 Choosing	Dec 18 1994	4 Breathing
Aug 1 1994	8 Listening	Oct 10 1994	13 Exploring	Dec 19 1994	5 Listening
Aug 2 1994	9 Planting	Oct 11 1994	1 Healing	Dec 20 1994	6 Planting
Aug 3 1994	10 Moving	Oct 12 1994	2 Seeing	Dec 21 1994	7 Moving
Aug 4 1994	11 Transcending	Oct 13 1994	3 Intuiting	Dec 22 1994	8 Transcending
Aug 5 1994	12 Remembering	Oct 14 1994	4 Evolving	Dec 23 1994	9 Remembering
Aug 6 1994	13 Loving	Oct 15 1994	5 Self-Regulating	Dec 24 1994	10 Loving
Aug 7 1994	1 Feeling	Oct 16 1994	6 Catalyzing	Dec 25 1994	11 Feeling
Aug 8 1994	2 Devoting	Oct 17 1994	7 Enlightening	Dec 26 1994	12 Devoting
Aug 9 1994	3 Illuminating	Oct 18 1994	8 Being	Dec 27 1994	13 Illuminating
Aug 10 1994	4 Choosing	Oct 19 1994	9 Breathing	Dec 28 1994	1 Choosing
Aug 11 1994	5 Exploring	Oct 20 1994	10 Listening	Dec 29 1994	2 Exploring
Aug 12 1994	6 Healing	Oct 21 1994	11 Planting	Dec 30 1994	3 Healing
Aug 13 1994	7 Seeing	Oct 22 1994	12 Moving	Dec 31 1994	4 Seeing
Aug 14 1994	8 Intuiting	Oct 23 1994	13 Transcending	Jan 1 1995	5 Intuiting
Aug 15 1994	9 Evolving	Oct 24 1994	1 Remembering	Jan 2 1995	6 Evolving
Aug 16 1994	10 Self-Regulating	Oct 25 1994	2 Loving	Jan 3 1995	7 Self-Regulating
Aug 17 1994	11 Catalyzing	Oct 26 1994	3 Feeling	Jan 4 1995	8 Catalyzing
Aug 18 1994	12 Enlightening	Oct 27 1994	4 Devoting	Jan 5 1995	9 Enlightening
Aug 19 1994	13 Being	Oct 28 1994	5 Illuminating	Jan 6 1995	10 Being
Aug 20 1994	1 Breathing	Oct 29 1994	6 Choosing	Jan 7 1995	11 Breathing
Aug 21 1994	2 Listening	Oct 30 1994	7 Exploring	Jan 8 1995	12 Listening
Aug 22 1994	3 Planting	Oct 31 1994	8 Healing	Jan 9 1995	13 Planting
Aug 23 1994	4 Moving	Nov 1 1994	9 Seeing	Jan 10 1995	1 Moving
Aug 24 1994	5 Transcending	Nov 2 1994	10 Intuiting	Jan 11 1995	2 Transcending
Aug 25 1994	6 Remembering	Nov 3 1994	11 Evolving	Jan 12 1995	3 Remembering
Aug 26 1994	7 Loving	Nov 4 1994	12 Self-Regulating	Jan 13 1995	4 Loving
Aug 27 1994	8 Feeling	Nov 5 1994	13 Catalyzing	Jan 14 1995	5 Feeling
Aug 28 1994	9 Devoting	Nov 6 1994	1 Enlightening	Jan 15 1995	6 Devoting
Aug 29 1994	10 Illuminating	Nov 7 1994	2 Being	Jan 16 1995	7 Illuminating
Aug 30 1994	11 Choosing	Nov 8 1994	3 Breathing	Jan 17 1995	8 Choosing
Aug 31 1994	12 Exploring	Nov 9 1994	4 Listening	Jan 18 1995	9 Exploring
Sep 1 1994	13 Healing	Nov 10 1994	5 Planting	Jan 19 1995	10 Healing
Sep 2 1994	1 Seeing	Nov 11 1994	6 Moving	Jan 20 1995	11 Seeing
Sep 3 1994	2 Intuiting	Nov 12 1994	7 Transcending	Jan 21 1995	12 Intuiting
Sep 4 1994	3 Evolving	Nov 13 1994	8 Remembering	Jan 22 1995	13 Evolving
Sep 5 1994	4 Self-Regulating	Nov 14 1994	9 Loving	Jan 23 1995	1 Self-Regulating
Sep 6 1994	5 Catalyzing	Nov 15 1994	10 Feeling	Jan 24 1995	2 Catalyzing
Sep 7 1994	6 Enlightening	Nov 16 1994	11 Devoting	Jan 25 1995	3 Enlightening
Sep 8 1994	7 Being	Nov 17 1994	12 Illuminating	Jan 26 1995	4 Being
Sep 9 1994	8 Breathing	Nov 18 1994	13 Choosing	Jan 27 1995	5 Breathing
Sep 10 1994	9 Listening	Nov 19 1994	1 Exploring	Jan 28 1995	6 Listening
Sep 11 1994	10 Planting	Nov 20 1994	2 Healing	Jan 29 1995	7 Planting
Sep 12 1994	11 Moving	Nov 21 1994	3 Seeing	Jan 30 1995	8 Moving
Sep 13 1994	12 Transcending	Nov 22 1994	4 Intuiting	Jan 31 1995	9 Transcending
Sep 14 1994	13 Remembering	Nov 23 1994	5 Evolving	Feb 1 1995	10 Remembering
Sep 15 1994	1 Loving	Nov 24 1994	6 Self-Regulating	Feb 2 1995	11 Loving
Sep 16 1994	2 Feeling	Nov 25 1994	7 Catalyzing	Feb 3 1995	12 Feeling
Sep 17 1994	3 Devoting	Nov 26 1994	8 Enlightening	Feb 4 1995	13 Devoting
Sep 18 1994	4 Illuminating	Nov 27 1994	9 Being	Feb 5 1995	1 Illuminating
Sep 19 1994	5 Choosing	Nov 28 1994	10 Breathing	Feb 6 1995	2 Choosing
Sep 20 1994	6 Exploring	Nov 29 1994	11 Listening	Feb 7 1995	3 Exploring
Sep 21 1994	7 Healing	Nov 30 1994	12 Planting	Feb 8 1995	4 Healing
Sep 22 1994	8 Seeing	Dec 1 1994	13 Moving	Feb 9 1995	5 Seeing
Sep 23 1994	9 Intuiting	Dec 2 1994	1 Transcending	Feb 10 1995	6 Intuiting
Sep 24 1994	10 Evolving	Dec 3 1994	2 Remembering	Feb 11 1995	7 Evolving
Sep 25 1994	11 Self-Regulating	Dec 4 1994	3 Loving	Feb 12 1995	8 Self-Regulating
Sep 26 1994	12 Catalyzing	Dec 5 1994	4 Feeling	Feb 13 1995	9 Catalyzing
Sep 27 1994	13 Enlightening	Dec 6 1994	5 Devoting	Feb 14 1995	10 Enlightening

Date	UE	Earth Energy	Date	UE	Earth Energy	Date	UE	Earth Energy
Feb 15 1995	11	Being	Apr 26 1995	3	Illuminating	Jul 5 1995	8	Being
Feb 16 1995	12	Breathing	Apr 27 1995	4	Choosing	Jul 6 1995	9	Breathing
Feb 17 1995	13	Listening	Apr 28 1995	5	Exploring	Jul 7 1995	10	Listening
Feb 18 1995	**1**	**Planting**	Apr 29 1995	6	Healing	Jul 8 1995	11	Planting
Feb 19 1995	2	Moving	Apr 30 1995	7	Seeing	Jul 9 1995	12	Moving
Feb 20 1995	3	Transcending	May 1 1995	8	Intuiting	Jul 10 1995	13	Transcending
Feb 21 1995	4	Remembering	May 2 1995	9	Evolving	Jul 11 1995	**1**	**Remembering**
Feb 22 1995	5	Loving	May 3 1995	10	Self-Regulating	Jul 12 1995	2	Loving
Feb 23 1995	6	Feeling	May 4 1995	11	Catalyzing	Jul 13 1995	3	Feeling
Feb 24 1995	7	Devoting	May 5 1995	12	Enlightening	Jul 14 1995	4	Devoting
Feb 25 1995	8	Illuminating	May 6 1995	13	Being	Jul 15 1995	5	Illuminating
Feb 26 1995	9	Choosing	May 7 1995	**1**	**Breathing**	Jul 16 1995	6	Choosing
Feb 27 1995	10	Exploring	May 8 1995	2	Listening	Jul 17 1995	7	Exploring
Feb 28 1995	11	Healing	May 9 1995	3	Planting	Jul 18 1995	8	Healing
Mar 1 1995	12	Seeing	May 10 1995	4	Moving	Jul 19 1995	9	Seeing
Mar 2 1995	13	Intuiting	May 11 1995	5	Transcending	Jul 20 1995	10	Intuiting
Mar 3 1995	**1**	**Evolving**	May 12 1995	6	Remembering	Jul 21 1995	11	Evolving
Mar 4 1995	2	Self-Regulating	May 13 1995	7	Loving	Jul 22 1995	12	Self-Regulating
Mar 5 1995	3	Catalyzing	May 14 1995	8	Feeling	Jul 23 1995	13	Catalyzing
Mar 6 1995	4	Enlightening	May 15 1995	9	Devoting	Jul 24 1995	**1**	**Enlightening**
Mar 7 1995	5	Being	May 16 1995	10	Illuminating	Jul 25 1995	2	Being
Mar 8 1995	6	Breathing	May 17 1995	11	Choosing	Jul 26 1995	3	Breathing
Mar 9 1995	7	Listening	May 18 1995	12	Exploring	Jul 27 1995	4	Listening
Mar 10 1995	8	Planting	May 19 1995	13	Healing	Jul 28 1995	5	Planting
Mar 11 1995	9	Moving	May 20 1995	**1**	**Seeing**	Jul 29 1995	6	Moving
Mar 12 1995	10	Transcending	May 21 1995	2	Intuiting	Jul 30 1995	7	Transcending
Mar 13 1995	11	Remembering	May 22 1995	3	Evolving	Jul 31 1995	8	Remembering
Mar 14 1995	12	Loving	May 23 1995	4	Self-Regulating	Aug 1 1995	9	Loving
Mar 15 1995	13	Feeling	May 24 1995	5	Catalyzing	Aug 2 1995	10	Feeling
Mar 16 1995	**1**	**Devoting**	May 25 1995	6	Enlightening	Aug 3 1995	11	Devoting
Mar 17 1995	2	Illuminating	May 26 1995	7	Being	Aug 4 1995	12	Illuminating
Mar 18 1995	3	Choosing	May 27 1995	8	Breathing	Aug 5 1995	13	Choosing
Mar 19 1995	4	Exploring	May 28 1995	9	Listening	Aug 6 1995	**1**	**Exploring**
Mar 20 1995	5	Healing	May 29 1995	10	Planting	Aug 7 1995	2	Healing
Mar 21 1995	6	Seeing	May 30 1995	11	Moving	Aug 8 1995	3	Seeing
Mar 22 1995	7	Intuiting	May 31 1995	12	Transcending	Aug 9 1995	4	Intuiting
Mar 23 1995	8	Evolving	Jun 1 1995	13	Remembering	Aug 10 1995	5	Evolving
Mar 24 1995	9	Self-Regulating	Jun 2 1995	**1**	**Loving**	Aug 11 1995	6	Self-Regulating
Mar 25 1995	10	Catalyzing	Jun 3 1995	2	Feeling	Aug 12 1995	7	Catalyzing
Mar 26 1995	11	Enlightening	Jun 4 1995	3	Devoting	Aug 13 1995	8	Enlightening
Mar 27 1995	12	Being	Jun 5 1995	4	Illuminating	Aug 14 1995	9	Being
Mar 28 1995	13	Breathing	Jun 6 1995	5	Choosing	Aug 15 1995	10	Breathing
Mar 29 1995	**1**	**Listening**	Jun 7 1995	6	Exploring	Aug 16 1995	11	Listening
Mar 30 1995	2	Planting	Jun 8 1995	7	Healing	Aug 17 1995	12	Planting
Mar 31 1995	3	Moving	Jun 9 1995	8	Seeing	Aug 18 1995	13	Moving
Apr 1 1995	4	Transcending	Jun 10 1995	9	Intuiting	Aug 19 1995	**1**	**Transcending**
Apr 2 1995	5	Remembering	Jun 11 1995	10	Evolving	Aug 20 1995	2	Remembering
Apr 3 1995	6	Loving	Jun 12 1995	11	Self-Regulating	Aug 21 1995	3	Loving
Apr 4 1995	7	Feeling	Jun 13 1995	12	Catalyzing	Aug 22 1995	4	Feeling
Apr 5 1995	8	Devoting	Jun 14 1995	13	Enlightening	Aug 23 1995	5	Devoting
Apr 6 1995	9	Illuminating	Jun 15 1995	**1**	**Being**	Aug 24 1995	6	Illuminating
Apr 7 1995	10	Choosing	Jun 16 1995	2	Breathing	Aug 25 1995	7	Choosing
Apr 8 1995	11	Exploring	Jun 17 1995	3	Listening	Aug 26 1995	8	Exploring
Apr 9 1995	12	Healing	Jun 18 1995	4	Planting	Aug 27 1995	9	Healing
Apr 10 1995	13	Seeing	Jun 19 1995	5	Moving	Aug 28 1995	10	Seeing
Apr 11 1995	**1**	**Intuiting**	Jun 20 1995	6	Transcending	Aug 29 1995	11	Intuiting
Apr 12 1995	2	Evolving	Jun 21 1995	7	Remembering	Aug 30 1995	12	Evolving
Apr 13 1995	3	Self-Regulating	Jun 22 1995	8	Loving	Aug 31 1995	13	Self-Regulating
Apr 14 1995	4	Catalyzing	Jun 23 1995	9	Feeling	Sep 1 1995	**1**	**Catalyzing**
Apr 15 1995	5	Enlightening	Jun 24 1995	10	Devoting	Sep 2 1995	2	Enlightening
Apr 16 1995	6	Being	Jun 25 1995	11	Illuminating	Sep 3 1995	3	Being
Apr 17 1995	7	Breathing	Jun 26 1995	12	Choosing	Sep 4 1995	4	Breathing
Apr 18 1995	8	Listening	Jun 27 1995	13	Exploring	Sep 5 1995	5	Listening
Apr 19 1995	9	Planting	Jun 28 1995	**1**	**Healing**	Sep 6 1995	6	Planting
Apr 20 1995	10	Moving	Jun 29 1995	2	Seeing	Sep 7 1995	7	Moving
Apr 21 1995	11	Transcending	Jun 30 1995	3	Intuiting	Sep 8 1995	8	Transcending
Apr 22 1995	12	Remembering	Jul 1 1995	4	Evolving	Sep 9 1995	9	Remembering
Apr 23 1995	13	Loving	Jul 2 1995	5	Self-Regulating	Sep 10 1995	10	Loving
Apr 24 1995	**1**	**Feeling**	Jul 3 1995	6	Catalyzing	Sep 11 1995	11	Feeling
Apr 25 1995	2	Devoting	Jul 4 1995	7	Enlightening	Sep 12 1995	12	Devoting

Date	UE	Earth Energy	Date	UE	Earth Energy	Date	UE	Earth Energy
Sep 13 1995	13	Illuminating	Nov 22 1995	5	Being	Jan 31 1996	10	Illuminating
Sep 14 1995	1	Choosing	Nov 23 1995	6	Breathing	Feb 1 1996	11	Choosing
Sep 15 1995	2	Exploring	Nov 24 1995	7	Listening	Feb 2 1996	12	Exploring
Sep 16 1995	3	Healing	Nov 25 1995	8	Planting	Feb 3 1996	13	Healing
Sep 17 1995	4	Seeing	Nov 26 1995	9	Moving	Feb 4 1996	1	Seeing
Sep 18 1995	5	Intuiting	Nov 27 1995	10	Transcending	Feb 5 1996	2	Intuiting
Sep 19 1995	6	Evolving	Nov 28 1995	11	Remembering	Feb 6 1996	3	Evolving
Sep 20 1995	7	Self-Regulating	Nov 29 1995	12	Loving	Feb 7 1996	4	Self-Regulating
Sep 21 1995	8	Catalyzing	Nov 30 1995	13	Feeling	Feb 8 1996	5	Catalyzing
Sep 22 1995	9	Enlightening	Dec 1 1995	1	Devoting	Feb 9 1996	6	Enlightening
Sep 23 1995	10	Being	Dec 2 1995	2	Illuminating	Feb 10 1996	7	Being
Sep 24 1995	11	Breathing	Dec 3 1995	3	Choosing	Feb 11 1996	8	Breathing
Sep 25 1995	12	Listening	Dec 4 1995	4	Exploring	Feb 12 1996	9	Listening
Sep 26 1995	13	Planting	Dec 5 1995	5	Healing	Feb 13 1996	10	Planting
Sep 27 1995	1	Moving	Dec 6 1995	6	Seeing	Feb 14 1996	11	Moving
Sep 28 1995	2	Transcending	Dec 7 1995	7	Intuiting	Feb 15 1996	12	Transcending
Sep 29 1995	3	Remembering	Dec 8 1995	8	Evolving	Feb 16 1996	13	Remembering
Sep 30 1995	4	Loving	Dec 9 1995	9	Self-Regulating	Feb 17 1996	1	Loving
Oct 1 1995	5	Feeling	Dec 10 1995	10	Catalyzing	Feb 18 1996	2	Feeling
Oct 2 1995	6	Devoting	Dec 11 1995	11	Enlightening	Feb 19 1996	3	Devoting
Oct 3 1995	7	Illuminating	Dec 12 1995	12	Being	Feb 20 1996	4	Illuminating
Oct 4 1995	8	Choosing	Dec 13 1995	13	Breathing	Feb 21 1996	5	Choosing
Oct 5 1995	9	Exploring	Dec 14 1995	1	Listening	Feb 22 1996	6	Exploring
Oct 6 1995	10	Healing	Dec 15 1995	2	Planting	Feb 23 1996	7	Healing
Oct 7 1995	11	Seeing	Dec 16 1995	3	Moving	Feb 24 1996	8	Seeing
Oct 8 1995	12	Intuiting	Dec 17 1995	4	Transcending	Feb 25 1996	9	Intuiting
Oct 9 1995	13	Evolving	Dec 18 1995	5	Remembering	Feb 26 1996	10	Evolving
Oct 10 1995	1	Self-Regulating	Dec 19 1995	6	Loving	Feb 27 1996	11	Self-Regulating
Oct 11 1995	2	Catalyzing	Dec 20 1995	7	Feeling	Feb 28 1996	12	Catalyzing
Oct 12 1995	3	Enlightening	Dec 21 1995	8	Devoting	Feb 29 1996	13	Enlightening
Oct 13 1995	4	Being	Dec 22 1995	9	Illuminating	Mar 1 1996	1	Being
Oct 14 1995	5	Breathing	Dec 23 1995	10	Choosing	Mar 2 1996	2	Breathing
Oct 15 1995	6	Listening	Dec 24 1995	11	Exploring	Mar 3 1996	3	Listening
Oct 16 1995	7	Planting	Dec 25 1995	12	Healing	Mar 4 1996	4	Planting
Oct 17 1995	8	Moving	Dec 26 1995	13	Seeing	Mar 5 1996	5	Moving
Oct 18 1995	9	Transcending	Dec 27 1995	1	Intuiting	Mar 6 1996	6	Transcending
Oct 19 1995	10	Remembering	Dec 28 1995	2	Evolving	Mar 7 1996	7	Remembering
Oct 20 1995	11	Loving	Dec 29 1995	3	Self-Regulating	Mar 8 1996	8	Loving
Oct 21 1995	12	Feeling	Dec 30 1995	4	Catalyzing	Mar 9 1996	9	Feeling
Oct 22 1995	13	Devoting	Dec 31 1995	5	Enlightening	Mar 10 1996	10	Devoting
Oct 23 1995	1	Illuminating	Jan 1 1996	6	Being	Mar 11 1996	11	Illuminating
Oct 24 1995	2	Choosing	Jan 2 1996	7	Breathing	Mar 12 1996	12	Choosing
Oct 25 1995	3	Exploring	Jan 3 1996	8	Listening	Mar 13 1996	13	Exploring
Oct 26 1995	4	Healing	Jan 4 1996	9	Planting	Mar 14 1996	1	Healing
Oct 27 1995	5	Seeing	Jan 5 1996	10	Moving	Mar 15 1996	2	Seeing
Oct 28 1995	6	Intuiting	Jan 6 1996	11	Transcending	Mar 16 1996	3	Intuiting
Oct 29 1995	7	Evolving	Jan 7 1996	12	Remembering	Mar 17 1996	4	Evolving
Oct 30 1995	8	Self-Regulating	Jan 8 1996	13	Loving	Mar 18 1996	5	Self-Regulating
Oct 31 1995	9	Catalyzing	Jan 9 1996	1	Feeling	Mar 19 1996	6	Catalyzing
Nov 1 1995	10	Enlightening	Jan 10 1996	2	Devoting	Mar 20 1996	7	Enlightening
Nov 2 1995	11	Being	Jan 11 1996	3	Illuminating	Mar 21 1996	8	Being
Nov 3 1995	12	Breathing	Jan 12 1996	4	Choosing	Mar 22 1996	9	Breathing
Nov 4 1995	13	Listening	Jan 13 1996	5	Exploring	Mar 23 1996	10	Listening
Nov 5 1995	1	Planting	Jan 14 1996	6	Healing	Mar 24 1996	11	Planting
Nov 6 1995	2	Moving	Jan 15 1996	7	Seeing	Mar 25 1996	12	Moving
Nov 7 1995	3	Transcending	Jan 16 1996	8	Intuiting	Mar 26 1996	13	Transcending
Nov 8 1995	4	Remembering	Jan 17 1996	9	Evolving	Mar 27 1996	1	Remembering
Nov 9 1995	5	Loving	Jan 18 1996	10	Self-Regulating	Mar 28 1996	2	Loving
Nov 10 1995	6	Feeling	Jan 19 1996	11	Catalyzing	Mar 29 1996	3	Feeling
Nov 11 1995	7	Devoting	Jan 20 1996	12	Enlightening	Mar 30 1996	4	Devoting
Nov 12 1995	8	Illuminating	Jan 21 1996	13	Being	Mar 31 1996	5	Illuminating
Nov 13 1995	9	Choosing	Jan 22 1996	1	Breathing	Apr 1 1996	6	Choosing
Nov 14 1995	10	Exploring	Jan 23 1996	2	Listening	Apr 2 1996	7	Exploring
Nov 15 1995	11	Healing	Jan 24 1996	3	Planting	Apr 3 1996	8	Healing
Nov 16 1995	12	Seeing	Jan 25 1996	4	Moving	Apr 4 1996	9	Seeing
Nov 17 1995	13	Intuiting	Jan 26 1996	5	Transcending	Apr 5 1996	10	Intuiting
Nov 18 1995	1	Evolving	Jan 27 1996	6	Remembering	Apr 6 1996	11	Evolving
Nov 19 1995	2	Self-Regulating	Jan 28 1996	7	Loving	Apr 7 1996	12	Self-Regulating
Nov 20 1995	3	Catalyzing	Jan 29 1996	8	Feeling	Apr 8 1996	13	Catalyzing
Nov 21 1995	4	Enlightening	Jan 30 1996	9	Devoting	Apr 9 1996	1	Enlightening

Date	UE	Earth Energy	Date	UE	Earth Energy	Date	UE	Earth Energy
Apr 10 1996	2	Being	Jun 19 1996	7	Illuminating	Aug 28 1996	12	Being
Apr 11 1996	3	Breathing	Jun 20 1996	8	Choosing	Aug 29 1996	13	Breathing
Apr 12 1996	4	Listening	Jun 21 1996	9	Exploring	Aug 30 1996	**1**	**Listening**
Apr 13 1996	5	Planting	Jun 22 1996	10	Healing	Aug 31 1996	2	Planting
Apr 14 1996	6	Moving	Jun 23 1996	11	Seeing	Sep 1 1996	3	Moving
Apr 15 1996	7	Transcending	Jun 24 1996	12	Intuiting	Sep 2 1996	4	Transcending
Apr 16 1996	8	Remembering	Jun 25 1996	13	Evolving	Sep 3 1996	5	Remembering
Apr 17 1996	9	Loving	Jun 26 1996	**1**	**Self-Regulating**	Sep 4 1996	6	Loving
Apr 18 1996	10	Feeling	Jun 27 1996	2	Catalyzing	Sep 5 1996	7	Feeling
Apr 19 1996	11	Devoting	Jun 28 1996	3	Enlightening	Sep 6 1996	8	Devoting
Apr 20 1996	12	Illuminating	Jun 29 1996	4	Being	Sep 7 1996	9	Illuminating
Apr 21 1996	13	Choosing	Jun 30 1996	5	Breathing	Sep 8 1996	10	Choosing
Apr 22 1996	**1**	**Exploring**	Jul 1 1996	6	Listening	Sep 9 1996	11	Exploring
Apr 23 1996	2	Healing	Jul 2 1996	7	Planting	Sep 10 1996	12	Healing
Apr 24 1996	3	Seeing	Jul 3 1996	8	Moving	Sep 11 1996	13	Seeing
Apr 25 1996	4	Intuiting	Jul 4 1996	9	Transcending	Sep 12 1996	**1**	**Intuiting**
Apr 26 1996	5	Evolving	Jul 5 1996	10	Remembering	Sep 13 1996	2	Evolving
Apr 27 1996	6	Self-Regulating	Jul 6 1996	11	Loving	Sep 14 1996	3	Self-Regulating
Apr 28 1996	7	Catalyzing	Jul 7 1996	12	Feeling	Sep 15 1996	4	Catalyzing
Apr 29 1996	8	Enlightening	Jul 8 1996	13	Devoting	Sep 16 1996	5	Enlightening
Apr 30 1996	9	Being	Jul 9 1996	**1**	**Illuminating**	Sep 17 1996	6	Being
May 1 1996	10	Breathing	Jul 10 1996	2	Choosing	Sep 18 1996	7	Breathing
May 2 1996	11	Listening	Jul 11 1996	3	Exploring	Sep 19 1996	8	Listening
May 3 1996	12	Planting	Jul 12 1996	4	Healing	Sep 20 1996	9	Planting
May 4 1996	13	Moving	Jul 13 1996	5	Seeing	Sep 21 1996	10	Moving
May 5 1996	**1**	**Transcending**	Jul 14 1996	6	Intuiting	Sep 22 1996	11	Transcending
May 6 1996	2	Remembering	Jul 15 1996	7	Evolving	Sep 23 1996	12	Remembering
May 7 1996	3	Loving	Jul 16 1996	8	Self-Regulating	Sep 24 1996	13	Loving
May 8 1996	4	Feeling	Jul 17 1996	9	Catalyzing	Sep 25 1996	**1**	**Feeling**
May 9 1996	5	Devoting	Jul 18 1996	10	Enlightening	Sep 26 1996	2	Devoting
May 10 1996	6	Illuminating	Jul 19 1996	11	Being	Sep 27 1996	3	Illuminating
May 11 1996	7	Choosing	Jul 20 1996	12	Breathing	Sep 28 1996	4	Choosing
May 12 1996	8	Exploring	Jul 21 1996	13	Listening	Sep 29 1996	5	Exploring
May 13 1996	9	Healing	Jul 22 1996	**1**	**Planting**	Sep 30 1996	6	Healing
May 14 1996	10	Seeing	Jul 23 1996	2	Moving	Oct 1 1996	7	Seeing
May 15 1996	11	Intuiting	Jul 24 1996	3	Transcending	Oct 2 1996	8	Intuiting
May 16 1996	12	Evolving	Jul 25 1996	4	Remembering	Oct 3 1996	9	Evolving
May 17 1996	13	Self-Regulating	Jul 26 1996	5	Loving	Oct 4 1996	10	Self-Regulating
May 18 1996	**1**	**Catalyzing**	Jul 27 1996	6	Feeling	Oct 5 1996	11	Catalyzing
May 19 1996	2	Enlightening	Jul 28 1996	7	Devoting	Oct 6 1996	12	Enlightening
May 20 1996	3	Being	Jul 29 1996	8	Illuminating	Oct 7 1996	13	Being
May 21 1996	4	Breathing	Jul 30 1996	9	Choosing	Oct 8 1996	**1**	**Breathing**
May 22 1996	5	Listening	Jul 31 1996	10	Exploring	Oct 9 1996	2	Listening
May 23 1996	6	Planting	Aug 1 1996	11	Healing	Oct 10 1996	3	Planting
May 24 1996	7	Moving	Aug 2 1996	12	Seeing	Oct 11 1996	4	Moving
May 25 1996	8	Transcending	Aug 3 1996	13	Intuiting	Oct 12 1996	5	Transcending
May 26 1996	9	Remembering	Aug 4 1996	**1**	**Evolving**	Oct 13 1996	6	Remembering
May 27 1996	10	Loving	Aug 5 1996	2	Self-Regulating	Oct 14 1996	7	Loving
May 28 1996	11	Feeling	Aug 6 1996	3	Catalyzing	Oct 15 1996	8	Feeling
May 29 1996	12	Devoting	Aug 7 1996	4	Enlightening	Oct 16 1996	9	Devoting
May 30 1996	13	Illuminating	Aug 8 1996	5	Being	Oct 17 1996	10	Illuminating
May 31 1996	**1**	**Choosing**	Aug 9 1996	6	Breathing	Oct 18 1996	11	Choosing
Jun 1 1996	2	Exploring	Aug 10 1996	7	Listening	Oct 19 1996	12	Exploring
Jun 2 1996	3	Healing	Aug 11 1996	8	Planting	Oct 20 1996	13	Healing
Jun 3 1996	4	Seeing	Aug 12 1996	9	Moving	Oct 21 1996	**1**	**Seeing**
Jun 4 1996	5	Intuiting	Aug 13 1996	10	Transcending	Oct 22 1996	2	Intuiting
Jun 5 1996	6	Evolving	Aug 14 1996	11	Remembering	Oct 23 1996	3	Evolving
Jun 6 1996	7	Self-Regulating	Aug 15 1996	12	Loving	Oct 24 1996	4	Self-Regulating
Jun 7 1996	8	Catalyzing	Aug 16 1996	13	Feeling	Oct 25 1996	5	Catalyzing
Jun 8 1996	9	Enlightening	Aug 17 1996	**1**	**Devoting**	Oct 26 1996	6	Enlightening
Jun 9 1996	10	Being	Aug 18 1996	2	Illuminating	Oct 27 1996	7	Being
Jun 10 1996	11	Breathing	Aug 19 1996	3	Choosing	Oct 28 1996	8	Breathing
Jun 11 1996	12	Listening	Aug 20 1996	4	Exploring	Oct 29 1996	9	Listening
Jun 12 1996	13	Planting	Aug 21 1996	5	Healing	Oct 30 1996	10	Planting
Jun 13 1996	**1**	**Moving**	Aug 22 1996	6	Seeing	Oct 31 1996	11	Moving
Jun 14 1996	2	Transcending	Aug 23 1996	7	Intuiting	Nov 1 1996	12	Transcending
Jun 15 1996	3	Remembering	Aug 24 1996	8	Evolving	Nov 2 1996	13	Remembering
Jun 16 1996	4	Loving	Aug 25 1996	9	Self-Regulating	Nov 3 1996	**1**	**Loving**
Jun 17 1996	5	Feeling	Aug 26 1996	10	Catalyzing	Nov 4 1996	2	Feeling
Jun 18 1996	6	Devoting	Aug 27 1996	11	Enlightening	Nov 5 1996	3	Devoting

Date	UE	Earth Energy	Date	UE	Earth Energy	Date	UE	Earth Energy
Nov 6 1996	4	Illuminating	Jan 15 1997	9	Being	Mar 26 1997	1	**Illuminating**
Nov 7 1996	5	Choosing	Jan 16 1997	10	Breathing	Mar 27 1997	2	Choosing
Nov 8 1996	6	Exploring	Jan 17 1997	11	Listening	Mar 28 1997	3	Exploring
Nov 9 1996	7	Healing	Jan 18 1997	12	Planting	Mar 29 1997	4	Healing
Nov 10 1996	8	Seeing	Jan 19 1997	13	Moving	Mar 30 1997	5	Seeing
Nov 11 1996	9	Intuiting	Jan 20 1997	1	**Transcending**	Mar 31 1997	6	Intuiting
Nov 12 1996	10	Evolving	Jan 21 1997	2	Remembering	Apr 1 1997	7	Evolving
Nov 13 1996	11	Self-Regulating	Jan 22 1997	3	Loving	Apr 2 1997	8	Self-Regulating
Nov 14 1996	12	Catalyzing	Jan 23 1997	4	Feeling	Apr 3 1997	9	Catalyzing
Nov 15 1996	13	Enlightening	Jan 24 1997	5	Devoting	Apr 4 1997	10	Enlightening
Nov 16 1996	1	**Being**	Jan 25 1997	6	Illuminating	Apr 5 1997	11	Being
Nov 17 1996	2	Breathing	Jan 26 1997	7	Choosing	Apr 6 1997	12	Breathing
Nov 18 1996	3	Listening	Jan 27 1997	8	Exploring	Apr 7 1997	13	Listening
Nov 19 1996	4	Planting	Jan 28 1997	9	Healing	Apr 8 1997	1	**Planting**
Nov 20 1996	5	Moving	Jan 29 1997	10	Seeing	Apr 9 1997	2	Moving
Nov 21 1996	6	Transcending	Jan 30 1997	11	Intuiting	Apr 10 1997	3	Transcending
Nov 22 1996	7	Remembering	Jan 31 1997	12	Evolving	Apr 11 1997	4	Remembering
Nov 23 1996	8	Loving	Feb 1 1997	13	Self-Regulating	Apr 12 1997	5	Loving
Nov 24 1996	9	Feeling	Feb 2 1997	1	**Catalyzing**	Apr 13 1997	6	Feeling
Nov 25 1996	10	Devoting	Feb 3 1997	2	Enlightening	Apr 14 1997	7	Devoting
Nov 26 1996	11	Illuminating	Feb 4 1997	3	Being	Apr 15 1997	8	Illuminating
Nov 27 1996	12	Choosing	Feb 5 1997	4	Breathing	Apr 16 1997	9	Choosing
Nov 28 1996	13	Exploring	Feb 6 1997	5	Listening	Apr 17 1997	10	Exploring
Nov 29 1996	1	**Healing**	Feb 7 1997	6	Planting	Apr 18 1997	11	Healing
Nov 30 1996	2	Seeing	Feb 8 1997	7	Moving	Apr 19 1997	12	Seeing
Dec 1 1996	3	Intuiting	Feb 9 1997	8	Transcending	Apr 20 1997	13	Intuiting
Dec 2 1996	4	Evolving	Feb 10 1997	9	Remembering	Apr 21 1997	1	**Evolving**
Dec 3 1996	5	Self-Regulating	Feb 11 1997	10	Loving	Apr 22 1997	2	Self-Regulating
Dec 4 1996	6	Catalyzing	Feb 12 1997	11	Feeling	Apr 23 1997	3	Catalyzing
Dec 5 1996	7	Enlightening	Feb 13 1997	12	Devoting	Apr 24 1997	4	Enlightening
Dec 6 1996	8	Being	Feb 14 1997	13	Illuminating	Apr 25 1997	5	Being
Dec 7 1996	9	Breathing	Feb 15 1997	1	**Choosing**	Apr 26 1997	6	Breathing
Dec 8 1996	10	Listening	Feb 16 1997	2	Exploring	Apr 27 1997	7	Listening
Dec 9 1996	11	Planting	Feb 17 1997	3	Healing	Apr 28 1997	8	Planting
Dec 10 1996	12	Moving	Feb 18 1997	4	Seeing	Apr 29 1997	9	Moving
Dec 11 1996	13	Transcending	Feb 19 1997	5	Intuiting	Apr 30 1997	10	Transcending
Dec 12 1996	1	**Remembering**	Feb 20 1997	6	Evolving	May 1 1997	11	Remembering
Dec 13 1996	2	Loving	Feb 21 1997	7	Self-Regulating	May 2 1997	12	Loving
Dec 14 1996	3	Feeling	Feb 22 1997	8	Catalyzing	May 3 1997	13	Feeling
Dec 15 1996	4	Devoting	Feb 23 1997	9	Enlightening	May 4 1997	1	**Devoting**
Dec 16 1996	5	Illuminating	Feb 24 1997	10	Being	May 5 1997	2	Illuminating
Dec 17 1996	6	Choosing	Feb 25 1997	11	Breathing	May 6 1997	3	Choosing
Dec 18 1996	7	Exploring	Feb 26 1997	12	Listening	May 7 1997	4	Exploring
Dec 19 1996	8	Healing	Feb 27 1997	13	Planting	May 8 1997	5	Healing
Dec 20 1996	9	Seeing	Feb 28 1997	1	**Moving**	May 9 1997	6	Seeing
Dec 21 1996	10	Intuiting	Mar 1 1997	2	Transcending	May 10 1997	7	Intuiting
Dec 22 1996	11	Evolving	Mar 2 1997	3	Remembering	May 11 1997	8	Evolving
Dec 23 1996	12	Self-Regulating	Mar 3 1997	4	Loving	May 12 1997	9	Self-Regulating
Dec 24 1996	13	Catalyzing	Mar 4 1997	5	Feeling	May 13 1997	10	Catalyzing
Dec 25 1996	1	**Enlightening**	Mar 5 1997	6	Devoting	May 14 1997	11	Enlightening
Dec 26 1996	2	Being	Mar 6 1997	7	Illuminating	May 15 1997	12	Being
Dec 27 1996	3	Breathing	Mar 7 1997	8	Choosing	May 16 1997	13	Breathing
Dec 28 1996	4	Listening	Mar 8 1997	9	Exploring	May 17 1997	1	**Listening**
Dec 29 1996	5	Planting	Mar 9 1997	10	Healing	May 18 1997	2	Planting
Dec 30 1996	6	Moving	Mar 10 1997	11	Seeing	May 19 1997	3	Moving
Dec 31 1996	7	Transcending	Mar 11 1997	12	Intuiting	May 20 1997	4	Transcending
Jan 1 1997	8	Remembering	Mar 12 1997	13	Evolving	May 21 1997	5	Remembering
Jan 2 1997	9	Loving	Mar 13 1997	1	**Self-Regulating**	May 22 1997	6	Loving
Jan 3 1997	10	Feeling	Mar 14 1997	2	Catalyzing	May 23 1997	7	Feeling
Jan 4 1997	11	Devoting	Mar 15 1997	3	Enlightening	May 24 1997	8	Devoting
Jan 5 1997	12	Illuminating	Mar 16 1997	4	Being	May 25 1997	9	Illuminating
Jan 6 1997	13	Choosing	Mar 17 1997	5	Breathing	May 26 1997	10	Choosing
Jan 7 1997	1	**Exploring**	Mar 18 1997	6	Listening	May 27 1997	11	Exploring
Jan 8 1997	2	Healing	Mar 19 1997	7	Planting	May 28 1997	12	Healing
Jan 9 1997	3	Seeing	Mar 20 1997	8	Moving	May 29 1997	13	Seeing
Jan 10 1997	4	Intuiting	Mar 21 1997	9	Transcending	May 30 1997	1	**Intuiting**
Jan 11 1997	5	Evolving	Mar 22 1997	10	Remembering	May 31 1997	2	Evolving
Jan 12 1997	6	Self-Regulating	Mar 23 1997	11	Loving	Jun 1 1997	3	Self-Regulating
Jan 13 1997	7	Catalyzing	Mar 24 1997	12	Feeling	Jun 2 1997	4	Catalyzing
Jan 14 1997	8	Enlightening	Mar 25 1997	13	Devoting	Jun 3 1997	5	Enlightening

Date	UE Earth Energy	Date	UE Earth Energy	Date	UE Earth Energy
Jun 4 1997	6 Being	Aug 13 1997	11 Illuminating	Oct 22 1997	3 Being
Jun 5 1997	7 Breathing	Aug 14 1997	12 Choosing	Oct 23 1997	4 Breathing
Jun 6 1997	8 Listening	Aug 15 1997	13 Exploring	Oct 24 1997	5 Listening
Jun 7 1997	9 Planting	Aug 16 1997	1 Healing	Oct 25 1997	6 Planting
Jun 8 1997	10 Moving	Aug 17 1997	2 Seeing	Oct 26 1997	7 Moving
Jun 9 1997	11 Transcending	Aug 18 1997	3 Intuiting	Oct 27 1997	8 Transcending
Jun 10 1997	12 Remembering	Aug 19 1997	4 Evolving	Oct 28 1997	9 Remembering
Jun 11 1997	13 Loving	Aug 20 1997	5 Self-Regulating	Oct 29 1997	10 Loving
Jun 12 1997	1 Feeling	Aug 21 1997	6 Catalyzing	Oct 30 1997	11 Feeling
Jun 13 1997	2 Devoting	Aug 22 1997	7 Enlightening	Oct 31 1997	12 Devoting
Jun 14 1997	3 Illuminating	Aug 23 1997	8 Being	Nov 1 1997	13 Illuminating
Jun 15 1997	4 Choosing	Aug 24 1997	9 Breathing	Nov 2 1997	1 Choosing
Jun 16 1997	5 Exploring	Aug 25 1997	10 Listening	Nov 3 1997	2 Exploring
Jun 17 1997	6 Healing	Aug 26 1997	11 Planting	Nov 4 1997	3 Healing
Jun 18 1997	7 Seeing	Aug 27 1997	12 Moving	Nov 5 1997	4 Seeing
Jun 19 1997	8 Intuiting	Aug 28 1997	13 Transcending	Nov 6 1997	5 Intuiting
Jun 20 1997	9 Evolving	Aug 29 1997	1 Remembering	Nov 7 1997	6 Evolving
Jun 21 1997	10 Self-Regulating	Aug 30 1997	2 Loving	Nov 8 1997	7 Self-Regulating
Jun 22 1997	11 Catalyzing	Aug 31 1997	3 Feeling	Nov 9 1997	8 Catalyzing
Jun 23 1997	12 Enlightening	Sep 1 1997	4 Devoting	Nov 10 1997	9 Enlightening
Jun 24 1997	13 Being	Sep 2 1997	5 Illuminating	Nov 11 1997	10 Being
Jun 25 1997	1 Breathing	Sep 3 1997	6 Choosing	Nov 12 1997	11 Breathing
Jun 26 1997	2 Listening	Sep 4 1997	7 Exploring	Nov 13 1997	12 Listening
Jun 27 1997	3 Planting	Sep 5 1997	8 Healing	Nov 14 1997	13 Planting
Jun 28 1997	4 Moving	Sep 6 1997	9 Seeing	Nov 15 1997	1 Moving
Jun 29 1997	5 Transcending	Sep 7 1997	10 Intuiting	Nov 16 1997	2 Transcending
Jun 30 1997	6 Remembering	Sep 8 1997	11 Evolving	Nov 17 1997	3 Remembering
Jul 1 1997	7 Loving	Sep 9 1997	12 Self-Regulating	Nov 18 1997	4 Loving
Jul 2 1997	8 Feeling	Sep 10 1997	13 Catalyzing	Nov 19 1997	5 Feeling
Jul 3 1997	9 Devoting	Sep 11 1997	1 Enlightening	Nov 20 1997	6 Devoting
Jul 4 1997	10 Illuminating	Sep 12 1997	2 Being	Nov 21 1997	7 Illuminating
Jul 5 1997	11 Choosing	Sep 13 1997	3 Breathing	Nov 22 1997	8 Choosing
Jul 6 1997	12 Exploring	Sep 14 1997	4 Listening	Nov 23 1997	9 Exploring
Jul 7 1997	13 Healing	Sep 15 1997	5 Planting	Nov 24 1997	10 Healing
Jul 8 1997	1 Seeing	Sep 16 1997	6 Moving	Nov 25 1997	11 Seeing
Jul 9 1997	2 Intuiting	Sep 17 1997	7 Transcending	Nov 26 1997	12 Intuiting
Jul 10 1997	3 Evolving	Sep 18 1997	8 Remembering	Nov 27 1997	13 Evolving
Jul 11 1997	4 Self-Regulating	Sep 19 1997	9 Loving	Nov 28 1997	1 Self-Regulating
Jul 12 1997	5 Catalyzing	Sep 20 1997	10 Feeling	Nov 29 1997	2 Catalyzing
Jul 13 1997	6 Enlightening	Sep 21 1997	11 Devoting	Nov 30 1997	3 Enlightening
Jul 14 1997	7 Being	Sep 22 1997	12 Illuminating	Dec 1 1997	4 Being
Jul 15 1997	8 Breathing	Sep 23 1997	13 Choosing	Dec 2 1997	5 Breathing
Jul 16 1997	9 Listening	Sep 24 1997	1 Exploring	Dec 3 1997	6 Listening
Jul 17 1997	10 Planting	Sep 25 1997	2 Healing	Dec 4 1997	7 Planting
Jul 18 1997	11 Moving	Sep 26 1997	3 Seeing	Dec 5 1997	8 Moving
Jul 19 1997	12 Transcending	Sep 27 1997	4 Intuiting	Dec 6 1997	9 Transcending
Jul 20 1997	13 Remembering	Sep 28 1997	5 Evolving	Dec 7 1997	10 Remembering
Jul 21 1997	1 Loving	Sep 29 1997	6 Self-Regulating	Dec 8 1997	11 Loving
Jul 22 1997	2 Feeling	Sep 30 1997	7 Catalyzing	Dec 9 1997	12 Feeling
Jul 23 1997	3 Devoting	Oct 1 1997	8 Enlightening	Dec 10 1997	13 Devoting
Jul 24 1997	4 Illuminating	Oct 2 1997	9 Being	Dec 11 1997	1 Illuminating
Jul 25 1997	5 Choosing	Oct 3 1997	10 Breathing	Dec 12 1997	2 Choosing
Jul 26 1997	6 Exploring	Oct 4 1997	11 Listening	Dec 13 1997	3 Exploring
Jul 27 1997	7 Healing	Oct 5 1997	12 Planting	Dec 14 1997	4 Healing
Jul 28 1997	8 Seeing	Oct 6 1997	13 Moving	Dec 15 1997	5 Seeing
Jul 29 1997	9 Intuiting	Oct 7 1997	1 Transcending	Dec 16 1997	6 Intuiting
Jul 30 1997	10 Evolving	Oct 8 1997	2 Remembering	Dec 17 1997	7 Evolving
Jul 31 1997	11 Self-Regulating	Oct 9 1997	3 Loving	Dec 18 1997	8 Self-Regulating
Aug 1 1997	12 Catalyzing	Oct 10 1997	4 Feeling	Dec 19 1997	9 Catalyzing
Aug 2 1997	13 Enlightening	Oct 11 1997	5 Devoting	Dec 20 1997	10 Enlightening
Aug 3 1997	1 Being	Oct 12 1997	6 Illuminating	Dec 21 1997	11 Being
Aug 4 1997	2 Breathing	Oct 13 1997	7 Choosing	Dec 22 1997	12 Breathing
Aug 5 1997	3 Listening	Oct 14 1997	8 Exploring	Dec 23 1997	13 Listening
Aug 6 1997	4 Planting	Oct 15 1997	9 Healing	Dec 24 1997	1 Planting
Aug 7 1997	5 Moving	Oct 16 1997	10 Seeing	Dec 25 1997	2 Moving
Aug 8 1997	6 Transcending	Oct 17 1997	11 Intuiting	Dec 26 1997	3 Transcending
Aug 9 1997	7 Remembering	Oct 18 1997	12 Evolving	Dec 27 1997	4 Remembering
Aug 10 1997	8 Loving	Oct 19 1997	13 Self-Regulating	Dec 28 1997	5 Loving
Aug 11 1997	9 Feeling	Oct 20 1997	1 Catalyzing	Dec 29 1997	6 Feeling
Aug 12 1997	10 Devoting	Oct 21 1997	2 Enlightening	Dec 30 1997	7 Devoting

Date	UE	Earth Energy	Date	UE	Earth Energy	Date	UE	Earth Energy
Dec 31 1997	8	Illuminating	Mar 11 1998	13	Being	May 20 1998	5	Illuminating
Jan 1 1998	9	Choosing	Mar 12 1998	**1**	**Breathing**	May 21 1998	6	Choosing
Jan 2 1998	10	Exploring	Mar 13 1998	2	Listening	May 22 1998	7	Exploring
Jan 3 1998	11	Healing	Mar 14 1998	3	Planting	May 23 1998	8	Healing
Jan 4 1998	12	Seeing	Mar 15 1998	4	Moving	May 24 1998	9	Seeing
Jan 5 1998	13	Intuiting	Mar 16 1998	5	Transcending	May 25 1998	10	Intuiting
Jan 6 1998	**1**	**Evolving**	Mar 17 1998	6	Remembering	May 26 1998	11	Evolving
Jan 7 1998	2	Self-Regulating	Mar 18 1998	7	Loving	May 27 1998	12	Self-Regulating
Jan 8 1998	3	Catalyzing	Mar 19 1998	8	Feeling	May 28 1998	13	Catalyzing
Jan 9 1998	4	Enlightening	Mar 20 1998	9	Devoting	May 29 1998	**1**	**Enlightening**
Jan 10 1998	5	Being	Mar 21 1998	10	Illuminating	May 30 1998	2	Being
Jan 11 1998	6	Breathing	Mar 22 1998	11	Choosing	May 31 1998	3	Breathing
Jan 12 1998	7	Listening	Mar 23 1998	12	Exploring	Jun 1 1998	4	Listening
Jan 13 1998	8	Planting	Mar 24 1998	13	Healing	Jun 2 1998	5	Planting
Jan 14 1998	9	Moving	Mar 25 1998	**1**	**Seeing**	Jun 3 1998	6	Moving
Jan 15 1998	10	Transcending	Mar 26 1998	2	Intuiting	Jun 4 1998	7	Transcending
Jan 16 1998	11	Remembering	Mar 27 1998	3	Evolving	Jun 5 1998	8	Remembering
Jan 17 1998	12	Loving	Mar 28 1998	4	Self-Regulating	Jun 6 1998	9	Loving
Jan 18 1998	13	Feeling	Mar 29 1998	5	Catalyzing	Jun 7 1998	10	Feeling
Jan 19 1998	**1**	**Devoting**	Mar 30 1998	6	Enlightening	Jun 8 1998	11	Devoting
Jan 20 1998	2	Illuminating	Mar 31 1998	7	Being	Jun 9 1998	12	Illuminating
Jan 21 1998	3	Choosing	Apr 1 1998	8	Breathing	Jun 10 1998	13	Choosing
Jan 22 1998	4	Exploring	Apr 2 1998	9	Listening	Jun 11 1998	**1**	**Exploring**
Jan 23 1998	5	Healing	Apr 3 1998	10	Planting	Jun 12 1998	2	Healing
Jan 24 1998	6	Seeing	Apr 4 1998	11	Moving	Jun 13 1998	3	Seeing
Jan 25 1998	7	Intuiting	Apr 5 1998	12	Transcending	Jun 14 1998	4	Intuiting
Jan 26 1998	8	Evolving	Apr 6 1998	13	Remembering	Jun 15 1998	5	Evolving
Jan 27 1998	9	Self-Regulating	Apr 7 1998	**1**	**Loving**	Jun 16 1998	6	Self-Regulating
Jan 28 1998	10	Catalyzing	Apr 8 1998	2	Feeling	Jun 17 1998	7	Catalyzing
Jan 29 1998	11	Enlightening	Apr 9 1998	3	Devoting	Jun 18 1998	8	Enlightening
Jan 30 1998	12	Being	Apr 10 1998	4	Illuminating	Jun 19 1998	9	Being
Jan 31 1998	13	Breathing	Apr 11 1998	5	Choosing	Jun 20 1998	10	Breathing
Feb 1 1998	**1**	**Listening**	Apr 12 1998	6	Exploring	Jun 21 1998	11	Listening
Feb 2 1998	2	Planting	Apr 13 1998	7	Healing	Jun 22 1998	12	Planting
Feb 3 1998	3	Moving	Apr 14 1998	8	Seeing	Jun 23 1998	13	Moving
Feb 4 1998	4	Transcending	Apr 15 1998	9	Intuiting	Jun 24 1998	**1**	**Transcending**
Feb 5 1998	5	Remembering	Apr 16 1998	10	Evolving	Jun 25 1998	2	Remembering
Feb 6 1998	6	Loving	Apr 17 1998	11	Self-Regulating	Jun 26 1998	3	Loving
Feb 7 1998	7	Feeling	Apr 18 1998	12	Catalyzing	Jun 27 1998	4	Feeling
Feb 8 1998	8	Devoting	Apr 19 1998	13	Enlightening	Jun 28 1998	5	Devoting
Feb 9 1998	9	Illuminating	Apr 20 1998	**1**	**Being**	Jun 29 1998	6	Illuminating
Feb 10 1998	10	Choosing	Apr 21 1998	2	Breathing	Jun 30 1998	7	Choosing
Feb 11 1998	11	Exploring	Apr 22 1998	3	Listening	Jul 1 1998	8	Exploring
Feb 12 1998	12	Healing	Apr 23 1998	4	Planting	Jul 2 1998	9	Healing
Feb 13 1998	13	Seeing	Apr 24 1998	5	Moving	Jul 3 1998	10	Seeing
Feb 14 1998	**1**	**Intuiting**	Apr 25 1998	6	Transcending	Jul 4 1998	11	Intuiting
Feb 15 1998	2	Evolving	Apr 26 1998	7	Remembering	Jul 5 1998	12	Evolving
Feb 16 1998	3	Self-Regulating	Apr 27 1998	8	Loving	Jul 6 1998	13	Self-Regulating
Feb 17 1998	4	Catalyzing	Apr 28 1998	9	Feeling	Jul 7 1998	**1**	**Catalyzing**
Feb 18 1998	5	Enlightening	Apr 29 1998	10	Devoting	Jul 8 1998	2	Enlightening
Feb 19 1998	6	Being	Apr 30 1998	11	Illuminating	Jul 9 1998	3	Being
Feb 20 1998	7	Breathing	May 1 1998	12	Choosing	Jul 10 1998	4	Breathing
Feb 21 1998	8	Listening	May 2 1998	13	Exploring	Jul 11 1998	5	Listening
Feb 22 1998	9	Planting	May 3 1998	**1**	**Healing**	Jul 12 1998	6	Planting
Feb 23 1998	10	Moving	May 4 1998	2	Seeing	Jul 13 1998	7	Moving
Feb 24 1998	11	Transcending	May 5 1998	3	Intuiting	Jul 14 1998	8	Transcending
Feb 25 1998	12	Remembering	May 6 1998	4	Evolving	Jul 15 1998	9	Remembering
Feb 26 1998	13	Loving	May 7 1998	5	Self-Regulating	Jul 16 1998	10	Loving
Feb 27 1998	**1**	**Feeling**	May 8 1998	6	Catalyzing	Jul 17 1998	11	Feeling
Feb 28 1998	2	Devoting	May 9 1998	7	Enlightening	Jul 18 1998	12	Devoting
Mar 1 1998	3	Illuminating	May 10 1998	8	Being	Jul 19 1998	13	Illuminating
Mar 2 1998	4	Choosing	May 11 1998	9	Breathing	Jul 20 1998	**1**	**Choosing**
Mar 3 1998	5	Exploring	May 12 1998	10	Listening	Jul 21 1998	2	Exploring
Mar 4 1998	6	Healing	May 13 1998	11	Planting	Jul 22 1998	3	Healing
Mar 5 1998	7	Seeing	May 14 1998	12	Moving	Jul 23 1998	4	Seeing
Mar 6 1998	8	Intuiting	May 15 1998	13	Transcending	Jul 24 1998	5	Intuiting
Mar 7 1998	9	Evolving	May 16 1998	**1**	**Remembering**	Jul 25 1998	6	Evolving
Mar 8 1998	10	Self-Regulating	May 17 1998	2	Loving	Jul 26 1998	7	Self-Regulating
Mar 9 1998	11	Catalyzing	May 18 1998	3	Feeling	Jul 27 1998	8	Catalyzing
Mar 10 1998	12	Enlightening	May 19 1998	4	Devoting	Jul 28 1998	9	Enlightening

Date	UE	Earth Energy	Date	UE	Earth Energy	Date	UE	Earth Energy
Jul 29 1998	10	Being	Oct 7 1998	2	Illuminating	Dec 16 1998	7	Being
Jul 30 1998	11	Breathing	Oct 8 1998	3	Choosing	Dec 17 1998	8	Breathing
Jul 31 1998	12	Listening	Oct 9 1998	4	Exploring	Dec 18 1998	9	Listening
Aug 1 1998	13	Planting	Oct 10 1998	5	Healing	Dec 19 1998	10	Planting
Aug 2 1998	**1**	**Moving**	Oct 11 1998	6	Seeing	Dec 20 1998	11	Moving
Aug 3 1998	2	Transcending	Oct 12 1998	7	Intuiting	Dec 21 1998	12	Transcending
Aug 4 1998	3	Remembering	Oct 13 1998	8	Evolving	Dec 22 1998	13	Remembering
Aug 5 1998	4	Loving	Oct 14 1998	9	Self-Regulating	Dec 23 1998	**1**	**Loving**
Aug 6 1998	5	Feeling	Oct 15 1998	10	Catalyzing	Dec 24 1998	2	Feeling
Aug 7 1998	6	Devoting	Oct 16 1998	11	Enlightening	Dec 25 1998	3	Devoting
Aug 8 1998	7	Illuminating	Oct 17 1998	12	Being	Dec 26 1998	4	Illuminating
Aug 9 1998	8	Choosing	Oct 18 1998	13	Breathing	Dec 27 1998	5	Choosing
Aug 10 1998	9	Exploring	Oct 19 1998	**1**	**Listening**	Dec 28 1998	6	Exploring
Aug 11 1998	10	Healing	Oct 20 1998	2	Planting	Dec 29 1998	7	Healing
Aug 12 1998	11	Seeing	Oct 21 1998	3	Moving	Dec 30 1998	8	Seeing
Aug 13 1998	12	Intuiting	Oct 22 1998	4	Transcending	Dec 31 1998	9	Intuiting
Aug 14 1998	13	Evolving	Oct 23 1998	5	Remembering	Jan 1 1999	10	Evolving
Aug 15 1998	**1**	**Self-Regulating**	Oct 24 1998	6	Loving	Jan 2 1999	11	Self-Regulating
Aug 16 1998	2	Catalyzing	Oct 25 1998	7	Feeling	Jan 3 1999	12	Catalyzing
Aug 17 1998	3	Enlightening	Oct 26 1998	8	Devoting	Jan 4 1999	13	Enlightening
Aug 18 1998	4	Being	Oct 27 1998	9	Illuminating	Jan 5 1999	**1**	**Being**
Aug 19 1998	5	Breathing	Oct 28 1998	10	Choosing	Jan 6 1999	2	Breathing
Aug 20 1998	6	Listening	Oct 29 1998	11	Exploring	Jan 7 1999	3	Listening
Aug 21 1998	7	Planting	Oct 30 1998	12	Healing	Jan 8 1999	4	Planting
Aug 22 1998	8	Moving	Oct 31 1998	13	Seeing	Jan 9 1999	5	Moving
Aug 23 1998	9	Transcending	Nov 1 1998	**1**	**Intuiting**	Jan 10 1999	6	Transcending
Aug 24 1998	10	Remembering	Nov 2 1998	2	Evolving	Jan 11 1999	7	Remembering
Aug 25 1998	11	Loving	Nov 3 1998	3	Self-Regulating	Jan 12 1999	8	Loving
Aug 26 1998	12	Feeling	Nov 4 1998	4	Catalyzing	Jan 13 1999	9	Feeling
Aug 27 1998	13	Devoting	Nov 5 1998	5	Enlightening	Jan 14 1999	10	Devoting
Aug 28 1998	**1**	**Illuminating**	Nov 6 1998	6	Being	Jan 15 1999	11	Illuminating
Aug 29 1998	2	Choosing	Nov 7 1998	7	Breathing	Jan 16 1999	12	Choosing
Aug 30 1998	3	Exploring	Nov 8 1998	8	Listening	Jan 17 1999	13	Exploring
Aug 31 1998	4	Healing	Nov 9 1998	9	Planting	Jan 18 1999	**1**	**Healing**
Sep 1 1998	5	Seeing	Nov 10 1998	10	Moving	Jan 19 1999	2	Seeing
Sep 2 1998	6	Intuiting	Nov 11 1998	11	Transcending	Jan 20 1999	3	Intuiting
Sep 3 1998	7	Evolving	Nov 12 1998	12	Remembering	Jan 21 1999	4	Evolving
Sep 4 1998	8	Self-Regulating	Nov 13 1998	13	Loving	Jan 22 1999	5	Self-Regulating
Sep 5 1998	9	Catalyzing	Nov 14 1998	**1**	**Feeling**	Jan 23 1999	6	Catalyzing
Sep 6 1998	10	Enlightening	Nov 15 1998	2	Devoting	Jan 24 1999	7	Enlightening
Sep 7 1998	11	Being	Nov 16 1998	3	Illuminating	Jan 25 1999	8	Being
Sep 8 1998	12	Breathing	Nov 17 1998	4	Choosing	Jan 26 1999	9	Breathing
Sep 9 1998	13	Listening	Nov 18 1998	5	Exploring	Jan 27 1999	10	Listening
Sep 10 1998	**1**	**Planting**	Nov 19 1998	6	Healing	Jan 28 1999	11	Planting
Sep 11 1998	2	Moving	Nov 20 1998	7	Seeing	Jan 29 1999	12	Moving
Sep 12 1998	3	Transcending	Nov 21 1998	8	Intuiting	Jan 30 1999	13	Transcending
Sep 13 1998	4	Remembering	Nov 22 1998	9	Evolving	Jan 31 1999	**1**	**Remembering**
Sep 14 1998	5	Loving	Nov 23 1998	10	Self-Regulating	Feb 1 1999	2	Loving
Sep 15 1998	6	Feeling	Nov 24 1998	11	Catalyzing	Feb 2 1999	3	Feeling
Sep 16 1998	7	Devoting	Nov 25 1998	12	Enlightening	Feb 3 1999	4	Devoting
Sep 17 1998	8	Illuminating	Nov 26 1998	13	Being	Feb 4 1999	5	Illuminating
Sep 18 1998	9	Choosing	Nov 27 1998	**1**	**Breathing**	Feb 5 1999	6	Choosing
Sep 19 1998	10	Exploring	Nov 28 1998	2	Listening	Feb 6 1999	7	Exploring
Sep 20 1998	11	Healing	Nov 29 1998	3	Planting	Feb 7 1999	8	Healing
Sep 21 1998	12	Seeing	Nov 30 1998	4	Moving	Feb 8 1999	9	Seeing
Sep 22 1998	13	Intuiting	Dec 1 1998	5	Transcending	Feb 9 1999	10	Intuiting
Sep 23 1998	**1**	**Evolving**	Dec 2 1998	6	Remembering	Feb 10 1999	11	Evolving
Sep 24 1998	2	Self-Regulating	Dec 3 1998	7	Loving	Feb 11 1999	12	Self-Regulating
Sep 25 1998	3	Catalyzing	Dec 4 1998	8	Feeling	Feb 12 1999	13	Catalyzing
Sep 26 1998	4	Enlightening	Dec 5 1998	9	Devoting	Feb 13 1999	**1**	**Enlightening**
Sep 27 1998	5	Being	Dec 6 1998	10	Illuminating	Feb 14 1999	2	Being
Sep 28 1998	6	Breathing	Dec 7 1998	11	Choosing	Feb 15 1999	3	Breathing
Sep 29 1998	7	Listening	Dec 8 1998	12	Exploring	Feb 16 1999	4	Listening
Sep 30 1998	8	Planting	Dec 9 1998	13	Healing	Feb 17 1999	5	Planting
Oct 1 1998	9	Moving	Dec 10 1998	**1**	**Seeing**	Feb 18 1999	6	Moving
Oct 2 1998	10	Transcending	Dec 11 1998	2	Intuiting	Feb 19 1999	7	Transcending
Oct 3 1998	11	Remembering	Dec 12 1998	3	Evolving	Feb 20 1999	8	Remembering
Oct 4 1998	12	Loving	Dec 13 1998	4	Self-Regulating	Feb 21 1999	9	Loving
Oct 5 1998	13	Feeling	Dec 14 1998	5	Catalyzing	Feb 22 1999	10	Feeling
Oct 6 1998	**1**	**Devoting**	Dec 15 1998	6	Enlightening	Feb 23 1999	11	Devoting

Date	UE	Earth Energy	Date	UE	Earth Energy	Date	UE	Earth Energy
Feb 24 1999	12	Illuminating	May 5 1999	4	Being	Jul 14 1999	9	Illuminating
Feb 25 1999	13	Choosing	May 6 1999	5	Breathing	Jul 15 1999	10	Choosing
Feb 26 1999	**1**	**Exploring**	May 7 1999	6	Listening	Jul 16 1999	11	Exploring
Feb 27 1999	2	Healing	May 8 1999	7	Planting	Jul 17 1999	12	Healing
Feb 28 1999	3	Seeing	May 9 1999	8	Moving	Jul 18 1999	13	Seeing
Mar 1 1999	4	Intuiting	May 10 1999	9	Transcending	Jul 19 1999	**1**	**Intuiting**
Mar 2 1999	5	Evolving	May 11 1999	10	Remembering	Jul 20 1999	2	Evolving
Mar 3 1999	6	Self-Regulating	May 12 1999	11	Loving	Jul 21 1999	3	Self-Regulating
Mar 4 1999	7	Catalyzing	May 13 1999	12	Feeling	Jul 22 1999	4	Catalyzing
Mar 5 1999	8	Enlightening	May 14 1999	13	Devoting	Jul 23 1999	5	Enlightening
Mar 6 1999	9	Being	May 15 1999	**1**	**Illuminating**	Jul 24 1999	6	Being
Mar 7 1999	10	Breathing	May 16 1999	2	Choosing	Jul 25 1999	7	Breathing
Mar 8 1999	11	Listening	May 17 1999	3	Exploring	Jul 26 1999	8	Listening
Mar 9 1999	12	Planting	May 18 1999	4	Healing	Jul 27 1999	9	Planting
Mar 10 1999	13	Moving	May 19 1999	5	Seeing	Jul 28 1999	10	Moving
Mar 11 1999	**1**	**Transcending**	May 20 1999	6	Intuiting	Jul 29 1999	11	Transcending
Mar 12 1999	2	Remembering	May 21 1999	7	Evolving	Jul 30 1999	12	Remembering
Mar 13 1999	3	Loving	May 22 1999	8	Self-Regulating	Jul 31 1999	13	Loving
Mar 14 1999	4	Feeling	May 23 1999	9	Catalyzing	Aug 1 1999	**1**	**Feeling**
Mar 15 1999	5	Devoting	May 24 1999	10	Enlightening	Aug 2 1999	2	Devoting
Mar 16 1999	6	Illuminating	May 25 1999	11	Being	Aug 3 1999	3	Illuminating
Mar 17 1999	7	Choosing	May 26 1999	12	Breathing	Aug 4 1999	4	Choosing
Mar 18 1999	8	Exploring	May 27 1999	13	Listening	Aug 5 1999	5	Exploring
Mar 19 1999	9	Healing	May 28 1999	**1**	**Planting**	Aug 6 1999	6	Healing
Mar 20 1999	10	Seeing	May 29 1999	2	Moving	Aug 7 1999	7	Seeing
Mar 21 1999	11	Intuiting	May 30 1999	3	Transcending	Aug 8 1999	8	Intuiting
Mar 22 1999	12	Evolving	May 31 1999	4	Remembering	Aug 9 1999	9	Evolving
Mar 23 1999	13	Self-Regulating	Jun 1 1999	5	Loving	Aug 10 1999	10	Self-Regulating
Mar 24 1999	**1**	**Catalyzing**	Jun 2 1999	6	Feeling	Aug 11 1999	11	Catalyzing
Mar 25 1999	2	Enlightening	Jun 3 1999	7	Devoting	Aug 12 1999	12	Enlightening
Mar 26 1999	3	Being	Jun 4 1999	8	Illuminating	Aug 13 1999	13	Being
Mar 27 1999	4	Breathing	Jun 5 1999	9	Choosing	Aug 14 1999	**1**	**Breathing**
Mar 28 1999	5	Listening	Jun 6 1999	10	Exploring	Aug 15 1999	2	Listening
Mar 29 1999	6	Planting	Jun 7 1999	11	Healing	Aug 16 1999	3	Planting
Mar 30 1999	7	Moving	Jun 8 1999	12	Seeing	Aug 17 1999	4	Moving
Mar 31 1999	8	Transcending	Jun 9 1999	13	Intuiting	Aug 18 1999	5	Transcending
Apr 1 1999	9	Remembering	Jun 10 1999	**1**	**Evolving**	Aug 19 1999	6	Remembering
Apr 2 1999	10	Loving	Jun 11 1999	2	Self-Regulating	Aug 20 1999	7	Loving
Apr 3 1999	11	Feeling	Jun 12 1999	3	Catalyzing	Aug 21 1999	8	Feeling
Apr 4 1999	12	Devoting	Jun 13 1999	4	Enlightening	Aug 22 1999	9	Devoting
Apr 5 1999	13	Illuminating	Jun 14 1999	5	Being	Aug 23 1999	10	Illuminating
Apr 6 1999	**1**	**Choosing**	Jun 15 1999	6	Breathing	Aug 24 1999	11	Choosing
Apr 7 1999	2	Exploring	Jun 16 1999	7	Listening	Aug 25 1999	12	Exploring
Apr 8 1999	3	Healing	Jun 17 1999	8	Planting	Aug 26 1999	13	Healing
Apr 9 1999	4	Seeing	Jun 18 1999	9	Moving	Aug 27 1999	**1**	**Seeing**
Apr 10 1999	5	Intuiting	Jun 19 1999	10	Transcending	Aug 28 1999	2	Intuiting
Apr 11 1999	6	Evolving	Jun 20 1999	11	Remembering	Aug 29 1999	3	Evolving
Apr 12 1999	7	Self-Regulating	Jun 21 1999	12	Loving	Aug 30 1999	4	Self-Regulating
Apr 13 1999	8	Catalyzing	Jun 22 1999	13	Feeling	Aug 31 1999	5	Catalyzing
Apr 14 1999	9	Enlightening	Jun 23 1999	**1**	**Devoting**	Sep 1 1999	6	Enlightening
Apr 15 1999	10	Being	Jun 24 1999	2	Illuminating	Sep 2 1999	7	Being
Apr 16 1999	11	Breathing	Jun 25 1999	3	Choosing	Sep 3 1999	8	Breathing
Apr 17 1999	12	Listening	Jun 26 1999	4	Exploring	Sep 4 1999	9	Listening
Apr 18 1999	13	Planting	Jun 27 1999	5	Healing	Sep 5 1999	10	Planting
Apr 19 1999	**1**	**Moving**	Jun 28 1999	6	Seeing	Sep 6 1999	11	Moving
Apr 20 1999	2	Transcending	Jun 29 1999	7	Intuiting	Sep 7 1999	12	Transcending
Apr 21 1999	3	Remembering	Jun 30 1999	8	Evolving	Sep 8 1999	13	Remembering
Apr 22 1999	4	Loving	Jul 1 1999	9	Self-Regulating	Sep 9 1999	**1**	**Loving**
Apr 23 1999	5	Feeling	Jul 2 1999	10	Catalyzing	Sep 10 1999	2	Feeling
Apr 24 1999	6	Devoting	Jul 3 1999	11	Enlightening	Sep 11 1999	3	Devoting
Apr 25 1999	7	Illuminating	Jul 4 1999	12	Being	Sep 12 1999	4	Illuminating
Apr 26 1999	8	Choosing	Jul 5 1999	13	Breathing	Sep 13 1999	5	Choosing
Apr 27 1999	9	Exploring	Jul 6 1999	**1**	**Listening**	Sep 14 1999	6	Exploring
Apr 28 1999	10	Healing	Jul 7 1999	2	Planting	Sep 15 1999	7	Healing
Apr 29 1999	11	Seeing	Jul 8 1999	3	Moving	Sep 16 1999	8	Seeing
Apr 30 1999	12	Intuiting	Jul 9 1999	4	Transcending	Sep 17 1999	9	Intuiting
May 1 1999	13	Evolving	Jul 10 1999	5	Remembering	Sep 18 1999	10	Evolving
May 2 1999	**1**	**Self-Regulating**	Jul 11 1999	6	Loving	Sep 19 1999	11	Self-Regulating
May 3 1999	2	Catalyzing	Jul 12 1999	7	Feeling	Sep 20 1999	12	Catalyzing
May 4 1999	3	Enlightening	Jul 13 1999	8	Devoting	Sep 21 1999	13	Enlightening

Date	UE Earth Energy	Date	UE Earth Energy	Date	UE Earth Energy
Sep 22 1999	1 Being	Dec 1 1999	6 Illuminating	Feb 9 2000	11 Being
Sep 23 1999	2 Breathing	Dec 2 1999	7 Choosing	Feb 10 2000	12 Breathing
Sep 24 1999	3 Listening	Dec 3 1999	8 Exploring	Feb 11 2000	13 Listening
Sep 25 1999	4 Planting	Dec 4 1999	9 Healing	Feb 12 2000	1 Planting
Sep 26 1999	5 Moving	Dec 5 1999	10 Seeing	Feb 13 2000	2 Moving
Sep 27 1999	6 Transcending	Dec 6 1999	11 Intuiting	Feb 14 2000	3 Transcending
Sep 28 1999	7 Remembering	Dec 7 1999	12 Evolving	Feb 15 2000	4 Remembering
Sep 29 1999	8 Loving	Dec 8 1999	13 Self-Regulating	Feb 16 2000	5 Loving
Sep 30 1999	9 Feeling	Dec 9 1999	1 Catalyzing	Feb 17 2000	6 Feeling
Oct 1 1999	10 Devoting	Dec 10 1999	2 Enlightening	Feb 18 2000	7 Devoting
Oct 2 1999	11 Illuminating	Dec 11 1999	3 Being	Feb 19 2000	8 Illuminating
Oct 3 1999	12 Choosing	Dec 12 1999	4 Breathing	Feb 20 2000	9 Choosing
Oct 4 1999	13 Exploring	Dec 13 1999	5 Listening	Feb 21 2000	10 Exploring
Oct 5 1999	1 Healing	Dec 14 1999	6 Planting	Feb 22 2000	11 Healing
Oct 6 1999	2 Seeing	Dec 15 1999	7 Moving	Feb 23 2000	12 Seeing
Oct 7 1999	3 Intuiting	Dec 16 1999	8 Transcending	Feb 24 2000	13 Intuiting
Oct 8 1999	4 Evolving	Dec 17 1999	9 Remembering	Feb 25 2000	1 Evolving
Oct 9 1999	5 Self-Regulating	Dec 18 1999	10 Loving	Feb 26 2000	2 Self-Regulating
Oct 10 1999	6 Catalyzing	Dec 19 1999	11 Feeling	Feb 27 2000	3 Catalyzing
Oct 11 1999	7 Enlightening	Dec 20 1999	12 Devoting	Feb 28 2000	4 Enlightening
Oct 12 1999	8 Being	Dec 21 1999	13 Illuminating	Feb 29 2000	5 Being
Oct 13 1999	9 Breathing	Dec 22 1999	1 Choosing	Mar 1 2000	6 Breathing
Oct 14 1999	10 Listening	Dec 23 1999	2 Exploring	Mar 2 2000	7 Listening
Oct 15 1999	11 Planting	Dec 24 1999	3 Healing	Mar 3 2000	8 Planting
Oct 16 1999	12 Moving	Dec 25 1999	4 Seeing	Mar 4 2000	9 Moving
Oct 17 1999	13 Transcending	Dec 26 1999	5 Intuiting	Mar 5 2000	10 Transcending
Oct 18 1999	1 Remembering	Dec 27 1999	6 Evolving	Mar 6 2000	11 Remembering
Oct 19 1999	2 Loving	Dec 28 1999	7 Self-Regulating	Mar 7 2000	12 Loving
Oct 20 1999	3 Feeling	Dec 29 1999	8 Catalyzing	Mar 8 2000	13 Feeling
Oct 21 1999	4 Devoting	Dec 30 1999	9 Enlightening	Mar 9 2000	1 Devoting
Oct 22 1999	5 Illuminating	Dec 31 1999	10 Being	Mar 10 2000	2 Illuminating
Oct 23 1999	6 Choosing	Jan 1 2000	11 Breathing	Mar 11 2000	3 Choosing
Oct 24 1999	7 Exploring	Jan 2 2000	12 Listening	Mar 12 2000	4 Exploring
Oct 25 1999	8 Healing	Jan 3 2000	13 Planting	Mar 13 2000	5 Healing
Oct 26 1999	9 Seeing	Jan 4 2000	1 Moving	Mar 14 2000	6 Seeing
Oct 27 1999	10 Intuiting	Jan 5 2000	2 Transcending	Mar 15 2000	7 Intuiting
Oct 28 1999	11 Evolving	Jan 6 2000	3 Remembering	Mar 16 2000	8 Evolving
Oct 29 1999	12 Self-Regulating	Jan 7 2000	4 Loving	Mar 17 2000	9 Self-Regulating
Oct 30 1999	13 Catalyzing	Jan 8 2000	5 Feeling	Mar 18 2000	10 Catalyzing
Oct 31 1999	1 Enlightening	Jan 9 2000	6 Devoting	Mar 19 2000	11 Enlightening
Nov 1 1999	2 Being	Jan 10 2000	7 Illuminating	Mar 20 2000	12 Being
Nov 2 1999	3 Breathing	Jan 11 2000	8 Choosing	Mar 21 2000	13 Breathing
Nov 3 1999	4 Listening	Jan 12 2000	9 Exploring	Mar 22 2000	1 Listening
Nov 4 1999	5 Planting	Jan 13 2000	10 Healing	Mar 23 2000	2 Planting
Nov 5 1999	6 Moving	Jan 14 2000	11 Seeing	Mar 24 2000	3 Moving
Nov 6 1999	7 Transcending	Jan 15 2000	12 Intuiting	Mar 25 2000	4 Transcending
Nov 7 1999	8 Remembering	Jan 16 2000	13 Evolving	Mar 26 2000	5 Remembering
Nov 8 1999	9 Loving	Jan 17 2000	1 Self-Regulating	Mar 27 2000	6 Loving
Nov 9 1999	10 Feeling	Jan 18 2000	2 Catalyzing	Mar 28 2000	7 Feeling
Nov 10 1999	11 Devoting	Jan 19 2000	3 Enlightening	Mar 29 2000	8 Devoting
Nov 11 1999	12 Illuminating	Jan 20 2000	4 Being	Mar 30 2000	9 Illuminating
Nov 12 1999	13 Choosing	Jan 21 2000	5 Breathing	Mar 31 2000	10 Choosing
Nov 13 1999	1 Exploring	Jan 22 2000	6 Listening	Apr 1 2000	11 Exploring
Nov 14 1999	2 Healing	Jan 23 2000	7 Planting	Apr 2 2000	12 Healing
Nov 15 1999	3 Seeing	Jan 24 2000	8 Moving	Apr 3 2000	13 Seeing
Nov 16 1999	4 Intuiting	Jan 25 2000	9 Transcending	Apr 4 2000	1 Intuiting
Nov 17 1999	5 Evolving	Jan 26 2000	10 Remembering	Apr 5 2000	2 Evolving
Nov 18 1999	6 Self-Regulating	Jan 27 2000	11 Loving	Apr 6 2000	3 Self-Regulating
Nov 19 1999	7 Catalyzing	Jan 28 2000	12 Feeling	Apr 7 2000	4 Catalyzing
Nov 20 1999	8 Enlightening	Jan 29 2000	13 Devoting	Apr 8 2000	5 Enlightening
Nov 21 1999	9 Being	Jan 30 2000	1 Illuminating	Apr 9 2000	6 Being
Nov 22 1999	10 Breathing	Jan 31 2000	2 Choosing	Apr 10 2000	7 Breathing
Nov 23 1999	11 Listening	Feb 1 2000	3 Exploring	Apr 11 2000	8 Listening
Nov 24 1999	12 Planting	Feb 2 2000	4 Healing	Apr 12 2000	9 Planting
Nov 25 1999	13 Moving	Feb 3 2000	5 Seeing	Apr 13 2000	10 Moving
Nov 26 1999	1 Transcending	Feb 4 2000	6 Intuiting	Apr 14 2000	11 Transcending
Nov 27 1999	2 Remembering	Feb 5 2000	7 Evolving	Apr 15 2000	12 Remembering
Nov 28 1999	3 Loving	Feb 6 2000	8 Self-Regulating	Apr 16 2000	13 Loving
Nov 29 1999	4 Feeling	Feb 7 2000	9 Catalyzing	Apr 17 2000	1 Feeling
Nov 30 1999	5 Devoting	Feb 8 2000	10 Enlightening	Apr 18 2000	2 Devoting

Date	UE	Earth Energy	Date	UE	Earth Energy	Date	UE	Earth Energy
Apr 19 2000	3	Illuminating	Jun 28 2000	8	Being	Sep 6 2000	13	Illuminating
Apr 20 2000	4	Choosing	Jun 29 2000	9	Breathing	Sep 7 2000	**1**	**Choosing**
Apr 21 2000	5	Exploring	Jun 30 2000	10	Listening	Sep 8 2000	2	Exploring
Apr 22 2000	6	Healing	Jul 1 2000	11	Planting	Sep 9 2000	3	Healing
Apr 23 2000	7	Seeing	Jul 2 2000	12	Moving	Sep 10 2000	4	Seeing
Apr 24 2000	8	Intuiting	Jul 3 2000	13	Transcending	Sep 11 2000	5	Intuiting
Apr 25 2000	9	Evolving	Jul 4 2000	**1**	**Remembering**	Sep 12 2000	6	Evolving
Apr 26 2000	10	Self-Regulating	Jul 5 2000	2	Loving	Sep 13 2000	7	Self-Regulating
Apr 27 2000	11	Catalyzing	Jul 6 2000	3	Feeling	Sep 14 2000	8	Catalyzing
Apr 28 2000	12	Enlightening	Jul 7 2000	4	Devoting	Sep 15 2000	9	Enlightening
Apr 29 2000	13	Being	Jul 8 2000	5	Illuminating	Sep 16 2000	10	Being
Apr 30 2000	**1**	**Breathing**	Jul 9 2000	6	Choosing	Sep 17 2000	11	Breathing
May 1 2000	2	Listening	Jul 10 2000	7	Exploring	Sep 18 2000	12	Listening
May 2 2000	3	Planting	Jul 11 2000	8	Healing	Sep 19 2000	13	Planting
May 3 2000	4	Moving	Jul 12 2000	9	Seeing	Sep 20 2000	**1**	**Moving**
May 4 2000	5	Transcending	Jul 13 2000	10	Intuiting	Sep 21 2000	2	Transcending
May 5 2000	6	Remembering	Jul 14 2000	11	Evolving	Sep 22 2000	3	Remembering
May 6 2000	7	Loving	Jul 15 2000	12	Self-Regulating	Sep 23 2000	4	Loving
May 7 2000	8	Feeling	Jul 16 2000	13	Catalyzing	Sep 24 2000	5	Feeling
May 8 2000	9	Devoting	Jul 17 2000	**1**	**Enlightening**	Sep 25 2000	6	Devoting
May 9 2000	10	Illuminating	Jul 18 2000	2	Being	Sep 26 2000	7	Illuminating
May 10 2000	11	Choosing	Jul 19 2000	3	Breathing	Sep 27 2000	8	Choosing
May 11 2000	12	Exploring	Jul 20 2000	4	Listening	Sep 28 2000	9	Exploring
May 12 2000	13	Healing	Jul 21 2000	5	Planting	Sep 29 2000	10	Healing
May 13 2000	**1**	**Seeing**	Jul 22 2000	6	Moving	Sep 30 2000	11	Seeing
May 14 2000	2	Intuiting	Jul 23 2000	7	Transcending	Oct 1 2000	12	Intuiting
May 15 2000	3	Evolving	Jul 24 2000	8	Remembering	Oct 2 2000	13	Evolving
May 16 2000	4	Self-Regulating	Jul 25 2000	9	Loving	Oct 3 2000	**1**	**Self-Regulating**
May 17 2000	5	Catalyzing	Jul 26 2000	10	Feeling	Oct 4 2000	2	Catalyzing
May 18 2000	6	Enlightening	Jul 27 2000	11	Devoting	Oct 5 2000	3	Enlightening
May 19 2000	7	Being	Jul 28 2000	12	Illuminating	Oct 6 2000	4	Being
May 20 2000	8	Breathing	Jul 29 2000	13	Choosing	Oct 7 2000	5	Breathing
May 21 2000	9	Listening	Jul 30 2000	**1**	**Exploring**	Oct 8 2000	6	Listening
May 22 2000	10	Planting	Jul 31 2000	2	Healing	Oct 9 2000	7	Planting
May 23 2000	11	Moving	Aug 1 2000	3	Seeing	Oct 10 2000	8	Moving
May 24 2000	12	Transcending	Aug 2 2000	4	Intuiting	Oct 11 2000	9	Transcending
May 25 2000	13	Remembering	Aug 3 2000	5	Evolving	Oct 12 2000	10	Remembering
May 26 2000	**1**	**Loving**	Aug 4 2000	6	Self-Regulating	Oct 13 2000	11	Loving
May 27 2000	2	Feeling	Aug 5 2000	7	Catalyzing	Oct 14 2000	12	Feeling
May 28 2000	3	Devoting	Aug 6 2000	8	Enlightening	Oct 15 2000	13	Devoting
May 29 2000	4	Illuminating	Aug 7 2000	9	Being	Oct 16 2000	**1**	**Illuminating**
May 30 2000	5	Choosing	Aug 8 2000	10	Breathing	Oct 17 2000	2	Choosing
May 31 2000	6	Exploring	Aug 9 2000	11	Listening	Oct 18 2000	3	Exploring
Jun 1 2000	7	Healing	Aug 10 2000	12	Planting	Oct 19 2000	4	Healing
Jun 2 2000	8	Seeing	Aug 11 2000	13	Moving	Oct 20 2000	5	Seeing
Jun 3 2000	9	Intuiting	Aug 12 2000	**1**	**Transcending**	Oct 21 2000	6	Intuiting
Jun 4 2000	10	Evolving	Aug 13 2000	2	Remembering	Oct 22 2000	7	Evolving
Jun 5 2000	11	Self-Regulating	Aug 14 2000	3	Loving	Oct 23 2000	8	Self-Regulating
Jun 6 2000	12	Catalyzing	Aug 15 2000	4	Feeling	Oct 24 2000	9	Catalyzing
Jun 7 2000	13	Enlightening	Aug 16 2000	5	Devoting	Oct 25 2000	10	Enlightening
Jun 8 2000	**1**	**Being**	Aug 17 2000	6	Illuminating	Oct 26 2000	11	Being
Jun 9 2000	2	Breathing	Aug 18 2000	7	Choosing	Oct 27 2000	12	Breathing
Jun 10 2000	3	Listening	Aug 19 2000	8	Exploring	Oct 28 2000	13	Listening
Jun 11 2000	4	Planting	Aug 20 2000	9	Healing	Oct 29 2000	**1**	**Planting**
Jun 12 2000	5	Moving	Aug 21 2000	10	Seeing	Oct 30 2000	2	Moving
Jun 13 2000	6	Transcending	Aug 22 2000	11	Intuiting	Oct 31 2000	3	Transcending
Jun 14 2000	7	Remembering	Aug 23 2000	12	Evolving	Nov 1 2000	4	Remembering
Jun 15 2000	8	Loving	Aug 24 2000	13	Self-Regulating	Nov 2 2000	5	Loving
Jun 16 2000	9	Feeling	Aug 25 2000	**1**	**Catalyzing**	Nov 3 2000	6	Feeling
Jun 17 2000	10	Devoting	Aug 26 2000	2	Enlightening	Nov 4 2000	7	Devoting
Jun 18 2000	11	Illuminating	Aug 27 2000	3	Being	Nov 5 2000	8	Illuminating
Jun 19 2000	12	Choosing	Aug 28 2000	4	Breathing	Nov 6 2000	9	Choosing
Jun 20 2000	13	Exploring	Aug 29 2000	5	Listening	Nov 7 2000	10	Exploring
Jun 21 2000	**1**	**Healing**	Aug 30 2000	6	Planting	Nov 8 2000	11	Healing
Jun 22 2000	2	Seeing	Aug 31 2000	7	Moving	Nov 9 2000	12	Seeing
Jun 23 2000	3	Intuiting	Sep 1 2000	8	Transcending	Nov 10 2000	13	Intuiting
Jun 24 2000	4	Evolving	Sep 2 2000	9	Remembering	Nov 11 2000	**1**	**Evolving**
Jun 25 2000	5	Self-Regulating	Sep 3 2000	10	Loving	Nov 12 2000	2	Self-Regulating
Jun 26 2000	6	Catalyzing	Sep 4 2000	11	Feeling	Nov 13 2000	3	Catalyzing
Jun 27 2000	7	Enlightening	Sep 5 2000	12	Devoting	Nov 14 2000	4	Enlightening

Date	UE	Earth Energy	Date	UE	Earth Energy	Date	UE	Earth Energy
Nov 15 2000	5	Being	Jan 24 2001	10	Illuminating	Apr 4 2001	2	Being
Nov 16 2000	6	Breathing	Jan 25 2001	11	Choosing	Apr 5 2001	3	Breathing
Nov 17 2000	7	Listening	Jan 26 2001	12	Exploring	Apr 6 2001	4	Listening
Nov 18 2000	8	Planting	Jan 27 2001	13	Healing	Apr 7 2001	5	Planting
Nov 19 2000	9	Moving	Jan 28 2001	**1**	**Seeing**	Apr 8 2001	6	Moving
Nov 20 2000	10	Transcending	Jan 29 2001	2	Intuiting	Apr 9 2001	7	Transcending
Nov 21 2000	11	Remembering	Jan 30 2001	3	Evolving	Apr 10 2001	8	Remembering
Nov 22 2000	12	Loving	Jan 31 2001	4	Self-Regulating	Apr 11 2001	9	Loving
Nov 23 2000	13	Feeling	Feb 1 2001	5	Catalyzing	Apr 12 2001	10	Feeling
Nov 24 2000	**1**	**Devoting**	Feb 2 2001	6	Enlightening	Apr 13 2001	11	Devoting
Nov 25 2000	2	Illuminating	Feb 3 2001	7	Being	Apr 14 2001	12	Illuminating
Nov 26 2000	3	Choosing	Feb 4 2001	8	Breathing	Apr 15 2001	13	Choosing
Nov 27 2000	4	Exploring	Feb 5 2001	9	Listening	Apr 16 2001	**1**	**Exploring**
Nov 28 2000	5	Healing	Feb 6 2001	10	Planting	Apr 17 2001	2	Healing
Nov 29 2000	6	Seeing	Feb 7 2001	11	Moving	Apr 18 2001	3	Seeing
Nov 30 2000	7	Intuiting	Feb 8 2001	12	Transcending	Apr 19 2001	4	Intuiting
Dec 1 2000	8	Evolving	Feb 9 2001	13	Remembering	Apr 20 2001	5	Evolving
Dec 2 2000	9	Self-Regulating	Feb 10 2001	**1**	**Loving**	Apr 21 2001	6	Self-Regulating
Dec 3 2000	10	Catalyzing	Feb 11 2001	2	Feeling	Apr 22 2001	7	Catalyzing
Dec 4 2000	11	Enlightening	Feb 12 2001	3	Devoting	Apr 23 2001	8	Enlightening
Dec 5 2000	12	Being	Feb 13 2001	4	Illuminating	Apr 24 2001	9	Being
Dec 6 2000	13	Breathing	Feb 14 2001	5	Choosing	Apr 25 2001	10	Breathing
Dec 7 2000	**1**	**Listening**	Feb 15 2001	6	Exploring	Apr 26 2001	11	Listening
Dec 8 2000	2	Planting	Feb 16 2001	7	Healing	Apr 27 2001	12	Planting
Dec 9 2000	3	Moving	Feb 17 2001	8	Seeing	Apr 28 2001	13	Moving
Dec 10 2000	4	Transcending	Feb 18 2001	9	Intuiting	Apr 29 2001	**1**	**Transcending**
Dec 11 2000	5	Remembering	Feb 19 2001	10	Evolving	Apr 30 2001	2	Remembering
Dec 12 2000	6	Loving	Feb 20 2001	11	Self-Regulating	May 1 2001	3	Loving
Dec 13 2000	7	Feeling	Feb 21 2001	12	Catalyzing	May 2 2001	4	Feeling
Dec 14 2000	8	Devoting	Feb 22 2001	13	Enlightening	May 3 2001	5	Devoting
Dec 15 2000	9	Illuminating	Feb 23 2001	**1**	**Being**	May 4 2001	6	Illuminating
Dec 16 2000	10	Choosing	Feb 24 2001	2	Breathing	May 5 2001	7	Choosing
Dec 17 2000	11	Exploring	Feb 25 2001	3	Listening	May 6 2001	8	Exploring
Dec 18 2000	12	Healing	Feb 26 2001	4	Planting	May 7 2001	9	Healing
Dec 19 2000	13	Seeing	Feb 27 2001	5	Moving	May 8 2001	10	Seeing
Dec 20 2000	**1**	**Intuiting**	Feb 28 2001	6	Transcending	May 9 2001	11	Intuiting
Dec 21 2000	2	Evolving	Mar 1 2001	7	Remembering	May 10 2001	12	Evolving
Dec 22 2000	3	Self-Regulating	Mar 2 2001	8	Loving	May 11 2001	13	Self-Regulating
Dec 23 2000	4	Catalyzing	Mar 3 2001	9	Feeling	May 12 2001	**1**	**Catalyzing**
Dec 24 2000	5	Enlightening	Mar 4 2001	10	Devoting	May 13 2001	2	Enlightening
Dec 25 2000	6	Being	Mar 5 2001	11	Illuminating	May 14 2001	3	Being
Dec 26 2000	7	Breathing	Mar 6 2001	12	Choosing	May 15 2001	4	Breathing
Dec 27 2000	8	Listening	Mar 7 2001	13	Exploring	May 16 2001	5	Listening
Dec 28 2000	9	Planting	Mar 8 2001	**1**	**Healing**	May 17 2001	6	Planting
Dec 29 2000	10	Moving	Mar 9 2001	2	Seeing	May 18 2001	7	Moving
Dec 30 2000	11	Transcending	Mar 10 2001	3	Intuiting	May 19 2001	8	Transcending
Dec 31 2000	12	Remembering	Mar 11 2001	4	Evolving	May 20 2001	9	Remembering
Jan 1 2001	13	Loving	Mar 12 2001	5	Self-Regulating	May 21 2001	10	Loving
Jan 2 2001	**1**	**Feeling**	Mar 13 2001	6	Catalyzing	May 22 2001	11	Feeling
Jan 3 2001	2	Devoting	Mar 14 2001	7	Enlightening	May 23 2001	12	Devoting
Jan 4 2001	3	Illuminating	Mar 15 2001	8	Being	May 24 2001	13	Illuminating
Jan 5 2001	4	Choosing	Mar 16 2001	9	Breathing	May 25 2001	**1**	**Choosing**
Jan 6 2001	5	Exploring	Mar 17 2001	10	Listening	May 26 2001	2	Exploring
Jan 7 2001	6	Healing	Mar 18 2001	11	Planting	May 27 2001	3	Healing
Jan 8 2001	7	Seeing	Mar 19 2001	12	Moving	May 28 2001	4	Seeing
Jan 9 2001	8	Intuiting	Mar 20 2001	13	Transcending	May 29 2001	5	Intuiting
Jan 10 2001	9	Evolving	Mar 21 2001	**1**	**Remembering**	May 30 2001	6	Evolving
Jan 11 2001	10	Self-Regulating	Mar 22 2001	2	Loving	May 31 2001	7	Self-Regulating
Jan 12 2001	11	Catalyzing	Mar 23 2001	3	Feeling	Jun 1 2001	8	Catalyzing
Jan 13 2001	12	Enlightening	Mar 24 2001	4	Devoting	Jun 2 2001	9	Enlightening
Jan 14 2001	13	Being	Mar 25 2001	5	Illuminating	Jun 3 2001	10	Being
Jan 15 2001	**1**	**Breathing**	Mar 26 2001	6	Choosing	Jun 4 2001	11	Breathing
Jan 16 2001	2	Listening	Mar 27 2001	7	Exploring	Jun 5 2001	12	Listening
Jan 17 2001	3	Planting	Mar 28 2001	8	Healing	Jun 6 2001	13	Planting
Jan 18 2001	4	Moving	Mar 29 2001	9	Seeing	Jun 7 2001	**1**	**Moving**
Jan 19 2001	5	Transcending	Mar 30 2001	10	Intuiting	Jun 8 2001	2	Transcending
Jan 20 2001	6	Remembering	Mar 31 2001	11	Evolving	Jun 9 2001	3	Remembering
Jan 21 2001	7	Loving	Apr 1 2001	12	Self-Regulating	Jun 10 2001	4	Loving
Jan 22 2001	8	Feeling	Apr 2 2001	13	Catalyzing	Jun 11 2001	5	Feeling
Jan 23 2001	9	Devoting	Apr 3 2001	**1**	**Enlightening**	Jun 12 2001	6	Devoting

Date UE Earth Energy	Date UE Earth Energy	Date UE Earth Energy
Jun 13 2001　7 Illuminating	Aug 22 2001　12 Being	Oct 31 2001　4 Illuminating
Jun 14 2001　8 Choosing	Aug 23 2001　13 Breathing	Nov 1 2001　5 Choosing
Jun 15 2001　9 Exploring	Aug 24 2001　**1 Listening**	Nov 2 2001　6 Exploring
Jun 16 2001　10 Healing	Aug 25 2001　2 Planting	Nov 3 2001　7 Healing
Jun 17 2001　11 Seeing	Aug 26 2001　3 Moving	Nov 4 2001　8 Seeing
Jun 18 2001　12 Intuiting	Aug 27 2001　4 Transcending	Nov 5 2001　9 Intuiting
Jun 19 2001　13 Evolving	Aug 28 2001　5 Remembering	Nov 6 2001　10 Evolving
Jun 20 2001　**1 Self-Regulating**	Aug 29 2001　6 Loving	Nov 7 2001　11 Self-Regulating
Jun 21 2001　2 Catalyzing	Aug 30 2001　7 Feeling	Nov 8 2001　12 Catalyzing
Jun 22 2001　3 Enlightening	Aug 31 2001　8 Devoting	Nov 9 2001　13 Enlightening
Jun 23 2001　4 Being	Sep 1 2001　9 Illuminating	Nov 10 2001　**1 Being**
Jun 24 2001　5 Breathing	Sep 2 2001　10 Choosing	Nov 11 2001　2 Breathing
Jun 25 2001　6 Listening	Sep 3 2001　11 Exploring	Nov 12 2001　3 Listening
Jun 26 2001　7 Planting	Sep 4 2001　12 Healing	Nov 13 2001　4 Planting
Jun 27 2001　8 Moving	Sep 5 2001　13 Seeing	Nov 14 2001　5 Moving
Jun 28 2001　9 Transcending	Sep 6 2001　**1 Intuiting**	Nov 15 2001　6 Transcending
Jun 29 2001　10 Remembering	Sep 7 2001　2 Evolving	Nov 16 2001　7 Remembering
Jun 30 2001　11 Loving	Sep 8 2001　3 Self-Regulating	Nov 17 2001　8 Loving
Jul 1 2001　12 Feeling	Sep 9 2001　4 Catalyzing	Nov 18 2001　9 Feeling
Jul 2 2001　13 Devoting	Sep 10 2001　5 Enlightening	Nov 19 2001　10 Devoting
Jul 3 2001　**1 Illuminating**	Sep 11 2001　6 Being	Nov 20 2001　11 Illuminating
Jul 4 2001　2 Choosing	Sep 12 2001　7 Breathing	Nov 21 2001　12 Choosing
Jul 5 2001　3 Exploring	Sep 13 2001　8 Listening	Nov 22 2001　13 Exploring
Jul 6 2001　4 Healing	Sep 14 2001　9 Planting	Nov 23 2001　**1 Healing**
Jul 7 2001　5 Seeing	Sep 15 2001　10 Moving	Nov 24 2001　2 Seeing
Jul 8 2001　6 Intuiting	Sep 16 2001　11 Transcending	Nov 25 2001　3 Intuiting
Jul 9 2001　7 Evolving	Sep 17 2001　12 Remembering	Nov 26 2001　4 Evolving
Jul 10 2001　8 Self-Regulating	Sep 18 2001　13 Loving	Nov 27 2001　5 Self-Regulating
Jul 11 2001　9 Catalyzing	Sep 19 2001　**1 Feeling**	Nov 28 2001　6 Catalyzing
Jul 12 2001　10 Enlightening	Sep 20 2001　2 Devoting	Nov 29 2001　7 Enlightening
Jul 13 2001　11 Being	Sep 21 2001　3 Illuminating	Nov 30 2001　8 Being
Jul 14 2001　12 Breathing	Sep 22 2001　4 Choosing	Dec 1 2001　9 Breathing
Jul 15 2001　13 Listening	Sep 23 2001　5 Exploring	Dec 2 2001　10 Listening
Jul 16 2001　**1 Planting**	Sep 24 2001　6 Healing	Dec 3 2001　11 Planting
Jul 17 2001　2 Moving	Sep 25 2001　7 Seeing	Dec 4 2001　12 Moving
Jul 18 2001　3 Transcending	Sep 26 2001　8 Intuiting	Dec 5 2001　13 Transcending
Jul 19 2001　4 Remembering	Sep 27 2001　9 Evolving	Dec 6 2001　**1 Remembering**
Jul 20 2001　5 Loving	Sep 28 2001　10 Self-Regulating	Dec 7 2001　2 Loving
Jul 21 2001　6 Feeling	Sep 29 2001　11 Catalyzing	Dec 8 2001　3 Feeling
Jul 22 2001　7 Devoting	Sep 30 2001　12 Enlightening	Dec 9 2001　4 Devoting
Jul 23 2001　8 Illuminating	Oct 1 2001　13 Being	Dec 10 2001　5 Illuminating
Jul 24 2001　9 Choosing	Oct 2 2001　**1 Breathing**	Dec 11 2001　6 Choosing
Jul 25 2001　10 Exploring	Oct 3 2001　2 Listening	Dec 12 2001　7 Exploring
Jul 26 2001　11 Healing	Oct 4 2001　3 Planting	Dec 13 2001　8 Healing
Jul 27 2001　12 Seeing	Oct 5 2001　4 Moving	Dec 14 2001　9 Seeing
Jul 28 2001　13 Intuiting	Oct 6 2001　5 Transcending	Dec 15 2001　10 Intuiting
Jul 29 2001　**1 Evolving**	Oct 7 2001　6 Remembering	Dec 16 2001　11 Evolving
Jul 30 2001　2 Self-Regulating	Oct 8 2001　7 Loving	Dec 17 2001　12 Self-Regulating
Jul 31 2001　3 Catalyzing	Oct 9 2001　8 Feeling	Dec 18 2001　13 Catalyzing
Aug 1 2001　4 Enlightening	Oct 10 2001　9 Devoting	Dec 19 2001　**1 Enlightening**
Aug 2 2001　5 Being	Oct 11 2001　10 Illuminating	Dec 20 2001　2 Being
Aug 3 2001　6 Breathing	Oct 12 2001　11 Choosing	Dec 21 2001　3 Breathing
Aug 4 2001　7 Listening	Oct 13 2001　12 Exploring	Dec 22 2001　4 Listening
Aug 5 2001　8 Planting	Oct 14 2001　13 Healing	Dec 23 2001　5 Planting
Aug 6 2001　9 Moving	Oct 15 2001　**1 Seeing**	Dec 24 2001　6 Moving
Aug 7 2001　10 Transcending	Oct 16 2001　2 Intuiting	Dec 25 2001　7 Transcending
Aug 8 2001　11 Remembering	Oct 17 2001　3 Evolving	Dec 26 2001　8 Remembering
Aug 9 2001　12 Loving	Oct 18 2001　4 Self-Regulating	Dec 27 2001　9 Loving
Aug 10 2001　13 Feeling	Oct 19 2001　5 Catalyzing	Dec 28 2001　10 Feeling
Aug 11 2001　**1 Devoting**	Oct 20 2001　6 Enlightening	Dec 29 2001　11 Devoting
Aug 12 2001　2 Illuminating	Oct 21 2001　7 Being	Dec 30 2001　12 Illuminating
Aug 13 2001　3 Choosing	Oct 22 2001　8 Breathing	Dec 31 2001　13 Choosing
Aug 14 2001　4 Exploring	Oct 23 2001　9 Listening	Jan 1 2002　**1 Exploring**
Aug 15 2001　5 Healing	Oct 24 2001　10 Planting	Jan 2 2002　2 Healing
Aug 16 2001　6 Seeing	Oct 25 2001　11 Moving	Jan 3 2002　3 Seeing
Aug 17 2001　7 Intuiting	Oct 26 2001　12 Transcending	Jan 4 2002　4 Intuiting
Aug 18 2001　8 Evolving	Oct 27 2001　13 Remembering	Jan 5 2002　5 Evolving
Aug 19 2001　9 Self-Regulating	Oct 28 2001　**1 Loving**	Jan 6 2002　6 Self-Regulating
Aug 20 2001　10 Catalyzing	Oct 29 2001　2 Feeling	Jan 7 2002　7 Catalyzing
Aug 21 2001　11 Enlightening	Oct 30 2001　3 Devoting	Jan 8 2002　8 Enlightening

Date	UE Earth Energy	Date	UE Earth Energy	Date	UE Earth Energy
Jan 9 2002	9 Being	Mar 20 2002	1 Illuminating	May 29 2002	6 Being
Jan 10 2002	10 Breathing	Mar 21 2002	2 Choosing	May 30 2002	7 Breathing
Jan 11 2002	11 Listening	Mar 22 2002	3 Exploring	May 31 2002	8 Listening
Jan 12 2002	12 Planting	Mar 23 2002	4 Healing	Jun 1 2002	9 Planting
Jan 13 2002	13 Moving	Mar 24 2002	5 Seeing	Jun 2 2002	10 Moving
Jan 14 2002	1 Transcending	Mar 25 2002	6 Intuiting	Jun 3 2002	11 Transcending
Jan 15 2002	2 Remembering	Mar 26 2002	7 Evolving	Jun 4 2002	12 Remembering
Jan 16 2002	3 Loving	Mar 27 2002	8 Self-Regulating	Jun 5 2002	13 Loving
Jan 17 2002	4 Feeling	Mar 28 2002	9 Catalyzing	Jun 6 2002	1 Feeling
Jan 18 2002	5 Devoting	Mar 29 2002	10 Enlightening	Jun 7 2002	2 Devoting
Jan 19 2002	6 Illuminating	Mar 30 2002	11 Being	Jun 8 2002	3 Illuminating
Jan 20 2002	7 Choosing	Mar 31 2002	12 Breathing	Jun 9 2002	4 Choosing
Jan 21 2002	8 Exploring	Apr 1 2002	13 Listening	Jun 10 2002	5 Exploring
Jan 22 2002	9 Healing	Apr 2 2002	1 Planting	Jun 11 2002	6 Healing
Jan 23 2002	10 Seeing	Apr 3 2002	2 Moving	Jun 12 2002	7 Seeing
Jan 24 2002	11 Intuiting	Apr 4 2002	3 Transcending	Jun 13 2002	8 Intuiting
Jan 25 2002	12 Evolving	Apr 5 2002	4 Remembering	Jun 14 2002	9 Evolving
Jan 26 2002	13 Self-Regulating	Apr 6 2002	5 Loving	Jun 15 2002	10 Self-Regulating
Jan 27 2002	1 Catalyzing	Apr 7 2002	6 Feeling	Jun 16 2002	11 Catalyzing
Jan 28 2002	2 Enlightening	Apr 8 2002	7 Devoting	Jun 17 2002	12 Enlightening
Jan 29 2002	3 Being	Apr 9 2002	8 Illuminating	Jun 18 2002	13 Being
Jan 30 2002	4 Breathing	Apr 10 2002	9 Choosing	Jun 19 2002	1 Breathing
Jan 31 2002	5 Listening	Apr 11 2002	10 Exploring	Jun 20 2002	2 Listening
Feb 1 2002	6 Planting	Apr 12 2002	11 Healing	Jun 21 2002	3 Planting
Feb 2 2002	7 Moving	Apr 13 2002	12 Seeing	Jun 22 2002	4 Moving
Feb 3 2002	8 Transcending	Apr 14 2002	13 Intuiting	Jun 23 2002	5 Transcending
Feb 4 2002	9 Remembering	Apr 15 2002	1 Evolving	Jun 24 2002	6 Remembering
Feb 5 2002	10 Loving	Apr 16 2002	2 Self-Regulating	Jun 25 2002	7 Loving
Feb 6 2002	11 Feeling	Apr 17 2002	3 Catalyzing	Jun 26 2002	8 Feeling
Feb 7 2002	12 Devoting	Apr 18 2002	4 Enlightening	Jun 27 2002	9 Devoting
Feb 8 2002	13 Illuminating	Apr 19 2002	5 Being	Jun 28 2002	10 Illuminating
Feb 9 2002	1 Choosing	Apr 20 2002	6 Breathing	Jun 29 2002	11 Choosing
Feb 10 2002	2 Exploring	Apr 21 2002	7 Listening	Jun 30 2002	12 Exploring
Feb 11 2002	3 Healing	Apr 22 2002	8 Planting	Jul 1 2002	13 Healing
Feb 12 2002	4 Seeing	Apr 23 2002	9 Moving	Jul 2 2002	1 Seeing
Feb 13 2002	5 Intuiting	Apr 24 2002	10 Transcending	Jul 3 2002	2 Intuiting
Feb 14 2002	6 Evolving	Apr 25 2002	11 Remembering	Jul 4 2002	3 Evolving
Feb 15 2002	7 Self-Regulating	Apr 26 2002	12 Loving	Jul 5 2002	4 Self-Regulating
Feb 16 2002	8 Catalyzing	Apr 27 2002	13 Feeling	Jul 6 2002	5 Catalyzing
Feb 17 2002	9 Enlightening	Apr 28 2002	1 Devoting	Jul 7 2002	6 Enlightening
Feb 18 2002	10 Being	Apr 29 2002	2 Illuminating	Jul 8 2002	7 Being
Feb 19 2002	11 Breathing	Apr 30 2002	3 Choosing	Jul 9 2002	8 Breathing
Feb 20 2002	12 Listening	May 1 2002	4 Exploring	Jul 10 2002	9 Listening
Feb 21 2002	13 Planting	May 2 2002	5 Healing	Jul 11 2002	10 Planting
Feb 22 2002	1 Moving	May 3 2002	6 Seeing	Jul 12 2002	11 Moving
Feb 23 2002	2 Transcending	May 4 2002	7 Intuiting	Jul 13 2002	12 Transcending
Feb 24 2002	3 Remembering	May 5 2002	8 Evolving	Jul 14 2002	13 Remembering
Feb 25 2002	4 Loving	May 6 2002	9 Self-Regulating	Jul 15 2002	1 Loving
Feb 26 2002	5 Feeling	May 7 2002	10 Catalyzing	Jul 16 2002	2 Feeling
Feb 27 2002	6 Devoting	May 8 2002	11 Enlightening	Jul 17 2002	3 Devoting
Feb 28 2002	7 Illuminating	May 9 2002	12 Being	Jul 18 2002	4 Illuminating
Mar 1 2002	8 Choosing	May 10 2002	13 Breathing	Jul 19 2002	5 Choosing
Mar 2 2002	9 Exploring	May 11 2002	1 Listening	Jul 20 2002	6 Exploring
Mar 3 2002	10 Healing	May 12 2002	2 Planting	Jul 21 2002	7 Healing
Mar 4 2002	11 Seeing	May 13 2002	3 Moving	Jul 22 2002	8 Seeing
Mar 5 2002	12 Intuiting	May 14 2002	4 Transcending	Jul 23 2002	9 Intuiting
Mar 6 2002	13 Evolving	May 15 2002	5 Remembering	Jul 24 2002	10 Evolving
Mar 7 2002	1 Self-Regulating	May 16 2002	6 Loving	Jul 25 2002	11 Self-Regulating
Mar 8 2002	2 Catalyzing	May 17 2002	7 Feeling	Jul 26 2002	12 Catalyzing
Mar 9 2002	3 Enlightening	May 18 2002	8 Devoting	Jul 27 2002	13 Enlightening
Mar 10 2002	4 Being	May 19 2002	9 Illuminating	Jul 28 2002	1 Being
Mar 11 2002	5 Breathing	May 20 2002	10 Choosing	Jul 29 2002	2 Breathing
Mar 12 2002	6 Listening	May 21 2002	11 Exploring	Jul 30 2002	3 Listening
Mar 13 2002	7 Planting	May 22 2002	12 Healing	Jul 31 2002	4 Planting
Mar 14 2002	8 Moving	May 23 2002	13 Seeing	Aug 1 2002	5 Moving
Mar 15 2002	9 Transcending	May 24 2002	1 Intuiting	Aug 2 2002	6 Transcending
Mar 16 2002	10 Remembering	May 25 2002	2 Evolving	Aug 3 2002	7 Remembering
Mar 17 2002	11 Loving	May 26 2002	3 Self-Regulating	Aug 4 2002	8 Loving
Mar 18 2002	12 Feeling	May 27 2002	4 Catalyzing	Aug 5 2002	9 Feeling
Mar 19 2002	13 Devoting	May 28 2002	5 Enlightening	Aug 6 2002	10 Devoting

Date	UE Earth Energy	Date	UE Earth Energy	Date	UE Earth Energy
Aug 7 2002	11 Illuminating	Oct 16 2002	3 Being	Dec 25 2002	8 Illuminating
Aug 8 2002	12 Choosing	Oct 17 2002	4 Breathing	Dec 26 2002	9 Choosing
Aug 9 2002	13 Exploring	Oct 18 2002	5 Listening	Dec 27 2002	10 Exploring
Aug 10 2002	**1 Healing**	Oct 19 2002	6 Planting	Dec 28 2002	11 Healing
Aug 11 2002	2 Seeing	Oct 20 2002	7 Moving	Dec 29 2002	12 Seeing
Aug 12 2002	3 Intuiting	Oct 21 2002	8 Transcending	Dec 30 2002	13 Intuiting
Aug 13 2002	4 Evolving	Oct 22 2002	9 Remembering	Dec 31 2002	**1 Evolving**
Aug 14 2002	5 Self-Regulating	Oct 23 2002	10 Loving	Jan 1 2003	2 Self-Regulating
Aug 15 2002	6 Catalyzing	Oct 24 2002	11 Feeling	Jan 2 2003	3 Catalyzing
Aug 16 2002	7 Enlightening	Oct 25 2002	12 Devoting	Jan 3 2003	4 Enlightening
Aug 17 2002	8 Being	Oct 26 2002	13 Illuminating	Jan 4 2003	5 Being
Aug 18 2002	9 Breathing	Oct 27 2002	**1 Choosing**	Jan 5 2003	6 Breathing
Aug 19 2002	10 Listening	Oct 28 2002	2 Exploring	Jan 6 2003	7 Listening
Aug 20 2002	11 Planting	Oct 29 2002	3 Healing	Jan 7 2003	8 Planting
Aug 21 2002	12 Moving	Oct 30 2002	4 Seeing	Jan 8 2003	9 Moving
Aug 22 2002	13 Transcending	Oct 31 2002	5 Intuiting	Jan 9 2003	10 Transcending
Aug 23 2002	**1 Remembering**	Nov 1 2002	6 Evolving	Jan 10 2003	11 Remembering
Aug 24 2002	2 Loving	Nov 2 2002	7 Self-Regulating	Jan 11 2003	12 Loving
Aug 25 2002	3 Feeling	Nov 3 2002	8 Catalyzing	Jan 12 2003	13 Feeling
Aug 26 2002	4 Devoting	Nov 4 2002	9 Enlightening	Jan 13 2003	**1 Devoting**
Aug 27 2002	5 Illuminating	Nov 5 2002	10 Being	Jan 14 2003	2 Illuminating
Aug 28 2002	6 Choosing	Nov 6 2002	11 Breathing	Jan 15 2003	3 Choosing
Aug 29 2002	7 Exploring	Nov 7 2002	12 Listening	Jan 16 2003	4 Exploring
Aug 30 2002	8 Healing	Nov 8 2002	13 Planting	Jan 17 2003	5 Healing
Aug 31 2002	9 Seeing	Nov 9 2002	**1 Moving**	Jan 18 2003	6 Seeing
Sep 1 2002	10 Intuiting	Nov 10 2002	2 Transcending	Jan 19 2003	7 Intuiting
Sep 2 2002	11 Evolving	Nov 11 2002	3 Remembering	Jan 20 2003	8 Evolving
Sep 3 2002	12 Self-Regulating	Nov 12 2002	4 Loving	Jan 21 2003	9 Self-Regulating
Sep 4 2002	13 Catalyzing	Nov 13 2002	5 Feeling	Jan 22 2003	10 Catalyzing
Sep 5 2002	**1 Enlightening**	Nov 14 2002	6 Devoting	Jan 23 2003	11 Enlightening
Sep 6 2002	2 Being	Nov 15 2002	7 Illuminating	Jan 24 2003	12 Being
Sep 7 2002	3 Breathing	Nov 16 2002	8 Choosing	Jan 25 2003	13 Breathing
Sep 8 2002	4 Listening	Nov 17 2002	9 Exploring	Jan 26 2003	**1 Listening**
Sep 9 2002	5 Planting	Nov 18 2002	10 Healing	Jan 27 2003	2 Planting
Sep 10 2002	6 Moving	Nov 19 2002	11 Seeing	Jan 28 2003	3 Moving
Sep 11 2002	7 Transcending	Nov 20 2002	12 Intuiting	Jan 29 2003	4 Transcending
Sep 12 2002	8 Remembering	Nov 21 2002	13 Evolving	Jan 30 2003	5 Remembering
Sep 13 2002	9 Loving	Nov 22 2002	**1 Self-Regulating**	Jan 31 2003	6 Loving
Sep 14 2002	10 Feeling	Nov 23 2002	2 Catalyzing	Feb 1 2003	7 Feeling
Sep 15 2002	11 Devoting	Nov 24 2002	3 Enlightening	Feb 2 2003	8 Devoting
Sep 16 2002	12 Illuminating	Nov 25 2002	4 Being	Feb 3 2003	9 Illuminating
Sep 17 2002	13 Choosing	Nov 26 2002	5 Breathing	Feb 4 2003	10 Choosing
Sep 18 2002	**1 Exploring**	Nov 27 2002	6 Listening	Feb 5 2003	11 Exploring
Sep 19 2002	2 Healing	Nov 28 2002	7 Planting	Feb 6 2003	12 Healing
Sep 20 2002	3 Seeing	Nov 29 2002	8 Moving	Feb 7 2003	13 Seeing
Sep 21 2002	4 Intuiting	Nov 30 2002	9 Transcending	Feb 8 2003	**1 Intuiting**
Sep 22 2002	5 Evolving	Dec 1 2002	10 Remembering	Feb 9 2003	2 Evolving
Sep 23 2002	6 Self-Regulating	Dec 2 2002	11 Loving	Feb 10 2003	3 Self-Regulating
Sep 24 2002	7 Catalyzing	Dec 3 2002	12 Feeling	Feb 11 2003	4 Catalyzing
Sep 25 2002	8 Enlightening	Dec 4 2002	13 Devoting	Feb 12 2003	5 Enlightening
Sep 26 2002	9 Being	Dec 5 2002	**1 Illuminating**	Feb 13 2003	6 Being
Sep 27 2002	10 Breathing	Dec 6 2002	2 Choosing	Feb 14 2003	7 Breathing
Sep 28 2002	11 Listening	Dec 7 2002	3 Exploring	Feb 15 2003	8 Listening
Sep 29 2002	12 Planting	Dec 8 2002	4 Healing	Feb 16 2003	9 Planting
Sep 30 2002	13 Moving	Dec 9 2002	5 Seeing	Feb 17 2003	10 Moving
Oct 1 2002	**1 Transcending**	Dec 10 2002	6 Intuiting	Feb 18 2003	11 Transcending
Oct 2 2002	2 Remembering	Dec 11 2002	7 Evolving	Feb 19 2003	12 Remembering
Oct 3 2002	3 Loving	Dec 12 2002	8 Self-Regulating	Feb 20 2003	13 Loving
Oct 4 2002	4 Feeling	Dec 13 2002	9 Catalyzing	Feb 21 2003	**1 Feeling**
Oct 5 2002	5 Devoting	Dec 14 2002	10 Enlightening	Feb 22 2003	2 Devoting
Oct 6 2002	6 Illuminating	Dec 15 2002	11 Being	Feb 23 2003	3 Illuminating
Oct 7 2002	7 Choosing	Dec 16 2002	12 Breathing	Feb 24 2003	4 Choosing
Oct 8 2002	8 Exploring	Dec 17 2002	13 Listening	Feb 25 2003	5 Exploring
Oct 9 2002	9 Healing	Dec 18 2002	**1 Planting**	Feb 26 2003	6 Healing
Oct 10 2002	10 Seeing	Dec 19 2002	2 Moving	Feb 27 2003	7 Seeing
Oct 11 2002	11 Intuiting	Dec 20 2002	3 Transcending	Feb 28 2003	8 Intuiting
Oct 12 2002	12 Evolving	Dec 21 2002	4 Remembering	Mar 1 2003	9 Evolving
Oct 13 2002	13 Self-Regulating	Dec 22 2002	5 Loving	Mar 2 2003	10 Self-Regulating
Oct 14 2002	**1 Catalyzing**	Dec 23 2002	6 Feeling	Mar 3 2003	11 Catalyzing
Oct 15 2002	2 Enlightening	Dec 24 2002	7 Devoting	Mar 4 2003	12 Enlightening

Date	UE Earth Energy	Date	UE Earth Energy	Date	UE Earth Energy
Mar 5 2003	13 Being	May 14 2003	5 Illuminating	Jul 23 2003	10 Being
Mar 6 2003	**1 Breathing**	May 15 2003	6 Choosing	Jul 24 2003	11 Breathing
Mar 7 2003	2 Listening	May 16 2003	7 Exploring	Jul 25 2003	12 Listening
Mar 8 2003	3 Planting	May 17 2003	8 Healing	Jul 26 2003	13 Planting
Mar 9 2003	4 Moving	May 18 2003	9 Seeing	Jul 27 2003	**1 Moving**
Mar 10 2003	5 Transcending	May 19 2003	10 Intuiting	Jul 28 2003	2 Transcending
Mar 11 2003	6 Remembering	May 20 2003	11 Evolving	Jul 29 2003	3 Remembering
Mar 12 2003	7 Loving	May 21 2003	12 Self-Regulating	Jul 30 2003	4 Loving
Mar 13 2003	8 Feeling	May 22 2003	13 Catalyzing	Jul 31 2003	5 Feeling
Mar 14 2003	9 Devoting	May 23 2003	**1 Enlightening**	Aug 1 2003	6 Devoting
Mar 15 2003	10 Illuminating	May 24 2003	2 Being	Aug 2 2003	7 Illuminating
Mar 16 2003	11 Choosing	May 25 2003	3 Breathing	Aug 3 2003	8 Choosing
Mar 17 2003	12 Exploring	May 26 2003	4 Listening	Aug 4 2003	9 Exploring
Mar 18 2003	13 Healing	May 27 2003	5 Planting	Aug 5 2003	10 Healing
Mar 19 2003	**1 Seeing**	May 28 2003	6 Moving	Aug 6 2003	11 Seeing
Mar 20 2003	2 Intuiting	May 29 2003	7 Transcending	Aug 7 2003	12 Intuiting
Mar 21 2003	3 Evolving	May 30 2003	8 Remembering	Aug 8 2003	13 Evolving
Mar 22 2003	4 Self-Regulating	May 31 2003	9 Loving	Aug 9 2003	**1 Self-Regulating**
Mar 23 2003	5 Catalyzing	Jun 1 2003	10 Feeling	Aug 10 2003	2 Catalyzing
Mar 24 2003	6 Enlightening	Jun 2 2003	11 Devoting	Aug 11 2003	3 Enlightening
Mar 25 2003	7 Being	Jun 3 2003	12 Illuminating	Aug 12 2003	4 Being
Mar 26 2003	8 Breathing	Jun 4 2003	13 Choosing	Aug 13 2003	5 Breathing
Mar 27 2003	9 Listening	Jun 5 2003	**1 Exploring**	Aug 14 2003	6 Listening
Mar 28 2003	10 Planting	Jun 6 2003	2 Healing	Aug 15 2003	7 Planting
Mar 29 2003	11 Moving	Jun 7 2003	3 Seeing	Aug 16 2003	8 Moving
Mar 30 2003	12 Transcending	Jun 8 2003	4 Intuiting	Aug 17 2003	9 Transcending
Mar 31 2003	13 Remembering	Jun 9 2003	5 Evolving	Aug 18 2003	10 Remembering
Apr 1 2003	**1 Loving**	Jun 10 2003	6 Self-Regulating	Aug 19 2003	11 Loving
Apr 2 2003	2 Feeling	Jun 11 2003	7 Catalyzing	Aug 20 2003	12 Feeling
Apr 3 2003	3 Devoting	Jun 12 2003	8 Enlightening	Aug 21 2003	13 Devoting
Apr 4 2003	4 Illuminating	Jun 13 2003	9 Being	Aug 22 2003	**1 Illuminating**
Apr 5 2003	5 Choosing	Jun 14 2003	10 Breathing	Aug 23 2003	2 Choosing
Apr 6 2003	6 Exploring	Jun 15 2003	11 Listening	Aug 24 2003	3 Exploring
Apr 7 2003	7 Healing	Jun 16 2003	12 Planting	Aug 25 2003	4 Healing
Apr 8 2003	8 Seeing	Jun 17 2003	13 Moving	Aug 26 2003	5 Seeing
Apr 9 2003	9 Intuiting	Jun 18 2003	**1 Transcending**	Aug 27 2003	6 Intuiting
Apr 10 2003	10 Evolving	Jun 19 2003	2 Remembering	Aug 28 2003	7 Evolving
Apr 11 2003	11 Self-Regulating	Jun 20 2003	3 Loving	Aug 29 2003	8 Self-Regulating
Apr 12 2003	12 Catalyzing	Jun 21 2003	4 Feeling	Aug 30 2003	9 Catalyzing
Apr 13 2003	13 Enlightening	Jun 22 2003	5 Devoting	Aug 31 2003	10 Enlightening
Apr 14 2003	**1 Being**	Jun 23 2003	6 Illuminating	Sep 1 2003	11 Being
Apr 15 2003	2 Breathing	Jun 24 2003	7 Choosing	Sep 2 2003	12 Breathing
Apr 16 2003	3 Listening	Jun 25 2003	8 Exploring	Sep 3 2003	13 Listening
Apr 17 2003	4 Planting	Jun 26 2003	9 Healing	Sep 4 2003	**1 Planting**
Apr 18 2003	5 Moving	Jun 27 2003	10 Seeing	Sep 5 2003	2 Moving
Apr 19 2003	6 Transcending	Jun 28 2003	11 Intuiting	Sep 6 2003	3 Transcending
Apr 20 2003	7 Remembering	Jun 29 2003	12 Evolving	Sep 7 2003	4 Remembering
Apr 21 2003	8 Loving	Jun 30 2003	13 Self-Regulating	Sep 8 2003	5 Loving
Apr 22 2003	9 Feeling	Jul 1 2003	**1 Catalyzing**	Sep 9 2003	6 Feeling
Apr 23 2003	10 Devoting	Jul 2 2003	2 Enlightening	Sep 10 2003	7 Devoting
Apr 24 2003	11 Illuminating	Jul 3 2003	3 Being	Sep 11 2003	8 Illuminating
Apr 25 2003	12 Choosing	Jul 4 2003	4 Breathing	Sep 12 2003	9 Choosing
Apr 26 2003	13 Exploring	Jul 5 2003	5 Listening	Sep 13 2003	10 Exploring
Apr 27 2003	**1 Healing**	Jul 6 2003	6 Planting	Sep 14 2003	11 Healing
Apr 28 2003	2 Seeing	Jul 7 2003	7 Moving	Sep 15 2003	12 Seeing
Apr 29 2003	3 Intuiting	Jul 8 2003	8 Transcending	Sep 16 2003	13 Intuiting
Apr 30 2003	4 Evolving	Jul 9 2003	9 Remembering	Sep 17 2003	**1 Evolving**
May 1 2003	5 Self-Regulating	Jul 10 2003	10 Loving	Sep 18 2003	2 Self-Regulating
May 2 2003	6 Catalyzing	Jul 11 2003	11 Feeling	Sep 19 2003	3 Catalyzing
May 3 2003	7 Enlightening	Jul 12 2003	12 Devoting	Sep 20 2003	4 Enlightening
May 4 2003	8 Being	Jul 13 2003	13 Illuminating	Sep 21 2003	5 Being
May 5 2003	9 Breathing	Jul 14 2003	**1 Choosing**	Sep 22 2003	6 Breathing
May 6 2003	10 Listening	Jul 15 2003	2 Exploring	Sep 23 2003	7 Listening
May 7 2003	11 Planting	Jul 16 2003	3 Healing	Sep 24 2003	8 Planting
May 8 2003	12 Moving	Jul 17 2003	4 Seeing	Sep 25 2003	9 Moving
May 9 2003	13 Transcending	Jul 18 2003	5 Intuiting	Sep 26 2003	10 Transcending
May 10 2003	**1 Remembering**	Jul 19 2003	6 Evolving	Sep 27 2003	11 Remembering
May 11 2003	2 Loving	Jul 20 2003	7 Self-Regulating	Sep 28 2003	12 Loving
May 12 2003	3 Feeling	Jul 21 2003	8 Catalyzing	Sep 29 2003	13 Feeling
May 13 2003	4 Devoting	Jul 22 2003	9 Enlightening	Sep 30 2003	**1 Devoting**

Date	UE Earth Energy	Date	UE Earth Energy	Date	UE Earth Energy
Oct 1 2003	2 Illuminating	Dec 10 2003	7 Being	Feb 18 2004	12 Illuminating
Oct 2 2003	3 Choosing	Dec 11 2003	8 Breathing	Feb 19 2004	13 Choosing
Oct 3 2003	4 Exploring	Dec 12 2003	9 Listening	Feb 20 2004	**1 Exploring**
Oct 4 2003	5 Healing	Dec 13 2003	10 Planting	Feb 21 2004	2 Healing
Oct 5 2003	6 Seeing	Dec 14 2003	11 Moving	Feb 22 2004	3 Seeing
Oct 6 2003	7 Intuiting	Dec 15 2003	12 Transcending	Feb 23 2004	4 Intuiting
Oct 7 2003	8 Evolving	Dec 16 2003	13 Remembering	Feb 24 2004	5 Evolving
Oct 8 2003	9 Self-Regulating	Dec 17 2003	**1 Loving**	Feb 25 2004	6 Self-Regulating
Oct 9 2003	10 Catalyzing	Dec 18 2003	2 Feeling	Feb 26 2004	7 Catalyzing
Oct 10 2003	11 Enlightening	Dec 19 2003	3 Devoting	Feb 27 2004	8 Enlightening
Oct 11 2003	12 Being	Dec 20 2003	4 Illuminating	Feb 28 2004	9 Being
Oct 12 2003	13 Breathing	Dec 21 2003	5 Choosing	Feb 29 2004	10 Breathing
Oct 13 2003	**1 Listening**	Dec 22 2003	6 Exploring	Mar 1 2004	11 Listening
Oct 14 2003	2 Planting	Dec 23 2003	7 Healing	Mar 2 2004	12 Planting
Oct 15 2003	3 Moving	Dec 24 2003	8 Seeing	Mar 3 2004	13 Moving
Oct 16 2003	4 Transcending	Dec 25 2003	9 Intuiting	Mar 4 2004	**1 Transcending**
Oct 17 2003	5 Remembering	Dec 26 2003	10 Evolving	Mar 5 2004	2 Remembering
Oct 18 2003	6 Loving	Dec 27 2003	11 Self-Regulating	Mar 6 2004	3 Loving
Oct 19 2003	7 Feeling	Dec 28 2003	12 Catalyzing	Mar 7 2004	4 Feeling
Oct 20 2003	8 Devoting	Dec 29 2003	13 Enlightening	Mar 8 2004	5 Devoting
Oct 21 2003	9 Illuminating	Dec 30 2003	**1 Being**	Mar 9 2004	6 Illuminating
Oct 22 2003	10 Choosing	Dec 31 2003	2 Breathing	Mar 10 2004	7 Choosing
Oct 23 2003	11 Exploring	Jan 1 2004	3 Listening	Mar 11 2004	8 Exploring
Oct 24 2003	12 Healing	Jan 2 2004	4 Planting	Mar 12 2004	9 Healing
Oct 25 2003	13 Seeing	Jan 3 2004	5 Moving	Mar 13 2004	10 Seeing
Oct 26 2003	**1 Intuiting**	Jan 4 2004	6 Transcending	Mar 14 2004	11 Intuiting
Oct 27 2003	2 Evolving	Jan 5 2004	7 Remembering	Mar 15 2004	12 Evolving
Oct 28 2003	3 Self-Regulating	Jan 6 2004	8 Loving	Mar 16 2004	13 Self-Regulating
Oct 29 2003	4 Catalyzing	Jan 7 2004	9 Feeling	Mar 17 2004	**1 Catalyzing**
Oct 30 2003	5 Enlightening	Jan 8 2004	10 Devoting	Mar 18 2004	2 Enlightening
Oct 31 2003	6 Being	Jan 9 2004	11 Illuminating	Mar 19 2004	3 Being
Nov 1 2003	7 Breathing	Jan 10 2004	12 Choosing	Mar 20 2004	4 Breathing
Nov 2 2003	8 Listening	Jan 11 2004	13 Exploring	Mar 21 2004	5 Listening
Nov 3 2003	9 Planting	Jan 12 2004	**1 Healing**	Mar 22 2004	6 Planting
Nov 4 2003	10 Moving	Jan 13 2004	2 Seeing	Mar 23 2004	7 Moving
Nov 5 2003	11 Transcending	Jan 14 2004	3 Intuiting	Mar 24 2004	8 Transcending
Nov 6 2003	12 Remembering	Jan 15 2004	4 Evolving	Mar 25 2004	9 Remembering
Nov 7 2003	13 Loving	Jan 16 2004	5 Self-Regulating	Mar 26 2004	10 Loving
Nov 8 2003	**1 Feeling**	Jan 17 2004	6 Catalyzing	Mar 27 2004	11 Feeling
Nov 9 2003	2 Devoting	Jan 18 2004	7 Enlightening	Mar 28 2004	12 Devoting
Nov 10 2003	3 Illuminating	Jan 19 2004	8 Being	Mar 29 2004	13 Illuminating
Nov 11 2003	4 Choosing	Jan 20 2004	9 Breathing	Mar 30 2004	**1 Choosing**
Nov 12 2003	5 Exploring	Jan 21 2004	10 Listening	Mar 31 2004	2 Exploring
Nov 13 2003	6 Healing	Jan 22 2004	11 Planting	Apr 1 2004	3 Healing
Nov 14 2003	7 Seeing	Jan 23 2004	12 Moving	Apr 2 2004	4 Seeing
Nov 15 2003	8 Intuiting	Jan 24 2004	13 Transcending	Apr 3 2004	5 Intuiting
Nov 16 2003	9 Evolving	Jan 25 2004	**1 Remembering**	Apr 4 2004	6 Evolving
Nov 17 2003	10 Self-Regulating	Jan 26 2004	2 Loving	Apr 5 2004	7 Self-Regulating
Nov 18 2003	11 Catalyzing	Jan 27 2004	3 Feeling	Apr 6 2004	8 Catalyzing
Nov 19 2003	12 Enlightening	Jan 28 2004	4 Devoting	Apr 7 2004	9 Enlightening
Nov 20 2003	13 Being	Jan 29 2004	5 Illuminating	Apr 8 2004	10 Being
Nov 21 2003	**1 Breathing**	Jan 30 2004	6 Choosing	Apr 9 2004	11 Breathing
Nov 22 2003	2 Listening	Jan 31 2004	7 Exploring	Apr 10 2004	12 Listening
Nov 23 2003	3 Planting	Feb 1 2004	8 Healing	Apr 11 2004	13 Planting
Nov 24 2003	4 Moving	Feb 2 2004	9 Seeing	Apr 12 2004	**1 Moving**
Nov 25 2003	5 Transcending	Feb 3 2004	10 Intuiting	Apr 13 2004	2 Transcending
Nov 26 2003	6 Remembering	Feb 4 2004	11 Evolving	Apr 14 2004	3 Remembering
Nov 27 2003	7 Loving	Feb 5 2004	12 Self-Regulating	Apr 15 2004	4 Loving
Nov 28 2003	8 Feeling	Feb 6 2004	13 Catalyzing	Apr 16 2004	5 Feeling
Nov 29 2003	9 Devoting	Feb 7 2004	**1 Enlightening**	Apr 17 2004	6 Devoting
Nov 30 2003	10 Illuminating	Feb 8 2004	2 Being	Apr 18 2004	7 Illuminating
Dec 1 2003	11 Choosing	Feb 9 2004	3 Breathing	Apr 19 2004	8 Choosing
Dec 2 2003	12 Exploring	Feb 10 2004	4 Listening	Apr 20 2004	9 Exploring
Dec 3 2003	13 Healing	Feb 11 2004	5 Planting	Apr 21 2004	10 Healing
Dec 4 2003	**1 Seeing**	Feb 12 2004	6 Moving	Apr 22 2004	11 Seeing
Dec 5 2003	2 Intuiting	Feb 13 2004	7 Transcending	Apr 23 2004	12 Intuiting
Dec 6 2003	3 Evolving	Feb 14 2004	8 Remembering	Apr 24 2004	13 Evolving
Dec 7 2003	4 Self-Regulating	Feb 15 2004	9 Loving	Apr 25 2004	**1 Self-Regulating**
Dec 8 2003	5 Catalyzing	Feb 16 2004	10 Feeling	Apr 26 2004	2 Catalyzing
Dec 9 2003	6 Enlightening	Feb 17 2004	11 Devoting	Apr 27 2004	3 Enlightening

Date	UE	Earth Energy	Date	UE	Earth Energy	Date	UE	Earth Energy
Apr 28 2004	4	Being	Jul 7 2004	9	Illuminating	Sep 15 2004	1	**Being**
Apr 29 2004	5	Breathing	Jul 8 2004	10	Choosing	Sep 16 2004	2	Breathing
Apr 30 2004	6	Listening	Jul 9 2004	11	Exploring	Sep 17 2004	3	Listening
May 1 2004	7	Planting	Jul 10 2004	12	Healing	Sep 18 2004	4	Planting
May 2 2004	8	Moving	Jul 11 2004	13	Seeing	Sep 19 2004	5	Moving
May 3 2004	9	Transcending	Jul 12 2004	1	**Intuiting**	Sep 20 2004	6	Transcending
May 4 2004	10	Remembering	Jul 13 2004	2	Evolving	Sep 21 2004	7	Remembering
May 5 2004	11	Loving	Jul 14 2004	3	Self-Regulating	Sep 22 2004	8	Loving
May 6 2004	12	Feeling	Jul 15 2004	4	Catalyzing	Sep 23 2004	9	Feeling
May 7 2004	13	Devoting	Jul 16 2004	5	Enlightening	Sep 24 2004	10	Devoting
May 8 2004	1	**Illuminating**	Jul 17 2004	6	Being	Sep 25 2004	11	Illuminating
May 9 2004	2	Choosing	Jul 18 2004	7	Breathing	Sep 26 2004	12	Choosing
May 10 2004	3	Exploring	Jul 19 2004	8	Listening	Sep 27 2004	13	Exploring
May 11 2004	4	Healing	Jul 20 2004	9	Planting	Sep 28 2004	1	**Healing**
May 12 2004	5	Seeing	Jul 21 2004	10	Moving	Sep 29 2004	2	Seeing
May 13 2004	6	Intuiting	Jul 22 2004	11	Transcending	Sep 30 2004	3	Intuiting
May 14 2004	7	Evolving	Jul 23 2004	12	Remembering	Oct 1 2004	4	Evolving
May 15 2004	8	Self-Regulating	Jul 24 2004	13	Loving	Oct 2 2004	5	Self-Regulating
May 16 2004	9	Catalyzing	Jul 25 2004	1	**Feeling**	Oct 3 2004	6	Catalyzing
May 17 2004	10	Enlightening	Jul 26 2004	2	Devoting	Oct 4 2004	7	Enlightening
May 18 2004	11	Being	Jul 27 2004	3	Illuminating	Oct 5 2004	8	Being
May 19 2004	12	Breathing	Jul 28 2004	4	Choosing	Oct 6 2004	9	Breathing
May 20 2004	13	Listening	Jul 29 2004	5	Exploring	Oct 7 2004	10	Listening
May 21 2004	1	**Planting**	Jul 30 2004	6	Healing	Oct 8 2004	11	Planting
May 22 2004	2	Moving	Jul 31 2004	7	Seeing	Oct 9 2004	12	Moving
May 23 2004	3	Transcending	Aug 1 2004	8	Intuiting	Oct 10 2004	13	Transcending
May 24 2004	4	Remembering	Aug 2 2004	9	Evolving	Oct 11 2004	1	**Remembering**
May 25 2004	5	Loving	Aug 3 2004	10	Self-Regulating	Oct 12 2004	2	Loving
May 26 2004	6	Feeling	Aug 4 2004	11	Catalyzing	Oct 13 2004	3	Feeling
May 27 2004	7	Devoting	Aug 5 2004	12	Enlightening	Oct 14 2004	4	Devoting
May 28 2004	8	Illuminating	Aug 6 2004	13	Being	Oct 15 2004	5	Illuminating
May 29 2004	9	Choosing	Aug 7 2004	1	**Breathing**	Oct 16 2004	6	Choosing
May 30 2004	10	Exploring	Aug 8 2004	2	Listening	Oct 17 2004	7	Exploring
May 31 2004	11	Healing	Aug 9 2004	3	Planting	Oct 18 2004	8	Healing
Jun 1 2004	12	Seeing	Aug 10 2004	4	Moving	Oct 19 2004	9	Seeing
Jun 2 2004	13	Intuiting	Aug 11 2004	5	Transcending	Oct 20 2004	10	Intuiting
Jun 3 2004	1	**Evolving**	Aug 12 2004	6	Remembering	Oct 21 2004	11	Evolving
Jun 4 2004	2	Self-Regulating	Aug 13 2004	7	Loving	Oct 22 2004	12	Self-Regulating
Jun 5 2004	3	Catalyzing	Aug 14 2004	8	Feeling	Oct 23 2004	13	Catalyzing
Jun 6 2004	4	Enlightening	Aug 15 2004	9	Devoting	Oct 24 2004	1	**Enlightening**
Jun 7 2004	5	Being	Aug 16 2004	10	Illuminating	Oct 25 2004	2	Being
Jun 8 2004	6	Breathing	Aug 17 2004	11	Choosing	Oct 26 2004	3	Breathing
Jun 9 2004	7	Listening	Aug 18 2004	12	Exploring	Oct 27 2004	4	Listening
Jun 10 2004	8	Planting	Aug 19 2004	13	Healing	Oct 28 2004	5	Planting
Jun 11 2004	9	Moving	Aug 20 2004	1	**Seeing**	Oct 29 2004	6	Moving
Jun 12 2004	10	Transcending	Aug 21 2004	2	Intuiting	Oct 30 2004	7	Transcending
Jun 13 2004	11	Remembering	Aug 22 2004	3	Evolving	Oct 31 2004	8	Remembering
Jun 14 2004	12	Loving	Aug 23 2004	4	Self-Regulating	Nov 1 2004	9	Loving
Jun 15 2004	13	Feeling	Aug 24 2004	5	Catalyzing	Nov 2 2004	10	Feeling
Jun 16 2004	1	**Devoting**	Aug 25 2004	6	Enlightening	Nov 3 2004	11	Devoting
Jun 17 2004	2	Illuminating	Aug 26 2004	7	Being	Nov 4 2004	12	Illuminating
Jun 18 2004	3	Choosing	Aug 27 2004	8	Breathing	Nov 5 2004	13	Choosing
Jun 19 2004	4	Exploring	Aug 28 2004	9	Listening	Nov 6 2004	1	**Exploring**
Jun 20 2004	5	Healing	Aug 29 2004	10	Planting	Nov 7 2004	2	Healing
Jun 21 2004	6	Seeing	Aug 30 2004	11	Moving	Nov 8 2004	3	Seeing
Jun 22 2004	7	Intuiting	Aug 31 2004	12	Transcending	Nov 9 2004	4	Intuiting
Jun 23 2004	8	Evolving	Sep 1 2004	13	Remembering	Nov 10 2004	5	Evolving
Jun 24 2004	9	Self-Regulating	Sep 2 2004	1	**Loving**	Nov 11 2004	6	Self-Regulating
Jun 25 2004	10	Catalyzing	Sep 3 2004	2	Feeling	Nov 12 2004	7	Catalyzing
Jun 26 2004	11	Enlightening	Sep 4 2004	3	Devoting	Nov 13 2004	8	Enlightening
Jun 27 2004	12	Being	Sep 5 2004	4	Illuminating	Nov 14 2004	9	Being
Jun 28 2004	13	Breathing	Sep 6 2004	5	Choosing	Nov 15 2004	10	Breathing
Jun 29 2004	1	**Listening**	Sep 7 2004	6	Exploring	Nov 16 2004	11	Listening
Jun 30 2004	2	Planting	Sep 8 2004	7	Healing	Nov 17 2004	12	Planting
Jul 1 2004	3	Moving	Sep 9 2004	8	Seeing	Nov 18 2004	13	Moving
Jul 2 2004	4	Transcending	Sep 10 2004	9	Intuiting	Nov 19 2004	1	**Transcending**
Jul 3 2004	5	Remembering	Sep 11 2004	10	Evolving	Nov 20 2004	2	Remembering
Jul 4 2004	6	Loving	Sep 12 2004	11	Self-Regulating	Nov 21 2004	3	Loving
Jul 5 2004	7	Feeling	Sep 13 2004	12	Catalyzing	Nov 22 2004	4	Feeling
Jul 6 2004	8	Devoting	Sep 14 2004	13	Enlightening	Nov 23 2004	5	Devoting

Date	UE Earth Energy	Date	UE Earth Energy	Date	UE Earth Energy
Nov 24 2004	6 Illuminating	Feb 2 2005	11 Being	Apr 13 2005	3 Illuminating
Nov 25 2004	7 Choosing	Feb 3 2005	12 Breathing	Apr 14 2005	4 Choosing
Nov 26 2004	8 Exploring	Feb 4 2005	13 Listening	Apr 15 2005	5 Exploring
Nov 27 2004	9 Healing	Feb 5 2005	1 Planting	Apr 16 2005	6 Healing
Nov 28 2004	10 Seeing	Feb 6 2005	2 Moving	Apr 17 2005	7 Seeing
Nov 29 2004	11 Intuiting	Feb 7 2005	3 Transcending	Apr 18 2005	8 Intuiting
Nov 30 2004	12 Evolving	Feb 8 2005	4 Remembering	Apr 19 2005	9 Evolving
Dec 1 2004	13 Self-Regulating	Feb 9 2005	5 Loving	Apr 20 2005	10 Self-Regulating
Dec 2 2004	1 Catalyzing	Feb 10 2005	6 Feeling	Apr 21 2005	11 Catalyzing
Dec 3 2004	2 Enlightening	Feb 11 2005	7 Devoting	Apr 22 2005	12 Enlightening
Dec 4 2004	3 Being	Feb 12 2005	8 Illuminating	Apr 23 2005	13 Being
Dec 5 2004	4 Breathing	Feb 13 2005	9 Choosing	Apr 24 2005	1 Breathing
Dec 6 2004	5 Listening	Feb 14 2005	10 Exploring	Apr 25 2005	2 Listening
Dec 7 2004	6 Planting	Feb 15 2005	11 Healing	Apr 26 2005	3 Planting
Dec 8 2004	7 Moving	Feb 16 2005	12 Seeing	Apr 27 2005	4 Moving
Dec 9 2004	8 Transcending	Feb 17 2005	13 Intuiting	Apr 28 2005	5 Transcending
Dec 10 2004	9 Remembering	Feb 18 2005	1 Evolving	Apr 29 2005	6 Remembering
Dec 11 2004	10 Loving	Feb 19 2005	2 Self-Regulating	Apr 30 2005	7 Loving
Dec 12 2004	11 Feeling	Feb 20 2005	3 Catalyzing	May 1 2005	8 Feeling
Dec 13 2004	12 Devoting	Feb 21 2005	4 Enlightening	May 2 2005	9 Devoting
Dec 14 2004	13 Illuminating	Feb 22 2005	5 Being	May 3 2005	10 Illuminating
Dec 15 2004	1 Choosing	Feb 23 2005	6 Breathing	May 4 2005	11 Choosing
Dec 16 2004	2 Exploring	Feb 24 2005	7 Listening	May 5 2005	12 Exploring
Dec 17 2004	3 Healing	Feb 25 2005	8 Planting	May 6 2005	13 Healing
Dec 18 2004	4 Seeing	Feb 26 2005	9 Moving	May 7 2005	1 Seeing
Dec 19 2004	5 Intuiting	Feb 27 2005	10 Transcending	May 8 2005	2 Intuiting
Dec 20 2004	6 Evolving	Feb 28 2005	11 Remembering	May 9 2005	3 Evolving
Dec 21 2004	7 Self-Regulating	Mar 1 2005	12 Loving	May 10 2005	4 Self-Regulating
Dec 22 2004	8 Catalyzing	Mar 2 2005	13 Feeling	May 11 2005	5 Catalyzing
Dec 23 2004	9 Enlightening	Mar 3 2005	1 Devoting	May 12 2005	6 Enlightening
Dec 24 2004	10 Being	Mar 4 2005	2 Illuminating	May 13 2005	7 Being
Dec 25 2004	11 Breathing	Mar 5 2005	3 Choosing	May 14 2005	8 Breathing
Dec 26 2004	12 Listening	Mar 6 2005	4 Exploring	May 15 2005	9 Listening
Dec 27 2004	13 Planting	Mar 7 2005	5 Healing	May 16 2005	10 Planting
Dec 28 2004	1 Moving	Mar 8 2005	6 Seeing	May 17 2005	11 Moving
Dec 29 2004	2 Transcending	Mar 9 2005	7 Intuiting	May 18 2005	12 Transcending
Dec 30 2004	3 Remembering	Mar 10 2005	8 Evolving	May 19 2005	13 Remembering
Dec 31 2004	4 Loving	Mar 11 2005	9 Self-Regulating	May 20 2005	1 Loving
Jan 1 2005	5 Feeling	Mar 12 2005	10 Catalyzing	May 21 2005	2 Feeling
Jan 2 2005	6 Devoting	Mar 13 2005	11 Enlightening	May 22 2005	3 Devoting
Jan 3 2005	7 Illuminating	Mar 14 2005	12 Being	May 23 2005	4 Illuminating
Jan 4 2005	8 Choosing	Mar 15 2005	13 Breathing	May 24 2005	5 Choosing
Jan 5 2005	9 Exploring	Mar 16 2005	1 Listening	May 25 2005	6 Exploring
Jan 6 2005	10 Healing	Mar 17 2005	2 Planting	May 26 2005	7 Healing
Jan 7 2005	11 Seeing	Mar 18 2005	3 Moving	May 27 2005	8 Seeing
Jan 8 2005	12 Intuiting	Mar 19 2005	4 Transcending	May 28 2005	9 Intuiting
Jan 9 2005	13 Evolving	Mar 20 2005	5 Remembering	May 29 2005	10 Evolving
Jan 10 2005	1 Self-Regulating	Mar 21 2005	6 Loving	May 30 2005	11 Self-Regulating
Jan 11 2005	2 Catalyzing	Mar 22 2005	7 Feeling	May 31 2005	12 Catalyzing
Jan 12 2005	3 Enlightening	Mar 23 2005	8 Devoting	Jun 1 2005	13 Enlightening
Jan 13 2005	4 Being	Mar 24 2005	9 Illuminating	Jun 2 2005	1 Being
Jan 14 2005	5 Breathing	Mar 25 2005	10 Choosing	Jun 3 2005	2 Breathing
Jan 15 2005	6 Listening	Mar 26 2005	11 Exploring	Jun 4 2005	3 Listening
Jan 16 2005	7 Planting	Mar 27 2005	12 Healing	Jun 5 2005	4 Planting
Jan 17 2005	8 Moving	Mar 28 2005	13 Seeing	Jun 6 2005	5 Moving
Jan 18 2005	9 Transcending	Mar 29 2005	1 Intuiting	Jun 7 2005	6 Transcending
Jan 19 2005	10 Remembering	Mar 30 2005	2 Evolving	Jun 8 2005	7 Remembering
Jan 20 2005	11 Loving	Mar 31 2005	3 Self-Regulating	Jun 9 2005	8 Loving
Jan 21 2005	12 Feeling	Apr 1 2005	4 Catalyzing	Jun 10 2005	9 Feeling
Jan 22 2005	13 Devoting	Apr 2 2005	5 Enlightening	Jun 11 2005	10 Devoting
Jan 23 2005	1 Illuminating	Apr 3 2005	6 Being	Jun 12 2005	11 Illuminating
Jan 24 2005	2 Choosing	Apr 4 2005	7 Breathing	Jun 13 2005	12 Choosing
Jan 25 2005	3 Exploring	Apr 5 2005	8 Listening	Jun 14 2005	13 Exploring
Jan 26 2005	4 Healing	Apr 6 2005	9 Planting	Jun 15 2005	1 Healing
Jan 27 2005	5 Seeing	Apr 7 2005	10 Moving	Jun 16 2005	2 Seeing
Jan 28 2005	6 Intuiting	Apr 8 2005	11 Transcending	Jun 17 2005	3 Intuiting
Jan 29 2005	7 Evolving	Apr 9 2005	12 Remembering	Jun 18 2005	4 Evolving
Jan 30 2005	8 Self-Regulating	Apr 10 2005	13 Loving	Jun 19 2005	5 Self-Regulating
Jan 31 2005	9 Catalyzing	Apr 11 2005	1 Feeling	Jun 20 2005	6 Catalyzing
Feb 1 2005	10 Enlightening	Apr 12 2005	2 Devoting	Jun 21 2005	7 Enlightening

Date	UE	Earth Energy	Date	UE	Earth Energy	Date	UE	Earth Energy
Jun 22 2005	8	Being	Aug 31 2005	13	Illuminating	Nov 9 2005	5	Being
Jun 23 2005	9	Breathing	Sep 1 2005	1	**Choosing**	Nov 10 2005	6	Breathing
Jun 24 2005	10	Listening	Sep 2 2005	2	Exploring	Nov 11 2005	7	Listening
Jun 25 2005	11	Planting	Sep 3 2005	3	Healing	Nov 12 2005	8	Planting
Jun 26 2005	12	Moving	Sep 4 2005	4	Seeing	Nov 13 2005	9	Moving
Jun 27 2005	13	Transcending	Sep 5 2005	5	Intuiting	Nov 14 2005	10	Transcending
Jun 28 2005	1	**Remembering**	Sep 6 2005	6	Evolving	Nov 15 2005	11	Remembering
Jun 29 2005	2	Loving	Sep 7 2005	7	Self-Regulating	Nov 16 2005	12	Loving
Jun 30 2005	3	Feeling	Sep 8 2005	8	Catalyzing	Nov 17 2005	13	Feeling
Jul 1 2005	4	Devoting	Sep 9 2005	9	Enlightening	Nov 18 2005	1	**Devoting**
Jul 2 2005	5	Illuminating	Sep 10 2005	10	Being	Nov 19 2005	2	Illuminating
Jul 3 2005	6	Choosing	Sep 11 2005	11	Breathing	Nov 20 2005	3	Choosing
Jul 4 2005	7	Exploring	Sep 12 2005	12	Listening	Nov 21 2005	4	Exploring
Jul 5 2005	8	Healing	Sep 13 2005	13	Planting	Nov 22 2005	5	Healing
Jul 6 2005	9	Seeing	Sep 14 2005	1	**Moving**	Nov 23 2005	6	Seeing
Jul 7 2005	10	Intuiting	Sep 15 2005	2	Transcending	Nov 24 2005	7	Intuiting
Jul 8 2005	11	Evolving	Sep 16 2005	3	Remembering	Nov 25 2005	8	Evolving
Jul 9 2005	12	Self-Regulating	Sep 17 2005	4	Loving	Nov 26 2005	9	Self-Regulating
Jul 10 2005	13	Catalyzing	Sep 18 2005	5	Feeling	Nov 27 2005	10	Catalyzing
Jul 11 2005	1	**Enlightening**	Sep 19 2005	6	Devoting	Nov 28 2005	11	Enlightening
Jul 12 2005	2	Being	Sep 20 2005	7	Illuminating	Nov 29 2005	12	Being
Jul 13 2005	3	Breathing	Sep 21 2005	8	Choosing	Nov 30 2005	13	Breathing
Jul 14 2005	4	Listening	Sep 22 2005	9	Exploring	Dec 1 2005	1	**Listening**
Jul 15 2005	5	Planting	Sep 23 2005	10	Healing	Dec 2 2005	2	Planting
Jul 16 2005	6	Moving	Sep 24 2005	11	Seeing	Dec 3 2005	3	Moving
Jul 17 2005	7	Transcending	Sep 25 2005	12	Intuiting	Dec 4 2005	4	Transcending
Jul 18 2005	8	Remembering	Sep 26 2005	13	Catalyzing	Dec 5 2005	5	Remembering
Jul 19 2005	9	Loving	Sep 27 2005	1	**Self-Regulating**	Dec 6 2005	6	Loving
Jul 20 2005	10	Feeling	Sep 28 2005	2	Catalyzing	Dec 7 2005	7	Feeling
Jul 21 2005	11	Devoting	Sep 29 2005	3	Enlightening	Dec 8 2005	8	Devoting
Jul 22 2005	12	Illuminating	Sep 30 2005	4	Being	Dec 9 2005	9	Illuminating
Jul 23 2005	13	Choosing	Oct 1 2005	5	Breathing	Dec 10 2005	10	Choosing
Jul 24 2005	1	**Exploring**	Oct 2 2005	6	Listening	Dec 11 2005	11	Exploring
Jul 25 2005	2	Healing	Oct 3 2005	7	Planting	Dec 12 2005	12	Healing
Jul 26 2005	3	Seeing	Oct 4 2005	8	Moving	Dec 13 2005	13	Seeing
Jul 27 2005	4	Intuiting	Oct 5 2005	9	Transcending	Dec 14 2005	1	**Intuiting**
Jul 28 2005	5	Evolving	Oct 6 2005	10	Remembering	Dec 15 2005	2	Evolving
Jul 29 2005	6	Self-Regulating	Oct 7 2005	11	Loving	Dec 16 2005	3	Self-Regulating
Jul 30 2005	7	Catalyzing	Oct 8 2005	12	Feeling	Dec 17 2005	4	Catalyzing
Jul 31 2005	8	Enlightening	Oct 9 2005	13	Devoting	Dec 18 2005	5	Enlightening
Aug 1 2005	9	Being	Oct 10 2005	1	**Illuminating**	Dec 19 2005	6	Being
Aug 2 2005	10	Breathing	Oct 11 2005	2	Choosing	Dec 20 2005	7	Breathing
Aug 3 2005	11	Listening	Oct 12 2005	3	Exploring	Dec 21 2005	8	Listening
Aug 4 2005	12	Planting	Oct 13 2005	4	Healing	Dec 22 2005	9	Planting
Aug 5 2005	13	Moving	Oct 14 2005	5	Seeing	Dec 23 2005	10	Moving
Aug 6 2005	1	**Transcending**	Oct 15 2005	6	Intuiting	Dec 24 2005	11	Transcending
Aug 7 2005	2	Remembering	Oct 16 2005	7	Evolving	Dec 25 2005	12	Remembering
Aug 8 2005	3	Loving	Oct 17 2005	8	Self-Regulating	Dec 26 2005	13	Loving
Aug 9 2005	4	Feeling	Oct 18 2005	9	Catalyzing	Dec 27 2005	1	**Feeling**
Aug 10 2005	5	Devoting	Oct 19 2005	10	Enlightening	Dec 28 2005	2	Devoting
Aug 11 2005	6	Illuminating	Oct 20 2005	11	Being	Dec 29 2005	3	Illuminating
Aug 12 2005	7	Choosing	Oct 21 2005	12	Breathing	Dec 30 2005	4	Choosing
Aug 13 2005	8	Exploring	Oct 22 2005	13	Listening	Dec 31 2005	5	Exploring
Aug 14 2005	9	Healing	Oct 23 2005	1	**Planting**	Jan 1 2006	6	Healing
Aug 15 2005	10	Seeing	Oct 24 2005	2	Moving	Jan 2 2006	7	Seeing
Aug 16 2005	11	Intuiting	Oct 25 2005	3	Transcending	Jan 3 2006	8	Intuiting
Aug 17 2005	12	Evolving	Oct 26 2005	4	Remembering	Jan 4 2006	9	Evolving
Aug 18 2005	13	Self-Regulating	Oct 27 2005	5	Loving	Jan 5 2006	10	Self-Regulating
Aug 19 2005	1	**Catalyzing**	Oct 28 2005	6	Feeling	Jan 6 2006	11	Catalyzing
Aug 20 2005	2	Enlightening	Oct 29 2005	7	Devoting	Jan 7 2006	12	Enlightening
Aug 21 2005	3	Being	Oct 30 2005	8	Illuminating	Jan 8 2006	13	Being
Aug 22 2005	4	Breathing	Oct 31 2005	9	Choosing	Jan 9 2006	1	**Breathing**
Aug 23 2005	5	Listening	Nov 1 2005	10	Exploring	Jan 10 2006	2	Listening
Aug 24 2005	6	Planting	Nov 2 2005	11	Healing	Jan 11 2006	3	Planting
Aug 25 2005	7	Moving	Nov 3 2005	12	Seeing	Jan 12 2006	4	Moving
Aug 26 2005	8	Transcending	Nov 4 2005	13	Intuiting	Jan 13 2006	5	Transcending
Aug 27 2005	9	Remembering	Nov 5 2005	1	**Evolving**	Jan 14 2006	6	Remembering
Aug 28 2005	10	Loving	Nov 6 2005	2	Self-Regulating	Jan 15 2006	7	Loving
Aug 29 2005	11	Feeling	Nov 7 2005	3	Catalyzing	Jan 16 2006	8	Feeling
Aug 30 2005	12	Devoting	Nov 8 2005	4	Enlightening	Jan 17 2006	9	Devoting

Date	UE Earth Energy	Date	UE Earth Energy	Date	UE Earth Energy
Jan 18 2006	10 Illuminating	Mar 29 2006	2 Being	Jun 7 2006	7 Illuminating
Jan 19 2006	11 Choosing	Mar 30 2006	3 Breathing	Jun 8 2006	8 Choosing
Jan 20 2006	12 Exploring	Mar 31 2006	4 Listening	Jun 9 2006	9 Exploring
Jan 21 2006	13 Healing	Apr 1 2006	5 Planting	Jun 10 2006	10 Healing
Jan 22 2006	**1 Seeing**	Apr 2 2006	6 Moving	Jun 11 2006	11 Seeing
Jan 23 2006	2 Intuiting	Apr 3 2006	7 Transcending	Jun 12 2006	12 Intuiting
Jan 24 2006	3 Evolving	Apr 4 2006	8 Remembering	Jun 13 2006	13 Evolving
Jan 25 2006	4 Self-Regulating	Apr 5 2006	9 Loving	Jun 14 2006	**1 Self-Regulating**
Jan 26 2006	5 Catalyzing	Apr 6 2006	10 Feeling	Jun 15 2006	2 Catalyzing
Jan 27 2006	6 Enlightening	Apr 7 2006	11 Devoting	Jun 16 2006	3 Enlightening
Jan 28 2006	7 Being	Apr 8 2006	12 Illuminating	Jun 17 2006	4 Being
Jan 29 2006	8 Breathing	Apr 9 2006	13 Choosing	Jun 18 2006	5 Breathing
Jan 30 2006	9 Listening	Apr 10 2006	**1 Exploring**	Jun 19 2006	6 Listening
Jan 31 2006	10 Planting	Apr 11 2006	2 Healing	Jun 20 2006	7 Planting
Feb 1 2006	11 Moving	Apr 12 2006	3 Seeing	Jun 21 2006	8 Moving
Feb 2 2006	12 Transcending	Apr 13 2006	4 Intuiting	Jun 22 2006	9 Transcending
Feb 3 2006	13 Remembering	Apr 14 2006	5 Evolving	Jun 23 2006	10 Remembering
Feb 4 2006	**1 Loving**	Apr 15 2006	6 Self-Regulating	Jun 24 2006	11 Loving
Feb 5 2006	2 Feeling	Apr 16 2006	7 Catalyzing	Jun 25 2006	12 Feeling
Feb 6 2006	3 Devoting	Apr 17 2006	8 Enlightening	Jun 26 2006	13 Devoting
Feb 7 2006	4 Illuminating	Apr 18 2006	9 Being	Jun 27 2006	**1 Illuminating**
Feb 8 2006	5 Choosing	Apr 19 2006	10 Breathing	Jun 28 2006	2 Choosing
Feb 9 2006	6 Exploring	Apr 20 2006	11 Listening	Jun 29 2006	3 Exploring
Feb 10 2006	7 Healing	Apr 21 2006	12 Planting	Jun 30 2006	4 Healing
Feb 11 2006	8 Seeing	Apr 22 2006	13 Moving	Jul 1 2006	5 Seeing
Feb 12 2006	9 Intuiting	Apr 23 2006	**1 Transcending**	Jul 2 2006	6 Intuiting
Feb 13 2006	10 Evolving	Apr 24 2006	2 Remembering	Jul 3 2006	7 Evolving
Feb 14 2006	11 Self-Regulating	Apr 25 2006	3 Loving	Jul 4 2006	8 Self-Regulating
Feb 15 2006	12 Catalyzing	Apr 26 2006	4 Feeling	Jul 5 2006	9 Catalyzing
Feb 16 2006	13 Enlightening	Apr 27 2006	5 Devoting	Jul 6 2006	10 Enlightening
Feb 17 2006	**1 Being**	Apr 28 2006	6 Illuminating	Jul 7 2006	11 Being
Feb 18 2006	2 Breathing	Apr 29 2006	7 Choosing	Jul 8 2006	12 Breathing
Feb 19 2006	3 Listening	Apr 30 2006	8 Exploring	Jul 9 2006	13 Listening
Feb 20 2006	4 Planting	May 1 2006	9 Healing	Jul 10 2006	**1 Planting**
Feb 21 2006	5 Moving	May 2 2006	10 Seeing	Jul 11 2006	2 Moving
Feb 22 2006	6 Transcending	May 3 2006	11 Intuiting	Jul 12 2006	3 Transcending
Feb 23 2006	7 Remembering	May 4 2006	12 Evolving	Jul 13 2006	4 Remembering
Feb 24 2006	8 Loving	May 5 2006	13 Self-Regulating	Jul 14 2006	5 Loving
Feb 25 2006	9 Feeling	May 6 2006	**1 Catalyzing**	Jul 15 2006	6 Feeling
Feb 26 2006	10 Devoting	May 7 2006	2 Enlightening	Jul 16 2006	7 Devoting
Feb 27 2006	11 Illuminating	May 8 2006	3 Being	Jul 17 2006	8 Illuminating
Feb 28 2006	12 Choosing	May 9 2006	4 Breathing	Jul 18 2006	9 Choosing
Mar 1 2006	13 Exploring	May 10 2006	5 Listening	Jul 19 2006	10 Exploring
Mar 2 2006	**1 Healing**	May 11 2006	6 Planting	Jul 20 2006	11 Healing
Mar 3 2006	2 Seeing	May 12 2006	7 Moving	Jul 21 2006	12 Seeing
Mar 4 2006	3 Intuiting	May 13 2006	8 Transcending	Jul 22 2006	13 Intuiting
Mar 5 2006	4 Evolving	May 14 2006	9 Remembering	Jul 23 2006	**1 Evolving**
Mar 6 2006	5 Self-Regulating	May 15 2006	10 Loving	Jul 24 2006	2 Self-Regulating
Mar 7 2006	6 Catalyzing	May 16 2006	11 Feeling	Jul 25 2006	3 Catalyzing
Mar 8 2006	7 Enlightening	May 17 2006	12 Devoting	Jul 26 2006	4 Enlightening
Mar 9 2006	8 Being	May 18 2006	13 Illuminating	Jul 27 2006	5 Being
Mar 10 2006	9 Breathing	May 19 2006	**1 Choosing**	Jul 28 2006	6 Breathing
Mar 11 2006	10 Listening	May 20 2006	2 Exploring	Jul 29 2006	7 Listening
Mar 12 2006	11 Planting	May 21 2006	3 Healing	Jul 30 2006	8 Planting
Mar 13 2006	12 Moving	May 22 2006	4 Seeing	Jul 31 2006	9 Moving
Mar 14 2006	13 Transcending	May 23 2006	5 Intuiting	Aug 1 2006	10 Transcending
Mar 15 2006	**1 Remembering**	May 24 2006	6 Evolving	Aug 2 2006	11 Remembering
Mar 16 2006	2 Loving	May 25 2006	7 Self-Regulating	Aug 3 2006	12 Loving
Mar 17 2006	3 Feeling	May 26 2006	8 Catalyzing	Aug 4 2006	13 Feeling
Mar 18 2006	4 Devoting	May 27 2006	9 Enlightening	Aug 5 2006	**1 Devoting**
Mar 19 2006	5 Illuminating	May 28 2006	10 Being	Aug 6 2006	2 Illuminating
Mar 20 2006	6 Choosing	May 29 2006	11 Breathing	Aug 7 2006	3 Choosing
Mar 21 2006	7 Exploring	May 30 2006	12 Listening	Aug 8 2006	4 Exploring
Mar 22 2006	8 Healing	May 31 2006	13 Planting	Aug 9 2006	5 Healing
Mar 23 2006	9 Seeing	Jun 1 2006	**1 Moving**	Aug 10 2006	6 Seeing
Mar 24 2006	10 Intuiting	Jun 2 2006	2 Transcending	Aug 11 2006	7 Intuiting
Mar 25 2006	11 Evolving	Jun 3 2006	3 Remembering	Aug 12 2006	8 Evolving
Mar 26 2006	12 Self-Regulating	Jun 4 2006	4 Loving	Aug 13 2006	9 Self-Regulating
Mar 27 2006	13 Catalyzing	Jun 5 2006	5 Feeling	Aug 14 2006	10 Catalyzing
Mar 28 2006	**1 Enlightening**	Jun 6 2006	6 Devoting	Aug 15 2006	11 Enlightening

Date	UE Earth Energy	Date	UE Earth Energy	Date	UE Earth Energy
Aug 16 2006	12 Being	Oct 25 2006	4 Illuminating	Jan 3 2007	9 Being
Aug 17 2006	13 Breathing	Oct 26 2006	5 Choosing	Jan 4 2007	10 Breathing
Aug 18 2006	1 Listening	Oct 27 2006	6 Exploring	Jan 5 2007	11 Listening
Aug 19 2006	2 Planting	Oct 28 2006	7 Healing	Jan 6 2007	12 Planting
Aug 20 2006	3 Moving	Oct 29 2006	8 Seeing	Jan 7 2007	13 Moving
Aug 21 2006	4 Transcending	Oct 30 2006	9 Intuiting	Jan 8 2007	1 Transcending
Aug 22 2006	5 Remembering	Oct 31 2006	10 Evolving	Jan 9 2007	2 Remembering
Aug 23 2006	6 Loving	Nov 1 2006	11 Self-Regulating	Jan 10 2007	3 Loving
Aug 24 2006	7 Feeling	Nov 2 2006	12 Catalyzing	Jan 11 2007	4 Feeling
Aug 25 2006	8 Devoting	Nov 3 2006	13 Enlightening	Jan 12 2007	5 Devoting
Aug 26 2006	9 Illuminating	Nov 4 2006	1 Being	Jan 13 2007	6 Illuminating
Aug 27 2006	10 Choosing	Nov 5 2006	2 Breathing	Jan 14 2007	7 Choosing
Aug 28 2006	11 Exploring	Nov 6 2006	3 Listening	Jan 15 2007	8 Exploring
Aug 29 2006	12 Healing	Nov 7 2006	4 Planting	Jan 16 2007	9 Healing
Aug 30 2006	13 Seeing	Nov 8 2006	5 Moving	Jan 17 2007	10 Seeing
Aug 31 2006	1 Intuiting	Nov 9 2006	6 Transcending	Jan 18 2007	11 Intuiting
Sep 1 2006	2 Evolving	Nov 10 2006	7 Remembering	Jan 19 2007	12 Evolving
Sep 2 2006	3 Self-Regulating	Nov 11 2006	8 Loving	Jan 20 2007	13 Self-Regulating
Sep 3 2006	4 Catalyzing	Nov 12 2006	9 Feeling	Jan 21 2007	1 Catalyzing
Sep 4 2006	5 Enlightening	Nov 13 2006	10 Devoting	Jan 22 2007	2 Enlightening
Sep 5 2006	6 Being	Nov 14 2006	11 Illuminating	Jan 23 2007	3 Being
Sep 6 2006	7 Breathing	Nov 15 2006	12 Choosing	Jan 24 2007	4 Breathing
Sep 7 2006	8 Listening	Nov 16 2006	13 Exploring	Jan 25 2007	5 Listening
Sep 8 2006	9 Planting	Nov 17 2006	1 Healing	Jan 26 2007	6 Planting
Sep 9 2006	10 Moving	Nov 18 2006	2 Seeing	Jan 27 2007	7 Moving
Sep 10 2006	11 Transcending	Nov 19 2006	3 Intuiting	Jan 28 2007	8 Transcending
Sep 11 2006	12 Remembering	Nov 20 2006	4 Evolving	Jan 29 2007	9 Remembering
Sep 12 2006	13 Loving	Nov 21 2006	5 Self-Regulating	Jan 30 2007	10 Loving
Sep 13 2006	1 Feeling	Nov 22 2006	6 Catalyzing	Jan 31 2007	11 Feeling
Sep 14 2006	2 Devoting	Nov 23 2006	7 Enlightening	Feb 1 2007	12 Devoting
Sep 15 2006	3 Illuminating	Nov 24 2006	8 Being	Feb 2 2007	13 Illuminating
Sep 16 2006	4 Choosing	Nov 25 2006	9 Breathing	Feb 3 2007	1 Choosing
Sep 17 2006	5 Exploring	Nov 26 2006	10 Listening	Feb 4 2007	2 Exploring
Sep 18 2006	6 Healing	Nov 27 2006	11 Planting	Feb 5 2007	3 Healing
Sep 19 2006	7 Seeing	Nov 28 2006	12 Moving	Feb 6 2007	4 Seeing
Sep 20 2006	8 Intuiting	Nov 29 2006	13 Transcending	Feb 7 2007	5 Intuiting
Sep 21 2006	9 Evolving	Nov 30 2006	1 Remembering	Feb 8 2007	6 Evolving
Sep 22 2006	10 Self-Regulating	Dec 1 2006	2 Loving	Feb 9 2007	7 Self-Regulating
Sep 23 2006	11 Catalyzing	Dec 2 2006	3 Feeling	Feb 10 2007	8 Catalyzing
Sep 24 2006	12 Enlightening	Dec 3 2006	4 Devoting	Feb 11 2007	9 Enlightening
Sep 25 2006	13 Being	Dec 4 2006	5 Illuminating	Feb 12 2007	10 Being
Sep 26 2006	1 Breathing	Dec 5 2006	6 Choosing	Feb 13 2007	11 Breathing
Sep 27 2006	2 Listening	Dec 6 2006	7 Exploring	Feb 14 2007	12 Listening
Sep 28 2006	3 Planting	Dec 7 2006	8 Healing	Feb 15 2007	13 Planting
Sep 29 2006	4 Moving	Dec 8 2006	9 Seeing	Feb 16 2007	1 Moving
Sep 30 2006	5 Transcending	Dec 9 2006	10 Intuiting	Feb 17 2007	2 Transcending
Oct 1 2006	6 Remembering	Dec 10 2006	11 Evolving	Feb 18 2007	3 Remembering
Oct 2 2006	7 Loving	Dec 11 2006	12 Self-Regulating	Feb 19 2007	4 Loving
Oct 3 2006	8 Feeling	Dec 12 2006	13 Catalyzing	Feb 20 2007	5 Feeling
Oct 4 2006	9 Devoting	Dec 13 2006	1 Enlightening	Feb 21 2007	6 Devoting
Oct 5 2006	10 Illuminating	Dec 14 2006	2 Being	Feb 22 2007	7 Illuminating
Oct 6 2006	11 Choosing	Dec 15 2006	3 Breathing	Feb 23 2007	8 Choosing
Oct 7 2006	12 Exploring	Dec 16 2006	4 Listening	Feb 24 2007	9 Exploring
Oct 8 2006	13 Healing	Dec 17 2006	5 Planting	Feb 25 2007	10 Healing
Oct 9 2006	1 Seeing	Dec 18 2006	6 Moving	Feb 26 2007	11 Seeing
Oct 10 2006	2 Intuiting	Dec 19 2006	7 Transcending	Feb 27 2007	12 Intuiting
Oct 11 2006	3 Evolving	Dec 20 2006	8 Remembering	Feb 28 2007	13 Evolving
Oct 12 2006	4 Self-Regulating	Dec 21 2006	9 Loving	Mar 1 2007	1 Self-Regulating
Oct 13 2006	5 Catalyzing	Dec 22 2006	10 Feeling	Mar 2 2007	2 Catalyzing
Oct 14 2006	6 Enlightening	Dec 23 2006	11 Devoting	Mar 3 2007	3 Enlightening
Oct 15 2006	7 Being	Dec 24 2006	12 Illuminating	Mar 4 2007	4 Being
Oct 16 2006	8 Breathing	Dec 25 2006	13 Choosing	Mar 5 2007	5 Breathing
Oct 17 2006	9 Listening	Dec 26 2006	1 Exploring	Mar 6 2007	6 Listening
Oct 18 2006	10 Planting	Dec 27 2006	2 Healing	Mar 7 2007	7 Planting
Oct 19 2006	11 Moving	Dec 28 2006	3 Seeing	Mar 8 2007	8 Moving
Oct 20 2006	12 Transcending	Dec 29 2006	4 Intuiting	Mar 9 2007	9 Transcending
Oct 21 2006	13 Remembering	Dec 30 2006	5 Evolving	Mar 10 2007	10 Remembering
Oct 22 2006	1 Loving	Dec 31 2006	6 Self-Regulating	Mar 11 2007	11 Loving
Oct 23 2006	2 Feeling	Jan 1 2007	7 Catalyzing	Mar 12 2007	12 Feeling
Oct 24 2006	3 Devoting	Jan 2 2007	8 Enlightening	Mar 13 2007	13 Devoting

Date	UE	Earth Energy	Date	UE	Earth Energy	Date	UE	Earth Energy
Mar 14 2007	1	Illuminating	May 23 2007	6	Being	Aug 1 2007	11	Illuminating
Mar 15 2007	2	Choosing	May 24 2007	7	Breathing	Aug 2 2007	12	Choosing
Mar 16 2007	3	Exploring	May 25 2007	8	Listening	Aug 3 2007	13	Exploring
Mar 17 2007	4	Healing	May 26 2007	9	Planting	Aug 4 2007	1	Healing
Mar 18 2007	5	Seeing	May 27 2007	10	Moving	Aug 5 2007	2	Seeing
Mar 19 2007	6	Intuiting	May 28 2007	11	Transcending	Aug 6 2007	3	Intuiting
Mar 20 2007	7	Evolving	May 29 2007	12	Remembering	Aug 7 2007	4	Evolving
Mar 21 2007	8	Self-Regulating	May 30 2007	13	Loving	Aug 8 2007	5	Self-Regulating
Mar 22 2007	9	Catalyzing	May 31 2007	1	Feeling	Aug 9 2007	6	Catalyzing
Mar 23 2007	10	Enlightening	Jun 1 2007	2	Devoting	Aug 10 2007	7	Enlightening
Mar 24 2007	11	Being	Jun 2 2007	3	Illuminating	Aug 11 2007	8	Being
Mar 25 2007	12	Breathing	Jun 3 2007	4	Choosing	Aug 12 2007	9	Breathing
Mar 26 2007	13	Listening	Jun 4 2007	5	Exploring	Aug 13 2007	10	Listening
Mar 27 2007	1	Planting	Jun 5 2007	6	Healing	Aug 14 2007	11	Planting
Mar 28 2007	2	Moving	Jun 6 2007	7	Seeing	Aug 15 2007	12	Moving
Mar 29 2007	3	Transcending	Jun 7 2007	8	Intuiting	Aug 16 2007	13	Transcending
Mar 30 2007	4	Remembering	Jun 8 2007	9	Evolving	Aug 17 2007	1	Remembering
Mar 31 2007	5	Loving	Jun 9 2007	10	Self-Regulating	Aug 18 2007	2	Loving
Apr 1 2007	6	Feeling	Jun 10 2007	11	Catalyzing	Aug 19 2007	3	Feeling
Apr 2 2007	7	Devoting	Jun 11 2007	12	Enlightening	Aug 20 2007	4	Devoting
Apr 3 2007	8	Illuminating	Jun 12 2007	13	Being	Aug 21 2007	5	Illuminating
Apr 4 2007	9	Choosing	Jun 13 2007	1	Breathing	Aug 22 2007	6	Choosing
Apr 5 2007	10	Exploring	Jun 14 2007	2	Listening	Aug 23 2007	7	Exploring
Apr 6 2007	11	Healing	Jun 15 2007	3	Planting	Aug 24 2007	8	Healing
Apr 7 2007	12	Seeing	Jun 16 2007	4	Moving	Aug 25 2007	9	Seeing
Apr 8 2007	13	Intuiting	Jun 17 2007	5	Transcending	Aug 26 2007	10	Intuiting
Apr 9 2007	1	Evolving	Jun 18 2007	6	Remembering	Aug 27 2007	11	Evolving
Apr 10 2007	2	Self-Regulating	Jun 19 2007	7	Loving	Aug 28 2007	12	Self-Regulating
Apr 11 2007	3	Catalyzing	Jun 20 2007	8	Feeling	Aug 29 2007	13	Catalyzing
Apr 12 2007	4	Enlightening	Jun 21 2007	9	Devoting	Aug 30 2007	1	Enlightening
Apr 13 2007	5	Being	Jun 22 2007	10	Illuminating	Aug 31 2007	2	Being
Apr 14 2007	6	Breathing	Jun 23 2007	11	Choosing	Sep 1 2007	3	Breathing
Apr 15 2007	7	Listening	Jun 24 2007	12	Exploring	Sep 2 2007	4	Listening
Apr 16 2007	8	Planting	Jun 25 2007	13	Healing	Sep 3 2007	5	Planting
Apr 17 2007	9	Moving	Jun 26 2007	1	Seeing	Sep 4 2007	6	Moving
Apr 18 2007	10	Transcending	Jun 27 2007	2	Intuiting	Sep 5 2007	7	Transcending
Apr 19 2007	11	Remembering	Jun 28 2007	3	Evolving	Sep 6 2007	8	Remembering
Apr 20 2007	12	Loving	Jun 29 2007	4	Self-Regulating	Sep 7 2007	9	Loving
Apr 21 2007	13	Feeling	Jun 30 2007	5	Catalyzing	Sep 8 2007	10	Feeling
Apr 22 2007	1	Devoting	Jul 1 2007	6	Enlightening	Sep 9 2007	11	Devoting
Apr 23 2007	2	Illuminating	Jul 2 2007	7	Being	Sep 10 2007	12	Illuminating
Apr 24 2007	3	Choosing	Jul 3 2007	8	Breathing	Sep 11 2007	13	Choosing
Apr 25 2007	4	Exploring	Jul 4 2007	9	Listening	Sep 12 2007	1	Exploring
Apr 26 2007	5	Healing	Jul 5 2007	10	Planting	Sep 13 2007	2	Healing
Apr 27 2007	6	Seeing	Jul 6 2007	11	Moving	Sep 14 2007	3	Seeing
Apr 28 2007	7	Intuiting	Jul 7 2007	12	Transcending	Sep 15 2007	4	Intuiting
Apr 29 2007	8	Evolving	Jul 8 2007	13	Remembering	Sep 16 2007	5	Evolving
Apr 30 2007	9	Self-Regulating	Jul 9 2007	1	Loving	Sep 17 2007	6	Self-Regulating
May 1 2007	10	Catalyzing	Jul 10 2007	2	Feeling	Sep 18 2007	7	Catalyzing
May 2 2007	11	Enlightening	Jul 11 2007	3	Devoting	Sep 19 2007	8	Enlightening
May 3 2007	12	Being	Jul 12 2007	4	Illuminating	Sep 20 2007	9	Being
May 4 2007	13	Breathing	Jul 13 2007	5	Choosing	Sep 21 2007	10	Breathing
May 5 2007	1	Listening	Jul 14 2007	6	Exploring	Sep 22 2007	11	Listening
May 6 2007	2	Planting	Jul 15 2007	7	Healing	Sep 23 2007	12	Planting
May 7 2007	3	Moving	Jul 16 2007	8	Seeing	Sep 24 2007	13	Moving
May 8 2007	4	Transcending	Jul 17 2007	9	Intuiting	Sep 25 2007	1	Transcending
May 9 2007	5	Remembering	Jul 18 2007	10	Evolving	Sep 26 2007	2	Remembering
May 10 2007	6	Loving	Jul 19 2007	11	Self-Regulating	Sep 27 2007	3	Loving
May 11 2007	7	Feeling	Jul 20 2007	12	Catalyzing	Sep 28 2007	4	Feeling
May 12 2007	8	Devoting	Jul 21 2007	13	Enlightening	Sep 29 2007	5	Devoting
May 13 2007	9	Illuminating	Jul 22 2007	1	Being	Sep 30 2007	6	Illuminating
May 14 2007	10	Choosing	Jul 23 2007	2	Breathing	Oct 1 2007	7	Choosing
May 15 2007	11	Exploring	Jul 24 2007	3	Listening	Oct 2 2007	8	Exploring
May 16 2007	12	Healing	Jul 25 2007	4	Planting	Oct 3 2007	9	Healing
May 17 2007	13	Seeing	Jul 26 2007	5	Moving	Oct 4 2007	10	Seeing
May 18 2007	1	Intuiting	Jul 27 2007	6	Transcending	Oct 5 2007	11	Intuiting
May 19 2007	2	Evolving	Jul 28 2007	7	Remembering	Oct 6 2007	12	Evolving
May 20 2007	3	Self-Regulating	Jul 29 2007	8	Loving	Oct 7 2007	13	Self-Regulating
May 21 2007	4	Catalyzing	Jul 30 2007	9	Feeling	Oct 8 2007	1	Catalyzing
May 22 2007	5	Enlightening	Jul 31 2007	10	Devoting	Oct 9 2007	2	Enlightening

Date	UE	Earth Energy
Oct 10 2007	3	Being
Oct 11 2007	4	Breathing
Oct 12 2007	5	Listening
Oct 13 2007	6	Planting
Oct 14 2007	7	Moving
Oct 15 2007	8	Transcending
Oct 16 2007	9	Remembering
Oct 17 2007	10	Loving
Oct 18 2007	11	Feeling
Oct 19 2007	12	Devoting
Oct 20 2007	13	Illuminating
Oct 21 2007	**1**	**Choosing**
Oct 22 2007	2	Exploring
Oct 23 2007	3	Healing
Oct 24 2007	4	Seeing
Oct 25 2007	5	Intuiting
Oct 26 2007	6	Evolving
Oct 27 2007	7	Self-Regulating
Oct 28 2007	8	Catalyzing
Oct 29 2007	9	Enlightening
Oct 30 2007	10	Being
Oct 31 2007	11	Breathing
Nov 1 2007	12	Listening
Nov 2 2007	13	Planting
Nov 3 2007	**1**	**Moving**
Nov 4 2007	2	Transcending
Nov 5 2007	3	Remembering
Nov 6 2007	4	Loving
Nov 7 2007	5	Feeling
Nov 8 2007	6	Devoting
Nov 9 2007	7	Illuminating
Nov 10 2007	8	Choosing
Nov 11 2007	9	Exploring
Nov 12 2007	10	Healing
Nov 13 2007	11	Seeing
Nov 14 2007	12	Intuiting
Nov 15 2007	13	Evolving
Nov 16 2007	**1**	**Self-Regulating**
Nov 17 2007	2	Catalyzing
Nov 18 2007	3	Enlightening
Nov 19 2007	4	Being
Nov 20 2007	5	Breathing
Nov 21 2007	6	Listening
Nov 22 2007	7	Planting
Nov 23 2007	8	Moving
Nov 24 2007	9	Transcending
Nov 25 2007	10	Remembering
Nov 26 2007	11	Loving
Nov 27 2007	12	Feeling
Nov 28 2007	13	Devoting
Nov 29 2007	**1**	**Illuminating**
Nov 30 2007	2	Choosing
Dec 1 2007	3	Exploring
Dec 2 2007	4	Healing
Dec 3 2007	5	Seeing
Dec 4 2007	6	Intuiting
Dec 5 2007	7	Evolving
Dec 6 2007	8	Self-Regulating
Dec 7 2007	9	Catalyzing
Dec 8 2007	10	Enlightening
Dec 9 2007	11	Being
Dec 10 2007	12	Breathing
Dec 11 2007	13	Listening
Dec 12 2007	**1**	**Planting**
Dec 13 2007	2	Moving
Dec 14 2007	3	Transcending
Dec 15 2007	4	Remembering
Dec 16 2007	5	Loving
Dec 17 2007	6	Feeling
Dec 18 2007	7	Devoting

Date	UE	Earth Energy
Dec 19 2007	8	Illuminating
Dec 20 2007	9	Choosing
Dec 21 2007	10	Exploring
Dec 22 2007	11	Healing
Dec 23 2007	12	Seeing
Dec 24 2007	13	Intuiting
Dec 25 2007	**1**	**Evolving**
Dec 26 2007	2	Self-Regulating
Dec 27 2007	3	Catalyzing
Dec 28 2007	4	Enlightening
Dec 29 2007	5	Being
Dec 30 2007	6	Breathing
Dec 31 2007	7	Listening
Jan 1 2008	8	Planting
Jan 2 2008	9	Moving
Jan 3 2008	10	Transcending
Jan 4 2008	11	Remembering
Jan 5 2008	12	Loving
Jan 6 2008	13	Feeling
Jan 7 2008	**1**	**Devoting**
Jan 8 2008	2	Illuminating
Jan 9 2008	3	Choosing
Jan 10 2008	4	Exploring
Jan 11 2008	5	Healing
Jan 12 2008	6	Seeing
Jan 13 2008	7	Intuiting
Jan 14 2008	8	Evolving
Jan 15 2008	9	Self-Regulating
Jan 16 2008	10	Catalyzing
Jan 17 2008	11	Enlightening
Jan 18 2008	12	Being
Jan 19 2008	13	Breathing
Jan 20 2008	**1**	**Listening**
Jan 21 2008	2	Planting
Jan 22 2008	3	Moving
Jan 23 2008	4	Transcending
Jan 24 2008	5	Remembering
Jan 25 2008	6	Loving
Jan 26 2008	7	Feeling
Jan 27 2008	8	Devoting
Jan 28 2008	9	Illuminating
Jan 29 2008	10	Choosing
Jan 30 2008	11	Exploring
Jan 31 2008	12	Healing
Feb 1 2008	13	Seeing
Feb 2 2008	**1**	**Intuiting**
Feb 3 2008	2	Evolving
Feb 4 2008	3	Self-Regulating
Feb 5 2008	4	Catalyzing
Feb 6 2008	5	Enlightening
Feb 7 2008	6	Being
Feb 8 2008	7	Breathing
Feb 9 2008	8	Listening
Feb 10 2008	9	Planting
Feb 11 2008	10	Moving
Feb 12 2008	11	Transcending
Feb 13 2008	12	Remembering
Feb 14 2008	13	Loving
Feb 15 2008	**1**	**Feeling**
Feb 16 2008	2	Devoting
Feb 17 2008	3	Illuminating
Feb 18 2008	4	Choosing
Feb 19 2008	5	Exploring
Feb 20 2008	6	Healing
Feb 21 2008	7	Seeing
Feb 22 2008	8	Intuiting
Feb 23 2008	9	Evolving
Feb 24 2008	10	Self-Regulating
Feb 25 2008	11	Catalyzing
Feb 26 2008	12	Enlightening

Date	UE	Earth Energy
Feb 27 2008	13	Being
Feb 28 2008	**1**	**Breathing**
Feb 29 2008	2	Listening
Mar 1 2008	3	Planting
Mar 2 2008	4	Moving
Mar 3 2008	5	Transcending
Mar 4 2008	6	Remembering
Mar 5 2008	7	Loving
Mar 6 2008	8	Feeling
Mar 7 2008	9	Devoting
Mar 8 2008	10	Illuminating
Mar 9 2008	11	Choosing
Mar 10 2008	12	Exploring
Mar 11 2008	13	Healing
Mar 12 2008	**1**	**Seeing**
Mar 13 2008	2	Intuiting
Mar 14 2008	3	Evolving
Mar 15 2008	4	Self-Regulating
Mar 16 2008	5	Catalyzing
Mar 17 2008	6	Enlightening
Mar 18 2008	7	Being
Mar 19 2008	8	Breathing
Mar 20 2008	9	Listening
Mar 21 2008	10	Planting
Mar 22 2008	11	Moving
Mar 23 2008	12	Transcending
Mar 24 2008	13	Remembering
Mar 25 2008	**1**	**Loving**
Mar 26 2008	2	Feeling
Mar 27 2008	3	Devoting
Mar 28 2008	4	Illuminating
Mar 29 2008	5	Choosing
Mar 30 2008	6	Exploring
Mar 31 2008	7	Healing
Apr 1 2008	8	Seeing
Apr 2 2008	9	Intuiting
Apr 3 2008	10	Evolving
Apr 4 2008	11	Self-Regulating
Apr 5 2008	12	Catalyzing
Apr 6 2008	13	Enlightening
Apr 7 2008	**1**	**Being**
Apr 8 2008	2	Breathing
Apr 9 2008	3	Listening
Apr 10 2008	4	Planting
Apr 11 2008	5	Moving
Apr 12 2008	6	Transcending
Apr 13 2008	7	Remembering
Apr 14 2008	8	Loving
Apr 15 2008	9	Feeling
Apr 16 2008	10	Devoting
Apr 17 2008	11	Illuminating
Apr 18 2008	12	Choosing
Apr 19 2008	13	Exploring
Apr 20 2008	**1**	**Healing**
Apr 21 2008	2	Seeing
Apr 22 2008	3	Intuiting
Apr 23 2008	4	Evolving
Apr 24 2008	5	Self-Regulating
Apr 25 2008	6	Catalyzing
Apr 26 2008	7	Enlightening
Apr 27 2008	8	Being
Apr 28 2008	9	Breathing
Apr 29 2008	10	Listening
Apr 30 2008	11	Planting
May 1 2008	12	Moving
May 2 2008	13	Transcending
May 3 2008	**1**	**Remembering**
May 4 2008	2	Loving
May 5 2008	3	Feeling
May 6 2008	4	Devoting

Date	UE	Earth Energy	Date	UE	Earth Energy	Date	UE	Earth Energy
May 7 2008	5	Illuminating	Jul 16 2008	10	Being	Sep 24 2008	2	Illuminating
May 8 2008	6	Choosing	Jul 17 2008	11	Breathing	Sep 25 2008	3	Choosing
May 9 2008	7	Exploring	Jul 18 2008	12	Listening	Sep 26 2008	4	Exploring
May 10 2008	8	Healing	Jul 19 2008	13	Planting	Sep 27 2008	5	Healing
May 11 2008	9	Seeing	Jul 20 2008	**1**	**Moving**	Sep 28 2008	6	Seeing
May 12 2008	10	Intuiting	Jul 21 2008	2	Transcending	Sep 29 2008	7	Intuiting
May 13 2008	11	Evolving	Jul 22 2008	3	Remembering	Sep 30 2008	8	Evolving
May 14 2008	12	Self-Regulating	Jul 23 2008	4	Loving	Oct 1 2008	9	Self-Regulating
May 15 2008	13	Catalyzing	Jul 24 2008	5	Feeling	Oct 2 2008	10	Catalyzing
May 16 2008	**1**	**Enlightening**	Jul 25 2008	6	Devoting	Oct 3 2008	11	Enlightening
May 17 2008	2	Being	Jul 26 2008	7	Illuminating	Oct 4 2008	12	Being
May 18 2008	3	Breathing	Jul 27 2008	8	Choosing	Oct 5 2008	13	Breathing
May 19 2008	4	Listening	Jul 28 2008	9	Exploring	Oct 6 2008	**1**	**Listening**
May 20 2008	5	Planting	Jul 29 2008	10	Healing	Oct 7 2008	2	Planting
May 21 2008	6	Moving	Jul 30 2008	11	Seeing	Oct 8 2008	3	Moving
May 22 2008	7	Transcending	Jul 31 2008	12	Intuiting	Oct 9 2008	4	Transcending
May 23 2008	8	Remembering	Aug 1 2008	13	Evolving	Oct 10 2008	5	Remembering
May 24 2008	9	Loving	Aug 2 2008	**1**	**Self-Regulating**	Oct 11 2008	6	Loving
May 25 2008	10	Feeling	Aug 3 2008	2	Catalyzing	Oct 12 2008	7	Feeling
May 26 2008	11	Devoting	Aug 4 2008	3	Enlightening	Oct 13 2008	8	Devoting
May 27 2008	12	Illuminating	Aug 5 2008	4	Being	Oct 14 2008	9	Illuminating
May 28 2008	13	Choosing	Aug 6 2008	5	Breathing	Oct 15 2008	10	Choosing
May 29 2008	**1**	**Exploring**	Aug 7 2008	6	Listening	Oct 16 2008	11	Exploring
May 30 2008	2	Healing	Aug 8 2008	7	Planting	Oct 17 2008	12	Healing
May 31 2008	3	Seeing	Aug 9 2008	8	Moving	Oct 18 2008	13	Seeing
Jun 1 2008	4	Intuiting	Aug 10 2008	9	Transcending	Oct 19 2008	**1**	**Intuiting**
Jun 2 2008	5	Evolving	Aug 11 2008	10	Remembering	Oct 20 2008	2	Evolving
Jun 3 2008	6	Self-Regulating	Aug 12 2008	11	Loving	Oct 21 2008	3	Self-Regulating
Jun 4 2008	7	Catalyzing	Aug 13 2008	12	Feeling	Oct 22 2008	4	Catalyzing
Jun 5 2008	8	Enlightening	Aug 14 2008	13	Devoting	Oct 23 2008	5	Enlightening
Jun 6 2008	9	Being	Aug 15 2008	**1**	**Illuminating**	Oct 24 2008	6	Being
Jun 7 2008	10	Breathing	Aug 16 2008	2	Choosing	Oct 25 2008	7	Breathing
Jun 8 2008	11	Listening	Aug 17 2008	3	Exploring	Oct 26 2008	8	Listening
Jun 9 2008	12	Planting	Aug 18 2008	4	Healing	Oct 27 2008	9	Planting
Jun 10 2008	13	Moving	Aug 19 2008	5	Seeing	Oct 28 2008	10	Moving
Jun 11 2008	**1**	**Transcending**	Aug 20 2008	6	Intuiting	Oct 29 2008	11	Transcending
Jun 12 2008	2	Remembering	Aug 21 2008	7	Evolving	Oct 30 2008	12	Remembering
Jun 13 2008	3	Loving	Aug 22 2008	8	Self-Regulating	Oct 31 2008	13	Loving
Jun 14 2008	4	Feeling	Aug 23 2008	9	Catalyzing	Nov 1 2008	**1**	**Feeling**
Jun 15 2008	5	Devoting	Aug 24 2008	10	Enlightening	Nov 2 2008	2	Devoting
Jun 16 2008	6	Illuminating	Aug 25 2008	11	Being	Nov 3 2008	3	Illuminating
Jun 17 2008	7	Choosing	Aug 26 2008	12	Breathing	Nov 4 2008	4	Choosing
Jun 18 2008	8	Exploring	Aug 27 2008	13	Listening	Nov 5 2008	5	Exploring
Jun 19 2008	9	Healing	Aug 28 2008	**1**	**Planting**	Nov 6 2008	6	Healing
Jun 20 2008	10	Seeing	Aug 29 2008	2	Moving	Nov 7 2008	7	Seeing
Jun 21 2008	11	Intuiting	Aug 30 2008	3	Transcending	Nov 8 2008	8	Intuiting
Jun 22 2008	12	Evolving	Aug 31 2008	4	Remembering	Nov 9 2008	9	Evolving
Jun 23 2008	13	Self-Regulating	Sep 1 2008	5	Loving	Nov 10 2008	10	Self-Regulating
Jun 24 2008	**1**	**Catalyzing**	Sep 2 2008	6	Feeling	Nov 11 2008	11	Catalyzing
Jun 25 2008	2	Enlightening	Sep 3 2008	7	Devoting	Nov 12 2008	12	Enlightening
Jun 26 2008	3	Being	Sep 4 2008	8	Illuminating	Nov 13 2008	13	Being
Jun 27 2008	4	Breathing	Sep 5 2008	9	Choosing	Nov 14 2008	**1**	**Breathing**
Jun 28 2008	5	Listening	Sep 6 2008	10	Exploring	Nov 15 2008	2	Listening
Jun 29 2008	6	Planting	Sep 7 2008	11	Healing	Nov 16 2008	3	Planting
Jun 30 2008	7	Moving	Sep 8 2008	12	Seeing	Nov 17 2008	4	Moving
Jul 1 2008	8	Transcending	Sep 9 2008	13	Intuiting	Nov 18 2008	5	Transcending
Jul 2 2008	9	Remembering	Sep 10 2008	**1**	**Evolving**	Nov 19 2008	6	Remembering
Jul 3 2008	10	Loving	Sep 11 2008	2	Self-Regulating	Nov 20 2008	7	Loving
Jul 4 2008	11	Feeling	Sep 12 2008	3	Catalyzing	Nov 21 2008	8	Feeling
Jul 5 2008	12	Devoting	Sep 13 2008	4	Enlightening	Nov 22 2008	9	Devoting
Jul 6 2008	13	Illuminating	Sep 14 2008	5	Being	Nov 23 2008	10	Illuminating
Jul 7 2008	**1**	**Choosing**	Sep 15 2008	6	Breathing	Nov 24 2008	11	Choosing
Jul 8 2008	2	Exploring	Sep 16 2008	7	Listening	Nov 25 2008	12	Exploring
Jul 9 2008	3	Healing	Sep 17 2008	8	Planting	Nov 26 2008	13	Healing
Jul 10 2008	4	Seeing	Sep 18 2008	9	Moving	Nov 27 2008	**1**	**Seeing**
Jul 11 2008	5	Intuiting	Sep 19 2008	10	Transcending	Nov 28 2008	2	Intuiting
Jul 12 2008	6	Evolving	Sep 20 2008	11	Remembering	Nov 29 2008	3	Evolving
Jul 13 2008	7	Self-Regulating	Sep 21 2008	12	Loving	Nov 30 2008	4	Self-Regulating
Jul 14 2008	8	Catalyzing	Sep 22 2008	13	Feeling	Dec 1 2008	5	Catalyzing
Jul 15 2008	9	Enlightening	Sep 23 2008	**1**	**Devoting**	Dec 2 2008	6	Enlightening

Date	UE	Earth Energy	Date	UE	Earth Energy	Date	UE	Earth Energy
Dec 3 2008	7	Being	Feb 11 2009	12	Illuminating	Apr 22 2009	4	Being
Dec 4 2008	8	Breathing	Feb 12 2009	13	Choosing	Apr 23 2009	5	Breathing
Dec 5 2008	9	Listening	Feb 13 2009	1	Exploring	Apr 24 2009	6	Listening
Dec 6 2008	10	Planting	Feb 14 2009	2	Healing	Apr 25 2009	7	Planting
Dec 7 2008	11	Moving	Feb 15 2009	3	Seeing	Apr 26 2009	8	Moving
Dec 8 2008	12	Transcending	Feb 16 2009	4	Intuiting	Apr 27 2009	9	Transcending
Dec 9 2008	13	Remembering	Feb 17 2009	5	Evolving	Apr 28 2009	10	Remembering
Dec 10 2008	1	Loving	Feb 18 2009	6	Self-Regulating	Apr 29 2009	11	Loving
Dec 11 2008	2	Feeling	Feb 19 2009	7	Catalyzing	Apr 30 2009	12	Feeling
Dec 12 2008	3	Devoting	Feb 20 2009	8	Enlightening	May 1 2009	13	Devoting
Dec 13 2008	4	Illuminating	Feb 21 2009	9	Being	May 2 2009	1	Illuminating
Dec 14 2008	5	Choosing	Feb 22 2009	10	Breathing	May 3 2009	2	Choosing
Dec 15 2008	6	Exploring	Feb 23 2009	11	Listening	May 4 2009	3	Exploring
Dec 16 2008	7	Healing	Feb 24 2009	12	Planting	May 5 2009	4	Healing
Dec 17 2008	8	Seeing	Feb 25 2009	13	Moving	May 6 2009	5	Seeing
Dec 18 2008	9	Intuiting	Feb 26 2009	1	Transcending	May 7 2009	6	Intuiting
Dec 19 2008	10	Evolving	Feb 27 2009	2	Remembering	May 8 2009	7	Evolving
Dec 20 2008	11	Self-Regulating	Feb 28 2009	3	Loving	May 9 2009	8	Self-Regulating
Dec 21 2008	12	Catalyzing	Mar 1 2009	4	Feeling	May 10 2009	9	Catalyzing
Dec 22 2008	13	Enlightening	Mar 2 2009	5	Devoting	May 11 2009	10	Enlightening
Dec 23 2008	1	Being	Mar 3 2009	6	Illuminating	May 12 2009	11	Being
Dec 24 2008	2	Breathing	Mar 4 2009	7	Choosing	May 13 2009	12	Breathing
Dec 25 2008	3	Listening	Mar 5 2009	8	Exploring	May 14 2009	13	Listening
Dec 26 2008	4	Planting	Mar 6 2009	9	Healing	May 15 2009	1	Planting
Dec 27 2008	5	Moving	Mar 7 2009	10	Seeing	May 16 2009	2	Moving
Dec 28 2008	6	Transcending	Mar 8 2009	11	Intuiting	May 17 2009	3	Transcending
Dec 29 2008	7	Remembering	Mar 9 2009	12	Evolving	May 18 2009	4	Remembering
Dec 30 2008	8	Loving	Mar 10 2009	13	Self-Regulating	May 19 2009	5	Loving
Dec 31 2008	9	Feeling	Mar 11 2009	1	Catalyzing	May 20 2009	6	Feeling
Jan 1 2009	10	Devoting	Mar 12 2009	2	Enlightening	May 21 2009	7	Devoting
Jan 2 2009	11	Illuminating	Mar 13 2009	3	Being	May 22 2009	8	Illuminating
Jan 3 2009	12	Choosing	Mar 14 2009	4	Breathing	May 23 2009	9	Choosing
Jan 4 2009	13	Exploring	Mar 15 2009	5	Listening	May 24 2009	10	Exploring
Jan 5 2009	1	Healing	Mar 16 2009	6	Planting	May 25 2009	11	Healing
Jan 6 2009	2	Seeing	Mar 17 2009	7	Moving	May 26 2009	12	Seeing
Jan 7 2009	3	Intuiting	Mar 18 2009	8	Transcending	May 27 2009	13	Intuiting
Jan 8 2009	4	Evolving	Mar 19 2009	9	Remembering	May 28 2009	1	Evolving
Jan 9 2009	5	Self-Regulating	Mar 20 2009	10	Loving	May 29 2009	2	Self-Regulating
Jan 10 2009	6	Catalyzing	Mar 21 2009	11	Feeling	May 30 2009	3	Catalyzing
Jan 11 2009	7	Enlightening	Mar 22 2009	12	Devoting	May 31 2009	4	Enlightening
Jan 12 2009	8	Being	Mar 23 2009	13	Illuminating	Jun 1 2009	5	Being
Jan 13 2009	9	Breathing	Mar 24 2009	1	Choosing	Jun 2 2009	6	Breathing
Jan 14 2009	10	Listening	Mar 25 2009	2	Exploring	Jun 3 2009	7	Listening
Jan 15 2009	11	Planting	Mar 26 2009	3	Healing	Jun 4 2009	8	Planting
Jan 16 2009	12	Moving	Mar 27 2009	4	Seeing	Jun 5 2009	9	Moving
Jan 17 2009	13	Transcending	Mar 28 2009	5	Intuiting	Jun 6 2009	10	Transcending
Jan 18 2009	1	Remembering	Mar 29 2009	6	Evolving	Jun 7 2009	11	Remembering
Jan 19 2009	2	Loving	Mar 30 2009	7	Self-Regulating	Jun 8 2009	12	Loving
Jan 20 2009	3	Feeling	Mar 31 2009	8	Catalyzing	Jun 9 2009	13	Feeling
Jan 21 2009	4	Devoting	Apr 1 2009	9	Enlightening	Jun 10 2009	1	Devoting
Jan 22 2009	5	Illuminating	Apr 2 2009	10	Being	Jun 11 2009	2	Illuminating
Jan 23 2009	6	Choosing	Apr 3 2009	11	Breathing	Jun 12 2009	3	Choosing
Jan 24 2009	7	Exploring	Apr 4 2009	12	Listening	Jun 13 2009	4	Exploring
Jan 25 2009	8	Healing	Apr 5 2009	13	Planting	Jun 14 2009	5	Healing
Jan 26 2009	9	Seeing	Apr 6 2009	1	Moving	Jun 15 2009	6	Seeing
Jan 27 2009	10	Intuiting	Apr 7 2009	2	Transcending	Jun 16 2009	7	Intuiting
Jan 28 2009	11	Evolving	Apr 8 2009	3	Remembering	Jun 17 2009	8	Evolving
Jan 29 2009	12	Self-Regulating	Apr 9 2009	4	Loving	Jun 18 2009	9	Self-Regulating
Jan 30 2009	13	Catalyzing	Apr 10 2009	5	Feeling	Jun 19 2009	10	Catalyzing
Jan 31 2009	1	Enlightening	Apr 11 2009	6	Devoting	Jun 20 2009	11	Enlightening
Feb 1 2009	2	Being	Apr 12 2009	7	Illuminating	Jun 21 2009	12	Being
Feb 2 2009	3	Breathing	Apr 13 2009	8	Choosing	Jun 22 2009	13	Breathing
Feb 3 2009	4	Listening	Apr 14 2009	9	Exploring	Jun 23 2009	1	Listening
Feb 4 2009	5	Planting	Apr 15 2009	10	Healing	Jun 24 2009	2	Planting
Feb 5 2009	6	Moving	Apr 16 2009	11	Seeing	Jun 25 2009	3	Moving
Feb 6 2009	7	Transcending	Apr 17 2009	12	Intuiting	Jun 26 2009	4	Transcending
Feb 7 2009	8	Remembering	Apr 18 2009	13	Evolving	Jun 27 2009	5	Remembering
Feb 8 2009	9	Loving	Apr 19 2009	1	Self-Regulating	Jun 28 2009	6	Loving
Feb 9 2009	10	Feeling	Apr 20 2009	2	Catalyzing	Jun 29 2009	7	Feeling
Feb 10 2009	11	Devoting	Apr 21 2009	3	Enlightening	Jun 30 2009	8	Devoting

Date	UE	Earth Energy
Jul 1 2009	9	Illuminating
Jul 2 2009	10	Choosing
Jul 3 2009	11	Exploring
Jul 4 2009	12	Healing
Jul 5 2009	13	Seeing
Jul 6 2009	1	**Intuiting**
Jul 7 2009	2	Evolving
Jul 8 2009	3	Self-Regulating
Jul 9 2009	4	Catalyzing
Jul 10 2009	5	Enlightening
Jul 11 2009	6	Being
Jul 12 2009	7	Breathing
Jul 13 2009	8	Listening
Jul 14 2009	9	Planting
Jul 15 2009	10	Moving
Jul 16 2009	11	Transcending
Jul 17 2009	12	Remembering
Jul 18 2009	13	Loving
Jul 19 2009	1	**Feeling**
Jul 20 2009	2	Devoting
Jul 21 2009	3	Illuminating
Jul 22 2009	4	Choosing
Jul 23 2009	5	Exploring
Jul 24 2009	6	Healing
Jul 25 2009	7	Seeing
Jul 26 2009	8	Intuiting
Jul 27 2009	9	Evolving
Jul 28 2009	10	Self-Regulating
Jul 29 2009	11	Catalyzing
Jul 30 2009	12	Enlightening
Jul 31 2009	13	Being
Aug 1 2009	1	**Breathing**
Aug 2 2009	2	Listening
Aug 3 2009	3	Planting
Aug 4 2009	4	Moving
Aug 5 2009	5	Transcending
Aug 6 2009	6	Remembering
Aug 7 2009	7	Loving
Aug 8 2009	8	Feeling
Aug 9 2009	9	Devoting
Aug 10 2009	10	Illuminating
Aug 11 2009	11	Choosing
Aug 12 2009	12	Exploring
Aug 13 2009	13	Healing
Aug 14 2009	1	**Seeing**
Aug 15 2009	2	Intuiting
Aug 16 2009	3	Evolving
Aug 17 2009	4	Self-Regulating
Aug 18 2009	5	Catalyzing
Aug 19 2009	6	Enlightening
Aug 20 2009	7	Being
Aug 21 2009	8	Breathing
Aug 22 2009	9	Listening
Aug 23 2009	10	Planting
Aug 24 2009	11	Moving
Aug 25 2009	12	Transcending
Aug 26 2009	13	Remembering
Aug 27 2009	1	**Loving**
Aug 28 2009	2	Feeling
Aug 29 2009	3	Devoting
Aug 30 2009	4	Illuminating
Aug 31 2009	5	Choosing
Sep 1 2009	6	Exploring
Sep 2 2009	7	Healing
Sep 3 2009	8	Seeing
Sep 4 2009	9	Intuiting
Sep 5 2009	10	Evolving
Sep 6 2009	11	Self-Regulating
Sep 7 2009	12	Catalyzing
Sep 8 2009	13	Enlightening

Date	UE	Earth Energy
Sep 9 2009	1	**Being**
Sep 10 2009	2	Breathing
Sep 11 2009	3	Listening
Sep 12 2009	4	Planting
Sep 13 2009	5	Moving
Sep 14 2009	6	Transcending
Sep 15 2009	7	Remembering
Sep 16 2009	8	Loving
Sep 17 2009	9	Feeling
Sep 18 2009	10	Devoting
Sep 19 2009	11	Illuminating
Sep 20 2009	12	Choosing
Sep 21 2009	13	Exploring
Sep 22 2009	1	**Healing**
Sep 23 2009	2	Seeing
Sep 24 2009	3	Intuiting
Sep 25 2009	4	Evolving
Sep 26 2009	5	Self-Regulating
Sep 27 2009	6	Catalyzing
Sep 28 2009	7	Enlightening
Sep 29 2009	8	Being
Sep 30 2009	9	Breathing
Oct 1 2009	10	Listening
Oct 2 2009	11	Planting
Oct 3 2009	12	Moving
Oct 4 2009	13	Transcending
Oct 5 2009	1	**Remembering**
Oct 6 2009	2	Loving
Oct 7 2009	3	Feeling
Oct 8 2009	4	Devoting
Oct 9 2009	5	Illuminating
Oct 10 2009	6	Choosing
Oct 11 2009	7	Exploring
Oct 12 2009	8	Healing
Oct 13 2009	9	Seeing
Oct 14 2009	10	Intuiting
Oct 15 2009	11	Evolving
Oct 16 2009	12	Self-Regulating
Oct 17 2009	13	Catalyzing
Oct 18 2009	1	**Enlightening**
Oct 19 2009	2	Being
Oct 20 2009	3	Breathing
Oct 21 2009	4	Listening
Oct 22 2009	5	Planting
Oct 23 2009	6	Moving
Oct 24 2009	7	Transcending
Oct 25 2009	8	Remembering
Oct 26 2009	9	Loving
Oct 27 2009	10	Feeling
Oct 28 2009	11	Devoting
Oct 29 2009	12	Illuminating
Oct 30 2009	13	Choosing
Oct 31 2009	1	**Exploring**
Nov 1 2009	2	Healing
Nov 2 2009	3	Seeing
Nov 3 2009	4	Intuiting
Nov 4 2009	5	Evolving
Nov 5 2009	6	Self-Regulating
Nov 6 2009	7	Catalyzing
Nov 7 2009	8	Enlightening
Nov 8 2009	9	Being
Nov 9 2009	10	Breathing
Nov 10 2009	11	Listening
Nov 11 2009	12	Planting
Nov 12 2009	13	Moving
Nov 13 2009	1	**Transcending**
Nov 14 2009	2	Remembering
Nov 15 2009	3	Loving
Nov 16 2009	4	Feeling
Nov 17 2009	5	Devoting

Date	UE	Earth Energy
Nov 18 2009	6	Illuminating
Nov 19 2009	7	Choosing
Nov 20 2009	8	Exploring
Nov 21 2009	9	Healing
Nov 22 2009	10	Seeing
Nov 23 2009	11	Intuiting
Nov 24 2009	12	Evolving
Nov 25 2009	13	Self-Regulating
Nov 26 2009	1	**Catalyzing**
Nov 27 2009	2	Enlightening
Nov 28 2009	3	Being
Nov 29 2009	4	Breathing
Nov 30 2009	5	Listening
Dec 1 2009	6	Planting
Dec 2 2009	7	Moving
Dec 3 2009	8	Transcending
Dec 4 2009	9	Remembering
Dec 5 2009	10	Loving
Dec 6 2009	11	Feeling
Dec 7 2009	12	Devoting
Dec 8 2009	13	Illuminating
Dec 9 2009	1	**Choosing**
Dec 10 2009	2	Exploring
Dec 11 2009	3	Healing
Dec 12 2009	4	Seeing
Dec 13 2009	5	Intuiting
Dec 14 2009	6	Evolving
Dec 15 2009	7	Self-Regulating
Dec 16 2009	8	Catalyzing
Dec 17 2009	9	Enlightening
Dec 18 2009	10	Being
Dec 19 2009	11	Breathing
Dec 20 2009	12	Listening
Dec 21 2009	13	Planting
Dec 22 2009	1	**Moving**
Dec 23 2009	2	Transcending
Dec 24 2009	3	Remembering
Dec 25 2009	4	Loving
Dec 26 2009	5	Feeling
Dec 27 2009	6	Devoting
Dec 28 2009	7	Illuminating
Dec 29 2009	8	Choosing
Dec 30 2009	9	Exploring
Dec 31 2009	10	Healing
Jan 1 2010	11	Seeing
Jan 2 2010	12	Intuiting
Jan 3 2010	13	Evolving
Jan 4 2010	1	**Self-Regulating**
Jan 5 2010	2	Catalyzing
Jan 6 2010	3	Enlightening
Jan 7 2010	4	Being
Jan 8 2010	5	Breathing
Jan 9 2010	6	Listening
Jan 10 2010	7	Planting
Jan 11 2010	8	Moving
Jan 12 2010	9	Transcending
Jan 13 2010	10	Remembering
Jan 14 2010	11	Loving
Jan 15 2010	12	Feeling
Jan 16 2010	13	Devoting
Jan 17 2010	1	**Illuminating**
Jan 18 2010	2	Choosing
Jan 19 2010	3	Exploring
Jan 20 2010	4	Healing
Jan 21 2010	5	Seeing
Jan 22 2010	6	Intuiting
Jan 23 2010	7	Evolving
Jan 24 2010	8	Self-Regulating
Jan 25 2010	9	Catalyzing
Jan 26 2010	10	Enlightening

Date	UE Earth Energy	Date	UE Earth Energy	Date	UE Earth Energy
Jan 27 2010	11 Being	Apr 7 2010	3 Illuminating	Jun 16 2010	8 Being
Jan 28 2010	12 Breathing	Apr 8 2010	4 Choosing	Jun 17 2010	9 Breathing
Jan 29 2010	13 Listening	Apr 9 2010	5 Exploring	Jun 18 2010	10 Listening
Jan 30 2010	**1 Planting**	Apr 10 2010	6 Healing	Jun 19 2010	11 Planting
Jan 31 2010	2 Moving	Apr 11 2010	7 Seeing	Jun 20 2010	12 Moving
Feb 1 2010	3 Transcending	Apr 12 2010	8 Intuiting	Jun 21 2010	13 Transcending
Feb 2 2010	4 Remembering	Apr 13 2010	9 Evolving	Jun 22 2010	**1 Remembering**
Feb 3 2010	5 Loving	Apr 14 2010	10 Self-Regulating	Jun 23 2010	2 Loving
Feb 4 2010	6 Feeling	Apr 15 2010	11 Catalyzing	Jun 24 2010	3 Feeling
Feb 5 2010	7 Devoting	Apr 16 2010	12 Enlightening	Jun 25 2010	4 Devoting
Feb 6 2010	8 Illuminating	Apr 17 2010	13 Being	Jun 26 2010	5 Illuminating
Feb 7 2010	9 Choosing	Apr 18 2010	**1 Breathing**	Jun 27 2010	6 Choosing
Feb 8 2010	10 Exploring	Apr 19 2010	2 Listening	Jun 28 2010	7 Exploring
Feb 9 2010	11 Healing	Apr 20 2010	3 Planting	Jun 29 2010	8 Healing
Feb 10 2010	12 Seeing	Apr 21 2010	4 Moving	Jun 30 2010	9 Seeing
Feb 11 2010	13 Intuiting	Apr 22 2010	5 Transcending	Jul 1 2010	10 Intuiting
Feb 12 2010	**1 Evolving**	Apr 23 2010	6 Remembering	Jul 2 2010	11 Evolving
Feb 13 2010	2 Self-Regulating	Apr 24 2010	7 Loving	Jul 3 2010	12 Self-Regulating
Feb 14 2010	3 Catalyzing	Apr 25 2010	8 Feeling	Jul 4 2010	13 Catalyzing
Feb 15 2010	4 Enlightening	Apr 26 2010	9 Devoting	Jul 5 2010	**1 Enlightening**
Feb 16 2010	5 Being	Apr 27 2010	10 Illuminating	Jul 6 2010	2 Being
Feb 17 2010	6 Breathing	Apr 28 2010	11 Choosing	Jul 7 2010	3 Breathing
Feb 18 2010	7 Listening	Apr 29 2010	12 Exploring	Jul 8 2010	4 Listening
Feb 19 2010	8 Planting	Apr 30 2010	13 Healing	Jul 9 2010	5 Planting
Feb 20 2010	9 Moving	May 1 2010	**1 Seeing**	Jul 10 2010	6 Moving
Feb 21 2010	10 Transcending	May 2 2010	2 Intuiting	Jul 11 2010	7 Transcending
Feb 22 2010	11 Remembering	May 3 2010	3 Evolving	Jul 12 2010	8 Remembering
Feb 23 2010	12 Loving	May 4 2010	4 Self-Regulating	Jul 13 2010	9 Loving
Feb 24 2010	13 Feeling	May 5 2010	5 Catalyzing	Jul 14 2010	10 Feeling
Feb 25 2010	**1 Devoting**	May 6 2010	6 Enlightening	Jul 15 2010	11 Devoting
Feb 26 2010	2 Illuminating	May 7 2010	7 Being	Jul 16 2010	12 Illuminating
Feb 27 2010	3 Choosing	May 8 2010	8 Breathing	Jul 17 2010	13 Choosing
Feb 28 2010	4 Exploring	May 9 2010	9 Listening	Jul 18 2010	**1 Exploring**
Mar 1 2010	5 Healing	May 10 2010	10 Planting	Jul 19 2010	2 Healing
Mar 2 2010	6 Seeing	May 11 2010	11 Moving	Jul 20 2010	3 Seeing
Mar 3 2010	7 Intuiting	May 12 2010	12 Transcending	Jul 21 2010	4 Intuiting
Mar 4 2010	8 Evolving	May 13 2010	13 Remembering	Jul 22 2010	5 Evolving
Mar 5 2010	9 Self-Regulating	May 14 2010	**1 Loving**	Jul 23 2010	6 Self-Regulating
Mar 6 2010	10 Catalyzing	May 15 2010	2 Feeling	Jul 24 2010	7 Catalyzing
Mar 7 2010	11 Enlightening	May 16 2010	3 Devoting	Jul 25 2010	8 Enlightening
Mar 8 2010	12 Being	May 17 2010	4 Illuminating	Jul 26 2010	9 Being
Mar 9 2010	13 Breathing	May 18 2010	5 Choosing	Jul 27 2010	10 Breathing
Mar 10 2010	**1 Listening**	May 19 2010	6 Exploring	Jul 28 2010	11 Listening
Mar 11 2010	2 Planting	May 20 2010	7 Healing	Jul 29 2010	12 Planting
Mar 12 2010	3 Moving	May 21 2010	8 Seeing	Jul 30 2010	13 Moving
Mar 13 2010	4 Transcending	May 22 2010	9 Intuiting	Jul 31 2010	**1 Transcending**
Mar 14 2010	5 Remembering	May 23 2010	10 Evolving	Aug 1 2010	2 Remembering
Mar 15 2010	6 Loving	May 24 2010	11 Self-Regulating	Aug 2 2010	3 Loving
Mar 16 2010	7 Feeling	May 25 2010	12 Catalyzing	Aug 3 2010	4 Feeling
Mar 17 2010	8 Devoting	May 26 2010	13 Enlightening	Aug 4 2010	5 Devoting
Mar 18 2010	9 Illuminating	May 27 2010	**1 Being**	Aug 5 2010	6 Illuminating
Mar 19 2010	10 Choosing	May 28 2010	2 Breathing	Aug 6 2010	7 Choosing
Mar 20 2010	11 Exploring	May 29 2010	3 Listening	Aug 7 2010	8 Exploring
Mar 21 2010	12 Healing	May 30 2010	4 Planting	Aug 8 2010	9 Healing
Mar 22 2010	13 Seeing	May 31 2010	5 Moving	Aug 9 2010	10 Seeing
Mar 23 2010	**1 Intuiting**	Jun 1 2010	6 Transcending	Aug 10 2010	11 Intuiting
Mar 24 2010	2 Evolving	Jun 2 2010	7 Remembering	Aug 11 2010	12 Evolving
Mar 25 2010	3 Self-Regulating	Jun 3 2010	8 Loving	Aug 12 2010	13 Self-Regulating
Mar 26 2010	4 Catalyzing	Jun 4 2010	9 Feeling	Aug 13 2010	**1 Catalyzing**
Mar 27 2010	5 Enlightening	Jun 5 2010	10 Devoting	Aug 14 2010	2 Enlightening
Mar 28 2010	6 Being	Jun 6 2010	11 Illuminating	Aug 15 2010	3 Being
Mar 29 2010	7 Breathing	Jun 7 2010	12 Choosing	Aug 16 2010	4 Breathing
Mar 30 2010	8 Listening	Jun 8 2010	13 Exploring	Aug 17 2010	5 Listening
Mar 31 2010	9 Planting	Jun 9 2010	**1 Healing**	Aug 18 2010	6 Planting
Apr 1 2010	10 Moving	Jun 10 2010	2 Seeing	Aug 19 2010	7 Moving
Apr 2 2010	11 Transcending	Jun 11 2010	3 Intuiting	Aug 20 2010	8 Transcending
Apr 3 2010	12 Remembering	Jun 12 2010	4 Evolving	Aug 21 2010	9 Remembering
Apr 4 2010	13 Loving	Jun 13 2010	5 Self-Regulating	Aug 22 2010	10 Loving
Apr 5 2010	**1 Feeling**	Jun 14 2010	6 Catalyzing	Aug 23 2010	11 Feeling
Apr 6 2010	2 Devoting	Jun 15 2010	7 Enlightening	Aug 24 2010	12 Devoting

Date	UE Earth Energy	Date	UE Earth Energy	Date	UE Earth Energy
Aug 25 2010	13 Illuminating	Nov 3 2010	5 Being	Jan 12 2011	10 Illuminating
Aug 26 2010	**1 Choosing**	Nov 4 2010	6 Breathing	Jan 13 2011	11 Choosing
Aug 27 2010	2 Exploring	Nov 5 2010	7 Listening	Jan 14 2011	12 Exploring
Aug 28 2010	3 Healing	Nov 6 2010	8 Planting	Jan 15 2011	13 Healing
Aug 29 2010	4 Seeing	Nov 7 2010	9 Moving	Jan 16 2011	**1 Seeing**
Aug 30 2010	5 Intuiting	Nov 8 2010	10 Transcending	Jan 17 2011	2 Intuiting
Aug 31 2010	6 Evolving	Nov 9 2010	11 Remembering	Jan 18 2011	3 Evolving
Sep 1 2010	7 Self-Regulating	Nov 10 2010	12 Loving	Jan 19 2011	4 Self-Regulating
Sep 2 2010	8 Catalyzing	Nov 11 2010	13 Feeling	Jan 20 2011	5 Catalyzing
Sep 3 2010	9 Enlightening	Nov 12 2010	**1 Devoting**	Jan 21 2011	6 Enlightening
Sep 4 2010	10 Being	Nov 13 2010	2 Illuminating	Jan 22 2011	7 Being
Sep 5 2010	11 Breathing	Nov 14 2010	3 Choosing	Jan 23 2011	8 Breathing
Sep 6 2010	12 Listening	Nov 15 2010	4 Exploring	Jan 24 2011	9 Listening
Sep 7 2010	13 Planting	Nov 16 2010	5 Healing	Jan 25 2011	10 Planting
Sep 8 2010	**1 Moving**	Nov 17 2010	6 Seeing	Jan 26 2011	11 Moving
Sep 9 2010	2 Transcending	Nov 18 2010	7 Intuiting	Jan 27 2011	12 Transcending
Sep 10 2010	3 Remembering	Nov 19 2010	8 Evolving	Jan 28 2011	13 Remembering
Sep 11 2010	4 Loving	Nov 20 2010	9 Self-Regulating	Jan 29 2011	**1 Loving**
Sep 12 2010	5 Feeling	Nov 21 2010	10 Catalyzing	Jan 30 2011	2 Feeling
Sep 13 2010	6 Devoting	Nov 22 2010	11 Enlightening	Jan 31 2011	3 Devoting
Sep 14 2010	7 Illuminating	Nov 23 2010	12 Being	Feb 1 2011	4 Illuminating
Sep 15 2010	8 Choosing	Nov 24 2010	13 Breathing	Feb 2 2011	5 Choosing
Sep 16 2010	9 Exploring	Nov 25 2010	**1 Listening**	Feb 3 2011	6 Exploring
Sep 17 2010	10 Healing	Nov 26 2010	2 Planting	Feb 4 2011	7 Healing
Sep 18 2010	11 Seeing	Nov 27 2010	3 Moving	Feb 5 2011	8 Seeing
Sep 19 2010	12 Intuiting	Nov 28 2010	4 Transcending	Feb 6 2011	9 Intuiting
Sep 20 2010	13 Evolving	Nov 29 2010	5 Remembering	Feb 7 2011	10 Evolving
Sep 21 2010	**1 Self-Regulating**	Nov 30 2010	6 Loving	Feb 8 2011	11 Self-Regulating
Sep 22 2010	2 Catalyzing	Dec 1 2010	7 Feeling	Feb 9 2011	12 Catalyzing
Sep 23 2010	3 Enlightening	Dec 2 2010	8 Devoting	Feb 10 2011	13 Enlightening
Sep 24 2010	4 Being	Dec 3 2010	9 Illuminating	Feb 11 2011	**1 Being**
Sep 25 2010	5 Breathing	Dec 4 2010	10 Choosing	Feb 12 2011	2 Breathing
Sep 26 2010	6 Listening	Dec 5 2010	11 Exploring	Feb 13 2011	3 Listening
Sep 27 2010	7 Planting	Dec 6 2010	12 Healing	Feb 14 2011	4 Planting
Sep 28 2010	8 Moving	Dec 7 2010	13 Seeing	Feb 15 2011	5 Moving
Sep 29 2010	9 Transcending	Dec 8 2010	**1 Intuiting**	Feb 16 2011	6 Transcending
Sep 30 2010	10 Remembering	Dec 9 2010	2 Evolving	Feb 17 2011	7 Remembering
Oct 1 2010	11 Loving	Dec 10 2010	3 Self-Regulating	Feb 18 2011	8 Loving
Oct 2 2010	12 Feeling	Dec 11 2010	4 Catalyzing	Feb 19 2011	9 Feeling
Oct 3 2010	13 Devoting	Dec 12 2010	5 Enlightening	Feb 20 2011	10 Devoting
Oct 4 2010	**1 Illuminating**	Dec 13 2010	6 Being	Feb 21 2011	11 Illuminating
Oct 5 2010	2 Choosing	Dec 14 2010	7 Breathing	Feb 22 2011	12 Choosing
Oct 6 2010	3 Exploring	Dec 15 2010	8 Listening	Feb 23 2011	13 Exploring
Oct 7 2010	4 Healing	Dec 16 2010	9 Planting	Feb 24 2011	**1 Healing**
Oct 8 2010	5 Seeing	Dec 17 2010	10 Moving	Feb 25 2011	2 Seeing
Oct 9 2010	6 Intuiting	Dec 18 2010	11 Transcending	Feb 26 2011	3 Intuiting
Oct 10 2010	7 Evolving	Dec 19 2010	12 Remembering	Feb 27 2011	4 Evolving
Oct 11 2010	8 Self-Regulating	Dec 20 2010	13 Loving	Feb 28 2011	5 Self-Regulating
Oct 12 2010	9 Catalyzing	Dec 21 2010	**1 Feeling**	Mar 1 2011	6 Catalyzing
Oct 13 2010	10 Enlightening	Dec 22 2010	2 Devoting	Mar 2 2011	7 Enlightening
Oct 14 2010	11 Being	Dec 23 2010	3 Illuminating	Mar 3 2011	8 Being
Oct 15 2010	12 Breathing	Dec 24 2010	4 Choosing	Mar 4 2011	9 Breathing
Oct 16 2010	13 Listening	Dec 25 2010	5 Exploring	Mar 5 2011	10 Listening
Oct 17 2010	**1 Planting**	Dec 26 2010	6 Healing	Mar 6 2011	11 Planting
Oct 18 2010	2 Moving	Dec 27 2010	7 Seeing	Mar 7 2011	12 Moving
Oct 19 2010	3 Transcending	Dec 28 2010	8 Intuiting	Mar 8 2011	13 Transcending
Oct 20 2010	4 Remembering	Dec 29 2010	9 Evolving	Mar 9 2011	**1 Remembering**
Oct 21 2010	5 Loving	Dec 30 2010	10 Self-Regulating	Mar 10 2011	2 Loving
Oct 22 2010	6 Feeling	Dec 31 2010	11 Catalyzing	Mar 11 2011	3 Feeling
Oct 23 2010	7 Devoting	Jan 1 2011	12 Enlightening	Mar 12 2011	4 Devoting
Oct 24 2010	8 Illuminating	Jan 2 2011	13 Being	Mar 13 2011	5 Illuminating
Oct 25 2010	9 Choosing	Jan 3 2011	**1 Breathing**	Mar 14 2011	6 Choosing
Oct 26 2010	10 Exploring	Jan 4 2011	2 Listening	Mar 15 2011	7 Exploring
Oct 27 2010	11 Healing	Jan 5 2011	3 Planting	Mar 16 2011	8 Healing
Oct 28 2010	12 Seeing	Jan 6 2011	4 Moving	Mar 17 2011	9 Seeing
Oct 29 2010	13 Intuiting	Jan 7 2011	5 Transcending	Mar 18 2011	10 Intuiting
Oct 30 2010	**1 Evolving**	Jan 8 2011	6 Remembering	Mar 19 2011	11 Intuiting
Oct 31 2010	2 Self-Regulating	Jan 9 2011	7 Loving	Mar 20 2011	12 Self-Regulating
Nov 1 2010	3 Catalyzing	Jan 10 2011	8 Feeling	Mar 21 2011	13 Catalyzing
Nov 2 2010	4 Enlightening	Jan 11 2011	9 Devoting	Mar 22 2011	**1 Enlightening**

Date	UE	Earth Energy	Date	UE	Earth Energy	Date	UE	Earth Energy
Mar 23 2011	2	Being	Jun 1 2011	7	Illuminating	Aug 10 2011	12	Being
Mar 24 2011	3	Breathing	Jun 2 2011	8	Choosing	Aug 11 2011	13	Breathing
Mar 25 2011	4	Listening	Jun 3 2011	9	Exploring	Aug 12 2011	**1**	**Listening**
Mar 26 2011	5	Planting	Jun 4 2011	10	Healing	Aug 13 2011	2	Planting
Mar 27 2011	6	Moving	Jun 5 2011	11	Seeing	Aug 14 2011	3	Moving
Mar 28 2011	7	Transcending	Jun 6 2011	12	Intuiting	Aug 15 2011	4	Transcending
Mar 29 2011	8	Remembering	Jun 7 2011	13	Evolving	Aug 16 2011	5	Remembering
Mar 30 2011	9	Loving	Jun 8 2011	**1**	**Self-Regulating**	Aug 17 2011	6	Loving
Mar 31 2011	10	Feeling	Jun 9 2011	2	Catalyzing	Aug 18 2011	7	Feeling
Apr 1 2011	11	Devoting	Jun 10 2011	3	Enlightening	Aug 19 2011	8	Devoting
Apr 2 2011	12	Illuminating	Jun 11 2011	4	Being	Aug 20 2011	9	Illuminating
Apr 3 2011	13	Choosing	Jun 12 2011	5	Breathing	Aug 21 2011	10	Choosing
Apr 4 2011	**1**	**Exploring**	Jun 13 2011	6	Listening	Aug 22 2011	11	Exploring
Apr 5 2011	2	Healing	Jun 14 2011	7	Planting	Aug 23 2011	12	Healing
Apr 6 2011	3	Seeing	Jun 15 2011	8	Moving	Aug 24 2011	13	Seeing
Apr 7 2011	4	Intuiting	Jun 16 2011	9	Transcending	Aug 25 2011	**1**	**Intuiting**
Apr 8 2011	5	Evolving	Jun 17 2011	10	Remembering	Aug 26 2011	2	Evolving
Apr 9 2011	6	Self-Regulating	Jun 18 2011	11	Loving	Aug 27 2011	3	Self-Regulating
Apr 10 2011	7	Catalyzing	Jun 19 2011	12	Feeling	Aug 28 2011	4	Catalyzing
Apr 11 2011	8	Enlightening	Jun 20 2011	13	Devoting	Aug 29 2011	5	Enlightening
Apr 12 2011	9	Being	Jun 21 2011	**1**	**Illuminating**	Aug 30 2011	6	Being
Apr 13 2011	10	Breathing	Jun 22 2011	2	Choosing	Aug 31 2011	7	Breathing
Apr 14 2011	11	Listening	Jun 23 2011	3	Exploring	Sep 1 2011	8	Listening
Apr 15 2011	12	Planting	Jun 24 2011	4	Healing	Sep 2 2011	9	Planting
Apr 16 2011	13	Moving	Jun 25 2011	5	Seeing	Sep 3 2011	10	Moving
Apr 17 2011	**1**	**Transcending**	Jun 26 2011	6	Intuiting	Sep 4 2011	11	Transcending
Apr 18 2011	2	Remembering	Jun 27 2011	7	Evolving	Sep 5 2011	12	Remembering
Apr 19 2011	3	Loving	Jun 28 2011	8	Self-Regulating	Sep 6 2011	13	Loving
Apr 20 2011	4	Feeling	Jun 29 2011	9	Catalyzing	Sep 7 2011	**1**	**Feeling**
Apr 21 2011	5	Devoting	Jun 30 2011	10	Enlightening	Sep 8 2011	2	Devoting
Apr 22 2011	6	Illuminating	Jul 1 2011	11	Being	Sep 9 2011	3	Illuminating
Apr 23 2011	7	Choosing	Jul 2 2011	12	Breathing	Sep 10 2011	4	Choosing
Apr 24 2011	8	Exploring	Jul 3 2011	13	Listening	Sep 11 2011	5	Exploring
Apr 25 2011	9	Healing	Jul 4 2011	**1**	**Planting**	Sep 12 2011	6	Healing
Apr 26 2011	10	Seeing	Jul 5 2011	2	Moving	Sep 13 2011	7	Seeing
Apr 27 2011	11	Intuiting	Jul 6 2011	3	Transcending	Sep 14 2011	8	Intuiting
Apr 28 2011	12	Evolving	Jul 7 2011	4	Remembering	Sep 15 2011	9	Evolving
Apr 29 2011	13	Self-Regulating	Jul 8 2011	5	Loving	Sep 16 2011	10	Self-Regulating
Apr 30 2011	**1**	**Catalyzing**	Jul 9 2011	6	Feeling	Sep 17 2011	11	Catalyzing
May 1 2011	2	Enlightening	Jul 10 2011	7	Devoting	Sep 18 2011	12	Enlightening
May 2 2011	3	Being	Jul 11 2011	8	Illuminating	Sep 19 2011	13	Being
May 3 2011	4	Breathing	Jul 12 2011	9	Choosing	Sep 20 2011	**1**	**Breathing**
May 4 2011	5	Listening	Jul 13 2011	10	Exploring	Sep 21 2011	2	Listening
May 5 2011	6	Planting	Jul 14 2011	11	Healing	Sep 22 2011	3	Planting
May 6 2011	7	Moving	Jul 15 2011	12	Seeing	Sep 23 2011	4	Moving
May 7 2011	8	Transcending	Jul 16 2011	13	Intuiting	Sep 24 2011	5	Transcending
May 8 2011	9	Remembering	Jul 17 2011	**1**	**Evolving**	Sep 25 2011	6	Remembering
May 9 2011	10	Loving	Jul 18 2011	2	Self-Regulating	Sep 26 2011	7	Loving
May 10 2011	11	Feeling	Jul 19 2011	3	Catalyzing	Sep 27 2011	8	Feeling
May 11 2011	12	Devoting	Jul 20 2011	4	Enlightening	Sep 28 2011	9	Devoting
May 12 2011	13	Illuminating	Jul 21 2011	5	Being	Sep 29 2011	10	Illuminating
May 13 2011	**1**	**Choosing**	Jul 22 2011	6	Breathing	Sep 30 2011	11	Choosing
May 14 2011	2	Exploring	Jul 23 2011	7	Listening	Oct 1 2011	12	Exploring
May 15 2011	3	Healing	Jul 24 2011	8	Planting	Oct 2 2011	13	Healing
May 16 2011	4	Seeing	Jul 25 2011	9	Moving	Oct 3 2011	**1**	**Seeing**
May 17 2011	5	Intuiting	Jul 26 2011	10	Transcending	Oct 4 2011	2	Intuiting
May 18 2011	6	Evolving	Jul 27 2011	11	Remembering	Oct 5 2011	3	Evolving
May 19 2011	7	Self-Regulating	Jul 28 2011	12	Loving	Oct 6 2011	4	Self-Regulating
May 20 2011	8	Catalyzing	Jul 29 2011	13	Feeling	Oct 7 2011	5	Catalyzing
May 21 2011	9	Enlightening	Jul 30 2011	**1**	**Devoting**	Oct 8 2011	6	Enlightening
May 22 2011	10	Being	Jul 31 2011	2	Illuminating	Oct 9 2011	7	Being
May 23 2011	11	Breathing	Aug 1 2011	3	Choosing	Oct 10 2011	8	Breathing
May 24 2011	12	Listening	Aug 2 2011	4	Exploring	Oct 11 2011	9	Listening
May 25 2011	13	Planting	Aug 3 2011	5	Healing	Oct 12 2011	10	Planting
May 26 2011	**1**	**Moving**	Aug 4 2011	6	Seeing	Oct 13 2011	11	Moving
May 27 2011	2	Transcending	Aug 5 2011	7	Intuiting	Oct 14 2011	12	Transcending
May 28 2011	3	Remembering	Aug 6 2011	8	Evolving	Oct 15 2011	13	Remembering
May 29 2011	4	Loving	Aug 7 2011	9	Self-Regulating	Oct 16 2011	**1**	**Loving**
May 30 2011	5	Feeling	Aug 8 2011	10	Catalyzing	Oct 17 2011	2	Feeling
May 31 2011	6	Devoting	Aug 9 2011	11	Enlightening	Oct 18 2011	3	Devoting

Date	UE	Earth Energy	Date	UE	Earth Energy	Date	UE	Earth Energy
Oct 19 2011	4	Illuminating	Dec 28 2011	9	Being	Mar 7 2012	1	**Illuminating**
Oct 20 2011	5	Choosing	Dec 29 2011	10	Breathing	Mar 8 2012	2	Choosing
Oct 21 2011	6	Exploring	Dec 30 2011	11	Listening	Mar 9 2012	3	Exploring
Oct 22 2011	7	Healing	Dec 31 2011	12	Planting	Mar 10 2012	4	Healing
Oct 23 2011	8	Seeing	Jan 1 2012	13	Moving	Mar 11 2012	5	Seeing
Oct 24 2011	9	Intuiting	Jan 2 2012	1	**Transcending**	Mar 12 2012	6	Intuiting
Oct 25 2011	10	Evolving	Jan 3 2012	2	Remembering	Mar 13 2012	7	Evolving
Oct 26 2011	11	Self-Regulating	Jan 4 2012	3	Loving	Mar 14 2012	8	Self-Regulating
Oct 27 2011	12	Catalyzing	Jan 5 2012	4	Feeling	Mar 15 2012	9	Catalyzing
Oct 28 2011	13	Enlightening	Jan 6 2012	5	Devoting	Mar 16 2012	10	Enlightening
Oct 29 2011	1	**Being**	Jan 7 2012	6	Illuminating	Mar 17 2012	11	Being
Oct 30 2011	2	Breathing	Jan 8 2012	7	Choosing	Mar 18 2012	12	Breathing
Oct 31 2011	3	Listening	Jan 9 2012	8	Exploring	Mar 19 2012	13	Listening
Nov 1 2011	4	Planting	Jan 10 2012	9	Healing	Mar 20 2012	1	**Planting**
Nov 2 2011	5	Moving	Jan 11 2012	10	Seeing	Mar 21 2012	2	Moving
Nov 3 2011	6	Transcending	Jan 12 2012	11	Intuiting	Mar 22 2012	3	Transcending
Nov 4 2011	7	Remembering	Jan 13 2012	12	Evolving	Mar 23 2012	4	Remembering
Nov 5 2011	8	Loving	Jan 14 2012	13	Self-Regulating	Mar 24 2012	5	Loving
Nov 6 2011	9	Feeling	Jan 15 2012	1	**Catalyzing**	Mar 25 2012	6	Feeling
Nov 7 2011	10	Devoting	Jan 16 2012	2	Enlightening	Mar 26 2012	7	Devoting
Nov 8 2011	11	Illuminating	Jan 17 2012	3	Being	Mar 27 2012	8	Illuminating
Nov 9 2011	12	Choosing	Jan 18 2012	4	Breathing	Mar 28 2012	9	Choosing
Nov 10 2011	13	Exploring	Jan 19 2012	5	Listening	Mar 29 2012	10	Exploring
Nov 11 2011	1	**Healing**	Jan 20 2012	6	Planting	Mar 30 2012	11	Healing
Nov 12 2011	2	Seeing	Jan 21 2012	7	Moving	Mar 31 2012	12	Seeing
Nov 13 2011	3	Intuiting	Jan 22 2012	8	Transcending	Apr 1 2012	13	Intuiting
Nov 14 2011	4	Evolving	Jan 23 2012	9	Remembering	Apr 2 2012	1	**Evolving**
Nov 15 2011	5	Self-Regulating	Jan 24 2012	10	Loving	Apr 3 2012	2	Self-Regulating
Nov 16 2011	6	Catalyzing	Jan 25 2012	11	Feeling	Apr 4 2012	3	Catalyzing
Nov 17 2011	7	Enlightening	Jan 26 2012	12	Devoting	Apr 5 2012	4	Enlightening
Nov 18 2011	8	Being	Jan 27 2012	13	Illuminating	Apr 6 2012	5	Being
Nov 19 2011	9	Breathing	Jan 28 2012	1	**Choosing**	Apr 7 2012	6	Breathing
Nov 20 2011	10	Listening	Jan 29 2012	2	Exploring	Apr 8 2012	7	Listening
Nov 21 2011	11	Planting	Jan 30 2012	3	Healing	Apr 9 2012	8	Planting
Nov 22 2011	12	Moving	Jan 31 2012	4	Seeing	Apr 10 2012	9	Moving
Nov 23 2011	13	Transcending	Feb 1 2012	5	Intuiting	Apr 11 2012	10	Transcending
Nov 24 2011	1	**Remembering**	Feb 2 2012	6	Evolving	Apr 12 2012	11	Remembering
Nov 25 2011	2	Loving	Feb 3 2012	7	Self-Regulating	Apr 13 2012	12	Loving
Nov 26 2011	3	Feeling	Feb 4 2012	8	Catalyzing	Apr 14 2012	13	Feeling
Nov 27 2011	4	Devoting	Feb 5 2012	9	Enlightening	Apr 15 2012	1	**Devoting**
Nov 28 2011	5	Illuminating	Feb 6 2012	10	Being	Apr 16 2012	2	Illuminating
Nov 29 2011	6	Choosing	Feb 7 2012	11	Breathing	Apr 17 2012	3	Choosing
Nov 30 2011	7	Exploring	Feb 8 2012	12	Listening	Apr 18 2012	4	Exploring
Dec 1 2011	8	Healing	Feb 9 2012	13	Planting	Apr 19 2012	5	Healing
Dec 2 2011	9	Seeing	Feb 10 2012	1	**Moving**	Apr 20 2012	6	Seeing
Dec 3 2011	10	Intuiting	Feb 11 2012	2	Transcending	Apr 21 2012	7	Intuiting
Dec 4 2011	11	Evolving	Feb 12 2012	3	Remembering	Apr 22 2012	8	Evolving
Dec 5 2011	12	Self-Regulating	Feb 13 2012	4	Loving	Apr 23 2012	9	Self-Regulating
Dec 6 2011	13	Catalyzing	Feb 14 2012	5	Feeling	Apr 24 2012	10	Catalyzing
Dec 7 2011	1	**Enlightening**	Feb 15 2012	6	Devoting	Apr 25 2012	11	Enlightening
Dec 8 2011	2	Being	Feb 16 2012	7	Illuminating	Apr 26 2012	12	Being
Dec 9 2011	3	Breathing	Feb 17 2012	8	Choosing	Apr 27 2012	13	Breathing
Dec 10 2011	4	Listening	Feb 18 2012	9	Exploring	Apr 28 2012	1	**Listening**
Dec 11 2011	5	Planting	Feb 19 2012	10	Healing	Apr 29 2012	2	Planting
Dec 12 2011	6	Moving	Feb 20 2012	11	Seeing	Apr 30 2012	3	Moving
Dec 13 2011	7	Transcending	Feb 21 2012	12	Intuiting	May 1 2012	4	Transcending
Dec 14 2011	8	Remembering	Feb 22 2012	13	Evolving	May 2 2012	5	Remembering
Dec 15 2011	9	Loving	Feb 23 2012	1	**Self-Regulating**	May 3 2012	6	Loving
Dec 16 2011	10	Feeling	Feb 24 2012	2	Catalyzing	May 4 2012	7	Feeling
Dec 17 2011	11	Devoting	Feb 25 2012	3	Enlightening	May 5 2012	8	Devoting
Dec 18 2011	12	Illuminating	Feb 26 2012	4	Being	May 6 2012	9	Illuminating
Dec 19 2011	13	Choosing	Feb 27 2012	5	Breathing	May 7 2012	10	Choosing
Dec 20 2011	1	**Exploring**	Feb 28 2012	6	Listening	May 8 2012	11	Exploring
Dec 21 2011	2	Healing	Feb 29 2012	7	Planting	May 9 2012	12	Healing
Dec 22 2011	3	Seeing	Mar 1 2012	8	Moving	May 10 2012	13	Seeing
Dec 23 2011	4	Intuiting	Mar 2 2012	9	Transcending	May 11 2012	1	**Intuiting**
Dec 24 2011	5	Evolving	Mar 3 2012	10	Remembering	May 12 2012	2	Evolving
Dec 25 2011	6	Self-Regulating	Mar 4 2012	11	Loving	May 13 2012	3	Self-Regulating
Dec 26 2011	7	Catalyzing	Mar 5 2012	12	Feeling	May 14 2012	4	Catalyzing
Dec 27 2011	8	Enlightening	Mar 6 2012	13	Devoting	May 15 2012	5	Enlightening

Date	UE	Earth Energy
May 16 2012	6	Being
May 17 2012	7	Breathing
May 18 2012	8	Listening
May 19 2012	9	Planting
May 20 2012	10	Moving
May 21 2012	11	Transcending
May 22 2012	12	Remembering
May 23 2012	13	Loving
May 24 2012	1	Feeling
May 25 2012	2	Devoting
May 26 2012	3	Illuminating
May 27 2012	4	Choosing
May 28 2012	5	Exploring
May 29 2012	6	Healing
May 30 2012	7	Seeing
May 31 2012	8	Intuiting
Jun 1 2012	9	Evolving
Jun 2 2012	10	Self-Regulating
Jun 3 2012	11	Catalyzing
Jun 4 2012	12	Enlightening
Jun 5 2012	13	Being
Jun 6 2012	1	Breathing
Jun 7 2012	2	Listening
Jun 8 2012	3	Planting
Jun 9 2012	4	Moving
Jun 10 2012	5	Transcending
Jun 11 2012	6	Remembering
Jun 12 2012	7	Loving
Jun 13 2012	8	Feeling
Jun 14 2012	9	Devoting
Jun 15 2012	10	Illuminating
Jun 16 2012	11	Choosing
Jun 17 2012	12	Exploring
Jun 18 2012	13	Healing
Jun 19 2012	1	Seeing
Jun 20 2012	2	Intuiting
Jun 21 2012	3	Evolving
Jun 22 2012	4	Self-Regulating
Jun 23 2012	5	Catalyzing
Jun 24 2012	6	Enlightening
Jun 25 2012	7	Being
Jun 26 2012	8	Breathing
Jun 27 2012	9	Listening
Jun 28 2012	10	Planting
Jun 29 2012	11	Moving
Jun 30 2012	12	Transcending
Jul 1 2012	13	Remembering
Jul 2 2012	1	Loving
Jul 3 2012	2	Feeling
Jul 4 2012	3	Devoting
Jul 5 2012	4	Illuminating
Jul 6 2012	5	Choosing
Jul 7 2012	6	Exploring
Jul 8 2012	7	Healing
Jul 9 2012	8	Seeing
Jul 10 2012	9	Intuiting
Jul 11 2012	10	Evolving
Jul 12 2012	11	Self-Regulating
Jul 13 2012	12	Catalyzing
Jul 14 2012	13	Enlightening
Jul 15 2012	1	Being
Jul 16 2012	2	Breathing
Jul 17 2012	3	Listening
Jul 18 2012	4	Planting
Jul 19 2012	5	Moving
Jul 20 2012	6	Transcending
Jul 21 2012	7	Remembering
Jul 22 2012	8	Loving
Jul 23 2012	9	Feeling
Jul 24 2012	10	Devoting
Jul 25 2012	11	Illuminating
Jul 26 2012	12	Choosing
Jul 27 2012	13	Exploring
Jul 28 2012	1	Healing
Jul 29 2012	2	Seeing
Jul 30 2012	3	Intuiting
Jul 31 2012	4	Evolving
Aug 1 2012	5	Self-Regulating
Aug 2 2012	6	Catalyzing
Aug 3 2012	7	Enlightening
Aug 4 2012	8	Being
Aug 5 2012	9	Breathing
Aug 6 2012	10	Listening
Aug 7 2012	11	Planting
Aug 8 2012	12	Moving
Aug 9 2012	13	Transcending
Aug 10 2012	1	Remembering
Aug 11 2012	2	Loving
Aug 12 2012	3	Feeling
Aug 13 2012	4	Devoting
Aug 14 2012	5	Illuminating
Aug 15 2012	6	Choosing
Aug 16 2012	7	Exploring
Aug 17 2012	8	Healing
Aug 18 2012	9	Seeing
Aug 19 2012	10	Intuiting
Aug 20 2012	11	Evolving
Aug 21 2012	12	Self-Regulating
Aug 22 2012	13	Catalyzing
Aug 23 2012	1	Enlightening
Aug 24 2012	2	Being
Aug 25 2012	3	Breathing
Aug 26 2012	4	Listening
Aug 27 2012	5	Planting
Aug 28 2012	6	Moving
Aug 29 2012	7	Transcending
Aug 30 2012	8	Remembering
Aug 31 2012	9	Loving
Sep 1 2012	10	Feeling
Sep 2 2012	11	Devoting
Sep 3 2012	12	Illuminating
Sep 4 2012	13	Choosing
Sep 5 2012	1	Exploring
Sep 6 2012	2	Healing
Sep 7 2012	3	Seeing
Sep 8 2012	4	Intuiting
Sep 9 2012	5	Evolving
Sep 10 2012	6	Self-Regulating
Sep 11 2012	7	Catalyzing
Sep 12 2012	8	Enlightening
Sep 13 2012	9	Being
Sep 14 2012	10	Breathing
Sep 15 2012	11	Listening
Sep 16 2012	12	Planting
Sep 17 2012	13	Moving
Sep 18 2012	1	Transcending
Sep 19 2012	2	Remembering
Sep 20 2012	3	Loving
Sep 21 2012	4	Feeling
Sep 22 2012	5	Devoting
Sep 23 2012	6	Illuminating
Sep 24 2012	7	Choosing
Sep 25 2012	8	Exploring
Sep 26 2012	9	Healing
Sep 27 2012	10	Seeing
Sep 28 2012	11	Intuiting
Sep 29 2012	12	Evolving
Sep 30 2012	13	Self-Regulating
Oct 1 2012	1	Catalyzing
Oct 2 2012	2	Enlightening
Oct 3 2012	3	Being
Oct 4 2012	4	Breathing
Oct 5 2012	5	Listening
Oct 6 2012	6	Planting
Oct 7 2012	7	Moving
Oct 8 2012	8	Transcending
Oct 9 2012	9	Remembering
Oct 10 2012	10	Loving
Oct 11 2012	11	Feeling
Oct 12 2012	12	Devoting
Oct 13 2012	13	Illuminating
Oct 14 2012	1	Choosing
Oct 15 2012	2	Exploring
Oct 16 2012	3	Healing
Oct 17 2012	4	Seeing
Oct 18 2012	5	Intuiting
Oct 19 2012	6	Evolving
Oct 20 2012	7	Self-Regulating
Oct 21 2012	8	Catalyzing
Oct 22 2012	9	Enlightening
Oct 23 2012	10	Being
Oct 24 2012	11	Breathing
Oct 25 2012	12	Listening
Oct 26 2012	13	Planting
Oct 27 2012	1	Moving
Oct 28 2012	2	Transcending
Oct 29 2012	3	Remembering
Oct 30 2012	4	Loving
Oct 31 2012	5	Feeling
Nov 1 2012	6	Devoting
Nov 2 2012	7	Illuminating
Nov 3 2012	8	Choosing
Nov 4 2012	9	Exploring
Nov 5 2012	10	Healing
Nov 6 2012	11	Seeing
Nov 7 2012	12	Intuiting
Nov 8 2012	13	Evolving
Nov 9 2012	1	Self-Regulating
Nov 10 2012	2	Catalyzing
Nov 11 2012	3	Enlightening
Nov 12 2012	4	Being
Nov 13 2012	5	Breathing
Nov 14 2012	6	Listening
Nov 15 2012	7	Planting
Nov 16 2012	8	Moving
Nov 17 2012	9	Transcending
Nov 18 2012	10	Remembering
Nov 19 2012	11	Loving
Nov 20 2012	12	Feeling
Nov 21 2012	13	Devoting
Nov 22 2012	1	Illuminating
Nov 23 2012	2	Choosing
Nov 24 2012	3	Exploring
Nov 25 2012	4	Healing
Nov 26 2012	5	Seeing
Nov 27 2012	6	Intuiting
Nov 28 2012	7	Evolving
Nov 29 2012	8	Self-Regulating
Nov 30 2012	9	Catalyzing
Dec 1 2012	10	Enlightening
Dec 2 2012	11	Being
Dec 3 2012	12	Breathing
Dec 4 2012	13	Listening
Dec 5 2012	1	Planting
Dec 6 2012	2	Moving
Dec 7 2012	3	Transcending
Dec 8 2012	4	Remembering
Dec 9 2012	5	Loving
Dec 10 2012	6	Feeling
Dec 11 2012	7	Devoting

Date	UE	Earth Energy	Date	UE	Earth Energy	Date	UE	Earth Energy
Dec 12 2012	8	Illuminating	Feb 20 2013	13	Being	May 1 2013	5	Illuminating
Dec 13 2012	9	Choosing	Feb 21 2013	1	Breathing	May 2 2013	6	Choosing
Dec 14 2012	10	Exploring	Feb 22 2013	2	Listening	May 3 2013	7	Exploring
Dec 15 2012	11	Healing	Feb 23 2013	3	Planting	May 4 2013	8	Healing
Dec 16 2012	12	Seeing	Feb 24 2013	4	Moving	May 5 2013	9	Seeing
Dec 17 2012	13	Intuiting	Feb 25 2013	5	Transcending	May 6 2013	10	Intuiting
Dec 18 2012	1	Evolving	Feb 26 2013	6	Remembering	May 7 2013	11	Evolving
Dec 19 2012	2	Self-Regulating	Feb 27 2013	7	Loving	May 8 2013	12	Self-Regulating
Dec 20 2012	3	Catalyzing	Feb 28 2013	8	Feeling	May 9 2013	13	Catalyzing
Dec 21 2012	4	Enlightening	Mar 1 2013	9	Devoting	May 10 2013	1	Enlightening
Dec 22 2012	5	Being	Mar 2 2013	10	Illuminating	May 11 2013	2	Being
Dec 23 2012	6	Breathing	Mar 3 2013	11	Choosing	May 12 2013	3	Breathing
Dec 24 2012	7	Listening	Mar 4 2013	12	Exploring	May 13 2013	4	Listening
Dec 25 2012	8	Planting	Mar 5 2013	13	Healing	May 14 2013	5	Planting
Dec 26 2012	9	Moving	Mar 6 2013	1	Seeing	May 15 2013	6	Moving
Dec 27 2012	10	Transcending	Mar 7 2013	2	Intuiting	May 16 2013	7	Transcending
Dec 28 2012	11	Remembering	Mar 8 2013	3	Evolving	May 17 2013	8	Remembering
Dec 29 2012	12	Loving	Mar 9 2013	4	Self-Regulating	May 18 2013	9	Loving
Dec 30 2012	13	Feeling	Mar 10 2013	5	Catalyzing	May 19 2013	10	Feeling
Dec 31 2012	1	Devoting	Mar 11 2013	6	Enlightening	May 20 2013	11	Devoting
Jan 1 2013	2	Illuminating	Mar 12 2013	7	Being	May 21 2013	12	Illuminating
Jan 2 2013	3	Choosing	Mar 13 2013	8	Breathing	May 22 2013	13	Choosing
Jan 3 2013	4	Exploring	Mar 14 2013	9	Listening	May 23 2013	1	Exploring
Jan 4 2013	5	Healing	Mar 15 2013	10	Planting	May 24 2013	2	Healing
Jan 5 2013	6	Seeing	Mar 16 2013	11	Moving	May 25 2013	3	Seeing
Jan 6 2013	7	Intuiting	Mar 17 2013	12	Transcending	May 26 2013	4	Intuiting
Jan 7 2013	8	Evolving	Mar 18 2013	13	Remembering	May 27 2013	5	Evolving
Jan 8 2013	9	Self-Regulating	Mar 19 2013	1	Loving	May 28 2013	6	Self-Regulating
Jan 9 2013	10	Catalyzing	Mar 20 2013	2	Feeling	May 29 2013	7	Catalyzing
Jan 10 2013	11	Enlightening	Mar 21 2013	3	Devoting	May 30 2013	8	Enlightening
Jan 11 2013	12	Being	Mar 22 2013	4	Illuminating	May 31 2013	9	Being
Jan 12 2013	13	Breathing	Mar 23 2013	5	Choosing	Jun 1 2013	10	Breathing
Jan 13 2013	1	Listening	Mar 24 2013	6	Exploring	Jun 2 2013	11	Listening
Jan 14 2013	2	Planting	Mar 25 2013	7	Healing	Jun 3 2013	12	Planting
Jan 15 2013	3	Moving	Mar 26 2013	8	Seeing	Jun 4 2013	13	Moving
Jan 16 2013	4	Transcending	Mar 27 2013	9	Intuiting	Jun 5 2013	1	Transcending
Jan 17 2013	5	Remembering	Mar 28 2013	10	Evolving	Jun 6 2013	2	Remembering
Jan 18 2013	6	Loving	Mar 29 2013	11	Self-Regulating	Jun 7 2013	3	Loving
Jan 19 2013	7	Feeling	Mar 30 2013	12	Catalyzing	Jun 8 2013	4	Feeling
Jan 20 2013	8	Devoting	Mar 31 2013	13	Enlightening	Jun 9 2013	5	Devoting
Jan 21 2013	9	Illuminating	Apr 1 2013	1	Being	Jun 10 2013	6	Illuminating
Jan 22 2013	10	Choosing	Apr 2 2013	2	Breathing	Jun 11 2013	7	Choosing
Jan 23 2013	11	Exploring	Apr 3 2013	3	Listening	Jun 12 2013	8	Exploring
Jan 24 2013	12	Healing	Apr 4 2013	4	Planting	Jun 13 2013	9	Healing
Jan 25 2013	13	Seeing	Apr 5 2013	5	Moving	Jun 14 2013	10	Seeing
Jan 26 2013	1	Intuiting	Apr 6 2013	6	Transcending	Jun 15 2013	11	Intuiting
Jan 27 2013	2	Evolving	Apr 7 2013	7	Remembering	Jun 16 2013	12	Evolving
Jan 28 2013	3	Self-Regulating	Apr 8 2013	8	Loving	Jun 17 2013	13	Self-Regulating
Jan 29 2013	4	Catalyzing	Apr 9 2013	9	Feeling	Jun 18 2013	1	Catalyzing
Jan 30 2013	5	Enlightening	Apr 10 2013	10	Devoting	Jun 19 2013	2	Enlightening
Jan 31 2013	6	Being	Apr 11 2013	11	Illuminating	Jun 20 2013	3	Being
Feb 1 2013	7	Breathing	Apr 12 2013	12	Choosing	Jun 21 2013	4	Breathing
Feb 2 2013	8	Listening	Apr 13 2013	13	Exploring	Jun 22 2013	5	Listening
Feb 3 2013	9	Planting	Apr 14 2013	1	Healing	Jun 23 2013	6	Planting
Feb 4 2013	10	Moving	Apr 15 2013	2	Seeing	Jun 24 2013	7	Moving
Feb 5 2013	11	Transcending	Apr 16 2013	3	Intuiting	Jun 25 2013	8	Transcending
Feb 6 2013	12	Remembering	Apr 17 2013	4	Evolving	Jun 26 2013	9	Remembering
Feb 7 2013	13	Loving	Apr 18 2013	5	Self-Regulating	Jun 27 2013	10	Loving
Feb 8 2013	1	Feeling	Apr 19 2013	6	Catalyzing	Jun 28 2013	11	Feeling
Feb 9 2013	2	Devoting	Apr 20 2013	7	Enlightening	Jun 29 2013	12	Devoting
Feb 10 2013	3	Illuminating	Apr 21 2013	8	Being	Jun 30 2013	13	Illuminating
Feb 11 2013	4	Choosing	Apr 22 2013	9	Breathing	Jul 1 2013	1	Choosing
Feb 12 2013	5	Exploring	Apr 23 2013	10	Listening	Jul 2 2013	2	Exploring
Feb 13 2013	6	Healing	Apr 24 2013	11	Planting	Jul 3 2013	3	Healing
Feb 14 2013	7	Seeing	Apr 25 2013	12	Moving	Jul 4 2013	4	Seeing
Feb 15 2013	8	Intuiting	Apr 26 2013	13	Transcending	Jul 5 2013	5	Intuiting
Feb 16 2013	9	Evolving	Apr 27 2013	1	Remembering	Jul 6 2013	6	Evolving
Feb 17 2013	10	Self-Regulating	Apr 28 2013	2	Loving	Jul 7 2013	7	Self-Regulating
Feb 18 2013	11	Catalyzing	Apr 29 2013	3	Feeling	Jul 8 2013	8	Catalyzing
Feb 19 2013	12	Enlightening	Apr 30 2013	4	Devoting	Jul 9 2013	9	Enlightening

Date	UE	Earth Energy	Date	UE	Earth Energy	Date	UE	Earth Energy
Jul 10 2013	10	Being	Sep 18 2013	2	Illuminating	Nov 27 2013	7	Being
Jul 11 2013	11	Breathing	Sep 19 2013	3	Choosing	Nov 28 2013	8	Breathing
Jul 12 2013	12	Listening	Sep 20 2013	4	Exploring	Nov 29 2013	9	Listening
Jul 13 2013	13	Planting	Sep 21 2013	5	Healing	Nov 30 2013	10	Planting
Jul 14 2013	**1**	**Moving**	Sep 22 2013	6	Seeing	Dec 1 2013	11	Moving
Jul 15 2013	2	Transcending	Sep 23 2013	7	Intuiting	Dec 2 2013	12	Transcending
Jul 16 2013	3	Remembering	Sep 24 2013	8	Evolving	Dec 3 2013	13	Remembering
Jul 17 2013	4	Loving	Sep 25 2013	9	Self-Regulating	Dec 4 2013	**1**	**Loving**
Jul 18 2013	5	Feeling	Sep 26 2013	10	Catalyzing	Dec 5 2013	2	Feeling
Jul 19 2013	6	Devoting	Sep 27 2013	11	Enlightening	Dec 6 2013	3	Devoting
Jul 20 2013	7	Illuminating	Sep 28 2013	12	Being	Dec 7 2013	4	Illuminating
Jul 21 2013	8	Choosing	Sep 29 2013	13	Breathing	Dec 8 2013	5	Choosing
Jul 22 2013	9	Exploring	Sep 30 2013	**1**	**Listening**	Dec 9 2013	6	Exploring
Jul 23 2013	10	Healing	Oct 1 2013	2	Planting	Dec 10 2013	7	Healing
Jul 24 2013	11	Seeing	Oct 2 2013	3	Moving	Dec 11 2013	8	Seeing
Jul 25 2013	12	Intuiting	Oct 3 2013	4	Transcending	Dec 12 2013	9	Intuiting
Jul 26 2013	13	Evolving	Oct 4 2013	5	Remembering	Dec 13 2013	10	Evolving
Jul 27 2013	**1**	**Self-Regulating**	Oct 5 2013	6	Loving	Dec 14 2013	11	Self-Regulating
Jul 28 2013	2	Catalyzing	Oct 6 2013	7	Feeling	Dec 15 2013	12	Catalyzing
Jul 29 2013	3	Enlightening	Oct 7 2013	8	Devoting	Dec 16 2013	13	Enlightening
Jul 30 2013	4	Being	Oct 8 2013	9	Illuminating	Dec 17 2013	**1**	**Being**
Jul 31 2013	5	Breathing	Oct 9 2013	10	Choosing	Dec 18 2013	2	Breathing
Aug 1 2013	6	Listening	Oct 10 2013	11	Exploring	Dec 19 2013	3	Listening
Aug 2 2013	7	Planting	Oct 11 2013	12	Healing	Dec 20 2013	4	Planting
Aug 3 2013	8	Moving	Oct 12 2013	13	Seeing	Dec 21 2013	5	Moving
Aug 4 2013	9	Transcending	Oct 13 2013	**1**	**Intuiting**	Dec 22 2013	6	Transcending
Aug 5 2013	10	Remembering	Oct 14 2013	2	Evolving	Dec 23 2013	7	Remembering
Aug 6 2013	11	Loving	Oct 15 2013	3	Self-Regulating	Dec 24 2013	8	Loving
Aug 7 2013	12	Feeling	Oct 16 2013	4	Catalyzing	Dec 25 2013	9	Feeling
Aug 8 2013	13	Devoting	Oct 17 2013	5	Enlightening	Dec 26 2013	10	Devoting
Aug 9 2013	**1**	**Illuminating**	Oct 18 2013	6	Being	Dec 27 2013	11	Illuminating
Aug 10 2013	2	Choosing	Oct 19 2013	7	Breathing	Dec 28 2013	12	Choosing
Aug 11 2013	3	Exploring	Oct 20 2013	8	Listening	Dec 29 2013	13	Exploring
Aug 12 2013	4	Healing	Oct 21 2013	9	Planting	Dec 30 2013	**1**	**Healing**
Aug 13 2013	5	Seeing	Oct 22 2013	10	Moving	Dec 31 2013	2	Seeing
Aug 14 2013	6	Intuiting	Oct 23 2013	11	Transcending	Jan 1 2014	3	Intuiting
Aug 15 2013	7	Evolving	Oct 24 2013	12	Remembering	Jan 2 2014	4	Evolving
Aug 16 2013	8	Self-Regulating	Oct 25 2013	13	Loving	Jan 3 2014	5	Self-Regulating
Aug 17 2013	9	Catalyzing	Oct 26 2013	**1**	**Feeling**	Jan 4 2014	6	Catalyzing
Aug 18 2013	10	Enlightening	Oct 27 2013	2	Devoting	Jan 5 2014	7	Enlightening
Aug 19 2013	11	Being	Oct 28 2013	3	Illuminating	Jan 6 2014	8	Being
Aug 20 2013	12	Breathing	Oct 29 2013	4	Choosing	Jan 7 2014	9	Breathing
Aug 21 2013	13	Listening	Oct 30 2013	5	Exploring	Jan 8 2014	10	Listening
Aug 22 2013	**1**	**Planting**	Oct 31 2013	6	Healing	Jan 9 2014	11	Planting
Aug 23 2013	2	Moving	Nov 1 2013	7	Seeing	Jan 10 2014	12	Moving
Aug 24 2013	3	Transcending	Nov 2 2013	8	Intuiting	Jan 11 2014	13	Transcending
Aug 25 2013	4	Remembering	Nov 3 2013	9	Evolving	Jan 12 2014	**1**	**Remembering**
Aug 26 2013	5	Loving	Nov 4 2013	10	Self-Regulating	Jan 13 2014	2	Loving
Aug 27 2013	6	Feeling	Nov 5 2013	11	Catalyzing	Jan 14 2014	3	Feeling
Aug 28 2013	7	Devoting	Nov 6 2013	12	Enlightening	Jan 15 2014	4	Devoting
Aug 29 2013	8	Illuminating	Nov 7 2013	13	Being	Jan 16 2014	5	Illuminating
Aug 30 2013	9	Choosing	Nov 8 2013	**1**	**Breathing**	Jan 17 2014	6	Choosing
Aug 31 2013	10	Exploring	Nov 9 2013	2	Listening	Jan 18 2014	7	Exploring
Sep 1 2013	11	Healing	Nov 10 2013	3	Planting	Jan 19 2014	8	Healing
Sep 2 2013	12	Seeing	Nov 11 2013	4	Moving	Jan 20 2014	9	Seeing
Sep 3 2013	13	Intuiting	Nov 12 2013	5	Transcending	Jan 21 2014	10	Intuiting
Sep 4 2013	**1**	**Evolving**	Nov 13 2013	6	Remembering	Jan 22 2014	11	Evolving
Sep 5 2013	2	Self-Regulating	Nov 14 2013	7	Loving	Jan 23 2014	12	Self-Regulating
Sep 6 2013	3	Catalyzing	Nov 15 2013	8	Feeling	Jan 24 2014	13	Catalyzing
Sep 7 2013	4	Enlightening	Nov 16 2013	9	Devoting	Jan 25 2014	**1**	**Enlightening**
Sep 8 2013	5	Being	Nov 17 2013	10	Illuminating	Jan 26 2014	2	Being
Sep 9 2013	6	Breathing	Nov 18 2013	11	Choosing	Jan 27 2014	3	Breathing
Sep 10 2013	7	Listening	Nov 19 2013	12	Exploring	Jan 28 2014	4	Listening
Sep 11 2013	8	Planting	Nov 20 2013	13	Healing	Jan 29 2014	5	Planting
Sep 12 2013	9	Moving	Nov 21 2013	**1**	**Seeing**	Jan 30 2014	6	Moving
Sep 13 2013	10	Transcending	Nov 22 2013	2	Intuiting	Jan 31 2014	7	Transcending
Sep 14 2013	11	Remembering	Nov 23 2013	3	Evolving	Feb 1 2014	8	Remembering
Sep 15 2013	12	Loving	Nov 24 2013	4	Self-Regulating	Feb 2 2014	9	Loving
Sep 16 2013	13	Feeling	Nov 25 2013	5	Catalyzing	Feb 3 2014	10	Feeling
Sep 17 2013	**1**	**Devoting**	Nov 26 2013	6	Enlightening	Feb 4 2014	11	Devoting

Date	UE Earth Energy	Date	UE Earth Energy	Date	UE Earth Energy
Feb 5 2014	12 Illuminating	Apr 16 2014	4 Being	Jun 25 2014	9 Illuminating
Feb 6 2014	13 Choosing	Apr 17 2014	5 Breathing	Jun 26 2014	10 Choosing
Feb 7 2014	**1 Exploring**	Apr 18 2014	6 Listening	Jun 27 2014	11 Exploring
Feb 8 2014	2 Healing	Apr 19 2014	7 Planting	Jun 28 2014	12 Healing
Feb 9 2014	3 Seeing	Apr 20 2014	8 Moving	Jun 29 2014	13 Seeing
Feb 10 2014	4 Intuiting	Apr 21 2014	9 Transcending	Jun 30 2014	**1 Intuiting**
Feb 11 2014	5 Evolving	Apr 22 2014	10 Remembering	Jul 1 2014	2 Evolving
Feb 12 2014	6 Self-Regulating	Apr 23 2014	11 Loving	Jul 2 2014	3 Self-Regulating
Feb 13 2014	7 Catalyzing	Apr 24 2014	12 Feeling	Jul 3 2014	4 Catalyzing
Feb 14 2014	8 Enlightening	Apr 25 2014	13 Devoting	Jul 4 2014	5 Enlightening
Feb 15 2014	9 Being	Apr 26 2014	**1 Illuminating**	Jul 5 2014	6 Being
Feb 16 2014	10 Breathing	Apr 27 2014	2 Choosing	Jul 6 2014	7 Breathing
Feb 17 2014	11 Listening	Apr 28 2014	3 Exploring	Jul 7 2014	8 Listening
Feb 18 2014	12 Planting	Apr 29 2014	4 Healing	Jul 8 2014	9 Planting
Feb 19 2014	13 Moving	Apr 30 2014	5 Seeing	Jul 9 2014	10 Moving
Feb 20 2014	**1 Transcending**	May 1 2014	6 Intuiting	Jul 10 2014	11 Transcending
Feb 21 2014	2 Remembering	May 2 2014	7 Evolving	Jul 11 2014	12 Remembering
Feb 22 2014	3 Loving	May 3 2014	8 Self-Regulating	Jul 12 2014	13 Loving
Feb 23 2014	4 Feeling	May 4 2014	9 Catalyzing	Jul 13 2014	**1 Feeling**
Feb 24 2014	5 Devoting	May 5 2014	10 Enlightening	Jul 14 2014	2 Devoting
Feb 25 2014	6 Illuminating	May 6 2014	11 Being	Jul 15 2014	3 Illuminating
Feb 26 2014	7 Choosing	May 7 2014	12 Breathing	Jul 16 2014	4 Choosing
Feb 27 2014	8 Exploring	May 8 2014	13 Listening	Jul 17 2014	5 Exploring
Feb 28 2014	9 Healing	May 9 2014	**1 Planting**	Jul 18 2014	6 Healing
Mar 1 2014	10 Seeing	May 10 2014	2 Moving	Jul 19 2014	7 Seeing
Mar 2 2014	11 Intuiting	May 11 2014	3 Transcending	Jul 20 2014	8 Intuiting
Mar 3 2014	12 Evolving	May 12 2014	4 Remembering	Jul 21 2014	9 Evolving
Mar 4 2014	13 Self-Regulating	May 13 2014	5 Loving	Jul 22 2014	10 Self-Regulating
Mar 5 2014	**1 Catalyzing**	May 14 2014	6 Feeling	Jul 23 2014	11 Catalyzing
Mar 6 2014	2 Enlightening	May 15 2014	7 Devoting	Jul 24 2014	12 Enlightening
Mar 7 2014	3 Being	May 16 2014	8 Illuminating	Jul 25 2014	13 Being
Mar 8 2014	4 Breathing	May 17 2014	9 Choosing	Jul 26 2014	**1 Breathing**
Mar 9 2014	5 Listening	May 18 2014	10 Exploring	Jul 27 2014	2 Listening
Mar 10 2014	6 Planting	May 19 2014	11 Healing	Jul 28 2014	3 Planting
Mar 11 2014	7 Moving	May 20 2014	12 Seeing	Jul 29 2014	4 Moving
Mar 12 2014	8 Transcending	May 21 2014	13 Intuiting	Jul 30 2014	5 Transcending
Mar 13 2014	9 Remembering	May 22 2014	**1 Evolving**	Jul 31 2014	6 Remembering
Mar 14 2014	10 Loving	May 23 2014	2 Self-Regulating	Aug 1 2014	7 Loving
Mar 15 2014	11 Feeling	May 24 2014	3 Catalyzing	Aug 2 2014	8 Feeling
Mar 16 2014	12 Devoting	May 25 2014	4 Enlightening	Aug 3 2014	9 Devoting
Mar 17 2014	13 Illuminating	May 26 2014	5 Being	Aug 4 2014	10 Illuminating
Mar 18 2014	**1 Choosing**	May 27 2014	6 Breathing	Aug 5 2014	11 Choosing
Mar 19 2014	2 Exploring	May 28 2014	7 Listening	Aug 6 2014	12 Exploring
Mar 20 2014	3 Healing	May 29 2014	8 Planting	Aug 7 2014	13 Healing
Mar 21 2014	4 Seeing	May 30 2014	9 Moving	Aug 8 2014	**1 Seeing**
Mar 22 2014	5 Intuiting	May 31 2014	10 Transcending	Aug 9 2014	2 Intuiting
Mar 23 2014	6 Evolving	Jun 1 2014	11 Remembering	Aug 10 2014	3 Evolving
Mar 24 2014	7 Self-Regulating	Jun 2 2014	12 Loving	Aug 11 2014	4 Self-Regulating
Mar 25 2014	8 Catalyzing	Jun 3 2014	13 Feeling	Aug 12 2014	5 Catalyzing
Mar 26 2014	9 Enlightening	Jun 4 2014	**1 Devoting**	Aug 13 2014	6 Enlightening
Mar 27 2014	10 Being	Jun 5 2014	2 Illuminating	Aug 14 2014	7 Being
Mar 28 2014	11 Breathing	Jun 6 2014	3 Choosing	Aug 15 2014	8 Breathing
Mar 29 2014	12 Listening	Jun 7 2014	4 Exploring	Aug 16 2014	9 Listening
Mar 30 2014	13 Planting	Jun 8 2014	5 Healing	Aug 17 2014	10 Planting
Mar 31 2014	**1 Moving**	Jun 9 2014	6 Seeing	Aug 18 2014	11 Moving
Apr 1 2014	2 Transcending	Jun 10 2014	7 Intuiting	Aug 19 2014	12 Transcending
Apr 2 2014	3 Remembering	Jun 11 2014	8 Evolving	Aug 20 2014	13 Remembering
Apr 3 2014	4 Loving	Jun 12 2014	9 Self-Regulating	Aug 21 2014	**1 Loving**
Apr 4 2014	5 Feeling	Jun 13 2014	10 Catalyzing	Aug 22 2014	2 Feeling
Apr 5 2014	6 Devoting	Jun 14 2014	11 Enlightening	Aug 23 2014	3 Devoting
Apr 6 2014	7 Illuminating	Jun 15 2014	12 Being	Aug 24 2014	4 Illuminating
Apr 7 2014	8 Choosing	Jun 16 2014	13 Breathing	Aug 25 2014	5 Choosing
Apr 8 2014	9 Exploring	Jun 17 2014	**1 Listening**	Aug 26 2014	6 Exploring
Apr 9 2014	10 Healing	Jun 18 2014	2 Planting	Aug 27 2014	7 Healing
Apr 10 2014	11 Seeing	Jun 19 2014	3 Moving	Aug 28 2014	8 Seeing
Apr 11 2014	12 Intuiting	Jun 20 2014	4 Transcending	Aug 29 2014	9 Intuiting
Apr 12 2014	13 Evolving	Jun 21 2014	5 Remembering	Aug 30 2014	10 Evolving
Apr 13 2014	**1 Self-Regulating**	Jun 22 2014	6 Loving	Aug 31 2014	11 Self-Regulating
Apr 14 2014	2 Catalyzing	Jun 23 2014	7 Feeling	Sep 1 2014	12 Catalyzing
Apr 15 2014	3 Enlightening	Jun 24 2014	8 Devoting	Sep 2 2014	13 Enlightening

Date	UE	Earth Energy
Sep 3 2014	1	Being
Sep 4 2014	2	Breathing
Sep 5 2014	3	Listening
Sep 6 2014	4	Planting
Sep 7 2014	5	Moving
Sep 8 2014	6	Transcending
Sep 9 2014	7	Remembering
Sep 10 2014	8	Loving
Sep 11 2014	9	Feeling
Sep 12 2014	10	Devoting
Sep 13 2014	11	Illuminating
Sep 14 2014	12	Choosing
Sep 15 2014	13	Exploring
Sep 16 2014	1	Healing
Sep 17 2014	2	Seeing
Sep 18 2014	3	Intuiting
Sep 19 2014	4	Evolving
Sep 20 2014	5	Self-Regulating
Sep 21 2014	6	Catalyzing
Sep 22 2014	7	Enlightening
Sep 23 2014	8	Being
Sep 24 2014	9	Breathing
Sep 25 2014	10	Listening
Sep 26 2014	11	Planting
Sep 27 2014	12	Moving
Sep 28 2014	13	Transcending
Sep 29 2014	1	Remembering
Sep 30 2014	2	Loving
Oct 1 2014	3	Feeling
Oct 2 2014	4	Devoting
Oct 3 2014	5	Illuminating
Oct 4 2014	6	Choosing
Oct 5 2014	7	Exploring
Oct 6 2014	8	Healing
Oct 7 2014	9	Seeing
Oct 8 2014	10	Intuiting
Oct 9 2014	11	Evolving
Oct 10 2014	12	Self-Regulating
Oct 11 2014	13	Catalyzing
Oct 12 2014	1	Enlightening
Oct 13 2014	2	Being
Oct 14 2014	3	Breathing
Oct 15 2014	4	Listening
Oct 16 2014	5	Planting
Oct 17 2014	6	Moving
Oct 18 2014	7	Transcending
Oct 19 2014	8	Remembering
Oct 20 2014	9	Loving
Oct 21 2014	10	Feeling
Oct 22 2014	11	Devoting
Oct 23 2014	12	Illuminating
Oct 24 2014	13	Choosing
Oct 25 2014	1	Exploring
Oct 26 2014	2	Healing
Oct 27 2014	3	Seeing
Oct 28 2014	4	Intuiting
Oct 29 2014	5	Evolving
Oct 30 2014	6	Self-Regulating
Oct 31 2014	7	Catalyzing
Nov 1 2014	8	Enlightening
Nov 2 2014	9	Being
Nov 3 2014	10	Breathing
Nov 4 2014	11	Listening
Nov 5 2014	12	Planting
Nov 6 2014	13	Moving
Nov 7 2014	1	Transcending
Nov 8 2014	2	Remembering
Nov 9 2014	3	Loving
Nov 10 2014	4	Feeling
Nov 11 2014	5	Devoting
Nov 12 2014	6	Illuminating
Nov 13 2014	7	Choosing
Nov 14 2014	8	Exploring
Nov 15 2014	9	Healing
Nov 16 2014	10	Seeing
Nov 17 2014	11	Intuiting
Nov 18 2014	12	Evolving
Nov 19 2014	13	Self-Regulating
Nov 20 2014	1	Catalyzing
Nov 21 2014	2	Enlightening
Nov 22 2014	3	Being
Nov 23 2014	4	Breathing
Nov 24 2014	5	Listening
Nov 25 2014	6	Planting
Nov 26 2014	7	Moving
Nov 27 2014	8	Transcending
Nov 28 2014	9	Remembering
Nov 29 2014	10	Loving
Nov 30 2014	11	Feeling
Dec 1 2014	12	Devoting
Dec 2 2014	13	Illuminating
Dec 3 2014	1	Choosing
Dec 4 2014	2	Exploring
Dec 5 2014	3	Healing
Dec 6 2014	4	Seeing
Dec 7 2014	5	Intuiting
Dec 8 2014	6	Evolving
Dec 9 2014	7	Self-Regulating
Dec 10 2014	8	Catalyzing
Dec 11 2014	9	Enlightening
Dec 12 2014	10	Being
Dec 13 2014	11	Breathing
Dec 14 2014	12	Listening
Dec 15 2014	13	Planting
Dec 16 2014	1	Moving
Dec 17 2014	2	Transcending
Dec 18 2014	3	Remembering
Dec 19 2014	4	Loving
Dec 20 2014	5	Feeling
Dec 21 2014	6	Devoting
Dec 22 2014	7	Illuminating
Dec 23 2014	8	Choosing
Dec 24 2014	9	Exploring
Dec 25 2014	10	Healing
Dec 26 2014	11	Seeing
Dec 27 2014	12	Intuiting
Dec 28 2014	13	Self-Regulating
Dec 29 2014	1	Self-Regulating
Dec 30 2014	2	Catalyzing
Dec 31 2014	3	Enlightening
Jan 1 2015	4	Being
Jan 2 2015	5	Breathing
Jan 3 2015	6	Listening
Jan 4 2015	7	Planting
Jan 5 2015	8	Moving
Jan 6 2015	9	Transcending
Jan 7 2015	10	Remembering
Jan 8 2015	11	Loving
Jan 9 2015	12	Feeling
Jan 10 2015	13	Devoting
Jan 11 2015	1	Illuminating
Jan 12 2015	2	Choosing
Jan 13 2015	3	Exploring
Jan 14 2015	4	Healing
Jan 15 2015	5	Seeing
Jan 16 2015	6	Intuiting
Jan 17 2015	7	Evolving
Jan 18 2015	8	Self-Regulating
Jan 19 2015	9	Catalyzing
Jan 20 2015	10	Enlightening
Jan 21 2015	11	Being
Jan 22 2015	12	Breathing
Jan 23 2015	13	Listening
Jan 24 2015	1	Planting
Jan 25 2015	2	Moving
Jan 26 2015	3	Transcending
Jan 27 2015	4	Remembering
Jan 28 2015	5	Loving
Jan 29 2015	6	Feeling
Jan 30 2015	7	Devoting
Jan 31 2015	8	Illuminating
Feb 1 2015	9	Choosing
Feb 2 2015	10	Exploring
Feb 3 2015	11	Healing
Feb 4 2015	12	Seeing
Feb 5 2015	13	Intuiting
Feb 6 2015	1	Evolving
Feb 7 2015	2	Self-Regulating
Feb 8 2015	3	Catalyzing
Feb 9 2015	4	Enlightening
Feb 10 2015	5	Being
Feb 11 2015	6	Breathing
Feb 12 2015	7	Listening
Feb 13 2015	8	Planting
Feb 14 2015	9	Moving
Feb 15 2015	10	Transcending
Feb 16 2015	11	Remembering
Feb 17 2015	12	Loving
Feb 18 2015	13	Feeling
Feb 19 2015	1	Devoting
Feb 20 2015	2	Illuminating
Feb 21 2015	3	Choosing
Feb 22 2015	4	Exploring
Feb 23 2015	5	Healing
Feb 24 2015	6	Seeing
Feb 25 2015	7	Intuiting
Feb 26 2015	8	Evolving
Feb 27 2015	9	Self-Regulating
Feb 28 2015	10	Catalyzing
Mar 1 2015	11	Enlightening
Mar 2 2015	12	Being
Mar 3 2015	13	Breathing
Mar 4 2015	1	Listening
Mar 5 2015	2	Planting
Mar 6 2015	3	Moving
Mar 7 2015	4	Transcending
Mar 8 2015	5	Remembering
Mar 9 2015	6	Loving
Mar 10 2015	7	Feeling
Mar 11 2015	8	Devoting
Mar 12 2015	9	Illuminating
Mar 13 2015	10	Choosing
Mar 14 2015	11	Exploring
Mar 15 2015	12	Healing
Mar 16 2015	13	Seeing
Mar 17 2015	1	Intuiting
Mar 18 2015	2	Evolving
Mar 19 2015	3	Self-Regulating
Mar 20 2015	4	Catalyzing
Mar 21 2015	5	Enlightening
Mar 22 2015	6	Being
Mar 23 2015	7	Breathing
Mar 24 2015	8	Listening
Mar 25 2015	9	Planting
Mar 26 2015	10	Moving
Mar 27 2015	11	Transcending
Mar 28 2015	12	Remembering
Mar 29 2015	13	Loving
Mar 30 2015	1	Feeling
Mar 31 2015	2	Devoting

Date	UE	Earth Energy	Date	UE	Earth Energy	Date	UE	Earth Energy
Apr 1 2015	3	Illuminating	Jun 10 2015	8	Being	Aug 19 2015	13	Illuminating
Apr 2 2015	4	Choosing	Jun 11 2015	9	Breathing	Aug 20 2015	**1**	**Choosing**
Apr 3 2015	5	Exploring	Jun 12 2015	10	Listening	Aug 21 2015	2	Exploring
Apr 4 2015	6	Healing	Jun 13 2015	11	Planting	Aug 22 2015	3	Healing
Apr 5 2015	7	Seeing	Jun 14 2015	12	Moving	Aug 23 2015	4	Seeing
Apr 6 2015	8	Intuiting	Jun 15 2015	13	Transcending	Aug 24 2015	5	Intuiting
Apr 7 2015	9	Evolving	Jun 16 2015	**1**	**Remembering**	Aug 25 2015	6	Evolving
Apr 8 2015	10	Self-Regulating	Jun 17 2015	2	Loving	Aug 26 2015	7	Self-Regulating
Apr 9 2015	11	Catalyzing	Jun 18 2015	3	Feeling	Aug 27 2015	8	Catalyzing
Apr 10 2015	12	Enlightening	Jun 19 2015	4	Devoting	Aug 28 2015	9	Enlightening
Apr 11 2015	13	Being	Jun 20 2015	5	Illuminating	Aug 29 2015	10	Being
Apr 12 2015	**1**	**Breathing**	Jun 21 2015	6	Choosing	Aug 30 2015	11	Breathing
Apr 13 2015	2	Listening	Jun 22 2015	7	Exploring	Aug 31 2015	12	Listening
Apr 14 2015	3	Planting	Jun 23 2015	8	Healing	Sep 1 2015	13	Planting
Apr 15 2015	4	Moving	Jun 24 2015	9	Seeing	Sep 2 2015	**1**	**Moving**
Apr 16 2015	5	Transcending	Jun 25 2015	10	Intuiting	Sep 3 2015	2	Transcending
Apr 17 2015	6	Remembering	Jun 26 2015	11	Evolving	Sep 4 2015	3	Remembering
Apr 18 2015	7	Loving	Jun 27 2015	12	Self-Regulating	Sep 5 2015	4	Loving
Apr 19 2015	8	Feeling	Jun 28 2015	13	Catalyzing	Sep 6 2015	5	Feeling
Apr 20 2015	9	Devoting	Jun 29 2015	**1**	**Enlightening**	Sep 7 2015	6	Devoting
Apr 21 2015	10	Illuminating	Jun 30 2015	2	Being	Sep 8 2015	7	Illuminating
Apr 22 2015	11	Choosing	Jul 1 2015	3	Breathing	Sep 9 2015	8	Choosing
Apr 23 2015	12	Exploring	Jul 2 2015	4	Listening	Sep 10 2015	9	Exploring
Apr 24 2015	13	Healing	Jul 3 2015	5	Planting	Sep 11 2015	10	Healing
Apr 25 2015	**1**	**Seeing**	Jul 4 2015	6	Moving	Sep 12 2015	11	Seeing
Apr 26 2015	2	Intuiting	Jul 5 2015	7	Transcending	Sep 13 2015	12	Intuiting
Apr 27 2015	3	Evolving	Jul 6 2015	8	Remembering	Sep 14 2015	13	Evolving
Apr 28 2015	4	Self-Regulating	Jul 7 2015	9	Loving	Sep 15 2015	**1**	**Self-Regulating**
Apr 29 2015	5	Catalyzing	Jul 8 2015	10	Feeling	Sep 16 2015	2	Catalyzing
Apr 30 2015	6	Enlightening	Jul 9 2015	11	Devoting	Sep 17 2015	3	Enlightening
May 1 2015	7	Being	Jul 10 2015	12	Illuminating	Sep 18 2015	4	Being
May 2 2015	8	Breathing	Jul 11 2015	13	Choosing	Sep 19 2015	5	Breathing
May 3 2015	9	Listening	Jul 12 2015	**1**	**Exploring**	Sep 20 2015	6	Listening
May 4 2015	10	Planting	Jul 13 2015	2	Healing	Sep 21 2015	7	Planting
May 5 2015	11	Moving	Jul 14 2015	3	Seeing	Sep 22 2015	8	Moving
May 6 2015	12	Transcending	Jul 15 2015	4	Intuiting	Sep 23 2015	9	Transcending
May 7 2015	13	Remembering	Jul 16 2015	5	Evolving	Sep 24 2015	10	Remembering
May 8 2015	**1**	**Loving**	Jul 17 2015	6	Self-Regulating	Sep 25 2015	11	Loving
May 9 2015	2	Feeling	Jul 18 2015	7	Catalyzing	Sep 26 2015	12	Feeling
May 10 2015	3	Devoting	Jul 19 2015	8	Enlightening	Sep 27 2015	13	Devoting
May 11 2015	4	Illuminating	Jul 20 2015	9	Being	Sep 28 2015	**1**	**Illuminating**
May 12 2015	5	Choosing	Jul 21 2015	10	Breathing	Sep 29 2015	2	Choosing
May 13 2015	6	Exploring	Jul 22 2015	11	Listening	Sep 30 2015	3	Exploring
May 14 2015	7	Healing	Jul 23 2015	12	Planting	Oct 1 2015	4	Healing
May 15 2015	8	Seeing	Jul 24 2015	13	Moving	Oct 2 2015	5	Seeing
May 16 2015	9	Intuiting	Jul 25 2015	**1**	**Transcending**	Oct 3 2015	6	Intuiting
May 17 2015	10	Evolving	Jul 26 2015	2	Remembering	Oct 4 2015	7	Evolving
May 18 2015	11	Self-Regulating	Jul 27 2015	3	Loving	Oct 5 2015	8	Self-Regulating
May 19 2015	12	Catalyzing	Jul 28 2015	4	Feeling	Oct 6 2015	9	Catalyzing
May 20 2015	13	Enlightening	Jul 29 2015	5	Devoting	Oct 7 2015	10	Enlightening
May 21 2015	**1**	**Being**	Jul 30 2015	6	Illuminating	Oct 8 2015	11	Being
May 22 2015	2	Breathing	Jul 31 2015	7	Choosing	Oct 9 2015	12	Breathing
May 23 2015	3	Listening	Aug 1 2015	8	Exploring	Oct 10 2015	13	Listening
May 24 2015	4	Planting	Aug 2 2015	9	Healing	Oct 11 2015	**1**	**Planting**
May 25 2015	5	Moving	Aug 3 2015	10	Seeing	Oct 12 2015	2	Moving
May 26 2015	6	Transcending	Aug 4 2015	11	Intuiting	Oct 13 2015	3	Transcending
May 27 2015	7	Remembering	Aug 5 2015	12	Evolving	Oct 14 2015	4	Remembering
May 28 2015	8	Loving	Aug 6 2015	13	Self-Regulating	Oct 15 2015	5	Loving
May 29 2015	9	Feeling	Aug 7 2015	**1**	**Catalyzing**	Oct 16 2015	6	Feeling
May 30 2015	10	Devoting	Aug 8 2015	2	Enlightening	Oct 17 2015	7	Devoting
May 31 2015	11	Illuminating	Aug 9 2015	3	Being	Oct 18 2015	8	Illuminating
Jun 1 2015	12	Choosing	Aug 10 2015	4	Breathing	Oct 19 2015	9	Choosing
Jun 2 2015	13	Exploring	Aug 11 2015	5	Listening	Oct 20 2015	10	Exploring
Jun 3 2015	**1**	**Healing**	Aug 12 2015	6	Planting	Oct 21 2015	11	Healing
Jun 4 2015	2	Seeing	Aug 13 2015	7	Moving	Oct 22 2015	12	Seeing
Jun 5 2015	3	Intuiting	Aug 14 2015	8	Transcending	Oct 23 2015	13	Intuiting
Jun 6 2015	4	Evolving	Aug 15 2015	9	Remembering	Oct 24 2015	**1**	**Evolving**
Jun 7 2015	5	Self-Regulating	Aug 16 2015	10	Loving	Oct 25 2015	2	Self-Regulating
Jun 8 2015	6	Catalyzing	Aug 17 2015	11	Feeling	Oct 26 2015	3	Catalyzing
Jun 9 2015	7	Enlightening	Aug 18 2015	12	Devoting	Oct 27 2015	4	Enlightening

Date	UE	Earth Energy	Date	UE	Earth Energy	Date	UE	Earth Energy
Oct 28 2015	5	Being	Jan 6 2016	10	Illuminating	Mar 16 2016	2	Being
Oct 29 2015	6	Breathing	Jan 7 2016	11	Choosing	Mar 17 2016	3	Breathing
Oct 30 2015	7	Listening	Jan 8 2016	12	Exploring	Mar 18 2016	4	Listening
Oct 31 2015	8	Planting	Jan 9 2016	13	Healing	Mar 19 2016	5	Planting
Nov 1 2015	9	Moving	Jan 10 2016	**1**	**Seeing**	Mar 20 2016	6	Moving
Nov 2 2015	10	Transcending	Jan 11 2016	2	Intuiting	Mar 21 2016	7	Transcending
Nov 3 2015	11	Remembering	Jan 12 2016	3	Evolving	Mar 22 2016	8	Remembering
Nov 4 2015	12	Loving	Jan 13 2016	4	Self-Regulating	Mar 23 2016	9	Loving
Nov 5 2015	13	Feeling	Jan 14 2016	5	Catalyzing	Mar 24 2016	10	Feeling
Nov 6 2015	**1**	**Devoting**	Jan 15 2016	6	Enlightening	Mar 25 2016	11	Devoting
Nov 7 2015	2	Illuminating	Jan 16 2016	7	Being	Mar 26 2016	12	Illuminating
Nov 8 2015	3	Choosing	Jan 17 2016	8	Breathing	Mar 27 2016	13	Choosing
Nov 9 2015	4	Exploring	Jan 18 2016	9	Listening	Mar 28 2016	**1**	**Exploring**
Nov 10 2015	5	Healing	Jan 19 2016	10	Planting	Mar 29 2016	2	Healing
Nov 11 2015	6	Seeing	Jan 20 2016	11	Moving	Mar 30 2016	3	Seeing
Nov 12 2015	7	Intuiting	Jan 21 2016	12	Transcending	Mar 31 2016	4	Intuiting
Nov 13 2015	8	Evolving	Jan 22 2016	13	Remembering	Apr 1 2016	5	Evolving
Nov 14 2015	9	Self-Regulating	Jan 23 2016	**1**	**Loving**	Apr 2 2016	6	Self-Regulating
Nov 15 2015	10	Catalyzing	Jan 24 2016	2	Feeling	Apr 3 2016	7	Catalyzing
Nov 16 2015	11	Enlightening	Jan 25 2016	3	Devoting	Apr 4 2016	8	Enlightening
Nov 17 2015	12	Being	Jan 26 2016	4	Illuminating	Apr 5 2016	9	Being
Nov 18 2015	13	Breathing	Jan 27 2016	5	Choosing	Apr 6 2016	10	Breathing
Nov 19 2015	**1**	**Listening**	Jan 28 2016	6	Exploring	Apr 7 2016	11	Listening
Nov 20 2015	2	Planting	Jan 29 2016	7	Healing	Apr 8 2016	12	Planting
Nov 21 2015	3	Moving	Jan 30 2016	8	Seeing	Apr 9 2016	13	Moving
Nov 22 2015	4	Transcending	Jan 31 2016	9	Intuiting	Apr 10 2016	**1**	**Transcending**
Nov 23 2015	5	Remembering	Feb 1 2016	10	Evolving	Apr 11 2016	2	Remembering
Nov 24 2015	6	Loving	Feb 2 2016	11	Self-Regulating	Apr 12 2016	3	Loving
Nov 25 2015	7	Feeling	Feb 3 2016	12	Catalyzing	Apr 13 2016	4	Feeling
Nov 26 2015	8	Devoting	Feb 4 2016	13	Enlightening	Apr 14 2016	5	Devoting
Nov 27 2015	9	Illuminating	Feb 5 2016	**1**	**Being**	Apr 15 2016	6	Illuminating
Nov 28 2015	10	Choosing	Feb 6 2016	2	Breathing	Apr 16 2016	7	Choosing
Nov 29 2015	11	Exploring	Feb 7 2016	3	Listening	Apr 17 2016	8	Exploring
Nov 30 2015	12	Healing	Feb 8 2016	4	Planting	Apr 18 2016	9	Healing
Dec 1 2015	13	Seeing	Feb 9 2016	5	Moving	Apr 19 2016	10	Seeing
Dec 2 2015	**1**	**Intuiting**	Feb 10 2016	6	Transcending	Apr 20 2016	11	Intuiting
Dec 3 2015	2	Evolving	Feb 11 2016	7	Remembering	Apr 21 2016	12	Evolving
Dec 4 2015	3	Self-Regulating	Feb 12 2016	8	Loving	Apr 22 2016	13	Self-Regulating
Dec 5 2015	4	Catalyzing	Feb 13 2016	9	Feeling	Apr 23 2016	**1**	**Catalyzing**
Dec 6 2015	5	Enlightening	Feb 14 2016	10	Devoting	Apr 24 2016	2	Enlightening
Dec 7 2015	6	Being	Feb 15 2016	11	Illuminating	Apr 25 2016	3	Being
Dec 8 2015	7	Breathing	Feb 16 2016	12	Choosing	Apr 26 2016	4	Breathing
Dec 9 2015	8	Listening	Feb 17 2016	13	Exploring	Apr 27 2016	5	Listening
Dec 10 2015	9	Planting	Feb 18 2016	**1**	**Healing**	Apr 28 2016	6	Planting
Dec 11 2015	10	Moving	Feb 19 2016	2	Seeing	Apr 29 2016	7	Moving
Dec 12 2015	11	Transcending	Feb 20 2016	3	Intuiting	Apr 30 2016	8	Transcending
Dec 13 2015	12	Remembering	Feb 21 2016	4	Evolving	May 1 2016	9	Remembering
Dec 14 2015	13	Loving	Feb 22 2016	5	Self-Regulating	May 2 2016	10	Loving
Dec 15 2015	**1**	**Feeling**	Feb 23 2016	6	Catalyzing	May 3 2016	11	Feeling
Dec 16 2015	2	Devoting	Feb 24 2016	7	Enlightening	May 4 2016	12	Devoting
Dec 17 2015	3	Illuminating	Feb 25 2016	8	Being	May 5 2016	13	Illuminating
Dec 18 2015	4	Choosing	Feb 26 2016	9	Breathing	May 6 2016	**1**	**Choosing**
Dec 19 2015	5	Exploring	Feb 27 2016	10	Listening	May 7 2016	2	Exploring
Dec 20 2015	6	Healing	Feb 28 2016	11	Planting	May 8 2016	3	Healing
Dec 21 2015	7	Seeing	Feb 29 2016	12	Moving	May 9 2016	4	Seeing
Dec 22 2015	8	Intuiting	Mar 1 2016	13	Transcending	May 10 2016	5	Intuiting
Dec 23 2015	9	Evolving	Mar 2 2016	**1**	**Remembering**	May 11 2016	6	Evolving
Dec 24 2015	10	Self-Regulating	Mar 3 2016	2	Loving	May 12 2016	7	Self-Regulating
Dec 25 2015	11	Catalyzing	Mar 4 2016	3	Feeling	May 13 2016	8	Catalyzing
Dec 26 2015	12	Enlightening	Mar 5 2016	4	Devoting	May 14 2016	9	Enlightening
Dec 27 2015	13	Being	Mar 6 2016	5	Illuminating	May 15 2016	10	Being
Dec 28 2015	**1**	**Breathing**	Mar 7 2016	6	Choosing	May 16 2016	11	Breathing
Dec 29 2015	2	Listening	Mar 8 2016	7	Exploring	May 17 2016	12	Listening
Dec 30 2015	3	Planting	Mar 9 2016	8	Healing	May 18 2016	13	Planting
Dec 31 2015	4	Moving	Mar 10 2016	9	Seeing	May 19 2016	**1**	**Moving**
Jan 1 2016	5	Transcending	Mar 11 2016	10	Intuiting	May 20 2016	2	Transcending
Jan 2 2016	6	Remembering	Mar 12 2016	11	Evolving	May 21 2016	3	Remembering
Jan 3 2016	7	Loving	Mar 13 2016	12	Self-Regulating	May 22 2016	4	Loving
Jan 4 2016	8	Feeling	Mar 14 2016	13	Catalyzing	May 23 2016	5	Feeling
Jan 5 2016	9	Devoting	Mar 15 2016	**1**	**Enlightening**	May 24 2016	6	Devoting

Date	UE	Earth Energy	Date	UE	Earth Energy	Date	UE	Earth Energy
May 25 2016	7	Illuminating	Aug 3 2016	12	Being	Oct 12 2016	4	Illuminating
May 26 2016	8	Choosing	Aug 4 2016	13	Breathing	Oct 13 2016	5	Choosing
May 27 2016	9	Exploring	Aug 5 2016	**1**	**Listening**	Oct 14 2016	6	Exploring
May 28 2016	10	Healing	Aug 6 2016	2	Planting	Oct 15 2016	7	Healing
May 29 2016	11	Seeing	Aug 7 2016	3	Moving	Oct 16 2016	8	Seeing
May 30 2016	12	Intuiting	Aug 8 2016	4	Transcending	Oct 17 2016	9	Intuiting
May 31 2016	13	Evolving	Aug 9 2016	5	Remembering	Oct 18 2016	10	Evolving
Jun 1 2016	**1**	**Self-Regulating**	Aug 10 2016	6	Loving	Oct 19 2016	11	Self-Regulating
Jun 2 2016	2	Catalyzing	Aug 11 2016	7	Feeling	Oct 20 2016	12	Catalyzing
Jun 3 2016	3	Enlightening	Aug 12 2016	8	Devoting	Oct 21 2016	13	Enlightening
Jun 4 2016	4	Being	Aug 13 2016	9	Illuminating	Oct 22 2016	**1**	**Being**
Jun 5 2016	5	Breathing	Aug 14 2016	10	Choosing	Oct 23 2016	2	Breathing
Jun 6 2016	6	Listening	Aug 15 2016	11	Exploring	Oct 24 2016	3	Listening
Jun 7 2016	7	Planting	Aug 16 2016	12	Healing	Oct 25 2016	4	Planting
Jun 8 2016	8	Moving	Aug 17 2016	13	Seeing	Oct 26 2016	5	Moving
Jun 9 2016	9	Transcending	Aug 18 2016	**1**	**Intuiting**	Oct 27 2016	6	Transcending
Jun 10 2016	10	Remembering	Aug 19 2016	2	Evolving	Oct 28 2016	7	Remembering
Jun 11 2016	11	Loving	Aug 20 2016	3	Self-Regulating	Oct 29 2016	8	Loving
Jun 12 2016	12	Feeling	Aug 21 2016	4	Catalyzing	Oct 30 2016	9	Feeling
Jun 13 2016	13	Devoting	Aug 22 2016	5	Enlightening	Oct 31 2016	10	Devoting
Jun 14 2016	**1**	**Illuminating**	Aug 23 2016	6	Being	Nov 1 2016	11	Illuminating
Jun 15 2016	2	Choosing	Aug 24 2016	7	Breathing	Nov 2 2016	12	Choosing
Jun 16 2016	3	Exploring	Aug 25 2016	8	Listening	Nov 3 2016	13	Exploring
Jun 17 2016	4	Healing	Aug 26 2016	9	Planting	Nov 4 2016	**1**	**Healing**
Jun 18 2016	5	Seeing	Aug 27 2016	10	Moving	Nov 5 2016	2	Seeing
Jun 19 2016	6	Intuiting	Aug 28 2016	11	Transcending	Nov 6 2016	3	Intuiting
Jun 20 2016	7	Evolving	Aug 29 2016	12	Remembering	Nov 7 2016	4	Evolving
Jun 21 2016	8	Self-Regulating	Aug 30 2016	13	Loving	Nov 8 2016	5	Self-Regulating
Jun 22 2016	9	Catalyzing	Aug 31 2016	**1**	**Feeling**	Nov 9 2016	6	Catalyzing
Jun 23 2016	10	Enlightening	Sep 1 2016	2	Devoting	Nov 10 2016	7	Enlightening
Jun 24 2016	11	Being	Sep 2 2016	3	Illuminating	Nov 11 2016	8	Being
Jun 25 2016	12	Breathing	Sep 3 2016	4	Choosing	Nov 12 2016	9	Breathing
Jun 26 2016	13	Listening	Sep 4 2016	5	Exploring	Nov 13 2016	10	Listening
Jun 27 2016	**1**	**Planting**	Sep 5 2016	6	Healing	Nov 14 2016	11	Planting
Jun 28 2016	2	Moving	Sep 6 2016	7	Seeing	Nov 15 2016	12	Moving
Jun 29 2016	3	Transcending	Sep 7 2016	8	Intuiting	Nov 16 2016	13	Transcending
Jun 30 2016	4	Remembering	Sep 8 2016	9	Evolving	Nov 17 2016	**1**	**Remembering**
Jul 1 2016	5	Loving	Sep 9 2016	10	Self-Regulating	Nov 18 2016	2	Loving
Jul 2 2016	6	Feeling	Sep 10 2016	11	Catalyzing	Nov 19 2016	3	Feeling
Jul 3 2016	7	Devoting	Sep 11 2016	12	Enlightening	Nov 20 2016	4	Devoting
Jul 4 2016	8	Illuminating	Sep 12 2016	13	Being	Nov 21 2016	5	Illuminating
Jul 5 2016	9	Choosing	Sep 13 2016	**1**	**Breathing**	Nov 22 2016	6	Choosing
Jul 6 2016	10	Exploring	Sep 14 2016	2	Listening	Nov 23 2016	7	Exploring
Jul 7 2016	11	Healing	Sep 15 2016	3	Planting	Nov 24 2016	8	Healing
Jul 8 2016	12	Seeing	Sep 16 2016	4	Moving	Nov 25 2016	9	Seeing
Jul 9 2016	13	Intuiting	Sep 17 2016	5	Transcending	Nov 26 2016	10	Intuiting
Jul 10 2016	**1**	**Evolving**	Sep 18 2016	6	Remembering	Nov 27 2016	11	Evolving
Jul 11 2016	2	Self-Regulating	Sep 19 2016	7	Loving	Nov 28 2016	12	Self-Regulating
Jul 12 2016	3	Catalyzing	Sep 20 2016	8	Feeling	Nov 29 2016	13	Catalyzing
Jul 13 2016	4	Enlightening	Sep 21 2016	9	Devoting	Nov 30 2016	**1**	**Enlightening**
Jul 14 2016	5	Being	Sep 22 2016	10	Illuminating	Dec 1 2016	2	Being
Jul 15 2016	6	Breathing	Sep 23 2016	11	Choosing	Dec 2 2016	3	Breathing
Jul 16 2016	7	Listening	Sep 24 2016	12	Exploring	Dec 3 2016	4	Listening
Jul 17 2016	8	Planting	Sep 25 2016	13	Healing	Dec 4 2016	5	Planting
Jul 18 2016	9	Moving	Sep 26 2016	**1**	**Seeing**	Dec 5 2016	6	Moving
Jul 19 2016	10	Transcending	Sep 27 2016	2	Intuiting	Dec 6 2016	7	Transcending
Jul 20 2016	11	Remembering	Sep 28 2016	3	Evolving	Dec 7 2016	8	Remembering
Jul 21 2016	12	Loving	Sep 29 2016	4	Self-Regulating	Dec 8 2016	9	Loving
Jul 22 2016	13	Feeling	Sep 30 2016	5	Catalyzing	Dec 9 2016	10	Feeling
Jul 23 2016	**1**	**Devoting**	Oct 1 2016	6	Enlightening	Dec 10 2016	11	Devoting
Jul 24 2016	2	Illuminating	Oct 2 2016	7	Being	Dec 11 2016	12	Illuminating
Jul 25 2016	3	Choosing	Oct 3 2016	8	Breathing	Dec 12 2016	13	Choosing
Jul 26 2016	4	Exploring	Oct 4 2016	9	Listening	Dec 13 2016	**1**	**Exploring**
Jul 27 2016	5	Healing	Oct 5 2016	10	Planting	Dec 14 2016	2	Healing
Jul 28 2016	6	Seeing	Oct 6 2016	11	Moving	Dec 15 2016	3	Seeing
Jul 29 2016	7	Intuiting	Oct 7 2016	12	Transcending	Dec 16 2016	4	Intuiting
Jul 30 2016	8	Evolving	Oct 8 2016	13	Remembering	Dec 17 2016	5	Evolving
Jul 31 2016	9	Self-Regulating	Oct 9 2016	**1**	**Loving**	Dec 18 2016	6	Self-Regulating
Aug 1 2016	10	Catalyzing	Oct 10 2016	2	Feeling	Dec 19 2016	7	Catalyzing
Aug 2 2016	11	Enlightening	Oct 11 2016	3	Devoting	Dec 20 2016	8	Enlightening

Date	UE	Earth Energy	Date	UE	Earth Energy	Date	UE	Earth Energy
Dec 21 2016	9	Being	Mar 1 2017	1	**Illuminating**	May 10 2017	6	Being
Dec 22 2016	10	Breathing	Mar 2 2017	2	Choosing	May 11 2017	7	Breathing
Dec 23 2016	11	Listening	Mar 3 2017	3	Exploring	May 12 2017	8	Listening
Dec 24 2016	12	Planting	Mar 4 2017	4	Healing	May 13 2017	9	Planting
Dec 25 2016	13	Moving	Mar 5 2017	5	Seeing	May 14 2017	10	Moving
Dec 26 2016	1	**Transcending**	Mar 6 2017	6	Intuiting	May 15 2017	11	Transcending
Dec 27 2016	2	Remembering	Mar 7 2017	7	Evolving	May 16 2017	12	Remembering
Dec 28 2016	3	Loving	Mar 8 2017	8	Self-Regulating	May 17 2017	13	Loving
Dec 29 2016	4	Feeling	Mar 9 2017	9	Catalyzing	May 18 2017	1	**Feeling**
Dec 30 2016	5	Devoting	Mar 10 2017	10	Enlightening	May 19 2017	2	Devoting
Dec 31 2016	6	Illuminating	Mar 11 2017	11	Being	May 20 2017	3	Illuminating
Jan 1 2017	7	Choosing	Mar 12 2017	12	Breathing	May 21 2017	4	Choosing
Jan 2 2017	8	Exploring	Mar 13 2017	13	Listening	May 22 2017	5	Exploring
Jan 3 2017	9	Healing	Mar 14 2017	1	**Planting**	May 23 2017	6	Healing
Jan 4 2017	10	Seeing	Mar 15 2017	2	Moving	May 24 2017	7	Seeing
Jan 5 2017	11	Intuiting	Mar 16 2017	3	Transcending	May 25 2017	8	Intuiting
Jan 6 2017	12	Evolving	Mar 17 2017	4	Remembering	May 26 2017	9	Evolving
Jan 7 2017	13	Self-Regulating	Mar 18 2017	5	Loving	May 27 2017	10	Self-Regulating
Jan 8 2017	1	**Catalyzing**	Mar 19 2017	6	Feeling	May 28 2017	11	Catalyzing
Jan 9 2017	2	Enlightening	Mar 20 2017	7	Devoting	May 29 2017	12	Enlightening
Jan 10 2017	3	Being	Mar 21 2017	8	Illuminating	May 30 2017	13	Being
Jan 11 2017	4	Breathing	Mar 22 2017	9	Choosing	May 31 2017	1	**Breathing**
Jan 12 2017	5	Listening	Mar 23 2017	10	Exploring	Jun 1 2017	2	Listening
Jan 13 2017	6	Planting	Mar 24 2017	11	Healing	Jun 2 2017	3	Planting
Jan 14 2017	7	Moving	Mar 25 2017	12	Seeing	Jun 3 2017	4	Moving
Jan 15 2017	8	Transcending	Mar 26 2017	13	Intuiting	Jun 4 2017	5	Transcending
Jan 16 2017	9	Remembering	Mar 27 2017	1	**Evolving**	Jun 5 2017	6	Remembering
Jan 17 2017	10	Loving	Mar 28 2017	2	Self-Regulating	Jun 6 2017	7	Loving
Jan 18 2017	11	Feeling	Mar 29 2017	3	Catalyzing	Jun 7 2017	8	Feeling
Jan 19 2017	12	Devoting	Mar 30 2017	4	Enlightening	Jun 8 2017	9	Devoting
Jan 20 2017	13	Illuminating	Mar 31 2017	5	Being	Jun 9 2017	10	Illuminating
Jan 21 2017	1	**Choosing**	Apr 1 2017	6	Breathing	Jun 10 2017	11	Choosing
Jan 22 2017	2	Exploring	Apr 2 2017	7	Listening	Jun 11 2017	12	Exploring
Jan 23 2017	3	Healing	Apr 3 2017	8	Planting	Jun 12 2017	13	Healing
Jan 24 2017	4	Seeing	Apr 4 2017	9	Moving	Jun 13 2017	1	**Seeing**
Jan 25 2017	5	Intuiting	Apr 5 2017	10	Transcending	Jun 14 2017	2	Intuiting
Jan 26 2017	6	Evolving	Apr 6 2017	11	Remembering	Jun 15 2017	3	Evolving
Jan 27 2017	7	Self-Regulating	Apr 7 2017	12	Loving	Jun 16 2017	4	Self-Regulating
Jan 28 2017	8	Catalyzing	Apr 8 2017	13	Feeling	Jun 17 2017	5	Catalyzing
Jan 29 2017	9	Enlightening	Apr 9 2017	1	**Devoting**	Jun 18 2017	6	Enlightening
Jan 30 2017	10	Being	Apr 10 2017	2	Illuminating	Jun 19 2017	7	Being
Jan 31 2017	11	Breathing	Apr 11 2017	3	Choosing	Jun 20 2017	8	Breathing
Feb 1 2017	12	Listening	Apr 12 2017	4	Exploring	Jun 21 2017	9	Listening
Feb 2 2017	13	Planting	Apr 13 2017	5	Healing	Jun 22 2017	10	Planting
Feb 3 2017	1	**Moving**	Apr 14 2017	6	Seeing	Jun 23 2017	11	Moving
Feb 4 2017	2	Transcending	Apr 15 2017	7	Intuiting	Jun 24 2017	12	Transcending
Feb 5 2017	3	Remembering	Apr 16 2017	8	Evolving	Jun 25 2017	13	Remembering
Feb 6 2017	4	Loving	Apr 17 2017	9	Self-Regulating	Jun 26 2017	1	**Loving**
Feb 7 2017	5	Feeling	Apr 18 2017	10	Catalyzing	Jun 27 2017	2	Feeling
Feb 8 2017	6	Devoting	Apr 19 2017	11	Enlightening	Jun 28 2017	3	Devoting
Feb 9 2017	7	Illuminating	Apr 20 2017	12	Being	Jun 29 2017	4	Illuminating
Feb 10 2017	8	Choosing	Apr 21 2017	13	Breathing	Jun 30 2017	5	Choosing
Feb 11 2017	9	Exploring	Apr 22 2017	1	**Listening**	Jul 1 2017	6	Exploring
Feb 12 2017	10	Healing	Apr 23 2017	2	Planting	Jul 2 2017	7	Healing
Feb 13 2017	11	Seeing	Apr 24 2017	3	Moving	Jul 3 2017	8	Seeing
Feb 14 2017	12	Intuiting	Apr 25 2017	4	Transcending	Jul 4 2017	9	Intuiting
Feb 15 2017	13	Evolving	Apr 26 2017	5	Remembering	Jul 5 2017	10	Evolving
Feb 16 2017	1	**Self-Regulating**	Apr 27 2017	6	Loving	Jul 6 2017	11	Self-Regulating
Feb 17 2017	2	Catalyzing	Apr 28 2017	7	Feeling	Jul 7 2017	12	Catalyzing
Feb 18 2017	3	Enlightening	Apr 29 2017	8	Devoting	Jul 8 2017	13	Enlightening
Feb 19 2017	4	Being	Apr 30 2017	9	Illuminating	Jul 9 2017	1	**Being**
Feb 20 2017	5	Breathing	May 1 2017	10	Choosing	Jul 10 2017	2	Breathing
Feb 21 2017	6	Listening	May 2 2017	11	Exploring	Jul 11 2017	3	Listening
Feb 22 2017	7	Planting	May 3 2017	12	Healing	Jul 12 2017	4	Planting
Feb 23 2017	8	Moving	May 4 2017	13	Seeing	Jul 13 2017	5	Moving
Feb 24 2017	9	Transcending	May 5 2017	1	**Intuiting**	Jul 14 2017	6	Transcending
Feb 25 2017	10	Remembering	May 6 2017	2	Evolving	Jul 15 2017	7	Remembering
Feb 26 2017	11	Loving	May 7 2017	3	Self-Regulating	Jul 16 2017	8	Loving
Feb 27 2017	12	Feeling	May 8 2017	4	Catalyzing	Jul 17 2017	9	Feeling
Feb 28 2017	13	Devoting	May 9 2017	5	Enlightening	Jul 18 2017	10	Devoting

Date	UE	Earth Energy	Date	UE	Earth Energy	Date	UE	Earth Energy
Jul 19 2017	11	Illuminating	Sep 27 2017	3	Being	Dec 6 2017	8	Illuminating
Jul 20 2017	12	Choosing	Sep 28 2017	4	Breathing	Dec 7 2017	9	Choosing
Jul 21 2017	13	Exploring	Sep 29 2017	5	Listening	Dec 8 2017	10	Exploring
Jul 22 2017	1	**Healing**	Sep 30 2017	6	Planting	Dec 9 2017	11	Healing
Jul 23 2017	2	Seeing	Oct 1 2017	7	Moving	Dec 10 2017	12	Seeing
Jul 24 2017	3	Intuiting	Oct 2 2017	8	Transcending	Dec 11 2017	13	Intuiting
Jul 25 2017	4	Evolving	Oct 3 2017	9	Remembering	Dec 12 2017	1	**Evolving**
Jul 26 2017	5	Self-Regulating	Oct 4 2017	10	Loving	Dec 13 2017	2	Self-Regulating
Jul 27 2017	6	Catalyzing	Oct 5 2017	11	Feeling	Dec 14 2017	3	Catalyzing
Jul 28 2017	7	Enlightening	Oct 6 2017	12	Devoting	Dec 15 2017	4	Enlightening
Jul 29 2017	8	Being	Oct 7 2017	13	Illuminating	Dec 16 2017	5	Being
Jul 30 2017	9	Breathing	Oct 8 2017	1	**Choosing**	Dec 17 2017	6	Breathing
Jul 31 2017	10	Listening	Oct 9 2017	2	Exploring	Dec 18 2017	7	Listening
Aug 1 2017	11	Planting	Oct 10 2017	3	Healing	Dec 19 2017	8	Planting
Aug 2 2017	12	Moving	Oct 11 2017	4	Seeing	Dec 20 2017	9	Moving
Aug 3 2017	13	Transcending	Oct 12 2017	5	Intuiting	Dec 21 2017	10	Transcending
Aug 4 2017	1	**Remembering**	Oct 13 2017	6	Evolving	Dec 22 2017	11	Remembering
Aug 5 2017	2	Loving	Oct 14 2017	7	Self-Regulating	Dec 23 2017	12	Loving
Aug 6 2017	3	Feeling	Oct 15 2017	8	Catalyzing	Dec 24 2017	13	Feeling
Aug 7 2017	4	Devoting	Oct 16 2017	9	Enlightening	Dec 25 2017	1	**Devoting**
Aug 8 2017	5	Illuminating	Oct 17 2017	10	Being	Dec 26 2017	2	Illuminating
Aug 9 2017	6	Choosing	Oct 18 2017	11	Breathing	Dec 27 2017	3	Choosing
Aug 10 2017	7	Exploring	Oct 19 2017	12	Listening	Dec 28 2017	4	Exploring
Aug 11 2017	8	Healing	Oct 20 2017	13	Planting	Dec 29 2017	5	Healing
Aug 12 2017	9	Seeing	Oct 21 2017	1	**Moving**	Dec 30 2017	6	Seeing
Aug 13 2017	10	Intuiting	Oct 22 2017	2	Transcending	Dec 31 2017	7	Intuiting
Aug 14 2017	11	Evolving	Oct 23 2017	3	Remembering	Jan 1 2018	8	Evolving
Aug 15 2017	12	Self-Regulating	Oct 24 2017	4	Loving	Jan 2 2018	9	Self-Regulating
Aug 16 2017	13	Catalyzing	Oct 25 2017	5	Feeling	Jan 3 2018	10	Catalyzing
Aug 17 2017	1	**Enlightening**	Oct 26 2017	6	Devoting	Jan 4 2018	11	Enlightening
Aug 18 2017	2	Being	Oct 27 2017	7	Illuminating	Jan 5 2018	12	Being
Aug 19 2017	3	Breathing	Oct 28 2017	8	Choosing	Jan 6 2018	13	Breathing
Aug 20 2017	4	Listening	Oct 29 2017	9	Exploring	Jan 7 2018	1	**Listening**
Aug 21 2017	5	Planting	Oct 30 2017	10	Healing	Jan 8 2018	2	Planting
Aug 22 2017	6	Moving	Oct 31 2017	11	Seeing	Jan 9 2018	3	Moving
Aug 23 2017	7	Transcending	Nov 1 2017	12	Intuiting	Jan 10 2018	4	Transcending
Aug 24 2017	8	Remembering	Nov 2 2017	13	Evolving	Jan 11 2018	5	Remembering
Aug 25 2017	9	Loving	Nov 3 2017	1	**Self-Regulating**	Jan 12 2018	6	Loving
Aug 26 2017	10	Feeling	Nov 4 2017	2	Catalyzing	Jan 13 2018	7	Feeling
Aug 27 2017	11	Devoting	Nov 5 2017	3	Enlightening	Jan 14 2018	8	Devoting
Aug 28 2017	12	Illuminating	Nov 6 2017	4	Being	Jan 15 2018	9	Illuminating
Aug 29 2017	13	Choosing	Nov 7 2017	5	Breathing	Jan 16 2018	10	Choosing
Aug 30 2017	1	**Exploring**	Nov 8 2017	6	Listening	Jan 17 2018	11	Exploring
Aug 31 2017	2	Healing	Nov 9 2017	7	Planting	Jan 18 2018	12	Healing
Sep 1 2017	3	Seeing	Nov 10 2017	8	Moving	Jan 19 2018	13	Seeing
Sep 2 2017	4	Intuiting	Nov 11 2017	9	Transcending	Jan 20 2018	1	**Intuiting**
Sep 3 2017	5	Evolving	Nov 12 2017	10	Remembering	Jan 21 2018	2	Evolving
Sep 4 2017	6	Self-Regulating	Nov 13 2017	11	Loving	Jan 22 2018	3	Self-Regulating
Sep 5 2017	7	Catalyzing	Nov 14 2017	12	Feeling	Jan 23 2018	4	Catalyzing
Sep 6 2017	8	Enlightening	Nov 15 2017	13	Devoting	Jan 24 2018	5	Enlightening
Sep 7 2017	9	Being	Nov 16 2017	1	**Illuminating**	Jan 25 2018	6	Being
Sep 8 2017	10	Breathing	Nov 17 2017	2	Choosing	Jan 26 2018	7	Breathing
Sep 9 2017	11	Listening	Nov 18 2017	3	Exploring	Jan 27 2018	8	Listening
Sep 10 2017	12	Planting	Nov 19 2017	4	Healing	Jan 28 2018	9	Planting
Sep 11 2017	13	Moving	Nov 20 2017	5	Seeing	Jan 29 2018	10	Moving
Sep 12 2017	1	**Transcending**	Nov 21 2017	6	Intuiting	Jan 30 2018	11	Transcending
Sep 13 2017	2	Remembering	Nov 22 2017	7	Evolving	Jan 31 2018	12	Remembering
Sep 14 2017	3	Loving	Nov 23 2017	8	Self-Regulating	Feb 1 2018	13	Loving
Sep 15 2017	4	Feeling	Nov 24 2017	9	Catalyzing	Feb 2 2018	1	**Feeling**
Sep 16 2017	5	Devoting	Nov 25 2017	10	Enlightening	Feb 3 2018	2	Devoting
Sep 17 2017	6	Illuminating	Nov 26 2017	11	Being	Feb 4 2018	3	Illuminating
Sep 18 2017	7	Choosing	Nov 27 2017	12	Breathing	Feb 5 2018	4	Choosing
Sep 19 2017	8	Exploring	Nov 28 2017	13	Listening	Feb 6 2018	5	Exploring
Sep 20 2017	9	Healing	Nov 29 2017	1	**Planting**	Feb 7 2018	6	Healing
Sep 21 2017	10	Seeing	Nov 30 2017	2	Moving	Feb 8 2018	7	Seeing
Sep 22 2017	11	Intuiting	Dec 1 2017	3	Transcending	Feb 9 2018	8	Intuiting
Sep 23 2017	12	Evolving	Dec 2 2017	4	Remembering	Feb 10 2018	9	Evolving
Sep 24 2017	13	Self-Regulating	Dec 3 2017	5	Loving	Feb 11 2018	10	Self-Regulating
Sep 25 2017	1	**Catalyzing**	Dec 4 2017	6	Feeling	Feb 12 2018	11	Catalyzing
Sep 26 2017	2	Enlightening	Dec 5 2017	7	Devoting	Feb 13 2018	12	Enlightening

Date	UE	Earth Energy	Date	UE	Earth Energy	Date	UE	Earth Energy
Feb 14 2018	13	Being	Apr 25 2018	5	Illuminating	Jul 4 2018	10	Being
Feb 15 2018	1	**Breathing**	Apr 26 2018	6	Choosing	Jul 5 2018	11	Breathing
Feb 16 2018	2	Listening	Apr 27 2018	7	Exploring	Jul 6 2018	12	Listening
Feb 17 2018	3	Planting	Apr 28 2018	8	Healing	Jul 7 2018	13	Planting
Feb 18 2018	4	Moving	Apr 29 2018	9	Seeing	Jul 8 2018	1	**Moving**
Feb 19 2018	5	Transcending	Apr 30 2018	10	Intuiting	Jul 9 2018	2	Transcending
Feb 20 2018	6	Remembering	May 1 2018	11	Evolving	Jul 10 2018	3	Remembering
Feb 21 2018	7	Loving	May 2 2018	12	Self-Regulating	Jul 11 2018	4	Loving
Feb 22 2018	8	Feeling	May 3 2018	13	Catalyzing	Jul 12 2018	5	Feeling
Feb 23 2018	9	Devoting	May 4 2018	1	**Enlightening**	Jul 13 2018	6	Devoting
Feb 24 2018	10	Illuminating	May 5 2018	2	Being	Jul 14 2018	7	Illuminating
Feb 25 2018	11	Choosing	May 6 2018	3	Breathing	Jul 15 2018	8	Choosing
Feb 26 2018	12	Exploring	May 7 2018	4	Listening	Jul 16 2018	9	Exploring
Feb 27 2018	13	Healing	May 8 2018	5	Planting	Jul 17 2018	10	Healing
Feb 28 2018	1	**Seeing**	May 9 2018	6	Moving	Jul 18 2018	11	Seeing
Mar 1 2018	2	Intuiting	May 10 2018	7	Transcending	Jul 19 2018	12	Intuiting
Mar 2 2018	3	Evolving	May 11 2018	8	Remembering	Jul 20 2018	13	Evolving
Mar 3 2018	4	Self-Regulating	May 12 2018	9	Loving	Jul 21 2018	1	**Self-Regulating**
Mar 4 2018	5	Catalyzing	May 13 2018	10	Feeling	Jul 22 2018	2	Catalyzing
Mar 5 2018	6	Enlightening	May 14 2018	11	Devoting	Jul 23 2018	3	Enlightening
Mar 6 2018	7	Being	May 15 2018	12	Illuminating	Jul 24 2018	4	Being
Mar 7 2018	8	Breathing	May 16 2018	13	Choosing	Jul 25 2018	5	Breathing
Mar 8 2018	9	Listening	May 17 2018	1	**Exploring**	Jul 26 2018	6	Listening
Mar 9 2018	10	Planting	May 18 2018	2	Healing	Jul 27 2018	7	Planting
Mar 10 2018	11	Moving	May 19 2018	3	Seeing	Jul 28 2018	8	Moving
Mar 11 2018	12	Transcending	May 20 2018	4	Intuiting	Jul 29 2018	9	Transcending
Mar 12 2018	13	Remembering	May 21 2018	5	Evolving	Jul 30 2018	10	Remembering
Mar 13 2018	1	**Loving**	May 22 2018	6	Self-Regulating	Jul 31 2018	11	Loving
Mar 14 2018	2	Feeling	May 23 2018	7	Catalyzing	Aug 1 2018	12	Feeling
Mar 15 2018	3	Devoting	May 24 2018	8	Enlightening	Aug 2 2018	13	Devoting
Mar 16 2018	4	Illuminating	May 25 2018	9	Being	Aug 3 2018	1	**Illuminating**
Mar 17 2018	5	Choosing	May 26 2018	10	Breathing	Aug 4 2018	2	Choosing
Mar 18 2018	6	Exploring	May 27 2018	11	Listening	Aug 5 2018	3	Exploring
Mar 19 2018	7	Healing	May 28 2018	12	Planting	Aug 6 2018	4	Healing
Mar 20 2018	8	Seeing	May 29 2018	13	Moving	Aug 7 2018	5	Seeing
Mar 21 2018	9	Intuiting	May 30 2018	1	**Transcending**	Aug 8 2018	6	Intuiting
Mar 22 2018	10	Evolving	May 31 2018	2	Remembering	Aug 9 2018	7	Evolving
Mar 23 2018	11	Self-Regulating	Jun 1 2018	3	Loving	Aug 10 2018	8	Self-Regulating
Mar 24 2018	12	Catalyzing	Jun 2 2018	4	Feeling	Aug 11 2018	9	Catalyzing
Mar 25 2018	13	Enlightening	Jun 3 2018	5	Devoting	Aug 12 2018	10	Enlightening
Mar 26 2018	1	**Being**	Jun 4 2018	6	Illuminating	Aug 13 2018	11	Being
Mar 27 2018	2	Breathing	Jun 5 2018	7	Choosing	Aug 14 2018	12	Breathing
Mar 28 2018	3	Listening	Jun 6 2018	8	Exploring	Aug 15 2018	13	Listening
Mar 29 2018	4	Planting	Jun 7 2018	9	Healing	Aug 16 2018	1	**Planting**
Mar 30 2018	5	Moving	Jun 8 2018	10	Seeing	Aug 17 2018	2	Moving
Mar 31 2018	6	Transcending	Jun 9 2018	11	Intuiting	Aug 18 2018	3	Transcending
Apr 1 2018	7	Remembering	Jun 10 2018	12	Evolving	Aug 19 2018	4	Remembering
Apr 2 2018	8	Loving	Jun 11 2018	13	Self-Regulating	Aug 20 2018	5	Loving
Apr 3 2018	9	Feeling	Jun 12 2018	1	**Catalyzing**	Aug 21 2018	6	Feeling
Apr 4 2018	10	Devoting	Jun 13 2018	2	Enlightening	Aug 22 2018	7	Devoting
Apr 5 2018	11	Illuminating	Jun 14 2018	3	Being	Aug 23 2018	8	Illuminating
Apr 6 2018	12	Choosing	Jun 15 2018	4	Breathing	Aug 24 2018	9	Choosing
Apr 7 2018	13	Exploring	Jun 16 2018	5	Listening	Aug 25 2018	10	Exploring
Apr 8 2018	1	**Healing**	Jun 17 2018	6	Planting	Aug 26 2018	11	Healing
Apr 9 2018	2	Seeing	Jun 18 2018	7	Moving	Aug 27 2018	12	Seeing
Apr 10 2018	3	Intuiting	Jun 19 2018	8	Transcending	Aug 28 2018	13	Intuiting
Apr 11 2018	4	Evolving	Jun 20 2018	9	Remembering	Aug 29 2018	1	**Evolving**
Apr 12 2018	5	Self-Regulating	Jun 21 2018	10	Loving	Aug 30 2018	2	Self-Regulating
Apr 13 2018	6	Catalyzing	Jun 22 2018	11	Feeling	Aug 31 2018	3	Catalyzing
Apr 14 2018	7	Enlightening	Jun 23 2018	12	Devoting	Sep 1 2018	4	Enlightening
Apr 15 2018	8	Being	Jun 24 2018	13	Illuminating	Sep 2 2018	5	Being
Apr 16 2018	9	Breathing	Jun 25 2018	1	**Choosing**	Sep 3 2018	6	Breathing
Apr 17 2018	10	Listening	Jun 26 2018	2	Exploring	Sep 4 2018	7	Listening
Apr 18 2018	11	Planting	Jun 27 2018	3	Healing	Sep 5 2018	8	Planting
Apr 19 2018	12	Moving	Jun 28 2018	4	Seeing	Sep 6 2018	9	Moving
Apr 20 2018	13	Transcending	Jun 29 2018	5	Intuiting	Sep 7 2018	10	Transcending
Apr 21 2018	1	**Remembering**	Jun 30 2018	6	Evolving	Sep 8 2018	11	Remembering
Apr 22 2018	2	Loving	Jul 1 2018	7	Self-Regulating	Sep 9 2018	12	Loving
Apr 23 2018	3	Feeling	Jul 2 2018	8	Catalyzing	Sep 10 2018	13	Feeling
Apr 24 2018	4	Devoting	Jul 3 2018	9	Enlightening	Sep 11 2018	1	**Devoting**

Date	UE	Earth Energy	Date	UE	Earth Energy	Date	UE	Earth Energy
Sep 12 2018	2	Illuminating	Nov 21 2018	7	Being	Jan 30 2019	12	Illuminating
Sep 13 2018	3	Choosing	Nov 22 2018	8	Breathing	Jan 31 2019	13	Choosing
Sep 14 2018	4	Exploring	Nov 23 2018	9	Listening	Feb 1 2019	**1**	**Exploring**
Sep 15 2018	5	Healing	Nov 24 2018	10	Planting	Feb 2 2019	2	Healing
Sep 16 2018	6	Seeing	Nov 25 2018	11	Moving	Feb 3 2019	3	Seeing
Sep 17 2018	7	Intuiting	Nov 26 2018	12	Transcending	Feb 4 2019	4	Intuiting
Sep 18 2018	8	Evolving	Nov 27 2018	13	Remembering	Feb 5 2019	5	Evolving
Sep 19 2018	9	Self-Regulating	Nov 28 2018	**1**	**Loving**	Feb 6 2019	6	Self-Regulating
Sep 20 2018	10	Catalyzing	Nov 29 2018	2	Feeling	Feb 7 2019	7	Catalyzing
Sep 21 2018	11	Enlightening	Nov 30 2018	3	Devoting	Feb 8 2019	8	Enlightening
Sep 22 2018	12	Being	Dec 1 2018	4	Illuminating	Feb 9 2019	9	Being
Sep 23 2018	13	Breathing	Dec 2 2018	5	Choosing	Feb 10 2019	10	Breathing
Sep 24 2018	**1**	**Listening**	Dec 3 2018	6	Exploring	Feb 11 2019	11	Listening
Sep 25 2018	2	Planting	Dec 4 2018	7	Healing	Feb 12 2019	12	Planting
Sep 26 2018	3	Moving	Dec 5 2018	8	Seeing	Feb 13 2019	13	Moving
Sep 27 2018	4	Transcending	Dec 6 2018	9	Intuiting	Feb 14 2019	**1**	**Transcending**
Sep 28 2018	5	Remembering	Dec 7 2018	10	Evolving	Feb 15 2019	2	Remembering
Sep 29 2018	6	Loving	Dec 8 2018	11	Self-Regulating	Feb 16 2019	3	Loving
Sep 30 2018	7	Feeling	Dec 9 2018	12	Catalyzing	Feb 17 2019	4	Feeling
Oct 1 2018	8	Devoting	Dec 10 2018	13	Enlightening	Feb 18 2019	5	Devoting
Oct 2 2018	9	Illuminating	Dec 11 2018	**1**	**Being**	Feb 19 2019	6	Illuminating
Oct 3 2018	10	Choosing	Dec 12 2018	2	Breathing	Feb 20 2019	7	Choosing
Oct 4 2018	11	Exploring	Dec 13 2018	3	Listening	Feb 21 2019	8	Exploring
Oct 5 2018	12	Healing	Dec 14 2018	4	Planting	Feb 22 2019	9	Healing
Oct 6 2018	13	Seeing	Dec 15 2018	5	Moving	Feb 23 2019	10	Seeing
Oct 7 2018	**1**	**Intuiting**	Dec 16 2018	6	Transcending	Feb 24 2019	11	Intuiting
Oct 8 2018	2	Evolving	Dec 17 2018	7	Remembering	Feb 25 2019	12	Evolving
Oct 9 2018	3	Self-Regulating	Dec 18 2018	8	Loving	Feb 26 2019	13	Self-Regulating
Oct 10 2018	4	Catalyzing	Dec 19 2018	9	Feeling	Feb 27 2019	**1**	**Catalyzing**
Oct 11 2018	5	Enlightening	Dec 20 2018	10	Devoting	Feb 28 2019	2	Enlightening
Oct 12 2018	6	Being	Dec 21 2018	11	Illuminating	Mar 1 2019	3	Being
Oct 13 2018	7	Breathing	Dec 22 2018	12	Choosing	Mar 2 2019	4	Breathing
Oct 14 2018	8	Listening	Dec 23 2018	13	Exploring	Mar 3 2019	5	Listening
Oct 15 2018	9	Planting	Dec 24 2018	**1**	**Healing**	Mar 4 2019	6	Planting
Oct 16 2018	10	Moving	Dec 25 2018	2	Seeing	Mar 5 2019	7	Moving
Oct 17 2018	11	Transcending	Dec 26 2018	3	Intuiting	Mar 6 2019	8	Transcending
Oct 18 2018	12	Remembering	Dec 27 2018	4	Evolving	Mar 7 2019	9	Remembering
Oct 19 2018	13	Loving	Dec 28 2018	5	Self-Regulating	Mar 8 2019	10	Loving
Oct 20 2018	**1**	**Feeling**	Dec 29 2018	6	Catalyzing	Mar 9 2019	11	Feeling
Oct 21 2018	2	Devoting	Dec 30 2018	7	Enlightening	Mar 10 2019	12	Devoting
Oct 22 2018	3	Illuminating	Dec 31 2018	8	Being	Mar 11 2019	13	Illuminating
Oct 23 2018	4	Choosing	Jan 1 2019	9	Breathing	Mar 12 2019	**1**	**Choosing**
Oct 24 2018	5	Exploring	Jan 2 2019	10	Listening	Mar 13 2019	2	Exploring
Oct 25 2018	6	Healing	Jan 3 2019	11	Planting	Mar 14 2019	3	Healing
Oct 26 2018	7	Seeing	Jan 4 2019	12	Moving	Mar 15 2019	4	Seeing
Oct 27 2018	8	Intuiting	Jan 5 2019	13	Transcending	Mar 16 2019	5	Intuiting
Oct 28 2018	9	Evolving	Jan 6 2019	**1**	**Remembering**	Mar 17 2019	6	Evolving
Oct 29 2018	10	Self-Regulating	Jan 7 2019	2	Loving	Mar 18 2019	7	Self-Regulating
Oct 30 2018	11	Catalyzing	Jan 8 2019	3	Feeling	Mar 19 2019	8	Catalyzing
Oct 31 2018	12	Enlightening	Jan 9 2019	4	Devoting	Mar 20 2019	9	Enlightening
Nov 1 2018	13	Being	Jan 10 2019	5	Illuminating	Mar 21 2019	10	Being
Nov 2 2018	**1**	**Breathing**	Jan 11 2019	6	Choosing	Mar 22 2019	11	Breathing
Nov 3 2018	2	Listening	Jan 12 2019	7	Exploring	Mar 23 2019	12	Listening
Nov 4 2018	3	Planting	Jan 13 2019	8	Healing	Mar 24 2019	13	Planting
Nov 5 2018	4	Moving	Jan 14 2019	9	Seeing	Mar 25 2019	**1**	**Moving**
Nov 6 2018	5	Transcending	Jan 15 2019	10	Intuiting	Mar 26 2019	2	Transcending
Nov 7 2018	6	Remembering	Jan 16 2019	11	Evolving	Mar 27 2019	3	Remembering
Nov 8 2018	7	Loving	Jan 17 2019	12	Self-Regulating	Mar 28 2019	4	Loving
Nov 9 2018	8	Feeling	Jan 18 2019	13	Catalyzing	Mar 29 2019	5	Feeling
Nov 10 2018	9	Devoting	Jan 19 2019	**1**	**Enlightening**	Mar 30 2019	6	Devoting
Nov 11 2018	10	Illuminating	Jan 20 2019	2	Being	Mar 31 2019	7	Illuminating
Nov 12 2018	11	Choosing	Jan 21 2019	3	Breathing	Apr 1 2019	8	Choosing
Nov 13 2018	12	Exploring	Jan 22 2019	4	Listening	Apr 2 2019	9	Exploring
Nov 14 2018	13	Healing	Jan 23 2019	5	Planting	Apr 3 2019	10	Healing
Nov 15 2018	**1**	**Seeing**	Jan 24 2019	6	Moving	Apr 4 2019	11	Seeing
Nov 16 2018	2	Intuiting	Jan 25 2019	7	Transcending	Apr 5 2019	12	Intuiting
Nov 17 2018	3	Evolving	Jan 26 2019	8	Remembering	Apr 6 2019	13	Evolving
Nov 18 2018	4	Self-Regulating	Jan 27 2019	9	Loving	Apr 7 2019	**1**	**Self-Regulating**
Nov 19 2018	5	Catalyzing	Jan 28 2019	10	Feeling	Apr 8 2019	2	Catalyzing
Nov 20 2018	6	Enlightening	Jan 29 2019	11	Devoting	Apr 9 2019	3	Enlightening

Date	UE	Earth Energy	Date	UE	Earth Energy	Date	UE	Earth Energy
Apr 10 2019	4	Being	Jun 19 2019	9	Illuminating	Aug 28 2019	1	**Being**
Apr 11 2019	5	Breathing	Jun 20 2019	10	Choosing	Aug 29 2019	2	Breathing
Apr 12 2019	6	Listening	Jun 21 2019	11	Exploring	Aug 30 2019	3	Listening
Apr 13 2019	7	Planting	Jun 22 2019	12	Healing	Aug 31 2019	4	Planting
Apr 14 2019	8	Moving	Jun 23 2019	13	Seeing	Sep 1 2019	5	Moving
Apr 15 2019	9	Transcending	Jun 24 2019	1	**Intuiting**	Sep 2 2019	6	Transcending
Apr 16 2019	10	Remembering	Jun 25 2019	2	Evolving	Sep 3 2019	7	Remembering
Apr 17 2019	11	Loving	Jun 26 2019	3	Self-Regulating	Sep 4 2019	8	Loving
Apr 18 2019	12	Feeling	Jun 27 2019	4	Catalyzing	Sep 5 2019	9	Feeling
Apr 19 2019	13	Devoting	Jun 28 2019	5	Enlightening	Sep 6 2019	10	Devoting
Apr 20 2019	1	**Illuminating**	Jun 29 2019	6	Being	Sep 7 2019	11	Illuminating
Apr 21 2019	2	Choosing	Jun 30 2019	7	Breathing	Sep 8 2019	12	Choosing
Apr 22 2019	3	Exploring	Jul 1 2019	8	Listening	Sep 9 2019	13	Exploring
Apr 23 2019	4	Healing	Jul 2 2019	9	Planting	Sep 10 2019	1	**Healing**
Apr 24 2019	5	Seeing	Jul 3 2019	10	Moving	Sep 11 2019	2	Seeing
Apr 25 2019	6	Intuiting	Jul 4 2019	11	Transcending	Sep 12 2019	3	Intuiting
Apr 26 2019	7	Evolving	Jul 5 2019	12	Remembering	Sep 13 2019	4	Evolving
Apr 27 2019	8	Self-Regulating	Jul 6 2019	13	Loving	Sep 14 2019	5	Self-Regulating
Apr 28 2019	9	Catalyzing	Jul 7 2019	1	**Feeling**	Sep 15 2019	6	Catalyzing
Apr 29 2019	10	Enlightening	Jul 8 2019	2	Devoting	Sep 16 2019	7	Enlightening
Apr 30 2019	11	Being	Jul 9 2019	3	Illuminating	Sep 17 2019	8	Being
May 1 2019	12	Breathing	Jul 10 2019	4	Choosing	Sep 18 2019	9	Breathing
May 2 2019	13	Listening	Jul 11 2019	5	Exploring	Sep 19 2019	10	Listening
May 3 2019	1	**Planting**	Jul 12 2019	6	Healing	Sep 20 2019	11	Planting
May 4 2019	2	Moving	Jul 13 2019	7	Seeing	Sep 21 2019	12	Moving
May 5 2019	3	Transcending	Jul 14 2019	8	Intuiting	Sep 22 2019	13	Transcending
May 6 2019	4	Remembering	Jul 15 2019	9	Evolving	Sep 23 2019	1	**Remembering**
May 7 2019	5	Loving	Jul 16 2019	10	Self-Regulating	Sep 24 2019	2	Loving
May 8 2019	6	Feeling	Jul 17 2019	11	Catalyzing	Sep 25 2019	3	Feeling
May 9 2019	7	Devoting	Jul 18 2019	12	Enlightening	Sep 26 2019	4	Devoting
May 10 2019	8	Illuminating	Jul 19 2019	13	Being	Sep 27 2019	5	Illuminating
May 11 2019	9	Choosing	Jul 20 2019	1	**Breathing**	Sep 28 2019	6	Choosing
May 12 2019	10	Exploring	Jul 21 2019	2	Listening	Sep 29 2019	7	Exploring
May 13 2019	11	Healing	Jul 22 2019	3	Planting	Sep 30 2019	8	Healing
May 14 2019	12	Seeing	Jul 23 2019	4	Moving	Oct 1 2019	9	Seeing
May 15 2019	13	Intuiting	Jul 24 2019	5	Transcending	Oct 2 2019	10	Intuiting
May 16 2019	1	**Evolving**	Jul 25 2019	6	Remembering	Oct 3 2019	11	Evolving
May 17 2019	2	Self-Regulating	Jul 26 2019	7	Loving	Oct 4 2019	12	Self-Regulating
May 18 2019	3	Catalyzing	Jul 27 2019	8	Feeling	Oct 5 2019	13	Catalyzing
May 19 2019	4	Enlightening	Jul 28 2019	9	Devoting	Oct 6 2019	1	**Enlightening**
May 20 2019	5	Being	Jul 29 2019	10	Illuminating	Oct 7 2019	2	Being
May 21 2019	6	Breathing	Jul 30 2019	11	Choosing	Oct 8 2019	3	Breathing
May 22 2019	7	Listening	Jul 31 2019	12	Exploring	Oct 9 2019	4	Listening
May 23 2019	8	Planting	Aug 1 2019	13	Healing	Oct 10 2019	5	Planting
May 24 2019	9	Moving	Aug 2 2019	1	**Seeing**	Oct 11 2019	6	Moving
May 25 2019	10	Transcending	Aug 3 2019	2	Intuiting	Oct 12 2019	7	Transcending
May 26 2019	11	Remembering	Aug 4 2019	3	Evolving	Oct 13 2019	8	Remembering
May 27 2019	12	Loving	Aug 5 2019	4	Self-Regulating	Oct 14 2019	9	Loving
May 28 2019	13	Feeling	Aug 6 2019	5	Catalyzing	Oct 15 2019	10	Feeling
May 29 2019	1	**Devoting**	Aug 7 2019	6	Enlightening	Oct 16 2019	11	Devoting
May 30 2019	2	Illuminating	Aug 8 2019	7	Being	Oct 17 2019	12	Illuminating
May 31 2019	3	Choosing	Aug 9 2019	8	Breathing	Oct 18 2019	13	Choosing
Jun 1 2019	4	Exploring	Aug 10 2019	9	Listening	Oct 19 2019	1	**Exploring**
Jun 2 2019	5	Healing	Aug 11 2019	10	Planting	Oct 20 2019	2	Healing
Jun 3 2019	6	Seeing	Aug 12 2019	11	Moving	Oct 21 2019	3	Seeing
Jun 4 2019	7	Intuiting	Aug 13 2019	12	Transcending	Oct 22 2019	4	Intuiting
Jun 5 2019	8	Evolving	Aug 14 2019	13	Remembering	Oct 23 2019	5	Evolving
Jun 6 2019	9	Self-Regulating	Aug 15 2019	1	**Loving**	Oct 24 2019	6	Self-Regulating
Jun 7 2019	10	Catalyzing	Aug 16 2019	2	Feeling	Oct 25 2019	7	Catalyzing
Jun 8 2019	11	Enlightening	Aug 17 2019	3	Devoting	Oct 26 2019	8	Enlightening
Jun 9 2019	12	Being	Aug 18 2019	4	Illuminating	Oct 27 2019	9	Being
Jun 10 2019	13	Breathing	Aug 19 2019	5	Choosing	Oct 28 2019	10	Breathing
Jun 11 2019	1	**Listening**	Aug 20 2019	6	Exploring	Oct 29 2019	11	Listening
Jun 12 2019	2	Planting	Aug 21 2019	7	Healing	Oct 30 2019	12	Planting
Jun 13 2019	3	Moving	Aug 22 2019	8	Seeing	Oct 31 2019	13	Moving
Jun 14 2019	4	Transcending	Aug 23 2019	9	Intuiting	Nov 1 2019	1	**Transcending**
Jun 15 2019	5	Remembering	Aug 24 2019	10	Evolving	Nov 2 2019	2	Remembering
Jun 16 2019	6	Loving	Aug 25 2019	11	Self-Regulating	Nov 3 2019	3	Loving
Jun 17 2019	7	Feeling	Aug 26 2019	12	Catalyzing	Nov 4 2019	4	Feeling
Jun 18 2019	8	Devoting	Aug 27 2019	13	Enlightening	Nov 5 2019	5	Devoting

Date	UE	Earth Energy	Date	UE	Earth Energy	Date	UE	Earth Energy
Nov 6 2019	6	Illuminating	Jan 15 2020	11	Being	Mar 25 2020	3	Illuminating
Nov 7 2019	7	Choosing	Jan 16 2020	12	Breathing	Mar 26 2020	4	Choosing
Nov 8 2019	8	Exploring	Jan 17 2020	13	Listening	Mar 27 2020	5	Exploring
Nov 9 2019	9	Healing	Jan 18 2020	**1**	**Planting**	Mar 28 2020	6	Healing
Nov 10 2019	10	Seeing	Jan 19 2020	2	Moving	Mar 29 2020	7	Seeing
Nov 11 2019	11	Intuiting	Jan 20 2020	3	Transcending	Mar 30 2020	8	Intuiting
Nov 12 2019	12	Evolving	Jan 21 2020	4	Remembering	Mar 31 2020	9	Evolving
Nov 13 2019	13	Self-Regulating	Jan 22 2020	5	Loving	Apr 1 2020	10	Self-Regulating
Nov 14 2019	**1**	**Catalyzing**	Jan 23 2020	6	Feeling	Apr 2 2020	11	Catalyzing
Nov 15 2019	2	Enlightening	Jan 24 2020	7	Devoting	Apr 3 2020	12	Enlightening
Nov 16 2019	3	Being	Jan 25 2020	8	Illuminating	Apr 4 2020	13	Being
Nov 17 2019	4	Breathing	Jan 26 2020	9	Choosing	Apr 5 2020	**1**	**Breathing**
Nov 18 2019	5	Listening	Jan 27 2020	10	Exploring	Apr 6 2020	2	Listening
Nov 19 2019	6	Planting	Jan 28 2020	11	Healing	Apr 7 2020	3	Planting
Nov 20 2019	7	Moving	Jan 29 2020	12	Seeing	Apr 8 2020	4	Moving
Nov 21 2019	8	Transcending	Jan 30 2020	13	Intuiting	Apr 9 2020	5	Transcending
Nov 22 2019	9	Remembering	Jan 31 2020	**1**	**Evolving**	Apr 10 2020	6	Remembering
Nov 23 2019	10	Loving	Feb 1 2020	2	Self-Regulating	Apr 11 2020	7	Loving
Nov 24 2019	11	Feeling	Feb 2 2020	3	Catalyzing	Apr 12 2020	8	Feeling
Nov 25 2019	12	Devoting	Feb 3 2020	4	Enlightening	Apr 13 2020	9	Devoting
Nov 26 2019	13	Illuminating	Feb 4 2020	5	Being	Apr 14 2020	10	Illuminating
Nov 27 2019	**1**	**Choosing**	Feb 5 2020	6	Breathing	Apr 15 2020	11	Choosing
Nov 28 2019	2	Exploring	Feb 6 2020	7	Listening	Apr 16 2020	12	Exploring
Nov 29 2019	3	Healing	Feb 7 2020	8	Planting	Apr 17 2020	13	Healing
Nov 30 2019	4	Seeing	Feb 8 2020	9	Moving	Apr 18 2020	**1**	**Seeing**
Dec 1 2019	5	Intuiting	Feb 9 2020	10	Transcending	Apr 19 2020	2	Intuiting
Dec 2 2019	6	Evolving	Feb 10 2020	11	Remembering	Apr 20 2020	3	Evolving
Dec 3 2019	7	Self-Regulating	Feb 11 2020	12	Loving	Apr 21 2020	4	Self-Regulating
Dec 4 2019	8	Catalyzing	Feb 12 2020	13	Feeling	Apr 22 2020	5	Catalyzing
Dec 5 2019	9	Enlightening	Feb 13 2020	**1**	**Devoting**	Apr 23 2020	6	Enlightening
Dec 6 2019	10	Being	Feb 14 2020	2	Illuminating	Apr 24 2020	7	Being
Dec 7 2019	11	Breathing	Feb 15 2020	3	Choosing	Apr 25 2020	8	Breathing
Dec 8 2019	12	Listening	Feb 16 2020	4	Exploring	Apr 26 2020	9	Listening
Dec 9 2019	13	Planting	Feb 17 2020	5	Healing	Apr 27 2020	10	Planting
Dec 10 2019	**1**	**Moving**	Feb 18 2020	6	Seeing	Apr 28 2020	11	Moving
Dec 11 2019	2	Transcending	Feb 19 2020	7	Intuiting	Apr 29 2020	12	Transcending
Dec 12 2019	3	Remembering	Feb 20 2020	8	Evolving	Apr 30 2020	13	Remembering
Dec 13 2019	4	Loving	Feb 21 2020	9	Self-Regulating	May 1 2020	**1**	**Loving**
Dec 14 2019	5	Feeling	Feb 22 2020	10	Catalyzing	May 2 2020	2	Feeling
Dec 15 2019	6	Devoting	Feb 23 2020	11	Enlightening	May 3 2020	3	Devoting
Dec 16 2019	7	Illuminating	Feb 24 2020	12	Being	May 4 2020	4	Illuminating
Dec 17 2019	8	Choosing	Feb 25 2020	13	Breathing	May 5 2020	5	Choosing
Dec 18 2019	9	Exploring	Feb 26 2020	**1**	**Listening**	May 6 2020	6	Exploring
Dec 19 2019	10	Healing	Feb 27 2020	2	Planting	May 7 2020	7	Healing
Dec 20 2019	11	Seeing	Feb 28 2020	3	Moving	May 8 2020	8	Seeing
Dec 21 2019	12	Intuiting	Feb 29 2020	4	Transcending	May 9 2020	9	Intuiting
Dec 22 2019	13	Evolving	Mar 1 2020	5	Remembering	May 10 2020	10	Loving
Dec 23 2019	**1**	**Self-Regulating**	Mar 2 2020	6	Loving	May 11 2020	11	Self-Regulating
Dec 24 2019	2	Catalyzing	Mar 3 2020	7	Feeling	May 12 2020	12	Catalyzing
Dec 25 2019	3	Enlightening	Mar 4 2020	8	Devoting	May 13 2020	13	Enlightening
Dec 26 2019	4	Being	Mar 5 2020	9	Illuminating	May 14 2020	**1**	**Being**
Dec 27 2019	5	Breathing	Mar 6 2020	10	Choosing	May 15 2020	2	Breathing
Dec 28 2019	6	Listening	Mar 7 2020	11	Exploring	May 16 2020	3	Listening
Dec 29 2019	7	Planting	Mar 8 2020	12	Healing	May 17 2020	4	Planting
Dec 30 2019	8	Moving	Mar 9 2020	13	Seeing	May 18 2020	5	Moving
Dec 31 2019	9	Transcending	Mar 10 2020	**1**	**Intuiting**	May 19 2020	6	Transcending
Jan 1 2020	10	Remembering	Mar 11 2020	2	Evolving	May 20 2020	7	Remembering
Jan 2 2020	11	Loving	Mar 12 2020	3	Self-Regulating	May 21 2020	8	Loving
Jan 3 2020	12	Feeling	Mar 13 2020	4	Catalyzing	May 22 2020	9	Feeling
Jan 4 2020	13	Devoting	Mar 14 2020	5	Enlightening	May 23 2020	10	Devoting
Jan 5 2020	**1**	**Illuminating**	Mar 15 2020	6	Being	May 24 2020	11	Illuminating
Jan 6 2020	2	Choosing	Mar 16 2020	7	Breathing	May 25 2020	12	Choosing
Jan 7 2020	3	Exploring	Mar 17 2020	8	Listening	May 26 2020	13	Exploring
Jan 8 2020	4	Healing	Mar 18 2020	9	Planting	May 27 2020	**1**	**Healing**
Jan 9 2020	5	Seeing	Mar 19 2020	10	Moving	May 28 2020	2	Seeing
Jan 10 2020	6	Intuiting	Mar 20 2020	11	Transcending	May 29 2020	3	Intuiting
Jan 11 2020	7	Evolving	Mar 21 2020	12	Remembering	May 30 2020	4	Evolving
Jan 12 2020	8	Self-Regulating	Mar 22 2020	13	Loving	May 31 2020	5	Self-Regulating
Jan 13 2020	9	Catalyzing	Mar 23 2020	**1**	**Feeling**	Jun 1 2020	6	Catalyzing
Jan 14 2020	10	Enlightening	Mar 24 2020	2	Devoting	Jun 2 2020	7	Enlightening

Date	UE	Earth Energy	Date	UE	Earth Energy	Date	UE	Earth Energy
Jun 3 2020	8	Being	Aug 12 2020	13	Illuminating	Oct 21 2020	5	Being
Jun 4 2020	9	Breathing	Aug 13 2020	**1**	**Choosing**	Oct 22 2020	6	Breathing
Jun 5 2020	10	Listening	Aug 14 2020	2	Exploring	Oct 23 2020	7	Listening
Jun 6 2020	11	Planting	Aug 15 2020	3	Healing	Oct 24 2020	8	Planting
Jun 7 2020	12	Moving	Aug 16 2020	4	Seeing	Oct 25 2020	9	Moving
Jun 8 2020	13	Transcending	Aug 17 2020	5	Intuiting	Oct 26 2020	10	Transcending
Jun 9 2020	**1**	**Remembering**	Aug 18 2020	6	Evolving	Oct 27 2020	11	Remembering
Jun 10 2020	2	Loving	Aug 19 2020	7	Self-Regulating	Oct 28 2020	12	Loving
Jun 11 2020	3	Feeling	Aug 20 2020	8	Catalyzing	Oct 29 2020	13	Feeling
Jun 12 2020	4	Devoting	Aug 21 2020	9	Enlightening	Oct 30 2020	**1**	**Devoting**
Jun 13 2020	5	Illuminating	Aug 22 2020	10	Being	Oct 31 2020	2	Illuminating
Jun 14 2020	6	Choosing	Aug 23 2020	11	Breathing	Nov 1 2020	3	Choosing
Jun 15 2020	7	Exploring	Aug 24 2020	12	Listening	Nov 2 2020	4	Exploring
Jun 16 2020	8	Healing	Aug 25 2020	13	Planting	Nov 3 2020	5	Healing
Jun 17 2020	9	Seeing	Aug 26 2020	**1**	**Moving**	Nov 4 2020	6	Seeing
Jun 18 2020	10	Intuiting	Aug 27 2020	2	Transcending	Nov 5 2020	7	Intuiting
Jun 19 2020	11	Evolving	Aug 28 2020	3	Remembering	Nov 6 2020	8	Evolving
Jun 20 2020	12	Self-Regulating	Aug 29 2020	4	Loving	Nov 7 2020	9	Self-Regulating
Jun 21 2020	13	Catalyzing	Aug 30 2020	5	Feeling	Nov 8 2020	10	Catalyzing
Jun 22 2020	**1**	**Enlightening**	Aug 31 2020	6	Devoting	Nov 9 2020	11	Enlightening
Jun 23 2020	2	Being	Sep 1 2020	7	Illuminating	Nov 10 2020	12	Being
Jun 24 2020	3	Breathing	Sep 2 2020	8	Choosing	Nov 11 2020	13	Breathing
Jun 25 2020	4	Listening	Sep 3 2020	9	Exploring	Nov 12 2020	**1**	**Listening**
Jun 26 2020	5	Planting	Sep 4 2020	10	Healing	Nov 13 2020	2	Planting
Jun 27 2020	6	Moving	Sep 5 2020	11	Seeing	Nov 14 2020	3	Moving
Jun 28 2020	7	Transcending	Sep 6 2020	12	Intuiting	Nov 15 2020	4	Transcending
Jun 29 2020	8	Remembering	Sep 7 2020	13	Evolving	Nov 16 2020	5	Remembering
Jun 30 2020	9	Loving	Sep 8 2020	**1**	**Self-Regulating**	Nov 17 2020	6	Loving
Jul 1 2020	10	Feeling	Sep 9 2020	2	Catalyzing	Nov 18 2020	7	Feeling
Jul 2 2020	11	Devoting	Sep 10 2020	3	Enlightening	Nov 19 2020	8	Devoting
Jul 3 2020	12	Illuminating	Sep 11 2020	4	Being	Nov 20 2020	9	Illuminating
Jul 4 2020	13	Choosing	Sep 12 2020	5	Breathing	Nov 21 2020	10	Choosing
Jul 5 2020	**1**	**Exploring**	Sep 13 2020	6	Listening	Nov 22 2020	11	Exploring
Jul 6 2020	2	Healing	Sep 14 2020	7	Planting	Nov 23 2020	12	Healing
Jul 7 2020	3	Seeing	Sep 15 2020	8	Moving	Nov 24 2020	13	Seeing
Jul 8 2020	4	Intuiting	Sep 16 2020	9	Transcending	Nov 25 2020	**1**	**Intuiting**
Jul 9 2020	5	Evolving	Sep 17 2020	10	Remembering	Nov 26 2020	2	Evolving
Jul 10 2020	6	Self-Regulating	Sep 18 2020	11	Loving	Nov 27 2020	3	Self-Regulating
Jul 11 2020	7	Catalyzing	Sep 19 2020	12	Feeling	Nov 28 2020	4	Catalyzing
Jul 12 2020	8	Enlightening	Sep 20 2020	13	Devoting	Nov 29 2020	5	Enlightening
Jul 13 2020	9	Being	Sep 21 2020	**1**	**Illuminating**	Nov 30 2020	6	Being
Jul 14 2020	10	Breathing	Sep 22 2020	2	Choosing	Dec 1 2020	7	Breathing
Jul 15 2020	11	Listening	Sep 23 2020	3	Exploring	Dec 2 2020	8	Listening
Jul 16 2020	12	Planting	Sep 24 2020	4	Healing	Dec 3 2020	9	Planting
Jul 17 2020	13	Moving	Sep 25 2020	5	Seeing	Dec 4 2020	10	Moving
Jul 18 2020	**1**	**Transcending**	Sep 26 2020	6	Intuiting	Dec 5 2020	11	Transcending
Jul 19 2020	2	Remembering	Sep 27 2020	7	Evolving	Dec 6 2020	12	Remembering
Jul 20 2020	3	Loving	Sep 28 2020	8	Self-Regulating	Dec 7 2020	13	Loving
Jul 21 2020	4	Feeling	Sep 29 2020	9	Catalyzing	Dec 8 2020	**1**	**Feeling**
Jul 22 2020	5	Devoting	Sep 30 2020	10	Enlightening	Dec 9 2020	2	Devoting
Jul 23 2020	6	Illuminating	Oct 1 2020	11	Being	Dec 10 2020	3	Illuminating
Jul 24 2020	7	Choosing	Oct 2 2020	12	Breathing	Dec 11 2020	4	Choosing
Jul 25 2020	8	Exploring	Oct 3 2020	13	Listening	Dec 12 2020	5	Exploring
Jul 26 2020	9	Healing	Oct 4 2020	**1**	**Planting**	Dec 13 2020	6	Healing
Jul 27 2020	10	Seeing	Oct 5 2020	2	Moving	Dec 14 2020	7	Seeing
Jul 28 2020	11	Intuiting	Oct 6 2020	3	Transcending	Dec 15 2020	8	Intuiting
Jul 29 2020	12	Evolving	Oct 7 2020	4	Remembering	Dec 16 2020	9	Evolving
Jul 30 2020	13	Self-Regulating	Oct 8 2020	5	Loving	Dec 17 2020	10	Self-Regulating
Jul 31 2020	**1**	**Catalyzing**	Oct 9 2020	6	Feeling	Dec 18 2020	11	Catalyzing
Aug 1 2020	2	Enlightening	Oct 10 2020	7	Devoting	Dec 19 2020	12	Enlightening
Aug 2 2020	3	Being	Oct 11 2020	8	Illuminating	Dec 20 2020	13	Being
Aug 3 2020	4	Breathing	Oct 12 2020	9	Choosing	Dec 21 2020	**1**	**Breathing**
Aug 4 2020	5	Listening	Oct 13 2020	10	Exploring	Dec 22 2020	2	Listening
Aug 5 2020	6	Planting	Oct 14 2020	11	Healing	Dec 23 2020	3	Planting
Aug 6 2020	7	Moving	Oct 15 2020	12	Seeing	Dec 24 2020	4	Moving
Aug 7 2020	8	Transcending	Oct 16 2020	13	Intuiting	Dec 25 2020	5	Transcending
Aug 8 2020	9	Remembering	Oct 17 2020	**1**	**Evolving**	Dec 26 2020	6	Remembering
Aug 9 2020	10	Loving	Oct 18 2020	2	Self-Regulating	Dec 27 2020	7	Loving
Aug 10 2020	11	Feeling	Oct 19 2020	3	Catalyzing	Dec 28 2020	8	Feeling
Aug 11 2020	12	Devoting	Oct 20 2020	4	Enlightening	Dec 29 2020	9	Devoting

Date	UE Earth Energy	Date	UE Earth Energy	Date	UE Earth Energy
Dec 30 2020	10 Illuminating	Mar 10 2021	2 Being	May 19 2021	7 Illuminating
Dec 31 2020	11 Choosing	Mar 11 2021	3 Breathing	May 20 2021	8 Choosing
Jan 1 2021	12 Exploring	Mar 12 2021	4 Listening	May 21 2021	9 Exploring
Jan 2 2021	13 Healing	Mar 13 2021	5 Planting	May 22 2021	10 Healing
Jan 3 2021	**1 Seeing**	Mar 14 2021	6 Moving	May 23 2021	11 Seeing
Jan 4 2021	2 Intuiting	Mar 15 2021	7 Transcending	May 24 2021	12 Intuiting
Jan 5 2021	3 Evolving	Mar 16 2021	8 Remembering	May 25 2021	13 Evolving
Jan 6 2021	4 Self-Regulating	Mar 17 2021	9 Loving	May 26 2021	**1 Self-Regulating**
Jan 7 2021	5 Catalyzing	Mar 18 2021	10 Feeling	May 27 2021	2 Catalyzing
Jan 8 2021	6 Enlightening	Mar 19 2021	11 Devoting	May 28 2021	3 Enlightening
Jan 9 2021	7 Being	Mar 20 2021	12 Illuminating	May 29 2021	4 Being
Jan 10 2021	8 Breathing	Mar 21 2021	13 Choosing	May 30 2021	5 Breathing
Jan 11 2021	9 Listening	Mar 22 2021	**1 Exploring**	May 31 2021	6 Listening
Jan 12 2021	10 Planting	Mar 23 2021	2 Healing	Jun 1 2021	7 Planting
Jan 13 2021	11 Moving	Mar 24 2021	3 Seeing	Jun 2 2021	8 Moving
Jan 14 2021	12 Transcending	Mar 25 2021	4 Intuiting	Jun 3 2021	9 Transcending
Jan 15 2021	13 Remembering	Mar 26 2021	5 Evolving	Jun 4 2021	10 Remembering
Jan 16 2021	**1 Loving**	Mar 27 2021	6 Self-Regulating	Jun 5 2021	11 Loving
Jan 17 2021	2 Feeling	Mar 28 2021	7 Catalyzing	Jun 6 2021	12 Feeling
Jan 18 2021	3 Devoting	Mar 29 2021	8 Enlightening	Jun 7 2021	13 Devoting
Jan 19 2021	4 Illuminating	Mar 30 2021	9 Being	Jun 8 2021	**1 Illuminating**
Jan 20 2021	5 Choosing	Mar 31 2021	10 Breathing	Jun 9 2021	2 Choosing
Jan 21 2021	6 Exploring	Apr 1 2021	11 Listening	Jun 10 2021	3 Exploring
Jan 22 2021	7 Healing	Apr 2 2021	12 Planting	Jun 11 2021	4 Healing
Jan 23 2021	8 Seeing	Apr 3 2021	13 Moving	Jun 12 2021	5 Seeing
Jan 24 2021	9 Intuiting	Apr 4 2021	**1 Transcending**	Jun 13 2021	6 Intuiting
Jan 25 2021	10 Evolving	Apr 5 2021	2 Remembering	Jun 14 2021	7 Evolving
Jan 26 2021	11 Self-Regulating	Apr 6 2021	3 Loving	Jun 15 2021	8 Self-Regulating
Jan 27 2021	12 Catalyzing	Apr 7 2021	4 Feeling	Jun 16 2021	9 Catalyzing
Jan 28 2021	13 Enlightening	Apr 8 2021	5 Devoting	Jun 17 2021	10 Enlightening
Jan 29 2021	**1 Being**	Apr 9 2021	6 Illuminating	Jun 18 2021	11 Being
Jan 30 2021	2 Breathing	Apr 10 2021	7 Choosing	Jun 19 2021	12 Breathing
Jan 31 2021	3 Listening	Apr 11 2021	8 Exploring	Jun 20 2021	13 Listening
Feb 1 2021	4 Planting	Apr 12 2021	9 Healing	Jun 21 2021	**1 Planting**
Feb 2 2021	5 Moving	Apr 13 2021	10 Seeing	Jun 22 2021	2 Moving
Feb 3 2021	6 Transcending	Apr 14 2021	11 Intuiting	Jun 23 2021	3 Transcending
Feb 4 2021	7 Remembering	Apr 15 2021	12 Evolving	Jun 24 2021	4 Remembering
Feb 5 2021	8 Loving	Apr 16 2021	13 Self-Regulating	Jun 25 2021	5 Loving
Feb 6 2021	9 Feeling	Apr 17 2021	**1 Catalyzing**	Jun 26 2021	6 Feeling
Feb 7 2021	10 Devoting	Apr 18 2021	2 Enlightening	Jun 27 2021	7 Devoting
Feb 8 2021	11 Illuminating	Apr 19 2021	3 Being	Jun 28 2021	8 Illuminating
Feb 9 2021	12 Choosing	Apr 20 2021	4 Breathing	Jun 29 2021	9 Choosing
Feb 10 2021	13 Exploring	Apr 21 2021	5 Listening	Jun 30 2021	10 Exploring
Feb 11 2021	**1 Healing**	Apr 22 2021	6 Planting	Jul 1 2021	11 Healing
Feb 12 2021	2 Seeing	Apr 23 2021	7 Moving	Jul 2 2021	12 Seeing
Feb 13 2021	3 Intuiting	Apr 24 2021	8 Transcending	Jul 3 2021	13 Intuiting
Feb 14 2021	4 Evolving	Apr 25 2021	9 Remembering	Jul 4 2021	**1 Evolving**
Feb 15 2021	5 Self-Regulating	Apr 26 2021	10 Loving	Jul 5 2021	2 Self-Regulating
Feb 16 2021	6 Catalyzing	Apr 27 2021	11 Feeling	Jul 6 2021	3 Catalyzing
Feb 17 2021	7 Enlightening	Apr 28 2021	12 Devoting	Jul 7 2021	4 Enlightening
Feb 18 2021	8 Being	Apr 29 2021	13 Illuminating	Jul 8 2021	5 Being
Feb 19 2021	9 Breathing	Apr 30 2021	**1 Choosing**	Jul 9 2021	6 Breathing
Feb 20 2021	10 Listening	May 1 2021	2 Exploring	Jul 10 2021	7 Listening
Feb 21 2021	11 Planting	May 2 2021	3 Healing	Jul 11 2021	8 Planting
Feb 22 2021	12 Moving	May 3 2021	4 Seeing	Jul 12 2021	9 Moving
Feb 23 2021	13 Transcending	May 4 2021	5 Intuiting	Jul 13 2021	10 Transcending
Feb 24 2021	**1 Remembering**	May 5 2021	6 Evolving	Jul 14 2021	11 Remembering
Feb 25 2021	2 Loving	May 6 2021	7 Self-Regulating	Jul 15 2021	12 Loving
Feb 26 2021	3 Feeling	May 7 2021	8 Catalyzing	Jul 16 2021	13 Feeling
Feb 27 2021	4 Devoting	May 8 2021	9 Enlightening	Jul 17 2021	**1 Devoting**
Feb 28 2021	5 Illuminating	May 9 2021	10 Being	Jul 18 2021	2 Illuminating
Mar 1 2021	6 Choosing	May 10 2021	11 Breathing	Jul 19 2021	3 Choosing
Mar 2 2021	7 Exploring	May 11 2021	12 Listening	Jul 20 2021	4 Exploring
Mar 3 2021	8 Healing	May 12 2021	13 Planting	Jul 21 2021	5 Healing
Mar 4 2021	9 Seeing	May 13 2021	**1 Moving**	Jul 22 2021	6 Seeing
Mar 5 2021	10 Intuiting	May 14 2021	2 Transcending	Jul 23 2021	7 Intuiting
Mar 6 2021	11 Evolving	May 15 2021	3 Remembering	Jul 24 2021	8 Evolving
Mar 7 2021	12 Self-Regulating	May 16 2021	4 Loving	Jul 25 2021	9 Self-Regulating
Mar 8 2021	13 Catalyzing	May 17 2021	5 Feeling	Jul 26 2021	10 Catalyzing
Mar 9 2021	**1 Enlightening**	May 18 2021	6 Devoting	Jul 27 2021	11 Enlightening

Date	UE	Earth Energy	Date	UE	Earth Energy	Date	UE	Earth Energy
Jul 28 2021	12	Being	Oct 6 2021	4	Illuminating	Dec 15 2021	9	Being
Jul 29 2021	13	Breathing	Oct 7 2021	5	Choosing	Dec 16 2021	10	Breathing
Jul 30 2021	1	**Listening**	Oct 8 2021	6	Exploring	Dec 17 2021	11	Listening
Jul 31 2021	2	Planting	Oct 9 2021	7	Healing	Dec 18 2021	12	Planting
Aug 1 2021	3	Moving	Oct 10 2021	8	Seeing	Dec 19 2021	13	Moving
Aug 2 2021	4	Transcending	Oct 11 2021	9	Intuiting	Dec 20 2021	1	**Transcending**
Aug 3 2021	5	Remembering	Oct 12 2021	10	Evolving	Dec 21 2021	2	Remembering
Aug 4 2021	6	Loving	Oct 13 2021	11	Self-Regulating	Dec 22 2021	3	Loving
Aug 5 2021	7	Feeling	Oct 14 2021	12	Catalyzing	Dec 23 2021	4	Feeling
Aug 6 2021	8	Devoting	Oct 15 2021	13	Enlightening	Dec 24 2021	5	Devoting
Aug 7 2021	9	Illuminating	Oct 16 2021	1	**Being**	Dec 25 2021	6	Illuminating
Aug 8 2021	10	Choosing	Oct 17 2021	2	Breathing	Dec 26 2021	7	Choosing
Aug 9 2021	11	Exploring	Oct 18 2021	3	Listening	Dec 27 2021	8	Exploring
Aug 10 2021	12	Healing	Oct 19 2021	4	Planting	Dec 28 2021	9	Healing
Aug 11 2021	13	Seeing	Oct 20 2021	5	Moving	Dec 29 2021	10	Seeing
Aug 12 2021	1	**Intuiting**	Oct 21 2021	6	Transcending	Dec 30 2021	11	Intuiting
Aug 13 2021	2	Evolving	Oct 22 2021	7	Remembering	Dec 31 2021	12	Evolving
Aug 14 2021	3	Self-Regulating	Oct 23 2021	8	Loving	Jan 1 2022	13	Self-Regulating
Aug 15 2021	4	Catalyzing	Oct 24 2021	9	Feeling	Jan 2 2022	1	**Catalyzing**
Aug 16 2021	5	Enlightening	Oct 25 2021	10	Devoting	Jan 3 2022	2	Enlightening
Aug 17 2021	6	Being	Oct 26 2021	11	Illuminating	Jan 4 2022	3	Being
Aug 18 2021	7	Breathing	Oct 27 2021	12	Choosing	Jan 5 2022	4	Breathing
Aug 19 2021	8	Listening	Oct 28 2021	13	Exploring	Jan 6 2022	5	Listening
Aug 20 2021	9	Planting	Oct 29 2021	1	**Healing**	Jan 7 2022	6	Planting
Aug 21 2021	10	Moving	Oct 30 2021	2	Seeing	Jan 8 2022	7	Moving
Aug 22 2021	11	Transcending	Oct 31 2021	3	Intuiting	Jan 9 2022	8	Transcending
Aug 23 2021	12	Remembering	Nov 1 2021	4	Evolving	Jan 10 2022	9	Remembering
Aug 24 2021	13	Loving	Nov 2 2021	5	Self-Regulating	Jan 11 2022	10	Loving
Aug 25 2021	1	**Feeling**	Nov 3 2021	6	Catalyzing	Jan 12 2022	11	Feeling
Aug 26 2021	2	Devoting	Nov 4 2021	7	Enlightening	Jan 13 2022	12	Devoting
Aug 27 2021	3	Illuminating	Nov 5 2021	8	Being	Jan 14 2022	13	Illuminating
Aug 28 2021	4	Choosing	Nov 6 2021	9	Breathing	Jan 15 2022	1	**Choosing**
Aug 29 2021	5	Exploring	Nov 7 2021	10	Listening	Jan 16 2022	2	Exploring
Aug 30 2021	6	Healing	Nov 8 2021	11	Planting	Jan 17 2022	3	Healing
Aug 31 2021	7	Seeing	Nov 9 2021	12	Moving	Jan 18 2022	4	Seeing
Sep 1 2021	8	Intuiting	Nov 10 2021	13	Transcending	Jan 19 2022	5	Intuiting
Sep 2 2021	9	Evolving	Nov 11 2021	1	**Remembering**	Jan 20 2022	6	Evolving
Sep 3 2021	10	Self-Regulating	Nov 12 2021	2	Loving	Jan 21 2022	7	Self-Regulating
Sep 4 2021	11	Catalyzing	Nov 13 2021	3	Feeling	Jan 22 2022	8	Catalyzing
Sep 5 2021	12	Enlightening	Nov 14 2021	4	Devoting	Jan 23 2022	9	Enlightening
Sep 6 2021	13	Being	Nov 15 2021	5	Illuminating	Jan 24 2022	10	Being
Sep 7 2021	1	**Breathing**	Nov 16 2021	6	Choosing	Jan 25 2022	11	Breathing
Sep 8 2021	2	Listening	Nov 17 2021	7	Exploring	Jan 26 2022	12	Listening
Sep 9 2021	3	Planting	Nov 18 2021	8	Healing	Jan 27 2022	13	Planting
Sep 10 2021	4	Moving	Nov 19 2021	9	Seeing	Jan 28 2022	1	**Moving**
Sep 11 2021	5	Transcending	Nov 20 2021	10	Intuiting	Jan 29 2022	2	Transcending
Sep 12 2021	6	Remembering	Nov 21 2021	11	Evolving	Jan 30 2022	3	Remembering
Sep 13 2021	7	Loving	Nov 22 2021	12	Self-Regulating	Jan 31 2022	4	Loving
Sep 14 2021	8	Feeling	Nov 23 2021	13	Catalyzing	Feb 1 2022	5	Feeling
Sep 15 2021	9	Devoting	Nov 24 2021	1	**Enlightening**	Feb 2 2022	6	Devoting
Sep 16 2021	10	Illuminating	Nov 25 2021	2	Being	Feb 3 2022	7	Illuminating
Sep 17 2021	11	Choosing	Nov 26 2021	3	Breathing	Feb 4 2022	8	Choosing
Sep 18 2021	12	Exploring	Nov 27 2021	4	Listening	Feb 5 2022	9	Exploring
Sep 19 2021	13	Healing	Nov 28 2021	5	Planting	Feb 6 2022	10	Healing
Sep 20 2021	1	**Seeing**	Nov 29 2021	6	Moving	Feb 7 2022	11	Seeing
Sep 21 2021	2	Intuiting	Nov 30 2021	7	Transcending	Feb 8 2022	12	Intuiting
Sep 22 2021	3	Evolving	Dec 1 2021	8	Remembering	Feb 9 2022	13	Evolving
Sep 23 2021	4	Self-Regulating	Dec 2 2021	9	Loving	Feb 10 2022	1	**Self-Regulating**
Sep 24 2021	5	Catalyzing	Dec 3 2021	10	Feeling	Feb 11 2022	2	Catalyzing
Sep 25 2021	6	Enlightening	Dec 4 2021	11	Devoting	Feb 12 2022	3	Enlightening
Sep 26 2021	7	Being	Dec 5 2021	12	Illuminating	Feb 13 2022	4	Being
Sep 27 2021	8	Breathing	Dec 6 2021	13	Choosing	Feb 14 2022	5	Breathing
Sep 28 2021	9	Listening	Dec 7 2021	1	**Exploring**	Feb 15 2022	6	Listening
Sep 29 2021	10	Planting	Dec 8 2021	2	Healing	Feb 16 2022	7	Planting
Sep 30 2021	11	Moving	Dec 9 2021	3	Seeing	Feb 17 2022	8	Moving
Oct 1 2021	12	Transcending	Dec 10 2021	4	Intuiting	Feb 18 2022	9	Transcending
Oct 2 2021	13	Remembering	Dec 11 2021	5	Evolving	Feb 19 2022	10	Remembering
Oct 3 2021	1	**Loving**	Dec 12 2021	6	Self-Regulating	Feb 20 2022	11	Loving
Oct 4 2021	2	Feeling	Dec 13 2021	7	Catalyzing	Feb 21 2022	12	Feeling
Oct 5 2021	3	Devoting	Dec 14 2021	8	Enlightening	Feb 22 2022	13	Devoting

Date	UE Earth Energy	Date	UE Earth Energy	Date	UE Earth Energy
Feb 23 2022	1 Illuminating	May 4 2022	6 Being	Jul 13 2022	11 Illuminating
Feb 24 2022	2 Choosing	May 5 2022	7 Breathing	Jul 14 2022	12 Choosing
Feb 25 2022	3 Exploring	May 6 2022	8 Listening	Jul 15 2022	13 Exploring
Feb 26 2022	4 Healing	May 7 2022	9 Planting	Jul 16 2022	1 Healing
Feb 27 2022	5 Seeing	May 8 2022	10 Moving	Jul 17 2022	2 Seeing
Feb 28 2022	6 Intuiting	May 9 2022	11 Transcending	Jul 18 2022	3 Intuiting
Mar 1 2022	7 Evolving	May 10 2022	12 Remembering	Jul 19 2022	4 Evolving
Mar 2 2022	8 Self-Regulating	May 11 2022	13 Loving	Jul 20 2022	5 Self-Regulating
Mar 3 2022	9 Catalyzing	May 12 2022	1 Feeling	Jul 21 2022	6 Catalyzing
Mar 4 2022	10 Enlightening	May 13 2022	2 Devoting	Jul 22 2022	7 Enlightening
Mar 5 2022	11 Being	May 14 2022	3 Illuminating	Jul 23 2022	8 Being
Mar 6 2022	12 Breathing	May 15 2022	4 Choosing	Jul 24 2022	9 Breathing
Mar 7 2022	13 Listening	May 16 2022	5 Exploring	Jul 25 2022	10 Listening
Mar 8 2022	1 Planting	May 17 2022	6 Healing	Jul 26 2022	11 Planting
Mar 9 2022	2 Moving	May 18 2022	7 Seeing	Jul 27 2022	12 Moving
Mar 10 2022	3 Transcending	May 19 2022	8 Intuiting	Jul 28 2022	13 Transcending
Mar 11 2022	4 Remembering	May 20 2022	9 Evolving	Jul 29 2022	1 Remembering
Mar 12 2022	5 Loving	May 21 2022	10 Self-Regulating	Jul 30 2022	2 Loving
Mar 13 2022	6 Feeling	May 22 2022	11 Catalyzing	Jul 31 2022	3 Feeling
Mar 14 2022	7 Devoting	May 23 2022	12 Enlightening	Aug 1 2022	4 Devoting
Mar 15 2022	8 Illuminating	May 24 2022	13 Being	Aug 2 2022	5 Illuminating
Mar 16 2022	9 Choosing	May 25 2022	1 Breathing	Aug 3 2022	6 Choosing
Mar 17 2022	10 Exploring	May 26 2022	2 Listening	Aug 4 2022	7 Exploring
Mar 18 2022	11 Healing	May 27 2022	3 Planting	Aug 5 2022	8 Healing
Mar 19 2022	12 Seeing	May 28 2022	4 Moving	Aug 6 2022	9 Seeing
Mar 20 2022	13 Intuiting	May 29 2022	5 Transcending	Aug 7 2022	10 Intuiting
Mar 21 2022	1 Evolving	May 30 2022	6 Remembering	Aug 8 2022	11 Evolving
Mar 22 2022	2 Self-Regulating	May 31 2022	7 Loving	Aug 9 2022	12 Self-Regulating
Mar 23 2022	3 Catalyzing	Jun 1 2022	8 Feeling	Aug 10 2022	13 Catalyzing
Mar 24 2022	4 Enlightening	Jun 2 2022	9 Devoting	Aug 11 2022	1 Enlightening
Mar 25 2022	5 Being	Jun 3 2022	10 Illuminating	Aug 12 2022	2 Being
Mar 26 2022	6 Breathing	Jun 4 2022	11 Choosing	Aug 13 2022	3 Breathing
Mar 27 2022	7 Listening	Jun 5 2022	12 Exploring	Aug 14 2022	4 Listening
Mar 28 2022	8 Planting	Jun 6 2022	13 Healing	Aug 15 2022	5 Planting
Mar 29 2022	9 Moving	Jun 7 2022	1 Seeing	Aug 16 2022	6 Moving
Mar 30 2022	10 Transcending	Jun 8 2022	2 Intuiting	Aug 17 2022	7 Transcending
Mar 31 2022	11 Remembering	Jun 9 2022	3 Evolving	Aug 18 2022	8 Remembering
Apr 1 2022	12 Loving	Jun 10 2022	4 Self-Regulating	Aug 19 2022	9 Loving
Apr 2 2022	13 Feeling	Jun 11 2022	5 Catalyzing	Aug 20 2022	10 Feeling
Apr 3 2022	1 Devoting	Jun 12 2022	6 Enlightening	Aug 21 2022	11 Devoting
Apr 4 2022	2 Illuminating	Jun 13 2022	7 Being	Aug 22 2022	12 Illuminating
Apr 5 2022	3 Choosing	Jun 14 2022	8 Breathing	Aug 23 2022	13 Choosing
Apr 6 2022	4 Exploring	Jun 15 2022	9 Listening	Aug 24 2022	1 Exploring
Apr 7 2022	5 Healing	Jun 16 2022	10 Planting	Aug 25 2022	2 Healing
Apr 8 2022	6 Seeing	Jun 17 2022	11 Moving	Aug 26 2022	3 Seeing
Apr 9 2022	7 Intuiting	Jun 18 2022	12 Transcending	Aug 27 2022	4 Intuiting
Apr 10 2022	8 Evolving	Jun 19 2022	13 Remembering	Aug 28 2022	5 Evolving
Apr 11 2022	9 Self-Regulating	Jun 20 2022	1 Loving	Aug 29 2022	6 Self-Regulating
Apr 12 2022	10 Catalyzing	Jun 21 2022	2 Feeling	Aug 30 2022	7 Catalyzing
Apr 13 2022	11 Enlightening	Jun 22 2022	3 Devoting	Aug 31 2022	8 Enlightening
Apr 14 2022	12 Being	Jun 23 2022	4 Illuminating	Sep 1 2022	9 Being
Apr 15 2022	13 Breathing	Jun 24 2022	5 Choosing	Sep 2 2022	10 Breathing
Apr 16 2022	1 Listening	Jun 25 2022	6 Exploring	Sep 3 2022	11 Listening
Apr 17 2022	2 Planting	Jun 26 2022	7 Healing	Sep 4 2022	12 Planting
Apr 18 2022	3 Moving	Jun 27 2022	8 Seeing	Sep 5 2022	13 Moving
Apr 19 2022	4 Transcending	Jun 28 2022	9 Intuiting	Sep 6 2022	1 Transcending
Apr 20 2022	5 Remembering	Jun 29 2022	10 Evolving	Sep 7 2022	2 Remembering
Apr 21 2022	6 Loving	Jun 30 2022	11 Self-Regulating	Sep 8 2022	3 Loving
Apr 22 2022	7 Feeling	Jul 1 2022	12 Catalyzing	Sep 9 2022	4 Feeling
Apr 23 2022	8 Devoting	Jul 2 2022	13 Enlightening	Sep 10 2022	5 Devoting
Apr 24 2022	9 Illuminating	Jul 3 2022	1 Being	Sep 11 2022	6 Illuminating
Apr 25 2022	10 Choosing	Jul 4 2022	2 Breathing	Sep 12 2022	7 Choosing
Apr 26 2022	11 Exploring	Jul 5 2022	3 Listening	Sep 13 2022	8 Exploring
Apr 27 2022	12 Healing	Jul 6 2022	4 Planting	Sep 14 2022	9 Healing
Apr 28 2022	13 Seeing	Jul 7 2022	5 Moving	Sep 15 2022	10 Seeing
Apr 29 2022	1 Intuiting	Jul 8 2022	6 Transcending	Sep 16 2022	11 Intuiting
Apr 30 2022	2 Evolving	Jul 9 2022	7 Remembering	Sep 17 2022	12 Evolving
May 1 2022	3 Self-Regulating	Jul 10 2022	8 Loving	Sep 18 2022	13 Self-Regulating
May 2 2022	4 Catalyzing	Jul 11 2022	9 Feeling	Sep 19 2022	1 Catalyzing
May 3 2022	5 Enlightening	Jul 12 2022	10 Devoting	Sep 20 2022	2 Enlightening

Date	UE	Earth Energy	Date	UE	Earth Energy	Date	UE	Earth Energy
Sep 21 2022	3	Being	Nov 30 2022	8	Illuminating	Feb 8 2023	13	Being
Sep 22 2022	4	Breathing	Dec 1 2022	9	Choosing	Feb 9 2023	1	**Breathing**
Sep 23 2022	5	Listening	Dec 2 2022	10	Exploring	Feb 10 2023	2	Listening
Sep 24 2022	6	Planting	Dec 3 2022	11	Healing	Feb 11 2023	3	Planting
Sep 25 2022	7	Moving	Dec 4 2022	12	Seeing	Feb 12 2023	4	Moving
Sep 26 2022	8	Transcending	Dec 5 2022	13	Intuiting	Feb 13 2023	5	Transcending
Sep 27 2022	9	Remembering	Dec 6 2022	1	**Evolving**	Feb 14 2023	6	Remembering
Sep 28 2022	10	Loving	Dec 7 2022	2	Self-Regulating	Feb 15 2023	7	Loving
Sep 29 2022	11	Feeling	Dec 8 2022	3	Catalyzing	Feb 16 2023	8	Feeling
Sep 30 2022	12	Devoting	Dec 9 2022	4	Enlightening	Feb 17 2023	9	Devoting
Oct 1 2022	13	Illuminating	Dec 10 2022	5	Being	Feb 18 2023	10	Illuminating
Oct 2 2022	1	**Choosing**	Dec 11 2022	6	Breathing	Feb 19 2023	11	Choosing
Oct 3 2022	2	Exploring	Dec 12 2022	7	Listening	Feb 20 2023	12	Exploring
Oct 4 2022	3	Healing	Dec 13 2022	8	Planting	Feb 21 2023	13	Healing
Oct 5 2022	4	Seeing	Dec 14 2022	9	Moving	Feb 22 2023	1	**Seeing**
Oct 6 2022	5	Intuiting	Dec 15 2022	10	Transcending	Feb 23 2023	2	Intuiting
Oct 7 2022	6	Evolving	Dec 16 2022	11	Remembering	Feb 24 2023	3	Evolving
Oct 8 2022	7	Self-Regulating	Dec 17 2022	12	Loving	Feb 25 2023	4	Self-Regulating
Oct 9 2022	8	Catalyzing	Dec 18 2022	13	Feeling	Feb 26 2023	5	Catalyzing
Oct 10 2022	9	Enlightening	Dec 19 2022	1	**Devoting**	Feb 27 2023	6	Enlightening
Oct 11 2022	10	Being	Dec 20 2022	2	Illuminating	Feb 28 2023	7	Being
Oct 12 2022	11	Breathing	Dec 21 2022	3	Choosing	Mar 1 2023	8	Breathing
Oct 13 2022	12	Listening	Dec 22 2022	4	Exploring	Mar 2 2023	9	Listening
Oct 14 2022	13	Planting	Dec 23 2022	5	Healing	Mar 3 2023	10	Planting
Oct 15 2022	1	**Moving**	Dec 24 2022	6	Seeing	Mar 4 2023	11	Moving
Oct 16 2022	2	Transcending	Dec 25 2022	7	Intuiting	Mar 5 2023	12	Transcending
Oct 17 2022	3	Remembering	Dec 26 2022	8	Evolving	Mar 6 2023	13	Remembering
Oct 18 2022	4	Loving	Dec 27 2022	9	Self-Regulating	Mar 7 2023	1	**Loving**
Oct 19 2022	5	Feeling	Dec 28 2022	10	Catalyzing	Mar 8 2023	2	Feeling
Oct 20 2022	6	Devoting	Dec 29 2022	11	Enlightening	Mar 9 2023	3	Devoting
Oct 21 2022	7	Illuminating	Dec 30 2022	12	Being	Mar 10 2023	4	Illuminating
Oct 22 2022	8	Choosing	Dec 31 2022	13	Breathing	Mar 11 2023	5	Choosing
Oct 23 2022	9	Exploring	Jan 1 2023	1	**Listening**	Mar 12 2023	6	Exploring
Oct 24 2022	10	Healing	Jan 2 2023	2	Planting	Mar 13 2023	7	Healing
Oct 25 2022	11	Seeing	Jan 3 2023	3	Moving	Mar 14 2023	8	Seeing
Oct 26 2022	12	Intuiting	Jan 4 2023	4	Transcending	Mar 15 2023	9	Intuiting
Oct 27 2022	13	Evolving	Jan 5 2023	5	Remembering	Mar 16 2023	10	Evolving
Oct 28 2022	1	**Self-Regulating**	Jan 6 2023	6	Loving	Mar 17 2023	11	Self-Regulating
Oct 29 2022	2	Catalyzing	Jan 7 2023	7	Feeling	Mar 18 2023	12	Catalyzing
Oct 30 2022	3	Enlightening	Jan 8 2023	8	Devoting	Mar 19 2023	13	Enlightening
Oct 31 2022	4	Being	Jan 9 2023	9	Illuminating	Mar 20 2023	1	**Being**
Nov 1 2022	5	Breathing	Jan 10 2023	10	Choosing	Mar 21 2023	2	Breathing
Nov 2 2022	6	Listening	Jan 11 2023	11	Exploring	Mar 22 2023	3	Listening
Nov 3 2022	7	Planting	Jan 12 2023	12	Healing	Mar 23 2023	4	Planting
Nov 4 2022	8	Moving	Jan 13 2023	13	Seeing	Mar 24 2023	5	Moving
Nov 5 2022	9	Transcending	Jan 14 2023	1	**Intuiting**	Mar 25 2023	6	Transcending
Nov 6 2022	10	Remembering	Jan 15 2023	2	Evolving	Mar 26 2023	7	Remembering
Nov 7 2022	11	Loving	Jan 16 2023	3	Self-Regulating	Mar 27 2023	8	Loving
Nov 8 2022	12	Feeling	Jan 17 2023	4	Catalyzing	Mar 28 2023	9	Feeling
Nov 9 2022	13	Devoting	Jan 18 2023	5	Enlightening	Mar 29 2023	10	Devoting
Nov 10 2022	1	**Illuminating**	Jan 19 2023	6	Being	Mar 30 2023	11	Illuminating
Nov 11 2022	2	Choosing	Jan 20 2023	7	Breathing	Mar 31 2023	12	Choosing
Nov 12 2022	3	Exploring	Jan 21 2023	8	Listening	Apr 1 2023	13	Exploring
Nov 13 2022	4	Healing	Jan 22 2023	9	Planting	Apr 2 2023	1	**Healing**
Nov 14 2022	5	Seeing	Jan 23 2023	10	Moving	Apr 3 2023	2	Seeing
Nov 15 2022	6	Intuiting	Jan 24 2023	11	Transcending	Apr 4 2023	3	Intuiting
Nov 16 2022	7	Evolving	Jan 25 2023	12	Remembering	Apr 5 2023	4	Evolving
Nov 17 2022	8	Self-Regulating	Jan 26 2023	13	Loving	Apr 6 2023	5	Self-Regulating
Nov 18 2022	9	Catalyzing	Jan 27 2023	1	**Feeling**	Apr 7 2023	6	Catalyzing
Nov 19 2022	10	Enlightening	Jan 28 2023	2	Devoting	Apr 8 2023	7	Enlightening
Nov 20 2022	11	Being	Jan 29 2023	3	Illuminating	Apr 9 2023	8	Being
Nov 21 2022	12	Breathing	Jan 30 2023	4	Choosing	Apr 10 2023	9	Breathing
Nov 22 2022	13	Listening	Jan 31 2023	5	Exploring	Apr 11 2023	10	Listening
Nov 23 2022	1	**Planting**	Feb 1 2023	6	Healing	Apr 12 2023	11	Planting
Nov 24 2022	2	Moving	Feb 2 2023	7	Seeing	Apr 13 2023	12	Moving
Nov 25 2022	3	Transcending	Feb 3 2023	8	Intuiting	Apr 14 2023	13	Transcending
Nov 26 2022	4	Remembering	Feb 4 2023	9	Evolving	Apr 15 2023	1	**Remembering**
Nov 27 2022	5	Loving	Feb 5 2023	10	Self-Regulating	Apr 16 2023	2	Loving
Nov 28 2022	6	Feeling	Feb 6 2023	11	Catalyzing	Apr 17 2023	3	Feeling
Nov 29 2022	7	Devoting	Feb 7 2023	12	Enlightening	Apr 18 2023	4	Devoting

Date	UE	Earth Energy	Date	UE	Earth Energy	Date	UE	Earth Energy
Apr 19 2023	5	Illuminating	Jun 28 2023	10	Being	Sep 6 2023	2	Illuminating
Apr 20 2023	6	Choosing	Jun 29 2023	11	Breathing	Sep 7 2023	3	Choosing
Apr 21 2023	7	Exploring	Jun 30 2023	12	Listening	Sep 8 2023	4	Exploring
Apr 22 2023	8	Healing	Jul 1 2023	13	Planting	Sep 9 2023	5	Healing
Apr 23 2023	9	Seeing	Jul 2 2023	**1**	**Moving**	Sep 10 2023	6	Seeing
Apr 24 2023	10	Intuiting	Jul 3 2023	2	Transcending	Sep 11 2023	7	Intuiting
Apr 25 2023	11	Evolving	Jul 4 2023	3	Remembering	Sep 12 2023	8	Evolving
Apr 26 2023	12	Self-Regulating	Jul 5 2023	4	Loving	Sep 13 2023	9	Self-Regulating
Apr 27 2023	13	Catalyzing	Jul 6 2023	5	Feeling	Sep 14 2023	10	Catalyzing
Apr 28 2023	**1**	**Enlightening**	Jul 7 2023	6	Devoting	Sep 15 2023	11	Enlightening
Apr 29 2023	2	Being	Jul 8 2023	7	Illuminating	Sep 16 2023	12	Being
Apr 30 2023	3	Breathing	Jul 9 2023	8	Choosing	Sep 17 2023	13	Breathing
May 1 2023	4	Listening	Jul 10 2023	9	Exploring	Sep 18 2023	**1**	**Listening**
May 2 2023	5	Planting	Jul 11 2023	10	Healing	Sep 19 2023	2	Planting
May 3 2023	6	Moving	Jul 12 2023	11	Seeing	Sep 20 2023	3	Moving
May 4 2023	7	Transcending	Jul 13 2023	12	Intuiting	Sep 21 2023	4	Transcending
May 5 2023	8	Remembering	Jul 14 2023	13	Evolving	Sep 22 2023	5	Remembering
May 6 2023	9	Loving	Jul 15 2023	**1**	**Self-Regulating**	Sep 23 2023	6	Loving
May 7 2023	10	Feeling	Jul 16 2023	2	Catalyzing	Sep 24 2023	7	Feeling
May 8 2023	11	Devoting	Jul 17 2023	3	Enlightening	Sep 25 2023	8	Devoting
May 9 2023	12	Illuminating	Jul 18 2023	4	Being	Sep 26 2023	9	Illuminating
May 10 2023	13	Choosing	Jul 19 2023	5	Breathing	Sep 27 2023	10	Choosing
May 11 2023	**1**	**Exploring**	Jul 20 2023	6	Listening	Sep 28 2023	11	Exploring
May 12 2023	2	Healing	Jul 21 2023	7	Planting	Sep 29 2023	12	Healing
May 13 2023	3	Seeing	Jul 22 2023	8	Moving	Sep 30 2023	13	Seeing
May 14 2023	4	Intuiting	Jul 23 2023	9	Transcending	Oct 1 2023	**1**	**Intuiting**
May 15 2023	5	Evolving	Jul 24 2023	10	Remembering	Oct 2 2023	2	Evolving
May 16 2023	6	Self-Regulating	Jul 25 2023	11	Loving	Oct 3 2023	3	Self-Regulating
May 17 2023	7	Catalyzing	Jul 26 2023	12	Feeling	Oct 4 2023	4	Catalyzing
May 18 2023	8	Enlightening	Jul 27 2023	13	Devoting	Oct 5 2023	5	Enlightening
May 19 2023	9	Being	Jul 28 2023	**1**	**Illuminating**	Oct 6 2023	6	Being
May 20 2023	10	Breathing	Jul 29 2023	2	Choosing	Oct 7 2023	7	Breathing
May 21 2023	11	Listening	Jul 30 2023	3	Exploring	Oct 8 2023	8	Listening
May 22 2023	12	Planting	Jul 31 2023	4	Healing	Oct 9 2023	9	Planting
May 23 2023	13	Moving	Aug 1 2023	5	Seeing	Oct 10 2023	10	Moving
May 24 2023	**1**	**Transcending**	Aug 2 2023	6	Intuiting	Oct 11 2023	11	Transcending
May 25 2023	2	Remembering	Aug 3 2023	7	Evolving	Oct 12 2023	12	Remembering
May 26 2023	3	Loving	Aug 4 2023	8	Self-Regulating	Oct 13 2023	13	Loving
May 27 2023	4	Feeling	Aug 5 2023	9	Catalyzing	Oct 14 2023	**1**	**Feeling**
May 28 2023	5	Devoting	Aug 6 2023	10	Enlightening	Oct 15 2023	2	Devoting
May 29 2023	6	Illuminating	Aug 7 2023	11	Being	Oct 16 2023	3	Illuminating
May 30 2023	7	Choosing	Aug 8 2023	12	Breathing	Oct 17 2023	4	Choosing
May 31 2023	8	Exploring	Aug 9 2023	13	Listening	Oct 18 2023	5	Exploring
Jun 1 2023	9	Healing	Aug 10 2023	**1**	**Planting**	Oct 19 2023	6	Healing
Jun 2 2023	10	Seeing	Aug 11 2023	2	Moving	Oct 20 2023	7	Seeing
Jun 3 2023	11	Intuiting	Aug 12 2023	3	Transcending	Oct 21 2023	8	Intuiting
Jun 4 2023	12	Evolving	Aug 13 2023	4	Remembering	Oct 22 2023	9	Evolving
Jun 5 2023	13	Self-Regulating	Aug 14 2023	5	Loving	Oct 23 2023	10	Self-Regulating
Jun 6 2023	**1**	**Catalyzing**	Aug 15 2023	6	Feeling	Oct 24 2023	11	Catalyzing
Jun 7 2023	2	Enlightening	Aug 16 2023	7	Devoting	Oct 25 2023	12	Enlightening
Jun 8 2023	3	Being	Aug 17 2023	8	Illuminating	Oct 26 2023	13	Being
Jun 9 2023	4	Breathing	Aug 18 2023	9	Choosing	Oct 27 2023	**1**	**Breathing**
Jun 10 2023	5	Listening	Aug 19 2023	10	Exploring	Oct 28 2023	2	Listening
Jun 11 2023	6	Planting	Aug 20 2023	11	Healing	Oct 29 2023	3	Planting
Jun 12 2023	7	Moving	Aug 21 2023	12	Seeing	Oct 30 2023	4	Moving
Jun 13 2023	8	Transcending	Aug 22 2023	13	Intuiting	Oct 31 2023	5	Transcending
Jun 14 2023	9	Remembering	Aug 23 2023	**1**	**Evolving**	Nov 1 2023	6	Remembering
Jun 15 2023	10	Loving	Aug 24 2023	2	Self-Regulating	Nov 2 2023	7	Loving
Jun 16 2023	11	Feeling	Aug 25 2023	3	Catalyzing	Nov 3 2023	8	Feeling
Jun 17 2023	12	Devoting	Aug 26 2023	4	Enlightening	Nov 4 2023	9	Devoting
Jun 18 2023	13	Illuminating	Aug 27 2023	5	Being	Nov 5 2023	10	Illuminating
Jun 19 2023	**1**	**Choosing**	Aug 28 2023	6	Breathing	Nov 6 2023	11	Choosing
Jun 20 2023	2	Exploring	Aug 29 2023	7	Listening	Nov 7 2023	12	Exploring
Jun 21 2023	3	Healing	Aug 30 2023	8	Planting	Nov 8 2023	13	Healing
Jun 22 2023	4	Seeing	Aug 31 2023	9	Moving	Nov 9 2023	**1**	**Seeing**
Jun 23 2023	5	Intuiting	Sep 1 2023	10	Transcending	Nov 10 2023	2	Intuiting
Jun 24 2023	6	Evolving	Sep 2 2023	11	Remembering	Nov 11 2023	3	Evolving
Jun 25 2023	7	Self-Regulating	Sep 3 2023	12	Loving	Nov 12 2023	4	Self-Regulating
Jun 26 2023	8	Catalyzing	Sep 4 2023	13	Feeling	Nov 13 2023	5	Catalyzing
Jun 27 2023	9	Enlightening	Sep 5 2023	**1**	**Devoting**	Nov 14 2023	6	Enlightening

Date	UE	Earth Energy	Date	UE	Earth Energy	Date	UE	Earth Energy
Nov 15 2023	7	Being	Jan 24 2024	12	Illuminating	Apr 3 2024	4	Being
Nov 16 2023	8	Breathing	Jan 25 2024	13	Choosing	Apr 4 2024	5	Breathing
Nov 17 2023	9	Listening	Jan 26 2024	1	**Exploring**	Apr 5 2024	6	Listening
Nov 18 2023	10	Planting	Jan 27 2024	2	Healing	Apr 6 2024	7	Planting
Nov 19 2023	11	Moving	Jan 28 2024	3	Seeing	Apr 7 2024	8	Moving
Nov 20 2023	12	Transcending	Jan 29 2024	4	Intuiting	Apr 8 2024	9	Transcending
Nov 21 2023	13	Remembering	Jan 30 2024	5	Evolving	Apr 9 2024	10	Remembering
Nov 22 2023	1	**Loving**	Jan 31 2024	6	Self-Regulating	Apr 10 2024	11	Loving
Nov 23 2023	2	Feeling	Feb 1 2024	7	Catalyzing	Apr 11 2024	12	Feeling
Nov 24 2023	3	Devoting	Feb 2 2024	8	Enlightening	Apr 12 2024	13	Devoting
Nov 25 2023	4	Illuminating	Feb 3 2024	9	Being	Apr 13 2024	1	**Illuminating**
Nov 26 2023	5	Choosing	Feb 4 2024	10	Breathing	Apr 14 2024	2	Choosing
Nov 27 2023	6	Exploring	Feb 5 2024	11	Listening	Apr 15 2024	3	Exploring
Nov 28 2023	7	Healing	Feb 6 2024	12	Planting	Apr 16 2024	4	Healing
Nov 29 2023	8	Seeing	Feb 7 2024	13	Moving	Apr 17 2024	5	Seeing
Nov 30 2023	9	Intuiting	Feb 8 2024	1	**Transcending**	Apr 18 2024	6	Intuiting
Dec 1 2023	10	Evolving	Feb 9 2024	2	Remembering	Apr 19 2024	7	Evolving
Dec 2 2023	11	Self-Regulating	Feb 10 2024	3	Loving	Apr 20 2024	8	Self-Regulating
Dec 3 2023	12	Catalyzing	Feb 11 2024	4	Feeling	Apr 21 2024	9	Catalyzing
Dec 4 2023	13	Enlightening	Feb 12 2024	5	Devoting	Apr 22 2024	10	Enlightening
Dec 5 2023	1	**Being**	Feb 13 2024	6	Illuminating	Apr 23 2024	11	Being
Dec 6 2023	2	Breathing	Feb 14 2024	7	Choosing	Apr 24 2024	12	Breathing
Dec 7 2023	3	Listening	Feb 15 2024	8	Exploring	Apr 25 2024	13	Listening
Dec 8 2023	4	Planting	Feb 16 2024	9	Healing	Apr 26 2024	1	**Planting**
Dec 9 2023	5	Moving	Feb 17 2024	10	Seeing	Apr 27 2024	2	Moving
Dec 10 2023	6	Transcending	Feb 18 2024	11	Intuiting	Apr 28 2024	3	Transcending
Dec 11 2023	7	Remembering	Feb 19 2024	12	Evolving	Apr 29 2024	4	Remembering
Dec 12 2023	8	Loving	Feb 20 2024	13	Self-Regulating	Apr 30 2024	5	Loving
Dec 13 2023	9	Feeling	Feb 21 2024	1	**Catalyzing**	May 1 2024	6	Feeling
Dec 14 2023	10	Devoting	Feb 22 2024	2	Enlightening	May 2 2024	7	Devoting
Dec 15 2023	11	Illuminating	Feb 23 2024	3	Being	May 3 2024	8	Illuminating
Dec 16 2023	12	Choosing	Feb 24 2024	4	Breathing	May 4 2024	9	Choosing
Dec 17 2023	13	Exploring	Feb 25 2024	5	Listening	May 5 2024	10	Exploring
Dec 18 2023	1	**Healing**	Feb 26 2024	6	Planting	May 6 2024	11	Healing
Dec 19 2023	2	Seeing	Feb 27 2024	7	Moving	May 7 2024	12	Seeing
Dec 20 2023	3	Intuiting	Feb 28 2024	8	Transcending	May 8 2024	13	Intuiting
Dec 21 2023	4	Evolving	Feb 29 2024	9	Remembering	May 9 2024	1	**Evolving**
Dec 22 2023	5	Self-Regulating	Mar 1 2024	10	Loving	May 10 2024	2	Self-Regulating
Dec 23 2023	6	Catalyzing	Mar 2 2024	11	Feeling	May 11 2024	3	Catalyzing
Dec 24 2023	7	Enlightening	Mar 3 2024	12	Devoting	May 12 2024	4	Enlightening
Dec 25 2023	8	Being	Mar 4 2024	13	Illuminating	May 13 2024	5	Being
Dec 26 2023	9	Breathing	Mar 5 2024	1	**Choosing**	May 14 2024	6	Breathing
Dec 27 2023	10	Listening	Mar 6 2024	2	Exploring	May 15 2024	7	Listening
Dec 28 2023	11	Planting	Mar 7 2024	3	Healing	May 16 2024	8	Planting
Dec 29 2023	12	Moving	Mar 8 2024	4	Seeing	May 17 2024	9	Moving
Dec 30 2023	13	Transcending	Mar 9 2024	5	Intuiting	May 18 2024	10	Transcending
Dec 31 2023	1	**Remembering**	Mar 10 2024	6	Evolving	May 19 2024	11	Remembering
Jan 1 2024	2	Loving	Mar 11 2024	7	Self-Regulating	May 20 2024	12	Loving
Jan 2 2024	3	Feeling	Mar 12 2024	8	Catalyzing	May 21 2024	13	Feeling
Jan 3 2024	4	Devoting	Mar 13 2024	9	Enlightening	May 22 2024	1	**Devoting**
Jan 4 2024	5	Illuminating	Mar 14 2024	10	Being	May 23 2024	2	Illuminating
Jan 5 2024	6	Choosing	Mar 15 2024	11	Breathing	May 24 2024	3	Choosing
Jan 6 2024	7	Exploring	Mar 16 2024	12	Listening	May 25 2024	4	Exploring
Jan 7 2024	8	Healing	Mar 17 2024	13	Planting	May 26 2024	5	Healing
Jan 8 2024	9	Seeing	Mar 18 2024	1	**Moving**	May 27 2024	6	Seeing
Jan 9 2024	10	Intuiting	Mar 19 2024	2	Transcending	May 28 2024	7	Intuiting
Jan 10 2024	11	Evolving	Mar 20 2024	3	Remembering	May 29 2024	8	Evolving
Jan 11 2024	12	Self-Regulating	Mar 21 2024	4	Loving	May 30 2024	9	Self-Regulating
Jan 12 2024	13	Catalyzing	Mar 22 2024	5	Feeling	May 31 2024	10	Catalyzing
Jan 13 2024	1	**Enlightening**	Mar 23 2024	6	Devoting	Jun 1 2024	11	Enlightening
Jan 14 2024	2	Being	Mar 24 2024	7	Illuminating	Jun 2 2024	12	Being
Jan 15 2024	3	Breathing	Mar 25 2024	8	Choosing	Jun 3 2024	13	Breathing
Jan 16 2024	4	Listening	Mar 26 2024	9	Exploring	Jun 4 2024	1	**Listening**
Jan 17 2024	5	Planting	Mar 27 2024	10	Healing	Jun 5 2024	2	Planting
Jan 18 2024	6	Moving	Mar 28 2024	11	Seeing	Jun 6 2024	3	Moving
Jan 19 2024	7	Transcending	Mar 29 2024	12	Intuiting	Jun 7 2024	4	Transcending
Jan 20 2024	8	Remembering	Mar 30 2024	13	Evolving	Jun 8 2024	5	Remembering
Jan 21 2024	9	Loving	Mar 31 2024	1	**Self-Regulating**	Jun 9 2024	6	Loving
Jan 22 2024	10	Feeling	Apr 1 2024	2	Catalyzing	Jun 10 2024	7	Feeling
Jan 23 2024	11	Devoting	Apr 2 2024	3	Enlightening	Jun 11 2024	8	Devoting

Date	UE	Earth Energy	Date	UE	Earth Energy	Date	UE	Earth Energy
Jun 12 2024	9	Illuminating	Aug 21 2024	1	**Being**	Oct 30 2024	6	Illuminating
Jun 13 2024	10	Choosing	Aug 22 2024	2	Breathing	Oct 31 2024	7	Choosing
Jun 14 2024	11	Exploring	Aug 23 2024	3	Listening	Nov 1 2024	8	Exploring
Jun 15 2024	12	Healing	Aug 24 2024	4	Planting	Nov 2 2024	9	Healing
Jun 16 2024	13	Seeing	Aug 25 2024	5	Moving	Nov 3 2024	10	Seeing
Jun 17 2024	1	**Intuiting**	Aug 26 2024	6	Transcending	Nov 4 2024	11	Intuiting
Jun 18 2024	2	Evolving	Aug 27 2024	7	Remembering	Nov 5 2024	12	Evolving
Jun 19 2024	3	Self-Regulating	Aug 28 2024	8	Loving	Nov 6 2024	13	Self-Regulating
Jun 20 2024	4	Catalyzing	Aug 29 2024	9	Feeling	Nov 7 2024	1	**Catalyzing**
Jun 21 2024	5	Enlightening	Aug 30 2024	10	Devoting	Nov 8 2024	2	Enlightening
Jun 22 2024	6	Being	Aug 31 2024	11	Illuminating	Nov 9 2024	3	Being
Jun 23 2024	7	Breathing	Sep 1 2024	12	Choosing	Nov 10 2024	4	Breathing
Jun 24 2024	8	Listening	Sep 2 2024	13	Exploring	Nov 11 2024	5	Listening
Jun 25 2024	9	Planting	Sep 3 2024	1	**Healing**	Nov 12 2024	6	Planting
Jun 26 2024	10	Moving	Sep 4 2024	2	Seeing	Nov 13 2024	7	Moving
Jun 27 2024	11	Transcending	Sep 5 2024	3	Intuiting	Nov 14 2024	8	Transcending
Jun 28 2024	12	Remembering	Sep 6 2024	4	Evolving	Nov 15 2024	9	Remembering
Jun 29 2024	13	Loving	Sep 7 2024	5	Self-Regulating	Nov 16 2024	10	Loving
Jun 30 2024	1	**Feeling**	Sep 8 2024	6	Catalyzing	Nov 17 2024	11	Feeling
Jul 1 2024	2	Devoting	Sep 9 2024	7	Enlightening	Nov 18 2024	12	Devoting
Jul 2 2024	3	Illuminating	Sep 10 2024	8	Being	Nov 19 2024	13	Illuminating
Jul 3 2024	4	Choosing	Sep 11 2024	9	Breathing	Nov 20 2024	1	**Choosing**
Jul 4 2024	5	Exploring	Sep 12 2024	10	Listening	Nov 21 2024	2	Exploring
Jul 5 2024	6	Healing	Sep 13 2024	11	Planting	Nov 22 2024	3	Healing
Jul 6 2024	7	Seeing	Sep 14 2024	12	Moving	Nov 23 2024	4	Seeing
Jul 7 2024	8	Intuiting	Sep 15 2024	13	Transcending	Nov 24 2024	5	Intuiting
Jul 8 2024	9	Evolving	Sep 16 2024	1	**Remembering**	Nov 25 2024	6	Evolving
Jul 9 2024	10	Self-Regulating	Sep 17 2024	2	Loving	Nov 26 2024	7	Self-Regulating
Jul 10 2024	11	Catalyzing	Sep 18 2024	3	Feeling	Nov 27 2024	8	Catalyzing
Jul 11 2024	12	Enlightening	Sep 19 2024	4	Devoting	Nov 28 2024	9	Enlightening
Jul 12 2024	13	Being	Sep 20 2024	5	Illuminating	Nov 29 2024	10	Being
Jul 13 2024	1	**Breathing**	Sep 21 2024	6	Choosing	Nov 30 2024	11	Breathing
Jul 14 2024	2	Listening	Sep 22 2024	7	Exploring	Dec 1 2024	12	Listening
Jul 15 2024	3	Planting	Sep 23 2024	8	Healing	Dec 2 2024	13	Planting
Jul 16 2024	4	Moving	Sep 24 2024	9	Seeing	Dec 3 2024	1	**Moving**
Jul 17 2024	5	Transcending	Sep 25 2024	10	Intuiting	Dec 4 2024	2	Transcending
Jul 18 2024	6	Remembering	Sep 26 2024	11	Evolving	Dec 5 2024	3	Remembering
Jul 19 2024	7	Loving	Sep 27 2024	12	Self-Regulating	Dec 6 2024	4	Loving
Jul 20 2024	8	Feeling	Sep 28 2024	13	Catalyzing	Dec 7 2024	5	Feeling
Jul 21 2024	9	Devoting	Sep 29 2024	1	**Enlightening**	Dec 8 2024	6	Devoting
Jul 22 2024	10	Illuminating	Sep 30 2024	2	Being	Dec 9 2024	7	Illuminating
Jul 23 2024	11	Choosing	Oct 1 2024	3	Breathing	Dec 10 2024	8	Choosing
Jul 24 2024	12	Exploring	Oct 2 2024	4	Listening	Dec 11 2024	9	Exploring
Jul 25 2024	13	Healing	Oct 3 2024	5	Planting	Dec 12 2024	10	Healing
Jul 26 2024	1	**Seeing**	Oct 4 2024	6	Moving	Dec 13 2024	11	Seeing
Jul 27 2024	2	Intuiting	Oct 5 2024	7	Transcending	Dec 14 2024	12	Intuiting
Jul 28 2024	3	Evolving	Oct 6 2024	8	Remembering	Dec 15 2024	13	Evolving
Jul 29 2024	4	Self-Regulating	Oct 7 2024	9	Loving	Dec 16 2024	1	**Self-Regulating**
Jul 30 2024	5	Catalyzing	Oct 8 2024	10	Feeling	Dec 17 2024	2	Catalyzing
Jul 31 2024	6	Enlightening	Oct 9 2024	11	Devoting	Dec 18 2024	3	Enlightening
Aug 1 2024	7	Being	Oct 10 2024	12	Illuminating	Dec 19 2024	4	Being
Aug 2 2024	8	Breathing	Oct 11 2024	13	Choosing	Dec 20 2024	5	Breathing
Aug 3 2024	9	Listening	Oct 12 2024	1	**Exploring**	Dec 21 2024	6	Listening
Aug 4 2024	10	Planting	Oct 13 2024	2	Healing	Dec 22 2024	7	Planting
Aug 5 2024	11	Moving	Oct 14 2024	3	Seeing	Dec 23 2024	8	Moving
Aug 6 2024	12	Transcending	Oct 15 2024	4	Intuiting	Dec 24 2024	9	Transcending
Aug 7 2024	13	Remembering	Oct 16 2024	5	Evolving	Dec 25 2024	10	Remembering
Aug 8 2024	1	**Loving**	Oct 17 2024	6	Self-Regulating	Dec 26 2024	11	Loving
Aug 9 2024	2	Feeling	Oct 18 2024	7	Catalyzing	Dec 27 2024	12	Feeling
Aug 10 2024	3	Devoting	Oct 19 2024	8	Enlightening	Dec 28 2024	13	Devoting
Aug 11 2024	4	Illuminating	Oct 20 2024	9	Being	Dec 29 2024	1	**Illuminating**
Aug 12 2024	5	Choosing	Oct 21 2024	10	Breathing	Dec 30 2024	2	Choosing
Aug 13 2024	6	Exploring	Oct 22 2024	11	Listening	Dec 31 2024	3	Exploring
Aug 14 2024	7	Healing	Oct 23 2024	12	Planting	Jan 1 2025	4	Healing
Aug 15 2024	8	Seeing	Oct 24 2024	13	Moving	Jan 2 2025	5	Seeing
Aug 16 2024	9	Intuiting	Oct 25 2024	1	**Transcending**	Jan 3 2025	6	Intuiting
Aug 17 2024	10	Evolving	Oct 26 2024	2	Remembering	Jan 4 2025	7	Evolving
Aug 18 2024	11	Self-Regulating	Oct 27 2024	3	Loving	Jan 5 2025	8	Self-Regulating
Aug 19 2024	12	Catalyzing	Oct 28 2024	4	Feeling	Jan 6 2025	9	Catalyzing
Aug 20 2024	13	Enlightening	Oct 29 2024	5	Devoting	Jan 7 2025	10	Enlightening

Date	UE Earth Energy	Date	UE Earth Energy	Date	UE Earth Energy
Jan 8 2025	11 Being	Mar 19 2025	3 Illuminating	May 28 2025	8 Being
Jan 9 2025	12 Breathing	Mar 20 2025	4 Choosing	May 29 2025	9 Breathing
Jan 10 2025	13 Listening	Mar 21 2025	5 Exploring	May 30 2025	10 Listening
Jan 11 2025	**1 Planting**	Mar 22 2025	6 Healing	May 31 2025	11 Planting
Jan 12 2025	2 Moving	Mar 23 2025	7 Seeing	Jun 1 2025	12 Moving
Jan 13 2025	3 Transcending	Mar 24 2025	8 Intuiting	Jun 2 2025	13 Transcending
Jan 14 2025	4 Remembering	Mar 25 2025	9 Evolving	Jun 3 2025	**1 Remembering**
Jan 15 2025	5 Loving	Mar 26 2025	10 Self-Regulating	Jun 4 2025	2 Loving
Jan 16 2025	6 Feeling	Mar 27 2025	11 Catalyzing	Jun 5 2025	3 Feeling
Jan 17 2025	7 Devoting	Mar 28 2025	12 Enlightening	Jun 6 2025	4 Devoting
Jan 18 2025	8 Illuminating	Mar 29 2025	13 Being	Jun 7 2025	5 Illuminating
Jan 19 2025	9 Choosing	Mar 30 2025	**1 Breathing**	Jun 8 2025	6 Choosing
Jan 20 2025	10 Exploring	Mar 31 2025	2 Listening	Jun 9 2025	7 Exploring
Jan 21 2025	11 Healing	Apr 1 2025	3 Planting	Jun 10 2025	8 Healing
Jan 22 2025	12 Seeing	Apr 2 2025	4 Moving	Jun 11 2025	9 Seeing
Jan 23 2025	13 Intuiting	Apr 3 2025	5 Transcending	Jun 12 2025	10 Intuiting
Jan 24 2025	**1 Evolving**	Apr 4 2025	6 Remembering	Jun 13 2025	11 Evolving
Jan 25 2025	2 Self-Regulating	Apr 5 2025	7 Loving	Jun 14 2025	12 Self-Regulating
Jan 26 2025	3 Catalyzing	Apr 6 2025	8 Feeling	Jun 15 2025	13 Catalyzing
Jan 27 2025	4 Enlightening	Apr 7 2025	9 Devoting	Jun 16 2025	**1 Enlightening**
Jan 28 2025	5 Being	Apr 8 2025	10 Illuminating	Jun 17 2025	2 Being
Jan 29 2025	6 Breathing	Apr 9 2025	11 Choosing	Jun 18 2025	3 Breathing
Jan 30 2025	7 Listening	Apr 10 2025	12 Exploring	Jun 19 2025	4 Listening
Jan 31 2025	8 Planting	Apr 11 2025	13 Healing	Jun 20 2025	5 Planting
Feb 1 2025	9 Moving	Apr 12 2025	**1 Seeing**	Jun 21 2025	6 Moving
Feb 2 2025	10 Transcending	Apr 13 2025	2 Intuiting	Jun 22 2025	7 Transcending
Feb 3 2025	11 Remembering	Apr 14 2025	3 Evolving	Jun 23 2025	8 Remembering
Feb 4 2025	12 Loving	Apr 15 2025	4 Self-Regulating	Jun 24 2025	9 Loving
Feb 5 2025	13 Feeling	Apr 16 2025	5 Catalyzing	Jun 25 2025	10 Feeling
Feb 6 2025	**1 Devoting**	Apr 17 2025	6 Enlightening	Jun 26 2025	11 Devoting
Feb 7 2025	2 Illuminating	Apr 18 2025	7 Being	Jun 27 2025	12 Illuminating
Feb 8 2025	3 Choosing	Apr 19 2025	8 Breathing	Jun 28 2025	13 Choosing
Feb 9 2025	4 Exploring	Apr 20 2025	9 Listening	Jun 29 2025	**1 Exploring**
Feb 10 2025	5 Healing	Apr 21 2025	10 Planting	Jun 30 2025	2 Healing
Feb 11 2025	6 Seeing	Apr 22 2025	11 Moving	Jul 1 2025	3 Seeing
Feb 12 2025	7 Intuiting	Apr 23 2025	12 Transcending	Jul 2 2025	4 Intuiting
Feb 13 2025	8 Evolving	Apr 24 2025	13 Remembering	Jul 3 2025	5 Evolving
Feb 14 2025	9 Self-Regulating	Apr 25 2025	**1 Loving**	Jul 4 2025	6 Self-Regulating
Feb 15 2025	10 Catalyzing	Apr 26 2025	2 Feeling	Jul 5 2025	7 Catalyzing
Feb 16 2025	11 Enlightening	Apr 27 2025	3 Devoting	Jul 6 2025	8 Enlightening
Feb 17 2025	12 Being	Apr 28 2025	4 Illuminating	Jul 7 2025	9 Being
Feb 18 2025	13 Breathing	Apr 29 2025	5 Choosing	Jul 8 2025	10 Breathing
Feb 19 2025	**1 Listening**	Apr 30 2025	6 Exploring	Jul 9 2025	11 Listening
Feb 20 2025	2 Planting	May 1 2025	7 Healing	Jul 10 2025	12 Planting
Feb 21 2025	3 Moving	May 2 2025	8 Seeing	Jul 11 2025	13 Moving
Feb 22 2025	4 Transcending	May 3 2025	9 Intuiting	Jul 12 2025	**1 Transcending**
Feb 23 2025	5 Remembering	May 4 2025	10 Evolving	Jul 13 2025	2 Remembering
Feb 24 2025	6 Loving	May 5 2025	11 Self-Regulating	Jul 14 2025	3 Loving
Feb 25 2025	7 Feeling	May 6 2025	12 Catalyzing	Jul 15 2025	4 Feeling
Feb 26 2025	8 Devoting	May 7 2025	13 Enlightening	Jul 16 2025	5 Devoting
Feb 27 2025	9 Illuminating	May 8 2025	**1 Being**	Jul 17 2025	6 Illuminating
Feb 28 2025	10 Choosing	May 9 2025	2 Breathing	Jul 18 2025	7 Choosing
Mar 1 2025	11 Exploring	May 10 2025	3 Listening	Jul 19 2025	8 Exploring
Mar 2 2025	12 Healing	May 11 2025	4 Planting	Jul 20 2025	9 Healing
Mar 3 2025	13 Seeing	May 12 2025	5 Moving	Jul 21 2025	10 Seeing
Mar 4 2025	**1 Intuiting**	May 13 2025	6 Transcending	Jul 22 2025	11 Intuiting
Mar 5 2025	2 Evolving	May 14 2025	7 Remembering	Jul 23 2025	12 Evolving
Mar 6 2025	3 Self-Regulating	May 15 2025	8 Loving	Jul 24 2025	13 Self-Regulating
Mar 7 2025	4 Catalyzing	May 16 2025	9 Feeling	Jul 25 2025	**1 Catalyzing**
Mar 8 2025	5 Enlightening	May 17 2025	10 Devoting	Jul 26 2025	2 Enlightening
Mar 9 2025	6 Being	May 18 2025	11 Illuminating	Jul 27 2025	3 Being
Mar 10 2025	7 Breathing	May 19 2025	12 Choosing	Jul 28 2025	4 Breathing
Mar 11 2025	8 Listening	May 20 2025	13 Exploring	Jul 29 2025	5 Listening
Mar 12 2025	9 Planting	May 21 2025	**1 Healing**	Jul 30 2025	6 Planting
Mar 13 2025	10 Moving	May 22 2025	2 Seeing	Jul 31 2025	7 Moving
Mar 14 2025	11 Transcending	May 23 2025	3 Intuiting	Aug 1 2025	8 Transcending
Mar 15 2025	12 Remembering	May 24 2025	4 Evolving	Aug 2 2025	9 Remembering
Mar 16 2025	13 Loving	May 25 2025	5 Self-Regulating	Aug 3 2025	10 Loving
Mar 17 2025	**1 Feeling**	May 26 2025	6 Catalyzing	Aug 4 2025	11 Feeling
Mar 18 2025	2 Devoting	May 27 2025	7 Enlightening	Aug 5 2025	12 Devoting

Date	UE	Earth Energy	Date	UE	Earth Energy	Date	UE	Earth Energy
Aug 6 2025	13	Illuminating	Oct 15 2025	5	Being	Dec 24 2025	10	Illuminating
Aug 7 2025	1	**Choosing**	Oct 16 2025	6	Breathing	Dec 25 2025	11	Choosing
Aug 8 2025	2	Exploring	Oct 17 2025	7	Listening	Dec 26 2025	12	Exploring
Aug 9 2025	3	Healing	Oct 18 2025	8	Planting	Dec 27 2025	13	Healing
Aug 10 2025	4	Seeing	Oct 19 2025	9	Moving	Dec 28 2025	1	**Seeing**
Aug 11 2025	5	Intuiting	Oct 20 2025	10	Transcending	Dec 29 2025	2	Intuiting
Aug 12 2025	6	Evolving	Oct 21 2025	11	Remembering	Dec 30 2025	3	Evolving
Aug 13 2025	7	Self-Regulating	Oct 22 2025	12	Loving	Dec 31 2025	4	Self-Regulating
Aug 14 2025	8	Catalyzing	Oct 23 2025	13	Feeling	Jan 1 2026	5	Catalyzing
Aug 15 2025	9	Enlightening	Oct 24 2025	1	**Devoting**	Jan 2 2026	6	Enlightening
Aug 16 2025	10	Being	Oct 25 2025	2	Illuminating	Jan 3 2026	7	Being
Aug 17 2025	11	Breathing	Oct 26 2025	3	Choosing	Jan 4 2026	8	Breathing
Aug 18 2025	12	Listening	Oct 27 2025	4	Exploring	Jan 5 2026	9	Listening
Aug 19 2025	13	Planting	Oct 28 2025	5	Healing	Jan 6 2026	10	Planting
Aug 20 2025	1	**Moving**	Oct 29 2025	6	Seeing	Jan 7 2026	11	Moving
Aug 21 2025	2	Transcending	Oct 30 2025	7	Intuiting	Jan 8 2026	12	Transcending
Aug 22 2025	3	Remembering	Oct 31 2025	8	Evolving	Jan 9 2026	13	Remembering
Aug 23 2025	4	Loving	Nov 1 2025	9	Self-Regulating	Jan 10 2026	1	**Loving**
Aug 24 2025	5	Feeling	Nov 2 2025	10	Catalyzing	Jan 11 2026	2	Feeling
Aug 25 2025	6	Devoting	Nov 3 2025	11	Enlightening	Jan 12 2026	3	Devoting
Aug 26 2025	7	Illuminating	Nov 4 2025	12	Being	Jan 13 2026	4	Illuminating
Aug 27 2025	8	Choosing	Nov 5 2025	13	Breathing	Jan 14 2026	5	Choosing
Aug 28 2025	9	Exploring	Nov 6 2025	1	**Listening**	Jan 15 2026	6	Exploring
Aug 29 2025	10	Healing	Nov 7 2025	2	Planting	Jan 16 2026	7	Healing
Aug 30 2025	11	Seeing	Nov 8 2025	3	Moving	Jan 17 2026	8	Seeing
Aug 31 2025	12	Intuiting	Nov 9 2025	4	Transcending	Jan 18 2026	9	Intuiting
Sep 1 2025	13	Evolving	Nov 10 2025	5	Remembering	Jan 19 2026	10	Evolving
Sep 2 2025	1	**Self-Regulating**	Nov 11 2025	6	Loving	Jan 20 2026	11	Self-Regulating
Sep 3 2025	2	Catalyzing	Nov 12 2025	7	Feeling	Jan 21 2026	12	Catalyzing
Sep 4 2025	3	Enlightening	Nov 13 2025	8	Devoting	Jan 22 2026	13	Enlightening
Sep 5 2025	4	Being	Nov 14 2025	9	Illuminating	Jan 23 2026	1	**Being**
Sep 6 2025	5	Breathing	Nov 15 2025	10	Choosing	Jan 24 2026	2	Breathing
Sep 7 2025	6	Listening	Nov 16 2025	11	Exploring	Jan 25 2026	3	Listening
Sep 8 2025	7	Planting	Nov 17 2025	12	Healing	Jan 26 2026	4	Planting
Sep 9 2025	8	Moving	Nov 18 2025	13	Seeing	Jan 27 2026	5	Moving
Sep 10 2025	9	Transcending	Nov 19 2025	1	**Intuiting**	Jan 28 2026	6	Transcending
Sep 11 2025	10	Remembering	Nov 20 2025	2	Evolving	Jan 29 2026	7	Remembering
Sep 12 2025	11	Loving	Nov 21 2025	3	Self-Regulating	Jan 30 2026	8	Loving
Sep 13 2025	12	Feeling	Nov 22 2025	4	Catalyzing	Jan 31 2026	9	Feeling
Sep 14 2025	13	Devoting	Nov 23 2025	5	Enlightening	Feb 1 2026	10	Devoting
Sep 15 2025	1	**Illuminating**	Nov 24 2025	6	Being	Feb 2 2026	11	Illuminating
Sep 16 2025	2	Choosing	Nov 25 2025	7	Breathing	Feb 3 2026	12	Choosing
Sep 17 2025	3	Exploring	Nov 26 2025	8	Listening	Feb 4 2026	13	Exploring
Sep 18 2025	4	Healing	Nov 27 2025	9	Planting	Feb 5 2026	1	**Healing**
Sep 19 2025	5	Seeing	Nov 28 2025	10	Moving	Feb 6 2026	2	Seeing
Sep 20 2025	6	Intuiting	Nov 29 2025	11	Transcending	Feb 7 2026	3	Intuiting
Sep 21 2025	7	Evolving	Nov 30 2025	12	Remembering	Feb 8 2026	4	Evolving
Sep 22 2025	8	Self-Regulating	Dec 1 2025	13	Loving	Feb 9 2026	5	Self-Regulating
Sep 23 2025	9	Catalyzing	Dec 2 2025	1	**Feeling**	Feb 10 2026	6	Catalyzing
Sep 24 2025	10	Enlightening	Dec 3 2025	2	Devoting	Feb 11 2026	7	Enlightening
Sep 25 2025	11	Being	Dec 4 2025	3	Illuminating	Feb 12 2026	8	Being
Sep 26 2025	12	Breathing	Dec 5 2025	4	Choosing	Feb 13 2026	9	Breathing
Sep 27 2025	13	Listening	Dec 6 2025	5	Exploring	Feb 14 2026	10	Listening
Sep 28 2025	1	**Planting**	Dec 7 2025	6	Healing	Feb 15 2026	11	Planting
Sep 29 2025	2	Moving	Dec 8 2025	7	Seeing	Feb 16 2026	12	Moving
Sep 30 2025	3	Transcending	Dec 9 2025	8	Intuiting	Feb 17 2026	13	Transcending
Oct 1 2025	4	Remembering	Dec 10 2025	9	Evolving	Feb 18 2026	1	**Remembering**
Oct 2 2025	5	Loving	Dec 11 2025	10	Self-Regulating	Feb 19 2026	2	Loving
Oct 3 2025	6	Feeling	Dec 12 2025	11	Catalyzing	Feb 20 2026	3	Feeling
Oct 4 2025	7	Devoting	Dec 13 2025	12	Enlightening	Feb 21 2026	4	Devoting
Oct 5 2025	8	Illuminating	Dec 14 2025	13	Being	Feb 22 2026	5	Illuminating
Oct 6 2025	9	Choosing	Dec 15 2025	1	**Breathing**	Feb 23 2026	6	Choosing
Oct 7 2025	10	Exploring	Dec 16 2025	2	Listening	Feb 24 2026	7	Exploring
Oct 8 2025	11	Healing	Dec 17 2025	3	Planting	Feb 25 2026	8	Healing
Oct 9 2025	12	Seeing	Dec 18 2025	4	Moving	Feb 26 2026	9	Seeing
Oct 10 2025	13	Intuiting	Dec 19 2025	5	Transcending	Feb 27 2026	10	Intuiting
Oct 11 2025	1	**Evolving**	Dec 20 2025	6	Remembering	Feb 28 2026	11	Evolving
Oct 12 2025	2	Self-Regulating	Dec 21 2025	7	Loving	Mar 1 2026	12	Self-Regulating
Oct 13 2025	3	Catalyzing	Dec 22 2025	8	Feeling	Mar 2 2026	13	Catalyzing
Oct 14 2025	4	Enlightening	Dec 23 2025	9	Devoting	Mar 3 2026	1	**Enlightening**

Date	UE	Earth Energy	Date	UE	Earth Energy	Date	UE	Earth Energy
Mar 4 2026	2	Being	May 13 2026	7	Illuminating	Jul 22 2026	12	Being
Mar 5 2026	3	Breathing	May 14 2026	8	Choosing	Jul 23 2026	13	Breathing
Mar 6 2026	4	Listening	May 15 2026	9	Exploring	Jul 24 2026	1	Listening
Mar 7 2026	5	Planting	May 16 2026	10	Healing	Jul 25 2026	2	Planting
Mar 8 2026	6	Moving	May 17 2026	11	Seeing	Jul 26 2026	3	Moving
Mar 9 2026	7	Transcending	May 18 2026	12	Intuiting	Jul 27 2026	4	Transcending
Mar 10 2026	8	Remembering	May 19 2026	13	Evolving	Jul 28 2026	5	Remembering
Mar 11 2026	9	Loving	May 20 2026	1	Self-Regulating	Jul 29 2026	6	Loving
Mar 12 2026	10	Feeling	May 21 2026	2	Catalyzing	Jul 30 2026	7	Feeling
Mar 13 2026	11	Devoting	May 22 2026	3	Enlightening	Jul 31 2026	8	Devoting
Mar 14 2026	12	Illuminating	May 23 2026	4	Being	Aug 1 2026	9	Illuminating
Mar 15 2026	13	Choosing	May 24 2026	5	Breathing	Aug 2 2026	10	Choosing
Mar 16 2026	1	Exploring	May 25 2026	6	Listening	Aug 3 2026	11	Exploring
Mar 17 2026	2	Healing	May 26 2026	7	Planting	Aug 4 2026	12	Healing
Mar 18 2026	3	Seeing	May 27 2026	8	Moving	Aug 5 2026	13	Seeing
Mar 19 2026	4	Intuiting	May 28 2026	9	Transcending	Aug 6 2026	1	Intuiting
Mar 20 2026	5	Evolving	May 29 2026	10	Remembering	Aug 7 2026	2	Evolving
Mar 21 2026	6	Self-Regulating	May 30 2026	11	Loving	Aug 8 2026	3	Self-Regulating
Mar 22 2026	7	Catalyzing	May 31 2026	12	Feeling	Aug 9 2026	4	Catalyzing
Mar 23 2026	8	Enlightening	Jun 1 2026	13	Devoting	Aug 10 2026	5	Enlightening
Mar 24 2026	9	Being	Jun 2 2026	1	Illuminating	Aug 11 2026	6	Being
Mar 25 2026	10	Breathing	Jun 3 2026	2	Choosing	Aug 12 2026	7	Breathing
Mar 26 2026	11	Listening	Jun 4 2026	3	Exploring	Aug 13 2026	8	Listening
Mar 27 2026	12	Planting	Jun 5 2026	4	Healing	Aug 14 2026	9	Planting
Mar 28 2026	13	Moving	Jun 6 2026	5	Seeing	Aug 15 2026	10	Moving
Mar 29 2026	1	Transcending	Jun 7 2026	6	Intuiting	Aug 16 2026	11	Transcending
Mar 30 2026	2	Remembering	Jun 8 2026	7	Evolving	Aug 17 2026	12	Remembering
Mar 31 2026	3	Loving	Jun 9 2026	8	Self-Regulating	Aug 18 2026	13	Loving
Apr 1 2026	4	Feeling	Jun 10 2026	9	Catalyzing	Aug 19 2026	1	Feeling
Apr 2 2026	5	Devoting	Jun 11 2026	10	Enlightening	Aug 20 2026	2	Devoting
Apr 3 2026	6	Illuminating	Jun 12 2026	11	Being	Aug 21 2026	3	Illuminating
Apr 4 2026	7	Choosing	Jun 13 2026	12	Breathing	Aug 22 2026	4	Choosing
Apr 5 2026	8	Exploring	Jun 14 2026	13	Listening	Aug 23 2026	5	Exploring
Apr 6 2026	9	Healing	Jun 15 2026	1	Planting	Aug 24 2026	6	Healing
Apr 7 2026	10	Seeing	Jun 16 2026	2	Moving	Aug 25 2026	7	Seeing
Apr 8 2026	11	Intuiting	Jun 17 2026	3	Transcending	Aug 26 2026	8	Intuiting
Apr 9 2026	12	Evolving	Jun 18 2026	4	Remembering	Aug 27 2026	9	Evolving
Apr 10 2026	13	Self-Regulating	Jun 19 2026	5	Loving	Aug 28 2026	10	Self-Regulating
Apr 11 2026	1	Catalyzing	Jun 20 2026	6	Feeling	Aug 29 2026	11	Catalyzing
Apr 12 2026	2	Enlightening	Jun 21 2026	7	Devoting	Aug 30 2026	12	Enlightening
Apr 13 2026	3	Being	Jun 22 2026	8	Illuminating	Aug 31 2026	13	Being
Apr 14 2026	4	Breathing	Jun 23 2026	9	Choosing	Sep 1 2026	1	Breathing
Apr 15 2026	5	Listening	Jun 24 2026	10	Exploring	Sep 2 2026	2	Listening
Apr 16 2026	6	Planting	Jun 25 2026	11	Healing	Sep 3 2026	3	Planting
Apr 17 2026	7	Moving	Jun 26 2026	12	Seeing	Sep 4 2026	4	Moving
Apr 18 2026	8	Transcending	Jun 27 2026	13	Intuiting	Sep 5 2026	5	Transcending
Apr 19 2026	9	Remembering	Jun 28 2026	1	Evolving	Sep 6 2026	6	Remembering
Apr 20 2026	10	Loving	Jun 29 2026	2	Self-Regulating	Sep 7 2026	7	Loving
Apr 21 2026	11	Feeling	Jun 30 2026	3	Catalyzing	Sep 8 2026	8	Feeling
Apr 22 2026	12	Devoting	Jul 1 2026	4	Enlightening	Sep 9 2026	9	Devoting
Apr 23 2026	13	Illuminating	Jul 2 2026	5	Being	Sep 10 2026	10	Illuminating
Apr 24 2026	1	Choosing	Jul 3 2026	6	Breathing	Sep 11 2026	11	Choosing
Apr 25 2026	2	Exploring	Jul 4 2026	7	Listening	Sep 12 2026	12	Exploring
Apr 26 2026	3	Healing	Jul 5 2026	8	Planting	Sep 13 2026	13	Healing
Apr 27 2026	4	Seeing	Jul 6 2026	9	Moving	Sep 14 2026	1	Seeing
Apr 28 2026	5	Intuiting	Jul 7 2026	10	Transcending	Sep 15 2026	2	Intuiting
Apr 29 2026	6	Evolving	Jul 8 2026	11	Remembering	Sep 16 2026	3	Evolving
Apr 30 2026	7	Self-Regulating	Jul 9 2026	12	Loving	Sep 17 2026	4	Self-Regulating
May 1 2026	8	Catalyzing	Jul 10 2026	13	Feeling	Sep 18 2026	5	Catalyzing
May 2 2026	9	Enlightening	Jul 11 2026	1	Devoting	Sep 19 2026	6	Enlightening
May 3 2026	10	Being	Jul 12 2026	2	Illuminating	Sep 20 2026	7	Being
May 4 2026	11	Breathing	Jul 13 2026	3	Choosing	Sep 21 2026	8	Breathing
May 5 2026	12	Listening	Jul 14 2026	4	Exploring	Sep 22 2026	9	Listening
May 6 2026	13	Planting	Jul 15 2026	5	Healing	Sep 23 2026	10	Planting
May 7 2026	1	Moving	Jul 16 2026	6	Seeing	Sep 24 2026	11	Moving
May 8 2026	2	Transcending	Jul 17 2026	7	Intuiting	Sep 25 2026	12	Transcending
May 9 2026	3	Remembering	Jul 18 2026	8	Evolving	Sep 26 2026	13	Remembering
May 10 2026	4	Loving	Jul 19 2026	9	Self-Regulating	Sep 27 2026	1	Loving
May 11 2026	5	Feeling	Jul 20 2026	10	Catalyzing	Sep 28 2026	2	Feeling
May 12 2026	6	Devoting	Jul 21 2026	11	Enlightening	Sep 29 2026	3	Devoting

Date	UE Earth Energy	Date	UE Earth Energy	Date	UE Earth Energy
Sep 30 2026	4 Illuminating	Dec 9 2026	9 Being	Feb 17 2027	1 **Illuminating**
Oct 1 2026	5 Choosing	Dec 10 2026	10 Breathing	Feb 18 2027	2 Choosing
Oct 2 2026	6 Exploring	Dec 11 2026	11 Listening	Feb 19 2027	3 Exploring
Oct 3 2026	7 Healing	Dec 12 2026	12 Planting	Feb 20 2027	4 Healing
Oct 4 2026	8 Seeing	Dec 13 2026	13 Moving	Feb 21 2027	5 Seeing
Oct 5 2026	9 Intuiting	Dec 14 2026	1 **Transcending**	Feb 22 2027	6 Intuiting
Oct 6 2026	10 Evolving	Dec 15 2026	2 Remembering	Feb 23 2027	7 Evolving
Oct 7 2026	11 Self-Regulating	Dec 16 2026	3 Loving	Feb 24 2027	8 Self-Regulating
Oct 8 2026	12 Catalyzing	Dec 17 2026	4 Feeling	Feb 25 2027	9 Catalyzing
Oct 9 2026	13 Enlightening	Dec 18 2026	5 Devoting	Feb 26 2027	10 Enlightening
Oct 10 2026	1 **Being**	Dec 19 2026	6 Illuminating	Feb 27 2027	11 Being
Oct 11 2026	2 Breathing	Dec 20 2026	7 Choosing	Feb 28 2027	12 Breathing
Oct 12 2026	3 Listening	Dec 21 2026	8 Exploring	Mar 1 2027	13 Listening
Oct 13 2026	4 Planting	Dec 22 2026	9 Healing	Mar 2 2027	1 **Planting**
Oct 14 2026	5 Moving	Dec 23 2026	10 Seeing	Mar 3 2027	2 Moving
Oct 15 2026	6 Transcending	Dec 24 2026	11 Intuiting	Mar 4 2027	3 Transcending
Oct 16 2026	7 Remembering	Dec 25 2026	12 Evolving	Mar 5 2027	4 Remembering
Oct 17 2026	8 Loving	Dec 26 2026	13 Self-Regulating	Mar 6 2027	5 Loving
Oct 18 2026	9 Feeling	Dec 27 2026	1 **Catalyzing**	Mar 7 2027	6 Feeling
Oct 19 2026	10 Devoting	Dec 28 2026	2 Enlightening	Mar 8 2027	7 Devoting
Oct 20 2026	11 Illuminating	Dec 29 2026	3 Being	Mar 9 2027	8 Illuminating
Oct 21 2026	12 Choosing	Dec 30 2026	4 Breathing	Mar 10 2027	9 Choosing
Oct 22 2026	13 Exploring	Dec 31 2026	5 Listening	Mar 11 2027	10 Exploring
Oct 23 2026	1 **Healing**	Jan 1 2027	6 Planting	Mar 12 2027	11 Healing
Oct 24 2026	2 Seeing	Jan 2 2027	7 Moving	Mar 13 2027	12 Seeing
Oct 25 2026	3 Intuiting	Jan 3 2027	8 Transcending	Mar 14 2027	13 Intuiting
Oct 26 2026	4 Evolving	Jan 4 2027	9 Remembering	Mar 15 2027	1 **Evolving**
Oct 27 2026	5 Self-Regulating	Jan 5 2027	10 Loving	Mar 16 2027	2 Self-Regulating
Oct 28 2026	6 Catalyzing	Jan 6 2027	11 Feeling	Mar 17 2027	3 Catalyzing
Oct 29 2026	7 Enlightening	Jan 7 2027	12 Devoting	Mar 18 2027	4 Enlightening
Oct 30 2026	8 Being	Jan 8 2027	13 Illuminating	Mar 19 2027	5 Being
Oct 31 2026	9 Breathing	Jan 9 2027	1 **Choosing**	Mar 20 2027	6 Breathing
Nov 1 2026	10 Listening	Jan 10 2027	2 Exploring	Mar 21 2027	7 Listening
Nov 2 2026	11 Planting	Jan 11 2027	3 Healing	Mar 22 2027	8 Planting
Nov 3 2026	12 Moving	Jan 12 2027	4 Seeing	Mar 23 2027	9 Moving
Nov 4 2026	13 Transcending	Jan 13 2027	5 Intuiting	Mar 24 2027	10 Transcending
Nov 5 2026	1 **Remembering**	Jan 14 2027	6 Evolving	Mar 25 2027	11 Remembering
Nov 6 2026	2 Loving	Jan 15 2027	7 Self-Regulating	Mar 26 2027	12 Loving
Nov 7 2026	3 Feeling	Jan 16 2027	8 Catalyzing	Mar 27 2027	13 Feeling
Nov 8 2026	4 Devoting	Jan 17 2027	9 Enlightening	Mar 28 2027	1 **Devoting**
Nov 9 2026	5 Illuminating	Jan 18 2027	10 Being	Mar 29 2027	2 Illuminating
Nov 10 2026	6 Choosing	Jan 19 2027	11 Breathing	Mar 30 2027	3 Choosing
Nov 11 2026	7 Exploring	Jan 20 2027	12 Listening	Mar 31 2027	4 Exploring
Nov 12 2026	8 Healing	Jan 21 2027	13 Planting	Apr 1 2027	5 Healing
Nov 13 2026	9 Seeing	Jan 22 2027	1 **Moving**	Apr 2 2027	6 Seeing
Nov 14 2026	10 Intuiting	Jan 23 2027	2 Transcending	Apr 3 2027	7 Intuiting
Nov 15 2026	11 Evolving	Jan 24 2027	3 Remembering	Apr 4 2027	8 Evolving
Nov 16 2026	12 Self-Regulating	Jan 25 2027	4 Loving	Apr 5 2027	9 Self-Regulating
Nov 17 2026	13 Catalyzing	Jan 26 2027	5 Feeling	Apr 6 2027	10 Catalyzing
Nov 18 2026	1 **Enlightening**	Jan 27 2027	6 Devoting	Apr 7 2027	11 Enlightening
Nov 19 2026	2 Being	Jan 28 2027	7 Illuminating	Apr 8 2027	12 Being
Nov 20 2026	3 Breathing	Jan 29 2027	8 Choosing	Apr 9 2027	13 Breathing
Nov 21 2026	4 Listening	Jan 30 2027	9 Exploring	Apr 10 2027	1 **Listening**
Nov 22 2026	5 Planting	Jan 31 2027	10 Healing	Apr 11 2027	2 Planting
Nov 23 2026	6 Moving	Feb 1 2027	11 Seeing	Apr 12 2027	3 Moving
Nov 24 2026	7 Transcending	Feb 2 2027	12 Intuiting	Apr 13 2027	4 Transcending
Nov 25 2026	8 Remembering	Feb 3 2027	13 Evolving	Apr 14 2027	5 Remembering
Nov 26 2026	9 Loving	Feb 4 2027	1 **Self-Regulating**	Apr 15 2027	6 Loving
Nov 27 2026	10 Feeling	Feb 5 2027	2 Catalyzing	Apr 16 2027	7 Feeling
Nov 28 2026	11 Devoting	Feb 6 2027	3 Enlightening	Apr 17 2027	8 Devoting
Nov 29 2026	12 Illuminating	Feb 7 2027	4 Being	Apr 18 2027	9 Illuminating
Nov 30 2026	13 Choosing	Feb 8 2027	5 Breathing	Apr 19 2027	10 Choosing
Dec 1 2026	1 **Exploring**	Feb 9 2027	6 Listening	Apr 20 2027	11 Exploring
Dec 2 2026	2 Healing	Feb 10 2027	7 Planting	Apr 21 2027	12 Healing
Dec 3 2026	3 Seeing	Feb 11 2027	8 Moving	Apr 22 2027	13 Seeing
Dec 4 2026	4 Intuiting	Feb 12 2027	9 Transcending	Apr 23 2027	1 **Intuiting**
Dec 5 2026	5 Evolving	Feb 13 2027	10 Remembering	Apr 24 2027	2 Evolving
Dec 6 2026	6 Self-Regulating	Feb 14 2027	11 Loving	Apr 25 2027	3 Self-Regulating
Dec 7 2026	7 Catalyzing	Feb 15 2027	12 Feeling	Apr 26 2027	4 Catalyzing
Dec 8 2026	8 Enlightening	Feb 16 2027	13 Devoting	Apr 27 2027	5 Enlightening

Date	UE Earth Energy	Date	UE Earth Energy	Date	UE Earth Energy
Apr 28 2027	6 Being	Jul 7 2027	11 Illuminating	Sep 15 2027	3 Being
Apr 29 2027	7 Breathing	Jul 8 2027	12 Choosing	Sep 16 2027	4 Breathing
Apr 30 2027	8 Listening	Jul 9 2027	13 Exploring	Sep 17 2027	5 Listening
May 1 2027	9 Planting	Jul 10 2027	1 Healing	Sep 18 2027	6 Planting
May 2 2027	10 Moving	Jul 11 2027	2 Seeing	Sep 19 2027	7 Moving
May 3 2027	11 Transcending	Jul 12 2027	3 Intuiting	Sep 20 2027	8 Transcending
May 4 2027	12 Remembering	Jul 13 2027	4 Evolving	Sep 21 2027	9 Remembering
May 5 2027	13 Loving	Jul 14 2027	5 Self-Regulating	Sep 22 2027	10 Loving
May 6 2027	1 Feeling	Jul 15 2027	6 Catalyzing	Sep 23 2027	11 Feeling
May 7 2027	2 Devoting	Jul 16 2027	7 Enlightening	Sep 24 2027	12 Devoting
May 8 2027	3 Illuminating	Jul 17 2027	8 Being	Sep 25 2027	13 Illuminating
May 9 2027	4 Choosing	Jul 18 2027	9 Breathing	Sep 26 2027	1 Choosing
May 10 2027	5 Exploring	Jul 19 2027	10 Listening	Sep 27 2027	2 Exploring
May 11 2027	6 Healing	Jul 20 2027	11 Planting	Sep 28 2027	3 Healing
May 12 2027	7 Seeing	Jul 21 2027	12 Moving	Sep 29 2027	4 Seeing
May 13 2027	8 Intuiting	Jul 22 2027	13 Transcending	Sep 30 2027	5 Intuiting
May 14 2027	9 Evolving	Jul 23 2027	1 Remembering	Oct 1 2027	6 Evolving
May 15 2027	10 Self-Regulating	Jul 24 2027	2 Loving	Oct 2 2027	7 Self-Regulating
May 16 2027	11 Catalyzing	Jul 25 2027	3 Feeling	Oct 3 2027	8 Catalyzing
May 17 2027	12 Enlightening	Jul 26 2027	4 Devoting	Oct 4 2027	9 Enlightening
May 18 2027	13 Being	Jul 27 2027	5 Illuminating	Oct 5 2027	10 Being
May 19 2027	1 Breathing	Jul 28 2027	6 Choosing	Oct 6 2027	11 Breathing
May 20 2027	2 Listening	Jul 29 2027	7 Exploring	Oct 7 2027	12 Listening
May 21 2027	3 Planting	Jul 30 2027	8 Healing	Oct 8 2027	13 Planting
May 22 2027	4 Moving	Jul 31 2027	9 Seeing	Oct 9 2027	1 Moving
May 23 2027	5 Transcending	Aug 1 2027	10 Intuiting	Oct 10 2027	2 Transcending
May 24 2027	6 Remembering	Aug 2 2027	11 Evolving	Oct 11 2027	3 Remembering
May 25 2027	7 Loving	Aug 3 2027	12 Self-Regulating	Oct 12 2027	4 Loving
May 26 2027	8 Feeling	Aug 4 2027	13 Catalyzing	Oct 13 2027	5 Feeling
May 27 2027	9 Devoting	Aug 5 2027	1 Enlightening	Oct 14 2027	6 Devoting
May 28 2027	10 Illuminating	Aug 6 2027	2 Being	Oct 15 2027	7 Illuminating
May 29 2027	11 Choosing	Aug 7 2027	3 Breathing	Oct 16 2027	8 Choosing
May 30 2027	12 Exploring	Aug 8 2027	4 Listening	Oct 17 2027	9 Exploring
May 31 2027	13 Healing	Aug 9 2027	5 Planting	Oct 18 2027	10 Healing
Jun 1 2027	1 Seeing	Aug 10 2027	6 Moving	Oct 19 2027	11 Seeing
Jun 2 2027	2 Intuiting	Aug 11 2027	7 Transcending	Oct 20 2027	12 Intuiting
Jun 3 2027	3 Evolving	Aug 12 2027	8 Remembering	Oct 21 2027	13 Evolving
Jun 4 2027	4 Self-Regulating	Aug 13 2027	9 Loving	Oct 22 2027	1 Self-Regulating
Jun 5 2027	5 Catalyzing	Aug 14 2027	10 Feeling	Oct 23 2027	2 Catalyzing
Jun 6 2027	6 Enlightening	Aug 15 2027	11 Devoting	Oct 24 2027	3 Enlightening
Jun 7 2027	7 Being	Aug 16 2027	12 Illuminating	Oct 25 2027	4 Being
Jun 8 2027	8 Breathing	Aug 17 2027	13 Choosing	Oct 26 2027	5 Breathing
Jun 9 2027	9 Listening	Aug 18 2027	1 Exploring	Oct 27 2027	6 Listening
Jun 10 2027	10 Planting	Aug 19 2027	2 Healing	Oct 28 2027	7 Planting
Jun 11 2027	11 Moving	Aug 20 2027	3 Seeing	Oct 29 2027	8 Moving
Jun 12 2027	12 Transcending	Aug 21 2027	4 Intuiting	Oct 30 2027	9 Transcending
Jun 13 2027	13 Remembering	Aug 22 2027	5 Evolving	Oct 31 2027	10 Remembering
Jun 14 2027	1 Loving	Aug 23 2027	6 Self-Regulating	Nov 1 2027	11 Loving
Jun 15 2027	2 Feeling	Aug 24 2027	7 Catalyzing	Nov 2 2027	12 Feeling
Jun 16 2027	3 Devoting	Aug 25 2027	8 Enlightening	Nov 3 2027	13 Devoting
Jun 17 2027	4 Illuminating	Aug 26 2027	9 Being	Nov 4 2027	1 Illuminating
Jun 18 2027	5 Choosing	Aug 27 2027	10 Breathing	Nov 5 2027	2 Choosing
Jun 19 2027	6 Exploring	Aug 28 2027	11 Listening	Nov 6 2027	3 Exploring
Jun 20 2027	7 Healing	Aug 29 2027	12 Planting	Nov 7 2027	4 Healing
Jun 21 2027	8 Seeing	Aug 30 2027	13 Moving	Nov 8 2027	5 Seeing
Jun 22 2027	9 Intuiting	Aug 31 2027	1 Transcending	Nov 9 2027	6 Intuiting
Jun 23 2027	10 Evolving	Sep 1 2027	2 Remembering	Nov 10 2027	7 Evolving
Jun 24 2027	11 Self-Regulating	Sep 2 2027	3 Loving	Nov 11 2027	8 Self-Regulating
Jun 25 2027	12 Catalyzing	Sep 3 2027	4 Feeling	Nov 12 2027	9 Catalyzing
Jun 26 2027	13 Enlightening	Sep 4 2027	5 Devoting	Nov 13 2027	10 Enlightening
Jun 27 2027	1 Being	Sep 5 2027	6 Illuminating	Nov 14 2027	11 Being
Jun 28 2027	2 Breathing	Sep 6 2027	7 Choosing	Nov 15 2027	12 Breathing
Jun 29 2027	3 Listening	Sep 7 2027	8 Exploring	Nov 16 2027	13 Listening
Jun 30 2027	4 Planting	Sep 8 2027	9 Healing	Nov 17 2027	1 Planting
Jul 1 2027	5 Moving	Sep 9 2027	10 Seeing	Nov 18 2027	2 Moving
Jul 2 2027	6 Transcending	Sep 10 2027	11 Intuiting	Nov 19 2027	3 Transcending
Jul 3 2027	7 Remembering	Sep 11 2027	12 Evolving	Nov 20 2027	4 Remembering
Jul 4 2027	8 Loving	Sep 12 2027	13 Self-Regulating	Nov 21 2027	5 Loving
Jul 5 2027	9 Feeling	Sep 13 2027	1 Catalyzing	Nov 22 2027	6 Feeling
Jul 6 2027	10 Devoting	Sep 14 2027	2 Enlightening	Nov 23 2027	7 Devoting

Date	UE	Earth Energy	Date	UE	Earth Energy	Date	UE	Earth Energy
Nov 24 2027	8	Illuminating	Feb 2 2028	13	Being	Apr 12 2028	5	Illuminating
Nov 25 2027	9	Choosing	Feb 3 2028	1	**Breathing**	Apr 13 2028	6	Choosing
Nov 26 2027	10	Exploring	Feb 4 2028	2	Listening	Apr 14 2028	7	Exploring
Nov 27 2027	11	Healing	Feb 5 2028	3	Planting	Apr 15 2028	8	Healing
Nov 28 2027	12	Seeing	Feb 6 2028	4	Moving	Apr 16 2028	9	Seeing
Nov 29 2027	13	Intuiting	Feb 7 2028	5	Transcending	Apr 17 2028	10	Intuiting
Nov 30 2027	1	**Evolving**	Feb 8 2028	6	Remembering	Apr 18 2028	11	Evolving
Dec 1 2027	2	Self-Regulating	Feb 9 2028	7	Loving	Apr 19 2028	12	Self-Regulating
Dec 2 2027	3	Catalyzing	Feb 10 2028	8	Feeling	Apr 20 2028	13	Catalyzing
Dec 3 2027	4	Enlightening	Feb 11 2028	9	Devoting	Apr 21 2028	1	**Enlightening**
Dec 4 2027	5	Being	Feb 12 2028	10	Illuminating	Apr 22 2028	2	Being
Dec 5 2027	6	Breathing	Feb 13 2028	11	Choosing	Apr 23 2028	3	Breathing
Dec 6 2027	7	Listening	Feb 14 2028	12	Exploring	Apr 24 2028	4	Listening
Dec 7 2027	8	Planting	Feb 15 2028	13	Healing	Apr 25 2028	5	Planting
Dec 8 2027	9	Moving	Feb 16 2028	1	**Seeing**	Apr 26 2028	6	Moving
Dec 9 2027	10	Transcending	Feb 17 2028	2	Intuiting	Apr 27 2028	7	Transcending
Dec 10 2027	11	Remembering	Feb 18 2028	3	Evolving	Apr 28 2028	8	Remembering
Dec 11 2027	12	Loving	Feb 19 2028	4	Self-Regulating	Apr 29 2028	9	Loving
Dec 12 2027	13	Feeling	Feb 20 2028	5	Catalyzing	Apr 30 2028	10	Feeling
Dec 13 2027	1	**Devoting**	Feb 21 2028	6	Enlightening	May 1 2028	11	Devoting
Dec 14 2027	2	Illuminating	Feb 22 2028	7	Being	May 2 2028	12	Illuminating
Dec 15 2027	3	Choosing	Feb 23 2028	8	Breathing	May 3 2028	13	Choosing
Dec 16 2027	4	Exploring	Feb 24 2028	9	Listening	May 4 2028	1	**Exploring**
Dec 17 2027	5	Healing	Feb 25 2028	10	Planting	May 5 2028	2	Healing
Dec 18 2027	6	Seeing	Feb 26 2028	11	Moving	May 6 2028	3	Seeing
Dec 19 2027	7	Intuiting	Feb 27 2028	12	Transcending	May 7 2028	4	Intuiting
Dec 20 2027	8	Evolving	Feb 28 2028	13	Remembering	May 8 2028	5	Evolving
Dec 21 2027	9	Self-Regulating	Feb 29 2028	1	**Loving**	May 9 2028	6	Self-Regulating
Dec 22 2027	10	Catalyzing	Mar 1 2028	2	Feeling	May 10 2028	7	Catalyzing
Dec 23 2027	11	Enlightening	Mar 2 2028	3	Devoting	May 11 2028	8	Enlightening
Dec 24 2027	12	Being	Mar 3 2028	4	Illuminating	May 12 2028	9	Being
Dec 25 2027	13	Breathing	Mar 4 2028	5	Choosing	May 13 2028	10	Breathing
Dec 26 2027	1	**Listening**	Mar 5 2028	6	Exploring	May 14 2028	11	Listening
Dec 27 2027	2	Planting	Mar 6 2028	7	Healing	May 15 2028	12	Planting
Dec 28 2027	3	Moving	Mar 7 2028	8	Seeing	May 16 2028	13	Moving
Dec 29 2027	4	Transcending	Mar 8 2028	9	Intuiting	May 17 2028	1	**Transcending**
Dec 30 2027	5	Remembering	Mar 9 2028	10	Evolving	May 18 2028	2	Remembering
Dec 31 2027	6	Loving	Mar 10 2028	11	Self-Regulating	May 19 2028	3	Loving
Jan 1 2028	7	Feeling	Mar 11 2028	12	Catalyzing	May 20 2028	4	Feeling
Jan 2 2028	8	Devoting	Mar 12 2028	13	Enlightening	May 21 2028	5	Devoting
Jan 3 2028	9	Illuminating	Mar 13 2028	1	**Being**	May 22 2028	6	Illuminating
Jan 4 2028	10	Choosing	Mar 14 2028	2	Breathing	May 23 2028	7	Choosing
Jan 5 2028	11	Exploring	Mar 15 2028	3	Listening	May 24 2028	8	Exploring
Jan 6 2028	12	Healing	Mar 16 2028	4	Planting	May 25 2028	9	Healing
Jan 7 2028	13	Seeing	Mar 17 2028	5	Moving	May 26 2028	10	Seeing
Jan 8 2028	1	**Intuiting**	Mar 18 2028	6	Transcending	May 27 2028	11	Intuiting
Jan 9 2028	2	Evolving	Mar 19 2028	7	Remembering	May 28 2028	12	Evolving
Jan 10 2028	3	Self-Regulating	Mar 20 2028	8	Loving	May 29 2028	13	Self-Regulating
Jan 11 2028	4	Catalyzing	Mar 21 2028	9	Feeling	May 30 2028	1	**Catalyzing**
Jan 12 2028	5	Enlightening	Mar 22 2028	10	Devoting	May 31 2028	2	Enlightening
Jan 13 2028	6	Being	Mar 23 2028	11	Illuminating	Jun 1 2028	3	Being
Jan 14 2028	7	Breathing	Mar 24 2028	12	Choosing	Jun 2 2028	4	Breathing
Jan 15 2028	8	Listening	Mar 25 2028	13	Exploring	Jun 3 2028	5	Listening
Jan 16 2028	9	Planting	Mar 26 2028	1	**Healing**	Jun 4 2028	6	Planting
Jan 17 2028	10	Moving	Mar 27 2028	2	Seeing	Jun 5 2028	7	Moving
Jan 18 2028	11	Transcending	Mar 28 2028	3	Intuiting	Jun 6 2028	8	Transcending
Jan 19 2028	12	Remembering	Mar 29 2028	4	Evolving	Jun 7 2028	9	Remembering
Jan 20 2028	13	Loving	Mar 30 2028	5	Self-Regulating	Jun 8 2028	10	Loving
Jan 21 2028	1	**Feeling**	Mar 31 2028	6	Catalyzing	Jun 9 2028	11	Feeling
Jan 22 2028	2	Devoting	Apr 1 2028	7	Enlightening	Jun 10 2028	12	Devoting
Jan 23 2028	3	Illuminating	Apr 2 2028	8	Being	Jun 11 2028	13	Illuminating
Jan 24 2028	4	Choosing	Apr 3 2028	9	Breathing	Jun 12 2028	1	**Choosing**
Jan 25 2028	5	Exploring	Apr 4 2028	10	Listening	Jun 13 2028	2	Exploring
Jan 26 2028	6	Healing	Apr 5 2028	11	Planting	Jun 14 2028	3	Healing
Jan 27 2028	7	Seeing	Apr 6 2028	12	Moving	Jun 15 2028	4	Seeing
Jan 28 2028	8	Intuiting	Apr 7 2028	13	Transcending	Jun 16 2028	5	Intuiting
Jan 29 2028	9	Evolving	Apr 8 2028	1	**Remembering**	Jun 17 2028	6	Evolving
Jan 30 2028	10	Self-Regulating	Apr 9 2028	2	Loving	Jun 18 2028	7	Self-Regulating
Jan 31 2028	11	Catalyzing	Apr 10 2028	3	Feeling	Jun 19 2028	8	Catalyzing
Feb 1 2028	12	Enlightening	Apr 11 2028	4	Devoting	Jun 20 2028	9	Enlightening

Date	UE	Earth Energy	Date	UE	Earth Energy	Date	UE	Earth Energy
Jun 21 2028	10	Being	Aug 30 2028	2	Illuminating	Nov 8 2028	7	Being
Jun 22 2028	11	Breathing	Aug 31 2028	3	Choosing	Nov 9 2028	8	Breathing
Jun 23 2028	12	Listening	Sep 1 2028	4	Exploring	Nov 10 2028	9	Listening
Jun 24 2028	13	Planting	Sep 2 2028	5	Healing	Nov 11 2028	10	Planting
Jun 25 2028	1	Moving	Sep 3 2028	6	Seeing	Nov 12 2028	11	Moving
Jun 26 2028	2	Transcending	Sep 4 2028	7	Intuiting	Nov 13 2028	12	Transcending
Jun 27 2028	3	Remembering	Sep 5 2028	8	Evolving	Nov 14 2028	13	Remembering
Jun 28 2028	4	Loving	Sep 6 2028	9	Self-Regulating	Nov 15 2028	1	**Loving**
Jun 29 2028	5	Feeling	Sep 7 2028	10	Catalyzing	Nov 16 2028	2	Feeling
Jun 30 2028	6	Devoting	Sep 8 2028	11	Enlightening	Nov 17 2028	3	Devoting
Jul 1 2028	7	Illuminating	Sep 9 2028	12	Being	Nov 18 2028	4	Illuminating
Jul 2 2028	8	Choosing	Sep 10 2028	13	Breathing	Nov 19 2028	5	Choosing
Jul 3 2028	9	Exploring	Sep 11 2028	1	**Listening**	Nov 20 2028	6	Exploring
Jul 4 2028	10	Healing	Sep 12 2028	2	Planting	Nov 21 2028	7	Healing
Jul 5 2028	11	Seeing	Sep 13 2028	3	Moving	Nov 22 2028	8	Seeing
Jul 6 2028	12	Intuiting	Sep 14 2028	4	Transcending	Nov 23 2028	9	Intuiting
Jul 7 2028	13	Evolving	Sep 15 2028	5	Remembering	Nov 24 2028	10	Evolving
Jul 8 2028	1	**Self-Regulating**	Sep 16 2028	6	Loving	Nov 25 2028	11	Self-Regulating
Jul 9 2028	2	Catalyzing	Sep 17 2028	7	Feeling	Nov 26 2028	12	Catalyzing
Jul 10 2028	3	Enlightening	Sep 18 2028	8	Devoting	Nov 27 2028	13	Enlightening
Jul 11 2028	4	Being	Sep 19 2028	9	Illuminating	Nov 28 2028	1	**Being**
Jul 12 2028	5	Breathing	Sep 20 2028	10	Choosing	Nov 29 2028	2	Breathing
Jul 13 2028	6	Listening	Sep 21 2028	11	Exploring	Nov 30 2028	3	Listening
Jul 14 2028	7	Planting	Sep 22 2028	12	Healing	Dec 1 2028	4	Planting
Jul 15 2028	8	Moving	Sep 23 2028	13	Seeing	Dec 2 2028	5	Moving
Jul 16 2028	9	Transcending	Sep 24 2028	1	**Intuiting**	Dec 3 2028	6	Transcending
Jul 17 2028	10	Remembering	Sep 25 2028	2	Evolving	Dec 4 2028	7	Remembering
Jul 18 2028	11	Loving	Sep 26 2028	3	Self-Regulating	Dec 5 2028	8	Loving
Jul 19 2028	12	Feeling	Sep 27 2028	4	Catalyzing	Dec 6 2028	9	Feeling
Jul 20 2028	13	Devoting	Sep 28 2028	5	Enlightening	Dec 7 2028	10	Devoting
Jul 21 2028	1	**Illuminating**	Sep 29 2028	6	Being	Dec 8 2028	11	Illuminating
Jul 22 2028	2	Choosing	Sep 30 2028	7	Breathing	Dec 9 2028	12	Choosing
Jul 23 2028	3	Exploring	Oct 1 2028	8	Listening	Dec 10 2028	13	Exploring
Jul 24 2028	4	Healing	Oct 2 2028	9	Planting	Dec 11 2028	1	**Healing**
Jul 25 2028	5	Seeing	Oct 3 2028	10	Moving	Dec 12 2028	2	Seeing
Jul 26 2028	6	Intuiting	Oct 4 2028	11	Transcending	Dec 13 2028	3	Intuiting
Jul 27 2028	7	Evolving	Oct 5 2028	12	Remembering	Dec 14 2028	4	Evolving
Jul 28 2028	8	Self-Regulating	Oct 6 2028	13	Loving	Dec 15 2028	5	Self-Regulating
Jul 29 2028	9	Catalyzing	Oct 7 2028	1	**Feeling**	Dec 16 2028	6	Catalyzing
Jul 30 2028	10	Enlightening	Oct 8 2028	2	Devoting	Dec 17 2028	7	Enlightening
Jul 31 2028	11	Being	Oct 9 2028	3	Illuminating	Dec 18 2028	8	Being
Aug 1 2028	12	Breathing	Oct 10 2028	4	Choosing	Dec 19 2028	9	Breathing
Aug 2 2028	13	Listening	Oct 11 2028	5	Exploring	Dec 20 2028	10	Listening
Aug 3 2028	1	**Planting**	Oct 12 2028	6	Healing	Dec 21 2028	11	Planting
Aug 4 2028	2	Moving	Oct 13 2028	7	Seeing	Dec 22 2028	12	Moving
Aug 5 2028	3	Transcending	Oct 14 2028	8	Intuiting	Dec 23 2028	13	Transcending
Aug 6 2028	4	Remembering	Oct 15 2028	9	Evolving	Dec 24 2028	1	**Remembering**
Aug 7 2028	5	Loving	Oct 16 2028	10	Self-Regulating	Dec 25 2028	2	Loving
Aug 8 2028	6	Feeling	Oct 17 2028	11	Catalyzing	Dec 26 2028	3	Feeling
Aug 9 2028	7	Devoting	Oct 18 2028	12	Enlightening	Dec 27 2028	4	Devoting
Aug 10 2028	8	Illuminating	Oct 19 2028	13	Being	Dec 28 2028	5	Illuminating
Aug 11 2028	9	Choosing	Oct 20 2028	1	**Breathing**	Dec 29 2028	6	Choosing
Aug 12 2028	10	Exploring	Oct 21 2028	2	Listening	Dec 30 2028	7	Exploring
Aug 13 2028	11	Healing	Oct 22 2028	3	Planting	Dec 31 2028	8	Healing
Aug 14 2028	12	Seeing	Oct 23 2028	4	Moving	Jan 1 2029	9	Seeing
Aug 15 2028	13	Intuiting	Oct 24 2028	5	Transcending	Jan 2 2029	10	Intuiting
Aug 16 2028	1	**Evolving**	Oct 25 2028	6	Remembering	Jan 3 2029	11	Evolving
Aug 17 2028	2	Self-Regulating	Oct 26 2028	7	Loving	Jan 4 2029	12	Self-Regulating
Aug 18 2028	3	Catalyzing	Oct 27 2028	8	Feeling	Jan 5 2029	13	Catalyzing
Aug 19 2028	4	Enlightening	Oct 28 2028	9	Devoting	Jan 6 2029	1	**Enlightening**
Aug 20 2028	5	Being	Oct 29 2028	10	Illuminating	Jan 7 2029	2	Being
Aug 21 2028	6	Breathing	Oct 30 2028	11	Choosing	Jan 8 2029	3	Breathing
Aug 22 2028	7	Listening	Oct 31 2028	12	Exploring	Jan 9 2029	4	Listening
Aug 23 2028	8	Planting	Nov 1 2028	13	Healing	Jan 10 2029	5	Planting
Aug 24 2028	9	Moving	Nov 2 2028	1	**Seeing**	Jan 11 2029	6	Moving
Aug 25 2028	10	Transcending	Nov 3 2028	2	Intuiting	Jan 12 2029	7	Transcending
Aug 26 2028	11	Remembering	Nov 4 2028	3	Evolving	Jan 13 2029	8	Remembering
Aug 27 2028	12	Loving	Nov 5 2028	4	Self-Regulating	Jan 14 2029	9	Loving
Aug 28 2028	13	Feeling	Nov 6 2028	5	Catalyzing	Jan 15 2029	10	Feeling
Aug 29 2028	1	**Devoting**	Nov 7 2028	6	Enlightening	Jan 16 2029	11	Planting

Date	UE Earth Energy	Date	UE Earth Energy	Date	UE Earth Energy
Jan 17 2029	12 Illuminating	Mar 28 2029	4 Being	Jun 6 2029	9 Illuminating
Jan 18 2029	13 Choosing	Mar 29 2029	5 Breathing	Jun 7 2029	10 Choosing
Jan 19 2029	**1 Exploring**	Mar 30 2029	6 Listening	Jun 8 2029	11 Exploring
Jan 20 2029	2 Healing	Mar 31 2029	7 Planting	Jun 9 2029	12 Healing
Jan 21 2029	3 Seeing	Apr 1 2029	8 Moving	Jun 10 2029	13 Seeing
Jan 22 2029	4 Intuiting	Apr 2 2029	9 Transcending	Jun 11 2029	**1 Intuiting**
Jan 23 2029	5 Evolving	Apr 3 2029	10 Remembering	Jun 12 2029	2 Evolving
Jan 24 2029	6 Self-Regulating	Apr 4 2029	11 Loving	Jun 13 2029	3 Self-Regulating
Jan 25 2029	7 Catalyzing	Apr 5 2029	12 Feeling	Jun 14 2029	4 Catalyzing
Jan 26 2029	8 Enlightening	Apr 6 2029	13 Devoting	Jun 15 2029	5 Enlightening
Jan 27 2029	9 Being	Apr 7 2029	**1 Illuminating**	Jun 16 2029	6 Being
Jan 28 2029	10 Breathing	Apr 8 2029	2 Choosing	Jun 17 2029	7 Breathing
Jan 29 2029	11 Listening	Apr 9 2029	3 Exploring	Jun 18 2029	8 Listening
Jan 30 2029	12 Planting	Apr 10 2029	4 Healing	Jun 19 2029	9 Planting
Jan 31 2029	13 Moving	Apr 11 2029	5 Seeing	Jun 20 2029	10 Moving
Feb 1 2029	**1 Transcending**	Apr 12 2029	6 Intuiting	Jun 21 2029	11 Transcending
Feb 2 2029	2 Remembering	Apr 13 2029	7 Evolving	Jun 22 2029	12 Remembering
Feb 3 2029	3 Loving	Apr 14 2029	8 Self-Regulating	Jun 23 2029	13 Loving
Feb 4 2029	4 Feeling	Apr 15 2029	9 Catalyzing	Jun 24 2029	**1 Feeling**
Feb 5 2029	5 Devoting	Apr 16 2029	10 Enlightening	Jun 25 2029	2 Devoting
Feb 6 2029	6 Illuminating	Apr 17 2029	11 Being	Jun 26 2029	3 Illuminating
Feb 7 2029	7 Choosing	Apr 18 2029	12 Breathing	Jun 27 2029	4 Choosing
Feb 8 2029	8 Exploring	Apr 19 2029	13 Listening	Jun 28 2029	5 Exploring
Feb 9 2029	9 Healing	Apr 20 2029	**1 Planting**	Jun 29 2029	6 Healing
Feb 10 2029	10 Seeing	Apr 21 2029	2 Moving	Jun 30 2029	7 Seeing
Feb 11 2029	11 Intuiting	Apr 22 2029	3 Transcending	Jul 1 2029	8 Intuiting
Feb 12 2029	12 Evolving	Apr 23 2029	4 Remembering	Jul 2 2029	9 Evolving
Feb 13 2029	13 Self-Regulating	Apr 24 2029	5 Loving	Jul 3 2029	10 Self-Regulating
Feb 14 2029	**1 Catalyzing**	Apr 25 2029	6 Feeling	Jul 4 2029	11 Catalyzing
Feb 15 2029	2 Enlightening	Apr 26 2029	7 Devoting	Jul 5 2029	12 Enlightening
Feb 16 2029	3 Being	Apr 27 2029	8 Illuminating	Jul 6 2029	13 Being
Feb 17 2029	4 Breathing	Apr 28 2029	9 Choosing	Jul 7 2029	**1 Breathing**
Feb 18 2029	5 Listening	Apr 29 2029	10 Exploring	Jul 8 2029	2 Listening
Feb 19 2029	6 Planting	Apr 30 2029	11 Healing	Jul 9 2029	3 Planting
Feb 20 2029	7 Moving	May 1 2029	12 Seeing	Jul 10 2029	4 Moving
Feb 21 2029	8 Transcending	May 2 2029	13 Intuiting	Jul 11 2029	5 Transcending
Feb 22 2029	9 Remembering	May 3 2029	**1 Evolving**	Jul 12 2029	6 Remembering
Feb 23 2029	10 Loving	May 4 2029	2 Self-Regulating	Jul 13 2029	7 Loving
Feb 24 2029	11 Feeling	May 5 2029	3 Catalyzing	Jul 14 2029	8 Feeling
Feb 25 2029	12 Devoting	May 6 2029	4 Enlightening	Jul 15 2029	9 Devoting
Feb 26 2029	13 Illuminating	May 7 2029	5 Being	Jul 16 2029	10 Illuminating
Feb 27 2029	**1 Choosing**	May 8 2029	6 Breathing	Jul 17 2029	11 Choosing
Feb 28 2029	2 Exploring	May 9 2029	7 Listening	Jul 18 2029	12 Exploring
Mar 1 2029	3 Healing	May 10 2029	8 Planting	Jul 19 2029	13 Healing
Mar 2 2029	4 Seeing	May 11 2029	9 Moving	Jul 20 2029	**1 Seeing**
Mar 3 2029	5 Intuiting	May 12 2029	10 Transcending	Jul 21 2029	2 Intuiting
Mar 4 2029	6 Evolving	May 13 2029	11 Remembering	Jul 22 2029	3 Evolving
Mar 5 2029	7 Self-Regulating	May 14 2029	12 Loving	Jul 23 2029	4 Self-Regulating
Mar 6 2029	8 Catalyzing	May 15 2029	13 Feeling	Jul 24 2029	5 Catalyzing
Mar 7 2029	9 Enlightening	May 16 2029	**1 Devoting**	Jul 25 2029	6 Enlightening
Mar 8 2029	10 Being	May 17 2029	2 Illuminating	Jul 26 2029	7 Being
Mar 9 2029	11 Breathing	May 18 2029	3 Choosing	Jul 27 2029	8 Breathing
Mar 10 2029	12 Listening	May 19 2029	4 Exploring	Jul 28 2029	9 Listening
Mar 11 2029	13 Planting	May 20 2029	5 Healing	Jul 29 2029	10 Planting
Mar 12 2029	**1 Moving**	May 21 2029	6 Seeing	Jul 30 2029	11 Moving
Mar 13 2029	2 Transcending	May 22 2029	7 Intuiting	Jul 31 2029	12 Transcending
Mar 14 2029	3 Remembering	May 23 2029	8 Evolving	Aug 1 2029	13 Remembering
Mar 15 2029	4 Loving	May 24 2029	9 Self-Regulating	Aug 2 2029	**1 Loving**
Mar 16 2029	5 Feeling	May 25 2029	10 Catalyzing	Aug 3 2029	2 Feeling
Mar 17 2029	6 Devoting	May 26 2029	11 Enlightening	Aug 4 2029	3 Devoting
Mar 18 2029	7 Illuminating	May 27 2029	12 Being	Aug 5 2029	4 Illuminating
Mar 19 2029	8 Choosing	May 28 2029	13 Breathing	Aug 6 2029	5 Choosing
Mar 20 2029	9 Exploring	May 29 2029	**1 Listening**	Aug 7 2029	6 Exploring
Mar 21 2029	10 Healing	May 30 2029	2 Planting	Aug 8 2029	7 Healing
Mar 22 2029	11 Seeing	May 31 2029	3 Moving	Aug 9 2029	8 Seeing
Mar 23 2029	12 Intuiting	Jun 1 2029	4 Transcending	Aug 10 2029	9 Intuiting
Mar 24 2029	13 Evolving	Jun 2 2029	5 Remembering	Aug 11 2029	10 Evolving
Mar 25 2029	**1 Self-Regulating**	Jun 3 2029	6 Loving	Aug 12 2029	11 Self-Regulating
Mar 26 2029	2 Catalyzing	Jun 4 2029	7 Feeling	Aug 13 2029	12 Catalyzing
Mar 27 2029	3 Enlightening	Jun 5 2029	8 Devoting	Aug 14 2029	13 Enlightening

Date	UE	Earth Energy	Date	UE	Earth Energy	Date	UE	Earth Energy
Aug 15 2029	**1**	**Being**	Oct 24 2029	6	Illuminating	Jan 2 2030	11	Being
Aug 16 2029	2	Breathing	Oct 25 2029	7	Choosing	Jan 3 2030	12	Breathing
Aug 17 2029	3	Listening	Oct 26 2029	8	Exploring	Jan 4 2030	13	Listening
Aug 18 2029	4	Planting	Oct 27 2029	9	Healing	Jan 5 2030	**1**	**Planting**
Aug 19 2029	5	Moving	Oct 28 2029	10	Seeing	Jan 6 2030	2	Moving
Aug 20 2029	6	Transcending	Oct 29 2029	11	Intuiting	Jan 7 2030	3	Transcending
Aug 21 2029	7	Remembering	Oct 30 2029	12	Evolving	Jan 8 2030	4	Remembering
Aug 22 2029	8	Loving	Oct 31 2029	13	Self-Regulating	Jan 9 2030	5	Loving
Aug 23 2029	9	Feeling	Nov 1 2029	**1**	**Catalyzing**	Jan 10 2030	6	Feeling
Aug 24 2029	10	Devoting	Nov 2 2029	2	Enlightening	Jan 11 2030	7	Devoting
Aug 25 2029	11	Illuminating	Nov 3 2029	3	Being	Jan 12 2030	8	Illuminating
Aug 26 2029	12	Choosing	Nov 4 2029	4	Breathing	Jan 13 2030	9	Choosing
Aug 27 2029	13	Exploring	Nov 5 2029	5	Listening	Jan 14 2030	10	Exploring
Aug 28 2029	**1**	**Healing**	Nov 6 2029	6	Planting	Jan 15 2030	11	Healing
Aug 29 2029	2	Seeing	Nov 7 2029	7	Moving	Jan 16 2030	12	Seeing
Aug 30 2029	3	Intuiting	Nov 8 2029	8	Transcending	Jan 17 2030	13	Intuiting
Aug 31 2029	4	Evolving	Nov 9 2029	9	Remembering	Jan 18 2030	**1**	**Evolving**
Sep 1 2029	5	Self-Regulating	Nov 10 2029	10	Loving	Jan 19 2030	2	Self-Regulating
Sep 2 2029	6	Catalyzing	Nov 11 2029	11	Feeling	Jan 20 2030	3	Catalyzing
Sep 3 2029	7	Enlightening	Nov 12 2029	12	Devoting	Jan 21 2030	4	Enlightening
Sep 4 2029	8	Being	Nov 13 2029	13	Illuminating	Jan 22 2030	5	Being
Sep 5 2029	9	Breathing	Nov 14 2029	**1**	**Choosing**	Jan 23 2030	6	Breathing
Sep 6 2029	10	Listening	Nov 15 2029	2	Exploring	Jan 24 2030	7	Listening
Sep 7 2029	11	Planting	Nov 16 2029	3	Healing	Jan 25 2030	8	Planting
Sep 8 2029	12	Moving	Nov 17 2029	4	Seeing	Jan 26 2030	9	Moving
Sep 9 2029	13	Transcending	Nov 18 2029	5	Intuiting	Jan 27 2030	10	Transcending
Sep 10 2029	**1**	**Remembering**	Nov 19 2029	6	Evolving	Jan 28 2030	11	Remembering
Sep 11 2029	2	Loving	Nov 20 2029	7	Self-Regulating	Jan 29 2030	12	Loving
Sep 12 2029	3	Feeling	Nov 21 2029	8	Catalyzing	Jan 30 2030	13	Feeling
Sep 13 2029	4	Devoting	Nov 22 2029	9	Enlightening	Jan 31 2030	**1**	**Devoting**
Sep 14 2029	5	Illuminating	Nov 23 2029	10	Being	Feb 1 2030	2	Illuminating
Sep 15 2029	6	Choosing	Nov 24 2029	11	Breathing	Feb 2 2030	3	Choosing
Sep 16 2029	7	Exploring	Nov 25 2029	12	Listening	Feb 3 2030	4	Exploring
Sep 17 2029	8	Healing	Nov 26 2029	13	Planting	Feb 4 2030	5	Healing
Sep 18 2029	9	Seeing	Nov 27 2029	**1**	**Moving**	Feb 5 2030	6	Seeing
Sep 19 2029	10	Intuiting	Nov 28 2029	2	Transcending	Feb 6 2030	7	Intuiting
Sep 20 2029	11	Evolving	Nov 29 2029	3	Remembering	Feb 7 2030	8	Evolving
Sep 21 2029	12	Self-Regulating	Nov 30 2029	4	Loving	Feb 8 2030	9	Self-Regulating
Sep 22 2029	13	Catalyzing	Dec 1 2029	5	Feeling	Feb 9 2030	10	Catalyzing
Sep 23 2029	**1**	**Enlightening**	Dec 2 2029	6	Devoting	Feb 10 2030	11	Enlightening
Sep 24 2029	2	Being	Dec 3 2029	7	Illuminating	Feb 11 2030	12	Being
Sep 25 2029	3	Breathing	Dec 4 2029	8	Choosing	Feb 12 2030	13	Breathing
Sep 26 2029	4	Listening	Dec 5 2029	9	Exploring	Feb 13 2030	**1**	**Listening**
Sep 27 2029	5	Planting	Dec 6 2029	10	Healing	Feb 14 2030	2	Planting
Sep 28 2029	6	Moving	Dec 7 2029	11	Seeing	Feb 15 2030	3	Moving
Sep 29 2029	7	Transcending	Dec 8 2029	12	Intuiting	Feb 16 2030	4	Transcending
Sep 30 2029	8	Remembering	Dec 9 2029	13	Evolving	Feb 17 2030	5	Remembering
Oct 1 2029	9	Loving	Dec 10 2029	**1**	**Self-Regulating**	Feb 18 2030	6	Loving
Oct 2 2029	10	Feeling	Dec 11 2029	2	Catalyzing	Feb 19 2030	7	Feeling
Oct 3 2029	11	Devoting	Dec 12 2029	3	Enlightening	Feb 20 2030	8	Devoting
Oct 4 2029	12	Illuminating	Dec 13 2029	4	Being	Feb 21 2030	9	Illuminating
Oct 5 2029	13	Choosing	Dec 14 2029	5	Breathing	Feb 22 2030	10	Choosing
Oct 6 2029	**1**	**Exploring**	Dec 15 2029	6	Listening	Feb 23 2030	11	Exploring
Oct 7 2029	2	Healing	Dec 16 2029	7	Planting	Feb 24 2030	12	Healing
Oct 8 2029	3	Seeing	Dec 17 2029	8	Moving	Feb 25 2030	13	Seeing
Oct 9 2029	4	Intuiting	Dec 18 2029	9	Transcending	Feb 26 2030	**1**	**Intuiting**
Oct 10 2029	5	Evolving	Dec 19 2029	10	Remembering	Feb 27 2030	2	Evolving
Oct 11 2029	6	Self-Regulating	Dec 20 2029	11	Loving	Feb 28 2030	3	Self-Regulating
Oct 12 2029	7	Catalyzing	Dec 21 2029	12	Feeling	Mar 1 2030	4	Catalyzing
Oct 13 2029	8	Enlightening	Dec 22 2029	13	Devoting	Mar 2 2030	5	Enlightening
Oct 14 2029	9	Being	Dec 23 2029	**1**	**Illuminating**	Mar 3 2030	6	Being
Oct 15 2029	10	Breathing	Dec 24 2029	2	Choosing	Mar 4 2030	7	Breathing
Oct 16 2029	11	Listening	Dec 25 2029	3	Exploring	Mar 5 2030	8	Listening
Oct 17 2029	12	Planting	Dec 26 2029	4	Healing	Mar 6 2030	9	Planting
Oct 18 2029	13	Moving	Dec 27 2029	5	Seeing	Mar 7 2030	10	Moving
Oct 19 2029	**1**	**Transcending**	Dec 28 2029	6	Intuiting	Mar 8 2030	11	Transcending
Oct 20 2029	2	Remembering	Dec 29 2029	7	Evolving	Mar 9 2030	12	Remembering
Oct 21 2029	3	Loving	Dec 30 2029	8	Self-Regulating	Mar 10 2030	13	Loving
Oct 22 2029	4	Feeling	Dec 31 2029	9	Catalyzing	Mar 11 2030	**1**	**Feeling**
Oct 23 2029	5	Devoting	Jan 1 2030	10	Enlightening	Mar 12 2030	2	Devoting

Date	UE Earth Energy	Date	UE Earth Energy	Date	UE Earth Energy
Mar 13 2030	3 Illuminating	May 22 2030	8 Being	Jul 31 2030	13 Illuminating
Mar 14 2030	4 Choosing	May 23 2030	9 Breathing	Aug 1 2030	**1 Choosing**
Mar 15 2030	5 Exploring	May 24 2030	10 Listening	Aug 2 2030	2 Exploring
Mar 16 2030	6 Healing	May 25 2030	11 Planting	Aug 3 2030	3 Healing
Mar 17 2030	7 Seeing	May 26 2030	12 Moving	Aug 4 2030	4 Seeing
Mar 18 2030	8 Intuiting	May 27 2030	13 Transcending	Aug 5 2030	5 Intuiting
Mar 19 2030	9 Evolving	May 28 2030	**1 Remembering**	Aug 6 2030	6 Evolving
Mar 20 2030	10 Self-Regulating	May 29 2030	2 Loving	Aug 7 2030	7 Self-Regulating
Mar 21 2030	11 Catalyzing	May 30 2030	3 Feeling	Aug 8 2030	8 Catalyzing
Mar 22 2030	12 Enlightening	May 31 2030	4 Devoting	Aug 9 2030	9 Enlightening
Mar 23 2030	13 Being	Jun 1 2030	5 Illuminating	Aug 10 2030	10 Being
Mar 24 2030	**1 Breathing**	Jun 2 2030	6 Choosing	Aug 11 2030	11 Breathing
Mar 25 2030	2 Listening	Jun 3 2030	7 Exploring	Aug 12 2030	12 Listening
Mar 26 2030	3 Planting	Jun 4 2030	8 Healing	Aug 13 2030	13 Planting
Mar 27 2030	4 Moving	Jun 5 2030	9 Seeing	Aug 14 2030	**1 Moving**
Mar 28 2030	5 Transcending	Jun 6 2030	10 Intuiting	Aug 15 2030	2 Transcending
Mar 29 2030	6 Remembering	Jun 7 2030	11 Evolving	Aug 16 2030	3 Remembering
Mar 30 2030	7 Loving	Jun 8 2030	12 Self-Regulating	Aug 17 2030	4 Loving
Mar 31 2030	8 Feeling	Jun 9 2030	13 Catalyzing	Aug 18 2030	5 Feeling
Apr 1 2030	9 Devoting	Jun 10 2030	**1 Enlightening**	Aug 19 2030	6 Devoting
Apr 2 2030	10 Illuminating	Jun 11 2030	2 Being	Aug 20 2030	7 Illuminating
Apr 3 2030	11 Choosing	Jun 12 2030	3 Breathing	Aug 21 2030	8 Choosing
Apr 4 2030	12 Exploring	Jun 13 2030	4 Listening	Aug 22 2030	9 Exploring
Apr 5 2030	13 Healing	Jun 14 2030	5 Planting	Aug 23 2030	10 Healing
Apr 6 2030	**1 Seeing**	Jun 15 2030	6 Moving	Aug 24 2030	11 Seeing
Apr 7 2030	2 Intuiting	Jun 16 2030	7 Transcending	Aug 25 2030	12 Intuiting
Apr 8 2030	3 Evolving	Jun 17 2030	8 Remembering	Aug 26 2030	13 Evolving
Apr 9 2030	4 Self-Regulating	Jun 18 2030	9 Loving	Aug 27 2030	**1 Self-Regulating**
Apr 10 2030	5 Catalyzing	Jun 19 2030	10 Feeling	Aug 28 2030	2 Catalyzing
Apr 11 2030	6 Enlightening	Jun 20 2030	11 Devoting	Aug 29 2030	3 Enlightening
Apr 12 2030	7 Being	Jun 21 2030	12 Illuminating	Aug 30 2030	4 Being
Apr 13 2030	8 Breathing	Jun 22 2030	13 Choosing	Aug 31 2030	5 Breathing
Apr 14 2030	9 Listening	Jun 23 2030	**1 Exploring**	Sep 1 2030	6 Listening
Apr 15 2030	10 Planting	Jun 24 2030	2 Healing	Sep 2 2030	7 Planting
Apr 16 2030	11 Moving	Jun 25 2030	3 Seeing	Sep 3 2030	8 Moving
Apr 17 2030	12 Transcending	Jun 26 2030	4 Intuiting	Sep 4 2030	9 Transcending
Apr 18 2030	13 Remembering	Jun 27 2030	5 Evolving	Sep 5 2030	10 Remembering
Apr 19 2030	**1 Loving**	Jun 28 2030	6 Self-Regulating	Sep 6 2030	11 Loving
Apr 20 2030	2 Feeling	Jun 29 2030	7 Catalyzing	Sep 7 2030	12 Feeling
Apr 21 2030	3 Devoting	Jun 30 2030	8 Enlightening	Sep 8 2030	13 Devoting
Apr 22 2030	4 Illuminating	Jul 1 2030	9 Being	Sep 9 2030	**1 Illuminating**
Apr 23 2030	5 Choosing	Jul 2 2030	10 Breathing	Sep 10 2030	2 Choosing
Apr 24 2030	6 Exploring	Jul 3 2030	11 Listening	Sep 11 2030	3 Exploring
Apr 25 2030	7 Healing	Jul 4 2030	12 Planting	Sep 12 2030	4 Healing
Apr 26 2030	8 Seeing	Jul 5 2030	13 Moving	Sep 13 2030	5 Seeing
Apr 27 2030	9 Intuiting	Jul 6 2030	**1 Transcending**	Sep 14 2030	6 Intuiting
Apr 28 2030	10 Evolving	Jul 7 2030	2 Remembering	Sep 15 2030	7 Evolving
Apr 29 2030	11 Self-Regulating	Jul 8 2030	3 Loving	Sep 16 2030	8 Self-Regulating
Apr 30 2030	12 Catalyzing	Jul 9 2030	4 Feeling	Sep 17 2030	9 Catalyzing
May 1 2030	13 Enlightening	Jul 10 2030	5 Devoting	Sep 18 2030	10 Enlightening
May 2 2030	**1 Being**	Jul 11 2030	6 Illuminating	Sep 19 2030	11 Being
May 3 2030	2 Breathing	Jul 12 2030	7 Choosing	Sep 20 2030	12 Breathing
May 4 2030	3 Listening	Jul 13 2030	8 Exploring	Sep 21 2030	13 Listening
May 5 2030	4 Planting	Jul 14 2030	9 Healing	Sep 22 2030	**1 Planting**
May 6 2030	5 Moving	Jul 15 2030	10 Seeing	Sep 23 2030	2 Moving
May 7 2030	6 Transcending	Jul 16 2030	11 Intuiting	Sep 24 2030	3 Transcending
May 8 2030	7 Remembering	Jul 17 2030	12 Evolving	Sep 25 2030	4 Remembering
May 9 2030	8 Loving	Jul 18 2030	13 Self-Regulating	Sep 26 2030	5 Loving
May 10 2030	9 Feeling	Jul 19 2030	**1 Catalyzing**	Sep 27 2030	6 Feeling
May 11 2030	10 Devoting	Jul 20 2030	2 Enlightening	Sep 28 2030	7 Devoting
May 12 2030	11 Illuminating	Jul 21 2030	3 Being	Sep 29 2030	8 Illuminating
May 13 2030	12 Choosing	Jul 22 2030	4 Breathing	Sep 30 2030	9 Choosing
May 14 2030	13 Exploring	Jul 23 2030	5 Listening	Oct 1 2030	10 Exploring
May 15 2030	**1 Healing**	Jul 24 2030	6 Planting	Oct 2 2030	11 Healing
May 16 2030	2 Seeing	Jul 25 2030	7 Moving	Oct 3 2030	12 Seeing
May 17 2030	3 Intuiting	Jul 26 2030	8 Transcending	Oct 4 2030	13 Intuiting
May 18 2030	4 Evolving	Jul 27 2030	9 Remembering	Oct 5 2030	**1 Evolving**
May 19 2030	5 Self-Regulating	Jul 28 2030	10 Loving	Oct 6 2030	2 Self-Regulating
May 20 2030	6 Catalyzing	Jul 29 2030	11 Feeling	Oct 7 2030	3 Catalyzing
May 21 2030	7 Enlightening	Jul 30 2030	12 Devoting	Oct 8 2030	4 Enlightening

Date	UE	Earth Energy
Oct 9 2030	5	Being
Oct 10 2030	6	Breathing
Oct 11 2030	7	Listening
Oct 12 2030	8	Planting
Oct 13 2030	9	Moving
Oct 14 2030	10	Transcending
Oct 15 2030	11	Remembering
Oct 16 2030	12	Loving
Oct 17 2030	13	Feeling
Oct 18 2030	1	Devoting
Oct 19 2030	2	Illuminating
Oct 20 2030	3	Choosing
Oct 21 2030	4	Exploring
Oct 22 2030	5	Healing
Oct 23 2030	6	Seeing
Oct 24 2030	7	Intuiting
Oct 25 2030	8	Evolving
Oct 26 2030	9	Self-Regulating
Oct 27 2030	10	Catalyzing
Oct 28 2030	11	Enlightening
Oct 29 2030	12	Being
Oct 30 2030	13	Breathing
Oct 31 2030	1	Listening
Nov 1 2030	2	Planting
Nov 2 2030	3	Moving
Nov 3 2030	4	Transcending
Nov 4 2030	5	Remembering
Nov 5 2030	6	Loving
Nov 6 2030	7	Feeling
Nov 7 2030	8	Devoting
Nov 8 2030	9	Illuminating
Nov 9 2030	10	Choosing
Nov 10 2030	11	Exploring
Nov 11 2030	12	Healing
Nov 12 2030	13	Seeing
Nov 13 2030	1	Intuiting
Nov 14 2030	2	Evolving
Nov 15 2030	3	Self-Regulating
Nov 16 2030	4	Catalyzing
Nov 17 2030	5	Enlightening
Nov 18 2030	6	Being
Nov 19 2030	7	Breathing
Nov 20 2030	8	Listening
Nov 21 2030	9	Planting
Nov 22 2030	10	Moving
Nov 23 2030	11	Transcending
Nov 24 2030	12	Remembering
Nov 25 2030	13	Loving
Nov 26 2030	1	Feeling
Nov 27 2030	2	Devoting
Nov 28 2030	3	Illuminating
Nov 29 2030	4	Choosing
Nov 30 2030	5	Exploring
Dec 1 2030	6	Healing
Dec 2 2030	7	Seeing
Dec 3 2030	8	Intuiting
Dec 4 2030	9	Evolving
Dec 5 2030	10	Self-Regulating
Dec 6 2030	11	Catalyzing
Dec 7 2030	12	Enlightening
Dec 8 2030	13	Being
Dec 9 2030	1	Breathing
Dec 10 2030	2	Listening
Dec 11 2030	3	Planting
Dec 12 2030	4	Moving
Dec 13 2030	5	Transcending
Dec 14 2030	6	Remembering
Dec 15 2030	7	Loving
Dec 16 2030	8	Feeling
Dec 17 2030	9	Devoting
Dec 18 2030	10	Illuminating
Dec 19 2030	11	Choosing
Dec 20 2030	12	Exploring
Dec 21 2030	13	Healing
Dec 22 2030	1	Seeing
Dec 23 2030	2	Intuiting
Dec 24 2030	3	Evolving
Dec 25 2030	4	Self-Regulating
Dec 26 2030	5	Catalyzing
Dec 27 2030	6	Enlightening
Dec 28 2030	7	Being
Dec 29 2030	8	Breathing
Dec 30 2030	9	Listening
Dec 31 2030	10	Planting
Jan 1 2031	11	Moving
Jan 2 2031	12	Transcending
Jan 3 2031	13	Remembering
Jan 4 2031	1	Loving
Jan 5 2031	2	Feeling
Jan 6 2031	3	Devoting
Jan 7 2031	4	Illuminating
Jan 8 2031	5	Choosing
Jan 9 2031	6	Exploring
Jan 10 2031	7	Healing
Jan 11 2031	8	Seeing
Jan 12 2031	9	Intuiting
Jan 13 2031	10	Evolving
Jan 14 2031	11	Self-Regulating
Jan 15 2031	12	Catalyzing
Jan 16 2031	13	Enlightening
Jan 17 2031	1	Being
Jan 18 2031	2	Breathing
Jan 19 2031	3	Listening
Jan 20 2031	4	Planting
Jan 21 2031	5	Moving
Jan 22 2031	6	Transcending
Jan 23 2031	7	Remembering
Jan 24 2031	8	Loving
Jan 25 2031	9	Feeling
Jan 26 2031	10	Devoting
Jan 27 2031	11	Illuminating
Jan 28 2031	12	Choosing
Jan 29 2031	13	Exploring
Jan 30 2031	1	Healing
Jan 31 2031	2	Seeing
Feb 1 2031	3	Intuiting
Feb 2 2031	4	Evolving
Feb 3 2031	5	Self-Regulating
Feb 4 2031	6	Catalyzing
Feb 5 2031	7	Enlightening
Feb 6 2031	8	Being
Feb 7 2031	9	Breathing
Feb 8 2031	10	Listening
Feb 9 2031	11	Planting
Feb 10 2031	12	Moving
Feb 11 2031	13	Transcending
Feb 12 2031	1	Remembering
Feb 13 2031	2	Loving
Feb 14 2031	3	Feeling
Feb 15 2031	4	Devoting
Feb 16 2031	5	Illuminating
Feb 17 2031	6	Choosing
Feb 18 2031	7	Exploring
Feb 19 2031	8	Healing
Feb 20 2031	9	Seeing
Feb 21 2031	10	Intuiting
Feb 22 2031	11	Evolving
Feb 23 2031	12	Self-Regulating
Feb 24 2031	13	Catalyzing
Feb 25 2031	1	Enlightening
Feb 26 2031	2	Being
Feb 27 2031	3	Breathing
Feb 28 2031	4	Listening
Mar 1 2031	5	Planting
Mar 2 2031	6	Moving
Mar 3 2031	7	Transcending
Mar 4 2031	8	Remembering
Mar 5 2031	9	Loving
Mar 6 2031	10	Feeling
Mar 7 2031	11	Devoting
Mar 8 2031	12	Illuminating
Mar 9 2031	13	Choosing
Mar 10 2031	1	Exploring
Mar 11 2031	2	Healing
Mar 12 2031	3	Seeing
Mar 13 2031	4	Intuiting
Mar 14 2031	5	Evolving
Mar 15 2031	6	Self-Regulating
Mar 16 2031	7	Catalyzing
Mar 17 2031	8	Enlightening
Mar 18 2031	9	Being
Mar 19 2031	10	Breathing
Mar 20 2031	11	Listening
Mar 21 2031	12	Planting
Mar 22 2031	13	Moving
Mar 23 2031	1	Transcending
Mar 24 2031	2	Remembering
Mar 25 2031	3	Loving
Mar 26 2031	4	Feeling
Mar 27 2031	5	Devoting
Mar 28 2031	6	Illuminating
Mar 29 2031	7	Choosing
Mar 30 2031	8	Exploring
Mar 31 2031	9	Healing
Apr 1 2031	10	Seeing
Apr 2 2031	11	Intuiting
Apr 3 2031	12	Evolving
Apr 4 2031	13	Self-Regulating
Apr 5 2031	1	Catalyzing
Apr 6 2031	2	Enlightening
Apr 7 2031	3	Being
Apr 8 2031	4	Breathing
Apr 9 2031	5	Listening
Apr 10 2031	6	Planting
Apr 11 2031	7	Moving
Apr 12 2031	8	Transcending
Apr 13 2031	9	Remembering
Apr 14 2031	10	Loving
Apr 15 2031	11	Feeling
Apr 16 2031	12	Devoting
Apr 17 2031	13	Illuminating
Apr 18 2031	1	Choosing
Apr 19 2031	2	Exploring
Apr 20 2031	3	Healing
Apr 21 2031	4	Seeing
Apr 22 2031	5	Intuiting
Apr 23 2031	6	Evolving
Apr 24 2031	7	Self-Regulating
Apr 25 2031	8	Catalyzing
Apr 26 2031	9	Enlightening
Apr 27 2031	10	Being
Apr 28 2031	11	Breathing
Apr 29 2031	12	Listening
Apr 30 2031	13	Planting
May 1 2031	1	Moving
May 2 2031	2	Transcending
May 3 2031	3	Remembering
May 4 2031	4	Loving
May 5 2031	5	Feeling
May 6 2031	6	Devoting

NOTES

2. DNA AND SPECIES EVOLUTION

1. Johnson et al., "System Genetics."
2. Hall, "Hidden Treasures in Junk DNA."
3. Rieper, Anders and Vedral, "Relevance of Continuous Variable Entanglement in DNA."
4. McCraty, *Science of the Heart,* 50.

5. VENUS AND DUALITY

1. Guttman, *Venus Star Rising.*
2. Guttman, *Venus Star Rising.*
3. Gainsburg, *Light of Venus.*

6. THE THIRTEEN UNIVERSAL ENERGIES

1. Authors' personal conversation with Bruce Scofield, March 2017.

8. LEVELS OF CONSCIOUSNESS IN EARTH ENERGIES

1. Authors' personal conversations with Cherokee, Dakota, and Navajo elders.
2. Seltzer, *Tenth Planet.*

9. THE RELATIONSHIP BETWEEN EARTH ENERGIES AND PERSONALITY

1. Scofield, *Day-Signs,* 1.
2. Orleane and Smith, *Conversations with Laarkmaa,* 12.

3. Orleane and Smith, *Remembering Who We Are*, 20.

4. Orleane and Smith, *Conversations with Laarkmaa*, 20.

5. Orleane and Smith, *Remembering Who We Are*, 25.

6. Authors' interview. More details from Laarkmaa about telepathic communication through water can be found in *Conversations with Laarkmaa*, 19.

11. SHADOW CYCLES OF EVOLUTION

1. Orleane and Smith, *Conversations with Laarkmaa*.

2. Tellinger, *Ubuntu Contributionism*.

3. Orleane and Smith, *Conversations with Laarkmaa*. See also Orleane and Smith, *Remembering Who We Are*.

13. A NEW CALENDAR BASED ON ENERGY, NOT TIME

1. Lyall Watson, in his foreword to Blair, *Rhythms of Vision*.

14. WHO ARE YOU REALLY?

1. Addey, *Harmonic Anthology*, 32–33.

2. Authors' personal conversation with Laarkmaa.

3. Childre, Martin, Rozman, and McCraty, *Heart Intelligence*.

BIBLIOGRAPHY

Addey, John. *Harmonic Anthology*. Tempe, Ariz.: American Federation of Astrologers, Inc., 1976.

Argüelles, José. *The Mayan Factor: Path beyond Technology*. Rochester, Vt.: Bear & Company, 1987.

Baring, Anne. *The Dream of the Cosmos: A Quest for the Soul*. Dorset, UK: Archive Publishing, 2013.

Berry, Thomas. *The Dream of the Earth*. San Francisco, Calif.: Sierra Club Books, 1988.

Blair, Lawrence. *Rhythms of Vision: The Changing Patterns of Belief*. London: Croom Helm, Ltd., 1975.

Capra, Fritjof. *The Web of Life: A New Scientific Understanding of Living Systems*. New York: Doubleday, 1996.

Childre, Doc, Howard Martin, Deborah Rozman, and Rollin McCraty. *Heart Intelligence: Connecting with the Intuitive Guidance of the Heart*. Lumsden, Canada: Waterfront Press, 2016.

Clow, Barbara Hand. *Chiron: Rainbow Bridge between Inner and Outer Planets*. 2nd ed. Woodbury, Minn.: Llewellyn Publications, 2016.

———. *The Mayan Code: Time Acceleration and Awakening*. Rochester, Vt.: Bear and Company, 2007

Coveney, Peter, and Roger Highfield. *The Arrow of Time: A Voyage through Science to Solve Time's Greatest Mystery*. New York: Ballantine Books, 1990.

Csikszentmihalyi, Mikhael. *Flow: The Psychology of Optimal Experience*. New York: Harper Perennial, 1990.

Davies, Paul. *About Time: Einstein's Unfinished Revolution*. New York: Simon and Schuster, 1995.

de Broglie, Louis. *The Current Interpretation of Wave Mechanics: A Critical Study.* Amsterdam: Elsevier Publications, 1964.

Dryer, Ronnie Gale. *Venus: The Evolution of the Goddess and Her Planet.* San Francisco: Aquarian Publishers, 1994.

Forrest, Steven. *The Book of Neptune.* Borrego Springs, Calif.: Seven Paws Press, 2016.

Gainsburg, Adam. *The Light of Venus: Embracing Your Deeper Feminine, Empowering Our Shared Future.* Fairfax, Va.: Soulsign Publishing, 2012.

Goswami, Amit. *The Everything Answer Book: How Quantum Science Explains Love, Death, and the Meaning of Life.* Charlottesville, Va.: Hampton Roads, 2017.

———. *Quantum Economics: Unleashing the Power of an Economics of Consciousness.* Faber, Va.: Rainbow Ridge Books, 2015.

———. *The Self-Aware Universe: How Consciousness Creates the Material World.* New York: Tarcher Perigee, 1995.

———. *The Visionary Window: A Quantum Physicist's Guide to Enlightenment.* Wheaton, Ill.: Quest Books. 2010.

Greene, Brian. *The Hidden Reality: Parallel Universes and the Deep Laws of the Cosmos.* New York: Alfred A. Knopf, 2011.

Guttman, Arielle. *Venus Star Rising: A New Cosmology for the 21st Century.* Santa Fe, N.Mex.: Sophia Venus Productions, 2011.

Hall, Stephen S. "Hidden Treasures in Junk DNA: What Was Once Known as Junk DNA Turns Out to Hold Hidden Treasures, Says Computational Biologist Ewan Birney." *Scientific American,* October 1, 2012. www .scientificamerican.com/article/hidden-treasures-in-junk-dna.

Herbert, Nick. *Elemental Mind: Consciousness and the New Physics.* New York: Plume, 1993.

Johnson, Kenneth. *Jaguar Wisdom: Mayan Calendar Magic.* Woodbury, Minn.: Llewellyn Worldwide, 1997.

Johnson, Michael R., Kirill Shkura, Sarah R. Langley, et al. "System Genetics Identifies a Convergent Gene Network for Cognition and Neuro-developmental Disease." *Nature Neuroscience* 19, no. 2 (February 2016): 223–32.

Kepler, Johann. *Concerning the More Certain Fundamentals of Astrology.* Whitefish, Mo.: Kessinger Publishing, 2003.

Lipton, Bruce H. *The Biology of Belief: Unleashing the Power of Consciousness, Matter, and Miracles.* Carlsbad, Calif.: Hay House Publishing, 2008.

McCraty, Rollin. *Science of the Heart: Exploring the Role of the Heart in Human Performance.* Vol. 2. Boulder Creek, Calif.: Heart Math Institute, 2015.

Miller, Hamish. *The Parallel Community: Joining Together as One* (DVD). Philippines: Reality Entertainment, 2008.

Orleane, Pia. *Sacred Retreat: Using Natural Cycles to Recharge Your Life.* Rochester, Vt.: Bear & Company, 2017.

Orleane, Pia, and Cullen Smith. *Conversations with Laarkmaa: A Pleiadian View of the New Reality.* Santa Fe, N.Mex.: Onewater Press, 2015.

———. *Remembering Who We Are: Laarkmaa's Guidance on Healing the Human Condition.* Santa Fe, N.Mex.: Onewater Press, 2015.

Rieper, Elisabeth, Janet Anders, and Vlatko Vedral. "The Relevance of Continuous Variable Entanglement in DNA." Mälardalen University, Sweden, June 21, 2010. www.idt.mdh.se/~gdc/work/ARTICLES/2014/5-IACAP %202014%20book/pdf-background/DNA-continuous-entanglement -1006.4053v1.pdf.

Rovelli, Carlo. *Reality Is Not What It Seems: The Journey to Quantum Gravity.* Sevierville, Tenn.: Insight Publishing, 2014.

———. *What is Time? What is Space?* Rome: Di Renzo Editore, 2006.

Rudhyar, Dane. *The Planetarization of Consciousness.* Santa Fe, N.Mex.: Aurora Press, 1995.

———. *The Galactic Dimension of Astrology: The Sun Is Also a Star.* Santa Fe, N.Mex.: Aurora Press, 1975.

Schwenk, Theodore. *Sensitive Chaos: Creation of Flowing Forms in Water and Air.* Herndon, Va.: Steiner Books, 1998.

Scofield, Bruce. *The Circuitry of the Self: Astrology and the Developmental Model.* Amherst, Mass.: One Reed Publications, 2001.

———. *Day-Signs: Native American Astrology from Ancient Mexico.* London: One Reed Publications, 1997.

Scofield, Bruce, and Barry Orr. *How to Practice Mayan Astrology: The Tzolkin Calendar and Your Life Path.* Rochester, Vt.: Bear and Company, 2007.

Seltzer, Henry. *The Tenth Planet: Revelations from the Astrological Eris.* Bournemouth, UK: The Wessex Astrologer, 2015.

Seymour, Percy. *Astrology: The Evidence of Science.* Luton, UK: Lennard Publishing, 1988.

———. *Cosmic Magnetism.* Bristol, UK: CRC Press, 1986.

Tellinger, Michael. *Ubuntu Contributionism.* Cape Town, S. Africa: Zulu Planet Publishing, 2014.

Yaxk'in, Aluna Joy. *Mayan Astrology: An Easy and Complete Guide.* Sedona, Ariz.: Center of the Sun, 1995.

INDEX

Numbers in *italics* preceded by *pl.* indicate color insert plate numbers.

ABOUT THE AUTHORS

Pia Orleane, Ph.D., is the author of *Sacred Retreat: Using Natural Cycles to Recharge Your Life* (Bear & Company) and two books coauthored with her husband, Cullen Baird Smith: *Conversations with Laarkmaa: A Pleiadian View of the New Reality* (Onewater Press) and *Remembering Who We Are: Laarkmaa's Guidance on Healing the Human Condition* (Onewater Press). When a group of Pleiadians began to speak to Orleane and Smith, they stopped their respective careers as a clinical psychologist and a whole systems consultant to bring a larger wisdom to the world. As international speakers, the authors have been lecturing together for decades on how to raise human consciousness. Aside from her professional background as a psychologist, Pia Orleane is a certified Venus Star Point astrologer and a Mayan Calendar researcher and is well versed in multiple systems of astrology. She provides Pleiadian-Earth Astrology Energy charts and consultations (https://www.piaorleane.com/energy-charts). Cullen Baird Smith has extensive training and background in Mayan anthropology and archeology.

Mayan elders accept that the information in the Mayan calendar was given to their people by a group of interstellar visitors from the Pleiades. The new voice of the Pleiadians is Laarkmaa, a loving group of interstellar beings who work with Pia Orleane and Cullen Baird Smith. As modern ambassadors to the Pleiadians, Orleane and Smith have dedicated their lives to supporting human evolution.

Pia Orleane is 1 *Healing;* Cullen Baird Smith is 12 *Healing.* Pia and Cullen both carry the 14th earth energy of *Healing.* Pia carries the universal energy of 1, *initiating,* and Cullen carries the universal energy of 12, *understanding.* Together, their relationship carries the 8th earth energy of *Loving* and the universal energy of 13, *completing,* as they join their energies to accomplish the work they came to Earth to complete.